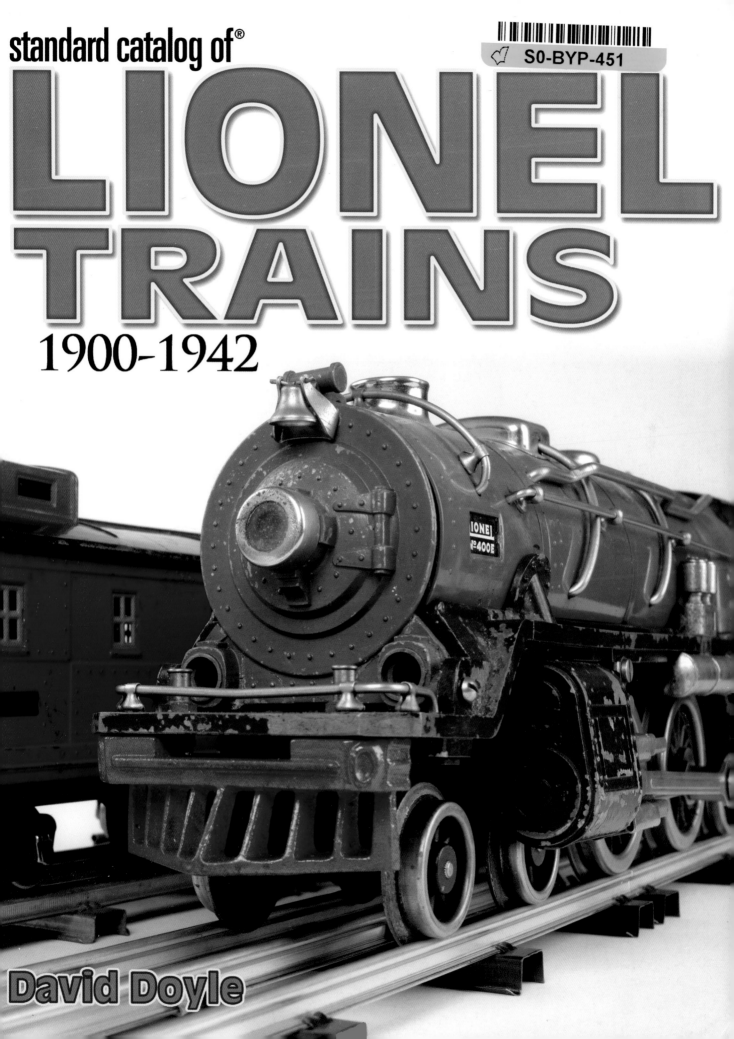

standard catalog of®
LIONEL TRAINS
1900-1942

S0-BYP-451

David Doyle

©2005 David Doyle
Published by

kp books
An Imprint of F+W Publications

700 East State Street • Iola, WI 54990-0001
715-445-2214 • 888-457-2873

Our toll-free number to place an order or obtain
a free catalog is (800) 258-0929.

Library of Congress Catalog Number: 2005924817
ISBN: 0-89689-239-5

Designed by Brian Brogaard
Edited by Dennis Thorton

Printed in China

DEDICATION

Dedicated to the memory of Gary W. Lavinus, Sr., Chairman of the TCA Education and Museum Committee, whose infectious enthusiasm for this hobby touched thousands, and without whose help this book would not have been possible.

CONTENTS

SECTION A
2 ⅞-INCH GAUGE

SECTION B
STANDARD GAUGE

SECTION C
O GAUGE

SECTION D
00 GAUGE

SECTION E
ACCESSORIES, CATALOGS & TOYS, ETC.

ACKNOWLEDGMENTS

When I worked on my first Lionel-related book, The Standard Catalog of Lionel Trains, 1945-1969, I had the assistance of a number of friends I had made through my years of collecting trains from that era. When I undertook this book, however, I realized that I would need to reach out for help to an even wider circle of collectors. As a result, not only has my knowledge been broadened, but so too has the circle of people that I call friends.

Many collectors and businesses shared photographs with me or allowed me to make my own images of rare and important pieces in their collections. Many knowledgeable collectors and dealers graciously reviewed the manuscript and offered corrections, criticism and commentary, and provided valuable insight on values for the items listed. Every effort has been made to present complete and accurate information here, and any errors are purely my own.

The late Gary Lavinous and his team of dedicated volunteers stayed until nearly midnight at the National Toy Train Museum helping me photograph many of the rarest pieces shown in this volume. Though their day was nearing 18 hours long, they dismantled display cases to allow access, not only without complaining, but with genuine enthusiasm.

Jan Athey, reference librarian for the Train Collector's Association, graciously located and allowed us to photograph many of Lionel's prewar catalogs. Former TCA president Dr. Paul Wassermann supplied additional images for that, and other chapters as well.

After long work days, Bill Blystone then worked well into the evening photographing items from his extensive prewar collection. Jim Nicholson allowed our photographer to spend two days in his home taking photos, then lent additional items for studio photography. With the date of the world's largest train show, the Eastern Division TCA meet in York, Pa., just around the corner–a show he runs as a volunteer–Clem Clement allowed us to photograph his wonderful Standard Gauge collection.

Barb Jones lent not only her photographic skills, but also her wonderful prewar collection and vast knowledge to this effort. Scott Douglas, another respected prewar collector, also provided photographs and information critical to this work.

The chapter on Lionel's smallest trains, and perhaps the smallest niche in prewar collecting, 00, would not have been possible without the help of Ken Shirey. Noted Standard Gauge aficionado Caryl Pettijohn provided much needed material in that area.

Dave McEntarfer contributed many photos, and much enthusiasm and experience, to this project. Joe Mania, who produces exquisite reproductions of some of Lionel's earliest, rarest and most valuable trains, provided photographs of these products as an aid in differentiating authentic pieces from reproductions. His integrity is to be commended.

Parts with Character shared much knowledge and experience with me, as well as allowing needed photos to be taken.

My old friend, Jeff Kane of www.ttender.com, sent needed photos of many individual items from his extensive inventory of prewar Lionel repair parts.

Barry Gilmore, who once gave the sage collecting advice, "Never buy a train you feel you should apologize for," opened his collection to our camera. Dennis Waldron answered many questions about Lionel's scale and semiscale production.

Train collecting is a passion for the entire Tschopp family, and they all pitched in on this project. Brothers Bob and John opened their collection for photography and shared their knowledge. Their sister, Mary Burns and her husband Terry put in a long, long day helping photograph the couple's fabulous prewar collection. Bob Senior provided several rare Standard Gauge pieces, and teen-ager Bobby, the newest collector of the family, tireless located trains for photography.

James D. Julia auctions provided photos of a few key pieces from their past sales.

Dr. Fred Bugg answered the first call I made on this project, and lent trains for the cover and other photographs.

Greg Stout of Stout Auctions, who arguably handles the largest train collections in the country, granted us unlimited access for photography, and as a result, saved many, many hours of work and miles of driving. His phenomenal knowledge and amazing memory were tremendous assets in this project.

A handful of collectors chose to remain anonymous. Their anonymity, however, does not lessen the value of their contributions of photographs and information to this work. Thank you.

OVERVIEW

CHAPTER 1
LIONEL TRAINS AND THE COLLECTING HOBBY

Lionel. Few brand names have the instantaneous recognition that Lionel enjoys early into its second century. Young or old, male or female, it seems almost everyone identifies the name with toy trains. In fact, to many people the two are synonymous.

The firm bears the middle name of its founder, Joshua Lionel Cohen, the son of immigrants, who was born Aug. 25, 1877. Young Cohen, a clever inventor and shameless self-promoter with a clear head for business, formed the company with Harry Grant on Sept. 5, 1900. Their first business was with the U.S. Navy, producing fuses for mines.

The Navy work completed, Cohen began tinkering, trying to find a product to keep he and his partner busy and his new company afloat. A motor he developed for a less-than-successful fan was installed under a gondola car. The car was placed on a circle of steel rails connected to dry cell batteries and, in 1900, the age of Lionel Electric Trains began.

As originally conceived the "train"—still only a motorized gondola car—was to be an animated window display for shopkeepers to use to promote other products. Immediately, though, it was apparent that there was more interest in the displays than the goods they held, and the transition from

merchandising aid to retail product was made.

In 1902, in addition to the gondola car, Lionel offered a miniature trolley, the first step towards realism. Like the gondola, the trolley ran on two-rail 2 7/8-inch gauge track. The first catalog was produced in 1900 and an American icon was born. Unfortunately, Cohen's partner Grant, though also a gifted inventor, was not a capable administrator. This led to a man joining the payroll who was arguably as influential to the company, and its trains, as Cohen himself; an Italian immigrant named Mario Caruso. Hired at age 18 as a laborer, Caruso rose to Secretary Treasurer, managing the company's factories, first in New York, then New Haven, followed by Newark—and ultimately the massive 15-acre Irvington plant—in a no-nonsense manner. Quality, production and cost control were always of great concern and skillfully balanced by Caruso.

In 1906, Lionel began producing trains that rolled on "Standard Gauge" track and, in 1915, this was supplemented by the smaller "0-gauge" trains. Though Lionel made forays into other sizes, namely 00 in 1938 and, after World War II, three attempts at HO, it was to be 0-gauge where Lionel ultimately rose to fame. It is also the predominate size of trains produced after World War II.

Price Guide Key: **VG** = Very Good, **EX** = Excellent, **LN** = Like New | *Values for each condition are in U.S. dollars.* | **Rarity** = Scale from 1-8 with 8 being the hardest to find.

7

During 1909, Lionel first used the slogan "Standard of the World," but it would be many years before the bold statement would become fact.

In 1910, for reasons unknown today, Cohen changed his last name to the one he is remembered by today, Cowen. A few years later, in 1918, the firm would change names as well, when the Lionel Manufacturing Company became The Lionel Corporation.

While toy train production continued in Lionel's plant during the First World War, alongside were defense products—after all, that is how the company was born—primarily signaling and navigational devices. This type of relationship would continue as long as The Lionel Corporation was in the manufacturing business during both war and peacetime.

In 1923, Lionel revamped its Standard Gauge offerings, replacing the somewhat realistic but dingy colors used previously with a veritable kaleidoscope of blues, greens, yellows and oranges…all augmented with bright brass, copper and nickel trim. These later trains constitute what is considered the classic era of Standard Gauge production.

The Great Depression was hard on Lionel, but harder on its competition. During the recession that preceded the Great Depression, Lionel, along with American Flyer, took over its bankrupt competitor Ives. In 1930, Lionel became the sole owner of Ives. Thirty-six years later, Lionel would take over American Flyer as well.

World War II would bring a halt to Lionel's toy production, with toy train production coming to a halt in June 1942. The Lionel plant, like countless others throughout the country, became totally devoted to manufacturing military products.

The complete cessation of train production for three years provided Lionel the opportunity to completely revamp its line. When production resumed in the fall of 1945, not only was Standard Gauge not mentioned, but the 0-gauge trains had newly designed trucks and couplers that were incompatible with the previous models and a newly designed plastic-bodied gondola car. Over the next few years, plastics would increasingly replace the previously used metals in Lionel's products.

Joshua Cowen resigned as Chairman of the Board at the end of 1958 and, less than a year later, sold his stock in the firm to a syndicate headed by his eccentric and controversial great-nephew, Roy Cohn.

Ultimately, in 1969, The Lionel Toy Corporation (as it had become known in 1965) exited the toy train business by licensing the name and selling the tooling to the Fundimensions Division of General Mills. Some production was moved immediately and, by the mid-1970s, Lionel trains

were no longer a presence in the huge Hillside plant.

With the exception of 1967, Lionel Trains have been, and are still, in production every year since 1945, and trains were available even in the bleak 1967. Today's Lionel trains have elaborate paint schemes and sophisticated electronics undreamed of at the dawn of the last century. Despite these advances they lack the mystique of the originals. Many of today's trains are manufactured as a collectible, to be displayed or operated. But rarely are they played with as Josh Cowen urged his young patrons. Perhaps it is memories of a small child remembering expectations of Christmases long ago, or sneaking the new catalog to school hidden in a tablet hoping to one day own that special item, that fuels today's interest in yesterday's toys. Countering what one may think by glancing at the prices in vintage catalogs, Lionel trains were always expensive, high-quality toys. They were built to last a lifetime and many have. Now that the baby boomers have reached adulthood, many of childhood's financial constraints are lifted—the toys of youthful dreams are at last within grasp.

COLLECTING

Toy train collectors are their own fraternity, eagerly welcoming new buffs who have a sincere interest in toy trains. Avail yourself of this knowledge base and friendship, no matter if you are an experienced collector or a rookie; something can always be learned. There is no substitute for experience in this hobby, as in any other. No book, no matter how complete, contains all the answers. Thousands of words and the best illustrations cannot equal the experience gained by holding a piece in your own hands. There is no finer place to do that than in the home of a friend and fellow collector. The piece that is not for sale can be examined unhurriedly, and questions answered honestly. It is an excellent preparation for seeking an item in the marketplace.

The advent of Internet auctions has been a boon for collectors in remote areas. But for those in more populous areas, there is no substitute for shopping in the company of fellow collectors at hobby shops and train shows, especially for the neophyte. Examining an item personally, with the counsel of more experienced collectors, is especially urged when purchasing expensive, often repaired or forged items.

However, after gaining some experience, working with a trusted and reputable train auction company can provide access to trains that may take years, or even decades, to acquire.

Enthusiasts have been collecting toy trains perhaps as long as they have been produced. In the United States, the largest and oldest collectors group is the Train Collectors Association (TCA). Founded in 1954 in Yardley, Pa., the group has grown to more than 31,000 members. An annual convention is held at various locations around the country each summer. Smaller, regional groups called Divisions and Chapters dot the nation. Twice each year, one such group,

L. MEHRAD MAYER

the Eastern Division, hosts the largest toy train show in the world. The York Fairgrounds, in York, Pa., becomes a veritable Mecca for the toy train buff, with several buildings encompassing more than 100,000 square feet of toy trains for sale, display or trade. Members of the TCA agree to abide by a code of conduct, assuring fair and honest dealings between members. The nationally recognized Grading Standards were developed by the TCA.

The TCA National Headquarters, and the associated National Toy Train Museum, is located in Strasburg, Pa. The Train Collectors Association can be reached at their Web site, www.traincollectors.org, or by writing to:

TRAIN COLLECTORS ASSOCIATION
P.O. Box 248
300 Paradise Lane
Strasburg, PA 17579
(717) 687-8623

The second-oldest organization is the Toy Train Operating Society, formed on the West Coast in 1966. Similar in style and purpose to the TCA, the bulk of the TTOS members and events traditionally have been in the West, but the group has been gradually spreading eastward. The TTOS can be contacted at:

TOY TRAIN OPERATING SOCIETY
25 W. Walnut St., Suite 308
Pasadena, CA 91103
Phone (626) 578-0673

One of the first, and certainly the largest, Lionel-specific clubs is the Lionel Collector's Club of America. Founded Aug. 1, 1970, by Jim Gates of Des Moines, Iowa, the organization has grown steadily since. The club was founded on the idea that collectors and operators of Lionel trains need an organization of their own. The club's mailing address is:

LCCA BUSINESS OFFICE
P.O. Box 479
La Salle, IL 61301-0479

The youngster of these groups is the Lionel Operating Train Society, or LOTS. Founded in 1979 by Larry Keller of Cincinnati, this club's purpose is providing a national train club for operators of Lionel trains and accessories. Like the others, it publishes magazines, swap-lists and a membership directory. LOTS can be reached at:

LOTS BUSINESS OFFICE
6376 West Fork Road
Cincinnati, OH 45247-5704

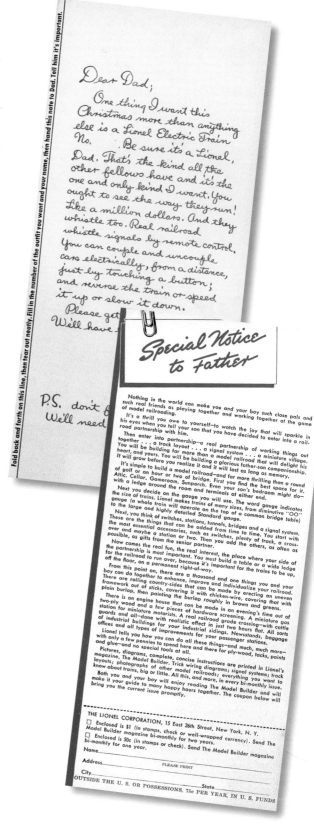

HOW TO USE

CHAPTER 2:
HOW TO USE THIS STANDARD CATALOG

This book is intended to aid both the novice and the experienced collector of Lionel products. The subject matter is broken down into groups: locomotives, freight and maintenance of way cars, passenger cars, accessories and others. Each group is then further broken down, such as steam locomotives and diesel locomotives. Within these subcategories, the items are arranged numerically by stock number. The stock number on the vast majority of Lionel's products was stamped either on the side or underside of the item.

Thus, if you pick up a Standard Gauge gondola car that is numbered 212, you can turn to the Standard Gauge gondola chapter and move through the listings until you reach the number 212. You will then find that this car was a Standard Gauge car produced from 1926 through 1940, and it was made in at least three distinct colors. Near most listings you will find a photo of the item described.

While Lionel produced many of these trains in distinct series, such as the 200- and 800-series freight cars, we have chosen to classify the trains by body type. A novice may not note the difference between a 10-series freight car and a 100-series freight car, but certainly will know the difference between a tank car and a caboose. The items are listed in numeric order in each chapter. The variations of each item are presented in chronological order, if known, or in increasing order of scarcity if the production sequence is unknown.

For items produced over a period of years, several details must be studied to accurately date each piece. Most of these dating clues involve the trucks and couplers on the cars, or boxes they were packaged in.

Lionel trains were built to provide a "lifetime of happiness," to quote one of the company's later advertising slogans; and with proper care they will do that and more. The first appendix contains tips on cleaning trains stored for years and properly preparing them for operation. Resist the temptation to simply pull them from the attic and put them on the track or grab the first household cleanser you find to clean them with. Either of these things could cause permanent, costly damage to an otherwise fine collectable and toy.

CONDITION AND RARITY

To the collector, condition is everything, and the Train Collector's Association, the world's oldest and largest train collector group, established very precise language for describing the condition of collectible trains in order to protect both the buyer and the seller. These standards have been used for so long by reputable dealers and collectors that their meaning is common knowledge in the hobby.

These grading standards are as follows:

Fair:
Well-scratched, chipped, dented, rusted, warped.

Good:
Small dents, scratches, dirty.

Very Good:
Few scratches, exceptionally clean, no major dents or rust.

Excellent:
Minute scratches or nicks, no dents or rust, all original, less than average wear.

Like New:
Only the slightest signs of handling and wheel wear, brilliant colors and crisp markings; literally like new. As a rule, Like New trains must have their original boxes in comparable condition to realize the prices listed in this guide.

Mint:
Brand new, absolutely unmarred, all original and unused. Items dusty or faded from display, or with fingerprints from handling, cannot be considered mint. Although Lionel test ran their locomotives briefly at the factory, items "test run" by consumers cannot be considered mint. Most collectors expect mint items to come with all associated packaging with which they were originally supplied.

As one can imagine, Mint pieces command premium prices. The supply is extremely limited, and the demand among collectors is great, so often the billfold of the buyer, rather than a more natural supply and demand situation, limits the price of such pieces.

In addition to the categories stated above, two other classifications are important in the toy train hobby: restored and reproduction.

Restored: A number of the trains found in the marketplace have been restored. The rugged steel construction of many of the items has insured that the item itself has survived, even if its brilliant enamel coating did not. Fortunately, many of these worn and scuffed items have been rescued from the trash bin, disassembled, stripped of their old finish and a new one applied. Coupled with mechanical repairs and polished or replaced brightwork, these items now shine with all their previous glory. Unfortunately, some of the more larcenous types of our society chose to represent these restored items as excellent condition originals—often painting them in the more desirable color combinations to boot. Under those circumstances, remember, it's not the train that is cheating, it's the seller.

No values are assigned in this book for restored items. The quality of restorations vary widely, ranging from spectroscopically matched paints applied to carefully stripped cars to "close enough" off the rack spray paints applied sometimes directly over the old paint. Also, some collectors loath restored items, no matter how well done, or how honestly marked as restored. These factors combine to make assigning values to restored items virtually impossible. Use your own judgment, and remember, no matter how scarce an original is in a given color, the value of a restored item is not affected by color.

Further, collecting prewar trains is becoming an old enough hobby that some early restorations are 50 years old, and have acquired a patina of their own. For neophytes contemplating a major purchase, it is extremely important that you have absolute confidence in the seller and, hopefully, the assistance of an experienced collector as well. If you are looking to add a specific item to your collection, it is extremely helpful to visit other collectors and carefully examine an original in advance. This will help you, much more than photos in this or any other book, know what an item should look like.

Reproduction: Reproductions allow enthusiasts to enjoy operating trains that otherwise they could not locate, could not afford or

would feel too risky to operate. A number of companies—Joe Mania Trains, Williams Reproductions, Kramer Reproductions, MTH and even Lionel itself—have built excellent reproductions of items from Lionel's prewar era. Their products are clearly, but discretely marked as reproductions. Unfortunately, other firms and individuals have reproduced items, particularly from Lionel's early years, without any indication that they are not of Lionel manufacture. These items are much more akin to being forgeries intended to deceive for great financial gain, rather than a reproduction built to permit enjoyment. None of the national train collecting organizations knowingly allow these items into their shows or meets, but occasionally they do slip in, as they often do at independent shows. Be especially wary of 2 7/8-inch items and early Standard Gauge—both prime areas for forgeries.

Values for forgeries are not given in this volume as they are worthless on the legitimate market.

Demand is one of the key factors influencing values. The postwar Santa Fe F-3 diesel was the most produced locomotive in Lionel's history, yet clean examples still command premium prices due to demand.

Rarity, or scarcity, is also a factor influencing the value of trains. Low production quantities or extreme fragility cause some items to be substantially more difficult to find than others. When scarcity is coupled with demand, the result is a premium price, while other items, extremely scarce, command only moderate prices due to lack of demand, or appreciation, on the part of collectors. In this guide we have rated each item on a scale of one to eight for rarity. One represents the most common items, such as the UTC lockon, while eight is assigned to those items hardest to find, such as the wooden 200 Electric Express gondola with Cowen's initials. It is hoped that this rarity rating will help the collector when having to choose which of similar priced items to buy by answering the proverbial "how likely am I to get this chance again?" question.

Supply, as a short-term extension of rarity, whether actual or temporary, also affects price. If only one sought after item is at a given show, the seller is unlikely to negotiate or reduce his price. If, however, multiple sellers at a given event have identical items, no matter how rare, the temporary market glut can bring about temporarily reduced prices.

Lastly, the **buyer's intent** will affect what he is willing to pay. A collector who intends to add a piece to their permanent collection will obviously pay more for an item than a dealer who is intending to resell the item.

Prices are given in this guide for trains in Good, Very Good and Excellent condition. Trains in less than Very Good condition are not generally considered collectible and Mint condition trains are too uncommon to establish pricing, as is the case for many prewar trains in Like New condition.

The prices listed are what a group of collectors would consider a reasonable market value when dealing at a train show or meet. Listed is a price they would be willing to pay to add that piece to their collections. When buying at a specialized train auction with Internet access, one can expect to pay more, as the pool of potential buyers is greater. The savings in fuel often offset this increased cost, by reducing lodging and time, that would otherwise be spent tracking a given item down, searching from show to show.

When contemplating a sale to a dealer, you should expect to receive 30 percent to 50 percent less than the value listed, with the poorer condition of the trains the greater the amount of discount, due to the greater difficulty the dealer will have selling them. Remember that these prices are only a guideline. You are spending your money. What an item is worth to you is of greater importance than what it is worth to the author. Conversely, the publisher does not sell trains, this is not a mail-order catalog and you should not expect a dealer or collector to "price match."

LIONEL BOXES

Lionel, like other manufacturers, boxed its products to ease handling and protect the trains en route and once at the market. They were strictly utilitarian, and throughout the prewar era, no thought was given to eye appeal. During the prewar era, it was intended that the trains be sold by attentive, trained salespeople. Self-service, and thus consumer-oriented packaging, was not in Lionel's marketing plan.

The box that most often comes to the mind's eye when thinking of Lionel trains is the traditional orange and blue box introduced just prior to World War II. However, from 1900 through 1942, Lionel used several types of boxes for its rolling stock. Most of these were comparatively drab. Scattered throughout this book are photos of selected pieces with their original packaging. Items produced over an extended period of time sometimes used a variety of boxes during their production run, so boxes for a given piece can legitimately vary from those shown in this book. Beware, however, that many unknowing (or uncaring) collectors and dealers often place items in the improper vintage box in an effort to "upgrade" the packaging.

One reason for this is that, relatively speaking, few boxes survive. The boxes, made of pasteboard, were more fragile than the sturdy trains and inherently would have a lower survival rate. Plus, people were buying TRAINS, not boxes, so many of the boxes went out with the trash Christmas morning. Even in the early days of collecting, boxes, especially set boxes and outer master cartons, were considered bulky nuisances and were thrown away. Today, any given box is scarcer than its intended contents, and clean trains in their original boxes command a premium price in the marketplace. Even the boxes themselves have developed a collector market, but remember, to be proper the box must be not only the same stock number, but also the same vintage as the train inside.

AIDS TO DATING TRAINS

Unlike certain other collectibles, the age of a Lionel train is not a factor in its value. That is, an older train is not inherently more valuable than a newer train. It is rather the variations in construction throughout an item's production run that affect its scarcity, and thus value. Some Lionel trains are marked on the sides with "New" or "Built" dates. These dates are totally irrelevant to when a piece was actually produced, and are decorative only.

Although a few collectors specialize in a specific year or two of Lionel production, they are the exception. Rather, establishing the production date of these trains is done more as a curiosity by most collectors, or when they are trying to properly and precisely recreate a given train set.

Among the key aids to dating trains are the construction techniques used in the manufacture of the trucks and couplers, and the type of original packaging used, if still present.

TRACK

Track forms the foundation of real and toy railroad

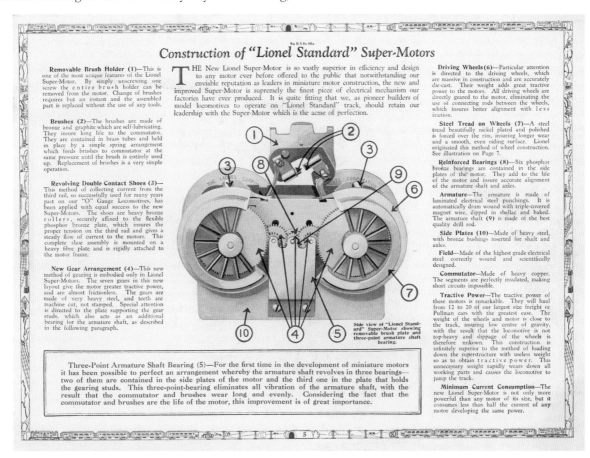

Construction of "Lionel Standard" Super-Motors

Removable Brush Holder (1)—This is one of the most unique features of the Lionel Super-Motor. By simply unscrewing one screw the entire brush holder can be removed from the motor. Change of brushes requires but an instant and the assembled part is replaced without the use of any tools.

Brushes (2)—The brushes are made of bronze and graphite which are self-lubricating. They insure longer life to the commutator. They are contained in brass tubes and held in place by a simple spring arrangement which feeds brushes to commutator at the same pressure until the brush is entirely used up. Replacement of brushes is a very simple operation.

Revolving Double Contact Shoes (3)—This method of collecting current from the third rail, so successfully used for many years past on our "O" Gauge Locomotives, has been applied with equal success to the new Super-Motors. The shoes are heavy bronze rollers, securely affixed to the flexible phosphor bronze plate, which insures the proper tension on the third rail and gives a steady flow of current to the motors. This complete shoe assembly is mounted on a heavy fibre plate and is rigidly attached to the motor frame.

New Gear Arrangement (4)—This new method of gearing is embodied only in Lionel Super-Motors. The seven gears in this new layout give the motor greater tractive power, and are almost frictionless. The gears are made of very heavy steel, and teeth are machine cut, not stamped. Special attention is directed to the plate supporting the gear studs, which also acts as an additional bearing for the armature shaft, as described in the following paragraph.

THE New Lionel Super-Motor is so vastly superior in efficiency and design to any motor ever before offered to the public that notwithstanding our enviable reputation as leaders in miniature motor construction, the new and improved Super-Motor is supremely the finest piece of electrical mechanism our factories have ever produced. It is quite fitting that we, as pioneer builders of model locomotives to operate on "Lionel Standard" track, should retain our leadership with the Super-Motor which is the acme of perfection.

Side view of "Lionel Standard" Super-Motor showing removable brush plate and three-point armature shaft bearing.

Driving Wheels (6)—Particular attention is directed to the driving wheels, which are massive in construction and are accurately die-cast. Their weight adds great tractive power to the motors. All driving wheels are directly geared to the motor, eliminating the use of connecting rods between the wheels, which insures better alignment with less friction.

Steel Tread on Wheels (7)—A steel tread beautifully nickel plated and polished is forced over the rim, insuring longer wear and a smooth, even riding surface. Lionel originated this method of wheel construction. See illustration on Page 7.

Reinforced Bearings (8)—Six phosphor bronze bearings are contained in the side plates of the motor. They add to the life of the motor and insure more accurate alignment of the armature shaft and axles.

Armature—The armature is made of laminated electrical steel punchings. It is automatically drum wound with triple-covered magnet wire, dipped in shellac and baked. The armature shaft (9) is made of the best quality drill rod.

Side Plates (10)—Made of heavy steel, with bronze bushings inserted for shaft and axles.

Field—Made of the highest grade electrical steel correctly wound and scientifically designed.

Commutator—Made of heavy copper. The segments are perfectly insulated, making short circuits impossible.

Tractive Power—The tractive power of these motors is remarkable. They will haul from 12 to 20 of our largest size freight or Pullman cars with the greatest ease. The weight of the wheels and motor is close to the track, insuring low centre of gravity, with the result that the locomotive is not top-heavy and slippage of the wheels is therefore unknown. This construction is infinitely superior to the method of loading down the superstructure with useless weight so as to obtain tractive power. This unnecessary weight rapidly wears down all working parts and causes the locomotive to jump the track.

Minimum Current Consumption—The new Lionel Super-Motor is not only more powerful than any motor of its size, but it consumes less than half the current of any motor developing the same power.

Three-Point Armature Shaft Bearing (5)—For the first time in the development of miniature motors it has been possible to perfect an arrangement whereby the armature shaft revolves in three bearings—two of them are contained in the side plates of the motor and the third one in the plate that holds the gearing studs. This three-point-bearing eliminates all vibration of the armature shaft, with the result that the commutator and brushes wear long and evenly. Considering the fact that the commutator and brushes are the life of the motor, this improvement is of great importance.

systems, so it is fitting that it also forms the basis for the principal sections of this book.

During the prewar era, Lionel produced four broad types of track systems. They were 2 7/8-inch gauge, Standard Gauge, 0 gauge and 00 gauge, and this book is divided accordingly.

The earliest was the 2 7/8-inch gauge two-rail track, which is described in the same-named chapter of this book. The other "odd" sized trackage was 00 gauge, which came in both two- and three-rail versions. Both are described in detail in the 00 chapter of this book.

The balance of Lionel's products operated on track with either 2 1/8" spacing between the rails or track with a 1 1/8" rail-to-rail spacing. The broader track, introduced to the product line in 1906, was dubbed Standard Gauge by Lionel.

The narrower track, referred to an 0 gauge, was first produced by Lionel in 1915 and came in a variety of styles. Initially, eight curved sections could be joined to form a circle 28 1/2" in diameter. In 1919, the radius of the track was increased, with a circle, still requiring eight sections, now 31 1/2" in diameter. Straight sections were 10 1/2" long.

When Lionel assimilated the former Ives product line into its line, with it came a smaller cross-sectioned, lighter weight track with a 27" diameter circle. Known alternately as Lionel-Ives, Winner or Lionel Junior track, ultimately

the moniker was bestowed by which it is still known today; 027. This size was even made in two-rail form for use with windup sets. Like the 0 gauge track, 027 track sections were connected by inserting steel pins protruding from one section into the hollow rails of the adjacent section.

In 1934, a wider-radius version of 0 gauge track was introduced. Known as 072, its broad curves lent themselves to the large streamlined passenger trains and scale-proportioned freight cars and locomotives that Lionel produced in the late 1930s and early 1940s. Sixteen of these curved sections were required to form a circle. Matching turnouts were produced, as well as 14" long straight sections for use with this track system.

The following year, Lionel introduced what was to be its finest trackage of the prewar era. Known as "T-rail," rather than the tubular cross section of the 0 and 027 tracks, which were formed from sheet metal, T-rail had solid steel rails that more closely resembled real railroad track. They were joined in a similar manner, with tiny fishplates being bolted to adjoining sections. T-rail straight and 72" diameter curved tracks, as well as turnouts, were offered through 1942. At that time their production, along with the rest of Lionel's train line, was interrupted by World War II. After the war, production of T-rail was not resumed.

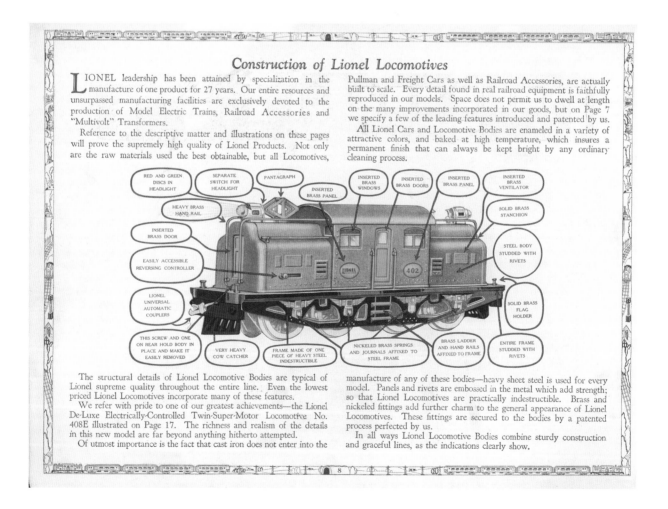

Construction of Lionel Locomotives

LIONEL leadership has been attained by specialization in the manufacture of one product for 27 years. Our entire resources and unsurpassed manufacturing facilities are exclusively devoted to the production of Model Electric Trains, Railroad Accessories and "Multivolt" Transformers.

Reference to the descriptive matter and illustrations on these pages will prove the supremely high quality of Lionel Products. Not only are the raw materials used the best obtainable, but all Locomotives,

Pullman and Freight Cars as well as Railroad Accessories, are actually built to scale. Every detail found in real railroad equipment is faithfully reproduced in our models. Space does not permit us to dwell at length on the many improvements incorporated in our goods, but on Page 7 we specify a few of the leading features introduced and patented by us.

All Lionel Cars and Locomotive Bodies are enameled in a variety of attractive colors, and baked at high temperature, which insures a permanent finish that can always be kept bright by any ordinary cleaning process.

The structural details of Lionel Locomotive Bodies are typical of Lionel supreme quality throughout the entire line. Even the lowest priced Lionel Locomotives incorporate many of these features.

We refer with pride to one of our greatest achievements—the Lionel De-Luxe Electrically-Controlled Twin-Super-Motor Locomotive No. 408E illustrated on Page 17. The richness and realism of the details in this new model are far beyond anything hitherto attempted.

Of utmost importance is the fact that cast iron does not enter into the

manufacture of any of these bodies—heavy sheet steel is used for every model. Panels and rivets are embossed in the metal which add strength; so that Lionel Locomotives are practically indestructible. Brass and nickeled fittings add further charm to the general appearance of Lionel Locomotives. These fittings are secured to the bodies by a patented process perfected by us.

In all ways Lionel Locomotive Bodies combine sturdy construction and graceful lines, as the indications clearly show.

HOW TO USE THIS STANDARD CATALOG
REFERENCE EXAMPLE

1. →

3. →

2. → **9E (Type II):** The orange 0-B-0 was also produced with the
4. → Bild-A-Loco motor, which was retained by two quick-release
levers.

5. →

VG	EX	LN	RARITY
600	850	1200	6

A.   B.   C.   D.

1.) Photo: In some listings, photos are supplied to better help identify and verify what Model and Type you possess.

2.) Listing Name/Type: Items will be listed by Model number and Variation number (Type).

3.) Photo Indicator: Items with a [icon] icon, indicates that this listing is accompanied by a photo. If the image is not directly above its given listing, it will more times than not be in an enlarged two-column format or on the following page.

4.) Listing Description: Located directly after the Listing Name/Type is a brief description of the listing, giving vital information to better help identification.

5.) Values Table: Below the Listing Description is the Values Table. Values for each condition are in U.S. Dollars.

Note: To better assist you, located on the bottom of every right hand page is a quick reference on how to use the Values Table.

A.) VG=*Very Good:* Few scratches, exceptionally clean, no major dents or rust.

B.) EX=*Excellent:* Minute scratches or nicks, no dents or rust, all original, less than average wear.

C.) LN=*Like New:* Only the slightest signs of handling and wheel wear, brilliant colors and crisp markings; literally like new. As a rule, Like New trains must have their original boxes in comparable condition to realize the prices listed in this guide.

D.) Rarity: On a scale of 1-8, this system will assess the accessibility and rarity of the particular listing. On occasion, an item may be so rare that there is not enough reference to place a price or rarity.

2 7/8-INCH GAUGE
OVERVIEW

When Lionel entered production of electric trains in 1901, it chose a track system with 2 7/8-inch spacing between the rails. Though bulky and crude by later standards, these trains were the foundation upon which the miniature railroad dynasty was built.

The track itself was made up of individual wooden crossties, routed to accept bands of steel that acted as the rails. Setup was considerably more time-consuming and awkward than that of later sectional track systems such as Standard and 0 Gauges. This was due not only to the infancy of Lionel's toy train production, but also to its original market–store window displays in retailers of other wares. Rather than a toy, the trains were to be merchandising aids – attention getters–for other products such as jewelry. Thus, they were expected to be set up and remain in place for some time, with the assembly done by adults.

By 1905, Lionel trains were becoming firmly entrenched as toys, and this was the final year 2 7/8-inch gauge trains were offered. Today, the early trains listed in this chapter are among the most difficult to find, and the most valuable trains of the prewar era. This has led to not only reproductions, but in some cases outright forgeries. Some of these reproductions are illustrated, along with their identifying marks.

These trains have been collectable since WWII, and reproductions have been produced for over 40 years. To inexperienced collectors, the patina of forty years aging resembles that of 100 years, especially when "enhanced" by unscrupulous sellers. Use extreme care when considering purchasing one of these items.

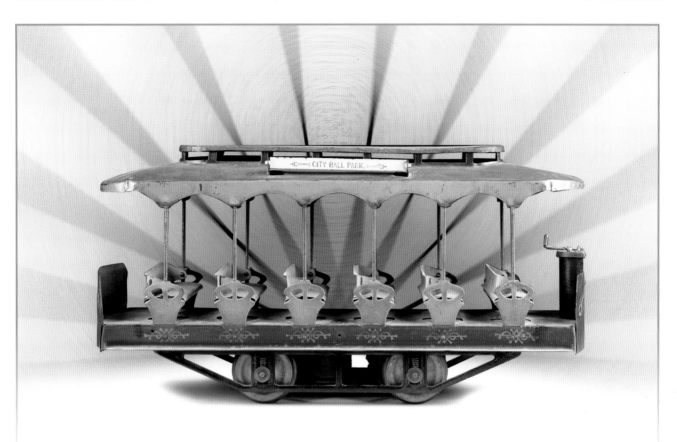

CHAPTER 3
2 7/8-INCH GAUGE

The 2 7/8-inch gauge trains described in this chapter are the roots from which the Lionel Corporation grew. The wooden 200 Gondola was the first electric train produced by Lionel, and it seems in this instance that means produced by Joshua Lionel Cowen himself, as the underside of some existing examples bear his initials in his own hand. All of the items in this chapter are extraordinarily rare; in some cases all known examples can be counted on the fingers of one hand. For this reason, rarity ratings are not included. Similarly, the pricing given for these items could be more accurately described as an estimate than as a result of experience as in the other chapters. These items rarely turn up at auction, almost never at train meets. Finding a buyer tends to amount to calling one of the leading collectors and offering the item for sale. Because of this, current pricing tends not to be widely known or public information.

Because of their extreme rarity, reproductions have been made by a variety of firms. Most of these are conspicuously marked as such by conscientious manufacturers, but some unscrupulous buyers attempt to alter them in order to represent them as authentic. So few exist that finding a knowledgeable collector to render an informed opinion is problematic.

Compounding this is the largely hand-crafted nature of many of these early items, leading to an inordinate number of variations. Because of the unique nature of 2 7/8-inch gauge collecting, the appropriate accessories are also listed in this chapter.

100 ELECTRIC LOCOMOTIVE: This was Lionel's attempt to create an authentic-looking replica of a GE LE-2 electric locomotive. The real locomotives were built for the B&O railroad to pull trains through tunnels beneath Baltimore. The 10 1/2" long, 4 1/4", and 6 5/8" tall number 100 appeared in the Lionel catalog from 1903 through 1905. Lionel's model always had "No. 5" stamped on its sides and ends, the number of one of the real locomotives.

Shown here is a reproduction made be Joe Mania Trains. Reproductions by this firm are carefully and permanently marked to avoid confusion with an original item. Others have made reproductions with removable identification, and still others have produced unmarked fraudulent pieces. Beware.

Price Guide Key: **VG** = Very Good, **EX** = Excellent, **LN** = Like New | *Values for each condition are in U.S. dollars.* | **Rarity** = Scale from 1-8 with 8 being the hardest to find.

17

100 ELECTRIC LOCOMOTIVE (Type I): It is believed the body of the earliest Lionel production was painted light green along with the roof, and mounted on a black-painted cast-iron frame. "B. & O." and "No. 5" were rubber-stamped in gold on both sides, with the number repeated on the ends. A simulated motorman's controller was installed inside the cab on one end, and it had gold-painted trim on it. The locomotive's two-inch diameter wheels were made of either hollow brass or cast-iron and turned in rectangular journals. "LIONEL MFG. CO. / N.Y." was pressed into the floor and is visible on the locomotive's underside. No screws were used to mount the body to the frame, and the reversing switch has tabs.

VG	EX	LN	RARITY
7000	21000	35000	—

100 ELECTRIC LOCOMOTIVE (Type II): Another early version of the electric locomotive was identical in construction to the Type I, but maroon paint replaced the light green on the cab sides, while the roof was now painted black.

VG	EX	LN	RARITY
7000	21000	35000	—

100 ELECTRIC LOCOMOTIVE (Type III): Fairly early in production the assembly process was changed, with the maroon and black body now being attached to the frame with machine screws. Apparently, at the same time, a new style reversing switch was introduced, which was circular and lacked the tabs of the earlier switch.

VG	EX	LN	RARITY
5000	16500	30000	—

100 ELECTRIC LOCOMOTIVE (Type IV): Near the end of production, the lettering was changed from gold to black.

VG	EX	LN	RARITY
5000	16500	30000	—

Shown here is a reproduction made be Joe Mania Trains. Reproductions by this firm are carefully and permanently marked to avoid confusion with an original item. Others have made reproductions with removable identification, and still others have produced unmarked fraudulent pieces. Beware.

100 ELECTRIC LOCOMOTIVE (Type V): Listed as a component of the number 700 Special Show Window Display cataloged in 1903-05, this version of the number 100 was supposed to have a phosphor-bronze mechanism and a nickel-plated body. No original examples have surfaced, however Lionel sales records indicate that sales of the 700 Window Display were made. Like the other versions of the 100, reproductions of this have been produced.

RARITY
No known examples.

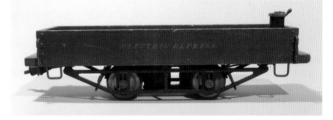

The upper photo above shows the original Lionel product, while the lower photo shows a properly marked reproduction made by Joe Mania Trains. This firm's reproductions are carefully and permanently marked, but beware, others have made unmarked reproductions.

200 GONDOLA (Type I): 🚃 A 15 1/8" long wooden-bodied motorized gondola was cataloged in 1901 only. It was 4 1/2" wide and 4 1/8" tall. The wooden body with mortise-and-tenon corners was stained red and lettered "Electric Express" in gold along both sides. The body was mounted on a cast-iron frame and the axles turned in round journals. An embossed aluminum tag tacked to the underside of the car read "MFG. BY - LIONEL MFG. CO. - NEW YORK". A simulated motorman's controller was installed inside the body at one end.

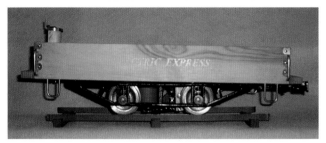

The upper photo above shows the original Lionel product, while the lower photo shows a properly marked reproduction made by Joe Mania Trains. This firm's reproductions are carefully and permanently marked, but beware, others have made unmarked reproductions.

200 GONDOLA (Type II): When the 1902 Lionel catalog appeared, the 200 gondola had grown to 17 1/2" long. The height and width, however, remained the same as in 1901. Its wooden body was now stained brown with gold "ELECTRIC EXPRESS" lettering on both sides. The corners now had brass reinforcements. The body was mounted on a cast-iron frame, and the axles turned in round journals. An embossed aluminum tag tacked to the underside of the car read "MFG. BY - LIONEL MFG. CO. - NEW YORK". A simulated motorman's controller was installed inside the body at one end.

VG	EX	LN	RARITY
15000	21000	35000	—

200 GONDOLA (Type III): When the 200 gondola returned in 1903, rather than having a wooden body it had an all-new steel body. Finished in apple green, the body was mounted on a cast iron frame painted black. The car was 12 1/4" long, 4 1/2" wide and 4 1/8" tall. Gold-painted handrails and steps were mounted on each corner and, in addition to the prominent "B. & O." lettering on both sides, there was also the marking "CAPACITY 80,000 LBS." rubber-stamped on the left lower corners of the sides. The legend "WEIGHT 35,000 LBS" appeared on the right lower corners of each side as well. Two vertical ribs were formed into either side of the body, and "LIONEL MFG. CO. - N.Y." was embossed into the bottom of the car.

VG	EX	LN	RARITY
8000	10000	15000	—

200 GONDOLA (Type IV): In late 1903 or possibly 1904, the metal-bodied self-propelled gondola underwent some changes. The body lost its ribs, "B. & O." was replaced with "LAKE SHORE" in gold lettering and the "35000 LBS." marking lost its comma.

VG	EX	LN	RARITY
8000	15000	25000	—

Shown here is a reproduction made be Joe Mania Trains. Reproductions by this firm are carefully and permanently marked to avoid confusion with an original item. Others have made reproductions with removable identification, and still others have produced unmarked fraudulent pieces. Beware.

200 GONDOLA (Type V): In late 1904 or early 1905, the motorized gondola was changed once again. Now, rather than green, the body was painted maroon with gold trim.

VG	EX	LN	RARITY
8000	15000	25000	—

This Converse push-toy trolley was the basis for Lionel's 300 series cars. Lionel purchased these bodies and installed their own mechanisms.

300 ELECTRIC TROLLEY CAR: The 300 trolley, along with the 200 gondola, were the first two electric trains offered by Lionel. Both appear in the 1901 Lionel catalog. The 300 remained in the catalog through 1905. The trolley utilized a body made by Morton E. Converse and Company. Converse offered its blue and yellow trolley as a push toy prior to the body being adopted by Lionel. Bodies purchased by Lionel were painted pea green, with maroon roof and ends and cream-colored trim. "CITY HALL PARK" and "175" were marked in yellow on both ends of the trolley. The reversible destination boards were marked "UNION DEPOT" and "CITY HALL PARK" in red or black on white backgrounds. Six seats were provided in the car, and they were actually reversible just like on real trolleys. A cast iron frame and wooden subbase supported the 16 1/2" long trolley. Most cars have an embossed aluminum

Price Guide Key: **VG** = Very Good, **EX** = Excellent, **LN** = Like New | *Values for each condition are in U.S. dollars.* | **Rarity** = Scale from 1-8 with 8 being the hardest to find.

19

plate tacked to the underside of the car reading "MFG. BY - LIONEL MFG. CO. - NEW YORK".

300 ELECTRIC TROLLEY CAR (Type I): It is believed the 1901 production trolleys included the 6" stamped-steel trolley pole that Converse used on its windup and push toy models. A string and hook were provided to secure the pole in the down position.

VG	EX	LN	RARITY
8000	10000	15000	—

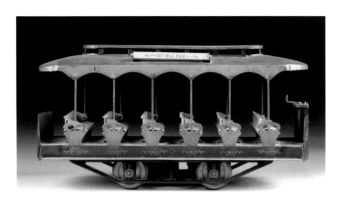

300 ELECTRIC TROLLEY CAR (Type II): From 1902 through 1903, the trolley was as described previously, only without the trolley pole.

VG	EX	LN	RARITY
5000	6500	10000	—

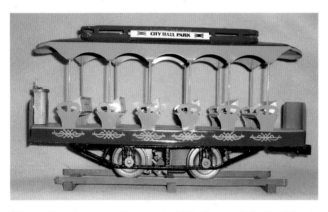

Shown here is a reproduction 300 Trolley made by Joe Mania Trains. This firm's reproductions are carefully and permanently marked as such, but beware, others have made unmarked reproductions.

300 ELECTRIC TROLLEY CAR (Type III): Beginning in 1904 and continuing until discontinued the next year, the 300 trolley was equipped with coupler pockets, enabling it to tow the unpowered 309 Trolley Trailer, which was introduced in 1904.

VG	EX	LN	RARITY
5000	6500	10000	—

301 BATTERIES: Home electric service was not common in the early years of the 20th century. For this reason, Lionel listed sets of four dry cell batteries in its 1903-05 catalogs. "Everbest Dry Cell" batteries were shown in the 1903 catalog; in 1904 the type changed to "Eastern dry cell No. 3" and in 1905, the "Climax Dry Cell" was shown.

RARITY
No known surviving examples.

302 PLUNGE BATTERY: Offered in 1901 and 1902, the plunge battery was described in the latter catalog as four glass jars containing a carbon cylinder and pencil-shaped zinc in a wood box. Water and three pounds of "electric sand" charged the four cells, which were connected in series.

RARITY
No known surviving examples.

303 CARBON CYLINDERS: This electrical component was listed in the 1902 catalog.

RARITY
No known surviving examples.

304 COMPOSITE ZINCS: This electrical component was listed in the 1902 catalog.

RARITY
No known surviving examples.

305 ELECTRIC SAND: This electrical component was listed in the 1902 catalog.

RARITY
No known surviving examples.

306 GLASS JARS: This electrical component was listed in the 1902 catalog.

RARITY
No known surviving examples.

309 ELECTRIC TROLLEY TRAILER: Introduced in 1904 and discontinued the following year, the 309 was a non-motorized companion to the 300. It was equipped with coupler pockets and cast-iron wheels.

VG	EX	LN	RARITY
8000	10000	15000	—

310 TRACK (Type I): The track available in 1901 and 1902 can best be described as primitive, and is the only Lionel track that can be truly termed rare. Loose tinplated straight steel rails about 13 3/8" long were furnished with wooden cross ties. The rails, which were all straight, were 3/8" high and 1/16" wide. The crossties were actually made of wood and stained red. They were 4" long, 1" wide, and 1/16" tall. Grooves were cut across the ties 2 7/8" apart to accept the rails.

Brass plates on the outer two of the five ties per "section" were equipped with brass plates that provided electrical contact to the next section. A tack held each brass plate in place. Curved track was created by bending the rails, then trimming the inner rail to the proper length.

RARITY
Too rarely, if ever, traded to establish market pricing.

310 TRACK (Type II): From 1903 through 1905, an improved version of the 2 7/8-inch gauge track was offered. Still assembled from component parts by the owner, it was now packaged as 24 tinplated steel rails with 60 wooden cross ties. Still 3/8" tall and 1/16" wide, the rails were shortened to about 12" long. The crossties were natural wood color and wood 4" long, 1/2" wide, and 1/2" tall. The ties continued to be routed to accept the steel rails.

The ends of the rails were now bent to form hooks that engaged abutting rail sections. The rails were now furnished in two different lengths, eliminating the need for the owner to trim the inner rail on curves to length, although the curve itself still had to be manually formed.

VG	EX	LN	RARITY
75	125	200	—

320 SWITCH AND SIGNAL: From 1902 through 1905, this 17 1/2" long turnout was marketed. A working cast iron switch stand was included, with red and white signal targets. A single lever moved both the points and the target, just as on a real turnout.

> **RARITY**
> Too rarely, if ever, traded to establish market pricing.

330 CROSSING: This 90-degree crossover was cataloged from 1902 through 1905. It mated with the Type II 310 track, and had a square solid base rather than individual crossties.

> **RARITY**
> Too rarely, if ever, traded to establish market pricing.

340 SUSPENSION BRIDGE: This hard to find 24" long bridge was sold unassembled during 1902-05. It was of cast iron and wooden construction. "LIONEL MFG. CO. — NEW YORK" was cast into the beams forming the top of the sides. Numbers to aid in assembly were also cast into the side members.

340 SUSPENSION BRIDGE (Type I): The 1902 edition of the 340 was 10" high, and the beams above the ends of the bridge were straight. The bridge was 6" wide.

> **RARITY**
> Too rarely, if ever, traded to establish market pricing.

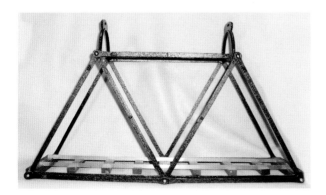

Shown here is a reproduction made be Joe Mania Trains. Reproductions by this firm are carefully and permanently marked to avoid confusion with an original item. Others have made reproductions with removable identification, and still others have produced unmarked fraudulent pieces. Beware.

340 SUSPENSION BRIDGE (Type II): From 1903-05; the height of the bridge was increased to 14" high in order to clear the derrick car. The beams over the ends of the bridge were arched on this version to permit greater clearance. The bridge continued to be 6" wide.

> **RARITY**
> Too rarely, if ever, traded to establish market pricing.

350 BUMPER: From 1902 through 1905, this end of track bumper was offered. Styled after bumpers found in contemporary big city terminals, it was about 4" tall and 4" long, and stood about 3" tall.

350 BUMPER (Type I): The 1902 edition came with a crosstie to be used instead of the normal end tie of the adjoining track. The new tie did not include the brass contact plate, creating an electrically dead section of track in order to stop the train.

> **RARITY**
> Too rarely, if ever, traded to establish market pricing.

Shown here is a reproduction made be Joe Mania Trains. Reproductions by this firm are carefully and permanently marked to avoid confusion with an original item. Others have made reproductions with removable identification, and still others have produced unmarked fraudulent pieces. Beware.

350 BUMPER (Type II): From 1903 through 1905, the bumper came pre-installed on a short straight section of track. Rather than insulating this section, a spring-loaded striker was incorporated to cushion the blow of the stopping train.

Price Guide Key: **VG** = Very Good, **EX** = Excellent, **LN** = Like New | *Values for each condition are in U.S. dollars.* | **Rarity** = Scale from 1-8 with 8 being the hardest to find.

21

370 JARS AND PLATES: During 1902 and 1903, Lionel offered a wet-cell battery consisting of two glass jars containing lead plates and electrolytes.

RARITY
No known surviving examples.

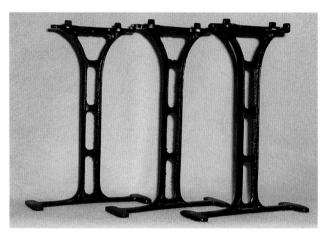

380 ELEVATED PILLARS: In 1904-05, Lionel sold 8 1/2" tall cast iron posts, with 12 in a set, to be used in creating an elevated railway. Hardware was included with which to attach the wooden 2 7/8-inch gauge crossties to the pillars.

VG	EX	LN	RARITY
450	850	1200	—

400 EXPRESS TRAILER CAR: From 1903-05, a non-motorized version of the 200 Electric Express gondola was offered as well.

400 EXPRESS TRAILER CAR (Type I): The 1903 trailers naturally were constructed to match the powered 200 cars built the same year, described earlier as the Type III.

VG	EX	LN	RARITY
6000	8000	12000	—

400 EXPRESS TRAILER CAR (Type II): As the 200 evolved in 1903-04, as described earlier as Type IV, so did the non-powered trailer.

VG	EX	LN	RARITY
6000	8000	12000	—

400 EXPRESS TRAILER CAR (Type III): When the final changes were made to the 200 in 1904-05, the 400 mimicked them.

VG	EX	LN	RARITY
5000	7000	12000	—

400 EXPRESS TRAILER CAR (Type IV): Cataloged in 1904-05 as part of the number 700 Special Show Window Display, this variation was to have had a nickeled body with "LAKE SHORE" lettering. No examples have surfaced, but sales records indicate that some of the Special Window Displays were sold.

RARITY
No known examples.

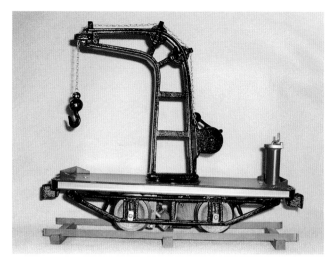

Shown here is a reproduction made be Joe Mania Trains. Reproductions by this firm are carefully and permanently marked to avoid confusion with an original item. Others have made reproductions with removable identification, and still others have produced unmarked fraudulent pieces. Beware.

500 ELECTRIC DERRICK CAR: This 12 1/4" long motorized flatcar had a manually operated cast derrick installed on its floor. Its cast iron frame was painted black, and its body was maroon and black with gold trim. "LIONEL MFG. — N.Y." was embossed on the bottom of the car. Due to the derrick, this car was a whopping 11 1/2" tall. A coupler pocket was installed on each end.

VG	EX	LN	RARITY
10000	13000	15000	—

600 DERRICK TRAILER: All 2 7/8-inch gauge items are hard to find, but this piece, offered in 1903 and 1904, seems to be especially difficult. It is essentially a non-motorized version of the 500.

Shown here is a reproduction made be Joe Mania Trains. Reproductions by this firm are carefully and permanently marked to avoid confusion with an original item. Others have made reproductions with removable identification, and still others have produced unmarked fraudulent pieces. Beware.

600 DERRICK TRAILER (Type I): The 1903 version appears to have been painted apple green with gold trim.

VG	EX	LN	RARITY
7500	10000	15000	—

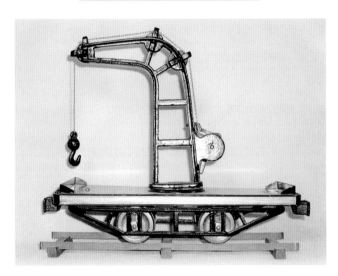

Shown here is a reproduction 600 Derrick made by Joe Mania Trains. This firm's reproductions are carefully and permanently marked as such, but beware, others have made unmarked reproductions.

600 DERRICK TRAILER (Type II): In 1904, the car was maroon and black with gold trim, like the powered version.

VG	EX	LN	RARITY
10000	14000	20000	—

700 SPECIAL SHOW WINDOW DISPLAY: Listed in Lionel's catalogs from 1903 through 1905, this special outfit was intended for use by retailers. It was to have included special nickel versions of the 100 Electric Locomotive and 400 Trailer. The mechanism of the locomotive was to be made

from phosphor-bronze. Also to be included in the outfit was a 340 Suspension Bridge and 24 feet of track. It carried the huge price of $25.

RARITY
No known examples.

The upper photo above shows the original Lionel product, while the lower photo shows a properly marked reproduction made by Joe Mania Trains. This firm's reproductions are carefully and permanently marked, but beware, others have made unmarked reproductions.

800 BOXCAR: Sometimes referred to by collectors as "jail cars" because of their unique bodies, these cars, as well as their unpowered 900 companions, were available in 1904 and 1905. The 14 1/2" long motorized boxcar had opening doors and a steel body painted maroon with a black roof and frame. Gold-painted doorknobs and bars on the windows trimmed the piece. "METROPOLITAN EXPRESS" was lettered on the side in black or gold, with the two words separated by the door. "Lionel" does not appear anywhere on the car.

VG	EX	LN	RARITY
5000	8000	10000	—

900 BOX TRAIL CAR: Also offered 1904-05 was this matching non-powered companion to the 800.

VG	EX	LN	RARITY
4000	7000	9000	—

1000 PASSENGER CAR: Introduced in 1905, the final year for Lionel's 2 7/8-inch gauge production, this 14 3/4" long trolley was maroon with a black roof and frame. In part due to its

Price Guide Key: **VG** = Very Good, **EX** = Excellent, **LN** = Like New | *Values for each condition are in U.S. dollars.* | **Rarity** = Scale from 1-8 with 8 being the hardest to find.

23

one-year production run, this car, and its matching trailer the 1050, are among the most difficult of the big trains to find. "Lionel" does not appear anywhere on the car, which has cast-iron wheels and frame. Examples have been found both with and without a factory-installed trolley pole.

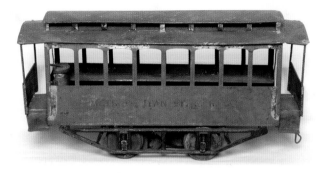

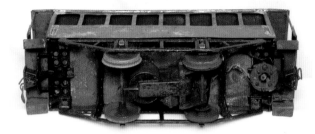

In the top two photos is shown an original, while the lower photo shows an excellent reproduction made by Joe Mania Trains.

1000 PASSENGER CAR (Type I): As shown in the catalog, the 1000 was lettered "METROPOLITAN ST. R. R. Co." in gold on both sides and on both ends.

VG	EX	LN	RARITY
8000	11000	15000	—

1000 PASSENGER CAR (Type II): A version was also produced in a brighter red with gold lettering reading "PHILADELPHIA R. T. CO."

VG	EX	LN	RARITY
9000	12000	16500	—

1000 PASSENGER CAR (Type III): A second uncataloged version was produced with "MARYLAND ST. RY. Co." on both sides in gold, and "BROADWAY" in gold on its ends.

VG	EX	LN	RARITY
8000	11000	15000	—

1050 PASSENGER CAR TRAILER: Also produced in 1905 was this non-powered matching companion to the 1000.

1050 PASSENGER CAR TRAILER (Type I): As shown in the catalog, the 1050 was lettered "METROPOLITAN ST. R. R. Co." in gold on both sides and on both ends.

VG	EX	LN	RARITY
9000	12000	16500	—

1050 PASSENGER CAR TRAILER (Type II): A version was also produced in a brighter red with gold lettering reading "PHILADELPHIA R. T. CO."

VG	EX	LN	RARITY
9000	12000	16500	—

1050 PASSENGER CAR TRAILER (Type III): A second uncataloged version was produced with "MARYLAND ST. RY. Co." on both sides in gold, and "BROADWAY" in gold on its ends.

VG	EX	LN	RARITY
9000	12000	16500	—

STANDARD GAUGE
OVERVIEW

Introduced in 1906, Standard Gauge offered two considerable advantages over the previously offered 2 7/8-inch gauge. Foremost was sectional track. This allowed the train display to be quickly and easily assembled and disassembled without tools, and by children. The second advantage was in its more compact size, measuring 2 1/8-inches between the rails. Perhaps the most obvious change, however, was the addition of the center third rail, which would remain a hallmark of Lionel trains to this day.

This third rail, while in most instances unrealistic, greatly simplified the operation of the trains, and permitted the creation of elaborate track layouts without the additional polarity reversing circuitry required of two-rail electric trains. First dubbed two-inch gauge in Lionel literature, in 1909, in a stroke of marketing genius, the new trackage began to be referred to as "Standard Gauge"–creating in the mind of the public the impression that anything else was substandard, or abnormal.

In time, both Ives and Chicago (later American) Flyer built trains that ran on 2 1/8-inch gauge track, but trademark law prevented the makers from referring to them as Standard Gauge. Lionel ceased producing Standard Gauge trains in 1940.

While when it was introduced Standard Gauge was a smaller size, in time these trains are viewed as large. When hefting one of these trains it is difficult to imagine that items of such mass were sold as children's toys. These factors lead to Lionel supplementing, and ultimately supplanting, Standard Gauge trains with 0 Gauge.

CHAPTER 4
STEAM LOCOMOTIVES

Steam locomotive replicas were first produced by Lionel in 1905. Previously, self-propelled rail cars, trolleys and reproductions of electric locomotives had provided the motive power. The early locomotives, 5, 6 and 7, had numerous wooden parts and were equipped with manual reverse mechanisms.

About 1929, Lionel began to make extensive use of die-cast components for its locomotives. Boiler fronts, frames and wheels were commonly made of die-cast zinc alloys. Unfortunately, die-casting technology at this time was in its infancy. The hazards of allowing impurities in the alloy slurry were not fully recognized until years later. The presence of these impurities is evidenced by swelling, warping and decaying castings. Longtime collectors have seen pieces destroyed over time, literally on their display shelves. This problem is so widespread that it is considered the norm to expect to have to replace the drive wheels on locomotives of this period, and it is not considered abnormal to have to replace the other die-cast components as well. While a premium is sometimes paid for pieces with their original components intact and undamaged, this is always approached with some apprehension, as this deterioration could still surface.

5: The 5 was introduced in 1906, and remained in the line through 1909. It had a 0-4-0 wheel arrangement and did not come with a tender, although the 5 Special, later known as the 51, did. The locomotives had blued steel boilers with turned wood boiler fronts, domes and smokestacks.

5 (Type I): In 1906-07, the 5 was rubber-stamped "N.Y.C. & H.R.R." Its headlight was non-functional, and at the rear of the locomotive was a large coal bunker. The driving wheels had thin rims and the locomotive was built on a two-piece frame.

VG	EX	LN	RARITY
800	1000	1200	5

5 (Type II): The next two years of production, 1908-1909, added a third R to the herald, becoming "N.Y.C. & H.R.R.R."

VG	EX	LN	RARITY
1000	1200	1500	6

5 (Type III): This engine is also known to exist with "B. & O. R.R." markings.

VG	EX	LN	RARITY
1500	1900	2500	8

5 (Type IV): "PENNSYLVANIA" was rubber-stamped on some examples of this engine.

VG	EX	LN	RARITY
1400	1800	2300	8

5 (Type V): In 1910, there were several changes made to the 5. It now had a one-piece frame, thin-rimmed drivers and an operating headlight. The "N.Y.C. & H.R.R.R." lettering was continued.

VG	EX	LN	RARITY
700	950	1350	7

5 (Type VI): The next year saw further electrical changes made as a terminal was added to the coal bunker to allow a feeder to illuminate passenger cars to be connected. The markings on the locomotive remained "N.Y.C. & H.R.R.R."

VG	EX	LN	RARITY
700	950	1350	7

5 (Type VII): In 1912, the locomotive began to be built with thick-rimmed drive wheels. It continued with these type rims and "N.Y.C. & H.R.R.R." rubber-stamped markings through 1920.

VG	EX	LN	RARITY
700	900	1100	6

5 Special: Initially the 5 Special was identical to the 5 but for the addition of a small tender. In fact, on these early models the box is required to positively identify which model of locomotive is being examined. Later, the coal bunker was eliminated from the 5 Special. Ultimately, in 1912, the 5 Special was assigned a new catalog number; 51.

5 Special (Type I): From 1906 though 1909, the 5 Special was rubber-stamped "N.Y.C. & H.R.R.R." Though it came with a tender, the locomotive itself continued to have an integral coal bunker. Despite catalog claims of authenticity, the slope-back tender looked almost ridiculous, with its single truck failing to stabilize its body properly.

VG	EX	LN	RARITY
1100	1300	1600	7

5 Special (Type II): Almost as if to add insult to injury, the 5 Special was also sold with a single-truck tender rubber-stamped "B. & O. R.R." despite the fact the locomotive continued to be lettered "N.Y.C. & H.R.R.R."

VG	EX	LN	RARITY
1100	1300	1600	7

5 Special (Type III): Aesthetically, the 1910 5 Special was a great improvement over the previous editions. Its tender was significantly larger and rode on two trucks rather than one. Embossed in the floor of the tender was "LIONEL MFG. CO." The flanks of the tender were rubber-stamped "N.Y.C. & H.R.R.R." to match the sides of the locomotive cab.

VG	EX	LN	RARITY
1100	1300	1600	7

5 Special (Type IV): The improved Special and tender were also produced with "PENNSYLVANIA" markings.

VG	EX	LN	RARITY
1100	1300	1600	7

5 Special: From 1912 through 1923, the locomotive and tender combination, which through 1911 was cataloged as the 5 Special, was renumbered as the 51. Additional production is listed in this volume accordingly.

6: The 4-4-0 wheel arrangement, known as the American, was in widespread use near the beginning of the 20th century. Not surprisingly then, Lionel chose to base a toy on this style locomotive. Measuring with its tender 18" long, the 6 was a much better looking locomotive than was the 5. It was a part of the Lionel product line from 1906 through 1923.

6 (Type I): When first built, these locomotives had thin-rimmed drivers and a split frame. Their pilot wheels and pilots were made of cast iron, and their headlights were non-operating.

Price Guide Key: **VG** = Very Good, **EX** = Excellent, **LN** = Like New | *Values for each condition are in U.S. dollars.* | **Rarity** = Scale from 1-8 with 8 being the hardest to find.

27

STEAM LOCOMOTIVE

6 TYPE III

The boiler was blued steel. Rubber-stamped lettering on the cab and tender read "N.Y.C. & H.R.R.R."

VG	EX	LN	RARITY
600	1000	1600	6

6 (Type II): In 1908, an operating headlight replaced the dummy headlight previously used. "N.Y.C. & H.R.R.R." continued to be rubber-stamped on the loco and tender.

VG	EX	LN	RARITY
600	1000	1600	6

6 (Type III):  Other locomotives and tenders were produced rubber-stamped "PENNSYLVANIA". Other than the markings, these were identical to the Type II.

VG	EX	LN	RARITY
900	1400	1900	7

6 (Type IV): Locomotives and tenders were also built with Baltimore and Ohio insignia. These were rubber-stamped "B. & O. R.R."

VG	EX	LN	RARITY
900	1400	1900	7

6 (Type V): Locomotive-tender combinations decorated for the Boston and Maine railroad were rubber-stamped "B. & M. R.R.".

VG	EX	LN	RARITY
900	1400	1900	7

6 (Type VI): About 1911, the 6 received a one-piece frame. This version is known to have been produced with "N.Y.C. & H.R.R.R." rubber-stamped lettering, and was likely to have been available in the previously listed road names as well.

VG	EX	LN	RARITY
600	1000	1600	6

6 (Type VII): Provision for attaching an electrical lead for passenger car lighting was added in 1911. It continued to be rubber-stamped with gold "N.Y.C. & H.R.R.R." lettering, which was now serif type.

VG	EX	LN	RARITY
600	1000	1600	6

6 (Type VIII): Beginning in 1912, the locomotive was equipped with thick-rimmed drive wheels. It continued to be gold rubber-stamped "N.Y.C. & H.R.R.R."

VG	EX	LN	RARITY
500	800	1200	5

6 TYPE VIII

6 (Type IX): About 1918, a significantly smaller bell began to be installed on the locomotive. Also, a strap-type headlight replaced the pedestal headlight previously used. The number "4351" was rubber-stamped in gold beneath "N.Y.C. & H.R.R.R." on the side of the tender. The locomotive continued to be produced this way through 1923.

VG	EX	LN	RARITY
500	800	1200	5

6 Special: This locomotive, indistinguishable from an early number 7, differed from the standard number 6 in that rather than steel it was made of brass, some of which was nickel plated. The locomotive cab and tender body were nickel plated, as were various trim items on the locomotive boiler. The boiler itself was brass. The cast iron pilot, pilot wheels and driver spokes were all painted red, as was a trim stripe on the tender. Thin nickel rims were on the drive wheels. No markings were stamped on the locomotive or tender. It was available in 1908 and 1909.

VG	EX	LN	RARITY
2000	2400	3000	7

7: In 1910, the brass and nickel 4-4-0 was renumbered 7. It remained in the product line through 1923.

7 (Type I): 🚂 The number 7 sold from 1910 through 1912 was indistinguishable from the number 6 Special of 1908-1909, as neither had any markings, and their construction was the same. Only the box was different.

VG	EX	LN	RARITY
2000	2400	3000	7

7 (Type II): 🚂 Probably in late 1912, the nickel rims used on the drive wheels became markedly thicker. These thicker rims were used for the balance of the production of the number 7.

VG	EX	LN	RARITY
1800	2000	2400	6

7 (Type III): Some of the number 7 locomotives were built with brass, rather than nickel-plated cabs. The cab windows on these locomotives were trimmed in red.

VG	EX	LN	RARITY
1800	2000	2400	6

7 (Type IV): The cab windows were trimmed in red on some of the nickel-cabbed locomotives as well.

VG	EX	LN	RARITY
1800	2000	2400	6

51: 🚂 Prior to 1912, this locomotive and tender was cataloged as the 5 Special. Renumbered in 1912, the combination remained in the product line through 1923. The 51 utilized the new in 1912 thick-rimmed drive wheels. It had a blued steel

7 TYPE I

Shown here is a reproduction made be Joe Mania Trains. Reproductions by this firm are carefully and permanently marked to avoid confusion with an original item. Others have made reproductions with removable identification, and still others have produced unmarked fraudulent pieces. Beware.

7 TYPE II

Price Guide Key: **VG** = Very Good, **EX** = Excellent, **LN** = Like New | *Values for each condition are in U.S. dollars.* | **Rarity** = Scale from 1-8 with 8 being the hardest to find.

29

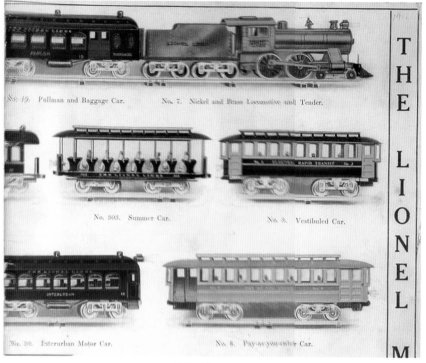

1910 CATALOG

Standard gauge is 2⅛ inches. Curved track forms a circle 40¾ inches in diameter. All Standard gauge outfits have built-in whistle. Extra track and switches are listed on page 41, cars on page 35.

No. 378W	No. 371W	No. 358W	No. 396W
$50.00	$55.00	$70.00	$75.00

LIONEL STANDARD GAUGE

No. 392EW LOCOMOTIVE-TENDER OUTFIT

Equipped with *whistle*. Nickel details. Locomotive has 4-4-2 wheel arrangement, and with tender, is 25 inches long. For use with car Nos. 420, 421, 422, 424, 425, 426 and the 500 series. Outfit includes whistle-controller. **Price $37.50**

No. 378W PASSENGER TRAIN OUTFIT

Everything but the size of a crack express! Locomotive *whistle*, focused headlight, running lights and a glow light from engine firebox. Cars have removable roofs and hinged doors. Outfit consists of: No. 392 Locomotive, No. 392W Tender, No. 424 Illuminated Pullman car, No. 425 Illuminated Pullman car, No. 426 Illuminated observation car, eight sections of C curved track, eight sections of S straight track, UTC Lockon and a whistling controller. Train is 79½ inches long. Track oval, 100⅜ by 43⅞ inches. **$50.00**

No. 371W FREIGHT TRAIN OUTFIT

This is "tops" in freight train outfits—America's finest, longest, fastest! Equipped with built-in *whistle*. Outfit consists of: No. 392 Locomotive, No. 392W Tender, No. 511 Flat car, No. 515 Oil tank car, No. 514R Refrigerator car, No. 516 Coal car, No. 517 Caboose, eight sections of C curved track, eight sections of S straight track, UTC Lockon and a whistling controller. Train is 93¾ inches long. Track supplied forms an oval 100⅜ by 43⅞ inches. **Price $55.00**

No. 400EW LOCOMOTIVE-TENDER OUTFIT

Equipped with super-motor and *whistle*. Locomotive and tender measure 29⅞ inches long, 5¾ inches high. For use with cars Nos. 420, 421, 422 and the 200 and 500 series freight cars. Outfit includes whistle-controller. **Price $45.00**

No. 358W WORK TRAIN OUTFIT

No more fun can be had with any outfit than with this train equipped with built-in *whistle*, many interesting cars and searchlights. Outfit consists of: No. 400 Locomotive, No. 400W Tender, No. 212 Gondola car with barrels and tools, No. 219 Work crane car, No. 220 Floodlight car, No. 217 Caboose, eight sections of C curved track, eight sections of S straight track, UTC Lockon and a whistling controller. Train is 88½ inches long. Track supplied forms an oval 100⅜ by 43⅞ inches. **Price $70.00**

No. 396W PASSENGER TRAIN OUTFIT

Lionel model of Jersey Central Railroad's famous Atlantic City Express, equipped with *whistle*. Outfit consists of: No. 400 Locomotive, No. 400W Tender, No. 420 Illuminated Pullman car, No. 421 Illuminated Pullman car, No. 422 Illuminated observation car, eight sections of C curved track, eight sections of S straight track, UTC Lockon and a whistling controller. Train is 91½ inches long. Track supplied forms an oval 100⅜ by 43⅞ inches. **Price $75.00**

1917 CATALOG

51

boiler and a black painted tender body. "N.Y.C. & H.R.R.R." was rubber-stamped in gold beneath the cab window and on the sides of the tender. Its slope-back tender rode on two 100-series trucks.

VG	EX	LN	RARITY
500	700	1000	5

384: This 2-4-0, introduced in 1930, was cataloged through 1932. Its sheet metal body was mounted on a one-piece die-cast frame. Copper piping was installed on the boiler, while the remainder of the trim, the dome, smokestack, handrails and bell, were made of brass. A brass nameplate, with "No. 384 LIONEL LINES" stamped on it in black, was mounted beneath the cab window. A Bild-A-Loco motor powered the 384, which was equipped with a manual reverse mechanism. The locomotive was usually furnished with a matching 384T tender. Some of these tenders had crackle-finish black paint, which warrants a $100 premium be added to the values listed below.

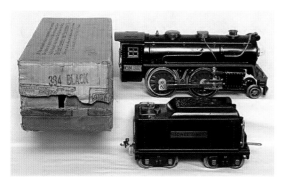

384 (Type I): Locomotive as described above, with brass cab windows.

VG	EX	LN	RARITY
350	475	650	2

384 (Type II): Some locomotives had the edge of their running boards painted green. The balance of the locomotive, except for the natural metal parts and red-spoked drivers, was painted black.

VG	EX	LN	RARITY
350	475	650	2

384 (Type III): Some of the green-striped engines had their cab windows painted the same color as the running board edge.

VG	EX	LN	RARITY
350	475	650	2

384 (Type IV): During 1931, some 384 locomotives were packaged with orange-striped 390T tenders as part of set 362.

VG	EX	LN	RARITY
400	525	700	5

384E: When equipped with the pendulum-type reverse unit, the suffix "E" was added to the 384 model number, and the printing on the cab side nameplate became red. The balance of the construction and trim were as described for the basic 384. This locomotive was offered from 1930 through 1932.

384E (Type I): The 384E had copper piping and brass trim. This version had an overall black boiler and frame, with brass windows in the cab.

VG	EX	LN	RARITY
350	475	650	2

384E (Type II): Considerably more attractive were versions with the running board edge painted green.

VG	EX	LN	RARITY
350	475	650	2

384E (Type III): Some of the locomotives with green running board edges also had green cab windows.

VG	EX	LN	RARITY
350	475	650	2

385E: This 23 1/2" long locomotive and tender was offered from 1933 through 1939. It used a sheet metal boiler and cab mounted on a die-cast frame. Its tenders had low mounted couplers for use with 500-series cars.

Price Guide Key: **VG** = Very Good, **EX** = Excellent, **LN** = Like New | *Values for each condition are in U.S. dollars.* | **Rarity** = Scale from 1-8 with 8 being the hardest to find.

31

385E (Type I): In 1933, the 385E was painted a dark gunmetal—nearly black—with copper and brass trim. It came with a 384T tender that was decorated with a brass plate stamped "LIONEL LINES". There was a "chugger" mechanism in the locomotive, and the locomotive rode on wheels with painted red centers.

VG	EX	LN	RARITY
400	550	750	6

385E (Type II): Some of these early locomotives with red driver centers had their 384T tenders painted with crackle-finish paint.

VG	EX	LN	RARITY
500	650	800	7

385E (Type III): 📷 During 1934, the wheel centers began to be painted black instead of red. The paint color was a slightly lighter shade of gunmetal. The trim, which up until now had been made of brass and copper, was now nickel-plated.

VG	EX	LN	RARITY
400	550	750	5

385E (Type IV): 📷 In 1935, a new tender, based on an Ives design and numbered 385TW was used. The "W" denoted whistle, indicating Lionel's newly developed air whistle was mounted inside. While most had a nickel-finished plate on the side of the tender reading "THE LIONEL RAILWAY LINES", a few produced early in the line had this plate made of brass. A chugger continued to be mounted in the locomotive, which itself was unchanged.

VG	EX	LN	RARITY
400	550	750	5

385E (Type V): In 1936, the tender's number was changed to simply 385W. The locomotive still had a chugger unit installed inside its boiler.

VG	EX	LN	RARITY
400	550	750	5

385E (Type VI): Beginning in 1937, the chugger unit was dropped. The tender furnished was still the whistle-equipped 385W.

VG	EX	LN	RARITY
400	550	750	5

390: This locomotive was produced only in 1929. This was largely due to its improbable coupling of a deluxe locomotive with a manual reverse unit. The 2-4-2 had a sheet metal boiler mounted on a die-cast frame. Both, like the 390T tender, were painted black. Brass and copper trim was installed on the locomotive, which had a Bild-A-Loco motor. Some of these locomotives have the sides of their running boards striped in orange, others do not, but this does not affect the value of the piece.

VG	EX	LN	RARITY
500	625	850	7

390E: This 2-4-2 was cataloged from 1929 through 1931, disappeared for a year, and returned for a final stand in 1933. It was equipped with a pendulum-type E-unit and a Bild-A-Loco motor. It had a die-cast frame and sheet metal boiler.

385 Type II

385E Type IV

LIONEL ELECTRIC TOY TRAINS *& Multivolt Transformers*

Electric and Steam-Type Trains for Standard Guage Track, 2¼ Inches Wide

ELECTRIC PULLMAN OUTFIT No. 34.

Outfit No. 34—Comprises No. 33 Locomotive, 1 No. 35 Pullman Car, 1 No. 36 Observation Car, 8 curved and 2 straight sections of track, making an oval 4 ft. 8 in. long by 3½ ft. wide. Length of train 34 in. Price, packed in strong box with full directions for operating.................$14.50

ELECTRIC FREIGHT TRAIN OUTFIT No. 37.

Outfit No. 37—Comprises No. 112 Gondola Car, 1 No. 117 Caboose, and 8 sections curved track, making a circle 3½ ft. in diameter. Length of train, 31 in. Price, packed in strong box with full directions for operating $12.00

ELECTRIC FREIGHT TRAIN OUTFIT No. 39.

Outfit No. 39—Comprises No. 38 Locomotive, 1 No. 116 Coal Car, 1 No. 117 Caboose and 8 sections curved track, making a circle 3½ ft. in diameter. Length of train 32 in. Price, packed in strong box with full directions for operating $13.00

ELECTRIC PULLMAN OUTFIT No. 40.

Outfit No. 40—Comprises No. 38 Locomotive, 2 No. 35 Pullman Cars, 1 No. 36 Observation Car, 8 curved and 4 straight sections of track, making an oval 5 ft. 9 in. long and 3½ ft. wide. Length of train, 4 ft. Price, packed in strong box with full directions for operating...................$20.00

ELECTRIC FREIGHT OUTFIT No. 41.

Outfit No. 41—Comprises No. 38 Locomotive, and 1 each Nos. 112 Gondola, 113 Cattle Car, 114 Box Car, 116 Coal Car, 117 Caboose, 8 curved and 4 straight sections of track, making an oval 5 ft. 9 in. long by 3½ ft. wide. Length of train, 5 ft. 4 in. Price, packed in strong box with full directions for operating..$18.00

ELECTRIC PASSENGER OUTFIT No. 44.

Outfit No. 44—Comprises No. 42 Locomotive, 2 No. 29 Day Coaches, 8 curved and 4 straight sections of track, making an oval 3½ ft. wide by 5 ft. 9 in. long. Length of train, 52 in. Price, packed in strong box with full directions for operating $25.00

OUTFITS No. 420 AND 421—PULLMAN TRAINS DE LUXE

Outfit No. 420—Passenger Train De Luxe. Comprises No. 42 Locomotive, 1 each Nos. 18 Pullman Car, 19 Pullman and Baggage Car, 190 Observation Car. 8 curved and 8 straight sections of track, making an oval 3½ ft. wide by 8 ft 2 in. long. The outfit also includes a series of 3 lights complete with cords for interior illumination of cars.

This train outfit is the most beautiful one made and considering the finish and the liberal equipment is big value for the price. The locomotive body and the cars are finished in handsome non-chipping enamel. All the wheels are nickeled and polished. The cars have seats in the interior, upon which minia- ture figures can be placed. The transoms in the roofs of the cars are fitted with imitation stained glass, as are also the windows; and the lights shining through them are wonderfully realistic. Length of train, 65 in. Price, packed in strong box with full directions for operating $35.00

Outfit No. 421—Similar in every respect to Outfit No. 420 above, but equipped with Locomotive No. 54, finished in nickel and brass. No better toy train can be obtained for the money. Price, packed in strong box and full directions for operating $42.50

STEAM-TYPE ELECTRIC PASSENGER OUTFIT No. 43.

Outfit No. 43—Comprises 1 No. 51 Locomotive and Tender, 2 No. 29 Day Coaches, 8 curved and 4 straight sections of track, making an oval 3½ ft. wide by 5 ft. 9 in. long. Length of train, 53 in. Price, packed in strong box with full directions for operating...................$21.00

ELECTRIC PULLMAN OUTFIT No. 52.

Outfit No. 52—Comprises No. 53 Locomotive, 1 No. 180 Pullman Car, 181 Pullman and Baggage Car, 182 Observation Car, 8 curved and 4 straight sections of track, making an oval 3½ ft. wide by 5 ft. 9 in. long. Length of train, 54 in. Price, packed in strong box with full directions for operating....$25.00

STEAM-TYPE ELECTRIC PULLMAN OUTFIT No. 50.

Outfit No. 50—Comprises No. 51 Locomotive and Tender, 1 each Nos. 180 Pullman Car, 181 Pullman and Baggage Car, 182 Observation Car, 8 curved and 4 straight sections of track, making an oval 3½ ft. wide by 5 ft. 9 in. long. Length of train, 5 ft. Price, packed in strong box with full directions for operating.$27.00

STEAM-TYPE ELECTRIC PULLMAN OUTFITS Nos. 620 and 621.

Outfit No. 620—Equipment and cars are same as described in Outfit No. 420, but has steam-type Locomotive No. 6 instead of the electric-type No. 42. A very handsome outfit, and represents very big value. Price, packed in strong box with full directions for operating...................$40.00

Outfit No. 621—Similar to Outfit No. 620 described above, but has steam- type Locomotive No. 7, finished in nickel and brass; a strong, beautiful outfit. Price, packed in strong box with full directions for operating...............$50.00

DE LUXE FREIGHT TRAIN OUTFITS.

Outfit No. 422—Comprises No. 42 Locomotive and the complete line of Freight Cars numbered 11 to 17 illustrated on another page of this pamphlet, together with 8 curved and 10 straight sections of track, making an oval 3½ ft. wide and 5 ft. 5 in. long. Complete train is 7 ft. in length. Price, complete, packed in strong box...................$35.00

Outfit No. 423—Similar to the above, but includes Locomotive No. 54, fin- ished in nickel and brass. Price, complete, packed in strong box........$45.00

Outfit No. 622—Same equipment as above outfits, but includes steam type Locomotive No. 6, with Tender, as described on another page of this pamphlet. Price, complete, packed in strong box...................$40.00

Outfit No. 623—Same equipment as above outfits, but includes steam type Locomotive No. 7 and Tender, finished in nickel and brass. Price, complete, packed in strong box...................$50.00

LOCOMOTIVE No. 33	LOCOMOTIVE No. 38	LOCOMOTIVE Nos. 42 & 54

No. 33—Length 11 in., width 3 in., height 4½ in. Outfit includes 8 sections curved track, making a circle 3½ ft. in diameter. Has Electric Headlight and connection for lighting interior of passenger cars. Price..............$10.00

No. 38—Length 12 in., width 3½ in., height 5 in. Outfit includes 8 sections curved track, making a circle 3½ ft. in diameter. Has Electric Headlight. Revers- ing Controller and connection for lighting interior of passenger cars. Price.$12.00

No. 53—Length 13 in., width 3½ in., height 5 in. Outfit includes 8 curved and 4 straight sections of track, making an oval 3½ ft. wide by 5 ft. 9 in. long. Has Electric Headlight, Reversing Controller and connection for lighting inte- rior of passenger cars. Price..................$13.50

No. 42—Length 15½ in., width 4 in., height 6 in. Outfit includes 8 curved and 4 straight sections of track, making an oval 3½ ft. wide by 5 ft. 9 in. long. Has Electric Headlight, Reversing Controller, and connection for lighting interior of passenger cars. Has 8 driving wheels, connected in pairs. Price...........$17.50

No. 54—Dimensions same as No. 42. Locomotive of nickel and brass, beau- tifully finished. Most elaborate electric-type locomotive we make. Price..$27.50

1917 Catalog

Price Guide Key: VG = Very Good, **EX** = Excellent, **LN** = Like New | *Values for each condition are in U.S. dollars.* | **Rarity** = Scale from 1-8 with 8 being the hardest to find.

33

Brass and copper trim adorned the locomotive and tender. The centers of the wheels of the locomotive were painted red.

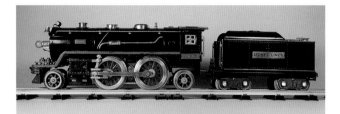

390E (Type I): The most common version of the 390E was painted black, with the side of the running board painted orange. It was produced in this configuration from 1929 through 1931.

VG	EX	LN	RARITY
400	550	750	5

390E (Type II): In addition to the common orange-striped black loco, in 1929 a much more colorful version was produced as well. Uncataloged, this version was painted two-tone green. The edge of the locomotive's running board was painted an even lighter, third shade of green. This apple green paint also highlighted upper and lower beads on the tender's flanks.

VG	EX	LN	RARITY
1000	1450	2000	8

390E (Type III): 🖼 A second uncataloged version of the 390E was made in 1929. Also two-tone green, the edge of this locomotive's running board was painted orange. The beads cast into the tender sides were also highlighted in orange.

VG	EX	LN	RARITY
1000	1450	2000	8

390E (Type IV): In 1930, a two-tone blue 390E was introduced. The sides of its running boards were painted cream, as were the beads on the tenders' sides.

VG	EX	LN	RARITY
600	900	1300	7

390E (Type V): In 1933, the black locomotive returned, only this time the running board edges were the same color as the rest of the boiler and frame.

VG	EX	LN	RARITY
400	550	750	6

392E: Introduced in 1932, and remaining in the catalog through 1939, the 392E was Lionel's next to the top of the line Lionel Standard Gauge steamer of the era. Its frame and hinged boiler front were die-cast.

392E (Type I): The first year's production was painted black with copper and brass trim. Its wheels had red centers, and its motor nickel sides. A two-position pendulum-type reverse unit was installed. The locomotive was paired with a 384T tender, which was trimmed with a green stripe.

VG	EX	LN	RARITY
700	900	1200	4

392E (Type II): The second year's production added a chugger to the locomotive, as well as the three-position drum type E-unit. The new, large 12-wheel 392T tender with whistle was introduced.

VG	EX	LN	RARITY
700	900	1200	4

392E (Type III): In 1934, the locomotive-tender combination continued unchanged.

VG	EX	LN	RARITY
700	900	1200	4

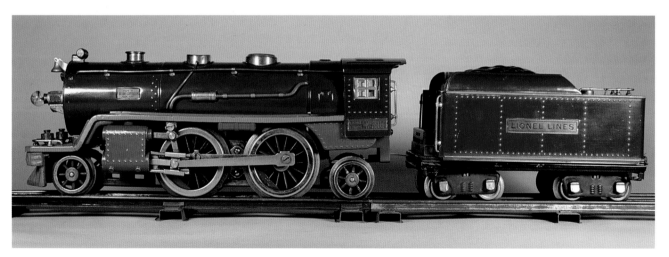

390E Type III

329E Type V

392E (Type IV): The pilot truck, which previously had been nickel-plated, was blackened in 1937. "LIONEL LINES" stood out against the black background on the brass plate on the tender side. The locomotive and tender remained black, and a chugger was mounted in the boiler. Some of the engines had red wheel centers, while others were black.

VG	EX	LN	RARITY
1000	1400	2000	6

392E (Type V): New for 1935 was a second color combination for the 392E/392T pair. Gun metal gray paint began to be used and the trim became nickel. The "Lionel Lines" plate on the tender became nickel as well, with its background color changing to red. Mechanically it was identical to the black locomotive.

VG	EX	LN	RARITY
1000	1400	2000	6

392E (Type VI): Nickel trim and plates were also used on the black locomotive and tender.

VG	EX	LN	RARITY
900	1250	1800	5

392E (Type VII): The chugger was dropped from the gunmetal version in 1937.

VG	EX	LN	RARITY
1000	1400	2000	6

400E: This was the top of the line steam locomotive during Lionel's "classic era" of Standard Gauge production. Measuring 31 3/8" long, this massive locomotive rode the rails from 1931 through 1939. It had a cast iron pilot, die-cast frame and sheet metal boiler. The locomotive was furnished with the 400T tender, which was of the Vanderbilt design, meaning its "water" compartment was cylindrical rather than rectangular.

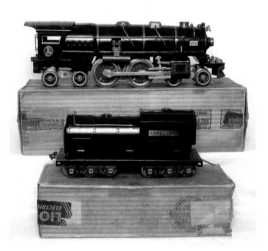

400E (Type I): In 1931 and 1932, the locomotive was available in black with copper and brass trim. It was powered by a Bild-A-Loco motor and equipped with a pendulum-type two-position reversing mechanism. White number boards with red lettering were installed near the front of the boiler.

VG	EX	LN	RARITY
1500	1750	2100	4

400E (Type II): During the same time period, a mechanically identical version of the 400E was offered, only this time finished in medium blue. The separately applied trim was made of either brass or copper.

VG	EX	LN	RARITY
2000	2500	3100	5

400E (Type III): Some of the blue 1931-33 400E locomotives had the sides of their running boards painted cream.

VG	EX	LN	RARITY
2000	2500	3100	5

400E (Type IV): Sometime in late 1933 or early 1934, turned stanchions began to be used instead of brass clips to retain the handrails on the black locomotives. Also in 1933, the drum-type three-position E-unit began to be used. At about the same time, the printing on the number boards changed to black. More important changes took place inside, as the three-position drum-type reversing unit came into use and a chugger mechanism was installed in the boiler.

VG	EX	LN	RARITY
1500	1750	2100	4

Price Guide Key: **VG** = Very Good, **EX** = Excellent, **LN** = Like New | *Values for each condition are in U.S. dollars.* | **Rarity** = Scale from 1-8 with 8 being the hardest to find.

35

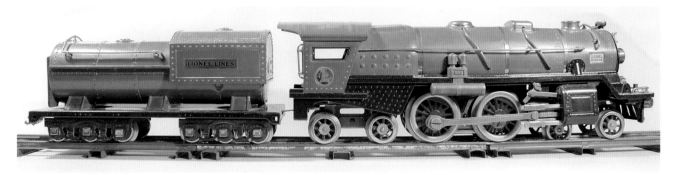

400E Type VIII

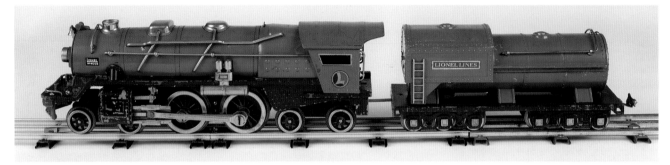

400E Type IX

400E (Type V): The same mechanical, as well as cosmetic, changes were made to the blue 400E as described previously for the black locomotive.

VG	EX	LN	RARITY
2000	2500	3100	5

400E (Type VI): A new color, dark gunmetal, was introduced during 1934. The locomotive had a three-position E-unit and a chugger mechanism installed. Its handrails were secured with turnings, and copper trim and brass boiler bands completed its decoration.

VG	EX	LN	RARITY
1800	2300	2800	4

400E (Type VII): In 1935, another version was introduced. It was painted a lighter shade of gunmetal, and had painted boiler bands and black wheels. Its pilot wheels were solid rather than spoked.

VG	EX	LN	RARITY
1800	2300	2800	4

400E (Type VIII): ◼ Beginning in 1935, and continuing through 1939, a lighter shade of blue was used on the two-tone blue locomotives. These also had nickel trim and brass boiler bands. The tender had nickel trim and aluminum nameplates.

VG	EX	LN	RARITY
2000	2500	3100	5

400E (Type IX): ◼ During 1935, the boiler bands on the blue locomotives, both with and without cream stripe, began to be painted the same medium blue color as the boiler. Previously they had been brass. At the same time, the wheel centers began to be painted black rather than red. The nameplate on the tender, which has nickel trim, began to have a red background painted on it.

VG	EX	LN	RARITY
2000	2500	3100	5

400E (Type X): Also in 1935, crackle-finish paint began to be used on the black locomotive. It had copper trim and boiler bands, and black number boards with white lettering.

VG	EX	LN	RARITY
3000	4200	6000	8

400E (Type XI): From 1936 through 1939, the gunmetal engine was built with nickel trim, including turned nickel handrail stanchions. Its boiler bands were painted the same color as the boiler. The chugger mechanism was deleted and the wheel centers were black.

VG	EX	LN	RARITY
1800	2300	2800	4

1835E TYPE 1

1835E TYPE III

1835E: At the time it was introduced in 1934, the 1835E was the least expensive Standard Gauge steamer in the Lionel lineup. Essentially a cheapened version of the 385E, the 1835E was finished in overall black. But for a single piece of nickel trim on each side, all the other piping and detail normally done as brightwork by Lionel was painted black, along with the boiler. It was not equipped with a chugger. The 1835E remained a part of the Lionel product line through 1939.

1835E (Type I): The 1934 production of the new locomotive was furnished with a 384T tender.

VG	EX	LN	RARITY
500	650	900	4

1835E (Type II): In 1935, the locomotive-tender combination began to come with an operating whistle. This required a new tender, which was the Ives-based 1835TW. There was a long brass plate on the tender reading "The Lionel Railway Lines". Sadly, the die-cast bodies of many of these tenders have deteriorated over time due to impurities in the zinc alloy.

VG	EX	LN	RARITY
550	700	950	4

1835E (Type III): In 1936, the number assigned to the tender was changed. Its product number was now 1835W, and its plates were now made of nickel. These tenders too are prone to disintegration.

VG	EX	LN	RARITY
550	700	950	4

Price Guide Key: **VG** = Very Good, **EX** = Excellent, **LN** = Like New | *Values for each condition are in U.S. dollars.* | **Rarity** = Scale from 1-8 with 8 being the hardest to find.

37

CHAPTER 5
ELECTRIC LOCOMOTIVES

In North America, steam locomotives are typically described using the Whyte classification system. An example of this would be 2-8-4, which describes a locomotive with a two-wheel pilot or leading truck, eight coupled driving wheels (four on each side) and a four-wheel trailing truck. An articulated locomotive, which essentially had two engines under one boiler, had an extra digit added for each set of coupled driving wheels. Union Pacific's famed Big Boy was a 4-8-8-4.

Electric locomotives are not classified by the Whyte system. Instead, a system of letters, numbers and signs was used to describe the axle arrangement, rather than the wheel arrangement used by Whyte. Letters represent the number of powered axles. B is two, C is three, etc. A plus sign (+) is used to represent multiple powered axle sets on separate articulated frames. Numerals are used to represent the number of non-powered axles on leading and trailing trucks. Therefore, in electric locomotive terms the two engines described would be a 1-D-2 and a 2-D+D-2 respectively. The two most common wheel arrangements used by Lionel during this period were 0-B-0 and 0-C-0, representative of 0-4-0 and 0-6-0.

In addition to being Lionel's home territory, New York has long been the most populous city in the country. It was natural then for Lionel to replicate a locomotive that was familiar not only to the company's principals, but also the largest pool of potential customers. This meant a model of an electric locomotive. In 1903, the New York state legislature, in response to a 1902 fatal accident due to steam locomotive exhaust, banned the operation of steam locomotives on Manhattan Island in New York City south of the Harlem River after June 30, 1908. This forced the railroads to electrify their lines in the city.

This situation was compounded in 1923 by the Kaufman Act. The text of that mandated: "No railroad or part thereof operating within the limits of the city of New York or within the limits of an adjoining city shall on or after Jan. 1, 1926, use any motive power in its operation within these cities except electricity, to be generated, transmitted and used in said operation in a manner to be approved by the Public Service Commission."

Thus, the electric locomotive came into its own, with Lionel's miniatures right on the heels of the real ones. New York Central, one of the major railroads serving the Big Apple, began purchasing the locomotives that were to become its class S-2 in 1904, and Lionel responded with not one, but three replicas, each targeting different price ranges, making this the most prolific of Lionel's Standard Gauge electric locomotives. While the full-sized locomotives were of the 2-D-2 wheel arrangement, Lionel mounted their bodies on a variety of chassis.

8 TYPE I

8: At 11" long, this 0-B-0 was the smallest of late-style Standard Gauge electrics when it was introduced in 1925. It was offered every year through 1932. With such a long production life, and being so inexpensive, it is natural that almost innumerable variations exist. The locomotive was designed to use the large-gear Super Motor, and the frame constructed so that the simulated springs and journals were placed equivalent to that motor's wheelbase. When the small-gear Super Motor, with its different wheelbase, was introduced the frame was not changed. Hence, the wheels were not centered behind the journals on the later locomotives.

8 (Type I): The earliest version of the 8 was painted maroon. On top of its body was mounted a small nickel pantograph and whistle, and a pair of strap-type headlights. Brass window inserts and trim were installed. In 1925, only a large single idler gear super motor, with a 1/2" shorter wheelbase than usual, was used.

VG	EX	LN	RARITY
175	215	250	2

8 (Type II): In 1926, the 8 began to be sprayed dark olive. The nickeled strap type headlights were retained, but the whistle and pantograph were changed to brass, matching the windows and other trim. Combination latch couplers began to be used.

VG	EX	LN	RARITY
150	175	200	2

8 (Type III): During 1927, the locomotive was available painted Mojave. Cast headlights were used and, though the pantograph always had a brass finish, it was sometimes made of steel. Both brass and nickel whistles were used on the Mojave locos.

VG	EX	LN	RARITY
150	175	200	2

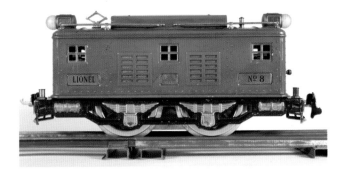

8 (Type IV): Olive green locomotives with brass decoration were offered from 1928 through 1930.

VG	EX	LN	RARITY
150	175	200	2

8E Type I

8 (Type V): Red was the dominant color for the 8 during 1930-32. Its window inserts were painted cream, and the rest of the trim was brass. Some examples exist that used carried-over brass window inserts with a cream bead around the base of the cab.

VG	EX	LN	RARITY
175	215	250	3

8 (Type VI): Occasionally, peacock number eights are found. These have orange window inserts and are well sought after.

VG	EX	LN	RARITY
500	600	750	7

8E: Reverse unit-equipped versions of the 8 began to be produced in 1926. By the time they were discontinued in 1932; the 11" 0-B-0 was using a drum-type E-unit, but the bulk of the production used the pendulum-type reversing unit.

8E (Type I): From 1926 through 1930, the 8E was painted olive green. The whistle and pantograph were brass, matching the windows and other trim. Cast headlights, painted gold, were installed beginning in 1927.

VG	EX	LN	RARITY
150	175	200	2

8E (Type II): During 1929, the locomotive was available painted Mojave. Cast headlights were used, and the pantograph and whistle were brass.

VG	EX	LN	RARITY
175	215	250	3

8E (Type III): As it was for the 8, red was the dominant color for the 8E during 1930-32. Its window inserts were painted cream, and the rest of the trim was brass. Some examples exist that used carried-over brass window inserts. Some examples have a cream bead around the cab base.

VG	EX	LN	RARITY
175	215	250	3

8E (Type IV): Occasionally, peacock examples of the 8E are found. These have orange window inserts and are well sought after. Some have an orange bead or stripe around the base of the cab.

VG	EX	LN	RARITY
350	350	600	6

8E (Type V): Another hard to find color combination for the 8E has a pea green body with cream-colored window inserts.

VG	EX	LN	RARITY
500	600	750	7

9: This 14 1/2" long 0-B-0 was only offered in 1929. It was painted dark green with a black frame. Its motor was secured to the frame by four screws.

VG	EX	LN	RARITY
1200	1600	2200	7

9E: This locomotive, naturally similar to the 9, was available in 1928-35. Early units were equipped with pendulum-type reverse units, while later production featured drum-type reverse mechanisms.

9U

9E (Type I): The initial production locomotives were painted orange and had two gray-painted cast headlights mounted on the roof. Four machine screws retained the motor.

VG	EX	LN	RARITY
600	850	1200	6

9E (Type II): The orange 0-B-0 was also produced with the Bild-A-Loco motor, which was retained by two quick-release levers.

VG	EX	LN	RARITY
600	850	1200	6

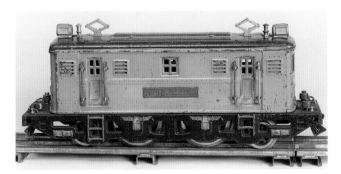

9E (Type III): In 1931, the body was changed, with its clerestory being lowered. Pilot trucks were also added, the wheel arrangement becoming 1-B-1. Its Bild-A-Loco Motor was mounted using two quick-release levers. The body was painted two-tone Stephen Girard green and dark green. It was available in this form through 1933.

VG	EX	LN	RARITY
900	1200	1600	7

9E (Type IV): In 1934-35, the color of the low-clerestory 1-B-1 was changed to gun-metal gray. Its nameplate is marked "No. 9E BILD-A-LOCO. LIONEL LINES".

VG	EX	LN	RARITY
800	1000	1300	6

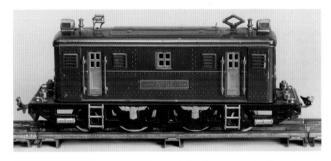

9E (Type V): The gunmetal gray 1-B-1 can also be found with an E-unit slot through the roof. On this version, the motor is secured with four machine screws. The nameplate on this version reads "LIONEL LINES, 9E".

VG	EX	LN	RARITY
800	1000	1300	6

Price Guide Key: **VG** = Very Good, **EX** = Excellent, **LN** = Like New | *Values for each condition are in U.S. dollars.* | **Rarity** = Scale from 1-8 with 8 being the hardest to find.

41

ELECTRIC LOCOMOTIVES

1939 CATALOG

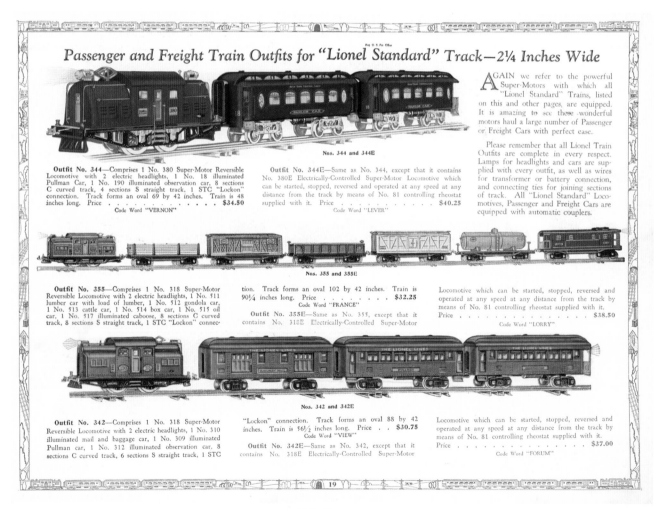

Passenger and Freight Train Outfits for "Lionel Standard" Track—2¼ Inches Wide

Nos. 344 and 344E

Outfit No. 344—Comprises 1 No. 380 Super-Motor Reversible Locomotive with 2 electric headlights, 1 No. 18 illuminated Pullman Car, 1 No. 190 illuminated observation car, 8 sections C curved track, 4 sections S straight track, 1 STC "Lockon" connection. Track forms an oval 69 by 42 inches. Train is 48 inches long. Price **$34.50**
Code Word "VERNON"

Outfit No. 344E—Same as No. 344, except that it contains No. 380E Electrically-Controlled Super-Motor Locomotive which can be started, stopped, reversed and operated at any speed at any distance from the track by means of No. 81 controlling rheostat supplied with it.   Price **$40.25**
Code Word "LEVER"

AGAIN we refer to the powerful Super-Motors with which all "Lionel Standard" Trains, listed on this and other pages, are equipped. It is amazing to see these wonderful motors haul a large number of Passenger or Freight Cars with perfect ease.

Please remember that all Lionel Train Outfits are complete in every respect. Lamps for headlights and cars are supplied with every outfit, as well as wires for transformer or battery connection, and connecting ties for joining sections of track. All "Lionel Standard" Locomotives, Passenger and Freight Cars are equipped with automatic couplers.

Nos. 355 and 355E

Outfit No. 355—Comprises 1 No. 318 Super-Motor Reversible Locomotive with 2 electric headlights, 1 No. 511 lumber car with load of lumber, 1 No. 512 gondola car, 1 No. 513 cattle car, 1 No. 514 box car, 1 No. 515 oil car, 1 No. 517 illuminated caboose, 8 sections C curved track, 8 sections S straight track, 1 STC "Lockon" connec-tion. Track forms an oval 102 by 42 inches. Train is 90¼ inches long. Price **$32.25**
Code Word "FRANCE"

Outfit No. 355E—Same as No. 355, except that it contains No. 318E Electrically-Controlled Super-Motor Locomotive which can be started, stopped, reversed and operated at any speed at any distance from the track by means of No. 81 controlling rheostat supplied with it. Price **$38.50**
Code Word "LORRY"

Nos. 342 and 342E

Outfit No. 342—Comprises 1 No. 318 Super-Motor Reversible Locomotive with 2 electric headlights, 1 No. 310 illuminated mail and baggage car, 1 No. 309 illuminated Pullman car, 1 No. 312 illuminated observation car. 8 sections C curved track, 6 sections S straight track, 1 STC "Lockon" connection. Track forms an oval 88 by 42 inches. Train is 56½ inches long. Price . . **$30.75**
Code Word "VIEW"

Outfit No. 342E—Same as No. 342, except that it contains No. 318E Electrically-Controlled Super-Motor Locomotive which can be started, stopped, reversed and operated at any speed at any distance from the track by means of No. 81 controlling rheostat supplied with it. Price **$37.00**
Code Word "FORUM"

19

1927 CATALOG

10 TYPE III

9U: In 1928 and 1929, the orange 0-B-0 9 was offered as a kit, with catalog number 9U. It had the tall clerestory and adapters to convert its motor to a stationary three-speed reversible unit. Eight sections of curved track were packed with the locomotive, which was lettered "9U". The price listed is for an unassembled example in its original box. Assembled examples without the box are worth about 50 percent less.

VG	EX	LN	RARITY
1500	2200	3000	7

10: Introduced in 1925, and remaining in the product line through 1929, this 11 1/2" long 0-B-0 was one of Lionel's most basic Standard Gauge electrics. It had unpainted brass window inserts, a hand reverse lever, one whistle and only one pantograph. Initially, a large-gear Super Motor powered the loco, but this was replaced in later versions with a small-gear Super Motor. Occasionally examples of this locomotive are found with frames painted dark green, but those are quite uncommon. Normal production locomotives had a black frame.

a nickel pantograph and whistle, and a pair of strap-type headlights. Combination latch couplers were used to connect it to its train.

VG	EX	LN	RARITY
150	175	200	2

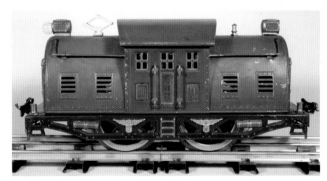

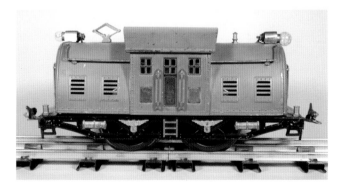

10 (Type I): Like many locos of the era, the earliest version of the 10 was painted Mojave. On top of its body was mounted

10 (Type II): Gray is believed to be the second color that the 10 was offered in. While this version retained the combination latch couplers, and nickel whistle and pantograph of its predecessor, a cast headlight, painted silver, replaced the previously used strap-type.

Price Guide Key: **VG** = Very Good, **EX** = Excellent, **LN** = Like New | *Values for each condition are in U.S. dollars.* | **Rarity** = Scale from 1-8 with 8 being the hardest to find.

43

MORE·THAN·A·TOY

AN ELECTRIC ACHIEVEMENT!

In construction, finish and general appearance, Lionel Electric Toys have no equal.

All locomotive bodies are of sheet steel, not cast iron. They are enameled and ornamented in gold, with hand rails, bells, headlights, and other fittings of nickeled steel. Every "Lionel" locomotive has an electric headlight.

The description below shows the perfection of construction and assembling. The motor is the most vital part of an electric train outfit. "Lionel" motors are built to last.

All cars are hand enameled, not lithographed. They are decorated in gold, have removable roofs, seats in the interior, and imitation glass in windows and transoms. Being made of a heavier gauge of metal, they are more durable than any others. Wheels are nickeled steel. Trucks are flexible, which enables cars to stay on track at high speed.

Track is very rigidly constructed. Track ties are wider than any others. Insulated third rail makes short circuits impossible.

Therefore, Lionel Electric Toys will last longer and give you the most fun.

DESCRIPTION OF PARTS.

Commutator (13)—One of the two most vital parts of a motor. Made of a solid bronze turning, with insulating material placed between the section (10) and the center, through which the armature shaft passes, held together with heavy fibre washers (12), and turned absolutely true when rigid on the armature shaft (11).

Brushes (5 & 6)—These are the vital parts of a motor. We have perfected a self-lubricating graphite brush. These brushes insure uniform speed and maximum power with very little current consumption. It is not necessary to lubricate commutators.

Brush Holders—(3 & 4)—Made of brass, with detachable tops, so that brushes may be easily reached. Contains brass compression spring (5), which feeds brush up to the commutator. This prevents sparking of the brushes and prolongs the life of the commutator.

Armature (8)—Made of electrical steel punchings mounted on drill rod shaft (11), and has fibre heads. Automatically drum-wound with proper size and amount of triple covered silk magnet wire (9), then dipped in shellac and baked, so that none of the coils become loose.

Field (1)—Made of best quality electrical steel, laminated throughout, and contains the winding properly insulated (2).

The Third Rail Shoe (14), which collects the current from the center insulated rail, is a steel punching with spring arrangement that regulates the pressure on the rail. It is case-hardened so that the friction against the third rail does not wear it through.

Pinions (17)—Made of steel, as perfect as the most delicate workmanship can produce.

The wheels are heavy steel castings, are die castings with steel shells forced over the face and tread to insure better wearing surface. On opposite page we show four illustrations of a locomotive wheel in different stages of completion. The die casting (19A) is accurate to the most minute detail. The steel ring (19B) is forced over tread of the wheel which by hydraulic pressure, which holds it in place indefinitely. Illustration (19B) shows the inside of the ring and (19C) the outside. Fig. (19) shows the completed wheel. They are substantial, and run absolutely true on the axles. The tread and flange are scientifically figured and aid the rolling stock in keeping on the rails all the time, even when traveling at very high rate of speed.

Gears (16)—Made of heavy steel discs, and mesh perfectly. Clock-work does not contain any more perfect workmanship.

Reversing Controller (15) is on all cars, with a few exceptions. Unique in construction. 15B is the reversing controller assembled without lever, wires, etc. 15C is a fibre disc showing hole for lever. On its face appear two flat brass contacts, on which the four spring contacts slide (15D). The tension of these brass springs against the brass cap insures perfect contact while controller is being reversed. These springs, while insuring good electrical contact, work with so little friction that controller may be reversed with our Automatic Trips, which can be attached to any part of the track.

Bearings (21)—These are made of heavy steel.

Car Couplers (28)—Once connected will not separate unless TAKEN apart. MADE OF STEEL NICKELED AND POLISHED.

Connecting Rods (23)—Are punched of heavy steel and are lined up accurately, as illustration shows.

Cowcatcher (29)—A heavy cast piece directly connected with the steel frame running entire length of locomotive. Will stand a lot of bumping without breaking or getting loose.

Simplicity Noticeable—The illustrations clearly show no complicated parts which add friction and prevent easy access for cleaning and replacing—if ever necessary.

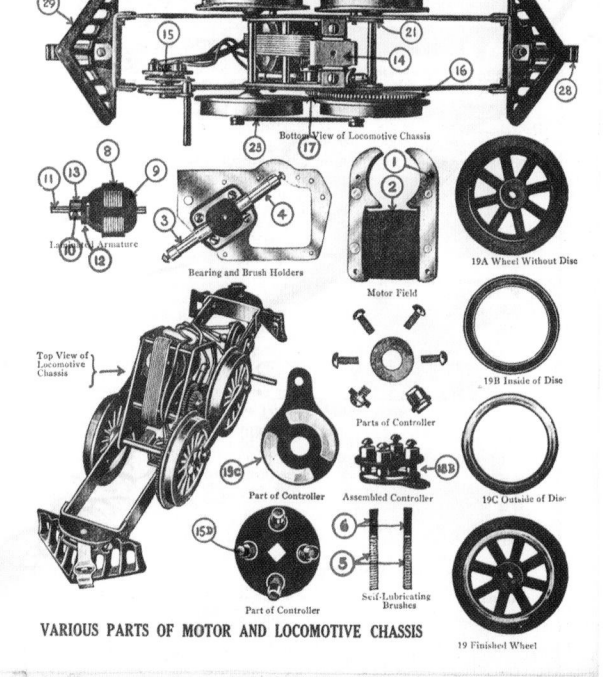

VARIOUS PARTS OF MOTOR AND LOCOMOTIVE CHASSIS

Bottom View of Locomotive Chassis

Bearing and Brush Holders

Motor Field

Laminated Armature

Top View of Locomotive Chassis

Parts of Controller

Part of Controller

Assembled Controller

Self-Lubricating Brushes

Part of Controller

19A Wheel Without Disc

19B Inside of Disc

19C Outside of Disc

19 Finished Wheel

STOP LOOK LISTEN

LIONEL ELECTRIC TOY TRAINS

And Multivolt Transformers

SOLD BY

CATALOG OF

1917

No. 88—**Rheostat**—This is for use with dry or storage batteries where a gradual increase or decrease of voltage is desired for operating miniature electric trains, motors, or other electrical devices. It can also be used with transformers that are not equipped with rheostats. Price, packed in box complete with connecting wires..**$1.00**

BATTERY RHEOSTAT.

No. 107, for 110 volts. Price, complete..........................**$8.00**
No. 170, for 220 volts. Price, complete..........................**$10.00**

Battery Rheostat

DIRECT CURRENT REDUCER.

This is constructed upon a substantial slate base, measuring 8 by 10 inches, and ¾-inch in thickness. The resistance wires are wound around 4 porcelain tubes and are protected by a perforated iron cover lined asbestos. The voltage that regulates the speed, and which is sufficient for operating any of our trains and other apparatus, is controled by a sliding lever. The reducer is connected with the house current by a screw plug, which, with 7 feet of flexible cord, as provided with the apparatus. The reducer can be fixed to wall or table by using the 4 porcelain knobs and screws which are supplied with it.

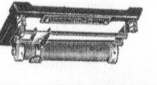

Direct Current Reducer

When ordering be sure to specify the number of cycles.

Prices: Type T (25 Cycles).........................7.00
Type B and T Transformers (25 Cycles).........................$4.00
Note—Types B and T Transformers will be made specially to order for 25-cycle current.

ALL THE ABOVE ARE FOR 60-CYCLE CURRENT.

Type	Price with Cord and Plug	No. of Voltages	Watts	
B	$3.40	2 Volt Steps 2 to 30 Volts	50	15 permanent and 15 with use of Rheostat [With Rheostat]
S	5.00	3 Volt Steps 1 to 15	50	30 15 permanent and 15 with use of Rheostat [With Rheostat]
T	6.50	1½ Volt Steps 1½ to 34	75	30 15 permanent and 15 with use of Rheostat [With Rheostat]
K	8.00	2 Volt Steps 2 to 30	150	30 15 permanent and 15 with use of Rheostat [With Rheostat]

PRICES AND SPECIFICATIONS.

With a Lionel "Multivolt" Transformer you can, when operating a Lionel Train, play the part of a motorman by moving the rheostat up high or low points, thus increasing or decreasing the speed without changing the wiring in any way. All other apparatus can be operated in the same manner.

Construction—The cores are made of the highest grade electrical silicon transformer sheets properly laminated. The primary and secondary coils are made of the correct size and amount of enameled wire, with insulation between the layers. The whole is embedded in an improved insulating compound, which makes the layers impervious to heat, air, oil or water. These coils are enclosed in a steel case handsomely finished in black enamel, having a brass index plate showing the various voltages obtainable. All other metal parts are nickel plated and polished.

Do not be misled into buying Transformers of doubtful make. Lionel "Multivolt" Transformers are expressly made to operate Lionel Trains, and are therefore the most efficient for this purpose. The prices alone should appeal to you, for they are lower than on any similar apparatus on sale.

Type B

Types S and T

Type K

LIONEL "MULTIVOLT" TOY TRANSFORMERS

10E Type III

VG	EX	LN	RARITY
150	175	200	2

VG	EX	LN	RARITY
600	750	900	7

10 (Type III): The most often found version of the 10 was painted peacock. Its cast headlights were painted gold, and matched nicely with its brass flag holders. A nickel pantograph and whistle were atop the loco, which continued to use combination latch couplers. Some of these have an orange stripe around the base of the cab.

VG	EX	LN	RARITY
125	160	180	1

10 (Type IV): Another peacock version is equally common. It was identical to the Type III except its pantograph and whistle were unpainted brass rather than nickel. Some of these have an orange stripe around the base of the cab.

VG	EX	LN	RARITY
125	160	180	1

10 (Type V): Macy's Department Stores had some passenger sets made especially for them, which were headed by number 10 locomotives. These hard to find locomotives had red bodies with a cream stripe running along the base of the cab. All the trim on the loco was brass.

10E: In 1926, a reversing unit was added to the 10, which then became the 10E. The 10E remained in the catalog through 1930. Like the 10, the 10E had a 0-B-0 wheel arrangement. Unless otherwise noted, the 10E came with a black frame and its name and number plates were marked in red.

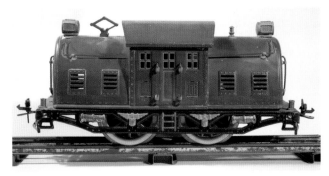

10E (Type I): Gray is believed to be the first color that the 10 was offered in. It had latch couplers, a cast headlight painted gold, and brass window and door inserts.

VG	EX	LN	RARITY
150	175	200	2

10E (Type II): The most often found version of the 10E was painted peacock with a black frame. Its cast headlights were painted gold, and matched nicely with its brass window and door inserts. Latch couplers continued to be used. Some of these have an orange stripe around the base of the cab.

VG	EX	LN	RARITY
125	160	180	1

10E (Type III): A much harder to find version also had a peacock body, but this time it was mounted on a dark green

Price Guide Key: **VG** = Very Good, **EX** = Excellent, **LN** = Like New | *Values for each condition are in U.S. dollars.* | **Rarity** = Scale from 1-8 with 8 being the hardest to find.

45

frame with an orange stripe. Whereas "normal" 10Es were powered by a Super Motor, this version had a Bild-A-Loco Motor secured by two quick release clips.

VG	EX	LN	RARITY
350	425	500	6

10E (Type IV): Not all the peacock-bodied, dark green-framed (Type III) locomotives had an orange stripe.

VG	EX	LN	RARITY
350	425	500	6

10E (Type V): The dark green frame, this time with a cream stripe, was also used under bodies painted State Brown. A Bild-A-Loco Motor powered this train, which was trimmed with a brass pantograph and whistle.

VG	EX	LN	RARITY
450	525	650	6

10E (Type VI): Macy's Department Stores had some passenger sets made especially for them, which were headed by number 10E locomotives. These hard to find locomotives had red bodies with a cream stripe running along the base of cab. All the trim on the loco was brass, and it was lettered in black.

VG	EX	LN	RARITY
600	750	900	7

10E (Type VII): A very few of these locomotives were produced in overall olive green.

RARITY
Too rarely, if ever, traded to establish pricing

33 (EARLY): Introduced early in 1913, this 10 3/8" long 0-C-0 was powered by what is known as a U-frame motor. This moniker was inspired by the profile of the stamped steel frame, which vaguely resembles a short, broad-based "U". The body had a rounded hood with gold-painted door vents and brass side vents. Its windows were outlined in red, and a nickel bell as well as a pedestal-style headlight were mounted atop the hoods. This locomotive was essentially the same as the late 1910.

33 (Type I): As originally produced, the 33 was painted dark olive green. Rubber-stamped in gold were the markings, either "NEW YORK - CENTRAL - LINES" in three lines of block lettering or the oval "NEW YORK – CENTRAL – LINES" logo.

VG	EX	LN	RARITY
400	600	900	4

33 (Type II): Some of these locomotives were painted black, but they were otherwise identical to the Type I.

VG	EX	LN	RARITY
500	750	1000	5

33 (Type III): Comparatively few of these locomotives were painted dark olive green and rubber-stamped "PENN R.R." in gold block letters.

VG	EX	LN	RARITY
700	1000	1300	7

33 (Type IV): In 1913, the 33 was redesigned, losing one axle to become a 0-B-0. It continued in this basic form through 1924. The 10 3/8" long locomotive had rounded hoods. This style 33 looks much more "finished" than does the previous style. Powered by a motor mounted in a U-shaped frame without hand reverse, the body was painted dark olive green and was rubber-stamped "NEW YORK - CENTRAL – LINES" inside an oval logo.

VG	EX	LN	RARITY
100	125	150	3

33 (Type V): With its midnight blue body, this extremely attractive and extremely hard to find version was produced for Montgomery Ward in 1913. In Ward's exclusive set, it towed 35 and 36 passenger cars.

VG	EX	LN	RARITY
750	1200	1600	7

33 (Type VI): About 1917, the frame was redesigned, becoming flatter, with one side of the frame having six rectangles punched into it and four punched into the other side. The plates on the ends read "THE LIONEL MFG. CO." The rubber-stamped markings were unchanged, but the body was now painted black.

VG	EX	LN	RARITY
100	125	150	3

33 (Type VII): After a year or so of production with the Type VI frame, there was another change. Now there were four rectangles punched into each side of the frame. The body continued to be black, and the end plates now read "THE LIONEL CORPORATION". A hand reverse switch was provided.

VG	EX	LN	RARITY
100	125	150	3

33 (Type VIII): Some locomotives with four rectangles punched into each side of the frame had dark olive green bodies. The end plates on these read "THE LIONEL CORPORATION" as well. A hand reverse switch was provided.

VG	EX	LN	RARITY
100	125	150	3

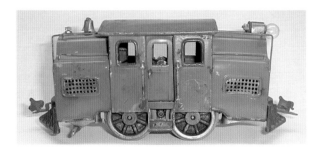

33 (Type IX): About 1923, the frame was changed again to accommodate the large-gear Super Motor. Rectangles were no longer punched from the frame. Combination latch couplers were installed and the end plates read "THE LIONEL CORPORATION". The bodies of these locomotives were commonly painted in one of three colors: dark green, gray and dark olive green. There is no difference in value or scarcity due to these color changes. The 33 was discontinued after 1924.

VG	EX	LN	RARITY
100	125	150	3

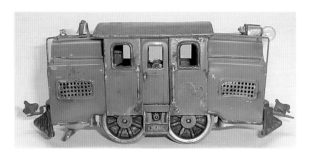

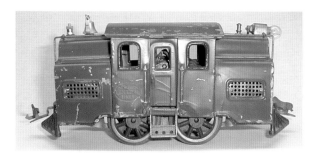

33 (Type X): During the mid-to-late 1920s, locomotives returned to Lionel for extensive repair were often repainted, typically in whatever colors were in use that day. As a result of this policy, examples of the 33 surface in unusual colors. Unfortunately, the faking of factory repaints is rampant, and appropriate caution should be used when contemplating a purchase. Known colors for these factory repaints, which are all valued equally, include red, maroon, peacock, and red with cream stripe.

VG	EX	LN	RARITY
300	450	600	7

34: Introduced in 1912; this locomotive was cataloged in 1912 and 1913, but the two years' production was vastly different.

34 (Type I): In 1912, the 34 was a 10 3/8" long 0-C-0 with a body similar to the one used by the early 33 locomotive. Its body was enameled dark olive green and its windows had dark red outlines. Its markings included "NEW YORK - CENTRAL – LINES" rubber-stamped in gold. Two different typefaces were used during the production run. Although it had three axles, only the center one was powered. It was equipped with long creased-hook couplers. Initially a slide-on headlight was used. This version had no terminal to supply power for passenger car lighting.

VG	EX	LN	RARITY
450	900	40	—

34 (Type II): Later production replaced the slide-on headlight with a pedestal-type, and added a car lighting terminal. These locomotives were supplied in passenger sets.

Price Guide Key: VG = Very Good, EX = Excellent, LN = Like New | *Values for each condition are in U.S. dollars.* | Rarity = Scale from 1-8 with 8 being the hardest to find.

47

ELECTRIC LOCOMOTIVES

VG	EX	LN	RARITY
400	600	800	7

34 (Type III): The final version of the 34 was a 0-B-0 with a U-frame. Despite losing an axle, its length remained 10 3/8". This was created by mounting the body developed for the 34 on the chassis of the number 33 0-B-0 with U-frame.

VG	EX	LN	RARITY
200	285	400	5

38: This was another long-running locomotive, cataloged every year from 1913 through 1924. Basically a renumbered late 1911, the 11 1/8" long locomotive had a 0-B-0 wheel arrangement. The bodies were usually rubber-stamped "NEW YORK - CENTRAL – LINES", either in block lettering or inside an oval logo.

Very broad aids in dating the production of specific locomotives are as follows. The earliest 38s have "Lionel Mfg." nameplates, turned handrail stanchions and vent holes in the end doors. Mid-production locomotives retained the door vents and "Lionel Mfg." markings, but the handrail stanchions were crimped. The final production locomotives had stamped Y-shaped handrail stanchions and plates replaced the vents in the doors. This version of the locomotive was made with either "Lionel Mfg." or "Lionel Corp." nameplates.

38 (Type I): A few of the locomotives were painted dark olive and rubber-stamped with "PENN R.R." lettering. These had red window and body edge trim, and vent holes in the doors. Small creased-hook couplers were used.

VG	EX	LN	RARITY
400	500	600	7

38 (Type II): Some of the NYC locomotives with turned handrail stanchions and vent holes in end doors were painted black.

VG	EX	LN	RARITY
100	120	150	4

38 (Type III): This locomotive was identical to the Type II, but was painted gray.

VG	EX	LN	RARITY
100	120	150	4

38 (Type IV): Some of the NYC engines were painted maroon.

VG	EX	LN	RARITY
150	210	275	5

38 (Type V): Dark green was also a popular color for the Type II locomotive.

VG	EX	LN	RARITY
250	300	350	5

38 (Type VI): Dark olive green examples of the Type I 38 with strap headlight were made as well.

VG	EX	LN	RARITY
250	300	350	5

38 (Type VII): Brown locomotives with strap headlights were also produced, which were similar to the Type I locomotives.

VG	EX	LN	RARITY
250	280	325	4

LIONEL ELECTRIC TOY TRAINS & Multivolt Transformers

Electric and Steam-Type Trains for Standard Guage Track, 2¼ Inches Wide

ELECTRIC PULLMAN OUTFIT No. 34.

Outfit No. 34—Comprises No. 33 Locomotive, 1 No. 35 Pullman Car, 1 No. 36 Observation Car, 8 curved and 2 straight sections of track, making an oval 4 ft. 8 in. long by 3½ ft. wide. Length of train 34 in. Price, packed in strong box with full directions for operating................$14.50

ELECTRIC FREIGHT TRAIN OUTFIT No. 37.

Outfit No. 37—Comprises No. 33 Locomotive, 1 No. 112 Gondola Car, 1 No. 117 Caboose, and 8 sections curved track, making a circle 3½ ft. in diameter. Length of train, 31 in. Price, packed in strong box with full directions for operating $12.00

ELECTRIC FREIGHT TRAIN OUTFIT No. 39.

Outfit No. 39—Comprises No. 38 Locomotive, 1 No. 116 Coal Car, 1 No. 117 Caboose and 8 sections curved track, making a circle 3½ ft. in diameter. Length of train 32 in. Price, packed in strong box with full directions for operating $13.00

ELECTRIC PULLMAN OUTFIT No. 40.

Outfit No. 40—Comprises No. 38 Locomotive, 2 No. 35 Pullman Cars, 1 No. 36 Observation Car, 8 curved and 4 straight sections of track, making an oval 5 ft. 9 in. long and 3½ ft. wide. Length of train, 4 ft. Price, packed in strong box with full directions for operating.................$20.00

ELECTRIC FREIGHT OUTFIT No. 41.

Outfit No. 41—Comprises No. 38 Locomotive, and 1 each Nos. 112 Gondola, 113 Cattle Car, 114 Box Car, 116 Coal Car, 117 Caboose, 8 curved and 4 straight sections of track, making an oval 5 ft. 9 in. long by 3½ ft. wide. Length of train, 5 ft. 4 in. Price, packed in strong box with full directions for operating..$18.00

ELECTRIC PASSENGER OUTFIT No. 44.

Outfit No. 44—Comprises No. 42 Locomotive, 2 No. 29 Day Coaches, 8 curved and 4 straight sections of track, making an oval 3½ ft. wide by 5 ft. 9 in. long. Length of train, 52 in. Price, packed in strong box with full directions for operating $25.00

OUTFITS No. 420 AND 421—PULLMAN TRAINS DE LUXE

Outfit No. 420—Passenger Train De Luxe. Comprises No. 42 Locomotive, 1 each Nos. 18 Pullman Car, 19 Pullman and Baggage Car, 190 Observation Car. 8 curved and 8 straight sections of track, making an oval 3½ ft. wide by 8 ft. 2 in. long. The outfit also includes a series of 3 lights complete with cords for interior illumination of cars.

This train outfit is the most beautiful one made and considering the finish and the liberal equipment is big value for the price. The locomotive body and the cars are finished in handsome non-chipping enamel. All the wheels are nickeled and polished. The cars have seats in the interior, upon which minia-ture figures can be placed. The transoms in the roofs of the cars are fitted with imitation stained glass, as are also the windows; and the lights shining through them are wonderfully realistic. Length of train, 65 in. Price, packed in strong box with full directions for operating..................$35.00

Outfit No. 421—Similar in every respect to Outfit No. 420 above, but equipped with Locomotive No. 7, finished in nickel and brass. No better toy train can be obtained for the money. Price, packed in strong box and full directions for operating..................$42.50

STEAM-TYPE ELECTRIC PASSENGER OUTFIT No. 43.

Outfit No. 43—Comprises 1 No. 51 Locomotive and Tender, 2 No. 29 Day Coaches, 8 curved and 4 straight sections of track, making an oval 3½ ft. wide by 5 ft. 9 in. long. Length of train, 53 in. Price, packed in strong box with full directions for operating..................$21.00

ELECTRIC PULLMAN OUTFIT No. 52.

Outfit No. 52—Comprises No. 53 Locomotive, 1 each Nos. 180 Pullman Car, 181 Pullman and Baggage Car, 182 Observation Car, 8 curved and 4 straight sections of track, making an oval 3½ ft. wide by 5 ft. 9 in. long. Length of train, 54 in. Price, packed in strong box with full directions for operating.....$25.00

STEAM-TYPE ELECTRIC PULLMAN OUTFITS Nos. 620 and 621.

Outfit No. 620—Equipment and cars are same as described in Outfit No. 420, but has steam-type Locomotive No. 6 instead of the electric-type No. 42. A very handsome outfit, and represents very big value. Price, packed in strong box with full directions for operating..................$40.00

Outfit No. 621—Similar to Outfit No. 620 described above, but has steam-type Locomotive No. 7, finished in nickel and brass; a strong, beautiful outfit. Price, packed in strong box with full directions for operating..................$50.00

STEAM-TYPE ELECTRIC PULLMAN OUTFIT No. 50.

Outfit No. 50—Comprises No. 51 Locomotive and Tender, 1 each Nos. 180 Pullman Car, 181 Pullman and Baggage Car, 182 Observation Car, 8 curved and 4 straight sections of track, making an oval 3½ ft. wide by 5 ft. 9 in. long. Length of train, 5 ft. Price, packed in strong box with full directions for operating..$27.00

DE LUXE FREIGHT TRAIN OUTFITS.

Outfit No. 422—Comprises No. 42 Locomotive and the complete line of Freight Cars numbered 11 to 17 illustrated on another page of this pamphlet, together with 8 curved and 10 straight sections of track, making an oval 3½ ft. wide and 5 ft. 5 in. long. Complete train is 7 ft. in length. Price, complete, packed in strong box..................$35.00

Outfit No. 423—Similar to the above, but includes Locomotive No. 54, finished in nickel and brass. Price, complete, packed in strong box........$45.00

Outfit No. 622—Same equipment as above outfits, but includes steam type Locomotive No. 6, with Tender, as described on another page of this pamphlet. Price, complete, packed in strong box..................$40.00

Outfit No. 623—Same equipment as above outfits, but includes steam type Locomotive No. 7 and Tender, finished in nickel and brass. Price, complete, packed in strong box..................$50.00

LOCOMOTIVE No. 33 LOCOMOTIVE No. 38 LOCOMOTIVE Nos. 42 & 54

No. 33—Length 11 in., width 3 in., height 4½ in. Outfit includes 8 sections curved track, making a circle 3½ ft. in diameter. Has Electric Headlight and connection for lighting interior of passenger cars. Price..................$10.00

No. 38—Length 12 in., width 3½ in., height 5 in. Outfit includes 8 sections curved track, making a circle 3½ ft. in diameter. Has Electric Headlight. Reversing Controller and connection for lighting interior of passenger cars. Price..$12.00

No. 53—Length 13 in., width 3½ in., height 5 in. Outfit includes 8 curved and 4 straight sections of track, making an oval 3½ ft. wide by 5 ft. 9 in. long. Has Electric Headlight, Reversing Controller and connection for lighting interior of passenger cars. Price..................$13.50

No. 42—Length 15½ in., width 4 in., height 6 in. Outfit includes 8 curved and 4 straight sections of track, making an oval 3½ ft. wide by 5 ft. 9 in. long. Has Electric Headlight, Reversing Controller, and connection for lighting interior of passenger cars. Has 8 driving wheels, connected in pairs. Price........$17.50

No. 54—Dimensions same as No. 42. Locomotive of nickel and brass, beautifully finished. Most elaborate electric-type locomotive we make. Price..$27.50

1917 CATALOG

42 Type III

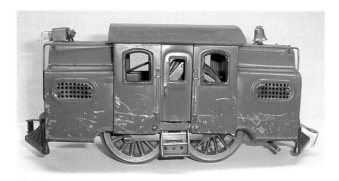

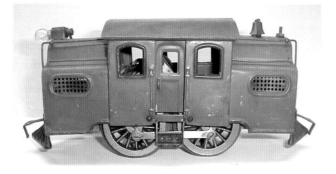

38 (Type VIII): During the mid- to late-1920s, locomotives returned to Lionel for extensive repair were often repainted, typically in whatever colors were in use that day. As a result of this policy, examples of the 38 surface in unusual colors. Unfortunately, the faking of factory repaints is rampant, and appropriate caution should be used when contemplating a purchase. Known colors for these factory repaints, which are all valued equally, include red, Mojave, pea green, peacock, and red with cream trim.

VG	EX	LN	RARITY
400	500	600	7

42 (Type I): Introduced in 1912; this large locomotive was 15 1/2" long and had a 0-B+B-0 wheel arrangement. It used the same body with square hood as the early 1912 locomotive. Side rods connected the drivers on both the dummy and powered motors. Dark green enamel coated the body; which was then rubber-stamped "NEW YORK - CENTRAL – LINES". Locomotives are known to exist with these markings in either block letters or inside the oval NYC logo.

VG	EX	LN	RARITY
700	1000	1500	7

42 (Type II): In 1913, the 42 was restyled, incorporating a round hood body that it would continue to use through 1923. It continued to have the same 0-B+B-0 as the earlier model. The first of the newly redesigned locomotives had its body painted olive. Through succeeding years the locomotive was built in a number of different colors as listed later. All had red trim and "NEW YORK - CENTRAL – LINES" markings.

These markings were rubber-stamped in either block letters, or included the oval logo. Three-tread steps were used on the loco through 1918, at which time they were replaced with a single step. At the same time, the sliding cab door was replaced with a fixed door. In 1921, a second powered motor replaced the dummy motor previously used in one position. Some, but not all, 42s were supplied with a Universal Current Controller switch. The body was painted black.

VG	EX	LN	RARITY
275	375	500	3

42 (Type III): Identical to the Type II but for the color, this locomotive was finished in gray.

VG	EX	LN	RARITY
275	375	500	3

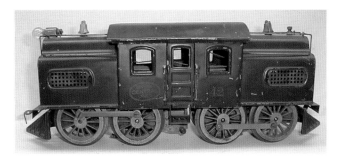

42 (Type IV): Some of the gray locomotives were painted in a notably darker shade.

VG	EX	LN	RARITY
375	475	600	4

42 (Type V): Identical to the Type II but for the color, this locomotive was finished in olive green.

VG	EX	LN	RARITY
600	900	1200	6

42 (Type VI): Some of the olive green locomotives were painted in a notably darker shade.

VG	EX	LN	RARITY
600	900	1200	6

42 (Type VII): Identical to the Type II but for the color, this locomotive was finished in dark green.

VG	EX	LN	RARITY
500	700	1000	5

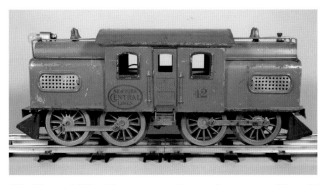

42 (Type VIII): Mojave was also used to paint Type II locomotives.

VG	EX	LN	RARITY
500	700	1000	5

42 (Type IX): Both maroon and peacock examples of the late-style 42 also exist, but these are suspected to be factory repaints.

VG	EX	LN	RARITY
1100	1500	2000	7

50: This little 11 1/8" long 0-B-0 was produced only in 1924. It shared its rounded hood and body with the 38. Red trim along the base and around the windows, along with a gold rubber-stamped "NEW YORK - CENTRAL – LINES"

Price Guide Key: **VG** = Very Good, **EX** = Excellent, **LN** = Like New | *Values for each condition are in U.S. dollars.* | **Rarity** = Scale from 1-8 with 8 being the hardest to find.

ELECTRIC LOCOMOTIVES

oval logo, accented the body. A nickel bell and whistle, two strap headlights and four brass ventilator screens, along with gold-painted handrails, completed the locomotive. Some locomotives had hook couplers, others had combination latch-hook couplers.

50 (Type I): As described above, it was painted dark green.

VG	EX	LN	RARITY
110	150	225	4

50 (Type II): This was the same as Type I, only painted maroon.

VG	EX	LN	RARITY
300	450	600	7

50 (Type III): This was the same as Type I, only painted dark gray.

VG	EX	LN	RARITY
110	150	225	4

50 (Type IV): As described above, this was painted Mojave.

VG	EX	LN	RARITY
150	210	300	5

53: Another of the locomotives whose wheel arrangement changed during the production run was the 53. When introduced in 1911, the 9 11/16" long loco was a 0-C-0. The following year, the locomotive became 12" long and had a 0-B+B-0 wheel arrangement, which remained the case until it was revised again in 1915. In that year, the wheel arrangement changed again, becoming 0-B-0, which it remained through 1919. The final version of the 53, offered in 1920 and 1921, was only 11 1/8" long and generally similar to the 38.

53 (Type I): The first year's version used the same body and motor as locomotive 1910. The body was painted maroon.

RARITY
Too infrequently traded to establish accurate pricing.

53 (Type II): The 1912-1914 edition had a maroon body with "NEW YORK - CENTRAL – LINES" rubber-stamped in oval with gold-colored ink. It was 12" long and had a 0-B+B-0 wheel arrangement.

VG	EX	LN	RARITY
1100	1600	2500	6

53: (Type III) Another variation of the 53 was identical to the Type II, but lacked the oval logo, having only gold block lettering.

VG	EX	LN	RARITY
1100	1600	2500	6

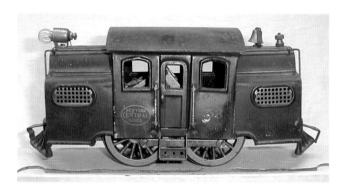

53 (Type IV): From 1915 through 1919, the 53 was a 12 1/2" long 0-B-0. It was rubber-stamped with the gold "NEW YORK - CENTRAL – LINES" oval logo. Unlike previous years when the hoods were rounded, they were now square. The maroon body color used on previous editions was carried over.

VG	EX	LN	RARITY
450	650	850	3

53 (Type V): In addition to the maroon that had by now become traditional for the 53, the locomotive was also produced in Mojave. Like the maroon version, this loco had its vents painted red.

VG	EX	LN	RARITY
650	1000	1400	6

53 (Type VI): A third color, dark olive green, was also produced.

VG	EX	LN	RARITY
600	900	1200	6

54 TYPE III

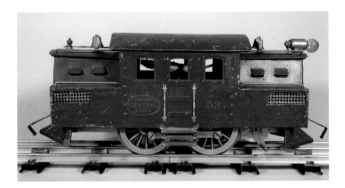

53 (Type VII): The 1920-21 version was still a 0-B-0, but was 11 1/8" long. The maroon body was still rubber-stamped with the oval "NEW YORK - CENTRAL – LINES" logo in gold, but the ventilators and handrails were now painted gold to match. This version was generally similar to the 38.

VG	EX	LN	RARITY
200	325	500	6

53 (Type VIII): The Type VII was also produced with an orange body.

VG	EX	LN	RARITY
200	325	500	6

54 (Type I): Produced only in 1912, this 15 1/2" long 0-B+B-0 locomotive was essentially a renumbering of the previous year's "1912 Special." The locomotive had an unlettered brass body with square hoods and eight "flap-type" ventilators as well as four red-painted vents on its sides. Its pilots and wheels were painted red also. It had one motor and a dummy motor. As a rule, thick rims on the drive wheels are indicative of a 54, while thin rimmed drivers are characteristic of the 1912 Special. However, it is possible that some of the late 1912s may have been equipped with the thicker rims.

This is a very attractive and fairly scarce locomotive. This has led to it having been reproduced. Any "brass" 54 that will attract a magnet is plated steel, and a reproduction. Unfortunately, very, very good forgeries exist that are made of brass. Use extreme caution when considering the purchase of one of these locomotives, and KNOW the seller.

VG	EX	LN	RARITY
2500	3200	4000	8

54 (Type II): In 1913, the 54 was restyled. Its brass hoods now had roundtops, but it continued to be a 15 1/2" long brass 0-B+B-0. Its vents, spoked wheels and pilots were still painted red, and no lettering was applied. A single motor as well as a dummy motor, both with thick-rimmed wheels, were installed. It continued to be produced in this form through 1920.

VG	EX	LN	RARITY
1800	2300	2800	6

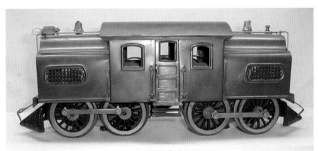

54 (Type III): In 1921, the 54 received a second motor. The dual-motored version was produced through 1923.

VG	EX	LN	RARITY
1900	2400	3000	7

60: In the mid-1910s, Lionel produced a run of its 33 0-B-0 locomotive especially for F.A.O. Schwartz. The "FAOS 60" markings were rubber-stamped in black.

RARITY
Too rarely, if ever, traded to establish pricing.

61: In the mid-1910s, Lionel produced a run of its 42 0-B+B-0 locomotive especially for F.A.O. Schwartz. The "FAOS 61" markings were rubber-stamped in black.

RARITY
Too rarely, if ever, traded to establish pricing.

62: In the mid-1910s, Lionel produced a run of its 38 0-B-0 locomotive especially for F.A.O. Schwartz. The "FAOS 62" markings were rubber-stamped in black.

RARITY
Too rarely, if ever, traded to establish pricing.

318: This 12 1/2" long 0-B-0 was introduced in the 1924 Lionel catalog. During its eight-year production run, it was made in a variety of colors, with pea green being the most common. Brass name and number plates, lettered in black, adorned the locomotive.

318 (Type I): The earliest versions were painted dark gray with red pilots. A nickel pantograph and whistle, and strap-type headlights were mounted atop the body. Inside the 1924 body was a large-gear Super Motor.

VG	EX	LN	RARITY
150	200	250	3

318 (Type II): The second version is believed to be this one, finished in Mojave, with brass trim and cast headlights. It was powered by a small-gear Super Motor.

VG	EX	LN	RARITY
150	200	250	3

318 (Type III): However, this lighter gray with strap headlights is suspected by some to predate the Mojave version. It features

combination latch couplers, and nickel pantograph and whistle. A small-gear Super motor propelled it.

VG	EX	LN	RARITY
150	200	250	3

318 (Type IV): Light gray examples exist that have brass handrails and trim. Like the nickel-trimmed version, these are powered by a small-gear Super Motor.

VG	EX	LN	RARITY
150	200	250	3

318 (Type V): As mentioned earlier, pea green with brass trim is the most abundant 318. Cast headlights and a small-gear Super Motor completed this locomotive.

VG	EX	LN	RARITY
150	200	250	2

318 (Type VI): In the early 1930s, a very attractive version of the 318 was made. Cream stripes and trim set off its State brown body. This version is found with pilots painted either the same color as the body, or red. The small-gear Super Motor and cast headlights were used on this variant. Later production eliminated the cream stripe, but the balance of the loco was unchanged.

VG	EX	LN	RARITY
250	325	425	6

318E: Beginning in 1926, versions of the 318 were built with a pendulum-type E-unit. This version was designated 318E. In 1933, the more modern drum-type reversing unit began to be used, but the designation was unchanged. Regardless of E-unit used, the 0-B-0 was powered by a small-gear Super Motor. In almost all instances, the lettering on the name and number plates was stamped in red.

318E (Type I): The earliest versions were painted Mojave with red pilots. A brass pantograph and whistle, and cast headlights were mounted atop the body.

VG	EX	LN	RARITY
150	200	250	3

318E (Type II): What is believed to be the second version of the 318E was painted gray, and was equipped with brass handrails and trim.

VG	EX	LN	RARITY
150	200	250	3

318E (Type III): The most common version was the pea green one with brass trim.

VG	EX	LN	RARITY
150	200	250	3

318E (Type IV): In 1929, an unusual black version with brass trim was built. This version came with the coal train set only.

VG	EX	LN	RARITY
600	775	1050	8

318E (Type V): In the early 1930s, a very attractive version of the 318E was made. Cream stripes and trim set off its State brown body. This version is found with pilots painted either the same color as the body, or red. The small-gear Super Motor and cast headlights were used on this variant.

VG	EX	LN	RARITY
275	350	450	6

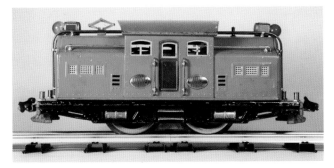

318E (Type VI): Later production of the State brown eliminated the cream stripe, but the balance of the loco was unchanged.

VG	EX	LN	RARITY
275	350	450	6

380: From 1923 through 1927, this 13 1/2" long 0-B-0 was splashed across the pages of the Lionel catalog. Brass letter and number plates, as well as brass doors and windows, decorated the body. Produced during a transition period, various coupler heights and styles were used. Both the large and small-gear Super Motors were used. As a rule, locos with the large-gear Super Motor had hook couplers; later ones with small-gear Super Motor had high-mounted couplers for use with 200-series cars. In most instances, the pilots were painted red and the brass plates had black lettering.

380 (Type I): The earliest versions were painted Mojave. Large celluloid insert headlights were mounted atop the body, along with one each extra-large simulated nickel bell and whistle. A large-gear Super Motor powered it.

VG	EX	LN	RARITY
450	525	650	6

380 (Type II): The most common version, and what was believed to have been the second version produced, had a maroon-painted body with large celluloid insert headlights. A large nickel bell was atop one end of the body, and a large nickel whistle was atop the opposite end. A large-gear Super Motor provided the power to pull the train through combination latch couplers.

VG	EX	LN	RARITY
300	350	400	3

380 (Type III): Another variation of the maroon locomotive had cast headlights, and an extra-large nickel whistle as well as a nickel pantograph. Underneath the cab of this version was a small-gear Super Motor, though it too used combination latch couplers.

VG	EX	LN	RARITY
300	350	400	3

380 (Type IV): A dark green version of the 380 was built as well, which had red lettering. It could come with either brass or nickel trim, and had combination latch couplers.

VG	EX	LN	RARITY
375	425	475	5

380E: A reverse unit-equipped version of the 380, the 380E, was introduced in 1926. Featuring a pendulum-type reversing unit, it remained in the product line through 1929. Some of the locomotive's frames included two weights in an effort to improve adhesion. These locos headed a set with the 428-429-430 cars. In most cases, the red-lettered numberplates were marked "380E", but in a few cases the "E" was stamped on the door and regular "380" plates were used. All the 380Es were powered by small-gear Super Motors.

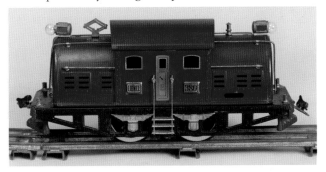

380E (Type I): The most common and earliest version of the 380E had a maroon-painted body topped with large celluloid-insert headlights. Combination latch couplers hung above red pilots on either end of the locomotive.

VG	EX	LN	RARITY
300	350	400	3

Price Guide Key: **VG** = Very Good, **EX** = Excellent, **LN** = Like New | *Values for each condition are in U.S. dollars.* | **Rarity** = Scale from 1-8 with 8 being the hardest to find.

55

380E (Type II): More difficult to find is a later version finished in dark green enamel. Like the maroon unit, it had red pilots and combination latch couplers. Occasionally one will be found without the weighted frame. This version warrants a $50 premium.

VG	EX	LN	RARITY
375	425	475	5

380E (Type III): Some locomotives were painted Mojave. They had red pilots; and cast headlights.

VG	EX	LN	RARITY
450	550	650	6

381: Though this locomotive, produced from 1928-29, and its reverse-unit equipped stable mate, the 381E, were the largest of Lionel's Standard Gauge electrics at 18" long, their single-motored 2-B-2 wheel arrangement made them disappointing pullers. The 381 had a State green body mounted to an apple green subframe, which in turn was attached to the locomotive's main frame, which was black. A Bild-A-Loco Motor was installed inside.

VG	EX	LN	RARITY
1600	1900	2200	6

381E: In 1928, a reversing unit was added to the 381. The new locomotive thus created was designated 381E. Like the 381, it had a 2-B-2 wheel arrangement but, unlike the 381 which had only a two-year production run, the 381E remained in the catalog through 1936. The number plate was stamped "381E", distinguishing it from its E-unit-less predecessor, whose plate merely read "381".

381E (Type I): The most common version had a State green body attached to an apple green subframe, just as the 381.

VG	EX	LN	RARITY
1500	2100	2700	6

381E (Type II): Less common was a version which utilized a red subframe to support the State green body.

VG	EX	LN	RARITY
2000	2500	3000	7

381U: The manual reverse dark State green/apple green 381 was offered as an assembly kit in 1928-29. In addition to the 18" long 2-B-2, the kit included eight sections of track. Also included were the components needed to use the motor as a stationary motor (aka Bild-A-Motor). Much of the value of this item is predicated on the presence of the original box and tools. Inclusion of these items can increase the value up to 50 percent.

381U (Type I): The more desirable version has number plates marked "381U".

VG	EX	LN	RARITY
1800	2800	4000	8

381U (Type II): Some used plates simply numbered "381".

VG	EX	LN	RARITY
1400	2400	3400	7

402: This magnificent locomotive debuted in 1923. Stretching 17 1/2" along the rails, the 0-B+B-0 was powered by two Super Motors. During its four-year production run, it was normally produced painted in Mojave. However, examples have surfaced in other colors, including mustard brown, cream and dark green. These are so scarce they are perhaps indicative of paint samples, rather than limited run department store specials or any other type of normal production. Thus, only the Mojave version is listed here. The earliest production had two holes near each end of the frame. The largest of these was to be used as a mounting point for an auxiliary lighting post, through which illuminated passenger cars received their power.

402 (Type I): The first year's production utilized large-gear Super Motors and featured strap headlights. The body was trimmed with two large nickel whistles and a pair of nickel bells. Hook-type couplers were used.

VG	EX	LN	RARITY
350	425	550	6

402 (Type II): During the next two years of production, combination or latch couplers replaced the hook-type, and a headlight with a celluloid insert began to be used.

VG	EX	LN	RARITY
350	425	550	6

402 (Type III): Some of these locomotives had latch couplers and standard large-sized whistles.

VG	EX	LN	RARITY
350	425	550	6

402 (Type IV): In 1926 and 1927, small gear Super Motors were used, along with latch couplers and cast headlights.

VG	EX	LN	RARITY
350	425	550	6

408E Type II

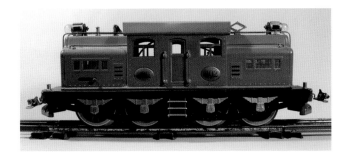

402 (Type V): Some of the 1926-27 production had a single nickel whistle and one brass bell in lieu of the two of each used previously.

VG	EX	LN	RARITY
350	425	550	6

402E: From 1926 through 1929, the 0-B+B-0 was also available with a pendulum-type reversing unit. These units all were powered by a pair of small-gear Super Motors. Once again, Mojave was selected as the body color. In most instances the number plates were stamped "402E", but occasional examples surface with standard "402" number plates and have "E" rubber-stamped on their cab door.

402E (Type I): Initially, celluloid insert headlights and combination couplers were used. The locos were trimmed with two nickel bells and two nickel whistles.

VG	EX	LN	RARITY
300	375	500	5

402E (Type II): Cast headlights began to be used in 1927, along with one pantograph, two whistles, one bell and combination couplers.

VG	EX	LN	RARITY
300	375	500	5

402E (Type III): This type has cast headlights, two pantographs, two whistles and latch couplers.

VG	EX	LN	RARITY
300	375	500	5

408E: In 1927, the 408E was introduced. This 17 1/2" long 0-B+B-0 was a spruced up version of the twin-motored 402E. A considerable amount of additional trim was installed, including a pair of large collapsible pantographs, additional handrails and a pair of additional lights on each end. The name and number plates were stamped in red.

408E (Type I): The earliest versions were painted Mojave with red pilots. Cast headlights were mounted atop the body, and either combination or latch couplers were installed.

VG	EX	LN	RARITY
700	900	1200	5

408E (Type II): What is believed to be the second version of the 408E has proven to be the most common. This version has a body painted apple green and pilots painted red.

VG	EX	LN	RARITY
700	900	1200	5

408E (Type III): A handsome version of the 408E was created by painting its body State brown and its roof dark brown. This version can be found with either two Super Motors or two

Price Guide Key: **VG** = Very Good, **EX** = Excellent, **LN** = Like New | *Values for each condition are in U.S. dollars.* | **Rarity** = Scale from 1-8 with 8 being the hardest to find.

57

Bild-A-Loco Motors. Bild-A-Loco Motors were used in the locomotives that came with the State sets, Super Motor locos were separate sale locomotives.

VG	EX	LN	RARITY
2100	2400	2700	7

408E (Type IV): Some of the State brown locomotives did not have the dark brown roof; rather, the roof was the same color as the rest of the body.

VG	EX	LN	RARITY
2000	2250	2500	6

408E (Type V): A limited number of 408E locomotives are believed to have been factory repainted in State car green to quell complaints from customers. The complaints came as a result of the inability of the 381E supplied in the four-car State sets to tow the train successfully.

VG	EX	LN	RARITY
2000	2700	3500	7

1910: As produced in 1910 and 1911, this 9 3/4" long dark olive green 0-C-0, locomotive was lettered "New York - New Haven - and Hartford" in gold script rubber stamping, despite being loosely based on the New York Central S-2 design. Its cast pilots (cowcatchers), and the four ventilator grilles as well as the eight ventilator flaps atop the square hoods were all painted red. A large nickel bell was mounted on one end of the body and a headlamp was on the other end. Only the two cast iron wheels on the center axle were powered. The other four wheels, which were pressed steel, were unpowered. The locomotive was not equipped with a reverse unit.

In 1912 the locomotive was redesigned. Its length was now 10 3/8", and the tops of its hoods were rounded.

1910 (Type I): The earliest production had handrails soldered by the door. Short creased-hook couplers were installed, as was a slide-on headlight.

VG	EX	LN	RARITY
800	1300	1900	6

1910 (Type II): In 1911, rather than having separately applied handrails, they were simply embossed beside the door.

VG	EX	LN	RARITY
800	1300	1900	6

1910 (Type III): In 1912, the locomotive got an extensive facelift. It was stretched to 10 3/8" long and the hood was rounded. A pedestal-type headlight began to be used. The ventilator grilles were painted gold, and the gold rubber-stamped lettering now read a realistic "NEW YORK-CENTRAL-LINES".

VG	EX	LN	RARITY
500	950	1400	5

1910 (Type IV): The "New York - New Haven -and Hartford" lettering soldiered on in fancy gold script lettering on some examples of the new body, however.

VG	EX	LN	RARITY
500	950	1400	5

1911 (EARLY): This 0-B-0 was available from 1910 through 1912. It was 11 3/8" long and the tops of its hoods were squared. Eight ventilator flaps lined the tops of the hoods, while four ventilator grilles were low on the locomotive's flanks. Some were furnished with an auxiliary lighting post. It had cast iron wheels and its pilots were painted red.

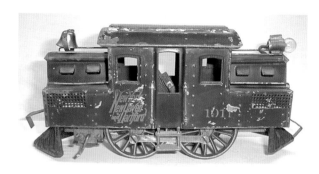

1911 (Type I): The initial production was painted dark olive green, with rubber-stamped "New York - New Haven - and Hartford" lettering. A slide-on type headlight was installed and it rode on thin-rimmed drivers. Short creased-hook couplers connected the locomotive to its train and a reversing mechanism was installed.

VG	EX	LN	RARITY
900	1200	1800	6

1911 (Type II): A second variation was identical mechanically, but it was painted maroon with gold rubber-stamped "NEW YORK - CENTRAL – LINES" in script lettering.

VG	EX	LN	RARITY
1000	1400	2000	7

1911 (Type III): The dark olive green "New York - New Haven - and Hartford" rubber-stamped locomotive was later built with thick-rimmed drivers.

VG	EX	LN	RARITY
900	1200	1800	6

1911 (Type IV): Dark olive green, gold-stamped, the "NEW YORK - CENTRAL – LINES" version was also produced with the gold lettering done in block letters. This version had a dark olive green body and was produced in both slide-on or pedestal headlight versions.

VG	EX	LN	RARITY
900	1200	1800	6

1911 (Type V): In 1913, locomotive 1911 was redesigned to incorporate rounded hoods. It was painted dark olive green with gold rubber-stamped "NEW YORK - CENTRAL – LINES" lettering. The window trim was painted red, as were the pilots, which were shorter than on previous models.

VG	EX	LN	RARITY
700	950	1200	5

1911 SPECIAL: This jumbo-size version of the 1911 was offered only in 1911-12. A full 12" long, an additional dummy motor was beneath the square hood, giving the 1911 Special a 0-B+B-0 wheel arrangement. Its maroon body was rubber-stamped "1911 – SPECIAL" in gold ink. Eight dark green ventilator flaps and long red pilots, along with a nickel bell and gold-painted handrails, trimmed the locomotive. A pedestal-type headlight was installed to light the way.

1911 SPECIAL (Type I): The gold rubber-stamped lettering on some of these locomotives read "New York - New Haven - and Hartford".

VG	EX	LN	RARITY
1000	1600	2500	7

1911 SPECIAL (Type II): Others were marked "NEW YORK - CENTRAL – LINES" in block-style gold rubber-stamped letters.

VG	EX	LN	RARITY
1000	1600	2500	7

1912: Beginning in 1910 and continuing through 1912, this15 1/2" long 0-B+B-0, with square hoods, graced the Lionel catalog. Its steel body was finished in dark olive green enamel with "1912" rubber-stamped in gold. It had eight red-painted ventilator flaps and four red-painted ventilator grilles with gold-painted handrails. Underneath the body was one motor with reversing switch, and one dummy motor. In addition to legitimate, plainly marked reproductions by a variety of manufacturers, unmarked forgeries of the 1912 exist. These are often identifiable by their lacquer finish, rather than the lead-laden enamel used on originals. Be particularly wary of maroon-finished locomotives.

1912 (Type I): The first year or so of production was rubber-stamped "New York - New Haven and Hartford" in fancy gold script. The motor trucks had thin rims and the locomotive was equipped with short straight-hook couplers. Slide-on headlights were mounted atop the hood.

VG	EX	LN	RARITY
1500	2200	3200	7

1912 (Type II): Later production was the same as Type I, but had short creased-hook couplers installed.

VG	EX	LN	RARITY
1200	1900	2600	6

1912 (Type III): During 1912, the lettering was changed to "NEW YORK - CENTRAL – LINES" and pedestal headlights began to be used. The picture shows a strap headlight, possibly a replacement.

VG	EX	LN	RARITY
1200	1900	2600	6

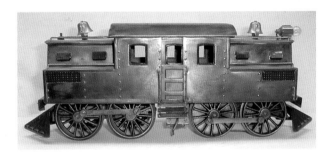

1912 (Type IV): During late 1912, thick rims began to appear on the drivers. "NEW YORK - CENTRAL - LINES" continued to be rubber-stamped on the cab.

VG	EX	LN	RARITY
1200	1900	2600	6

1912 (Type V): Some of the 1912 production had thick driver rims and "New York - New Haven - and Hartford" lettering in fancy gold rubber-stamped script.

VG	EX	LN	RARITY
1500	2200	3200	7

1912 SPECIAL: During 1911, the 1912 Special was offered. Essentially the same as the normal 1912, this locomotive had a polished brass body. It featured sliding cab doors and a soldered-on headlamp. Two large brass bells were mounted, one atop each hood.

VG	EX	LN	RARITY
2300	3500	4500	6

ELECTRIC LOCOMOTIVES

Price Guide Key: **VG** = Very Good, **EX** = Excellent, **LN** = Like New | *Values for each condition are in U.S. dollars.* | **Rarity** = Scale from 1-8 with 8 being the hardest to find.

59

Twin-Super-Motor Locomotives

FOR "LIONEL STANDARD" TRACK—2¼ INCHES WIDE

AS the American boy expects Lionel to introduce model railroad equipment that is in keeping with electric railroad development, we offer the new Electrically-Controlled Locomotives, made in six different types as illustrated on these pages. They are the result of years of experiment and research by Lionel engineers.

The new Electrically-Controlled Locomotives are the only ones made that will operate on direct current as well as on alternating current, dry cells or storage batteries. A patented electrical device makes it possible to operate or reverse these locomotives without using more current than models that are reversed by hand. When the Electrically-Controlled Locomotive is running forward, front headlight is illuminated—when it is reversed, rear one shines brilliantly and forward one is automatically cut out.

All "Lionel Standard" Locomotives are made either with hand reversing controller, or with electrically-controlled reversing mechanism that also can be operated by hand.

We are proud to show the De-Luxe Locomotive No. 408E illustrated on this page. It is one of Lionel's greatest achievements. The illustration clearly shows the great amount of realistic detail incorporated in it. In addition to the details of construction indicated on Page 8, this locomotive includes two operating pantagraphs, two illuminated signal lanterns on front of locomotive, two flags, and an enormous amount of extra special detail in the superstructure. It is indeed a triumph of model engineering skill.

The locomotives shown on this page are for use with Passenger Cars Nos. 428, 429, 430, 431, 418, 419 and 490, illustrated on Page 31; also with Freight Cars Nos. 211 to 219, illustrated on Pages 27 and 28.

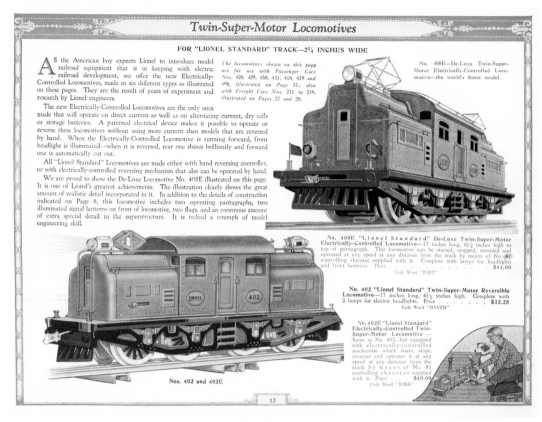

No. 408E—De-Luxe Twin-Super-Motor Electrically-Controlled Locomotive—the world's finest model.

No. 408E "Lionel Standard" De-Luxe Twin-Super-Motor Electrically-Controlled Locomotive—17 inches long, 8½ inches high to top of pantagraph. This locomotive can be started, stopped, reversed and operated at any speed at any distance from the track by means of No. 81 controlling rheostat supplied with it. Complete with lamps for headlights and front lanterns. Price $44.00
Code Word "FAST"

No. 402 "Lionel Standard" Twin-Super-Motor Reversible Locomotive—17 inches long, 6½ inches high. Complete with 2 lamps for electric headlights. Price $32.25
Code Word "HAVEN"

No. 402E "Lionel Standard" Electrically-Controlled Twin-Super-Motor Locomotive — Same as No. 402, but equipped with electrically-controlled mechanism which starts, stops, reverses and operates it at any speed at any distance from the track by means of No. 81 controlling rheostat supplied with it. Price $40.00
Code Word "YORK"

Nos. 402 and 402E

17

1927 CATALOG

Super-Motor Locomotives for "Lionel Standard" Track

— 2¼ INCHES WIDE —

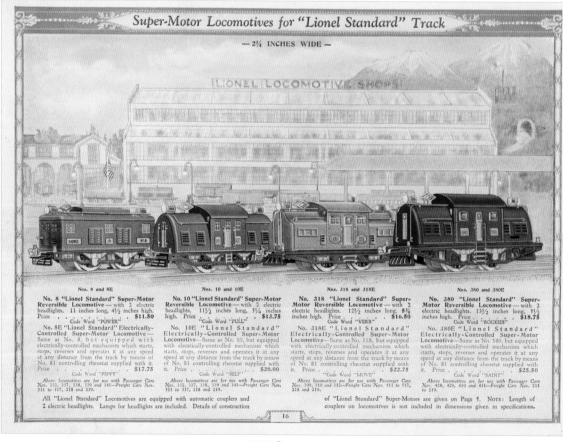

Nos. 8 and 8E

No. 8 "Lionel Standard" Super-Motor Reversible Locomotive — with 2 electric headlights. 11 inches long, 4½ inches high. Price $11.50
Code Word "POWER"

No. 8E "Lionel Standard" Electrically-Controlled Super-Motor Locomotive— Same as No. 8, but equipped with electrically-controlled mechanism which starts, stops, reverses and operates it at any distance from the track by means of No. 81 controlling rheostat supplied with it. Price $17.75
Code Word "PEPPY"

Above locomotives are for use with Passenger Cars Nos. 332, 337, 338, 339 and 341—Freight Cars Nos. 511 to 517, 218 and 219.

Nos. 10 and 10E

No. 10 "Lionel Standard" Super-Motor Reversible Locomotive — with 2 electric headlights. 11½ inches long, 5¼ inches high. Price . . . . . . "Code Word "PULL"" . . . $13.75

No. 10E "Lionel Standard" Electrically-Controlled Super-Motor Locomotive—Same as No. 10, but equipped with electrically-controlled mechanism which starts, stops, reverses and operates it at any speed at any distance from the track by means of No. 81 controlling rheostat supplied with it. Price $20.00
Code Word "SELF"

Above locomotives are for use with Passenger Cars Nos. 332, 337, 338 and 341—Freight Cars Nos. 511 to 517, 218 and 219.

Nos. 318 and 318E

No. 318 "Lionel Standard" Super-Motor Reversible Locomotive — with 2 electric headlights. 12½ inches long. 8¾ inches high. Price $16.50
Code Word "VERB"

No. 318E "Lionel Standard" Electrically-Controlled Super-Motor Locomotive—Same as No. 318, but equipped with electrically-controlled mechanism which starts, stops, reverses and operates it at any speed at any distance from the track by means of No. 81 controlling rheostat supplied with it. Price . . . . . "Code Word "MOVE"" . . $22.75

Above locomotives are for use with Passenger Cars Nos. 309, 310 and 312—Freight Cars Nos. 511 to 517, 218 and 219.

Nos. 380 and 380E

No. 380 "Lionel Standard" Super-Motor Reversible Locomotive — with 2 electric headlights. 13½ inches long, 5½ inches high. Price $18.75
Code Word "ROCKIES"

No. 380E "Lionel Standard" Electrically-Controlled Super-Motor Locomotive—Same as No. 380, but equipped with electrically-controlled mechanism which starts, stops, reverses and operates it at any speed at any distance from the track by means of No. 81 controlling rheostat supplied with it. Price $25.50
Code Word "SAINT"

Above locomotives are for use with Passenger Cars Nos. 428, 429, 430 and 431—Freight Cars Nos. 211 to 219.

All "Lionel Standard" Locomotives are equipped with automatic couplers and 2 electric headlights. Lamps for headlights are included. Details of construction of "Lionel Standard" Super-Motors are given on Page 5. NOTE: Length of couplers on locomotives is not included in dimensions given in specifications.

16

1927 CATALOG

CHAPTER 6
TROLLEYS

The trolleys (actually streetcars, but the catalog used the word "trolley") made by Lionel prior to World War II are today among the most valuable items of that time period. Not surprisingly then, exquisite reproductions of these items have been made, as well as outright forgeries. Due caution is urged when contemplating the purchase of one of these items.

1 TROLLEY: Introduced in 1906, this four-wheel trolley remained in the Lionel product line through 1914. Not surprisingly, during those years there were many manufacturing variations.

1 Trolley (Type I): The earliest version of the trolley used a 5 1/8" frame, with an 8 1/2" long roof topping its cream body. A broad orange band provided contrast, as did an orange roof. The clerestory was cream. "No.1 Electric-Rapid Transit No. 1" was rubber-stamped above the five side windows. An early New Departure motor with friction drive powered this version. Solid, L-shaped steps were mounted on the frame.

VG	EX	LN	RARITY
2000	3500	5000	7

1 Trolley (Type II): Probably during the second year of the number 1's production, the frame was lengthened 1/2", now totaling 5 5/8" overall. An 8 1/2" roof, painted blue with a white clerestory, was mounted atop the car. A band of blue paint wrapped around the white body. Rubber-stamped markings reading "No. 1 Electric-Rapid Transit No. 1" were applied. Though a New Departure motor was still used, it now drove the trolley through a gear drive. A matching non-powered trailer was offered.

VG	EX	LN	RARITY
1800	3300	4800	6

1 Trolley (Type III): During the same time period, another variation of the trolley was built which differed by having dark olive replace the blue in the paint scheme.

VG	EX	LN	RARITY
2000	3500	5000	7

Price Guide Key: **VG** = Very Good, **EX** = Excellent, **LN** = Like New | *Values for each condition are in U.S. dollars.* | **Rarity** = Scale from 1-8 with 8 being the hardest to find.

61

1 Trolley (Type IV): In 1908, the trolley got another facelift. Not only did its frame grow again, to 5 7/8" long, but its roof did as well, becoming 9 9/16" long. The body, which now had six windows on each side, was now painted blue with a cream band. The roof was painted blue and its solid clerestory was painted. The rubber-stamped markings were unchanged from the previous year. A conventional motor powered the trolley and a matching non-powered trailer was available.

VG	EX	LN	RARITY
1500	2500	4000	5

1 Trolley (Type V): In about 1910, the roof was further lengthened, to 10 15/16" long, while the frame remained at 5 7/8". The body was painted blue with a cream window band. The roof was also blue and the clerestory continued to be cream-colored, but differed from previous production by having the clerestory windows actually punched out. The lettering was unchanged, however the steps now had open rungs.

VG	EX	LN	RARITY
1500	2500	4000	5

1 Trolley (Type VI): Maryland Electrical Supply Company, a prominent early Lionel dealer, had Lionel specially make trolleys lettered for Baltimore streetcar lines. Lettered "No. 1 CURTIS BAY No. 1", the car had a cream body with a blue band and roof, and a cream solid clerestory. These cars used the six window-type bodies with L-shaped solid steps.

RARITY
Too infrequently traded to accurately establish pricing.

1 TRAILER: This companion item was also later offered with the new stock number of 111.

VG	EX	LN	RARITY
1000	1900	2800	7

2 TROLLEY: The number 2 trolley was introduced in 1906 and the four-wheeled car remained in the catalog through 1916. Powered by a conventional motor and mounted on a 5 7/8" long frame, the car was rubber-stamped "No. 2 ELECTRIC RAPID TRANSIT No. 2" above its six windows.

2 TROLLEY (Type I): When first offered in 1906, the trolley had a yellow body trimmed with a red belt. Its light blue roof was capped with a yellow clerestory, which had actual window openings. Above the window opening punched in the body was rubber-stamped "No. 2 ELECTRIC RAPID TRANSIT No. 2" in gold. Open-rung steps led to an open platform with light blue posts. A matching non-powered trailer was available.

VG	EX	LN	RARITY
1200	1600	2200	7

2 TROLLEY (Type II): Beginning in about 1908, the ends of the roof became rounded (previously the ends had been squared), while still having open clerestory windows. The body was still painted yellow with a red belt. The steps were now L-shaped and wire-suspended. The most noticeable change, however, was the enclosure of the end platforms, making this a truly handsome piece. A matching trailer was available, and could be connected via the long couplers, which were of either the straight-hook or long creased hook type.

VG	EX	LN	RARITY
1200	1600	2200	7

2 TROLLEY (Type III): Beginning in 1910 and continuing through 1916, the trolley's colors were reversed, with the body now being red with a yellow window belt. Long creased-

2 TROLLEY TYPE III

hook or straight-hook couplers were provided for towing the available matching non-powered trailer.

VG	EX	LN	RARITY
1200	1600	2200	7

2 TROLLEY (Type IV): Like the number 1 trolley, the number 2 was also produced in an uncataloged variation for Maryland Electrical Supply Company. The cars were lettered "No. 2 EDMONDSON AVE. No. 2".

RARITY
Too infrequently traded to accurately establish pricing.

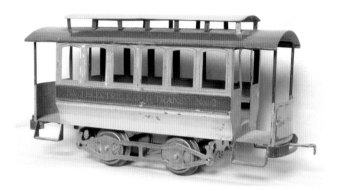

2 TRAILER: This companion item was also later offered with the new stock number of 200.

VG	EX	LN	RARITY
1000	1500	2000	8

3 TROLLEY: The number 3 trolley was introduced in 1906 and remained in the catalog through 1913. Powered by a conventional motor and equipped with a 13 7/8" long roof, the trolley rode on two four-wheel trucks.

3 TROLLEY (Type I): During 1906-07, the trolley, which was rubber-stamped "No. 3 ELECTRIC RAPID TRANSIT No. 3" had an orange band decorating its cream body. The open clerestory-type roof had straight ends and was painted orange. Its windows did not have embossed frames.

VG	EX	LN	RARITY
1500	2500	3500	8

3 TROLLEY (Type II): In 1908 and 1909, the orange was a lighter shade, but the balance of the car was unchanged.

VG	EX	LN	RARITY
1500	2500	3500	8

3 TROLLEY (Type III): Some cars were made which were identical to those listed earlier, except the orange paint was replaced with dark olive. The windows of these cars have embossed frames.

VG	EX	LN	RARITY
1500	2500	3500	8

3 TROLLEY (Type IV): In 1910, the trolley was revised. The ends became enclosed, rather than open as previously used, and the roof was now 15 1/4" long. Its body was painted dark green, as were the lower platform ends as well as its roof. The embossed window frames were cream as were the doors and clerestory roof. Above the roof was rubber-stamped "No. 3 ELECTRIC RAPID TRANSIT No. 3". The windows on the enclosed platform were offset.

VG	EX	LN	RARITY
1500	2500	3500	8

3 TROLLEY (Type V): In 1913, the closed ends of the green and cream trolley became flush, rather than offset. The balance of the car was essentially unchanged.

VG	EX	LN	RARITY
1500	2500	3500	8

3 TROLLEY (Type VI): The Maryland Electrical Supply Company also had some number 3s decorated specially for them. Similar to the Type V listed earlier, they were rubber-stamped "No. 3 BAY SHORE No. 3".

RARITY
Too infrequently traded to accurately establish pricing.

3 TRAILER: Two types of non-powered trailers were produced, which matched either the Type I or Type III trolleys listed earlier. These were later assigned catalog number 300.

VG	EX	LN	RARITY
1200	2200	3200	8

4 TROLLEY: First released in 1906, the "No. 4 ELECTRIC RAPID TRANSIT No. 4" was part of the Lionel lineup for six years. It rode on two four-wheel trucks and had two standard streetcar motors. It was discontinued in 1912.

4 TROLLEY (Type I): This cream-colored trolley was decorated with dark olive green bands and roof. A cream clerestory accented the 13 7/8" long roof. It came both with and without interior and head lights.

VG	EX	LN	RARITY
2500	4000	5500	8

4 TROLLEY (Type II): The number 4 was also offered its body painted in a reverse scheme, with a dark olive green body and cream windows. Its open platform ends and its roof were olive, but the clerestory roof was cream.

VG	EX	LN	RARITY
2500	4000	5500	8

4 TROLLEY (Type III): About 1913, the trolley was changed. Its roof became 15 1/4" long. The body, roof and closed platform ends were painted green, while the clerestory roof, doors and windows were cream.

VG	EX	LN	RARITY
2500	4000	5500	8

8 TROLLEY: Offered from 1908 through 1914, the number 8 was one of the most attractive trolleys offered by Lionel. Today, it is one of the most sought after. Powered by a standard streetcar motor, it rode on two four-wheel 10-series open trucks.

Price Guide Key: **VG** = Very Good, **EX** = Excellent, **LN** = Like New | *Values for each condition are in U.S. dollars.* | **Rarity** = Scale from 1-8 with 8 being the hardest to find.

TROLLEYS

1938 Catalog

Construction of Lionel "O" Gauge Motors

DRIVING GEARS ("A") — They are made of heavy steel blanks, machine-cut. They mesh without friction and are far superior to gears with punched teeth.

Field ("B") — The field is made of a number of specially prepared transformer steel laminations. This construction represents a much stronger field than if a single piece of steel were used.

Third Rail Shoe Support ("C") — Made of heavy fibre to which the third rail contact rollers are attached. Our construction protects rollers from injury, for the brackets can be bent against the fibre without disturbing the arc of the spring that gives them the correct tension against the third rail.

Wheels ("D") — Lionel was first to introduce die-cast wheels. They are absolutely balanced. A nickel-plated steel rim is forced over the tread of the wheel to insure long wear.

Collecting Shoes ("E") — They collect current from the third rail. Made of solid brass turnings and revolve on steel shafts which pass through phosphor bronze supports. They insure perfect contact with the third rail at all times so that locomotives will run at uniform speed.

Frame ("F") — Made of very heavy steel punchings, embodying great detail. Will withstand more than the ordinary amount of wear and tear.

Journals ("G") — Made of heavy brass, nickel-plated. Attached to the frames by mechanical means. They add greatly to the appearance of the structure.

Cowcatchers ("H") — The construction of the cowcatchers varies with the type of locomotive on which they are used. Many of them are part of the steel frame which is made in one piece, and others are heavy castings rigidly attached to the frame.

Flag Posts ("J") — All our locomotives are equipped with four flag posts, two at each end of the frame; a very realistic detail.

Tanks ("K") — These tanks are made of brass, nickel-plated, and are separable pieces attached to the frame, which further accentuates the great detail.

Lionel Automatic Couplers ("L") — Made of heavy steel, nickel-plated and polished. They are scientifically constructed so that cars cannot become detached when in motion, but are easily taken apart when desired. The new improved Lionel Coupler with invisible spring arrangement is a great advance over any similar device ever made.

Illustration shows the type of motor used in "O" gauge Locomotives Nos. 248, 252 and 253.

THE NEW LIONEL "O" GAUGE ELECTRICALLY-CONTROLLED SUPER-MOTOR

This marvelous new motor will haul twice as many cars as any other "O" Gauge Motor now on sale. The illustration below shows some of the remarkable features that make this possible. Notice the new system of gearing which gives maximum hauling power with minimum current consumption.

The electric-controlling mechanism is built right into the motor, and is completely protected against injury. This new "O" Gauge Super-Motor, a triumph of engineering skill, is one of Lionel's greatest achievements.

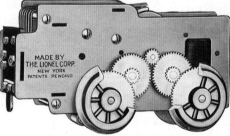

Illustration above shows Electrically-Controlled Super-Motor used in "O" Gauge Locomotives Nos. 254E and 251E.

The same Super-Motor with hand reversing mechanism is used in "O" Gauge Locomotives Nos. 254, 251 and in Twin-Super-Motor No. 256.

Reversing Controllers ("M") — Lionel Reversing Controllers have been in use for many years during which time they have given thorough satisfaction. They are the only controllers in use that cannot get out of order. They operate very easily and due to the brass cups and spring tension, the electrical contact is always permanent.

Frame Support ("N") — The frame is supported to the motor with only four screws. This simple method of construction was originally introduced by us in 1913. All parts of Lionel Locomotives can be easily reached for cleaning.

Side Plates ("P") — Made of heavy gauge steel and support all working parts. All bearing holes are reinforced with phosphor bronze bushings. The alignment of these holes is absolutely perfect so that gears work with minimum friction. All holes are drilled and reamed to proper diameter. The accuracy of these plates compares with the frame work of a very fine clock.

Brush Plate ("Q") — The unique construction permits rapid change of brushes after motor has been in use for a considerable period. The brushes fit in brass cups. Two properly tempered steel springs give the correct pressure of the brush on the commutator until brushes are worn down to the end. Brushes are replaced by simply raising the springs, lifting up worn-out brushes and dropping in new ones.

Brushes ("R") — We were the first manufacturers of model trains to equip our motors with combination gauze and graphite brushes that wear long and are self-lubricating.

Removable Locomotive Body ("S") — The bodies of all Lionel Locomotives are held in place on the frame with only two screws, one at each end of the locomotive. Supporting members are placed at several points of the frame that rigidly hold the body in place.

Commutator — Made of bronze, and perfectly turned when connected to armature so that it is absolutely parallel with brushes. Commutator surface is polished so as to reduce all friction when in contact with brushes.

Armature — Made of specially prepared electrical sheets mounted on a drill rod shaft. It is perfectly insulated and wound with the correct amount of triple insulated wire.

1927 Catalog

8 TROLLEY (Type I): During the first two years of production, the number 8 used a modified Number 3 trolley body with a roof 17 3/4" long. The body was modified by the addition of long vestibules on each end. Nine windows ran alongside its cream body, which was trimmed with an orange band and roof. The clerestory roof and platform ends were painted cream, and the slogan, "No. 8 PAY AS YOU ENTER No. 8", was rubber-stamped on each side.

VG	EX	LN	RARITY
3000	4200	6000	8

8 TROLLEY (Type II): In 1910, the trolley got a longer body with a roof 20 1/4" long with 11 cream-colored windows on each of its dark green sides. Except for the clerestory, which was cream, the roof, the platforms and lower panels were all painted dark green. The steps and coupler supports came in either maroon or green. Despite this being the largest trolley ever made by Lionel, like the 1908-1909 version it was still powered by only one motor.

Some of these cars lacked the "No." preceding the "8" in the rubber-stamped lettering.

VG	EX	LN	RARITY
3000	4200	6000	8

9 MOTOR CAR: First offered in 1909, the number 9 addressed the problem of the huge number 8 only having a single

motor. Made through 1912, the 9 used the same bodies as the corresponding year's 8, but was double motored.

9 MOTOR CAR (Type I): The 1909 production used the same smaller body as the 1908-09 number 8. It was painted in the cream and orange color scheme, and was rubber-stamped "No. 9 PAY AS YOU ENTER No. 9". It was powered by two motors.

VG	EX	LN	RARITY
3000	4200	6000	8

9 MOTOR CAR (Type II): Like the number 8, in 1910 the number 9 began to use a larger green and cream body. It continued to have two motors and be rubber-stamped "No. 9 PAY AS YOU ENTER No. 9".

VG	EX	LN	RARITY
3000	4200	6000	8

10 INTERURBAN: Like an actual interurban, this 15 5/16" long car more closely resembled a motorized passenger car than it did a trolley. Of course, in the case of these miniatures, this is due in no small part to Lionel reusing components of the passenger cars to manufacture these pieces. With one exception, all these cars were rubber-stamped "NEW YORK CENTRAL LINES" in gold above the seven side windows. The number 10 was available from 1910 through 1916.

10 INTERURBAN (Type I): What is believed to be the first version of the number 10 had a body painted maroon with a maroon roof, to which were soldered three black-painted ventilator "knobs." The window inserts were painted gold, as were the handrails, coupler supports and steps. "INTERURBAN" was rubber-stamped beneath the windows on each side.

VG	EX	LN	RARITY
2000	3100	4200	8

10 INTERURBAN (Type II): The maroon car was also built with green and gold window trim and green doors. The gold rubber-stamping on these cars read "10 INTERURBAN 10".

VG	EX	LN	RARITY
1000	1600	2200	7

10 INTERURBAN (Type III): The number 10 was also made in a dark olive green body with a matching roof. Again, onto the

10 INTERURBAN TYPE IV

Price Guide Key: **VG** = Very Good, **EX** = Excellent, **LN** = Like New | *Values for each condition are in U.S. dollars.* | **Rarity** = Scale from 1-8 with 8 being the hardest to find.

65

TROLLEYS

1010 TRAILER TYPE II

roof were soldered three black ventilator "knobs." However, these knobs, always installed in matching sets, were made in both high and low versions. The windows of the interurban were trimmed in maroon and gold, and it had maroon doors. Below the windows, rubber-stamped in gold, was "10 INTERURBAN 10".

VG	EX	LN	RARITY
1000	1600	2200	7

10 INTERURBAN (Type IV): Soldering the ventilators on the roofs of these cars was a time-consuming task and added negligible value to the car in the minds of shoppers nine decades ago. Very probably that is why they were discontinued, making the cars look even more like simple passenger cars. Perhaps the earliest version of the "knobless" interurban is this dark olive green car. Its roof, also olive green, was retained by a single thumbscrew.

The body was rubber-stamped "10 INTERURBAN 10" in gold below the windows, the upper portion of which were covered in red celluloid. The doors were painted red. The clerestory windows, which were actually stamped open, were covered with blue-painted celluloid.

VG	EX	LN	RARITY
800	1100	1600	6

10 INTERURBAN (Type V): Once again, the Maryland Electrical Supply Company had some trolleys specially made. Its version of the 10 was painted olive and decorated just like the Type IV car, except it was rubber-stamped "10 W. B. & A. 10" below the windows, and "INTERURBAN" above. Both markings were in gold. W.B. & A. stood for the Washington, Baltimore and Annapolis, an interurban line that operated from 1908 through 1935.

RARITY
Too infrequently traded to accurately establish pricing.

1010 Trailer: This non-powered interurban was made in a variety of colors and styles in order to match the various cars listed earlier. A trailer is not known to exist for the W.B. & A. interurban.

1010 Trailer (Type I): This model is similar, with knobs on the roof.

RARITY
Value equal to power car, harder to find.

1010 Trailer (Type II): This model came without knobs on the roof.

VG	EX	LN	RARITY
800	1100	1600	7

100 TROLLEY: Produced from 1910 through 1916, these cars were a reasonable representation of a Double Ended, Single Truck trolley, styled similar to real cars made by Barney and Smith. This is the design of trolley immortalized by Fontaine Fox in his "Toonerville Folks" comic strips.

100 TROLLEY (Type I): During its first year, the 100 sported a blue body, roof and ends, with five white windows, door and clerestory. Maroon steps and coupler supports, along with gold rubber-stamped "100 Electric Rapid Transit 100", completed the color combination. Its roof was 10 7/8" long. The windows on the closed platform ends were offset and turned knobs graced the doors.

VG	EX	LN	RARITY
1100	1800	2600	6

100 TROLLEY (Type II): In 1911, the length of the roof was reduced to 10 7/16". While the body, roof and ends remained blue, the windows, doors and clerestory became cream. The steps and coupler supports continued to be maroon. The windows on the closed end platforms were now flush, and beneath the five side windows was rubber-stamped "100 Electric Rapid Transit".

VG	EX	LN	RARITY
1100	1800	2600	6

100 TROLLEY (Type III): During 1912-14, Maryland Electrical Supply Company sold number 100 trolleys that Lionel had custom decorated. They were identical to the type II listed earlier, except the gold rubber-stamped lettering read "100 LINDEN AVE. 100".

RARITY
Too infrequently traded to accurately establish pricing.

100 TROLLEY (Type IV): Yet another version was made, again identical to the Type II, but with red replacing blue throughout the color scheme. It was rubber-stamped "100 Electric Rapid Transit".

VG	EX	LN	RARITY
1100	1800	2600	6

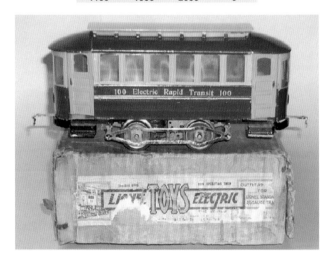

100 TROLLEY (Type V): In 1914, the red-bodied trolley received a makeover. Its roof was now 11 1/2" long, its turned doorknobs were replaced with stampings and it now had six embossed windows along each side. The rubber-stamped lettering read "100 Electric Rapid Transit", and the car continued this way through 1915.

VG	EX	LN	RARITY
1100	1800	2600	6

100 TROLLEY (Type VI): Also in 1915, the trolleys with 11 1/2" roofs began to have their bodies, roofs and ends painted blue once again. Like the red version, the windows, doors and clerestory were cream, and its suspended L-shaped steps and coupler supports were maroon.

VG	EX	LN	RARITY
1100	1800	2600	6

1000 TRAILER: This non-powered version of the 100 was built to complement the 1910 version of the 100.

VG	EX	LN	RARITY
1100	1800	2600	8

101 SUMMER TROLLEY: From 1910 to 1913, the"101 ELECTRIC RAPID TRANSIT 101" trolley was offered. This was an open summer-type car with five benches. Its 10 3/8" long roof had a yellow clerestory. The car's lettering was applied with gold rubber-stamping.

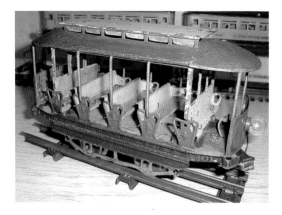

101 SUMMER TROLLEY (Type I): One early version had a blue roof supported by cream posts. The car's ends and bench ends were painted blue, its side sill was maroon.

VG	EX	LN	RARITY
1200	1900	2600	7

101 SUMMER TROLLEY (Type II): An identical car was produced, with the exception of the roof posts and side sill, which were maroon.

VG	EX	LN	RARITY
1200	1900	2600	7

101 SUMMER TROLLEY (Type III): A third version was also produced, attractively decorated with red car ends and roof. Yellow posts supported the roof above the black side sills.

VG	EX	LN	RARITY
1200	1900	2600	7

101 SUMMER TROLLEY (Type IV): By far the most difficult to find version of the 101 is this one. Rubber-stamped "101 WILKENS AVENUE 101", like most of the unusually lettered trolleys, it was made especially for the Maryland Electrical Supply Company and decorated with the name of a Baltimore streetcar line.

RARITY
Too infrequently traded to accurately establish pricing.

1100 TRAILER: Matching non-powered trailers were made to pair with each of the first two versions of the 101 listed earlier.

RARITY
Too infrequently traded to accurately establish pricing.

202 SUMMER TROLLEY: A second summer trolley was also available in 1910-13. With a roof 11 1/2" long and six benches inside, the 202 was slightly larger than the 101. Its side sills were painted black, as were its ends. The roof was red with a yellow clerestory, and the ends of both the car itself and the benches were painted red. It was powered with a standard motor and had a manual reverse.

202 SUMMER TROLLEY (Type I): The bulk of the production was decorated with gold rubber-stamped "202 ELECTRIC RAPID TRANSIT 202" lettering.

VG	EX	LN	RARITY
1200	2100	3200	8

202 SUMMER TROLLEY (Type II): Once again, Maryland Electrical Supply Company ordered cars made that were marked for a Baltimore streetcar line. In this case, the rubber-stamping read "202 PRESTON St. 202", and today this is the most difficult version of the 202 to locate.

Price Guide Key: VG = Very Good, EX = Excellent, LN = Like New | *Values for each condition are in U.S. dollars.* | **Rarity** = Scale from 1-8 with 8 being the hardest to find.

67

2200 TRAILER: A matching non-powered trailer was made to pair with the 202 (Type I).

VG	EX	LN	RARITY
1100	2000	3000	8

303 SUMMER TROLLEY: The biggest of Lionel's summer trolleys, again offered 1910-13, was the 303. Its dark olive green roof stretched 15", and covered eight cream benches. The ends of the car were painted the same dark olive as the roof, while the side sills and floor were maroon. A yellow clerestory and posts set off the other colors. While the car rode on two four-wheel trucks; only one was powered, via a standard motor.

303 SUMMER TROLLEY (Type I): Most Lionel dealers were shipped trolleys with gold rubber-stamped markings reading "303 ELECTRIC RAPID TRANSIT 303".

VG	EX	LN	RARITY
1500	2500	3500	8

303 SUMMER TROLLEY (Type II): As was the case with many other early trolleys, those shipped to Maryland Electrical Supply Company were custom lettered for that firm by special order. Their rubber-stamped lettering read "303 MADISON AVE 303".

3300 TRAILER: A matching non-powered trailer was made to pair with the 303 (Type I).

VG	EX	LN	RARITY
1200	1900	2600	7

1938 CATALOG

CHAPTER 7
CABOOSES

Though today we have an entire generation of adults who have never seen a caboose in actual railroad service, for previous generations the caboose, along with the locomotive, comprised an essential building block of a freight train. Stock cars, gondola cars, tank cars–none of those were essential, some trains had them, others were all box cars or hopper cars–but *every* freight train had a caboose.

Accordingly, every Lionel freight outfit included a caboose. Naturally, this makes the caboose likely the most singularly abundant car type made by Lionel. Even though only four catalog numbers of Standard Gauge cabooses were made–17, 117, 217 and 517–there are many, many manufacturing variations to be found.

17 Caboose: The earliest series of cabooses produced by Lionel was the 17. This car was introduced in 1906 and was shown in every catalog through 1925. In 1926, it was a component of an uncataloged set. Also in 1926, American Flyer began using the body of the 17 for its 4011 caboose.

17 Caboose (Type I): When production of the 17 began in 1906, its body was soldered together from several parts. Neither the car body nor its underframe were embossed. The car was primed, using either red or yellow primer, then the sides painted red. The primer is visible on the underside of

various areas. The roof was black. Black vertical lines were painted on the flanks of the car to simulate the appearance of tongue and groove car siding. Two benches, with pins to accept figures, were inside the car. There were awnings over the main side windows. The car was numbered "5906" and lettered "NYC & H.R.R.R."

VG	EX	LN	RARITY
200	325	450	8

17 Caboose (Type II): Probably the next year, the construction technique of the car was changed. Fewer parts were involved in the body as more sophisticated metal stamping and braking (folding) techniques were used. The painting and decoration was similar to that of the earlier car, although it appears that the use of yellow primer was discontinued. The awnings were painted black. The number was altered to "51906". The car continued to have awnings on the main side windows and two benches inside.

VG	EX	LN	RARITY
200	300	425	7

17 Caboose (Type III): For reasons now unknown, the number of the Type II car reverted to "5906", apparently around 1910.

VG	EX	LN	RARITY
200	300	425	7

Price Guide Key: **VG** = Very Good, **EX** = Excellent, **LN** = Like New | *Values for each condition are in U.S. dollars.* | **Rarity** = Scale from 1-8 with 8 being the hardest to find.

69

17 CABOOSE TYPE VI

17 Caboose (Type IV): In about 1911, the entire "10-series" of cars (11, 12, 13, 14, 15, 16) as well as the 17 caboose received a facelift. "LIONEL MFG. CO N.Y." began to be embossed on the underside. At the same time, the sides began to be embossed, giving some texture to the car. This was to be the case with all the subsequent 17 cabooses. The cupola windows now had awnings, although the main windows no longer did. The roof, awnings and steps were painted black. The car sides were painted red, with black vertical striping. The number reverted to "51906", and the rubber-stamped lettering was altered to "NYC & H.R.RR."

VG	EX	LN	RARITY
150	200	275	6

17 Caboose (Type V): The embossed-side 17 was also produced with a brown body. The steps and roof were painted black, while the entire cupola was brown. It was rubber-stamped "NYC & HRR 4351" and embossed "LIONEL MFG. CO N.Y." on the underside.

VG	EX	LN	RARITY
100	150	200	5

17 Caboose (Type VI):  The number 5906 reappeared on a maroon-bodied caboose with a black roof and embossed sides. "LIONEL MFG. CO N.Y." was embossed on the underside.

VG	EX	LN	RARITY
100	150	200	5

17 Caboose (Type VII): About 1916, the 342715 caboose began to be produced on frames that were not embossed "LIONEL MFG. CO N.Y." In fact, "Lionel" does not appear at all on these cars. The car body and cupola were red, and both roofs were black, as were the steps. These cars were produced both with and without the figure pins on the benches.

VG	EX	LN	RARITY
150	200	275	6

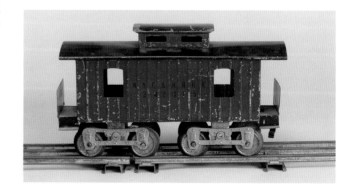

17 Caboose (Type VIII): Yet another number was stamped on the sides of this red caboose, this time "342715". The railroad name rubber-stamping read "NYC & HRRR" on this version. "LIONEL MFG. CO N.Y." continued to be embossed on the underside of the car.

VG	EX	LN	RARITY
100	150	200	5

17 Caboose (Type IX):  The brown "NYC & HRR 4351" caboose was also built without the Lionel name on the car. Both the main and cupola roof were painted black, as were the steps.

VG	EX	LN	RARITY
100	150	200	5

17 Caboose (Type X): Another version of the brown caboose was built as well. This time, the caboose was overall brown, including the roof. The rubber-stamped markings were altered slightly as well, now reading "NYC & H.R.R.R. 4351". No Lionel name was on the car.

VG	EX	LN	RARITY
100	150	200	5

17 Caboose (Type XI): In 1918, "Lionel" returned to the caboose. Reflecting a change in business, rubber-stamped on the underside of the car was "MADE IN U.S.A. - THE LIONEL CORPORATION – NEW YORK". The catalog number, 17, was also rubber-stamped on the underside, marking its first appearance on the actual product. The corporate name would appear on the balance of the 17 production, as would the catalog number in most cases. The body was painted brown with a black roof. The cupola sides were not embossed, nor did they have awnings. "NYC & HRRR 4351" was rubber-stamped in two lines on the sides of the caboose.

VG	EX	LN	RARITY
45	70	100	3

17 Caboose (Type XII): The "Corporation" caboose was also produced with its body painted maroon. The balance of the car was identical to the Type XI car.

VG	EX	LN	RARITY
45	70	100	3

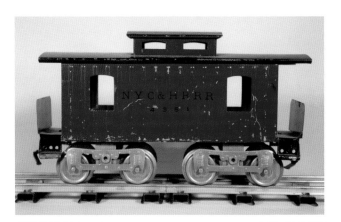

17 Caboose (Type XIII): Perhaps stereotypically, the 17 was also available in red, with the words "MADE IN U.S.A. - THE LIONEL CORPORATION – NEW YORK" rubber-stamped on the bottom. The roof of both the car and the

17 CABOOSE TYPE IX

Price Guide Key: **VG** = Very Good, **EX** = Excellent, **LN** = Like New | *Values for each condition are in U.S. dollars.* | **Rarity** = Scale from 1-8 with 8 being the hardest to find.

71

No. 385EW LOCOMOTIVE - TENDER OUTFIT
Built-in whistle. Rolled steel boiler. Gun metal finish. Nickel details. Locomotive is 14½ inches long, 5½ inches high. Tender is 8½ inches long. For use with cars Nos. 332, 339, 341, 424, 425, 426, 309, 310, 312, 1766, 1767, 1768 and the 500 series freight cars. Locomotive and tender, with a remote control for operating the whistle and reversing the train. Price $30.00

No. 369W STANDARD GAUGE REMOTE CONTROL FREIGHT TRAIN
Fitting for the boy who wants his railroad to be the best—for nothing has been spared in this model. Locomotive whistles as a real one does. Outfit consists of: No. 385E Locomotive, No. 385W Tender, No. 514 Box car, No. 511 Flat car, No. 515 Oil car, No. 517 Caboose, eight sections of C straight track, four sections of S straight track, Lockon and a remote control for operating the whistle and reversing the train. Train is 77 inches long. Track forms oval 71 by 43 inches. Price $40.00

Type "T" Lionel Multivolt Transformer will operate this train. Type "K", of greater capacity, will operate this train and a number of accessories.

STANDARD GAUGE ★ Track Width, Between Running Rails, 2⅛"

No. 367W STANDARD GAUGE REMOTE CONTROL PASSENGER TRAIN
Six feet of model craftsmanship with a racing, whistle-equipped engine leading three accurately proportioned, illuminated twelve-wheel cars. Outfit consists of: No. 385E Locomotive, No. 385W Tender, No. 1767 Illuminated baggage car with sliding doors, No. 1766 Illuminated Pullman car, No. 1768 Illuminated observation car, eight sections of C curved track, four sections of S straight track, Lockon and a remote control for operating the whistle and reversing the train. Train is 73¼ inches long. Track forms oval 71 by 43 inches. Price $40.00

Type "T" Lionel Multivolt Transformer will operate this train. Type "K", of greater capacity, will operate this train and a number of accessories.

1938 CATALOG

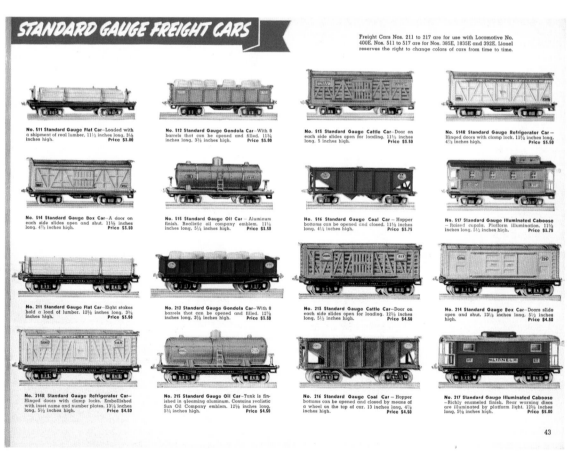

STANDARD GAUGE FREIGHT CARS

Freight Cars Nos. 211 to 217 are for use with Locomotive No. 400E. Nos. 511 to 517 are for Nos. 385E, 1835E and 392E. Lionel reserves the right to change colors of cars from time to time.

No. 511 Standard Gauge Flat Car—Loaded with a shipment of real lumber. 11½ inches long. 3½ inches high. Price $5.00

No. 512 Standard Gauge Gondola Car—With 8 barrels that can be opened and filled. 11¾ inches long, 3½ inches high. Price $5.00

No. 513 Standard Gauge Cattle Car—Door on each side slides open for loading. 11½ inches long, 5 inches high. Price $5.50

No. 514R Standard Gauge Refrigerator Car—Hinged doors with clamp lock. 11⅝ inches long, 4⅞ inches high. Price $5.50

No. 514 Standard Gauge Box Car—A door on each side slides open and shut. 11⅝ inches long, 4⅞ inches high. Price $5.50

No. 515 Standard Gauge Oil Car—Aluminum finish. Realistic oil company emblem. 11⅝ inches long, 5¼ inches high. Price $5.50

No. 516 Standard Gauge Coal Car—Hopper bottoms can be opened and closed. 11½ inches long, 4¼ inches high. Price $5.75

No. 517 Standard Gauge Illuminated Caboose—Raised cupola. Platform illumination. 11½ inches long, 5½ inches high. Price $5.75

No. 211 Standard Gauge Flat Car—Eight stakes hold a load of lumber. 12½ inches long, 3¼ inches high. Price $5.50

No. 212 Standard Gauge Gondola Car—With 8 barrels that can be opened and filled. 12½ inches long, 3½ inches high. Price $5.50

No. 213 Standard Gauge Cattle Car—Door on each side slides open for loading. 12½ inches long, 5½ inches high. Price $4.50

No. 214 Standard Gauge Box Car—Doors slide open and shut. 13½ inches long, 5½ inches high. Price $4.50

No. 214R Standard Gauge Refrigerator Car—Hinged doors with clamp locks. Embellished with inset name and number plates. 13½ inches long, 5½ inches high. Price $4.50

No. 215 Standard Gauge Oil Car—Tank is finished in gleaming aluminum. Contains realistic Sun Oil Company emblem. 12½ inches long, 5¼ inches high. Price $4.50

No. 216 Standard Gauge Coal Car—Hopper bottoms can be opened and closed by means of a wheel on the top of car. 13 inches long, 4½ inches high. Price $4.50

No. 217 Standard Gauge Illuminated Caboose—Richly enameled finish. Rear warning discs are illuminated by platform light. 12½ inches long, 5½ inches high. Price $5.00

43

1938 CATALOG

117 CABOOSE

cupola was black. On these cars the "NYC & HRRR 4351" was rubber-stamped in either gold or black.

VG	EX	LN	RARITY
40	60	90	2

117 Caboose: 🔲 The 117s, like the rest of the 100 series cars, were introduced as slightly smaller and less expensive alternatives to the 10-series cars. While the line debuted in 1910, the caboose was not added until 1912. The flanks of the 117 were embossed with 15 vertical ribs simulating planks, and are rubber-stamped "NYC & HRRR 4351". The 117 was dropped after 1926.

117 Caboose (Type I): The cars that are believed to be the first production of the 117 were painted dark red. The main roof was painted black, although the entire cupola was painted the same dark red color as the body.

VG	EX	LN	RARITY
35	50	70	7

117 Caboose (Type II): Very early in the production of the 117, "LIONEL MFG. CO." began to be embossed in the floor. Its main roof was painted black, but the balance of the upper portion of the car was painted dark brown.

VG	EX	LN	RARITY
30	40	60	6

117 Caboose (Type III): The dark brown car was also made with both the main and cupola roof painted black. The "LIONEL MFG. CO." markings continued to be pressed into the floor. Slight variations in the spacing of the side windows of this car exist, but they do not affect the value of the piece.

VG	EX	LN	RARITY
30	40	60	6

117 Caboose (Type IV): The brown car with both roofs black was also produced with additional lettering. Some of these cars have "LIONEL LINES – N.Y. – MADE IN USA" rubber-stamped on one end in black.

VG	EX	LN	RARITY
30	40	60	6

117 Caboose (Type V): Between 1916 and 1918, Lionel stopped embossing "LIONEL MFG. CO." in the car floors. Instead, in most cases, "LIONEL LINES – N.Y. – MADE IN USA" was rubber-stamped on one end in black. The car remained brown with black main and cupola roofs.

VG	EX	LN	RARITY
30	40	60	6

117 Caboose (Type VI): Some of these cars had "117" rubber-stamped on their ends in addition to the black "LIONEL LINES – N.Y. – MADE IN USA". There were numerous slight variances in the size of the "NYC & HRRR 4351" side stampings, none of which have any effect on the car's collectibility. These cars too were brown with black cupola and main roofs.

VG	EX	LN	RARITY
30	40	60	6

117 Caboose (Type VII): Some of the brown cars had their cupola roofs painted brown. The main roof remained black.

VG	EX	LN	RARITY
30	40	60	6

117 Caboose (Type VIII): Tuscan replaced the brown on some of the later cars with black main roofs. The cupola roofs on these cars were also Tuscan. A variety of typefaces were used on the lettering of these cars during the course of production, with no effect on today's values.

VG	EX	LN	RARITY
30	40	60	6

117 Caboose (Type IX): In 1918, the text of the rubber stamping was changed, a result of a change in the firm's name.

Price Guide Key: **VG** = Very Good, **EX** = Excellent, **LN** = Like New | *Values for each condition are in U.S. dollars.* | **Rarity** = Scale from 1-8 with 8 being the hardest to find.

117 CABOOSE TYPE XVI

The maker's stamping was also moved from the car ends to the underside, where it now read: "MADE IN U.S.A. - THE LIONEL CORPORATION – NEW YORK". The catalog number, 117, was also rubber-stamped on the underside during much of the final production. The body and cupola were dark red, with black cupola and main roofs.

VG	EX	LN	RARITY
30	40	60	6

117 Caboose (Type X): Other cars were otherwise identical to the Type X, but the roof of the cupola was painted the same color as the car's side, rather than black.

VG	EX	LN	RARITY
30	40	60	6

117 Caboose (Type XI): The "Corporation" 117 was also produced in maroon, with gold rather than black "NYC & HRRR 4351" rubber-stampings on its sides. The main roof was black, with the balance of the car's upper works painted maroon.

VG	EX	LN	RARITY
25	35	50	4

117 Caboose (Type XII): Another version was built that differed from the previously listed caboose in having its cupola roof painted black.

VG	EX	LN	RARITY
25	35	50	4

117 Caboose (Type XIII): On some of these cars, the bottom lettering in addition to the side lettering was rubber-stamped in gold.

VG	EX	LN	RARITY
25	35	50	4

117 Caboose (Type XIV): In other cases, all the rubber stamping on the car was black. The cupola roof remained black, as did the main roof, while the vertical surfaces continued to be maroon.

VG	EX	LN	RARITY
25	35	50	4

117 Caboose (Type XV): Red returned as the color of choice for the caboose before production stopped in 1926. In addition to the body, the cupola and cupola roof were red, but the main roof was black. Although the maker's identification was stamped on the bottom of the car, the catalog number was not.

VG	EX	LN	RARITY
25	35	50	4

117 Caboose (Type XVI):  A slightly more common red caboose had both the cupola and main roof painted black.

VG	EX	LN	RARITY
25	35	50	3

117 Caboose (Type XVII): Some of the red cars with double black roofs had their catalog numbers rubber-stamped on the ends of the car.

VG	EX	LN	RARITY
25	35	50	3

117 Caboose (Type XVIII): Still other cars with both black main and cupola roofs did have their catalog numbers rubber-stamped on the bottom, along with the builder information.

VG	EX	LN	RARITY
25	35	50	3

217 Caboose: When Lionel introduced the 200-series cars in 1926, what is now considered the "Classic" era of its Standard Gauge production began. Whereas previous series of cars were painted in the somewhat drab colors of their full-sized counterparts and rubber-stamped with the markings of actual railroads, both of these attributes were about to change. Unrealistic but bright colors were introduced, and the lettering was stamped on separately installed inserts. These inserts, either painted a contrasting color or unpainted brass or aluminum plates, were visible through stampings in the caboose side. Invariably, one of these plates bore the name of the famous railroad "Lionel Lines."

217 Caboose (Type I): The earliest version of the 217 had an orange body with maroon trim insert including roof, doors, cupola and inserts. The lettering was applied with gold rubber-stamping. The end railings were painted dark green. The car rode on trucks, retained with cotter pins, that have both dimples and slots in their bolster on either side of the mounting stud. Nickel journal boxes decorated the trucks. An oiling instruction label, printed in red block lettering and illustrating a 10-series truck, was applied to the bottom of the car. This car was also produced with black handrails.

VG	EX	LN	RARITY
250	400	550	7

217 Caboose (Type II): Another early version of the 217, hard to find today, had a light olive green body with a dark

217 Caboose Type I

217 Caboose Type IV

CABOOSES

olive green roof and cupola. This car had dark red inserts with gold rubber-stamped lettering and peacock-colored railings. Other construction details are identical to those listed for the 217 (Type I).

VG	EX	LN	RARITY
275	450	600	8

217 Caboose (Type III): A pea green version of the 217 was created as well. It had a red roof and doors, and a dark green cupola. Its markings were rubber-stamped in black on gold-painted inserts. Its trucks, retained with cotter pins, had both dimples and slots in their bolster on either side of their mounting stud. The railings on its ends were painted orange.

VG	EX	LN	RARITY
250	400	550	7

217 Caboose (Type IV): Beginning in 1927, the body and cupola of the 217 were painted red, with a peacock roof and doors. Brass railings were installed at each end. An oiling instruction label, printed in red block lettering and illustrating a 10-series truck, was pasted between the two trucks. In most cases, these trucks were retained with cotter pins, though in 1927 screws were used. Both dimples and slots were present in the truck bolsters on either side of their mounting studs. The new window trim, as well as the letter boards, was unpainted brass. The lettering was stamped on these inserts in black.

VG	EX	LN	RARITY
125	175	250	3

Price Guide Key: **VG** = Very Good, **EX** = Excellent, **LN** = Like New | *Values for each condition are in U.S. dollars.* | **Rarity** = Scale from 1-8 with 8 being the hardest to find.

75

217 Caboose (Type V): The red caboose with peacock roof was also made with a peacock cupola. The balance of its decoration, including its oiling label, was identical to that of the Type III. However, it rode on slightly different trucks. Though still retained with cotter pins, these trucks have no dimples but do have slots in their bolster on either side of the mounting stud. Nickel journal boxes were attached to the truck sides.

VG	EX	LN	RARITY
125	200	275	4

217 Caboose (Type VI): The 217 with red body and cupola and peacock roof sometimes appeared with a cream-colored door. Its trucks have nickel journal boxes. Railings on each end of the car were formed of brass.

VG	EX	LN	RARITY
125	200	275	4

217 Caboose (Type VII): About 1931, the red caboose with peacock roof and door, and red cupola, was equipped with trucks retained with horseshoe washers. These trucks have no slots but do have dimples in their bolster on either side of the mounting stud. Copper journal boxes decorated the trucks. These cars do not have the lubrication label pasted on the underside. The railings on the end of this car were made of brass.

VG	EX	LN	RARITY
125	175	250	3

217 Caboose (Type VIII): Sometime in the 1935-1936 time span, the shade of red used on the 217 got noticeably lighter. This color was used on the roof, body and cupola, while the door was an ivory color. Its trucks, retained with horseshoe washers, have no slots but do have dimples in their bolster on either side of the mounting stud. Copper journal boxes decorated the trucks. The lettering was stamped on separately installed inserts that initially were made of brass, but later, aluminum was used. Its end railings were nickel and the window inserts were painted silver.

VG	EX	LN	RARITY
175	250	325	5

217 Caboose (Type IX): As production of the light red caboose continued, the color of the door shifted to cream, and aluminum lettering inserts began to be used exclusively. The silver-painted window inserts continued to be used, although the final production was done with nickel window inserts. The car was last cataloged in 1940.

VG	EX	LN	RARITY
175	250	325	5

517 Caboose: First cataloged in 1927 along with the rest of the 500-series cars, the 517 became the last new Standard Gauge caboose introduced by Lionel. Painted in bright colors like the 217, the 517 stayed in the catalog through 1940.

517 Caboose (Type I): The most commonly found color for the 517 is pea green with a red roof and pea green cupola.

It was produced in these colors from 1927 through 1934. However, there were further variations. Some had orange-painted windows, while others had unpainted brass windows. While nickel journal boxes were used on both, apparently only those with the orange windows had a lubrication label applied. The car's markings were stamped on brass plates.

VG	EX	LN	RARITY
50	75	100	2

517 Caboose (Type II): In 1929, the 517 was offered in red with a black roof and red cupola. Its windows were orange and its nameplates brass. It did have a lubrication label and its trucks, which were retained with cotter pins, had decorative nickel journal boxes. This car was only available in the coal train set headed by the black 318 or the 390 steamer.

VG	EX	LN	RARITY
350	500	800	8

517 Caboose (Type III): An extremely unusual variation of the 517 had an apple green body with red roof and pea green cupola. Orange window inserts, and brass plates and railings, were used on this car.

RARITY
Too infrequently traded to establish pricing.

517 Caboose (Type IV): About 1931, the journal boxes became copper-colored. The body and cupola were pea green, while the roof was red. Its railings and nameplates were

brass, but the window inserts could be either painted orange or unpainted brass with black stamping. Most of these cars, including all the orange-windowed ones, had their trucks retained with cotter pins, but some used horseshoe clips instead.

VG	EX	LN	RARITY
50	75	100	2

517 Caboose (Type V): In 1935, the 517 was revamped. Its roof, body and cupola all became a uniform color, red. Nickel journals and windows were used across the board. The number and letter plates were made of aluminum, which were stamped in black. While most had railings painted silver, some cars were made with nickel railings. Early 1935 versions of this car had copper journal boxes.

VG	EX	LN	RARITY
100	125	150	2

517 Caboose (Type VI): Some of these late all-red cars with silver painted railings had another interesting variation. They had plates reading "Lionel Lines" installed in the position formerly occupied by the number plate. These cars were rubber-stamped "517" on their bottoms.

VG	EX	LN	RARITY
150	175	225	6

CABOOSES

Price Guide Key: **VG** = Very Good, **EX** = Excellent, **LN** = Like New | *Values for each condition are in U.S. dollars.* | **Rarity** = Scale from 1-8 with 8 being the hardest to find.

77

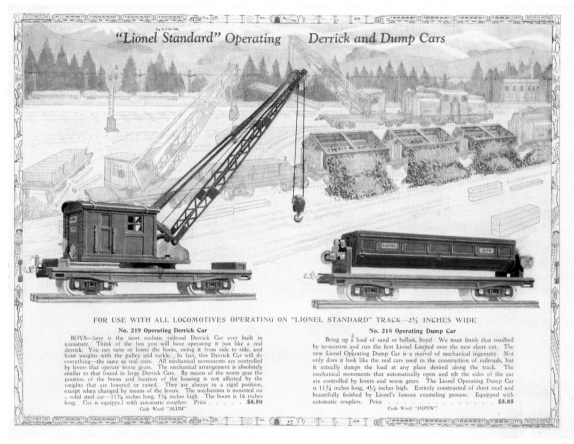

1927 CATALOG

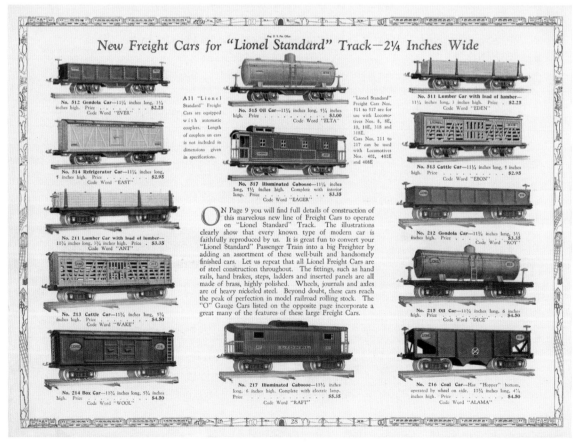

1927 CATALOG

CHAPTER 8
DERRICK & CRANE CARS

219 Crane Car: Referred to alternately as a crane or derrick car, regardless of its name, this is an impressive piece of equipment. It was offered every year from 1926 through 1940 and, though it is relatively common, its ageless appeal makes the car remain popular and moderately pricey. Unlike postwar Lionel crane cars, which were hard-pressed to actually lift anything, the 219 came with nickel support frame that clamped it to the track when in use, thereby allowing its operator to actually lift other cars with the hand-operated hoist

All the 219 cranes were built with black sheet-metal frames. Cranes with peacock cabs had dark green toolboxes installed on either end of their frames. Cranes with other color cabs used red toolboxes.

219 Crane Car (Type I): The earliest version of the 219 had a crane cab that was painted peacock, covered with a dark green roof. A dark red window was installed in both sides of the cab and its boom was dark red as well. Its trim plates were brass with black lettering and its handrails, knobs and other trim were brass as well. The journal boxes on the trucks were nickel.

VG	EX	LN	RARITY
150	200	250	3

Price Guide Key: **VG** = Very Good, **EX** = Excellent, **LN** = Like New | *Values for each condition are in U.S. dollars.* | **Rarity** = Scale from 1-8 with 8 being the hardest to find.

79

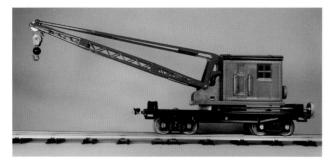

219 Crane Car (Type II): An identically decorated crane was built with a noticeably lighter shade of red paint on its boom.

VG	EX	LN	RARITY
150	200	250	3

219 Crane Car (Type III): The peacock crane with dark red boom was also made with window inserts painted peacock rather than dark red. All other construction details were unchanged.

VG	EX	LN	RARITY
175	225	275	4

219 Crane Car (Type IV): About 1931-1932, the derrick, along with the rest of Lionel's 200-series cars, was slightly revamped. Among the changes were mounting the trucks, which had copper journals, with horseshoe clips and introducing aluminum operating knobs for the crane. Even more noticeable than these, however, was the change in the crane cab color to a lighter shade of peacock.

VG	EX	LN	RARITY
175	225	275	4

219 Crane Car (Type V): Another color of 219 also appeared in 1935. Its color is somewhat controversial, being alternately described as ivory, cream or white. Much of this discussion revolves around the potential for color shifts due to differing paint batches, sun fading, general wear and exposure to tobacco smoke. Perhaps at one time all these were the same color, perhaps not. In any event, they are referred to here simply as white. This white-cabbed crane had nickel journal boxes on its trucks, a red roof and windows, and a light green boom. Its control knobs were turned brass.

VG	EX	LN	RARITY
200	375	625	7

219 Crane Car (Type VI): White cranes were also produced with black die-cast control knobs. The balance of these cranes was identical to those described as Type V.

VG	EX	LN	RARITY
200	375	625	7

219 Crane Car (Type VII): About 1936, cranes began to be made with yellow cabs. The roofs and windows of these cabs were red, and their booms were light green. The trim plates continued to be brass; handrails and other trim were now nickel. Its control knobs were turned aluminum. Nickel journal boxes were used on its trucks.

VG	EX	LN	RARITY
250	350	475	5

219 Crane Car (Type VIII): A 1935 version of the yellow 219 had copper journal boxes on its trucks and aluminum trim plates with black stamping. Otherwise it was a duplicate of the Type VII car.

VG	EX	LN	RARITY
250	350	475	5

219 Crane Car (Type IX): By 1936, production of the yellow 219 had become a bit more standardized. The cars had nickel journal boxes, nickel trim, aluminum plates with black lettering, red roofs and windows, and light green booms. Variations continued to occur for the control knobs, as both turned aluminum and black die-cast parts were used.

VG	EX	LN	RARITY
250	350	475	5

219 Crane Car (Type X): A final white version of the crane was also built using aluminum trim plates, and black die-cast knobs and gears. It had a light green boom, a red roof and red windows. Its handrails and trim were nickel.

VG	EX	LN	RARITY
200	375	625	7

CHAPTER 9
FLATCARS & SEARCHLIGHT CARS

For real railroads, flatcars have long provided a means of transporting bulky cargo that is largely impervious to weather. Machinery, including vehicles such as tractors and bulldozers, as well as such bulk goods as pipe and lumber, were and are carried on flats.

For toymakers, flatcars are often the least expensive type of rolling stock to produce. Not only is the fabrication of the body simple, the decoration process as well is very basic. And, in the case of Lionel, the flatcar also formed an ideal base for its searchlight cars.

For children, who often were the owners of the toy trains discussed in this book, the flat car and the gondola usually held the greatest play value. Other toys could be intermingled with the trains through these cars, with toy tractors or Lincoln Logs serving as the payload.

Today, evidence of such use is often seen in the form of scratched paint and even a few dents…just as there is on real flatcars.

11 Flatcar: Lionel's first Standard Gauge flatcar was this car, which was produced for 20 years beginning in 1906. In the early years, handrails ran the length of each side of the car, but these were ultimately eliminated.

11 Flatcar (Type I): When production of the 11 began in 1906, its 11 1/4" long body was not embossed. The car was primed, using either red or yellow primer, then painted maroon. Two vertically mounted brakewheels were found on the car, as were handrails along each side. The primer is visible on the underside of the car.

VG	EX	LN	RARITY
225	275	350	8

11 Flatcar (Type II): An identical car was also produced, but lacking the handrails.

VG	EX	LN	RARITY
125	175	250	8

11 Flatcar (Type III): About 1911, there were several changes made to the 11. "LIONEL MFG. CO. - NY" was embossed in the underside, where the red primer was also visible. The body was painted orange. Rubber-stamped in black on the sides of the car was "PENNSYLVANIA R.R." This car did not have handrails, but did have two brakewheels mounted on vertical shafts.

VG	EX	LN	RARITY
75	125	175	6

11 FLATCAR TYPE IV

11 Flatcar (Type IV):  The car was also produced painted red with two brakewheels, no handrails and no rubber-stamping. The bottom of the car was embossed "LIONEL MFG. CO. - NY".

VG	EX	LN	RARITY
50	75	100	5

11 Flatcar (Type V): A brown version of the flatcar was made with handrails and brakewheels. "LIONEL MFG. CO." was embossed in the underside of the car. Rubber-stamped on the sides of the car was "PENNSYLVANIA R.R."

VG	EX	LN	RARITY
50	75	100	5

11 Flatcar (Type VI): The unlettered handrail-equipped car was also available in maroon. Stamped into its metal bottom was "LIONEL MFG. CO."

VG	EX	LN	RARITY
50	75	100	5

11 Flatcar (Type VII): During 1916, Lionel stopped embossing its name in the car bottoms. In fact, "Lionel" did not appear anywhere on the car, which was now painted brown with black trim. Rubber-stamped on the sides of the car was a sans-serif "PENNSYLVANIA R.R."

VG	EX	LN	RARITY
50	75	100	5

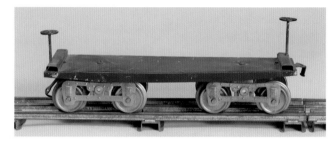

11 Flatcar (Type VIII): Some brown cars were produced, which, though otherwise identical to the ones listed as Type VII, lacked the rubber-stamped railroad markings.

VG	EX	LN	RARITY
50	75	100	5

11 Flatcar (Type IX): For 1918, Lionel returned to marking its cars, perhaps to emphasize the new name for the company. Rubber-stamped on the underside of the cars was the legend "MADE IN U.S.A. – THE LIONEL CORPORATION – NEW YORK". One type of car had a gray body with no handrails, two brakewheels and no railroad markings.

VG	EX	LN	RARITY
50	75	100	5

11 Flatcar (Type X): Another version was painted brown and, except for the maker's identification stamped on the bottom, was devoid of markings. It was otherwise identical to the Type IX.

VG	EX	LN	RARITY
50	75	100	5

11 Flatcar (Type XI): The brown car with the legend rubber-stamped on the bottom was also made with "PENNSYLVANIA R.R." rubber-stamped on the side in black.

VG	EX	LN	RARITY
50	75	100	5

11 Flatcar (Type XII): Still with "MADE IN U.S.A. – THE LIONEL CORPORATION – NEW YORK" stamped on the bottom, a car was made that was painted maroon. Two brass brakewheels were on this car, but again no handrails were present. "PENNSYLVANIA R.R." was rubber-stamped on the side in black.

1939 CATALOG

VG	EX	LN	RARITY
50	75	100	5

11 Flatcar (Type XIII):
Otherwise identical to the Type XII, this car did not have the "PENNSYLVANIA" lettering.

VG	EX	LN	RARITY
35	55	75	4

211 Flatcar:
Lionel's 211 series of flatcars, much like Henry Ford's Model T, could be had in any color you wanted, so long as you wanted black. Production began in 1926 and continued through 1940. Beyond the color, other constants through the car's production were the use of nickel stakes and "211 THE LIONEL LINES 211" being rubber-stamped in gold on the car sides. Despite this, a surprising variety of cars were built with this catalog number. A simulated load of lumber, made from wood, was carried on the car. The two chief variations of these loads have to do with the length of the top "layer" of wood. On the bulk of these loads, this top layer is 1/2" shorter than the lower layers, while a few are a full inch shorter. The loads (and stakes) have been reproduced with great accuracy. The position of the brakewheels varied from side to side, depending on which side was "up" when the metal body blank was inserted in the forming die. While this aspect does add some variety to a collection, the brakewheel orientation does not affect the value, and so is not distinguished in the listings.

211 Flatcar (Type I):
The trucks on the first year's production were retained with cotter pins and had nickel journals.

VG	EX	LN	RARITY
100	150	225	3

211 Flatcar (Type II):
Sometime between 1927 and 1929, the trucks began to be mounted using screws.

VG	EX	LN	RARITY
100	150	225	3

211 Flatcar (Type III):
In 1930, copper journals began to be used on the trucks. Some trucks were retained with horseshoe washers, while other trucks were retained with cotter pins.

VG	EX	LN	RARITY
100	150	225	3

211 Flatcar (Type IV):
About 1935, the journal boxes reverted to nickel construction. By this time, all the trucks were mounted with horseshoe washers.

VG	EX	LN	RARITY
100	150	225	3

Price Guide Key: **VG** = Very Good, **EX** = Excellent, **LN** = Like New | *Values for each condition are in U.S. dollars.* | **Rarity** = Scale from 1-8 with 8 being the hardest to find.

83

11 Flatcar Type IV

220 Searchlight Car Type I

220 Searchlight Car: This car joined the product line in 1931. It was created by mounting the searchlight and platform assembly designed for the 0-gauge 800/2800-series cars on the 211 flatcar. The cars were rubber-stamped "220 THE LIONEL LINES 220" in gold on their sides

220 Searchlight Car (Type I):  When first produced, the light platform was painted terracotta, and the lamps and handrails were brass. The journals were copper.

VG	EX	LN	RARITY
225	300	375	4

220 Searchlight Car (Type II): During 1935, the journals began to be nickel. The lamps and handrails continued to be brass, and the light base remained painted in terracotta.

VG	EX	LN	RARITY
225	300	375	4

220 Searchlight Car (Type III): Probably in 1936, the light bases began to be painted light green. At the same time, the handrails and lamps began to be finished in nickel, matching the journals.

VG	EX	LN	RARITY
350	425	550	6

220 Searchlight Car (Type IV): An unusual variation of this car occurred when Lionel repainted some terracotta lamp bases in the new light green color. This resulted in a slightly different shade and texture to the paint.

VG	EX	LN	RARITY
450	525	650	7

511 Flatcar: Offered from 1927 through 1940, this car came in a few more varieties than did the 211. The rubber-stamped "LIONEL LINES" on the sides of the car was usually done in gold, but it is in silver on some variations produced after 1935. Earlier cars that appear to have silver stamping actually have faded gold markings. The paint itself is green, most often a dark green, slightly less often a medium green, and occasionally a very dark green that sometimes appears black. Usually the simulated lumber load is a single large block of wood with "planks" milled in, but near the end of production eight individual pieces of lumber were supplied with the car.

511 Flatcar (Type I): The trucks on the first year's production were retained with cotter pins and had nickel journals. Gold rubber-stamped lettering was applied to the sides of the dark green car. Brass stakes secured the load.

VG	EX	LN	RARITY
50	70	100	3

511 Flatcar (Type II): In 1928, nickel began to be used for the stakes. The remainder of the car was unchanged.

VG	EX	LN	RARITY
50	70	100	3

220 Searchlight Car Type III

511 Flatcar Type I

511 Flatcar (Type III): At about the same time as the nickel stakes were introduced, a group of cars was produced painted a medium shade of green.

VG	EX	LN	RARITY
50	70	100	3

511 Flatcar (Type IV): During 1930, the nickel journals on the trucks were replaced with copper. The color reverted to dark green, and the gold rubber-stamping was unchanged. A few of these cars had brass stakes, but most had nickel. Because stakes are so easily interchanged, there is no difference in value warranted based on this variation.

VG	EX	LN	RARITY
50	70	100	3

511 Flatcar (Type V): It is believed that 1930 was also the year that the very dark green–almost black–car was produced. It had copper journals, nickel stakes and gold rubber-stamping.

VG	EX	LN	RARITY
50	70	100	3

511 Flatcar (Type VI): Yet another version of the 511 built in 1930 had silver, rather than gold, colored rubber-stamped lettering on its dark green flanks. Once again the journals were copper and the stakes nickel.

VG	EX	LN	RARITY
50	70	100	3

511 Flatcar (Type VII): In 1931, horseshoe washers began to be used to retain the trucks on the 511. Dark green continued to be the color of the car, and nickel stakes remained in use. The journals were copper.

VG	EX	LN	RARITY
50	70	100	3

511 Flatcar (Type VIII): An uncommon variation exists, made in 1932. It is a standard green car with all of the normal features of the previous car including the Lionel Lines script on the side and the trucks are held on with a cotter pin, but is stamped 1771 on the bottom instead of 511. The number 1771 is used for the Ives car that Lionel made for that line of trains, so this should be considered a factory error.

VG	EX	LN	RARITY
70	100	125	5

511 Flatcar (Type IX): From 1936 onward, the color of the car was a medium green. Nickel journals were used on the trucks, and nickel stakes retained the load. The rubber-stamped lettering was either gold or silver, but no difference in value or scarcity is associated with this variation.

VG	EX	LN	RARITY
50	70	100	3

520 Searchlight Car: Like the 220, this car joined the product line in 1931. It was created by mounting the searchlight and platform assembly designed for the 0-gauge 800/2800-series cars on the 511 flatcar. The cars were rubber-stamped "LIONEL LINES" in gold on their sides.

Price Guide Key: VG = Very Good, EX = Excellent, LN = Like New | *Values for each condition are in U.S. dollars.* | Rarity = Scale from 1-8 with 8 being the hardest to find.

85

520 SEARCHLIGHT CAR TYPE II

520 Searchlight Car (Type I): When first produced, the light platform was painted terra cotta, and the lamps and handrails were brass. The journals were copper.

VG	EX	LN	RARITY
100	150	200	3

520 Searchlight Car (Type II): Probably in 1936, the light bases began to be painted bright light green. At the same time the handrails and lamps began to be finished in nickel, as were the journals.

VG	EX	LN	RARITY
105	160	225	4

520 Searchlight Car (Type III): On other cars, the light bases were painted a darker, less bright, light green. Nickel handrails, journals and lamps were used.

VG	EX	LN	RARITY
105	160	225	3

520 Searchlight Car (Type IV): An unusual variation of this car occurred when Lionel repainted some terra-cotta lamp bases in the new light green color. This resulted in a slightly different shade and texture to the paint.

VG	EX	LN	RARITY
200	300	425	7

CHAPTER 10
GONDOLA & DUMP CARS

Gondola cars, along with flatcars, no doubt were the least interesting cars in the eyes of train buyers prior to World War II, just as they are today. However, despite this lack of immediate appeal, these cars probably did more to foster enjoyment of the trains by children than did the more elegant Pullmans.

These simple cars gave the child an opportunity to interact with the trains. Lincoln Logs, marbles, sticks and rocks suddenly became valuable commodities in transit in the child's mind. Creativity was fostered, finding other toys that could be integrated into the trains as well, adding to the cargo.

Perhaps for this reason, or perhaps due to their relatively low manufacturing costs, gondolas were included in many starter sets. While this makes these cars on a whole fairly common today, at the same time such mass production gave ample opportunity for many variations to be produced, and they were.

12 Gondola (Type I): The 12 was Lionel's first standard guage Gondola. It was offered from 1906 through 1926. When production of the 12 began in 1906, its 10 3/4" long body was soldered together from four parts. Neither the car body nor its underframe were embossed. The car was primed, using either red or yellow primer, then painted red. Two black vertically-mounted handrails were found on the car, mounted

on red shafts. The primer is visible on the underside of the car. Rubber-stamped in black on the side of the car were "CAPACITY 80,000 LBS.", "Lake Shore" and "WEIGHT 35,000 LBS."

VG	EX	LN	RARITY
125	175	250	8

12 Gondola (Type II): About 1911, there were several changes made to the 12. "LIONEL MFG. CO." was embossed in the underside, where the red primer was also visible. The body, which was painted dark olive green, was now made of only two parts, rather than the previous four. Rubber-stamped in black on the sides of the car were "CAPACITY 80,000 LBS.", "Lake Shore" and "WEIGHT 35,000 LBS." Four columns of simulated rivets were embossed into the sides of the car. Mounted on red vertical shafts were two black brakewheels.

VG	EX	LN	RARITY
125	175	250	8

12 Gondola (Type III): The embossed car was also produced painted red with a dark green stripe. It was rubber-stamped in black "CAPACITY 80,000 LBS.", "Lake Shore" and "WEIGHT 35,000 LBS." The black brakewheels on red vertical shafts were used on this car as well.

VG	EX	LN	RARITY
40	65	100	6

Price Guide Key: **VG** = Very Good, **EX** = Excellent, **LN** = Like New | *Values for each condition are in U.S. dollars.* | **Rarity** = Scale from 1-8 with 8 being the hardest to find.

87

12 GONDOLA TYPE III

VG	EX	LN	RARITY
40	65	100	6

12 Gondola (Type VII): When 1918 rolled around, Lionel chose to resume putting its name on the 10-series cars, including the 12. However, its name had changed and now the rubber-stamping on the underside of the cars read "MADE IN U.S.A. – THE LIONEL CORPORATION – NEW YORK". One type of car had a gray body with pea green trim. The rubber-stamped lettering on the sides of this car read "LAKE SHORE" and "65784", and in much smaller print "CAPACITY 20000 WEIGHT 10000".

VG	EX	LN	RARITY
40	65	100	6

12 Gondola (Type IV): Some of these embossed cars were painted brown. This version was rubber-stamped on the sides of this car with "LAKE SHORE" and "65784", and in much smaller print "CAPACITY 60000 WEIGHT 34500 – LENGTH INSIDE 36 FT – M.C.B. COUPLERS – AIR BRAKE".

VG	EX	LN	RARITY
40	65	100	6

12 Gondola (Type V): Some of the brown cars had dark olive green stripes rather than black. These cars had embossed into their sides four columns of simulated rivets. The brakewheels were black and their shafts were brown. "LAKE SHORE 65784" was rubber-stamped on each side in black.

VG	EX	LN	RARITY
40	65	100	6

12 Gondola (Type VI): A new color, gray, was introduced to the car, as well as a new railroad name, Rock Island. Gold rubber-stamping spelled out the logo in all caps: "ROCK ISLAND LINES".

12 Gondola (Type VIII): A second version of the green-trimmed gray gondola was also produced. This version was rubber-stamped on the sides of this car with "LAKE SHORE"

and "65784", and in much smaller print "CAPACITY WEIGHT 34500 – LENGTH INSIDE 36 FT – M.C.B. COUPLERS – AIR BRAKE".

VG	EX	LN	RARITY
40	65	100	6

12 Gondola (Type IX): A third variation of the gray Lake Shore gondola with green trim was rubber-stamped in this manner: "LAKE SHORE", "65784", with smaller "CAPACITY 60000 WEIGHT 36500".

VG	EX	LN	RARITY
40	65	100	6

12 Gondola (Type X): "ROCK ISLAND LINES" was rubber-stamped in gold on some of the gray cars. They had dark green trim, and additional lettering reading "CAPACITY 20000 WEIGHT 10000".

VG	EX	LN	RARITY
40	65	100	6

12 Gondola (Type XI): The dark green trimmed gray body was also sometimes rubber-stamped simply "LAKE SHORE" and "65784" in black.

VG	EX	LN	RARITY
40	65	100	6

12 Gondola (Type XII): "CAPACITY 60000 WEIGHT 34500 – LENGTH INSIDE 36 FT – M.C.B. COUPLERS – AIR BRAKE" was rubber-stamped in black on some of the gray "LAKE SHORE" and "65784" gondolas. These cars had olive upper and lower stripes.

VG	EX	LN	RARITY
40	65	100	6

12 Gondola (Type XIII): Slightly more difficult to find is a brown car with olive upper and lower trim. These cars bore black rubber-stamped markings reading "LAKE SHORE" and "65784", and in much smaller print "CAPACITY 60000 WEIGHT 34500".

VG	EX	LN	RARITY
50	80	125	7

16 Ballast Car: Traditionally thought of by collectors as a hopper car, stylistically this car, produced from 1906 through 1926, has more in common with a gondola. Levers on the ends of this 10 3/4" long car were used to open the car sides, allowing the cargo to be discharged.

16 Ballast Car (Type I): One of the earliest versions of this car had a maroon body with green trim. It had a yellow frame and was decorated with black serif "PENNSYLVANIA 65784" rubber-stamped lettering.

VG	EX	LN	RARITY
200	275	375	6

16 Ballast Car (Type II): An identical car was made with a brown body trimmed in black.

VG	EX	LN	RARITY
200	275	375	6

16 Ballast Car (Type III): About 1911, "LIONEL MFG. CO." began to be embossed in the underframe of the car, which was now painted black. The brown body was trimmed in black. Rubber-stamped in gold sans-serif lettering were "PENNSYLVANIA 65784", "CAPACITY 20000 LBS. WEIGHT 10000 LBS."

VG	EX	LN	RARITY
125	200	275	5

16 Ballast Car (Type IV): The car described as Type III above was also made with a maroon body trimmed in dark green. The rubber-stamping was like that of the Type III.

VG	EX	LN	RARITY
90	125	175	3

16 Ballast Car (Type V): A brown car was also made with black trim as well as frame. Rubber-stamped in gold sans-serif lettering were "PENNSYLVANIA 65784", "CAPACITY 20000 LBS. WEIGHT 34500 LBS."

VG	EX	LN	RARITY
125	200	275	5

16 Ballast Car (Type VI): Black trim also came to the maroon ballast cars, joining a black frame. "PENNSYLVANIA R.R." was rubber-stamped in gold sans-serif lettering on the flanks of the car.

VG	EX	LN	RARITY
90	125	175	3

16 Ballast Car (Type VII): During the 1911-1912 time period, the ballast car was also made with a dark green body trimmed in maroon. The frame of this car was also painted maroon. "PENNSYLVANIA R.R." was rubber-stamped in gold sans-serif lettering on the sides of this version.

VG	EX	LN	RARITY
90	125	175	3

16 Ballast Car (Type VIII): During 1916, Lionel stopped embossing its name in the car bottoms. In fact, "Lionel" did not appear anywhere on the ballast car, which was now painted red with black trim. "PENNSYLVANIA 76399" was rubber-stamped in gold sans-serif lettering on the sides of this version.

VG	EX	LN	RARITY
90	125	175	3

16 Ballast Car (Type IX): Some of the 1916-18 cars without Lionel markings were painted maroon with black trim. Rubber-stamped in black on these cars was "PENNSYLVANIA

Price Guide Key: **VG** = Very Good, **EX** = Excellent, **LN** = Like New | *Values for each condition are in U.S. dollars.* | **Rarity** = Scale from 1-8 with 8 being the hardest to find.

89

16 BALLAST CAR TYPE XI

65784" and "CAPACITY 20000 LBS. - WEIGHT 10000 LBS."

VG	EX	LN	RARITY
90	125	175	3

16 Ballast Car (Type X): When 1918 rolled around, Lionel chose to resume rubber-stamping its name on its products. However, its name had changed, and now the underside of the cars read "MADE IN U.S.A. – THE LIONEL CORPORATION – NEW YORK". It was maroon with dark green trim and a black frame. On the sides of the car was rubber-stamped "PENNSYLVANIA 65784" in black.

VG	EX	LN	RARITY
90	125	175	3

16 Ballast Car (Type XI): The "Corporation" cars were also produced in dark green with maroon trim and a green frame. Black "PENNSYLVANIA 65784" and "CAPACITY 20000 LBS. - WEIGHT 10000 LBS." rubber-stamped lettering was used on these cars as well. The catalog number, 16, was stamped on one end of the car body.

VG	EX	LN	RARITY
90	125	175	3

112 Gondola: Lionel's next generation of gondola car was introduced in 1910, and by the time it was discontinued in 1926, it had been produced in an even greater variety than had been the 12. For the first two years of its production run, the car was 6 1/2" long. In 1912, this was increased to 9 1/2".

112 Gondola (Type I): This 6 1/2" long car was painted dark olive green. The lip around the top of the body was painted red, and gold "N.Y.N.H. & H." lettering was rubber-stamped on its side. "CAPACITY 80000 LBS." and "WEIGHT 30000 LBS." were also rubber-stamped on the sides in gold. "LIONEL MFG. CO." was embossed in the underside of the car.

VG	EX	LN	RARITY
200	275	375	7

112 Gondola (Type II): Some cars were produced that, though otherwise identical to the previous car, had red interiors.

VG	EX	LN	RARITY
200	275	375	7

112 Gondola (Type III): Yet another variant of the basic Type I car had an olive interior.

VG	EX	LN	RARITY
200	275	375	7

112 Gondola (Type IV): The short car was also produced with a dark gray body trimmed in red. Its gold rubber-stamped lettering read "LAKE SHORE" and "CAPACITY 80000 LBS.", "WEIGHT 30000 LBS."

VG	EX	LN	RARITY
200	275	375	7

112 Gondola (Type V): In 1912, the car was lengthened to 9 1/2" long. The "LAKE SHORE" lettering continued, as did

112 GONDOLA TYPE XI

the red body. However, now the lettering was rubber-stamped in black and the body had dark olive trim. "CAPACITY 80000 LBS." and "WEIGHT 35000 LBS." were also rubber-stamped on the sides in black.

VG	EX	LN	RARITY
50	60	75	4

112 Gondola (Type VI): For some reason, a number of these cars were made that, otherwise identical to the Type V, were marked "CAPACITY 20000 LBS." and "WEIGHT 30000 LBS."

VG	EX	LN	RARITY
75	100	135	6

112 Gondola (Type VII): On some 112 gondolas, the rubber-stamped lettering was presented as "Lake Shore". The capacity stamping was "CAPACITY 80000 LBS.", "WEIGHT 35000 LBS."

VG	EX	LN	RARITY
50	60	75	4

112 Gondola (Type VIII): "WEIGHT 35000 LBS" was rubber-stamped on the lower left of some of these red "LAKE SHORE" cars, while "CAPACITY 60000 LBS" was stamped on the lower right.

VG	EX	LN	RARITY
50	60	75	4

112 Gondola (Type IX): Another variation had the "CAPACITY 60000 LBS" stamped on the lower left, while "WEIGHT 35000 LBS" was applied to the lower right. "LAKE SHORE" remained the largest marking on the sides of these red cars.

VG	EX	LN	RARITY
50	60	75	4

112 Gondola (Type X): Some brown cars were made with dark olive trim. The largest lettering on their sides was the black two-line rubber-stamping "LAKE SHORE" – "65784". The reporting marks, "CAPACITY 60000 WEIGHT 34500 – LENGTH INSIDE 36 FT – M.C.B. COUPLERS – AIR BRAKE", were also rubber-stamped in black.

VG	EX	LN	RARITY
50	60	75	4

112 Gondola (Type XI): Simplified lettering was applied to some of the dark brown "LAKE SHORE" 112 gondolas. This consisted merely of a black "CAPACITY 20000 LBS"

rubber-stamped above "WEIGHT 10000 LBS". The cars were numbered "65784" in black above the capacity.

VG	EX	LN	RARITY
50	60	75	4

112 Gondola (Type XII): A dark brown version of the 112 was built, trimmed with a dark olive painted upper rim. This car was marked with black rubber-stamped lettering reading "NYC & HRRR", with the number "76399" beneath the road name. "CAPACITY 60000 WEIGHT 34500 – LENGTH INSIDE 36 FT – M.C.B. COUPLERS – AIR BRAKE", were also rubber-stamped in black on the cars' sides.

VG	EX	LN	RARITY
50	60	75	4

112 Gondola (Type XIII): Simplified lettering was applied to some of the dark brown "NYC & HRRR" 112 gondolas. This consisted merely of a black "CAPACITY 20000 LBS" rubber-stamped above "WEIGHT 10000 LBS". The cars were numbered "65784" in black beneath the road name.

VG	EX	LN	RARITY
50	60	75	4

112 Gondola (Type XIV): Beginning in 1916, the Lionel markings were no longer embossed on the car floors. The brown body 112 with dark olive trim continued to be produced with the simplified capacity markings as listed earlier. Even the "65784" number continued, but the road name reverted to "LAKE SHORE".

VG	EX	LN	RARITY
50	60	75	4

112 Gondola (Type XV): In 1918, "MADE IN U.S.A. – THE LIONEL CORPORATION – NEW YORK" began to be rubber-stamped on the underside of the cars, which were now painted dark gray with a dark olive rim. Also rubber-stamped on the bottom was the catalog number, 112. On the sides of the car, rubber-stamped in black, were "LAKE SHORE", and on the right end; "CAPACITY 20000 LBS" and "WEIGHT 10000 LBS" were rubber-stamped beneath "65784" in black.

VG	EX	LN	RARITY
50	60	75	4

Price Guide Key: **VG** = Very Good, **EX** = Excellent, **LN** = Like New | *Values for each condition are in U.S. dollars.* | **Rarity** = Scale from 1-8 with 8 being the hardest to find.

91

112 Gondola (Type XVI): In some cases, the rim was trimmed in dark green rather than dark olive, but the rest of the car was identical to the Type XV.

VG	EX	LN	RARITY
50	60	75	4

112 Gondola (Type XVII): Some cars, while similar to the Type XVI, were painted a noticeably lighter shade of gray, and had all their lettering rubber-stamped in gold rather than black.

VG	EX	LN	RARITY
50	60	75	4

112 Gondola (Type XVIII): The lighter shade of gray was also used for some cars, which were rubber-stamped "ROCK ISLAND LINES". This stamping was in gold, as was all the rubber-stamping on this car, including the catalog number on the bottom.

VG	EX	LN	RARITY
50	60	75	4

112 Gondola (Type XIX): The "LAKE SHORE" "65784" cars were also produced with red bodies with green trim. Their lettering was rubber-stamped in black.

VG	EX	LN	RARITY
60	75	100	5

212 Gondola: The 212 debuted in 1926, and remained in Lionel's product line through 1940. During this time, it was produced in numerous variations. All of these cars had a black frame, onto which were attached sides of various colors. It is the color of these sides that are used when referring to the color of the cars.

212 Gondola (Type I): The earliest of these cars were painted gray. They had brass trim, and brass letter and number plates. Their journal boxes were nickel. The markings on the plates were stamped in black. The trucks were retained by cotter pins.

VG	EX	LN	RARITY
100	150	200	6

212 Gondola (Type II): A maroon-bodied car replaced the gray car, likely in 1927. The decoration and trim of these cars was identical to that of the gray cars. Most have their trucks retained by cotter pins, though occasionally one will surface which has screws mounting its trucks.

VG	EX	LN	RARITY
75	115	150	3

212 GONDOLA TYPE II

212 GONDOLA TYPE IV

212 Gondola (Type III): About 1930, the nickel journal boxes were replaced with copper ones.

VG	EX	LN	RARITY
75	115	150	3

212 Gondola (Type IV): 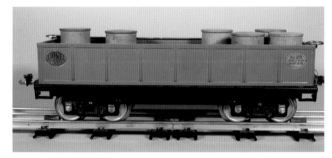 In 1935, the color of the gondola changed again, with the maroon giving way to a medium shade of light green. These cars had nickel journals and black-lettered brass plates. Their trucks were retained with horseshoe washers.

VG	EX	LN	RARITY
100	150	200	6

212 Gondola (Type V): The 212 is known to exist in a darker shade of light green as well. These cars have copper journals and black-stamped aluminum plates.

VG	EX	LN	RARITY
100	150	200	6

212 Gondola (Type VI): Probably during 1936, the 212 became more or less standardized. Horseshoe washers retained their trucks, which had nickel journal boxes. The plates, which were lettered in black, were made of aluminum. The color of the car sides was green, although a variety of shades and lusters of paint are known to have been used.

VG	EX	LN	RARITY
100	150	200	5

218 Dump Car: This operating car was an offering from 1926 through 1938. The dump body was mounted on a black-painted frame, and its markings were stamped in black on brass plates. Brass trim adorned the car.

218 Dump Car (Type I): The most common version of this car has a Mojave-painted dump bin. Like most of the cars in this series, its trucks were retained by cotter pins, and had nickel journals. Two brass knobs were used to operate the car. Brass supports were used on each end to mount the dump bin.

VG	EX	LN	RARITY
200	275	350	3

218 Dump Car (Type II): Some, very few actually, of these cars had peacock-colored dump bins. The remainder of the car was the same as listed.

RARITY
Too rarely traded to establish accurate pricing.

218 Dump Car (Type III): Another hard to find version was built with a dump bin painted pea green.

RARITY
Too rarely traded to establish accurate pricing.

218 Dump Car (Type IV): A gray version of the dump bin was also used and, like any of the colors but Mojave, is today difficult to locate. All of these "odd colored" cars used brass supports for the dump bin.

RARITY
Too rarely traded to establish accurate pricing.

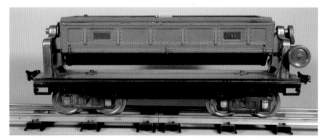

Price Guide Key: **VG** = Very Good, **EX** = Excellent, **LN** = Like New | *Values for each condition are in U.S. dollars.* | **Rarity** = Scale from 1-8 with 8 being the hardest to find.

93

218 Dump Car (Type V): As production of the Mojave car continued, only one brass control knob was used. The rest of the car was unchanged.

VG	EX	LN	RARITY
175	225	325	3

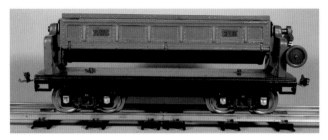

218 Dump Car (Type VI): About 1929, the brass supports were replaced with painted steel supports. Usually the supports were painted to match the bin. In some instances, the brass supports were painted as well.

VG	EX	LN	RARITY
175	225	325	3

218 Dump Car (Type VII): Near the end of the Mojave car's 12-year production run, copper journals were used on its trucks.

VG	EX	LN	RARITY
175	225	325	3

512 Gondola: Cataloged from 1927 through 1939, the 512 gondola was included in many sets. Like the 212, it always had a black frame, and the colors listed refer to the color of the cars' sides. The values listed assume the presence of a cargo of barrels, which were supplied with most cars. Some cars were furnished with a set of miniature tools. Add a premium for that load.

512 Gondola (Type I): 🔲 Riding on cotter pin-retained trucks with nickel journals, the first of the 512 series were painted peacock. They had brass trim, and their name and number plates were brass with black printing. A lubrication label was attached to the bottom of the car.

VG	EX	LN	RARITY
30	40	50	4

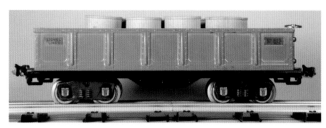

512 Gondola (Type II): About 1930, copper journals replaced the nickel ones and the lubrication label was no longer applied. The trucks were now secured with horseshoe washers.

VG	EX	LN	RARITY
30	40	50	2

512 Gondola (Type III): Nickel journals reappeared about 1935. Brass plates continued to be used, still marked in black.

VG	EX	LN	RARITY
30	40	50	2

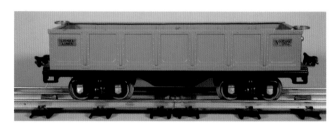

512 Gondola (Type IV): Probably in the latter part of 1935, the 512 body began to be painted light green rather than peacock. At the same time, aluminum began to be used for the plates in lieu of brass, although the markings continued to be black. Various shades and lusters of light green paint were used.

VG	EX	LN	RARITY
30	40	50	2

512 GONDOLA TYPE I

CHAPTER 11
HOPPER & BALLAST CARS

Two types of hopper cars are used by real railroads to move bulk commodities. Covered hopper cars are totally enclosed. They are used to transport products such as grains and dry chemicals that must be sheltered from the weather. These cars are loaded through hatches in the roof. Open hoppers lack this roof, and are used to haul cargo that does not need protection from the weather, such as coal or gravel.

Both types of cars are customarily unloaded by opening doors in the bottom of the car body, allowing gravity and the sloping sides of the car to force the contents out. Lionel did not produce a Standard Gauge version of a covered hopper.

16 Ballast Car: From 1906 through 1926, this 10 3/4" long manually-operated car was available. Levers on the ends of the car were used to open the car sides, allowing the cargo to be discharged.

16 Ballast Car (Type I): One of the earliest versions of this car had a maroon body with green trim. It had a yellow frame and was decorated with black serif "PENNSYLVANIA 65784" rubber-stamped lettering.

VG	EX	LN	RARITY
200	275	375	6

16 Ballast Car (Type II): An identical car was made with a brown body trimmed in black.

VG	EX	LN	RARITY
200	275	375	6

16 Ballast Car (Type III): About 1911, "LIONEL MFG. CO." began to be embossed in the underframe of the car, which was now painted black. The brown body was trimmed in black. Rubber-stamped in gold sans-serif lettering were "PENNSYLVANIA 65784", "CAPACITY 20000 LBS. WEIGHT 10000 LBS."

VG	EX	LN	RARITY
125	200	275	5

16 Ballast Car (Type IV): The car described as Type III was also made with a maroon body trimmed in dark green. The rubber-stamping was like that of the Type III.

VG	EX	LN	RARITY
90	125	175	3

16 Ballast Car (Type V): A brown car was also made with black trim as well as frame. Rubber-stamped in gold sans-serif lettering were "PENNSYLVANIA 65784", "CAPACITY 20000 LBS. WEIGHT 34500 LBS."

VG	EX	LN	RARITY
125	200	275	5

16 Ballast Car (Type VI): Black trim also came to the maroon ballast cars, joining a black frame. "PENNSYLVANIA R.R."

Price Guide Key: **VG** = Very Good, **EX** = Excellent, **LN** = Like New | *Values for each condition are in U.S. dollars.* | **Rarity** = Scale from 1-8 with 8 being the hardest to find.

95

16 BALLAST CAR TYPE IX

was rubber-stamped in gold sans-serif lettering on the flanks of the car.

VG	EX	LN	RARITY
90	125	175	3

16 Ballast Car (Type VII): During the 1911-1912 time period, the ballast car was also made with a dark green body trimmed in maroon. The frame of this car was also painted maroon. "PENNSYLVANIA R.R." was rubber-stamped in gold sans-serif lettering on the sides of this version.

VG	EX	LN	RARITY
90	125	175	3

16 Ballast Car (Type VIII): During 1916, Lionel stopped embossing its name in the car bottoms. In fact, "Lionel" did not appear anywhere on the ballast car, which was now painted red with black trim. "PENNSYLVANIA 76399" was rubber-stamped in gold sans-serif lettering on the sides of this version.

VG	EX	LN	RARITY
90	125	175	3

16 Ballast Car (Type IX): 🖼 Some of the 1916-1918 cars without Lionel markings were painted maroon with black trim. Rubber-stamped in black on these cars was "PENNSYLVANIA 65784" and "CAPACITY 20000 LBS. - WEIGHT 10000 LBS."

VG	EX	LN	RARITY
90	125	175	3

16 Ballast Car (Type X): When 1918 rolled around, Lionel chose to resume rubber-stamping its name on its products. However, the name had changed, and now the underside

of the cars read "MADE IN U.S.A. – THE LIONEL CORPORATION – NEW YORK". It was a maroon car with dark green trim and a black frame. On the sides of the car was rubber-stamped "PENNSYLVANIA 65784" in black.

VG	EX	LN	RARITY
90	125	175	3

16 Ballast Car (Type XI): The "Corporation" cars were also produced in dark green with maroon trim and a green frame. Black "PENNSYLVANIA 65784" and "CAPACITY 20000 LBS. - WEIGHT 10000 LBS." rubber-stamped lettering was used on these cars as well. The catalog number, 16, was stamped on one end of the car body.

VG	EX	LN	RARITY
90	125	175	3

116 Ballast Car: When the smaller 100-series cars were introduced in 1910, naturally an equivalent to the popular 16 was part of the line. Stylistically, this car was much more like a hopper car than was the 16, which was a gondola-like design. The side-mounted control lever opened two doors, which discharged the cargo onto the rails beneath the car. The 116 was produced through 1926, and in many variations. However with a single exception, none of the variations are significantly harder to find or more valuable than any of the others.

116 Ballast Car (Type I): The notation "LIONEL MFG. CO." was embossed on the underside of the earliest cars. These cars had maroon bodies trimmed in black, with gold rubber-stamped lettering reading "N.Y.N.H & H." centered on the car sides. To the left, it was stamped "CAPACITY

116 BALLAST CAR TYPE III

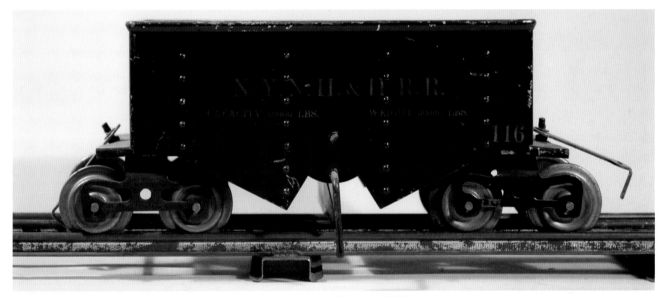

116 BALLAST CAR TYPE XIII

80,000 LBS", while on the right was stamped "WEIGHT 30,000 LBS".

VG	EX	LN	RARITY
60	80	110	3

116 Ballast Car (Type II): Other cars were made that were identical to the ones described above, except the weight legend stamped on them read "WEIGHT 35,000 LBS".

VG	EX	LN	RARITY
50	75	100	3

116 Ballast Car (Type III):  A third version of weight and capacity lettering was rubber-stamped in black on some cars. This lettering was stamped "CAPACITY 50,000 LBS" on the left, while on the right was stamped "WEIGHT 30,000 LBS".

VG	EX	LN	RARITY
50	75	100	3

116 Ballast Car (Type IV): The 116 ballast car was also produced in overall brown. In addition to the "N.Y.N.H & H." lettering, this car was stamped "CAPACITY 50,000

LBS" on the left, and "WEIGHT 30,000 LBS" on the right. Gold colored sans-serif type was used for these.

VG	EX	LN	RARITY
50	75	100	3

116 Ballast Car (Type V): The brown car was also made with black rubber-stamped lettering.

VG	EX	LN	RARITY
50	75	100	3

116 Ballast Car (Type VI): A third brown version was made, which had a distinctly red tint. Some of these cars also had their upper rim painted black.

VG	EX	LN	RARITY
50	75	100	3

116 Ballast Car (Type VII): In 1916, the Lionel data ceased to be embossed into the car. The red-brown car continued to be made, but now its rim was dark olive. "N.Y.N.H & H.", "CAPACITY 50,000 LBS" and "WEIGHT 30,000 LBS" were rubber-stamped in black on the car.

Price Guide Key: **VG** = Very Good, **EX** = Excellent, **LN** = Like New | *Values for each condition are in U.S. dollars.* | **Rarity** = *Scale from 1-8 with 8 being the hardest to find.*

97

216 HOPPER CAR TYPE I

VG	EX	LN	RARITY
50	75	100	3

116 Ballast Car (Type VIII): Some of these cars also had their catalog number, 116, rubber-stamped on their ends.

VG	EX	LN	RARITY
50	75	100	3

116 Ballast Car (Type IX): Cars identical to Type VII were made, with maroon replacing red-brown as the primary color.

VG	EX	LN	RARITY
50	75	100	3

116 Ballast Car (Type X): Maroon versions of the Type VIII were made as well.

VG	EX	LN	RARITY
50	75	100	3

116 Ballast Car (Type XI): From 1918 through 1926, the 116 was marked as a product of "THE LIONEL CORP." The bodies of these cars were dark green, with black rubber-stamped lettering. On the end of the car was rubber-stamped the product number. The upper rim of the car was painted red.

VG	EX	LN	RARITY
50	75	100	3

116 Ballast Car (Type XII): Some of the dark green cars had their lettering applied with gold rubber-stamping. They were otherwise identical, but for the omission of the car number on the end.

VG	EX	LN	RARITY
50	75	100	3

116 Ballast Car (Type XIII): 🖼 The sole premium-priced 116 is this car. Dark green with red rim, and rubber-stamped in gold, this car also has its number stamped on its side, rather than its end.

VG	EX	LN	RARITY
75	100	125	7

116 Ballast Car (Type XIV): The ballast car was also made with a dark gray body trimmed in green. Black rubber-stamping was used for both its side and end lettering.

VG	EX	LN	RARITY
50	75	100	3

216 Hopper Car: The 216 hopper car was offered from 1926 through 1938. Unlike most of Lionel's products from this time period, production of the 216 was remarkably uniform. The car body was always dark green and it was always mounted on a black frame. Only its trucks, trim and plates varied.

216 Hopper Car (Type I): 🖼 As originally produced, the car had brass trim and red lettered brass plates. It rode on trucks with nickel journals.

VG	EX	LN	RARITY
200	275	375	5

216 Hopper Car (Type II): About 1928, the lettering on the brass plates changed from red to black. The trim was still brass and the journals were still nickel.

VG	EX	LN	RARITY
200	275	375	5

216 Hopper Car (Type III): 🖼 Copper journals appeared in 1930 or 1931. The rest of the car continued unchanged.

VG	EX	LN	RARITY
200	275	375	5

216 Hopper Car (Type IV): Strangely, some of the copper journal equipped cars were also produced with red lettered brass plates.

VG	EX	LN	RARITY
200	275	375	5

216 Hopper Car (Type V): In 1935, the trim on the 216 began to be nickel. This included the journal, which reverted to nickel. The plates, however, remained brass with black lettering.

VG	EX	LN	RARITY
200	275	375	5

216 Hopper Car (Type VI): 🖼 Probably in early 1936, the plates began to be made of aluminum, with black lettering. The trim and journals were nickel.

VG	EX	LN	RARITY
500	1000	1600	8

216 HOPPER CAR TYPE III

216 HOPPER CAR TYPE VI

516 Hopper Car: Much like the 216, the 516 that was cataloged from 1928 through 1940 was remarkably consistent throughout its production run. The cars were always painted red and, in most cases, had a black sheet metal simulated coal load installed in them.

516 Hopper Car (Type I): As originally produced, the cars had trucks with nickel journals, brass trim and brass plates with black lettering.

VG	EX	LN	RARITY
150	225	275	4

516 Hopper Car (Type II): As part of what was believed to be a special production run intended for use in special "coal train" sets in 1929-30, some of the cars had reporting marks and various other data rubber-stamped in gold on their sides. The rest of the car's construction was identical to the Type I.

VG	EX	LN	RARITY
200	275	375	5

516 Hopper Car (Type III): Copper journals appeared in 1930 or 1931. The rest of the car continued unchanged.

VG	EX	LN	RARITY
150	225	275	4

516 Hopper Car (Type IV): Separate sale cars were produced without simulated coal loads. As a rule, cars that were originally produced with loads will have evidence of these, either through wear or damage from the removal of the load.

VG	EX	LN	RARITY
150	225	275	5

516 Hopper Car (Type V): In about 1935, the journals reverted to nickel. The trim remained brass, as did the black-lettered plates.

VG	EX	LN	RARITY
150	225	275	4

Price Guide Key: **VG** = Very Good, **EX** = Excellent, **LN** = Like New | *Values for each condition are in U.S. dollars.* | **Rarity** = Scale from 1-8 with 8 being the hardest to find.

99

516 HOPPER CAR TYPE VI

516 HOPPER CAR TYPE VIII

516 Hopper Car (Type VI): Some of the Type V cars were also rubber-stamped with the gold reporting marks. Again, this was believed to have been done for inclusion in special sets.

VG	EX	LN	RARITY
200	275	375	5

516 Hopper Car (Type VII): Strangely, some of the copper journal equipped cars were also produced with nickel trim and black-lettered brass plates.

VG	EX	LN	RARITY
150	225	275	4

516 Hopper Car (Type VIII): In 1936 or 1937, the plates began to be made of aluminum, with black lettering. The trim and journals were nickel.

VG	EX	LN	RARITY
225	325	450	6

CHAPTER 12
BOX, STOCK & REFRIGERATOR CARS

During the first half of the 20th century, most goods shipped in the United States traveled in what railroads termed "house cars." "House car" is a term used for enclosed freight cars such as boxcars, stock, refrigerator and poultry cars. These cars are used for lading requiring protection from weather.

All of these cars are built much like a house, with permanently installed roof and sides, and are equipped with side or side and end doors. They vaguely resemble a house as well.

To assist the layman in locating a specific car, the item listings in this book group all house cars together in numeric order, rather than separating them into specific categories such as stock, box, refrigerator, etc., although a brief overview of the three main types is given.

BOXCARS

Boxcars were the dominant means of shipping goods that needed protection. Everything from clothing and appliances to automobiles was shipped inside boxcars. Lionel produced four primary types of Standard Gauge boxcars: the 10-series, and the 100-, 200- and 500-series.

REFRIGERATOR CARS

Also known as reefers, these cars were found in two major varieties in real rail yards. The earliest cars were chilled with ice. Compartments, known as bunkers, were built into each end of the car. Massive blocks of ice were loaded into these bunkers through rooftop hatches. The air inside was circulated to maintain an even temperature throughout the cargo and thick insulation was provided to prolong the cooling. Replicated by Lionel in the 200- and 500-series cars, an R suffix was often, but not always, added to a catalog number to denote refrigerator.

The necessity of maintaining extensive ice plants and docks, and the large workforce required to keep these cars serviced, was a considerable expense for railroads. The mechanical refrigerator car, which came into widespread use after World War II, dispensed with much of this expense. Mechanical refrigerator cars work much like your home refrigerator or air conditioner, with the power to drive them being supplied in most cases by a diesel engine.

STOCK CARS

The third category of house car Lionel produced in

Price Guide Key: **VG** = Very Good, **EX** = Excellent, **LN** = Like New | *Values for each condition are in U.S. dollars.* | **Rarity** = Scale from 1-8 with 8 being the hardest to find.

101

13 CATTLE CAR TYPE VIII

large numbers was the stock car. These types of railroad cars were used to transport live animals, from horses and cattle to poultry. Lionel distinguished stock cars by assigning the last two digits 13 to the catalog number.

13 Cattle Car: This green stock car was part of the Lionel product line from 1906 through 1926. During its 20-year production run, assorted details were changed, resulting in the variations listed.

13 Cattle Car (Type I): Cars produced prior to 1911 typically have yellow primer exposed on their undersides, while the upper, exposed portion of the car was painted green. Its sides were flat, with numerous cutouts to simulate open-sided construction. There were five slots in each door. The roof was made of two pieces of steel.

VG	EX	LN	RARITY
275	350	450	7

13 Cattle Car (Type II): During 1911, Lionel began embossing "LIONEL MFG. Co." into the metal of the underside of the car. The roof continued to be constructed from two pieces of steel, and the sides were still flat.

VG	EX	LN	RARITY
275	350	450	7

13 Cattle Car (Type III): Eventually, perhaps as early as 1912 or 1913, the roof began to be made from a single piece of steel.

VG	EX	LN	RARITY
125	175	225	5

13 Cattle Car (Type IV): Ultimately, a darker shade of green was used for the paint. Both the doors and the sides continued to have five horizontal slots cut in them.

VG	EX	LN	RARITY
50	75	100	3

13 Cattle Car (Type V): Some of the dark green cars had doors with only four horizontal slots cut in them.

VG	EX	LN	RARITY
50	75	100	3

13 Cattle Car (Type VI): During 1916, Lionel ceased to emboss its name in the car bottom. In fact, no Lionel markings whatsoever appeared on the cars from 1916 through 1918. The sides of the car were now embossed, giving it a more three-dimensional look. It continued to be painted dark green, and had five slots in the sides and four in the door.

VG	EX	LN	RARITY
50	75	100	3

13 Cattle Car (Type VII): The embossed-side dark green car was also made with six slots in the door and sides sometime in 1916 or earlier.

VG	EX	LN	RARITY
50	75	100	3

13 Cattle Car (Type VIII): Beginning sometime in 1918, and continuing until the 13 was discontinued in 1926, "MADE IN U.S.A. – THE LIONEL CORPORATION – NEW YORK" was rubber-stamped on the underside of the car, along with the catalog number, 13. The sides continued to be embossed and were now painted pea green. Both the sides and the doors had five slots punched out of them, yielding four slats.

VG	EX	LN	RARITY
50	75	100	3

13 Cattle Car (Type IX): Sometimes the catalog number was not stamped on the bottom of the car, which was otherwise identical to the Type VIII.

VG	EX	LN	RARITY
50	75	100	3

13 Cattle Car (Type X): Some of these late production cars were painted a darker than normal shade of green–nearly as dark as Type IV cars.

VG	EX	LN	RARITY
50	75	100	3

14 Boxcar: The first Standard Gauge boxcar offered by Lionel was the 14. This sheet metal car was produced from 1906 through 1926, and was made in many variations.

14 Boxcar (Type I): When production of the boxcar began in 1906, its body was soldered together from several parts. Neither the car body nor its underframe were embossed. The car was primed, using yellow primer, then the sides painted red. The primer is visible on the underside of various areas. The roof was black. Black vertical lines were painted on the flanks of the car to simulate the appearance of tongue and groove car siding. On each end of the car was mounted a

brakewheel, which was painted black. On either side of the doors was rubber-stamped "C.M. & ST. P –19050" in black.

VG	EX	LN	RARITY
200	325	450	7

14 Boxcar (Type II): Cars made a little later had their brakewheels painted red.

VG	EX	LN	RARITY
200	325	450	7

14 Boxcar (Type III): Another version of the car, also painted red, lacked the black vertical striping. These cars were rubber-stamped "NYC & H.R.R.R. – 54087".

VG	EX	LN	RARITY
200	325	450	7

14 Boxcar (Type IV): About 1909 or 1910, the sides began to be embossed with simulated boards, giving some texture to the car. The car continued to be red. The rubber-stamped lettering on either side of the door read "NYC & H.R.R.R. – 5906".

VG	EX	LN	RARITY
200	325	450	6

14 Boxcar (Type V): The embossed-side car body was also painted yellow-orange and rubber-stamped "NYC & H.R.R.R. – 4351".

VG	EX	LN	RARITY
200	325	450	6

14 Boxcar (Type VI): In about 1911, the entire "10-series" of cars, including the 14, began to have "LIONEL MFG. CO. - N.Y." embossed on their undersides. Yellow primer was no longer used. The number on the yellow-orange car changed to "98237".

VG	EX	LN	RARITY
50	75	100	3

14 BOXCAR TYPE VIII

Price Guide Key: **VG** = Very Good, **EX** = Excellent, **LN** = Like New | *Values for each condition are in U.S. dollars.* | **Rarity** = Scale from 1-8 with 8 being the hardest to find.

103

14 Boxcar Type X

14 Boxcar (Type VII): 🔲 The boxcar was also made in dark red, with embossed sides. This car was rubber-stamped "C.M. & ST. P – 54087" in black.

VG	EX	LN	RARITY
50	75	100	3

14 Boxcar (Type VIII): On some of these red cars, black vertical striping was painted on the embossments.

VG	EX	LN	RARITY
50	75	100	3

14 Boxcar (Type IX): Some of the cars with the black stripes were numbered "19050" rather than 54087.

VG	EX	LN	RARITY
50	75	100	3

14 Boxcar (Type X): About 1916, the boxcar began to be produced on frames that were not embossed with the Lionel name. Actually, "Lionel" did not appear anywhere on the car. These cars had embossed sides and were painted orange. They did not have the black vertical striping. The black rubber-stamped lettering applied to this car read "C.M. & ST. P. - 98237".

VG	EX	LN	RARITY
50	75	100	3

14 Boxcar (Type XI): In 1918, "MADE IN U.S.A. - THE LIONEL CORPORATION – NEW YORK" began to be rubber-stamped on the bottom of the cars. However, with the car upright, it looked just like the Type X car.

VG	EX	LN	RARITY
50	75	100	3

14 Boxcar (Type XII): Comparatively few of these cars were made, which were rubber-stamped on the bottom "Made and Guaranteed By – The Lionel Corporation – New York, U.S.A." The balance of the car was identical to the Type XI.

VG	EX	LN	RARITY
75	100	175	5

14 Boxcar (Type XIII): About 1920, a special run of boxcars was made for the Harmony Creamery. These cars, which had embossed sides, were painted dark green. A decal reading "BALTIMORE AND OHIO" in gold was placed high on the sides of the car. To the left of the door was rubber-stamped "MILK INSULATED TANK – SERVICE" in gold, while to the right of the door, also in gold, was rubber-stamped "HARMONY CREAMERY – PITTSBURGH, PA".

RARITY
Too infrequently traded to establish value.

14 Boxcar Type X

113 Cattle Car: The 113 was part of the Lionel product line from 1912 through 1926. During this time, it came first in medium and later in light green. Five horizontal rows of slots were punched out of the car sides, leaving four slats. Some cars have square-cut roof corners, others are angle cut, but because of these with which roofs are interchanged, this feature is not distinguished in the following listings.

113 Cattle Car (Type I): As first made, the cattle car was painted medium green. "LIONEL MFG CO." was embossed into the car floor. The guides that retained the opening doors had a flat cross section.

VG	EX	LN	RARITY
40	50	60	4

113 Cattle Car (Type II): The green paint used on some cars had a definite flat finish. These cars also had door guides that were rounded.

VG	EX	LN	RARITY
40	50	60	4

113 Cattle Car (Type III): Glossy green paint was used on other cars.

VG	EX	LN	RARITY
40	50	60	4

113 Cattle Car (Type IV): Pea green paint was also used, it is believed, about 1915.

VG	EX	LN	RARITY
40	50	60	4

113 Cattle Car (Type V): Like the other cars, in about 1916 the cattle cars were no longer embossed "LIONEL MFG. CO." In fact, "Lionel" does not appear at all on these cars. These cars were painted a light pea green. These and all subsequent 113 cattle cars had rounded door guides and square-cut roof ends.

VG	EX	LN	RARITY
40	50	60	4

113 Cattle Car (Type VI): Beginning in 1918, rubber-stamped on the underside of the car was "MADE IN U.S.A. - THE LIONEL CORPORATION – NEW YORK". The catalog number, 113, was also rubber-stamped on the underside, marking its first appearance on the actual product. Both a lighter and a darker shade of pea green have been found on this car, with no difference in value or scarcity.

VG	EX	LN	RARITY
40	50	60	4

113 Cattle Car (Type VII): The product number, 113, was omitted from the rubber stamping on some cars.

VG	EX	LN	RARITY
40	50	60	4

114 Boxcar: This boxcar was a part of the Lionel product line from 1912 through 1926. Through the years, it was painted red, yellow-orange and orange, but it always had "CM & ST. P" rubber-stamped in black on either side of the doorway. It appears that in most cases either Roman or sans-serif lettering could be found. Exceptions are noted in the listings.

114 Boxcar (Type I): When first sold, the 114 was painted red. In addition to the railroad initials, it had "54087" rubber-stamped on the car sides, in either serif or sans-serif lettering. "LIONEL MFG CO." was embossed into the car floor. The door handle was painted black.

VG	EX	LN	RARITY
80	125	180	6

114 Boxcar (Type II): An otherwise identical car was produced, however the body was painted yellow-orange rather than red. The door handles, however, were red. The markings were the same.

VG	EX	LN	RARITY
50	100	150	6

114 Boxcar (Type III): Some of the yellow-orange cars were numbered 62976 rather than 54087.

Price Guide Key: **VG** = Very Good, **EX** = Excellent, **LN** = Like New | *Values for each condition are in U.S. dollars.* | **Rarity** = Scale from 1-8 with 8 being the hardest to find.

105

114 Boxcar Type VI

VG	EX	LN	RARITY
50	100	150	6

114 Boxcar (Type IV): The number 98237 was also used on some of the yellow-orange cars. This car used Roman block lettering.

VG	EX	LN	RARITY
50	100	150	6

114 Boxcar (Type V): Sometime during 1916, the Lionel information ceased to be embossed into the floor of the car. The car continued to be painted yellow-orange, and wore the number 54087 on its side.

VG	EX	LN	RARITY
40	50	60	4

114 Boxcar (Type VI):  Cars were also made that were otherwise like the Type V, except that they were stamped with the number 98237 rather than 54087.

VG	EX	LN	RARITY
40	50	60	4

114 Boxcar (Type VII): Some of these 54087 cars were rubber-stamped "LIONEL – LINES – N.Y. – MADE IN USA" on one end. Over time, two different sizes of print were used for this.

VG	EX	LN	RARITY
40	50	60	4

114 Boxcar (Type VIII): In 1918, the maker's information began to be rubber-stamped on the underside of the car, which now read: "MADE IN U.S.A. - THE LIONEL CORPORATION – NEW YORK". These cars were orange, with black rubber-stamped lettering. The number on the side was 98237. The door handles were painted dark red.

VG	EX	LN	RARITY
40	50	60	4

114 Boxcar (Type IX): Some of these cars had their catalog numbers rubber-stamped on the ends.

VG	EX	LN	RARITY
40	50	60	4

114 Boxcar (Type X): This car was identical to the Type VIII, except its door handle was painted the same color as the body.

VG	EX	LN	RARITY
40	50	60	4

213 Cattle Car: The 213 first appeared in the 1926 Lionel catalog. It remained in the catalog through 1940. During its production span, four different paint color combinations were used on the car, as well as the usual variation in plates and trim.

213 CATTLE CAR TYPE III

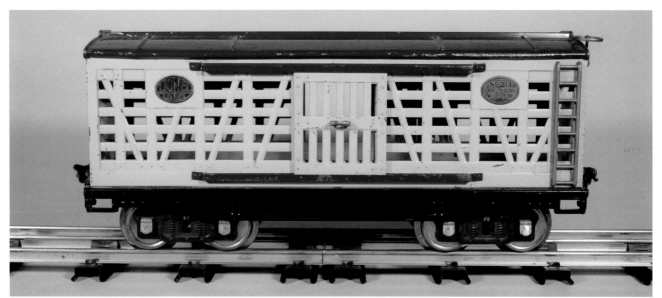

213 CATTLE CAR TYPE IV

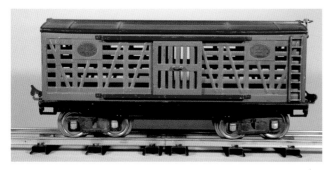

213 Cattle Car (Type I): The earliest car of this type was also the least attractive, though perhaps the most realistic. It had a Mojave body and a maroon roof and brass trim. Brass lettering plates with black printing was installed. Nickel journal boxes were installed on the trucks.

VG	EX	LN	RARITY
175	275	400	6

213 Cattle Car (Type II): Somewhat more colorful were terra-cotta cars with maroon roofs. The trim on these cars was identical to that on the Type I.

VG	EX	LN	RARITY
125	200	300	5

213 Cattle Car (Type III): Even brighter were terra-cotta cars, which had pea green roofs installed. These cars also had nickel journal boxes, brass trim and black-lettered brass plates.

VG	EX	LN	RARITY
125	200	275	3

213 Cattle Car (Type IV): In 1930, Lionel began installing copper journal boxes on the 213. The car itself continued to have a terra-cotta body and pea green roof, and was decorated with brass trim and plates, which had black lettering.

VG	EX	LN	RARITY
125	200	275	3

Price Guide Key: **VG** = Very Good, **EX** = Excellent, **LN** = Like New | *Values for each condition are in U.S. dollars.* | **Rarity** = Scale from 1-8 with 8 being the hardest to find.

107

214 BOXCAR TYPE I

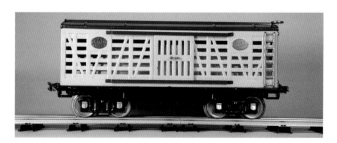

213 Cattle Car (Type V): About 1935, nickel journal boxes began to be used again, and the colors of the car changed to a cream body with a maroon roof. At the same time, the trim on the 213 became nickel. Brass nameplates with black print continued to be used.

VG	EX	LN	RARITY
200	350	600	8

213 Cattle Car (Type VI): Probably in 1937, aluminum nameplates replaced the brass ones previously used. The car continued to be cream with a maroon roof, and had nickel trim.

VG	EX	LN	RARITY
200	350	600	8

214 Boxcar: Though commonly referred to as a boxcar, the plate on the side of this car had printed on it in black: "NO. 214 – AUTOMOBILE – FURNITURE". Its double doors would be indicative of this type of service as well. No matter what color of body was used, all of these cars had a black frame. This car was available from 1926 through 1940.

214 Boxcar (Type I): When production of the 214 began in 1926, its body was painted terracotta and its roof black. Brass trim and black-lettered brass nameplates adorned the car. Trucks, retained by cotter pins and equipped with nickel journals, supported the car.

VG	EX	LN	RARITY
175	225	300	6

214 Boxcar (Type II): Sometime in the late 1920s, the color of the car body was changed to cream. An orange roof was used, along with brass trim and brass plates. Nickel journal boxes were used through 1930.

VG	EX	LN	RARITY
125	175	250	4

214 Boxcar (Type III): In late 1930 or 1931, the journal boxes became copper. The rest of the car was unchanged, however some cars had their trucks retained with horseshoe washers.

VG	EX	LN	RARITY
125	175	250	4

214 Boxcar (Type IV): About 1935, nickel journals reappeared. At the same time, the color of the body changed to yellow, and the roof began to be painted brown.

VG	EX	LN	RARITY
300	400	525	6

214 Boxcar (Type V): More than likely also in 1935, nickel trim replaced the brass, although brass plates continued to be used. The body and roof remained yellow and brown respectively.

VG	EX	LN	RARITY
300	400	525	6

513 CATTLE CAR TYPE II

214 Boxcar (Type VI): Probably in 1937, aluminum nameplates began to be used. The car continued to be yellow with a brown roof and had nickel trim.

VG	EX	LN	RARITY
300	400	525	6

214R Refrigerator Car: The 214R was available from 1929 through 1940. It was unique among the 200-series freight cars in that it was never included in a cataloged set. The car always had a black frame and black lettering on its plates.

214R Refrigerator Car (Type I): The earliest cars had dark pearl body paint with a peacock roof. The bodies were trimmed in brass and they had brass nameplates. The trucks were retained with cotter pins and had nickel journals.

VG	EX	LN	RARITY
250	375	500	6

214R Refrigerator Car (Type II): An identical car was made that was painted in a lighter shade of pearl. Careful examination indicates that these cars have uniform colors inside and out, so this color shift is not a result of age.

VG	EX	LN	RARITY
250	375	500	6

214R Refrigerator Car (Type III): A still lighter pearl car was also made, although its trucks were retained by screws.

VG	EX	LN	RARITY
250	375	500	6

214R Refrigerator Car (Type IV): In late 1930 or 1931, the journal boxes became copper. The body of this car was painted white, while the rest of the car was unchanged.

VG	EX	LN	RARITY
250	375	500	6

214R Refrigerator Car (Type V): About 1935, nickel journals reappeared. At the same time, nickel trim replaced the brass. Although small brass plates continued to be used, the long plate was now aluminum. The body remained white, but the roof was now painted light blue. The trucks were retained by horseshoe washers.

VG	EX	LN	RARITY
400	550	725	8

Price Guide Key: VG = Very Good, EX = Excellent, LN = Like New | *Values for each condition are in U.S. dollars.* | Rarity = Scale from 1-8 with 8 being the hardest to find.

109

214R REFRIGERATOR CAR TYPE I

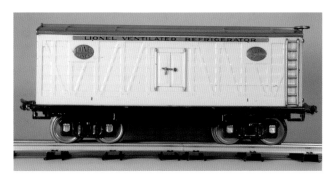

214R Refrigerator Car (Type VI): Probably in 1937, aluminum nameplates replaced the brass ones previously used. The car continued to be white with a light blue roof. The trucks were retained by horseshoe washers.

VG	EX	LN	RARITY
400	550	725	8

513 Cattle Car: This car appeared in Lionel's catalogs from 1927 through 1938, and in several variations. Consistencies were the use of a black frame, and the black legends on the nameplates. One plate was lettered "LIONEL LINES" while the other plate was stamped "CAPACITY – 60000 – WEIGHT – 20000".

513 Cattle Car (Type I): The first version of the 513 was painted olive green. Its roof and door guides were painted orange. The trim and nameplates were brass, and sans serif

lettering was used. The trucks had nickel journal boxes and were secured to the frame by using cotter pins.

VG	EX	LN	RARITY
75	110	150	5

513 Cattle Car (Type II): During 1928 or 1929, the color of the car was changed to orange, and pea green was used for the roof and the door guides. The remainder of its characteristics were unchanged.

VG	EX	LN	RARITY
50	75	100	3

513 Cattle Car (Type III): In late 1930 or early 1931, the journal boxes became copper. The colors of the car were unchanged, but serif lettering was now used on the plates. Most of these cars have their trucks retained with horseshoe washers, but a few cars were made using cotter-pin retainers.

VG	EX	LN	RARITY
50	75	100	3

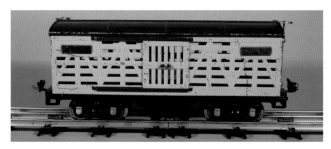

513 Cattle Car (Type IV): About 1935 the body color changed to cream, and the roof was now painted maroon. At the same time nickel journals reappeared and nickel trim replaced the brass. Also aluminum nameplates began to be used. The trucks were retained by horseshoe washers.

VG	EX	LN	RARITY
80	115	150	6

514 Boxcar: Available from 1929 through 1940, this car always had a black frame. One of its plates always read "CAPACITY

514 Boxcar Type III

514 Boxcar Type IV

60000 – No 514 – WEIGHT 20000". The other plate usually read "LIONEL LINES".

514 Boxcar (Type I): When first introduced, the color of the car body was cream and an orange roof was used. Brass trim and brass plates were installed. Nickel journal boxes were used through 1930.

VG	EX	LN	RARITY
100	125	150	3

514 Boxcar (Type II): In late 1930 or 1931, the journal boxes became copper. The rest of the car was unchanged.

VG	EX	LN	RARITY
100	125	150	3

514 Boxcar (Type III): About 1935, the color of the body changed to yellow and the roof began to be painted brown. Nickel journals reappeared, and at the same time nickel trim began to be used. The plates, however, continued to be brass.

VG	EX	LN	RARITY
125	200	300	6

514 Boxcar (Type IV): Probably in 1937, aluminum nameplates replaced the brass ones previously used. The car continued to be yellow with a brown roof, and nickel trim and journal boxes were used.

Price Guide Key: **VG** = Very Good, **EX** = Excellent, **LN** = Like New | *Values for each condition are in U.S. dollars.* | **Rarity** = Scale from 1-8 with 8 being the hardest to find.

111

514R REFRIGERATOR CAR

VG	EX	LN	RARITY
125	200	300	6

514 Boxcar (Type V): Sometime, likely near the end of production, cars were built that had two "LIONEL LINES" plates and no capacity/number plate. These cars were rubber-stamped "514" on the bottom.

VG	EX	LN	RARITY
125	200	300	7

514 Refrigerator Car: This car was offered in 1927 and 1928. After that time, it was replaced by the essentially identical 514R. The 514 refrigerator always had a black frame, brass plates with black lettering, brass trim and nickel journal boxes. A long plate along the top of the car side read "LIONEL VENTILATED REFRIGERATOR". Their bodies were painted a dark pearl color and a peacock roof was installed.

VG	EX	LN	RARITY
200	300	400	5

514R Refrigerator Car: ▓ When the 514 boxcar was introduced in 1929, the number of the refrigerator was changed to 514R, although the basic construction of the car did not change. The 514R was offered through 1940.

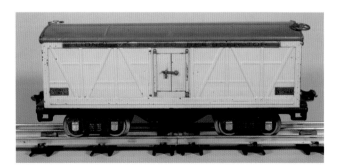

514R Refrigerator Car (Type I): The initial cars were identical to the previous 514 refrigerator car, except for the number and being painted in a lighter shade of pearl.

VG	EX	LN	RARITY
100	200	300	4

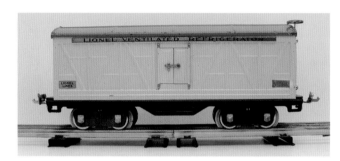

514R Refrigerator Car (Type II): In late 1930 or 1931, the journal boxes became copper. The body of this car was painted white, while the rest of the car was unchanged.

VG	EX	LN	RARITY
100	200	300	4

514R Refrigerator Car (Type III): The car was also produced in ivory, with a roof painted a lighter shade of peacock.

VG	EX	LN	RARITY
100	200	300	4

514R Refrigerator Car (Type IV): Some of the ivory-painted cars had roofs painted the "normal" shade of peacock.

VG	EX	LN	RARITY
100	200	300	4

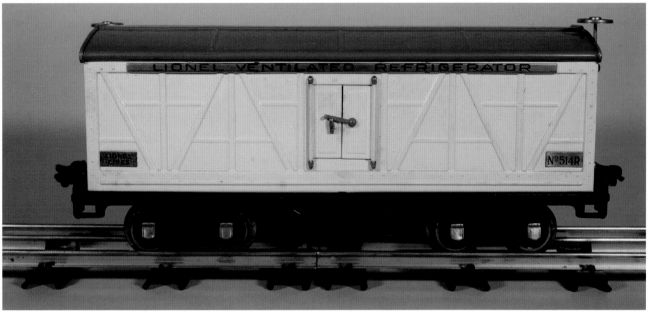

514R Refrigerator Car Type VII

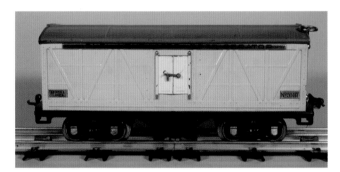

514R Refrigerator Car (Type V): About 1935, nickel journals reappeared. At the same time, nickel trim replaced the brass and, although brass continued to be used for the "LIONEL VENTILATED REFRIGERATOR" plates, the other plates were aluminum. The body remained ivory, but the roof was now painted light blue. The trucks were retained by horseshoe washers.

VG	EX	LN	RARITY
350	450	600	6

514R Refrigerator Car (Type VI): Some of the cars with nickel journals used all brass plates. These cars had nickel trim, white bodies and light blue roofs.

VG	EX	LN	RARITY
250	350	500	7

514R Refrigerator Car (Type VII): Probably by 1937, aluminum nameplates had completely replaced the brass ones previously used. The car continued to be white with a light blue roof. The trucks were retained by horseshoe washers.

VG	EX	LN	RARITY
350	450	600	6

BOX, STOCK & REFRIGERATOR CARS

Price Guide Key: **VG** = Very Good, **EX** = Excellent, **LN** = Like New | *Values for each condition are in U.S. dollars.* | **Rarity** = Scale from 1-8 with 8 being the hardest to find.

113

CHAPTER 13
OIL & TANK CARS

The cars that today we refer to as tank cars were called "Oil Cars" by Lionel, at least through the first two generations of production. This was probably a reflection of the times. While today most real tank cars seem be used hauling chemicals or corn syrup, and most petroleum products move by pipeline or truck, that was not always the case. At the time these replicas were introduced, many tank cars were used to transport crude oil, home heating oil and gasoline. Not surprisingly, the later production cars carried the markings of two large oil companies: Sun Oil Company and Shell.

15 Oil Car: The 15 was Lionel's first tank car. Although its wooden dome and the wooden ends used in early versions gave it a somewhat crude look, its substructure, consisting only of a center sill, was somewhat more realistic than the full frame used on subsequent tankers. Two gold-painted handrails trimmed the car. The 15 was available from 1906 through 1926.

15 Oil Car (Type I): The earliest tank cars were painted red. A wooden dome and wooden ends were mounted in the tank before it was painted. U-shaped steps were attached to the car and short hook couplers were provided. "PENNSYLVANIA RR 416" was rubber-stamped in black on the sides of the tank.

VG	EX	LN	RARITY
175	250	350	7

15 Oil Car (Type II): A second early version of the 15 was identical to the previous car listed. However, rather than red, its body, ends and dome were painted maroon.

VG	EX	LN	RARITY
150	225	325	6

15 Oil Car (Type III): A slightly later version of the maroon 15 had long, creased-hook couplers. It also had four-piece steps rather than the U-shaped steps. "PENNSYLVANIA RR 416" continued to be rubber-stamped in black on the tank, as it was on the previous versions.

VG	EX	LN	RARITY
50	75	110	5

15 Oil Car (Type IV): Another variation of the maroon 15 had wooden ends and dome, but the dome was painted black. "PENNSYLVANIA" was rubber-stamped in gold sans-serif lettering on the sides of the tank.

VG	EX	LN	RARITY
50	75	110	5

15 Oil Car (Type V): About 1911, "LIONEL MFG. CO N.Y." began to be embossed on the underside of the tank cars. At the same time, the dome of the red tank car began

15 Oil Car Type XII

to be painted black, and the black rubber-stamped lettering read simply "PENNSYLVANIA RR". The car was trimmed with two gold-painted handrails and steps pierced with three holes. Significantly, the ends of the tank began to be formed from metal.

VG	EX	LN	RARITY
50	75	110	5

15 Oil Car (Type VI): Similar changes were made to the maroon-bodied tank car. In addition to its dome being painted black, so were its metal ends. "PENNSYLVANIA" was rubber-stamped in gold serif lettering on the sides of the tank. The dome was somewhat taller than it had been previously.

VG	EX	LN	RARITY
50	70	100	3

15 Oil Car (Type VII): The maroon car was also made with sans serif gold "PENNSYLVANIA" rubber-stamped lettering. This version had four-piece steps.

VG	EX	LN	RARITY
50	70	100	3

15 Oil Car (Type VIII): A brown version of the gold sans-serif lettered "PENNSYLVANIA" tanker was made as well.

Its black dome was wood, its ends were metal painted black and its steps were four-piece.

VG	EX	LN	RARITY
50	70	100	3

15 Oil Car (Type IX): Some of the cars had their domes painted brown to match their bodies, rather than black. These cars did not have the "Lionel" information embossed in their undercarriage, though the rest of the car was identical to the Type VIII.

VG	EX	LN	RARITY
50	70	100	3

15 Oil Car (Type X): Later cars were similar to the type VIII cars, but had steps with three holes in them. These cars also lacked the "LIONEL" embossing on their undersides.

VG	EX	LN	RARITY
50	70	100	3

15 Oil Car (Type XI): Around 1916, the red cars also lost their "LIONEL" embossing. Their dome, which was wooden, as well as their frame, couplers and metal ends were all painted black. One side of the frame had "LIONEL – LINES – N.Y. – MADE IN U.S.A." rubber-stamped on it in gold ink. Both sides of the tank had "PENNSYLVANIA RR" applied in gold rubber-stamping. Both serif and sans serif type were used through time.

VG	EX	LN	RARITY
50	70	100	3

15 Oil Car (Type XII): ▦ Red tank cars were also built that were devoid of the Lionel name anywhere. These cars had a sans serif "PENNSYLVANIA RR" rubber-stamped in black. The steps on these cars were the three-hole type.

VG	EX	LN	RARITY
50	70	100	3

15 Oil Car (Type XIV): During the final years of production, the red 15 began to be rubber-stamped "MADE IN U.S.A. - THE LIONEL CORPORATION – NEW YORK" on its

OIL & TANK CARS

Price Guide Key: **VG** = Very Good, **EX** = Excellent, **LN** = Like New | *Values for each condition are in U.S. dollars.* | **Rarity** = Scale from 1-8 with 8 being the hardest to find.

115

215 Oil Car Type I

215 Oil Car Type III

underside. Up top, the dome and ends continued to be painted black, and "PENNSYLVANIA", in either serif or sans serif type, was rubber-stamped in gold on its sides. The steps on these cars were of the three-hole type.

VG	EX	LN	RARITY
50	70	100	3

215 Oil Car: As mentioned elsewhere, the 1926 introduction of the 200-series freight cars began the "Classic" age of Lionel Standard Gauge trains. Though the colors on these tank or "oil" cars were somewhat more subdued that those of some other 200-series cars, they were nevertheless brighter than the previous 15 tank cars had been. Their lettering was stamped on separately installed plates of unpainted brass, or aluminum plates onto which the lettering was stamped in either black or red. Invariably, one of these plates bore the name of the famous railroad "Lionel Lines." These cars all had exposed black frames.

215 Oil Car (Type I): As initially produced, the tank was painted pea green and topped with turned solid brass domes, one large and two small. The small domes were press-fit into the tank, while the large dome was screwed into place. A brass handrail encircled the tank and a pair of brass ladders led to the dome. Brass name plates, lettered in red, were installed in the tank. The car rode on trucks, retained with cotter pins, that had both dimples and slots in their bolster on either side of the mounting stud. Nickel journal boxes were installed on these trucks. A 5/8" diameter brass brakewheel was installed on the left side of the frame at either end.

VG	EX	LN	RARITY
175	225	275	2

215 Oil Car (Type II): Near 1929, all three of the turned brass domes began to be secured with screws. A 3/4" brake wheel, referred to in this volume as Type II HW, was mounted on each end. The balance of the car was unchanged.

VG	EX	LN	RARITY
150	200	250	2

215 Oil Car (Type III):  Stamping is a much less expensive process than is turning, which no doubt is what led Lionel to introduce stamped brass domes to their tanker. At the same time, probably late 1929, the trucks were changed as well. Retained with cotter pins, they had slots in their bolster on either side of the mounting stud, but no dimples. Nickel journal boxes decorated the trucks.

VG	EX	LN	RARITY
150	200	250	2

215 Oil Car (Type IV): At nearly the same time the stamped domes were introduced, so was the first major color variation of the 215. The tank was now painted an ivory or buff color, but the rest of the car was unchanged from the Type III.

VG	EX	LN	RARITY
200	275	350	4

215 Oil Car (Type V): During 1930, the journal boxes on the trucks began to be copper rather than nickel, though the rest of the car was unchanged.

VG	EX	LN	RARITY
200	275	350	4

215 Oil Car (Type VI): In the early 1930s, the plates decorating the 215 began to change. Now, on some cars, the brass plate with the number on it was stamped in red, while the "Lionel Lines" plate was stamped in black. On other cars, both plates were lettered in red. The trucks had copper journals, and both Type II HW and Type III HW 3/4" brake wheels are known to be used on these cars.

VG	EX	LN	RARITY
200	275	350	4

215 Oil Car (Type VII): Toward the mid-1930s, the ivory tanker was dressed up a bit with the application of a "Sunoco" decal on the upper left tank surface. Both cars with all-red lettered plates and those with mixed red and black lettered plates were affected by this change.

VG	EX	LN	RARITY
225	300	400	4

215 Oil Car (Type VIII): Shortly after the "Sunoco" decals were introduced, the color of the tank was changed to silver. The type III brakewheel was installed on these cars and their trucks, which were retained by horseshoe washers, had copper journals. The lettering plates were brass, with the numbers in red and letters in black. Its handrail continued to be brass.

VG	EX	LN	RARITY
275	350	450	6

215 OIL CAR TYPE IV

Price Guide Key: **VG** = Very Good, **EX** = Excellent, **LN** = Like New | *Values for each condition are in U.S. dollars.* | **Rarity** = Scale from 1-8 with 8 being the hardest to find.

117

515 Tank Car Type III

215 Oil Car (Type IX): Arguably the most difficult to find version of the 215 had a silver tank, "Sunoco" decal, brass number plates lettered in red, aluminum nameplate lettered in black, and nickel handrails and trim. Its trucks were retained by cotter pins and have nickel journal boxes. Type IV brakewheels were installed.

VG	EX	LN	RARITY
325	400	525	7

215 Oil Car (Type X): As the end of production neared, the nickel handrails reverted to brass, yet the rest of the trim remained nickel. The brass data plates gave way to aluminum plates with black stampings. The trucks, which had nickel journals, were held into place by cotter pins.

VG	EX	LN	RARITY
225	300	400	4

515 Tank Car: Like the larger 215, the 515 tank car consisted of a black-painted sheet metal frame supporting the colorful tank itself, which in turn was trimmed with three brass domes. It was produced from 1927 through 1940.

515 Tank Car (Type I):  When first introduced, the tank of the 515 was painted terra cotta–the color it was when cataloged for separate sale through 1938. Its trim, handrail and plates were brass, with the lettering stamped in black. Its trucks, retained with cotter pins, had nickel journals.

VG	EX	LN	RARITY
80	125	175	3

515 Tank Car (Type II): About 1930, the cars actually being produced began to have their tanks painted a cream color. The trim, handrails and plates were unchanged. Copper journal boxes appeared on the trucks.

VG	EX	LN	RARITY
80	125	175	3

515 Tank Car (Type III): In the early 1930s, a few cars were made that were painted a distinctly different shade, more of an ivory color rather than cream. These cars had copper journals, but the balance of the trim and handrails, as well as the nameplates, were brass.

VG	EX	LN	RARITY
100	150	225	4

515 Tank Car (Type IV): A Sunoco herald decal was added to the upper left side of the ivory tank, adding a bit of color to the car. At the same time horseshoe washers began to

515 TANK CAR TYPE IV

515 TANK CAR TYPE VII

be used to retain the trucks. These would continue to be used throughout the rest of the 515 production. The balance of the car was unchanged.

VG	EX	LN	RARITY
90	140	200	4

515 Tank Car (Type V): The 1931 catalog showed the 515, with its "Sunoco" decal, with a silver tank as part of set 363E. It was in fact produced in that color, with copper journals and copper handrails. The rest of its trim and its plates were brass.

VG	EX	LN	RARITY
90	140	200	4

515 Tank Car (Type VI): The silver Sunoco was also built with nickel handrails, with the rest of the car being unchanged from the Type V.

VG	EX	LN	RARITY
90	140	200	4

515 Tank Car (Type VII): 🔲 Nickel journals reappeared, replacing the copper journals, in 1935. The tank continued to be painted silver, and the remaining trim was brass, except for the handrails, which were copper.

VG	EX	LN	RARITY
90	140	200	4

515 Tank Car (Type VIII): 🔲 Shortly after the journals became nickel, so did the handrails and trim. The plates continued to be brass with black lettering and a Sunoco decal continued to be applied to the silver tank.

VG	EX	LN	RARITY
90	140	200	4

Price Guide Key: **VG** = Very Good, **EX** = Excellent, **LN** = Like New | *Values for each condition are in U.S. dollars.* | **Rarity** = Scale from 1-8 with 8 being the hardest to find.

119

515 Tank Car Type VIII

515 Tank Car Type IX

515 Tank Car (Type IX):  Probably around 1936, the brass plates with black lettering were replaced with aluminum plates, still with black lettering. The rest of the car continued as before.

VG	EX	LN	RARITY
90	140	200	4

515 Tank Car (Type X): The 1939 catalog showed a very changed look for the 515. Its tank was now painted a bright orange, and the "Sunoco" herald was replaced with a red "Shell" decal. Trim, journal boxes and handrails were all nickel, while the plates were aluminum with black lettering.

VG	EX	LN	RARITY
350	525	725	6

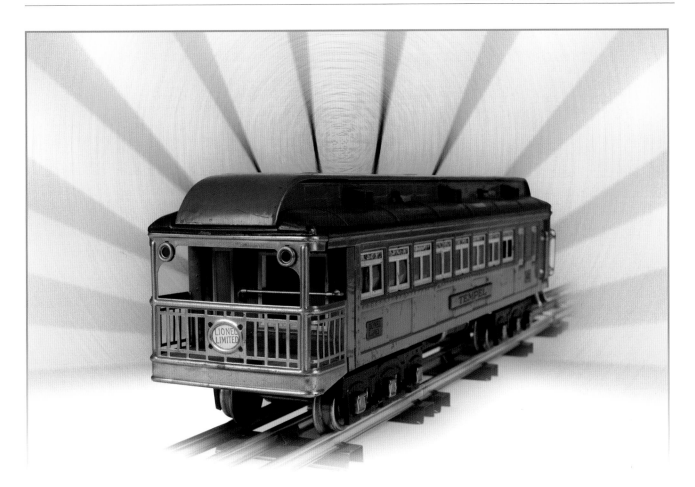

CHAPTER 14
PASSENGER CARS

Although Lionel catalogs show passenger cars as far back as 1906, it is generally believed that no such cars were actually produced until the following year. Many of these cars are offered for sale separately, but most were sold in the form of sets. The cars are listed in numeric order, with notations about what cars match to form a "set."

18 Pullman: This car was first shown in the 1906 catalog, but construction characteristics for this car indicate that, more than likely, assembly did not actually take place until 1909 or 1910. The 18 remained a part of Lionel's offerings through 1927. The 19 combine, and later the 190 observation, matched these cars.

18 Pullman (Type I): Cars produced in 1910 (or perhaps earlier) were painted dark olive green over red primer. This primer was exposed on the bottom of the car. The doors and windowsills were painted a contrasting maroon color, with the windows having gold-tone dividers. The main windows were glazed with clear celluloid, while the upper and toilet windows used red-speckled celluloid.

Gold rubber-stamped lettering reading "NEW YORK CENTRAL LINES" was applied above the windows, while centered below the windows, again stamped in gold, was "18

PULLMAN 18". Variously, serif and sans serif lettering was used on these cars.

VG	EX	LN	RARITY
800	1500	2400	8

18 Pullman (Type II): Beginning about 1913, the bottom of the car was painted the same dark olive green as the sides and roof. The bottom was also embossed "LIONEL MFG. CO. – N.Y." The rest of the paint and decoration was the same as it had been previously, except now serif lettering was used exclusively. The clerestory windows were punched open on these cars, unlike the earlier cars that omitted these windows. The roofs of these cars also began to be removable, and the doors would actually open.

VG	EX	LN	RARITY
100	150	200	5

18 Pullman (Type III): Starting about 1915, and continuing through 1918, the Lionel name appeared nowhere on the car. Other than this change, the car was identical to the Type II.

VG	EX	LN	RARITY
100	150	200	5

18 Pullman (Type IV): During this time period, the 18 was also produced with a yellow-orange body and roof. Those components that were normally painted maroon were instead painted cream.

Price Guide Key: **VG** = Very Good, **EX** = Excellent, **LN** = Like New | *Values for each condition are in U.S. dollars.* | **Rarity** = Scale from 1-8 with 8 being the hardest to find.

121

PASSENGER CARS

18 PULLMAN TYPE V

VG	EX	LN	RARITY
300	550	900	7

18 Pullman (Type V): 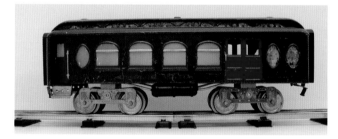 Though the basic olive color scheme of the car remained the same as prior models, starting in 1918 there were significant changes to the rubber-stamping on the car. While above the windows "NEW YORK CENTRAL LINES" continued to be rubber-stamped in gold serif letters, the print below the windows was different. It now read "18 PARLOR CAR 18". Additionally, on the underside of the car was rubber-stamped "MADE IN U.S.A. – THE LIONEL CORPORATION – NEW YORK". The celluloid used for the upper windows and lavatories, which previously had always been red-speckled, was now blue-speckled.

VG	EX	LN	RARITY
125	200	300	4

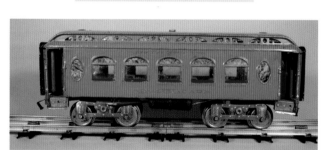

18 Pullman (Type VI): The changes described previously that were made to the dark olive and maroon cars were also made to the yellow-orange and cream cars. Also, the orange hue became stronger.

VG	EX	LN	RARITY
125	200	300	5

18 Pullman (Type VII): From 1923 through 1926, the dark olive cars were factory equipped with interior illumination. The balance of the car remained unchanged.

VG	EX	LN	RARITY
125	200	300	4

18 Pullman (Type VIII): The orange cars also received interior illumination in 1923.

VG	EX	LN	RARITY
125	200	300	5

18 Pullman (Type IX): The illuminated cars were also produced in Mojave with maroon trim.

VG	EX	LN	RARITY
300	550	900	7

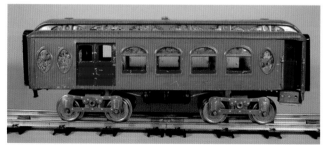

19 Combine: In the world of real railroads, combination cars, or combines, combined multiple functions, such as baggage and RPO (Railway Post Office), baggage and coach, or even three functions, such as baggage, RPO and coach. In most cases, the portion of the car with seating was intended to serve as a "rider car" for use by the train crew. In some

29 DAY COACH TYPE I

cases, however, revenue passengers were hauled in this space.

A 19 combine was produced that had features matching each variation of the 18 listed earlier. Discontinued two years earlier than the 18 and 190, the late combines are slightly more difficult to locate than the equivalent parlor car or observation car. Nevertheless, all the 19 combines are valued equally with their matching 18.

29 Day Coach: Although the 18 and 19 were cataloged as far back as 1906, they aren't believed to have been produced prior to 1909 or 1910. That makes the 29, first offered in 1907, the first passenger car actually produced by Lionel. The 29 used the body of the 3 trolley, painted dark olive green.

29 Day Coach (Type I): 🖼 As initially produced, the 29 had a 13 7/8" long dark olive green body with cream interior. Rubber-stamped in gold on its sides was "No. 29 N.Y.C. & H.R.R.R. CO. No. 29". Four passengers and a conductor were provided, which were held in place by pins. Nine windows were punched in each side, and the lower halves of the car ends were solid.

VG	EX	LN	RARITY
1200	2000	3100	8

29 Day Coach (Type II): In 1908 or 1909, some of these closed-end cars were built with Pennsylvania lettering.

VG	EX	LN	RARITY
1200	2000	3100	8

29 Day Coach (Type III): About 1909, the car was changed, with open platforms replacing the half-enclosed ends. A split railing decorated the ends.

VG	EX	LN	RARITY
1200	2000	3100	8

29 Day Coach (Type IV): In 1910, the car was lengthened to 15 1/4". At the same time, an additional window was added to each side, raising the per side total to 10. The roof was no longer removable. Three high ventilators decorated the roof. "No. 29

N.Y.C. & H.R.R.R. CO. No. 29" continued to be rubber-stamped in gold on the sides of the dark olive green body.

VG	EX	LN	RARITY
550	750	1000	6

29 Day Coach (Type V): An otherwise identical car was manufactured, except its body and roof were painted maroon.

VG	EX	LN	RARITY
1000	1200	1500	7

29 Day Coach (Type VI): During 1911, some dark green cars were built that were numbered "No. 29" on each side near the ends below the windows. Above the windows was stamped "NEW YORK CENTRAL LINES". All the rubber-stamping was done in gold. A thin gold stripe ran beneath the windows.

VG	EX	LN	RARITY
550	750	1000	6

29 Day Coach (Type VII): From 1912 through 1914, the car had a removable roof. The dark olive body had a maroon window band. "29 NEW YORK CENTRAL LINES 29" was rubber-stamped in gold beneath the windows. Some cars had a thin gold stripe under the windows as well.

VG	EX	LN	RARITY
550	750	1000	6

29 Day Coach (Type VIII): Cars, otherwise identical to the Type VI, were built lettered for the Pennsylvania Railroad as well.

VG	EX	LN	RARITY
1000	1200	1500	7

Price Guide Key: VG = Very Good, EX = Excellent, LN = Like New | *Values for each condition are in U.S. dollars.* | Rarity = Scale from 1-8 with 8 being the hardest to find.

123

PASSENGER CARS

31 Combine Type IV

31 Combine: This car, along with the 32 Mail Car, was added to the product line in 1921. Matching the 35 Pullman and 36 Observation, the 31 was offered through 1925.

31 Combine (Type I): This dark olive car matches the Type VIII 35 Pullman. The opening baggage door has simulated wood grain.

VG	EX	LN	RARITY
60	70	80	3

31 Combine (Type II): This orange car matches the Type IX 35 Pullman. The opening baggage door was painted maroon.

VG	EX	LN	RARITY
100	120	150	6

31 Combine (Type III): This brown car matches the Type X 35 Pullman. The opening baggage door has simulated wood grain.

VG	EX	LN	RARITY
60	70	80	3

31 Combine (Type IV):  This maroon car matches the Type XI 35 Pullman. The opening baggage door has simulated wood grain.

VG	EX	LN	RARITY
60	70	80	3

32 Mail Car: This car, along with the 31 Combine, was added to the product line in 1921. Matching the 35 Pullman and 36 Observation, the 32 was offered through 1925.

VG	EX	LN	RARITY
60	70	80	3

32 Mail Car (Type I): This maroon car matches the Type IV 31 Combine and Type XI 35 Pullman. Its four opening baggage doors have simulated wood grain. There are no passenger doors.

VG	EX	LN	RARITY
70	80	95	4

32 Mail Car (Type II): This maroon car matches the Type IV 31 Combine and Type XI 35 Pullman. Its four opening baggage doors have simulated wood grain. Unlike the car listed previously, this car has passenger doors at each end of its sides.

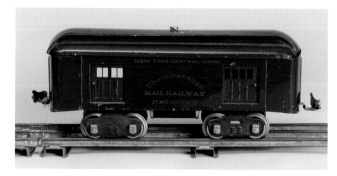

32 Mail Car (Type III): This dark olive car matches the Type I 31 Combine and Type VIII 35 Pullman.

VG	EX	LN	RARITY
50	60	75	3

35 PULLMAN TYPE I

32 Mail Car (Type IV): This brown car matches the Type III 31 Combine and Type X 35 Pullman.

VG	EX	LN	RARITY
60	70	80	3

32 Mail Car (Type V): This orange car matches the Type II 31 Combine and Type IX 35 Pullman. Its four opening baggage doors have simulated wood grain.

VG	EX	LN	RARITY
100	120	150	6

35 Pullman: First offered in 1912, the 35 Pullman car, along with its companion the 36 Observation car, continued to be cataloged through 1926. With such a long production run, it is not surprising that these 10 1/2" long cars exist in many colors and variations.

35 Pullman (Type I): 🔲 When first introduced in 1912, the 35 had two horizontal ribs embossed beneath the windows. Embossed in the underside of the car was "LIONEL MFG. CO. – N.Y." The cars were painted dark olive green. Gold rubber-stamped lettering reading "NEW YORK CENTRAL LINES" was applied above the windows. Rubber-stamped in gold between the ribs was "35 PULLMAN 35".

VG	EX	LN	RARITY
120	150	180	5

35 Pullman (Type II): Except for the "PENNSYLVANIA LINES" lettering in lieu of the New York Central markings, these cars were identical to the Type I.

VG	EX	LN	RARITY
120	150	180	5

35 Pullman (Type III): A hard to find variation of the early 35 is the midnight-blue version produced for Montgomery Ward.

VG	EX	LN	RARITY
450	700	1000	8

35 Pullman (Type IV): About 1914, the embossed ribs were eliminated from the sides of the cars, which were dark olive green with maroon windowsills. At the same time, the car number was moved to the ends, and a decorative gold rubber-stamped box surrounded the word "PULLMAN" on the car sides. The celluloid used for the upper windows, which had previously been red-speckled, was now blue-speckled. Gold "NEW YORK CENTRAL LINES" lettering was rubber-stamped above the windows.

VG	EX	LN	RARITY
50	60	75	3

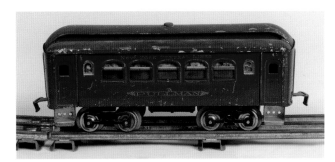

35 Pullman (Type V): During the same time period, the 35 was also painted maroon with green windowsills. This car's construction otherwise duplicated the Type IV.

VG	EX	LN	RARITY
70	80	90	5

PASSENGER CARS

Price Guide Key: **VG** = Very Good, **EX** = Excellent, **LN** = Like New | *Values for each condition are in U.S. dollars.* | **Rarity** = Scale from 1-8 with 8 being the hardest to find.

125

35 Pullman (Type VI): About 1916, the Lionel identification ceased to be embossed in the car bottoms. The dark olive car was gold rubber-stamped "35 PULLMAN 35" beneath its windows, without the decorative box. "NEW YORK CENTRAL LINES" was applied above the windows. The ends of the cars were gold stamped "LIONEL – LINES".

VG	EX	LN	RARITY
50	60	75	3

35 Pullman (Type VII): About the same time, the 35 began to be offered in orange with maroon windowsills.

VG	EX	LN	RARITY
110	140	180	5

35 Pullman (Type VIII): About 1918, the underside of the car began to be rubber-stamped "MADE IN U.S.A. – THE LIONEL CORPORATION – NEW YORK". The decorative gold rubber-stamped box reappeared surrounding the "PULLMAN" applied under the windows. "NEW YORK CENTRAL LINES" continued to be rubber-stamped above the windows, and "35" began to be stamped on one end of the car. The basic color continued to be dark olive with maroon windowsills.

VG	EX	LN	RARITY
25	35	45	2

35 Pullman (Type IX): The orange car with maroon windowsills received the same marking changes as did the olive car listed previously.

VG	EX	LN	RARITY
100	140	200	5

35 Pullman (Type X): A brown car with green windowsills joined the orange and olive cars on the roster.

VG	EX	LN	RARITY
25	35	45	2

35 Pullman (Type XI): 🔲 Near the end of production, a maroon car with green windowsills also was produced. Many of these cars have metal simulated air tanks, rather than the previously used wooden tanks.

VG	EX	LN	RARITY
25	35	45	2

36 Observation (Type I): Matches Type I 35 Pullman.

VG	EX	LN	RARITY
120	150	180	5

36 Observation (Type II): Matches Type II 35 Pullman.

VG	EX	LN	RARITY
120	150	180	5

36 Observation (Type III): Matches Type III 35 Pullman.

VG	EX	LN	RARITY
450	700	1000	8

35 PULLMAN TYPE XI

36 OBSERVATION TYPE VIII

36 Observation (Type IV): Matches Type IV 35 Pullman.

VG	EX	LN	RARITY
50	60	75	3

36 Observation (Type V): Matches maroon Type V 35 Pullman.

VG	EX	LN	RARITY
70	80	90	5

36 Observation (Type VI): Matches Type VI 35 Pullman.

VG	EX	LN	RARITY
50	60	75	3

36 Observation (Type VII): Matches Type VII 35 Pullman.

VG	EX	LN	RARITY
110	140	180	5

36 Observation (Type VIII): 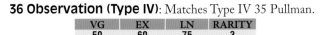 Matches Type VIII 35 Pullman.

VG	EX	LN	RARITY
25	35	45	2

36 Observation (Type IX): Matches Type IX 35 Pullman.

VG	EX	LN	RARITY
100	140	200	5

36 Observation (Type X): Matches Type X 35 Pullman.

VG	EX	LN	RARITY
25	35	45	2

36 Observation (Type XI): Matches Type XI 35 Pullman.

VG	EX	LN	RARITY
25	35	45	2

180 Pullman: Introduced in 1911, and remaining in the product line through 1921, the 180 was the first of Lionel's medium-sized Standard Gauge passenger cars. During their production, these 12 1/2" long cars were offered in several variations.

180 Pullman (Type I): The first cars produced were painted maroon over red primer. This primer was exposed on the bottom of the car. The doors were painted dark olive green, and the windows had gold-tone dividers. The main windows were glazed with clear celluloid, while the upper windows used red celluloid.

Gold rubber-stamped lettering reading "NEW YORK CENTRAL LINES" was applied above the windows, while centered below the windows, again stamped in gold, was "180 PULLMAN 180". Perforated steps were used on these cars.

VG	EX	LN	RARITY
100	130	175	4

180 Pullman (Type II): Beginning in 1913, the bottom of the car was painted the same shade of maroon as the rest of the body. The bottom was also embossed "LIONEL MFG. CO. – N.Y." The steps were replaced with a three-hole variety at

PASSENGER CARS

Price Guide Key: **VG** = Very Good, **EX** = Excellent, **LN** = Like New | *Values for each condition are in U.S. dollars.* | **Rarity** = Scale from 1-8 with 8 being the hardest to find.

127

180 PULLMAN TYPE IV

the same time. The lettering of the car was unchanged from the type I.

VG	EX	LN	RARITY
100	130	175	4

180 Pullman (Type III): Very early in the Type II production, the car number was moved to the ends, and a decorative gold rubber-stamped box surrounded the word "PULLMAN" on the car sides. This resulted in the Type III car. The celluloid used for the upper windows, which previously had always been red, was now blue-speckled.

VG	EX	LN	RARITY
75	110	150	3

180 Pullman (Type IV): 🔲 In 1915, the embossing was deleted from the underside of the car. These cars were lettered "180 PULLMAN 180" in gold.

VG	EX	LN	RARITY
75	110	150	3

180 Pullman (Type V): Similar cars were also made, except their bodies and roofs were painted brown rather than maroon.

VG	EX	LN	RARITY
100	140	200	5

180 Pullman (Type VI): About 1916, the 180 was also offered decorated for the Canadian Pacific. These cars, painted maroon, were gold rubber-stamped "CANADIAN PACIFIC

RAILWAY" above the window strip. On one end "LIONEL – LINES – N.Y. – Made in U.S.A." was stamped to the left of the diaphragm, while to the right of the diaphragm was stamped "NO. – 180".

RARITY
Not traded frequently enough to establish value.

180 Pullman (Type VII): Beginning in 1918, the underside of the maroon car was rubber-stamped "MADE IN U.S.A. – THE LIONEL CORPORATION – NEW YORK".

VG	EX	LN	RARITY
75	100	125	3

180 Pullman (Type VIII): The Type VII-style car was also produced in brown.

VG	EX	LN	RARITY
100	125	150	4

181 Combine (Type I): Matches Type I 180 Pullman cars and 182 Observation cars and has similar value.

181 Combine (Type II): Matches Type II 180 Pullman cars and 182 Observation cars, and has similar value.

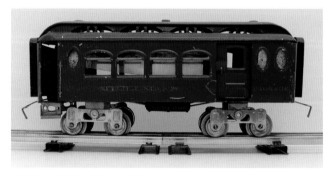

181 Combine (Type III): Matches Type III 180 Pullman cars and 182 Observation cars, and has similar value.

182 Observation Type IV

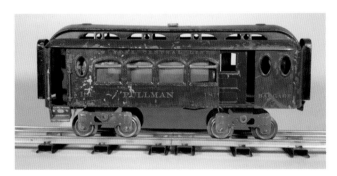

182 Observation (Type II): Matches Type II 180 Pullman cars and 181 Combine cars, and has similar value.

181 Combine (Type IV): Matches Type IV 180 Pullman cars and 182 Observation cars, and has similar value.

181 Combine (Type V): Matches Type V 180 Pullman cars and 182 Observation cars, and has similar value.

181 Combine (Type VI): Matches Type VI 180 Pullman cars and 182 Observation cars, and has similar value.

181 Combine (Type VII): Matches Type VII 180 Pullman cars and 182 Observation cars, and has similar value.

181 Combine (Type VIII): Matches Type VIII 180 Pullman cars and 182 Observation cars, and has similar value.

181 Combine (Type IX): A yellow-orange version of the 181 was built about 1916. These cars lacked Lionel identification. They were rubber-stamped "NEW YORK CENTRAL LINES" above the windows, and "PULLMAN" inside a decorative rubber-stamped box. The doors of these cars were painted orange and the diaphragms black. Strangely, though a matching 182 observation was made, apparently a matching 180 Pullman was not.

VG	EX	LN	RARITY
300	400	525	5

182 Observation (Type I): Matches Type I 180 Pullman cars and 181 Combine cars, and has similar value.

182 Observation (Type III): Matches Type III 180 Pullman cars and 181 Combine cars, and has similar value.

182 Observation (Type IV): Matches Type IV 180 Pullman cars and 181 Combine cars, and has similar value.

182 Observation (Type V): Matches Type V 180 Pullman cars and 181 Combine cars, and has similar value.

182 Observation (Type VI): Matches Type VI 180 Pullman cars and 181 Combine cars, and has similar value.

182 Observation (Type VII): Matches Type VII 180 Pullman cars and 181 Combine cars, and has similar value.

182 Observation (Type VIII): Matches Type VIII 180 Pullman cars and 181 Combine cars, and has similar value.

182 Observation (Type IX): Matches Type IX 181 Combines and has similar value.

VG	EX	LN	RARITY
300	400	525	5

PASSENGER CARS

Price Guide Key: **VG** = Very Good, **EX** = Excellent, **LN** = Like New | *Values for each condition are in U.S. dollars.* | **Rarity** = Scale from 1-8 with 8 being the hardest to find.

129

309 Pullman Type I

190 Observation: Produced from 1910 through 1927, the 190 was offered in each of the color combinations, with all the same characteristics, as the matching 18 Pullman/parlor cars and 19 combination cars. Because most collectors want to display these cars as a set of three–combine, parlor and observation–the demand for all three car types, and hence the value, is approximately equal.

309 Pullman: This 13 1/4" long illuminated passenger car was added to the line in 1926. It, and its companions the 310 and 312, remained in the catalog through 1939. During its production run, two styles of doors were used, early doors having larger windows than the later doors. Although collectors tend to prefer matched sets, Lionel included both styles in many factory-assembled train sets. While "THE LIONEL LINES" was rubber-stamped directly on the body above the windows, the "PULLMAN" lettering was rubber-stamped on a separately installed plate. Through the years, two styles of lettering were used: one contained within scrollwork, the other simply stamped on the plate.

309 Pullman (Type I): As first produced, the Pullman body was painted Mojave, as was the roof. Its doors were lithographed with simulated wood grain, and its window/plate insert was maroon.

VG	EX	LN	RARITY
100	125	150	3

309 Pullman (Type II): In 1927, the color of the car changed to pea green. At the same time, both the insert and the doors began to be painted orange. This color combination was used through 1930.

VG	EX	LN	RARITY
50	75	100	1

309 Pullman (Type III): New in 1930 was the 309 painted State brown with a dark brown roof. The cream doors and window inserts made this a handsome car. This color combination was available through 1933.

VG	EX	LN	RARITY
125	160	200	6

309 Pullman (Type IV): Produced only in 1934, this attractive version had a medium blue body and doors accented by cream window inserts. The roof was painted dark blue.

VG	EX	LN	RARITY
125	160	200	6

310 Baggage Type I

309 Pullman (Type V): Also introduced in 1934, and continuing the next year, was a car painted Stephen Girard green. The doors were painted the same color as the body, while the roof was dark green and the inserts cream.

VG	EX	LN	RARITY
150	200	275	7

309 Pullman (Type VI): In 1935, what would be the final version of the car began to be produced. This car had a light blue body, while its roof, inserts and doors were painted silver. It continued unchanged through 1939.

VG	EX	LN	RARITY
100	125	150	3

309 Pullman (Type VII): An unusual version was made in 1931. It had a maroon body, cream doors and inserts, and a terra-cotta roof. Rather than being rubber-stamped "THE LIONEL LINES", it was stamped "NEW YORK CENTRAL LINES".

VG	EX	LN	RARITY
150	200	275	7

310 Baggage: A companion to the 309 and 312, the 310 was rubber-stamped "BAGGAGE" on its nameplate.

310 Baggage (Type I): Matching the 309 Type I, this car was painted Mojave and had dark green baggage doors.

VG	EX	LN	RARITY
100	125	150	3

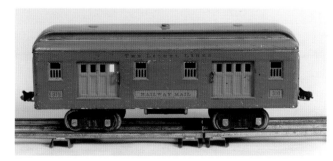

310 Baggage (Type II): A companion to the pea green Type II 309 was also made. In addition to being produced as shown

in the catalog, with orange baggage doors, some were also made with dark green baggage doors.

VG	EX	LN	RARITY
50	75	100	1

310 Baggage (Type III): Dark green baggage doors were also used on the cars built to match the State brown Type III Pullmans.

VG	EX	LN	RARITY
125	160	200	6

310 Baggage (Type IV): The mate to the Type IV Pullman had a light blue baggage door.

VG	EX	LN	RARITY
125	160	200	6

310 Baggage (Type V): The cars built to match the Stephen Girard green Type V Pullman used doors the same color as the body.

VG	EX	LN	RARITY
150	200	275	7

Price Guide Key: **VG** = Very Good, **EX** = Excellent, **LN** = Like New | *Values for each condition are in U.S. dollars.* | **Rarity** = Scale from 1-8 with 8 being the hardest to find.

131

PASSENGER CARS

310 BAGGAGE TYPE I

310 Baggage (Type VI): The light blue baggage car had silver doors, matching the Type VI Pullman.

VG	EX	LN	RARITY
100	125	150	3

310 Baggage (Type VII): Lettered "Lionel Electric Railroad", the maroon baggage car had a terra-cotta roof and cream doors.

RARITY
Too infrequently traded to establish value.

312 Observation: A companion to the 309 and 310, the 312 was rubber-stamped "OBSERVATION" on its nameplate.

312 Observation (Type I): Matches the 309 and 310 Type I.

VG	EX	LN	RARITY
100	125	150	3

312 Observation (Type II): 🔲 Matches the pea green 309 and 310 Type II.

VG	EX	LN	RARITY
50	75	100	1

312 Observation (Type III): Matches the State brown 309 and 310 Type III.

VG	EX	LN	RARITY
125	160	200	6

312 Observation (Type IV): Matches the 309 and 310 Type IV.

VG	EX	LN	RARITY
125	160	200	6

312 Observation (Type V): Matches the Stephen Girard Green 309 and 310 Type V.

VG	EX	LN	RARITY
150	200	275	7

319 PULLMAN TYPE II

312 Observation (Type VI): Matches the light blue 309 and 310 Type VI.

VG	EX	LN	RARITY
100	125	150	3

312 Observation (Type VII): Built to match the 309 Type IV, this car has a maroon body, cream inserts and a terra-cotta roof. However, strangely, on its body is rubber-stamped in gold "THE LIONEL LINES".

VG	EX	LN	RARITY
150	200	275	7

319 Pullman: These cars, which were made with the same metal forming dies used to produce the 309, were produced from 1924 through 1930, although they were not illustrated in the catalog during their final two years. They differed from the 309 by using the taller 200-series trucks (with few exceptions), and were intended for use with more expensive locomotives. The cars had a maroon body and roof and Mojave

inserts. The doors were either wood-grain lithographed or painted Mojave.

319 Pullman (Type I): The first cars produced in 1924 were exceptions to the use of the 200-series trucks. Instead, these cars had 100-series trucks installed on them. The inserts were gold rubber-stamped "319 PULLMAN 319", while above the windows "NEW YORK CENTRAL LINES" was rubber-stamped.

VG	EX	LN	RARITY
95	120	160	3

319 Pullman (Type II): For the remainder of 1924, and continuing through 1927, the car rode on 200-series trucks.

VG	EX	LN	RARITY
95	120	160	3

319 Pullman (Type III): Identical cars were offered from 1925 through 1927, with "LIONEL LINES" replacing the New York Central markings.

VG	EX	LN	RARITY
175	250	350	5

319 Pullman (Type IV): After it was dropped from the catalog in 1927, production of the 319 resumed in 1929 for a final two-year run, but it did not reappear on the catalog pages. Now, however, it rode on 500-series trucks like the 309. It continued to be lettered "LIONEL LINES" in gold on the body.

VG	EX	LN	RARITY
175	250	350	5

320 Baggage: Introduced a year after the 319, the 320 was cataloged from 1925 through 1927, then continued in production for two more years.

Price Guide Key: **VG** = Very Good, **EX** = Excellent, **LN** = Like New | *Values for each condition are in U.S. dollars.* | **Rarity** = Scale from 1-8 with 8 being the hardest to find.

133

Construction of "Lionel Standard" Super-Motors

Removable Brush Holder (1)—This is one of the most unique features of the Lionel Super-Motor. By simply unscrewing one screw the entire brush holder can be removed from the motor. Change of brushes requires but an instant and the assembled part is replaced without the use of any tools.

Brushes (2)—The brushes are made of bronze and graphite which are self-lubricating. They insure long life to the commutator. They are contained in brass tubes and held in place by a simple spring arrangement which feeds brushes to commutator at the same pressure until the brush is entirely used up. Replacement of brushes is a very simple operation.

Revolving Double Contact Shoes (3)—This method of collecting current from the third rail, so successfully used for many years past on our "O" Gauge Locomotives, has been applied with equal success to the new Super-Motors. The shoes are heavy bronze rollers, securely affixed to the flexible phosphor bronze plate, which insures the proper tension on the third rail and gives a steady flow of current to the motors. This complete shoe assembly is mounted on a heavy fibre plate and is rigidly attached to the motor frame.

New Gear Arrangement (4)—This new method of gearing is embodied only in Lionel Super-Motors. The seven gears in this new layout give the motor greater tractive power, and are almost frictionless. The gears are made of very heavy steel, and teeth are machine cut, not stamped. Special attention is directed to the plate supporting the gear studs, which also acts as an additional bearing for the armature shaft, as described in the following paragraph.

THE New Lionel Super-Motor is so vastly superior in efficiency and design to any motor ever before offered to the public that notwithstanding our enviable reputation as leaders in miniature motor construction, the new and improved Super-Motor is supremely the finest piece of electrical mechanism our factories have ever produced. It is quite fitting that we, as pioneer builders of model locomotives to operate on "Lionel Standard" track, should retain our leadership with the Super-Motor which is the acme of perfection.

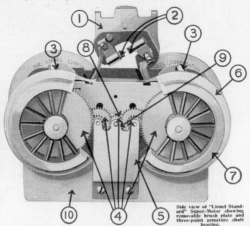

Side view of "Lionel Standard" Super-Motor showing removable brush plate and three-point armature shaft bearing.

Driving Wheels (6)—Particular attention is directed to the driving wheels, which are massive in construction and are accurately die-cast. Their weight adds great tractive power to the motors. All driving wheels are directly geared to the motor, eliminating the use of connecting rods between the wheels, which insures better alignment with less friction.

Steel Tread on Wheels (7)—A steel tread beautifully nickel plated and polished is forced over the rim, insuring longer wear and a smooth, even riding surface. Lionel originated this method of wheel construction. See illustration on Page 7.

Reinforced Bearings (8)—Six phosphor bronze bearings are contained in the side plates of the motor. They add to the life of the motor and insure accurate alignment of the armature shaft and axles.

Armature—The armature is made of laminated electrical steel punchings. It is automatically drum wound with triple-covered magnet wire, dipped in shellac and baked. The armature shaft (9) is made of the best quality drill rod.

Side Plates (10)—Made of heavy steel, with bronze bushings inserted for shaft and axles.

Field—Made of the highest grade electrical steel correctly wound and scientifically designed.

Commutator—Made of heavy copper. The segments are perfectly insulated, making short circuits impossible.

Tractive Power—The tractive power of these motors is remarkable. They will haul from 12 to 20 of our largest size freight or Pullman cars with the greatest ease. The weight of the wheels and motor is close to the track, insuring low centre of gravity, with the result that the locomotive is not top-heavy and slippage of the wheels is therefore unknown. This construction is infinitely superior to the method of loading down the superstructure with useless weight so as to obtain tractive power. This unnecessary weight rapidly wears down all working parts and causes the locomotive to jump the track.

Minimum Current Consumption—The new Lionel Super-Motor is not only more powerful than any motor of its size, but it consumes less than half the current of any motor developing the same power.

Three-Point Armature Shaft Bearing (5)—For the first time in the development of miniature motors it has been possible to perfect an arrangement whereby the armature shaft revolves in three bearings—two of them are contained in the side plates of the motor and the third one in the plate that holds the gearing studs. This three-point-bearing eliminates all vibration of the armature shaft, with the result that the commutator and brushes wear long and evenly. Considering the fact that the commutator and brushes are the life of the motor, this improvement is of great importance.

1927 CATALOG

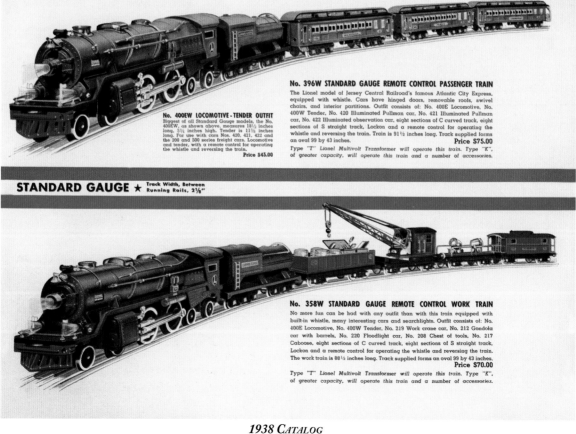

No. 400EW LOCOMOTIVE-TENDER OUTFIT
Biggest of all Standard Gauge models, the No. 400EW, as shown above, measures 18½ inches long, 5¼ inches high. Tender is 11⅝ inches long. For use with cars Nos. 420, 421, 422 and the 200 and 500 series freight cars. Locomotive and tender, with a remote control for operating the whistle and reversing the train.
Price $45.00

No. 396W STANDARD GAUGE REMOTE CONTROL PASSENGER TRAIN
The Lionel model of Jersey Central Railroad's famous Atlantic City Express, equipped with whistle. Cars have hinged doors, removable roofs, swivel chairs, and interior partitions. Outfit consists of: No. 400E Locomotive, No. 400W Tender, No. 420 Illuminated Pullman car, No. 421 Illuminated Pullman car, No. 422 Illuminated observation car, eight sections of C curved track, eight sections of S straight track, Lockon and a remote control for operating the whistle and reversing the train. Train is 91½ inches long. Track supplied forms an oval 99 by 43 inches.
Price $75.00
Type "T" Lionel Multivolt Transformer will operate this train. Type "K", of greater capacity, will operate this train and a number of accessories.

STANDARD GAUGE ★ Track Width, Between Running Rails, 2⅛"

No. 358W STANDARD GAUGE REMOTE CONTROL WORK TRAIN
No more fun can be had with any outfit than with this train equipped with built-in whistle, many interesting cars and searchlights. Outfit consists of: No. 400E Locomotive, No. 400W Tender, No. 219 Work crane car, No. 212 Gondola car with barrels, No. 220 Floodlight car, No. 208 Chest of tools, No. 217 Caboose, eight sections of C curved track, eight sections of S straight track, Lockon and a remote control for operating the whistle and reversing the train. The work train is 88½ inches long. Track supplied forms an oval 99 by 43 inches.
Price $70.00
Type "T" Lionel Multivolt Transformer will operate this train. Type "K", of greater capacity, will operate this train and a number of accessories.

1938 CATALOG

320 Baggage Type II

320 Baggage (Type I): Matches Type II 319 and Type I 322.

VG	EX	LN	RARITY
95	120	160	3

320 Baggage (Type II):  Matches Type III 319 and Type II 322, except rubber-stamped "LIONEL ELECTRIC RAILROAD".

VG	EX	LN	RARITY
95	120	160	3

320 Baggage (Type III): Matches Type IV 319 and Type III 322, except rubber-stamped "LIONEL ELECTRIC RAILROAD".

VG	EX	LN	RARITY
175	250	350	5

320 Baggage (Type IV): Also produced in 1929 or 1930 was a car that matched the Type IV 319 and 322, except it was rubber-stamped "ILLINOIS CENTRAL".

VG	EX	LN	RARITY
175	250	350	5

322 Observation: Like the 319, the 322 was shown in the catalog from 1924 to 1927, before being dropped, only to resume production–albeit uncataloged–after a one-year hiatus.

322 Observation (Type I): Matches Type II 319 and Type I 320.

VG	EX	LN	RARITY
95	120	160	3

322 Observation (Type II): Matches Type III 319 and Type II 320.

VG	EX	LN	RARITY
95	120	160	3

322 Observation (Type III): Matches Type IV 319 and Type III 320.

VG	EX	LN	RARITY
175	250	350	5

322 Observation (Type IV): Matches Type V 319 and Type IV 320.

VG	EX	LN	RARITY
175	250	350	5

332 Baggage: Introduced in 1926, this 12" long car was produced through 1933 and was a companion to two different series of passenger cars.

332 Baggage (Type I): As first produced, the baggage body was painted Mojave, as was the roof. Its doors were painted maroon, and its window/plate inserts were maroon as well. It continued with this color scheme through 1927.

PASSENGER CARS

Price Guide Key: **VG** = Very Good, **EX** = Excellent, **LN** = Like New | *Values for each condition are in U.S. dollars.* | **Rarity** = Scale from 1-8 with 8 being the hardest to find.

135

332 BAGGAGE TYPE VI

332 Baggage (Type II): Also introduced in 1926 was a car with a gray body and roof. Its doors were painted maroon, and its window/plate inserts were maroon as well. It continued with this color scheme through 1928.

VG	EX	LN	RARITY
70	95	125	3

332 Baggage (Type III): Also produced from 1926 to 1928 was a version with an olive green body and roof, which was available for separate sale only. This car had red inserts and doors.

VG	EX	LN	RARITY
100	140	190	6

332 Baggage (Type IV): Between 1928 and 1930, the 332 was painted peacock. Its windows and number boards were painted orange. Matching sets of either orange or red baggage doors were installed.

VG	EX	LN	RARITY
70	95	125	3

332 Baggage (Type V): In 1930, some cars were produced for Macy's that were painted State brown with dark brown roofs. These cars had cream-colored inserts and doors.

VG	EX	LN	RARITY
175	275	300	8

332 Baggage (Type VI): Introduced in 1930, cars with red bodies and roofs were available through 1932. These cars had cream-colored inserts and doors.

VG	EX	LN	RARITY
70	95	125	3

337 PULLMAN TYPE II

332 Baggage (Type VII): In 1931, the peacock-bodied car with orange trim returned, although with some major changes. The roof was now dark green, and covering the "THE LIONEL LINES" rubber-stamping was a decal reading "IVES LINES". On the bottom of the cars, which were offered again in 1932, was a paper label marked "MANUFACTURED BY – THE IVES CORPORATION – IRVINGTON, N.J."

VG	EX	LN	RARITY
100	140	190	6

332 Baggage (Type VIII): For 1933, the peacock/dark green cars lost their Ives decal, once again displaying rubber-stamped "THE LIONEL LINES".

VG	EX	LN	RARITY
70	95	125	5

332 Baggage (Type IX): During 1934, unsold cars with the Ives decal were re-decaled. A decal reading THE LIONEL RAILWAY LINES" was applied, positioned to obscure the previously installed Ives decal.

VG	EX	LN	RARITY
100	140	190	6

337 Pullman: This 12" long Pullman, and the matching 338 Observation car, was produced from 1925 through 1932. Its decoration was simple, with contrasting inserts for the windows, name and number boards installed, as well as contrasting doors. Black air tanks and brass steps were mounted on the underside of the car.

337 Pullman (Type I): As first produced, the Pullman body was painted Mojave, as was the roof. Its doors were painted maroon, and its window/plate inserts were maroon as well.

"THE LIONEL LINES" was rubber-stamped above the windows.

VG	EX	LN	RARITY
80	100	125	3

337 Pullman (Type II): A second version was built as well, identical to the Type I except for "NEW YORK CENTRAL LINES" rubber-stamping being used rather than Lionel Lines.

VG	EX	LN	RARITY
80	100	125	3

337 Pullman (Type III): The Lionel Lines Pullman was also painted olive green (a prototypical color) with red trim.

VG	EX	LN	RARITY
100	140	190	3

337 Pullman (Type IV): Maroon trim was also used on some olive green Lionel Lines cars.

VG	EX	LN	RARITY
80	100	125	2

337 Pullman (Type V): Olive green with maroon trim was also used as the color scheme for cars lettered "ILLINOIS CENTRAL" used in a set.

RARITY
Too infrequently traded to establish accurate values.

Price Guide Key: **VG** = Very Good, **EX** = Excellent, **LN** = Like New | *Values for each condition are in U.S. dollars.* | **Rarity** = Scale from 1-8 with 8 being the hardest to find.

137

PASSENGER CARS

338 OBSERVATION TYPE I

337 Pullman (Type VI): Pullmans were also made in red with cream trim. These cars were rubber-stamped "THE LIONEL LINES" and matched the 332 Type VI.

VG	EX	LN	RARITY
125	175	225	5

337 Pullman (Type VII): Some Lionel Lines Pullmans were painted pea green with cream trim.

VG	EX	LN	RARITY
175	225	275	6

338 Observation: This 12" long Observation car, and the matching 337 Pullman, were produced from 1925 through 1932. A brass railing surrounded the observation platform. The car had contrasting inserts for the windows, name and number boards installed, as well as contrasting doors. Black air tanks and brass steps were mounted on the underside of the car.

338 Observation (Type I):  Matches 337 Mojave Lionel Lines Pullman Type I.

VG	EX	LN	RARITY
80	100	125	3

338 Observation (Type II): Matches Mojave NYC 337 Pullman Type II.

VG	EX	LN	RARITY
80	100	125	3

338 Observation (Type III): Matches 337 Pullman Type III.

VG	EX	LN	RARITY
100	140	190	3

338 Observation (Type IV): Matches 337 Pullman Type IV.

VG	EX	LN	RARITY
80	100	125	2

338 Observation (Type V): Matches 337 Pullman Type V.

RARITY
Too infrequently traded to establish accurate values.

339 PULLMAN TYPE III

338 Observation (Type VI): Matches 337 red Pullman Type VI.

VG	EX	LN	RARITY
125	175	225	5

338 Observation (Type VII): Matches 337 Pullman Type VII.

VG	EX	LN	RARITY
175	225	275	6

339 Pullman: These illuminated passenger cars were introduced in 1925 and remained part of the Lionel product line through 1933. They were similar to the 337, however they had fewer, and much more elaborate, windows.

339 Pullman (Type I): The 339 was offered in gray with maroon trim from 1926 through 1928. Its markings, including "THE LIONEL LINES" which was printed directly on the body above the roof, were rubber-stamped in gold.

VG	EX	LN	RARITY
40	60	90	1

339 Pullman (Type II): Between 1928 and 1930, the body and roof of the 339 were painted peacock. Its windows, doors and number boards were painted orange. Its markings, including "THE LIONEL LINES" which was printed directly on the body above the roof, were rubber-stamped in gold.

VG	EX	LN	RARITY
40	60	90	1

339 Pullman (Type III): The peacock cars were also made with a dark green roof.

VG	EX	LN	RARITY
60	90	125	2

339 Pullman (Type IV): In 1931, the peacock car with dark green roof was redecorated. Covering the "THE LIONEL LINES" rubber-stamping was a decal reading "IVES LINES". On the bottom of the cars, which were offered again in 1932, was a paper label marked "MANUFACTURED BY – THE IVES CORPORATION – IRVINGTON, N.J."

VG	EX	LN	RARITY
100	140	190	6

339 Pullman (Type V): In 1930, some cars were produced for Macy's that were painted State brown with dark brown roofs. These cars had cream-colored inserts and doors.

VG	EX	LN	RARITY
175	275	300	8

341 Observation: This illuminated 12" long Observation car, and the matching 339 Pullman, were produced from 1925 through 1933. A brass railing surrounded the observation platform. The car had contrasting inserts for the windows,

Price Guide Key: **VG** = Very Good, **EX** = Excellent, **LN** = Like New | *Values for each condition are in U.S. dollars.* | **Rarity** = Scale from 1-8 with 8 being the hardest to find.

PASSENGER CARS

139

412 CALIFORNIA TYPE I

name and number boards installed, as well as contrasting doors. Black air tanks and brass steps were mounted on the underside of the car.

341 Observation (Type I): Matches gray 339 Pullman Type I.

VG	EX	LN	RARITY
40	60	90	1

341 Observation (Type II): Matches peacock Lionel Lines 339 Pullman Type II.

VG	EX	LN	RARITY
40	60	90	1

341 Observation (Type III): Matches the peacock 339 Pullman Type III with dark green roof.

VG	EX	LN	RARITY
60	90	125	2

341 Observation (Type IV): Matches Ives Railway 339 Pullman Type IV.

VG	EX	LN	RARITY
100	140	190	6

341 Observation (Type V): Matches 339 Pullman Type V.

VG	EX	LN	RARITY
175	275	300	8

412 Pullman, California: This 21 1/2" long car, along with its companions the 413 Colorado, 414 Illinois and 416 Observation, comprise what is known as the State Set. These were Lionel's largest, most elaborate and most expensive Standard Gauge passenger cars. They were available from 1929 through 1935, and always had interior lighting and six-wheel trucks. The roofs of these cars were hinged to reveal a complete interior, including interior walls, seats, toilets and sinks.

412 California (Type I): Some of these cars were painted in what was known as State green. These cars had a dark green roof, with apple green window inserts. The restroom and upper windows were covered with blue-speckled celluloid.

VG	EX	LN	RARITY
800	1250	1800	6

412 California (Type II): The green cars were also made with cream window inserts.

VG	EX	LN	RARITY
1200	1700	2300	8

416 Illinois Type I

412 California (Type III): This magnificent car was also available painted "State brown," and with a dark brown roof.

VG	EX	LN	RARITY
1000	1500	2000	7

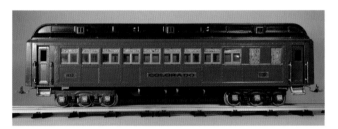

413 Colorado (Type I): This Pullman matches the Type I 412.

VG	EX	LN	RARITY
800	1250	1800	6

413 Colorado (Type II): This Pullman matches the Type II 412.

VG	EX	LN	RARITY
1200	1700	2300	8

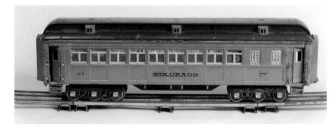

413 Colorado (Type III): This Pullman matches the Type III 412.

VG	EX	LN	RARITY
1000	1500	2000	7

414 Illinois (Type I): This Pullman matches the Type I 412.

VG	EX	LN	RARITY
1000	1500	2000	7

414 Illinois (Type II): This Pullman matches the Type II 412.

VG	EX	LN	RARITY
1700	2300	2900	8

414 Illinois (Type III): This Pullman matches the Type III 412.

VG	EX	LN	RARITY
1200	1700	2300	8

416 Observation, New York: Naturally, a train consisting of three magnificent Pullmans had to have an equally magnificent observation car at its end. The New York performed this function admirably. Its construction details were similar to those of the Pullmans, but in addition to the ornate brass handrails and steps of those cars, there was a fancy brass railing on an observation platform on the tail end of the car. A large glazed window looked out over this platform, also revealing the detailed interior. A drumhead on the rear railing proclaimed either "LIONEL LIMITED" or "TRANSCONTINENTAL LIMITED".

416 New York (Type I): This observation matches the Type I 412, 413 and 414 Pullmans.

VG	EX	LN	RARITY
800	1250	1800	6

416 New York (Type II): This observation matches the Type II 412, 413 and 414 Pullmans.

VG	EX	LN	RARITY
1200	1700	2300	8

PASSENGER CARS

Price Guide Key: VG = Very Good, EX = Excellent, LN = Like New | *Values for each condition are in U.S. dollars.* | Rarity = Scale from 1-8 with 8 being the hardest to find.

141

418 PULLMAN TYPE VII

416 New York (Type III): This observation matches the Type III 412, 413 and 414 Pullmans.

VG	EX	LN	RARITY
1000	1500	2000	7

418 Pullman: These attractive cars were first produced in 1923. Two years later, their appearance was further enhanced by the addition of six-wheel trucks in place of the previously used four-wheel trucks. These early four-wheel trucks were similar to the ones used on 10-series freight cars. They remained in the product line through 1932. With one exception, these cars were painted Mojave and have gold rubber-stamped markings, including the catalog number, which is stamped on one end. Black-painted steel air tanks with nickel ends are mounted on the underside of the cars, along with brass steps. The interiors of the cars are illuminated.

418 Pullman (Type I): "NEW YORK CENTRAL LINES" was rubber-stamped above the windows, while centered below the windows and stamped in gold was "PULLMAN". These cars, built in 1923, were equipped with maroon window trim and lithographed wooden doors.

VG	EX	LN	RARITY
150	225	325	4

418 Pullman (Type II): Other cars, built in 1923-1924, were identical to the Type I, except "PARLOR CAR" replaced the "Pullman" lettering. This was to be the case for the rest of the 418's production.

VG	EX	LN	RARITY
150	225	325	4

418 Pullman (Type III): Rather than being lithographed to simulate wood, the doors on some cars were painted maroon to match the window trim.

VG	EX	LN	RARITY
150	225	325	4

418 Pullman (Type IV): In 1925, six-wheel trucks with nickel journal boxes began to be used on the 418, including cars with lithographed doors.

VG	EX	LN	RARITY
175	250	350	4

418 Pullman (Type V): The new six-wheel trucks were also mounted on cars with maroon-painted doors.

VG	EX	LN	RARITY
175	250	350	4

418 Pullman (Type VI): Some of the cars with six-wheel trucks and maroon doors were built with orange window trim rather than the customary maroon.

VG	EX	LN	RARITY
175	250	350	4

418 Pullman (Type VII): A further variation was created by lettering some of the orange-trimmed Mojave cars "THE LIONEL LINES" rather than New York Central. The doors of these cars were maroon, and they rode on six-wheel trucks.

VG	EX	LN	RARITY
175	250	350	4

418 Pullman (Type VIII): Rather than the somewhat drab Mojave of the other 418 Pullmans, this car was painted apple green. Its doors remained maroon, but the windows were trimmed in red.

VG	EX	LN	RARITY
300	400	500	7

418 Pullman Illinois Central: Some 418s were built lettered Illinois Central rather than New York Central or Lionel Lines. These cars are substantially harder to find, and more valuable, than the cars listed previously.

419 Combination: A companion to the 418 listed previously, the lower sides of these cars were lettered "PARLOR CAR" and "BAGGAGE".

419 Combination (Type I): Paint, decoration and construction detail were comparable to the 418 Type II.

VG	EX	LN	RARITY
150	225	325	4

419 Combination (Type II): Paint, decoration and construction detail were comparable to the 418 Type III.

VG	EX	LN	RARITY
150	225	325	4

419 Combination (Type III): Paint, decoration and construction detail were comparable to the 418 Type IV.

VG	EX	LN	RARITY
175	250	350	4

419 Combination (Type IV): Paint, decoration and construction detail were comparable to the 418 Type V.

VG	EX	LN	RARITY
175	250	350	4

419 Combination (Type V): Paint, decoration and construction detail were comparable to the 418 Type VI.

VG	EX	LN	RARITY
175	250	350	4

419 Combination (Type VI): Paint, decoration and construction detail were comparable to the 418 Type VII.

VG	EX	LN	RARITY
175	250	350	4

419 Combination (Type VII): Apple green paint, decoration and construction detail, including six-wheel trucks, were comparable to the 418 Type VIII.

VG	EX	LN	RARITY
300	400	500	7

420 Pullman, Faye: This car, along with the 421 Westphal Pullman and 422 Tempel Observation, comprised the magnificent Blue Comet. At 18 3/4" long, these cars were only slightly smaller than the State cars and mimicked many of their construction details, including six-wheel trucks and complete interiors. The names of the cars, and their colors, were taken from the fastest and most famous train from Central Railroad of New Jersey (CNJ). The real Blue Comet ran between Jersey City, N.J., and the Atlantic City resort area during the 1930s.

420 Faye (Type I): The earliest cars are distinguished by their die-cast journal boxes. Like the real train, the car bodies were medium blue. The removable roof was painted dark blue and the roof trim was cream colored. The steps, handrails and plates were brass.

VG	EX	LN	RARITY
600	800	1000	6

420 Faye (Type II): Stamped brass journals replaced the castings early on, but the balance of the car remained unchanged.

VG	EX	LN	RARITY
600	800	1000	6

420 Faye (Type III): In the mid-1930s, nickel trim began to be used, leaving only the plates brass. At the same time, a lighter shade of blue began to be used as the body color. Ironically, given the detailed interior in this car, frosted window glazing also began to be used.

VG	EX	LN	RARITY
800	1000	1250	7

420 Faye (Type IV): Some of these lighter blue cars had their diaphragms painted the same color as the body. Previously they had matched the roof.

VG	EX	LN	RARITY
1000	1200	1500	8

421 Westphal (Type I): Matches 420 Type I.

VG	EX	LN	RARITY
600	800	1000	6

421 Westphal (Type II): Matches 420 Type II.

VG	EX	LN	RARITY
600	800	1000	6

421 Westphal (Type III): Matches 420 Type III.

VG	EX	LN	RARITY
800	1000	1250	7

421 Westphal (Type IV): Matches 420 Type IV.

VG	EX	LN	RARITY
1000	1200	1500	8

422 Observation, Tempel: Bringing up the rear of the Blue Comet was this ornate observation car. At the rear of the car was an observation platform, its railing of either brass or nickel (to match the rest of the car's trim) and the drumhead reading "LIONEL LIMITED".

PASSENGER CARS

Price Guide Key: VG = Very Good, EX = Excellent, LN = Like New | *Values for each condition are in U.S. dollars.* | Rarity = Scale from 1-8 with 8 being the hardest to find.

143

422 TEMPEL TYPE II

422 Tempel (Type I): Matches 420 Type I, brass observation railing.

VG	EX	LN	RARITY
600	800	1000	6

422 Tempel (Type II):  Matches 420 Type II, brass observation railing.

VG	EX	LN	RARITY
600	800	1000	6

422 Tempel (Type III): Matches 420 Type III, nickel observation railing.

VG	EX	LN	RARITY
800	1000	1250	7

422 Tempel (Type IV): Matches 420 Type IV, nickel observation railing.

VG	EX	LN	RARITY
1000	1200	1500	8

424 Pullman, Liberty Bell: This handsome car, along with the matching 425 Stephen Girard and 426 Coral Isle observation, had a body painted in what is known to collectors as "Stephen Girard green." Their roofs were dark green, as were their diaphragms. Brass plates, along with cream-colored window inserts, adorned the 16" car. These cars were manufactured from 1931 through 1940.

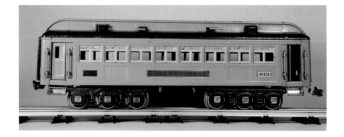

424 Liberty Bell (Type I): The early cars had brass steps and trim.

VG	EX	LN	RARITY
450	550	675	5

424 Liberty Bell (Type II): In the mid-1930s, nickel steps and trim began to be used.

VG	EX	LN	RARITY
575	675	800	6

425 Pullman, Stephen Girard: The green color of this series is named for this car, which in turn was named for a real man. Stephen Girard was a Revolutionary War-era merchant and shipper whose business interests later turned to banking. In fact, it was Girard's loan of $8 million that kept the U.S. government solvent during the War of 1812.

425 Stephen Girard (Type I): The early cars had brass steps and trim.

VG	EX	LN	RARITY
450	550	675	5

425 Stephen Girard (Type II):  In the mid-1930s, nickel steps and trim began to be used.

VG	EX	LN	RARITY
575	675	800	6

425 STEPHEN GIRARD TYPE II

426 Observation, Coral Isle: Bringing up the rear of this two-tone green passenger train was the Coral Isle observation car. Its platform railing was made of brass or nickel, as appropriate to match the rest of the car, and its keystone-shaped drumhead read "PENNSYLVANIA LIMITED".

426 Coral Isle (Type I): Matches Type I 424 and 425.

VG	EX	LN	RARITY
450	550	675	5

426 Coral Isle (Type II): Matches Type II 424 and 425.

VG	EX	LN	RARITY
575	675	800	6

427 Diner: Cataloged in 1930, this car never entered mass production.

428 Pullman: In 1926, a year after the 418-series was upgraded to six-wheel trucks, four-wheel trucks were reinstalled underneath that body type. The new series of cars, riding on 200-series trucks, was dubbed 428, 429 and 430. The Pullman of this series was the 428. It remained part of the product line through 1930.

428 Pullman (Type I): The roof and body of the new car were initially painted dark green and trimmed with maroon window inserts. Its doors were lithographed with simulated wood grain, and the catalog number was rubber-stamped on one end of the car. That rubber-stamping was gold, as were the "THE LIONEL LINES" and "PARLOR CAR" markings on the upper and lower car sides, respectively.

VG	EX	LN	RARITY
225	280	350	3

428 Pullman (Type II): Some cars had maroon-painted doors rather than the lithographed doors.

VG	EX	LN	RARITY
225	280	350	3

428 Pullman (Type III): Orange window inserts were used along with the maroon doors on some cars.

VG	EX	LN	RARITY
225	280	350	4

428 Pullman (Type IV): A few cars were painted orange rather than dark green. These cars had apple green doors and

Price Guide Key: **VG** = Very Good, **EX** = Excellent, **LN** = Like New | *Values for each condition are in U.S. dollars.* | **Rarity** = Scale from 1-8 with 8 being the hardest to find.

145

PASSENGER CARS

429 COMBINATION TYPE II

window inserts. The rubber-stamped markings, however, were unchanged from those of the other versions.

VG	EX	LN	RARITY
575	675	800	6

429 Combination: A companion to the 428 listed previously, the lower sides of these cars were lettered "PARLOR CAR" and "BAGGAGE". The catalog number was stamped on one end. "THE LIONEL LINES" appears above the windows.

429 Combination (Type I): Paint, decoration and construction detail were comparable to the 428 Type I.

VG	EX	LN	RARITY
225	280	350	3

429 Combination (Type II): Paint, decoration and construction detail were comparable to the 428 Type II.

VG	EX	LN	RARITY
225	280	350	3

429 Combination (Type III): Paint, decoration and construction detail were comparable to the 428 Type III.

VG	EX	LN	RARITY
225	280	350	4

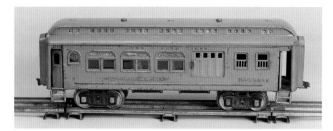

429 Combination (Type IV): Orange paint, decoration and construction detail were comparable to the 428 Type IV.

VG	EX	LN	RARITY
575	675	800	6

430 Observation: A companion to the previously listed 428 Pullman and 429 combine, the lower sides of these 17 5/8" long cars were lettered "OBSERVATION" inside an ornate rubber-stamped box. At the rear of the car was an open observation platform with brass railing.

430 Observation (Type I): Matches 428 Pullman and 429 combination Type I.

VG	EX	LN	RARITY
225	280	350	3

430 Observation (Type II): Matches 428 Pullman and 429 combination Type II.

VG	EX	LN	RARITY
225	280	350	3

430 Observation (Type III): Matches 428 Pullman and 429 combination Type III.

VG	EX	LN	RARITY
225	280	350	3

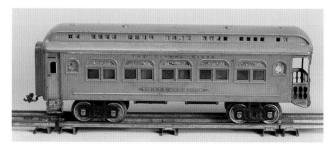

430 Observation (Type IV): Orange paint matches 428 Pullman and 429 combination Type IV.

VG	EX	LN	RARITY
575	675	800	6

431 Dining Car: Unlike the comparable 418, 419 and 490, the 431 dining car was usually a separate sale-only item, and hence is much more difficult to find today than its companion pieces. Introduced in 1927, with one exception, the 431 always had six-wheel trucks. Like its companion cars, it was discontinued in 1932.

431 Dining Car (Type I): Mojave with orange trim, matches Type VII 418.

VG	EX	LN	RARITY
400	500	600	6

431 Dining Car (Type II): Identical to the Type I 431 dining car, but for maroon rather than orange window inserts.

VG	EX	LN	RARITY
400	500	600	6

431 Dining Car (Type III): Apple green, matches Type VIII 418 Pullman.

VG	EX	LN	RARITY
450	575	750	8

431 Dining Car (Type IV): Some 431 diners were painted orange with apple green window inserts.

VG	EX	LN	RARITY
450	575	750	8

431 Dining Car (Type V): The sole version of the 431 equipped with four-wheel trucks was painted dark green. Its window inserts were orange.

VG	EX	LN	RARITY
450	575	750	8

490 Observation: A companion to the previously listed 418 Pullman and 419 combine, the lower sides of these 17 5/8" long cars were lettered "OBSERVATION" inside an ornate rubber-stamped box. At the rear of the car was an open observation platform with brass railing.

490 Observation (Type I): Paint, decoration and construction detail were comparable to the Type II 418 and Type I 419 cars.

VG	EX	LN	RARITY
125	200	300	4

490 Observation (Type II): Paint, decoration and construction detail were comparable to the Type III 418 and Type II 419 cars.

VG	EX	LN	RARITY
125	200	300	4

490 Observation (Type III): Paint, decoration and construction detail, including six-wheel trucks, were comparable to the Type IV 418 and Type III 419 cars.

VG	EX	LN	RARITY
175	250	350	4

490 Observation (Type IV): Paint, decoration and construction detail, including six-wheel trucks, were comparable to the Type V 418 and Type IV 419 cars.

VG	EX	LN	RARITY
175	250	350	4

490 Observation (Type V): Paint, decoration and construction detail, including six-wheel trucks, were comparable to the Type VI 418 and Type V 419 cars.

VG	EX	LN	RARITY
175	250	350	4

490 Observation (Type VI): Paint, decoration and construction detail, including six-wheel trucks, were comparable to the Type VII 418 and Type VI 419 cars.

VG	EX	LN	RARITY
175	250	350	4

490 Observation (Type VII): Paint, decoration and construction detail, including six-wheel trucks, were comparable to the Type VIII 418 and Type VII 419 cars.

VG	EX	LN	RARITY
300	400	500	7

1766 Pullman: This car, along with its companions the 1767 and 1768, was originally developed for use by Lionel's Ives subsidiary in 1932. Beginning in 1934, they were re-badged for the Lionel market. They remained part of the Lionel product line until Standard Gauge was discontinued in 1940.

1766 Pullman (Type I): As first produced, and as always shown in the catalog, the cars had terra-cotta sides and maroon roofs. Cream window inserts were used. Brass plates and trim decorated the 15" long car, which rode on six-wheel trucks.

VG	EX	LN	RARITY
350	500	700	6

Price Guide Key: **VG** = Very Good, **EX** = Excellent, **LN** = Like New | *Values for each condition are in U.S. dollars.* | **Rarity** = Scale from 1-8 with 8 being the hardest to find.

PASSENGER CARS

147

1766 Pullman (Type II): Later, uncataloged versions of the car had red sides and maroon roofs, as well as silver colored doors and window inserts. The trim on these cars was nickel.

VG	EX	LN	RARITY
450	600	800	7

1767 Pullman (Type I): Matches 1766 Type I Pullman.

VG	EX	LN	RARITY
350	500	700	6

1767 Pullman (Type II): Matches 1766 Type II Pullman.

VG	EX	LN	RARITY
450	600	800	7

1768 Observation (Type I): Matches 1766 and 1767 Type I Pullmans.

VG	EX	LN	RARITY
350	500	700	6

1768 Observation (Type II): Matches 1766 and 1767 Type II Pullmans.

VG	EX	LN	RARITY
450	600	800	7

1910 Pullman: About 1910, this uncataloged passenger car was offered. It was 16 1/4" long, with a dark olive body and roof. Gold rubber-stamped markings reading simply "1910 PULLMAN 1910" were applied to the car sides. Its doors and windowsills were maroon.

VG	EX	LN	RARITY
900	1250	1700	8

SECTION C

O GAUGE
OVERVIEW

In 1915, a new size of trains appeared in the catalog. Unlike the 1906 replacement of 2 7/8-inch trains with Standard Gauge, the new line, known as 0 gauge, was an addition to the then-current Standard Gauge line.

Riding on rails spaced 1 1/4 inches apart, the purpose of the new size was similar to the purpose of Standard Gauge nine years previous – to offer a more compact train,, thus appealing to a broader market. The smaller size also allowed another benefit – lower cost. The track itself was constructed much like its Standard Gauge counterpart – even the rails themselves had the same cross section – with three rails permanently attached to steel crossties.

Lionel was not the first to make trains in this size, but in time the name "Lionel" would become virtually synonymous with "0 gauge train." In a mere two decades, this newcomer would totally eclipse Standard Gauge in sales and, even today, is the most popular size of trains made by Lionel.

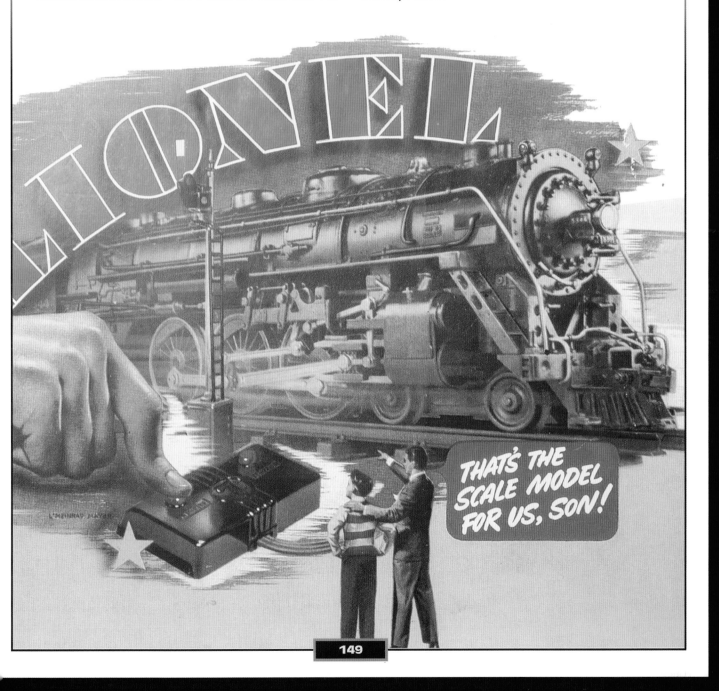

THAT'S THE SCALE MODEL FOR US, SON!

CHAPTER 15
O GAUGE STEAM LOCOMOTIVES

The steam locomotives of Lionel's prewar era went through a remarkable evolutionary process and a long gestation period. Lionel introduced the smaller 0 gauge trains to its product line in 1915 but, despite advertisements of that year and again in 1921, steam locomotives weren't produced in this size until 1930. From 1915 through 1929, the 0 gauge Lionel Lines relied exclusively on replicas of electric locomotives. The catalog numbers 258 and 259 introduced at that time were of sheet metal construction with die-cast frames, clearly toys rather than models despite the catalog's promotions. Within two years, the steam types had forced all but one of the electric-pattern locomotives from the catalog. The final one capitulated in 1936.

Even more incredible was the advance in design and manufacturing, from the tin toy-like beginning to the amazing, die-cast, scale-detailed 700E in just seven years! Die-casting had been in use by Lionel for some time for such items as locomotive frames, but never before in such a widespread manner as the 700E. Die-casting was also used to manufacture the boilers and other major components of several smaller steam locomotives beginning in 1938, although sheet-metal steam locomotives were not totally forced from the product line until after World War II.

201: This somewhat reduced-sized version of Lionel's scale-proportioned 701T switcher, a replica of the Pennsylvania Railroad's B-6 0-6-0, was introduced in 1940. It remained a part of the product line through the 1942 catalog. The wiring for the reversing unit (E-unit) of these locomotives was routed through a DC-activated relay. This allowed it to be operated on the same track with conventional locomotives, yet have independent directional control. This system was known as "Magic Electrol."

201 (Type I): Some of these 0-6-0 switchers were furnished with a 2201T tender, which lacked a bell.

VG	EX	LN	RARITY
350	500	700	6

201 (Type II): Others came with a 2201B tender.

VG	EX	LN	RARITY
400	550	750	6

201 (Type III): Some of the switchers with 2201T tender also had the "201" on the cab sides, stamped smaller than usual.

VG	EX	LN	RARITY
375	525	725	6

201 (Type IV): The smaller-number boiler was also used on some of these 0-6-0 switchers with 2201B bell-ringing tenders.

VG	EX	LN	RARITY
425	575	775	6

203: This locomotive and tender was essentially identical to the 201, but lacked the DC control circuitry. The 203 was offered in 1940 and 1941.

203 (Type I): Like the 201, some of these 0-6-0 switchers were furnished with 2203T tenders, which did not have a bell mechanism.

VG	EX	LN	RARITY
325	400	500	6

203 (Type II): The 2203B bell-ringing tender-equipped locomotives were more heavily promoted, however.

VG	EX	LN	RARITY
375	450	550	5

203 (Type III): The lettering on the cab sides of some of the 203T tender-equipped locomotives was smaller than the norm.

VG	EX	LN	RARITY
350	425	525	6

203 (Type IV): The bell-ringing 2203B tender was supplied with some of the small-number locomotives, also.

VG	EX	LN	RARITY
400	475	575	5

204: The smallest of the prewar die-cast steamers was the 204. The locomotive rolled on nickel-rimmed Baldwin disc drivers. Its boiler would go on to be the basis for the famous, or infamous, postwar "Scout" series. Though uncataloged, it was assembled in 1940-41.

204 (Type I): An attractive version of the 204 was painted gunmetal, as was its latch coupler-equipped 1689T tender.

VG	EX	LN	RARITY
75	110	150	5

204 (Type II): Some of the gunmetal 204 locomotives came with the electric box coupler-equipped 2689T tender.

VG	EX	LN	RARITY
75	110	150	5

204 (Type III): More commonly, the 204 and its 1689T were painted black.

VG	EX	LN	RARITY
50	70	100	3

204 (Type IV): Electric coupler-equipped 2689T tender and 204 locomotive combinations are also more abundant in black.

VG	EX	LN	RARITY
50	70	100	3

224 (Type I): This well-proportioned 2-6-2 was identical mechanically to the 224E, only the "E" suffix was dropped midway through production as reversing, or "E units," came to be considered standard equipment. This version was painted gunmetal and was sold with a die-cast 2224 tender.

Price Guide Key: VG = Very Good, EX = Excellent, LN = Like New | *Values for each condition are in U.S. dollars.* | Rarity = Scale from 1-8 with 8 being the hardest to find.

151

224E Type III

VG	EX	LN	RARITY
500	850	1200	7

224 (Type II): The 224 with 2224 die-cast tender was also offered in black.

VG	EX	LN	RARITY
125	165	225	3

224 (Type III): In 1941, the black 224 was furnished with a plastic-bodied 2224 tender. Locomotives produced in 1941 also lacked the simulated hatch detail previously cast into the top of the sand dome.

VG	EX	LN	RARITY
75	125	175	3

224E (Type I): As initially produced, the die-cast 2-6-2 later known as the 224 bore nameplates reading 224E. During 1938, its first year of production, the locomotive and accompanying 2689W tender with sheet metal body were painted gunmetal.

VG	EX	LN	RARITY
125	165	225	4

224E (Type II): The next year the gunmetal 224E was furnished with the much more detailed, die-cast bodied 2224 tender.

VG	EX	LN	RARITY
500	850	1200	7

224E (Type III): ■ The 224E with 2224 die-cast tender was also produced wearing a black paint scheme.

VG	EX	LN	RARITY
125	165	225	3

225 (Type I): Somewhat larger than the 224, the 225 was also a die-cast 2-6-2. It was furnished with a black 2235 die-cast tender.

VG	EX	LN	RARITY
200	280	400	4

225 (Type II): Some of the black 225s came with high-truck 2245 die-cast tenders.

VG	EX	LN	RARITY
200	280	400	4

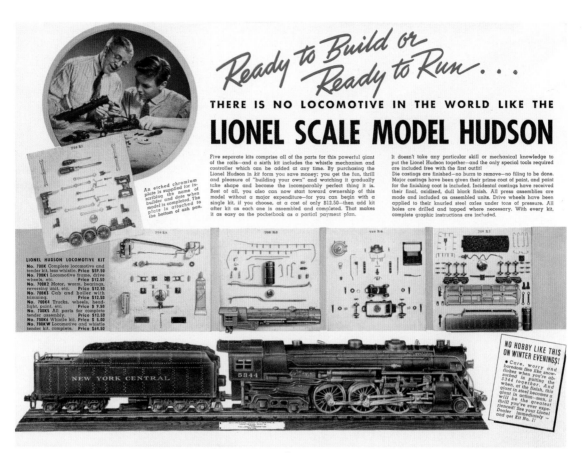

Ready to Build or Ready to Run . . .

THERE IS NO LOCOMOTIVE IN THE WORLD LIKE THE

LIONEL SCALE MODEL HUDSON

Five separate kits comprise all of the parts for this powerful giant of the rails—and a sixth kit includes the whistle mechanism and controller which can be added at any time. By purchasing the Lionel Hudson in *kit* form you save money; you get the fun, thrill and pleasure of "building your own" and watching it gradually take shape and become the incomparably perfect thing it is. Best of all, you also can now start toward ownership of this model without a major expenditure—for you can begin with a single kit, if you choose, at a cost of only $12.50—then add kit after kit as each one is assembled and completed. That makes it as easy on the pocketbook as a partial payment plan.

It doesn't take any particular skill or mechanical knowledge to put the Lionel Hudson together—and the only special tools required are included free with the first outfit!

Die castings are finished—no burrs to remove—no filing to be done. Major castings have been given their prime coat of paint, and paint for the finishing coat is included. Incidental castings have received their final, oxidized, dull black finish. All press assemblies are made and included as assembled units. Drive wheels have been applied to their knurled steel axles under tons of pressure. All holes are drilled and tapped where necessary. With every kit, complete graphic instructions are included.

An etched chromium plate is supplied for inscribing the name of builder and date when model is completed. The plate is attached to the bottom of ash pan.

LIONEL HUDSON LOCOMOTIVE KIT
No. 700K Complete locomotive and tender kit, less whistle. Price $59.50
No. 700K1 Locomotive frame, drive wheels, etc. Price $12.50
No. 700K2 Motor, worm, bearings, reversing unit, etc. Price $12.50
No. 700K3 Cab and boiler with trimming. Price $12.50
No. 700K4 Trucks, wheels, headlight, paint, etc. Price $9.50
No. 700K5 All parts for complete tender assembly. Price $12.50
No. 700K6 Whistle kit. Price $5.00
No. 700KW Locomotive and whistle tender kit, complete. Price $64.50

NEW YORK CENTRAL 5344

NO HOBBY LIKE THIS ON WINTER EVENINGS!
● Care, worry and boredom flee like snowflakes when you're absorbed in putting the 5344 together. And when, at the finish, this giant in steel becomes a giant in action-man, it will be the greatest thrill you've ever experienced! See your Lionel Dealer immediately—and get Kit No. 1!

1939 Catalog

No. 145W $29.50   No. 143 $18.00   No. 143W $21.75   LIONEL O GAUGE

Coal car can be unloaded electrically —by remote control.

145W

143W

No. 145W FREIGHT TRAIN OUTFIT WITH BUILT-IN WHISTLE

Three cars that can be unloaded *electrically* and a useful operating crane, *electric couplers* and *built-in whistle* combine to make this outfit unusually attractive. Outfit consists of: No. 224 Locomotive, No. 2224W Tender, No. 3659 Electric dump car, No. 3652 Electric gondola car, No. 2660 Crane car, No. 3651 Electric lumber car, No. 2657 Caboose, eight sections OC curved track, three sections of OS straight track, R.C.S. track set, UTC Lockon, whistling controller, three No. 160 Unloading bins. Train is 60¾ inches long. Track supplied forms an oval 51⅛ by 30⅞ inches. **Price $29.50**

In both outfits illustrated above, the flat cars can be unloaded electrically, by remote control.

No. 143W FREIGHT TRAIN OUTFIT WITH BUILT-IN WHISTLE

A fast freight with a lumber car that can be unloaded *electrically*. Equipped with *built-in whistle*. All cars have *electric couplers*. Outfit consists of No. 224 Locomotive, No. 2224W Tender, No. 2652 Gondola car, No. 2654 Oil tank car, No. 3651 Electric lumber car, No. 2657 Caboose, No. 160 Unloading bin, eight sections of OC curved track, three sections of OS straight track, R.C.S. track set, UTC Lockon and whistle-controller. Train is 52¼ inches long. Track supplied forms oval 51⅛ by 30⅞ inches. **Price $21.75**

To unload the gondola car in outfit 145W, you touch a remote control button. The side of the car swings open and barrels tumble out.

No. 143. Similar to No. 143W outfit, as described above, but without built-in whistle and whistle-controller. **Price $18.00**

ELECTRIC REMOTE CONTROL COUPLERS

Type "Q" Transformer will operate either train, above. Type "R" will provide for many accessories.

1939 Catalog

Price Guide Key: VG = Very Good, EX = Excellent, LN = Like New | *Values for each condition are in U.S. dollars.* | Rarity = Scale from 1-8 with 8 being the hardest to find.

153

225E TYPE I

225 (Type III): The later production 224 locomotives came with a black 2235 tender with plastic body.

VG	EX	LN	RARITY
175	250	350	3

225E (Type I): When introduced to the product line in 1938, the 225 carried the E suffix on its catalog number and nameplate. The first year the locomotive, which was furnished with the "waffle top" sheet metal 2225 tender, was painted gunmetal.

VG	EX	LN	RARITY
225	300	425	5

225E (Type II): Some of the waffle top tenders packaged with gunmetal 225E locomotives had high trucks, and the number 2265.

VG	EX	LN	RARITY
200	280	400	4

225E (Type III): Later production gunmetal 225E came with 2235 die-cast tenders.

VG	EX	LN	RARITY
175	250	350	3

225E (Type IV): The final production version of the 225E was painted black and came with a 2235 tender with plastic body.

VG	EX	LN	RARITY
150	225	300	3

226 (Type I): Like most of the large die-cast steam locomotives, the "E" suffix was dropped from the nameplate of Lionel's largest 2-6-2. The journal boxes on the 2226W tender began to be blackened rather than nickel plated.

VG	EX	LN	RARITY
350	475	650	4

226 (Type II): Some of the 226 locomotives were built without the model number appearing on the nameplate at all. Instead, the plate below the cab window read only Lionel Lines.

VG	EX	LN	RARITY
400	525	700	6

226E: The 226E was the biggest die-cast steamer Lionel produced, except for the Hudson. Like the 224E and 225E, the 226E had 2-6-2 wheel arrangement. Introduced in 1938, it came with a large die-cast bodied 2226W tender, which rode on six-wheel trucks with nickel journal boxes.

VG	EX	LN	RARITY
350	475	650	4

227: Utilizing many of the castings developed for the 701 scale switcher, Lionel created this semi-scale switcher in 1939. Remaining in the product line through 1942, a number of variations were created, as outlined subsequently. All were equipped with "Teledyne" couplers. This system used a DC relay, similar to that used to activate the whistle on most Lionel steamers, to operate the couplers. The height of the couplers of the 227 matched that of the 2650, 2750 and 2950 series cars. Available as an option was a bell-ringing tender. An off-on lever beneath the tender floor energized a bimetallic strip, which controlled the striker mechanism that sounded the bell. Lionel's catalog number for the 227 locomotive tender combination when not equipped with a bell was 902. Adding a bell resulted in the number being changed to 902B.

227 (Type I): As introduced in 1939, this semi-scale 0-6-0 had the number 8976 rubber-stamped beneath the cab window. The number 227 appeared on the boiler front, and the locomotive was furnished with a 2227T tender.

VG	EX	LN	RARITY
500	700	950	4

227 (Type II): Some of the catalog number 227 0-6-0 locomotives built in 1939 came with 2227B tenders.

VG	EX	LN	RARITY
550	750	975	5

227 (Type III): In 1940, the couplers were redesigned, and now cast into the top of the "box" was a representation of a real railroad knuckle coupler. The numberplate on the front of the locomotive continued to read "227" and the number rubber-stamped beneath the cab window was 8976. The locomotive continued to be available with the 2227T tender.

VG	EX	LN	RARITY
500	700	950	4

227 (Type IV): Locomotives with the bell-equipped 2227B tender received the same coupler upgrades outlined previously.

VG	EX	LN	RARITY
550	750	975	5

227 (Type V): During 1941, the numbers beneath the cab windows began to be heat-stamped rather than rubber-stamped. This technique results in crisper lettering, and oftentimes results in the lettering being slightly recessed into the underlying surface. The boiler front number plate continued to read 227, and the locomotive was still offered with the non bell-equipped 2227T tender.

VG	EX	LN	RARITY
500	700	950	4

227 (Type VI): Heat-stamped lettering was also applied to locomotives sold with the bell-ringing 2227B tender beginning in 1941.

VG	EX	LN	RARITY
550	750	975	5

227 (Type VII): Apparently late in the production life of the 0-6-0 with 2227B tender, in late 1941 or 1942, Lionel exhausted its supply of 227 boiler front number plates. Locomotives continued to be produced and shipped without these plates, with the head of a rivet being exposed on the boiler front as a result of this omission.

VG	EX	LN	RARITY
550	750	975	5

228: The general description of the 228 is the same as that of the 227, except the coupler height of the 228 matches that of the 2800-series cars. Lionel's catalog number for the 228 locomotive-tender combination, when not equipped with a bell, was 903. Adding a bell resulted in the number being changed to 903B.

228 (Type I): As introduced in 1939, this semi-scale 0-6-0 had the number 8976 rubber-stamped beneath the cab window. The number 228 appeared on the boiler front, and the locomotive was furnished with a 2228T tender.

VG	EX	LN	RARITY
500	700	950	4

228 (Type II): Some of the catalog number 228 0-6-0 locomotives built in 1939 came with 2228B tenders.

VG	EX	LN	RARITY
550	750	975	5

228 (Type III): In 1940, the couplers were redesigned. Now cast into the top of the "box" was a representation of a real railroad knuckle coupler. The numberplate on the front of the locomotive continued to read "228" and the number rubber-stamped beneath the cab window was 8976. The locomotive continued to be available with the 2228T tender.

VG	EX	LN	RARITY
500	700	950	4

228 (Type IV): Locomotives with the bell-equipped 2228B tender received the same coupler upgrades outlined previously.

VG	EX	LN	RARITY
550	750	975	5

Price Guide Key: **VG** = Very Good, **EX** = Excellent, **LN** = Like New | *Values for each condition are in U.S. dollars.* | **Rarity** = Scale from 1-8 with 8 being the hardest to find.

155

229 TYPE IV

228 (Type V): During 1941, the numbers beneath the cab windows began to be heat-stamped rather than rubber-stamped. This technique results in crisper lettering, and oftentimes results in the lettering being slightly recessed into the underlying surface. The boiler front number plate continued to read 228, and the locomotive was still offered with the non bell-equipped 2228T tender.

VG	EX	LN	RARITY
500	700	950	4

228 (Type VI): Heat-stamped lettering was also applied to locomotives sold with the bell-ringing 2228B tender beginning in 1941.

VG	EX	LN	RARITY
550	750	975	5

229: This 2-4-2 was created by mounting a four-wheel mechanism into the boiler casting designed for the 224 2-6-2. The 229 was cataloged from 1939 through 1942. Mid-production, the mechanism was redesigned so that the E-unit was moved from a position behind the armature to a position forward of the armature. This, of course, required relocating the slot in the boiler casting through which the E-unit's lockout lever protruded.

229 (Type I): When initially offered, the locomotive was supplied with a 2689T sheet metal tender, and both were painted gunmetal.

VG	EX	LN	RARITY
100	130	175	3

229 (Type II): The 229/2689T locomotive-tender combination was also produced in an overall black paint scheme.

VG	EX	LN	RARITY
100	130	175	3

229 (Type III): Black was also the color of choice when the 229 was paired with the whistle-equipped 2689W tender.

VG	EX	LN	RARITY
125	175	250	3

229 (Type IV): Probably in 1941, the cabs' side number plates began to be omitted from the black locomotive, although the mounting slots for the plates remained. The locomotives' numbers were rubber-stamped directly on the cab beneath the windows. A plastic-bodied, whistle-equipped 2666W tender accompanied the locomotive.

VG	EX	LN	RARITY
125	175	250	4

229 (Type V): Some black locomotives without number plates, but with their mounting slots, were shipped with non-whistling 2666T tenders.

VG	EX	LN	RARITY
100	150	225	4

229 (Type VI): Near the end of production, the number plate mounting slots were eliminated from the casting, providing a smooth, even surface for the rubber-stamped lettering. Some of these black locomotives were shipped with whistle-equipped 2666W tenders.

VG	EX	LN	RARITY
125	175	250	4

229 (Type VII): Other black locomotives without the number plate mounting slots were supplied with non-whistling 2666T tenders.

VG	EX	LN	RARITY
100	150	225	4

229E (Type I): When initially offered, the number plate was marked with the full "229E" catalog number. They were supplied with a 2689T sheet metal tender, and both were painted gunmetal.

VG	EX	LN	RARITY
100	150	225	4

229E (Type II): Locomotives with 229E number plates and 2689T non-whistling sheet-metal tenders were also produced in black.

VG	EX	LN	RARITY
100	150	225	4

229E (Type III): Some of the black 229E locomotives came with whistle-equipped 2689W sheet-metal tenders.

VG	EX	LN	RARITY
125	175	250	4

230: Like its stablemates, the 227, 228 and 231, the 230 used many of the castings developed for the 701 scale switcher. Produced for only one year, 1939, the height of the couplers of the 230 matched that of the 2650, 2750 and 2950 series cars. Available as an option was a bell-ringing tender. An off-on lever beneath the tender floor energized a bimetallic strip, which controlled the striker mechanism that sounded the bell.

230 (Type I): The 0-6-0 switcher was furnished with a 2230T tender. A plate was installed on the boiler front reading 230, while beneath the cab window was rubber-stamped 8976. This combination was listed in the Lionel catalog under number 900.

VG	EX	LN	RARITY
800	1300	1900	6

230 (Type II): When equipped with the bell-ringing 2230B tender, the catalog number assigned to the locomotive-tender pair was 900B.

VG	EX	LN	RARITY
800	1300	1900	6

231: Like its stablemates, the 227, 228 and 230, the 231 used many of the castings developed for the 701 scale switcher. Produced for only one year, 1939, the height of the high couplers of the 231 matched that of the 2800 series cars. Available as an option was a bell-ringing tender. An off-on

lever beneath the tender floor energized a bimetallic strip, which controlled the striker mechanism that sounded the bell.

231 (Type I): Some locomotives were sold with bell-less 2231T tenders. The number 231 was on the boiler front, and 8976 was rubber-stamped beneath the cab windows.

VG	EX	LN	RARITY
650	1200	1800	5

231 (Type II): Other 231 0-6-0 switchers came with the bell-equipped 2231B tender. They too had 231 on their boiler fronts, and 8976 beneath the cab windows.

VG	EX	LN	RARITY
650	1200	1800	5

232: Utilizing many of the castings developed for the 701 scale switcher, Lionel created this semi-scale switcher in 1940. It remained in the product line through 1941. The wiring for the reversing unit (E-unit) of these locomotives was routed through a DC-activated relay. This allowed it to be operated on the same track with conventional locomotives, yet have independent directional control. This system was known as "Magic Electrol." The height of the electric box couplers of the 232 matched that of the 2650, 2750 and 2950 series cars.

232 (Type I): As introduced in 1940, this semi-scale 0-6-0 had the number 8976 rubber-stamped beneath the cab window. The number 232 appeared on the boiler front, and the locomotive was furnished with a bell-ringing 2232B tender.

VG	EX	LN	RARITY
650	1200	1800	5

232 (Type II): During 1941-42, the cab-side 8976 were applied with heat-stamping rather than rubber-stamping.

VG	EX	LN	RARITY
650	1200	1800	5

233: The 233, cataloged from 1940 through 1942, was essentially a 232 with high couplers for use with 2800-series cars. The number 233 appeared on the boiler front, and the locomotive was furnished with a bell-ringing 2233B tender.

Price Guide Key: **VG** = Very Good, **EX** = Excellent, **LN** = Like New | *Values for each condition are in U.S. dollars.* | **Rarity** = Scale from 1-8 with 8 being the hardest to find.

157

238E Type II

233 (Type I): As introduced in 1940, this semi-scale 0-6-0 had the number 8976 rubber-stamped beneath the cab window. The number 233 appeared on the boiler front and the locomotive was furnished with a bell-ringing 2233B tender.

VG	EX	LN	RARITY
650	1200	1800	5

233 (Type II): During 1941-42, the cab-side 8976 were applied with heat-stamping rather than rubber-stamping.

VG	EX	LN	RARITY
650	1200	1800	5

238/238E: Though stylistically based on the streamlined shrouding Raymon Loewy designed for a select few of the Pennsylvania Railroad's K4 Pacifics, the 238 had a 4-4-2 wheel arrangement. A Pacific steam locomotive has a 4-6-2 wheel arrangement.

238E (Type I): From 1936 through 1937, the 238E locomotive was painted gunmetal and came with a matching sheet metal 265T tender.

VG	EX	LN	RARITY
225	275	350	3

238E (Type II): Also available in 1936 and 1937 were gunmetal locomotives with 265W whistling tenders.

VG	EX	LN	RARITY
250	300	375	3

238E (Type III): In 1938, the gunmetal locomotive towed a high-truck equipped, whistling 2265W tender.

VG	EX	LN	RARITY
250	300	375	3

238E (Type IV): Some of the 1938 production gunmetal 238E locomotives were furnished with a gunmetal 2225W tender.

VG	EX	LN	RARITY
250	300	375	3

238E (Type V): In 1939, the 238E began to be painted black and they were accompanied with 265W tenders.

VG	EX	LN	RARITY
250	300	375	3

238 (Type I): From 1936 through 1937, the locomotive was painted gunmetal and came with a matching sheet metal 265W whistling tender.

VG	EX	LN	RARITY
250	300	375	3

238 (Type II): During 1939-40, the 238 was made in black and came with a 2225 tender.

VG	EX	LN	RARITY
250	300	375	3

249/249E: This locomotive was of composite die-cast and sheet metal construction. Though the "E" suffix did not appear on all the numberplates, all were equipped with a three-position E unit.

249E (Type I): As originally offered, the 249E was finished in gunmetal. It was prominently featured in the 1936 catalog with a 265T tender.

VG	EX	LN	RARITY
75	125	200	3

249E Type I

249E (Type II): At a slight additional expense, 1936 sets pulled by the gunmetal 249E could be purchased with the whistle-equipped 265W tender in lieu of the 265T.

VG	EX	LN	RARITY
75	125	200	3

249E (Type III): In 1937, the 249E was also produced in gloss black, with a 265T tender.

VG	EX	LN	RARITY
75	125	200	3

249 (Type I): Gloss black was also the color of choice for 249, no-"E" locomotives with 265T tenders in 1937.

VG	EX	LN	RARITY
75	125	200	3

249 (Type II): Some of the gloss black 249 locos pulled whistling 265W tenders in 1937.

VG	EX	LN	RARITY
75	125	200	3

249 (Type III): Apparently sometime in late 1937 or 1938, and continuing into 1939, matte black paint began to be used on the 249. The same paint was used on its accompanying 265T tender.

VG	EX	LN	RARITY
75	125	200	3

249 (Type IV): Matte black was used on locos equipped with 265W whistle tenders during the same time period.

VG	EX	LN	RARITY
75	125	200	3

250E: Arguably the most colorful 0-gauge steam locomotive built by Lionel, the 250E, introduced in 1935, was a replica of the locomotives used to pull the Milwaukee Road's Hiawatha passenger train. Its die-cast boiler houses a 4-4-2 mechanism and is finished in gloss orange, black and gray. When combined with its 12-wheel tender, it stretches 13 1/2" along the rails.

250E (Type I): Although styled after the Hiawatha's passenger locomotive, Lionel also paired the 250E with the 250W tender for use in pulling freight cars.

VG	EX	LN	RARITY
600	1000	1600	5

250E (Type II): When supplied with passenger cars, the similar-looking 250WX tender was used.

VG	EX	LN	RARITY
600	1000	1600	5

250E (Type III): When not equipped with a whistle, the freight-hauling 250E came with a 250T tender.

VG	EX	LN	RARITY
600	1000	1600	5

250E (Type IV): Some of the non-whistling tenders had electric couplers, resulting in them having the number 2250T assigned.

VG	EX	LN	RARITY
600	1000	1600	5

250E (Type V): The deluxe freight version of the Hiawatha came with an electric coupler-equipped, whistling 2250W tender.

VG	EX	LN	RARITY
600	1000	1600	5

255E: Produced in 1935 and 1936 only, and not available for separate sale, this 2-4-2 was paired with a 263W whistle tender in sets.

VG	EX	LN	RARITY
500	700	1000	5

257 (Type I): Although it was available from 1930 through 1932, this black 2-4-0 with black 257T tender appeared only in the 1930 catalog. These locomotives run forward only.

VG	EX	LN	RARITY
125	200	300	3

Price Guide Key: **VG** = Very Good, **EX** = Excellent, **LN** = Like New | *Values for each condition are in U.S. dollars.* | **Rarity** = Scale from 1-8 with 8 being the hardest to find.

159

249E Type I

257 (Type II): Some of 257T tenders accompanying the 2-4-0 were finished with black crackle paint.

VG	EX	LN	RARITY
225	300	400	5

257 (Type III): An orange stripe ran along the running board edge on some of the locomotives, with orange striping on the 257T as well.

VG	EX	LN	RARITY
125	200	300	3

257 (Type IV): Others of the black 2-4-0 locomotives had a red stripe.

VG	EX	LN	RARITY
125	200	300	3

257 (Type V): Some of the uncataloged all-black 2-4-0 locomotives came with a 259T tender.

VG	EX	LN	RARITY
125	200	300	3

258 (Type I): Beyond its number, this black 2-4-0 differed from the 257 by including a manual reverse switch. It came with a black 257T tender. It was produced only in 1930.

VG	EX	LN	RARITY
70	125	200	4

258 (Type II): An orange stripe was present on the flanks of some of the 258 locomotives, and their 257T tenders as well. This combination was produced only in 1930.

VG	EX	LN	RARITY
70	125	200	4

258 (Type III): A cream stripe ran along the running board edge on some of the locomotives. This was only made in 1930.

VG	EX	LN	RARITY
70	125	200	4

258 (Type IV): In 1941, a totally different locomotive design was assigned the number 258. This 2-4-2 was based on the 259E design. It was painted gunmetal and came with a 1689T tender.

VG	EX	LN	RARITY
50	80	125	3

258 (Type V): The new style gunmetal locomotive also came with a whistling 1689W tender.

VG	EX	LN	RARITY
75	110	150	3

258 (Type VI): Some of this second style of 258, along with their 1689T tenders, were painted black.

VG	EX	LN	RARITY
40	75	100	2

259: Only produced in 1932, this black 2-4-2 with 259T lacked both a whistle and electric reversing.

VG	EX	LN	RARITY
50	80	125	4

259E (Type I): This gloss black 2-4-2 had red-spoked drive wheels, and copper and brass trim. It came with a black 259T with copper journal boxes.

VG	EX	LN	RARITY
75	100	125	3

259E (Type II): Beginning in 1934, the black 2-4-2 had black wheels and nickel trim. This version came with a die-cast 262T tender.

VG	EX	LN	RARITY
75	100	125	3

259E (Type III): From 1936 through 1938, the 2-4-2 was also painted gunmetal and came with a 1689T.

VG	EX	LN	RARITY
75	100	125	3

259E (Type IV): An electric coupler was provided on the rear of some of the tenders packaged with the gunmetal tenders from 1936-38. This resulted in the tender having the number 2689T.

VG	EX	LN	RARITY
75	100	125	3

259E (Type V): An uncataloged version of the 259E was made in black from 1936 through 1940. Some of these came with 1689W tenders.

VG	EX	LN	RARITY
75	100	125	3

259E (Type VI): Some of the black 259E made from 1936 through 1940 came with 1689T tenders.

VG	EX	LN	RARITY
75	100	125	3

259E (Type VII): An electric coupler-equipped 2689T was supplied with some of the black locomotives between 1936-1940.

VG	EX	LN	RARITY
75	100	125	3

259E (Type VIII): The inexpensive four-wheel 1588TX tender was also used with the uncataloged version of the 259E sometime between 1936 and 1940.

VG	EX	LN	RARITY
75	100	125	3

260E: At the time of its 1930 introduction, the 260E was Lionel's top of the line 0 gauge locomotive. It had a die-cast frame and was initially equipped with a two-position, pendulum-type E-unit. Later production utilized a three-position, drum-type E-unit.

260E (Type I): The glossy black 260E, as built in 1930, had a cream stripe painted on the side of the running board. The running board itself was cast as an integral part of the die-cast frame, and a groove was formed in it to aid in positioning the stripe. A 260T was provided with the locomotive.

VG	EX	LN	RARITY
350	450	550	4

Price Guide Key: **VG** = Very Good, **EX** = Excellent, **LN** = Like New | *Values for each condition are in U.S. dollars.* | **Rarity** = Scale from 1-8 with 8 being the hardest to find.

161

260E Type III

261

260E (Type II): In 1931, the stripe on the running board of the glossy black locomotive was changed to green. The locomotive and 260T eight-wheel tender continued like this through the next year. Operationally, locomotives produced beginning in 1931 included a switch that could be used to disable the automatic sequencing of the reversing unit.

VG	EX	LN	RARITY
350	450	550	4

260E (Type III): In 1933, the stripe alongside the frame became green and the groove was removed from the edge of the running board. At the same time, a chugger mechanism was added to the locomotive. Like its predecessors, this variant of the 260E rolled on red wheels. Behind the locomotive was a 260T tender, now with 12 wheels.

VG	EX	LN	RARITY
350	450	550	4

260E (Type IV): In 1934, the 260E received quite a facelift. The locomotive was now painted gunmetal and rode on black wheels. The trim on the locomotive, which previously had been yellow metal, was now nickel. The tender was upgraded, too. Now the 263T 12-wheel tender was used.

VG	EX	LN	RARITY
450	550	650	5

260E (Type V): In 1935, the gunmetal 260E became even louder. Now, in addition to the chugger mechanism located in the locomotive boiler, the tender housed a whistle. The new designation for the tender was 263W.

VG	EX	LN	RARITY
450	550	650	5

261: This black 2-4-2 with red wheels was produced only in 1931. It came with a black 257T tender, and was trimmed in brass and copper. The locomotive was wired to run forward only.

VG	EX	LN	RARITY
125	175	225	4

261E (Type I): Built only in 1935, this black 2-4-2 with 261T tender was equipped with a reversing unit. Its wheels were black and the locomotive had nickel trim.

VG	EX	LN	RARITY
150	200	250	3

261E (Type II): Some of the 261Es were decorated with a red stripe.

VG	EX	LN	RARITY
150	200	250	3

262 (Type I): During 1931-32, Lionel offered this glossy black 2-4-2 with die-cast 262T tender. The locomotive had a hand-reversing lever mounted in the cab, and copper and brass trim.

VG	EX	LN	RARITY
200	250	325	3

262 (Type II): Rather than gloss black, some of these 2-4-2 locomotives and 262T tenders were painted flat black during 1931-32.

VG	EX	LN	RARITY
200	250	325	3

262 (Type III): The most attractive variation of this mid-sized 2-4-2 was painted gloss black, with an orange stripe along its running board, and small orange stripes on the accompanying 262T tender. This version was available sometime during 1931-32.

VG	EX	LN	RARITY
200	250	325	3

262 (Type IV): Some of the 262T tenders provided with the 262 were finished with crackle black paint.

VG	EX	LN	RARITY
250	300	375	3

262E (Type I): In 1933, an electronic reversing unit began to be installed in the 262, resulting in its number being changed to 262E. The 2-4-2 was finished in gloss black with an orange stripe. It was apparently produced the same way the following year as well.

VG	EX	LN	RARITY
100	140	200	3

262E (Type II): The gloss black 2-4-2 was reportedly also sometimes supplied with sheet metal 261T tenders.

VG	EX	LN	RARITY
100	140	200	3

262E (Type III): Some of the die-cast 262T tender-equipped 2-4-2 locomotives sported red striping on their gloss black paint.

VG	EX	LN	RARITY
100	140	200	3

262E (Type IV): The black 262E continued to be produced in 1935 and 1936, even though it was not shown in the catalog during those years. During this time, many of the 2-4-2 locomotives came with streamlined sheet metal 265T tenders.

VG	EX	LN	RARITY
100	140	200	3

262E (Type V): The balance of the uncataloged production was shipped with two-whistling 265W tenders.

VG	EX	LN	RARITY
100	140	200	3

263: The 263E was an E-unit equipped 2-4-2 along the lines of the 255E and 260E. It was produced from 1936-1939, with the plate on the tender being brass initially and silver-colored on later production.

Price Guide Key: **VG** = Very Good, **EX** = Excellent, **LN** = Like New | *Values for each condition are in U.S. dollars.* | **Rarity** = Scale from 1-8 with 8 being the hardest to find.

163

263E Type III

263E (Type I): The 263E was initially offered in gunmetal with a matching 263W 12-wheel tender.

VG	EX	LN	RARITY
300	450	625	5

263E (Type II): Some of the gunmetal locomotives came with electric coupler-equipped 2263W whistling tenders.

VG	EX	LN	RARITY
300	450	625	5

263E (Type III): More attractive was a two-tone blue version of the 263E with matching 2263W tender dubbed the baby Blue Comet.

VG	EX	LN	RARITY
400	650	1000	6

264E: Although its wheel arrangement was only 2-4-2, the 264E took its styling from streamlined versions of New York Central's famed 4-6-4 Hudson locomotives. In fact, this style of streamlining, designed by the now almost-forgotten Carl F. Kantola, was the first applied to a real steam locomotive. The locomotive chosen for this shrouding by the New York Central was none other than J-1E Hudson 5344–the same locomotive in non-streamlined form that was immortalized as Lionel's famed 700E. Dubbed the Commodore Vanderbilt, this style streamlining was short-lived on the real railroad. In 1939, this streamlined casing was removed and replaced with a bullet nose design by Henry Dreyfuss, but the Commodore Vanderbilt was widely used by Lionel. Lionel's replica had a die-cast cab and steam chests, but the boiler and shrouding were sheet metal.

264E (Type I): In 1935, the new 264E, along with its companion 261T tender, was given an overall red paint job and headed a set dubbed The Red Comet.

VG	EX	LN	RARITY
125	200	300	4

264E (Type II): In 1936, the appearance of the red combination was considerably improved by replacing the 261T with a 265T tender.

VG	EX	LN	RARITY
125	200	300	4

264E (Type III): In 1936, a black version of the 264E was produced. It came with a 265T tender, and was available again, although uncataloged, in 1940.

VG	EX	LN	RARITY
200	275	375	5

265E: The 265E was a deluxe version of the 264E. Introduced in the same year, the two locomotives differed in that the 265E incorporated an eccentric crank and associated rods, giving it a more pleasing and realistic appearance.

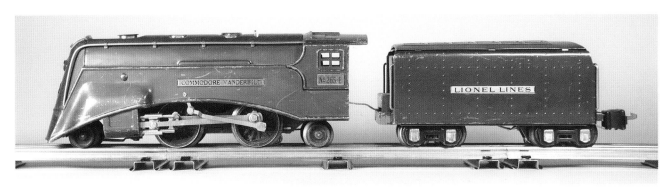

265E TYPE VIII

289E TYPE III

265E (Type I): As first issued, the 265E was painted black and was supplied with a 261TX tender. This tender did not include a rear coupler, but instead had a second drawbar that was used to connect the string of chrome articulated passenger cars that came with it.

VG	EX	LN	RARITY
150	225	350	4

265E (Type II): In 1936, United Drug Company (Rexall) chartered a special train that toured 47 states and Canada. Named the Rexall Train, it showcased Rexall's extensive line of products to druggists and the public. The unique blue and white train's arrival garnered media and public attention wherever it went. Motive power for this train was a New York Central L-2a 4-8-2 Mohawk. This locomotive was shrouded in a streamlined casing designed by Carl F. Kantola, the same man who designed the Commodore Vanderbilt. Naturally, the styling was very similar. Not surprisingly, in 1936 Lionel offered a blue and white train it called The Blue Streak. It was pulled by a blue 265E with 265TX with rear drawbar. This combination was only cataloged in 1936.

VG	EX	LN	RARITY
425	625	850	6

265E (Type III): The blue locomotive was also equipped with a whistling 265WX tender with rear drawbar. Lionel offered this combination from 1936 through 1938.

VG	EX	LN	RARITY
425	625	850	6

265E (Type IV): The black 265E was carried over into 1936, then coming with a 265W whistling tender.

VG	EX	LN	RARITY
150	225	350	4

265E (Type V): For those not wanting a whistle, in 1936 the black loco was also available with the 265T tender.

VG	EX	LN	RARITY
150	225	350	4

265E (Type VI): In 1936, the 265E was offered, along with its 265T tender, painted gunmetal. This combination was carried over into 1937.

VG	EX	LN	RARITY
150	225	350	4

265E (Type VII): Some of the gunmetal locomotives came with whistling 265W tenders in 1936 and 1937.

Price Guide Key: **VG** = Very Good, **EX** = Excellent, **LN** = Like New | *Values for each condition are in U.S. dollars.* | **Rarity** = Scale from 1-8 with 8 being the hardest to find.

THERE IS NO LOCOMOTIVE IN THE WORLD LIKE THE
LIONEL SCALE MODEL HUDSON

Five separate kits comprise all of the parts for this powerful giant of the rails—and a sixth kit includes the whistle mechanism and controller which can be added at any time. By purchasing the Lionel Hudson in *kit* form you save money; you get the fun, thrill and pleasure of "building your own" and watching it gradually take shape and become the incomparably perfect thing it is. Best of all, you also can now start toward ownership of this model without a major expenditure—for you can begin with a single kit, if you choose, at a cost of $12.50—then add kit after kit as each one is assembled and completed. That makes it as easy on the pocketbook as a partial payment plan.

It doesn't take any particular skill or mechanical knowledge to put the Lionel Hudson together—and the only special tools required are included free with the first outfit! Die castings are finished—no burrs to remove—no filing to be done. Major castings have been given their prime coat of paint, and paint for the finishing coat is included. Incidental castings have received their final, oxidized, dull black finish. All press assemblies are made and included as assembled units. Drive wheels have been applied to their knurled steel axles under tons of pressure. All holes are drilled and tapped where necessary. With every kit, complete graphic instructions are included.

An etched chromium plate is supplied for inscribing the name of builder and date when model is completed. The plate is attached to the bottom of ash pan.

LIONEL HUDSON LOCOMOTIVE KIT
No. 700K Complete locomotive and tender kit, less whistle. Price $59.50
No. 700K1 Locomotive frame, drive wheels, etc. Price $12.50
No. 700K2 Motor, worm, bearings, reversing unit, etc. Price $12.50
No. 700K3 Cab and boiler with trimming. Price $12.50
No. 700K4 Trucks, wheels, headlight, paint, etc. Price $ 9.50
No. 700K5 All parts for complete tender assembly. Price $12.50
No. 700K6 Whistle kit. Price $ 5.00
No. 700KW Locomotive and whistle tender kit, complete. Price $64.50

NO HOBBY LIKE THIS ON WINTER EVENINGS!
• Care, worry and boredom flee like snowflakes when you're absorbed in putting the 5344 together. And when, at the finish, this giant in steel becomes a giant in action—as it will be the greatest thrill you've ever experienced! See your Lionel Dealer immediately—and get Kit No. 1!

1938 CATALOG

MIGHTY ENGINE OF THE CENTURY, PRESSURE DIE CAST, 1/48 ACTUAL SIZE
DRIVEN BY WORM GEARS—EQUIPPED WITH OIL-LESS BRONZE BEARINGS

Whether your fingers are fidgeting to build a railroad engine of your own—or your heart is set on the most perfectly finished locomotive that can be produced—Lionel 5344 is your number, sir!

For, this year this greatest of all models can be bought two ways—in kits, ready for assembly; or assembled and ready for service.

And what an engine it is! None other than the ace of the New York Central's fleet of rail giants, exactly quarter-inch-scale by every measurement. Driven by worm gears and powered by a heavy duty AC-DC motor—with a 10 to 1 gear reduction. Equipped with stainless steel handrails and die-cast, chromium plated rods. Headlight is projected in parallel beams through a Lucite lens. Headlight lamp is concealed inside boiler-front, accessible through a smoke box door that is hinged and can be opened as real ones do. The headlight housing swings with the door.

Drive wheels are die cast and pressed on knurled steel shafts, the bearing surface of which is polished to within a quarter mil, which is one fourth of one thousandth of an inch.

The central crank pin holds an accurately shaped eccentric crank. Complete Baker reversing gear is reproduced and, when locomotive is running, it presents a flawless kinematic action.

Pipes and control rods, the crank pins and the crosshead guides are cold drawn steel. The alligator crossheads are cast and finished in black. The rods and cranks of the driving gear are also cast and then chromium plated to provide the permanent, non-tarnishing appearance of polished steel.

Sixteen hundred rivets cover the sides and end of the tender, a single ribbed casting, into which has been built model railroading's most thrilling feature — the remote control whistle.

Wheel flanges are so made that the engine may be operated on any style of solid rail "O" Gauge track with curves having a radius of not less than three feet. In addition to inside third-rail shoes, two outside third-rail collectors are included, with runners of phosphor bronze, built to N. M. R. A. standard specifications.

Locomotive measures 24½ inches overall and is complete with walnut finish stand pictured on page 26, and with a controller for operation of the whistle and for reversing the locomotive.

No. 700EW Scale Model Locomotive and Tender, completely assembled. **Price $75.00**

Down around the cylinders are where the eyes of the veteran go first, to judge the faithfulness and accuracy of a model engine. For here is the center of speed and motion. And here it is where Lionel has excelled anything ever done before in scale model building. The alligator crossheads in the Lionel model, for instance, are studded with hexhead bolts accurately shaped 'though they are smaller than a pin-head. The interesting action of the valve is derived from the combined motions of the valve gear and piston crosshead through the combination lever. On the engineer's side of the locomotive are the minute linkages of the automatic lubricator, motivated by rod connections. The eccentric crank is an absolute reproduction. There is only one way of making drive rods that look like drive rods and that is by casting them. In the Lionel model, drive rods are die cast under intense pressure to obtain accuracy of form, then chromium plated to obtain accuracy of finish, and finally they are bushed with oil-less bronze bearings to obtain perfect, enduring performance.

1938 CATALOG

700E

VG	EX	LN	RARITY
150	225	350	4

265E (Type VIII):  The gunmetal locomotive with whistle tender was given an electric coupler in 1938. The new number assigned the tender was 2225W and it continued to be offered through 1940.

VG	EX	LN	RARITY
150	225	350	4

265E (Type IX): The non-whistling gunmetal tenders were also equipped with the new coupler and, with it, a new number as well: 2225T.

VG	EX	LN	RARITY
150	225	350	4

265E (Type X): A handful of these locomotives with 265T tenders were reportedly chrome plated for Lionel, but far more have been plated by collectors. Use caution.

RATITY
Too rarely traded to establish pricing

265E (Type XI): Like the gunmetal locomotives, the black 265E also was equipped with electric couplers. Like the gunmetal version, the black non-whistling tender was given the number 2225T. This combination was available from 1938 to 1940.

VG	EX	LN	RARITY
150	225	350	4

265E (Type XII): The black tender with whistle and electric coupler was numbered 2225W and was offered from 1938 to 1940.

VG	EX	LN	RARITY
150	225	350	4

289E: This was Lionel's attempt at an economy 0 gauge streamlined steam locomotive in 1937. For this uncataloged locomotive, they shoehorned a 0 gauge motor into a small 027 streamlined boiler. Some correspondents believe this uncataloged locomotive was built in 1936, others believe in 1937, still others think both.

289E (Type I): Some of these hybrid locomotives were painted gunmetal and came with 1689T tenders.

VG	EX	LN	RARITY
100	200	325	5

289E (Type II): The whistle-equipped 1689W tender accompanied other gunmetal 289E locomotives.

VG	EX	LN	RARITY
100	200	325	5

289E (Type III):  Other engines were finished in black, as were their 1588 tenders.

VG	EX	LN	RARITY
100	200	325	5

289E (Type IV): Locomotives equipped with 1688T tenders were also sometimes painted black.

VG	EX	LN	RARITY
100	200	325	5

289E (Type V): Black was also the color of choice for some 1688W whistling tenders and the 289E locomotives that pulled them.

VG	EX	LN	RARITY
100	200	325	5

700E:  Known to collectors as the 700E, but listed consistently in the catalog as a 700EW, by any name this was Lionel's premier locomotive. Dealer-only promotional literature in 1937 listed the locomotive-tender combination as also being available without whistle as the 700E. Regardless of their era of interest–prewar, postwar or modern–this is the one product number that is universally recognized by Lionel buffs. When introduced, this replica of a New York Central class J1-E 4-6-4 Hudson was touted as being full-scale. It was very close to hitting that mark, and set a standard for detail that was not reached again by three-rail train manufacturers for 50 years. So complicated was the design and manufacturing of this locomotive that work on this project was begun by Lionel in 1935, yet delivery of finished locomotives did not begin until 1937. The 700E and 700EW were designed to operate on rails formed to National Model Railroad Association (NMRA) standards, such as Lionel's T-rail, rather than traditional tubular rails.

700EW (Type I): Principal tooling for the 1937 700EW and 1937 763EW was made by Societa Meccanica La Precisa in Italy. This firm had been formed in 1924 by Joshua Cowen and plant superintendent Mario Caruso to manufacture tooling for Lionel. Locomotives produced in 1937 differ from later production. In 1937, a small box was just above the forward on each of the running boards on each side of the locomotive. In 1938, this "box" was a continuation of the running board, without the clear separation previously seen. The frames used in 1937 lack the screw-plugged axle oil holes found on later locomotives. Other differences exist as noted later.

VG	EX	LN	RARITY
1300	2000	2800	5

700EW (Type II): Problems with casting impurities had begun to surface as early as 1937, which were causing the boiler and

Price Guide Key: **VG** = Very Good, **EX** = Excellent, **LN** = Like New | *Values for each condition are in U.S. dollars.* | **Rarity** = Scale from 1-8 with 8 being the hardest to find.

167

700K

frame to distort. This sometimes caused the pilot to touch the center rail, creating short circuits. As an expedient solution, Lionel ground down the thickness of the lower lip of the pilot.

VG	EX	LN	RARITY
1300	2000	2800	5

700EW (Type III): New major tooling was created for the 1938 and later production of the 700EW, 700K, 700KW and 763EW by the New York plant of the Swedish firm Scandia Tool and Die. The 1938 and later production 700EW can be distinguished from the 1937 production by careful examination of select areas.

The 1938 and later cab window mullins measured .060", which was larger than the previous model. The 1938 frame design was modified to include screw-covered oilers for the drive axles, absent on earlier frames. Further, 1937 frames were serially numbered with a 01 prefix; in 1938, the prefix was changed to 38.

VG	EX	LN	RARITY
1300	2000	2800	5

700EW (Type IV): Locomotives produced in 1940 or later lack serial numbers.

VG	EX	LN	RARITY
1300	2000	2800	4

700EWX: A number of customers liked the scale detailed appearance of Lionel's Hudson, but had extensive model railroad systems made of conventional tubular track. The 700EWX, available by special order, had blind (lacking flanges) center drivers, while the profile of the flanges of the other drivers was also slightly different. Many collectors, however, place great emphasis on the box to distinguish this variation.

VG	EX	LN	RARITY
1500	2250	3000	6

700K: From 1938 through 1942, Lionel offered its scale Hudson in kit form as well. While some, no doubt, were bought by hobbyists who derived pleasure from assembling their own locomotives, that probably wasn't the major incentive for most customers. The kit version, or 700K, was also less expensive than the ready to run model. Further, it could be bought on an installment plan, so to speak, as each of the six major parts groups were sold individually. Today, an unassembled set of kits, in their boxes, still in gray primer, commands a substantial premium.

Assembled:

VG	EX	LN	RARITY
2500	1000	4000	6

Unassembled:

VG	EX	LN	RARITY
5000	8000	12000	8

701: Though billed as full-scale like the Hudson, this attractive 0-6-0 switcher, while styled along the line of a Pennsylvania B6, was not an accurate replica. The actual B6 had an asymmetrical axle spacing. And the 701 included details that, though individually proper, weren't proper in the combination as built by Lionel. Cab shape, headlight style, blind center axle and cab side number (8976) are not believed to have coexisted simultaneously on the prototype. Nevertheless, this locomotive, when coupled with its 701T tender, makes an attractive combination and was available from 1939 to 1942.

VG	EX	LN	RARITY
350	500	700	6

763: The 763EW underwent many of these same changes (except for those involving serial numbers, which all 763 locomotives lacked), although apparently at later dates. This could be a result of Lionel having an excess inventory of 1937-produced 763 locomotives, or at least boiler and frame components.

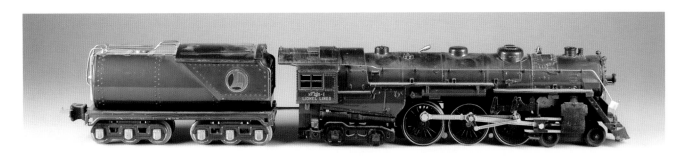

763E Type II

763E (Type I): This variation was gunmetal, with 263W oil tender made from 1937 to 1940.

VG	EX	LN	RARITY
1100	1800	2750	4

763E (Type II): This type was gunmetal, with 2263W oil tender, made from 1937 to 1940.

VG	EX	LN	RARITY
1200	1900	2850	4

763E (Type III): This type was gunmetal, with 2226W coal tender, made in 1940.

VG	EX	LN	RARITY
1200	1900	2850	4

763E (Type IV): This type was gunmetal, with 2226WX coal tender, made in 1940.

VG	EX	LN	RARITY
1200	1900	2850	4

763E (Type V): This type was black, with 2226W coal tender, made in 1941-42.

VG	EX	LN	RARITY
1100	1800	2750	4

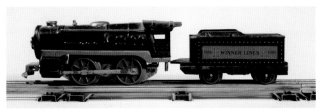

1015: This black sheet metal 0-4-0 and its 1016 tender were available in 1931-32. The locomotive ran forward only and had copper trim.

VG	EX	LN	RARITY
100	150	200	3

1035 (Type I): A member of Lionel's inexpensive Winner line, this black 0-4-0 with copper trim and black and red tender was made in 1931-32.

VG	EX	LN	RARITY
75	100	125	4

1035 (Type II): The Winner 0-4-0 also came with a black and orange tender.

VG	EX	LN	RARITY
75	100	125	4

1506: This clockwork-powered 0-4-0, with Mickey Mouse riding in its 1509 tender, was a component of the 1935 1532 outfit.

VG	EX	LN	RARITY
225	325	450	6

1506L: This black clockwork-powered 0-4-0 included a battery-operated headlight. Its frame was red and its trim copper. It came with a 1502 Lionel Lines tender during 1933-34. No Mickey Mouse rode on this version.

VG	EX	LN	RARITY
80	100	125	4

1508: This red streamlined clockwork-powered 0-4-0 had Mickey Mouse acting as its fireman from its 1509 tender. It had a battery-powered headlight and nickel trim, and was included in set 1536 made only in 1935.

VG	EX	LN	RARITY
325	450	600	6

1511 (Type I): This black 0-4-0 clockwork locomotive was styled along the lines of the Commodore Vanderbilt. It came with a 1516T oil-style tender and was packaged in 1936-37 sets.

VG	EX	LN	RARITY
100	125	150	2

Price Guide Key: **VG** = Very Good, **EX** = Excellent, **LN** = Like New | *Values for each condition are in U.S. dollars.* | **Rarity** = Scale from 1-8 with 8 being the hardest to find.

169

1511 (Type II): The 1511/1516T combination was also made in red sometime during 1936-37.

VG	EX	LN	RARITY
100	125	150	2

1588: This die-cast 9 1/2" long locomotive was more elaborate than most of Lionel clockwork locomotives. The black locomotive came in sets with a 1588T tender during the period 1936-37.

VG	EX	LN	RARITY
125	175	225	3

1661E: Produced in 1933 for use in inexpensive sets, this 2-4-0 was equipped with a three-position reversing unit. The locomotive, which had a red frame, was painted black and was furnished with a lithographed 1661T tender.

VG	EX	LN	RARITY
70	100	150	2

1662 (Type I): Introduced in 1940, this 0-4-0 came with a 2201T tender with backup light. Its low-height couplers aligned with those on 2650-series cars.

VG	EX	LN	RARITY
225	300	400	4

1662 (Type II): Some of the locomotives were supplied with the 2203B bell-ringing tender between 1940 and 1942.

VG	EX	LN	RARITY
250	325	425	4

1663: This 0-4-0 switcher followed no particular prototype. It was introduced in 1940 and remained a part of the product line through the 1942 catalog. The wiring for the reversing unit (E-unit) of these locomotives was routed through a DC-activated relay. This allowed it to be operated on the same track with conventional locomotives, yet have independent directional control. This system was known as "Magic Electrol." The locomotive came with a 2201T tender with backup light.

VG	EX	LN	RARITY
200	300	400	5

1664/1664E: These locomotives, produced between 1938 and 1942, utilized the same boiler and cab castings as did the 2-6-2 1666, but had only a 2-4-2 wheel arrangement.

1664E (Type I): This type was gunmetal 2-4-2 with nickel number plates on cab and 1689W whistling tender, available in this form in 1938-39.

VG	EX	LN	RARITY
50	75	100	2

1664E (Type II): Nickel number plates were also used on black locomotives with 1689W during 1939-40.

VG	EX	LN	RARITY
50	75	100	2

1664E (Type III): The black locomotive with nickel plates was also supplied with the 1689T tender in the 1939-40 period.

VG	EX	LN	RARITY
50	75	100	2

1664 (Type I): Probably during 1939, some of the gunmetal locomotives lacked the "E" on their model number. These locomotives came with 1689W tenders.

VG	EX	LN	RARITY
50	75	100	2

1664 (Type II): Black locomotives were also made without the E appearing on the number plate. Probably shipped in 1940 or 1941, some of them were supplied with 1689W tenders.

VG	EX	LN	RARITY
50	75	100	2

1664 (Type III): Other black 1664 locomotives without the E were shipped with the less-expensive, non-whistling 1689T tender in the 1940-41 time frame.

VG	EX	LN	RARITY
50	75	100	2

1664 (Type IV): Ultimately the numbers began to be rubber-stamped directly on the side of the black locomotives. This was likely the case in late 1941, as well as 1942, during which time the plastic-bodied 2666T tender began to accompany the 1664.

VG	EX	LN	RARITY
50	75	100	2

1664 (Type V): Some of these black rubber-stamped 2-4-2 locomotives came with 2666W whistle tenders with plastic shells. This was the case in 1942 and perhaps in late 1941.

1666E TYPE *I*

1666 TYPE *II*

VG	EX	LN	RARITY
50	75	100	2

1666/1666E: One of the few die-cast steamers to be produced both prewar and postwar was this 2-6-2. Prewar versions have a square-cast rear to their cab floor, while on postwar versions this area is rounded, with the apex reaching further to the rear of the locomotive. The simulated bell on prewar versions was a moveable unit as well.

1666E (Type I): This well-proportioned 2-6-2 was first produced in 1938. At that time it was painted gunmetal and came with a 1689W tender.

VG	EX	LN	RARITY
100	130	175	4

1666E (Type II): In 1938-39, the gunmetal 1666E was often furnished with a matching 2689W tender.

VG	EX	LN	RARITY
100	130	175	4

1666E (Type III): Not all of the gunmetal locomotives came with whistling tenders during 1938-1939. Some had the 2689T tender instead.

VG	EX	LN	RARITY
100	130	175	4

1666E (Type IV): Nickel number plates were also used on black locomotives with 2689W during 1939-40.

VG	EX	LN	RARITY
75	100	125	3

1666E (Type V): The black locomotive with nickel plates was also supplied with the 2689T tender in the 1939-40 period.

VG	EX	LN	RARITY
75	100	125	3

1666 (Type I): Black locomotives were also made without the E appearing on the number plate. Probably shipped in 1940, some of them were supplied with 2689W tenders.

VG	EX	LN	RARITY
75	100	125	3

1666 (Type II): Other black 1666 locomotives without the E were shipped with the less-expensive, non-whistling 2689T tender during 1940.

VG	EX	LN	RARITY
75	100	125	3

1666 (Type III): Ultimately the numbers began to be rubber-stamped directly on the side of the black locomotives. This was likely the case in 1941, as well as 1942, during which time the plastic-bodied 2666T tender began to accompany the 1666.

VG	EX	LN	RARITY
75	100	125	4

1666 (Type IV): Some of these black rubber-stamped 2-6-2 locomotives came with 2666W whistle tenders with plastic shells. This was the case in 1942, and perhaps late 1941.

VG	EX	LN	RARITY
75	100	125	3

1668/1668E: These locomotives, produced between 1937 and 1941, used the Pennsylvania streamlined boiler and cab castings as did the 2-4-2 1688 and 1588 locomotives.

1668E: This type was a gunmetal 2-6-2 with nickel number plates on boiler and 1689W whistling tender, available in this form in 1937-38.

VG	EX	LN	RARITY
75	100	125	2

1668 (Type I): Probably during 1938, some of the gunmetal locomotives lacked the "E" on their model number. Some of these locomotives came with 1689W whistling tenders.

Price Guide Key: **VG** = Very Good, **EX** = Excellent, **LN** = Like New | *Values for each condition are in U.S. dollars.* | **Rarity** = Scale from 1-8 with 8 being the hardest to find.

171

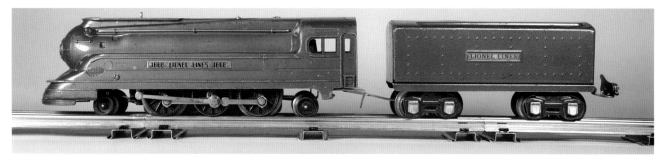

1669 TYPE II

1668 TYPE III

1681E TYPE I

VG	EX	LN	RARITY
75	100	125	2

1668 (Type II): 🖼 Again, probably in 1938, some of the gunmetal locomotives without the "E" designation were shipped with plain 1689T tenders.

VG	EX	LN	RARITY
75	100	125	2

1668 (Type III): 🖼 Nickel number plates were also used on black locomotives with 1689W during 1939-40.

VG	EX	LN	RARITY
75	100	125	2

1668 (Type IV): The black locomotive with nickel plates was also supplied with the 1689T tender in the 1939-40 period.

VG	EX	LN	RARITY
75	100	125	2

1681E (Type I): 🖼 Produced in 1934 as part of the Lionel Junior line, this 2-4-0 was equipped with a three-position reversing unit. The locomotive, which had a red frame, was painted black and was furnished with a lithographed 1661T tender.

VG	EX	LN	RARITY
50	80	110	3

1681E (Type II): In 1935, the color of the body was changed to red. The rest of the 2-4-0 and 1661 tender were unchanged.

VG	EX	LN	RARITY
75	100	150	5

1681 (Type I): Produced in 1934 for use in inexpensive sets, this 2-4-0 had a red frame and black body. It was furnished with a lithographed 1661T tender.

VG	EX	LN	RARITY
50	80	110	3

1681 (Type II): In 1935, the color of the body was changed to red. The rest of the 2-4-0 and 1661 tender were unchanged.

VG	EX	LN	RARITY
75	100	150	5

1688 TYPE III

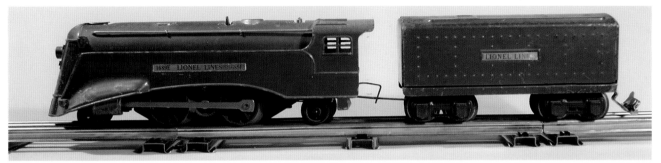

1689E TYPE II

1684 (Type I): This die-cast 2-4-2 with three-position reverse unit was produced in the 1941-42 time frame, finished in gunmetal.

VG	EX	LN	RARITY
40	55	75	3

1684 (Type II): The same rubber-stamped locomotive was also made in black.

VG	EX	LN	RARITY
40	55	75	3

1688/1688E: These 2-4-2 locomotives, produced from 1936 through 1940, used the Pennsylvania streamlined boiler and cab castings as did the 2-6-2 1688 and clockwork 2-4-2 1588.

1688E: This was a gunmetal 2-4-2 with nickel number plates on the boiler and a 1689W whistling tender. Available in this form in 1936-38.

VG	EX	LN	RARITY
40	55	75	3

1688 (Type I): Probably during 1938, the "E" began to be omitted from the nameplate of the gunmetal locomotives. Some of these locomotives came with 1689W whistling tenders.

VG	EX	LN	RARITY
40	55	75	3

1688 (Type II): Again, probably in 1938, some of the gunmetal locomotives without the "E" designation were shipped with plain 1689T tenders.

VG	EX	LN	RARITY
40	55	75	3

1688 (Type III): During 1939 and 1940, the now uncataloged locomotive was painted black. Nickel number plates with the "E" were used on these black locomotives, some of which came with 1689W tenders.

VG	EX	LN	RARITY
40	55	75	3

1688 (Type IV): The black locomotive with nickel plates was also supplied with the 1689T tender in the 1939-40 period.

VG	EX	LN	RARITY
40	55	75	3

1689E: This was Lionel's attempt at an economy Commodore Vanderbilt-style streamlined locomotive for 027. For this uncataloged locomotive, its die-cast body housed a 2-4-2 mechanism, with the lock-out lever for the three-position E-unit protruding through the top of the casting. It was shown in the 1936 and 1937 catalogs as part of the Lionel Jr. and 027 lines.

1689E (Type I): The whistle-equipped 1689W tender accompanied some gunmetal 1689E locomotives.

VG	EX	LN	RARITY
75	100	125	3

1689E (Type II): Other locomotives were painted gunmetal and came with 1689T tenders.

VG	EX	LN	RARITY
65	90	115	2

1689E (Type III): Locomotives equipped with 1688T tenders were sometimes painted black.

VG	EX	LN	RARITY
50	75	100	2

1689E (Type IV): Black was also the color of choice for some 1688W whistling tenders and the 1689E locomotives that pulled them.

VG	EX	LN	RARITY
60	80	110	2

CHAPTER 16
O GAUGE ELECTRIC LOCOMOTIVES

Replicas of electric locomotives powered Lionel's 0 gauge line from its inception until 1930. The steam locomotives, which eclipsed them, did not debut until 1930. The electrics last appeared in the catalog in 1936. Despite Lionel's vigorous advertising claims, its 0 gauge electric locomotives fell far short of being authentic models; stylized replicas would have been a more accurate description.

In North America, steam locomotives are typically described using the Whyte classification system. An example of this would be 2-8-4, which describes a locomotive with a two-wheel pilot or leading truck, eight coupled driving wheels (four on each side) and a four-wheel trailing truck. An articulated locomotive, which essentially had two engines under one boiler, had an extra digit added for each set of coupled driving wheels. Union Pacific's famed Big Boy was a 4-8-8-4.

Electric locomotives are not classified by the Whyte system. Instead, a system of letters, numbers and signs was used to describe the axle arrangement, rather than the wheel arrangement used by Whyte. Letters represent the number of powered axles. B is two, C is three, etc. A plus sign (+) is used to represent multiple powered axle sets on separate articulated frames. Numerals are used to represent the number of non-powered axles on leading and trailing trucks. Therefore, in

electric locomotive terms, the two engines described above would be a 1-D-2 and a 2-D+D-2 respectively. The two most common wheel arrangements used by Lionel during this period were 0-B-0 and 0-C-0, representative of 0-4-0 and 0-6-0.

4: This locomotive, produced from 1928 through 1932 was a greatly stylized, foreshortened version of the Milwaukee Road's famed EP-2 Bi-Polar electrics. The Bi-Polar name of the original was derived from each traction motors, which each had only two poles. While the massive real locomotives had an incredible 1-B+D+D+B-1 wheel arrangement, in Lionel's world this became a 1-B-1. The Lionel version had brass trim, except for the simulated leaf springs and journal boxes attached to the frame, which were aluminum.

4 (Type I): The most common version of the 4 had a body painted orange, which was mounted on a black frame.

VG	EX	LN	RARITY
450	650	900	6

4 (Type II): The 4 was also built with a gray body, which was trimmed with an apple green stripe where it met the black frame.

VG	EX	LN	RARITY
600	900	1300	7

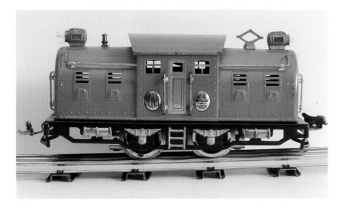

4U: The orange 4 was also offered in kit form as the 4U in 1928 and 1929. To attain the values listed here, the kit must be unassembled and complete with all packaging.

VG	EX	LN	RARITY
1200	2000	4000	8

150: Produced from 1917 through 1925, the number 150 was assigned to locomotives with two different body styles, both resembling the New York Central's class S-2. However, the real locomotives had a 2-D-2 wheel arrangement, which Lionel truncated to 0-B-0.

150 (Type I): The earliest version of the 150 used the 700-type body, and was painted dark green with red window trim. The body was attached to a black frame, and decorated with nickel-finished headlight and bell. The rubber-stamped markings consisted of an oval "NEW YORK CENTRAL LINES" logo on the left side of the door and "150" to the right. This is the only case of this style body being used by the 150.

VG	EX	LN	RARITY
115	150	200	6

150 (Type II): A new 5" body was used on later 1917 and subsequent production. The dark green body was decorated in the same manner as the earlier 150.

VG	EX	LN	RARITY
50	75	110	3

150 (Type III): Dark olive paint was used on some of the newer style 150 locomotives. These too had their embossed window frames painted red.

VG	EX	LN	RARITY
50	75	110	3

150 (Type IV): Brown locomotives with dark olive window trim were also made.

VG	EX	LN	RARITY
100	130	175	5

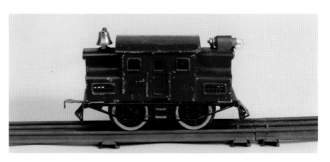

150 (Type V): Some of these locomotives were painted maroon with dark olive window frames. The frames continued to be black and the cab was decorated with a nickel-finished headlight and bell.

VG	EX	LN	RARITY
50	75	110	3

150 (Type VI): The embossed window frames of some of the maroon locomotives were painted brown.

VG	EX	LN	RARITY
50	75	110	3

150 (Type VII): Peacock, gray, mojave and olive are among other colors the 150 reportedly exists in. It is possible that Lionel produced short runs in these colors for special customers, or locomotives returned to the factory for repair could have been refinished in one of these colors. However, almost certainly, more fakes than originals of these variations exist, and due caution is urged.

VG	EX	LN	RARITY
100	200	300	7-8

152: Like the 150, the 152 was loosely based on the New York Central S-2 locomotive, but once again Lionel's version had a 0-B-0 wheel arrangement. This locomotive was available from 1917 through 1927.

152 (Type I): The first year's production had a black frame and a body painted dark green. A nickel pedestal headlight was mounted atop one end of the locomotive, a nickel bell atop the other. The plate on the bottom of this locomotive read "THE LIONEL MANUFACTURING COMPANY".

VG	EX	LN	RARITY
50	75	110	3

152 (Type II): A dark olive green locomotive entered production in 1918 and was continued into the 1920s. The name-

Price Guide Key: VG = Very Good, EX = Excellent, LN = Like New | Values for each condition are in U.S. dollars. | Rarity = Scale from 1-8 with 8 being the hardest to find.

175

O GAUGE ELECTRIC LOCOMOTIVES

plate on the bottom of the motor read "THE LIONEL CORPORATION".

VG	EX	LN	RARITY
50	75	110	3

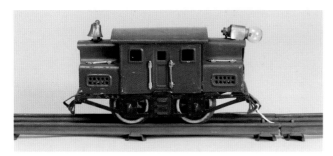

152 (Type III): The 0-B-0 was also produced in dark gray.

VG	EX	LN	RARITY
50	75	110	3

152 (Type IV): Near the end of the production, a light gray enamel was used on some of the locomotives.

VG	EX	LN	RARITY
60	90	125	4

152 (Type V): Pea green 0-B-0 have also been reported.

VG	EX	LN	RARITY
60	90	125	4

152 (Type VI): Mojave examples have surfaced that have late production characteristics such as strap headlights and "CORPORATION" nameplates.

VG	EX	LN	RARITY
300	400	550	6

152 (Type VII): Authentic examples of the 152 painted peacock do exist, but are outnumbered by repainted units.

VG	EX	LN	RARITY
400	550	700	8

153: Although some of the uncataloged late production 152 locomotives came equipped with hand reverse units, it was the presence of these mechanisms that differentiated the 153 from the 152. Built only in 1924 and 1925, the locomotive was decorated with a rubber-stamped "NEW YORK CENTRAL LINES" oval logo to the left of the side door, and the catalog number "153" to the right of the door. Like the 152, it had S-2 styling and a 0-B-0 wheel arrangement. Despite its short production life, the 153 was produced in a variety of colors.

153 (Type I): The first year's production had a black frame and a body painted dark green. A nickel strap headlight was mounted atop one end of the locomotive, a nickel bell atop the other.

VG	EX	LN	RARITY
80	110	150	4

153 (Type II): Dark olive green 153 locomotives were also produced. Like the dark green units, they had black frames.

VG	EX	LN	RARITY
100	125	165	5

153 (Type III): Another color the locomotive was painted was gray.

VG	EX	LN	RARITY
100	125	165	5

153 (Type IV): Maroon 0-B-0 units were built.

VG	EX	LN	RARITY
80	110	150	4

153 (Type V): As was the case with many of Lionel's electric locomotives, a mojave version was produced as well.

VG	EX	LN	RARITY
115	150	200	6

153 (Type VI): The miniature S2 was also available painted peacock.

VG	EX	LN	RARITY
80	110	150	4

154: Yet another incarnation of the S2, again in the abbreviated 0-B-0 format, was this locomotive offered from 1917 through 1923. A rubber-stamped "NEW YORK CENTRAL LINES" oval logo was to the left of the side door, and the catalog number "154" to the door's right.

154 (Type I): In 1917, the 154 had a dark green body mounted on a black frame. A pedestal headlight sat atop one hood, a nickel bell atop the other. The hook couplers were attached to the frame with rivets.

VG	EX	LN	RARITY
80	110	150	4

154 (Type II): Starting in 1918, the dark green locomotive had nickel strap headlights and the couplers were twisted into slots in the frame.

VG	EX	LN	RARITY
115	150	200	6

156: Once again, Lionel turned to the New York Central S2 class locomotives for styling inspiration when creating the 156. While still not replicating the prototype's 2-D-2 wheel arrangement, the 156 got closer, with a 2-B-2 arrangement. The S2 was not a poor choice for a pattern, as these were widely used in New York City, obviously a prime market for toys. The 156 was available from 1917 through 1923.

156 (Type I): As built in 1917, the dark green 2-B-2 had a pedestal headlight.

VG	EX	LN	RARITY
400	550	725	7

156 (Type II): The next year, several changes were made to the dark green 2-B-2. Although the method of coupler mounting and the motor style changed, the most noticeable change was the move to a strap headlight.

VG	EX	LN	RARITY
400	550	725	7

156 (Type III): Some of the post 1917 locomotives were finished in olive green.

VG	EX	LN	RARITY
550	700	875	7

156 (Type IV): The later 2-B-2 locos were also made in gray.

VG	EX	LN	RARITY
750	900	1100	8

156 (Type V): The 156 sometimes was painted maroon. The 2-B-2 always came with a nickel-finished bell, regardless of body color.

VG	EX	LN	RARITY
400	550	725	7

156 (Type VI): Mojave 2-B-2 156 locomotives are also known to exist.

VG	EX	LN	RARITY
750	900	1100	8

156 (Type VII): In 1922, a less-expensive version of the locomotive was made. Shorn of its pilot and trailing trucks, the dark green locomotive became a 0-B-0. In subsequent years, the 0-B-0 variation was known as the 156X.

VG	EX	LN	RARITY
550	700	900	8

156X (Type I): The less expensive 0-B-0 version of the 156 was designated 156X in 1923 and 1924. Among the colors it was produced in was olive green.

VG	EX	LN	RARITY
350	425	550	6

156X (Type II): The 0-B-0 156 was also made in gray.

VG	EX	LN	RARITY
300	375	500	5

156X (Type III): Maroon 0-B-0 versions were built as well.

VG	EX	LN	RARITY
350	425	550	6

156X (Type IV): Not surprisingly, a mojave version of the 0-B-0 was produced.

VG	EX	LN	RARITY
300	375	500	5

156X (Type V): Though the standard 156 was not made in brown, the 0-B-0 version was.

VG	EX	LN	RARITY
350	425	550	6

158: This locomotive, offered from 1919 through 1923, was a bare-bones version of the 150. It had a dummy headlight instead of an operating unit. The decorative bell was omitted, as were the decorative springs and journal boxes. Like the 150, it had a 0-B-0 wheel arrangement and was decorated in New York Central markings.

158 (Type I): The economy 0-B-0 was made in dark green with its windows trimmed in red.

VG	EX	LN	RARITY
100	140	200	4

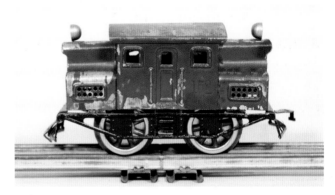

158 (Type II): A gray version was produced as well, also with red window trim.

VG	EX	LN	RARITY
80	125	175	3

158 (Type III): The basic 0-B-0 was also fittingly offered in basic black.

VG	EX	LN	RARITY
100	140	200	4

203 Armored locomotive: While this toy is not actually a replica, even stylized, of any actual locomotive, electric or otherwise, it is included in this chapter because Lionel powered the unit with the same mechanism used in the 154 electric. The toy, with its simulated armored body, was topped with the same style of turret as used on U.S. pre-dreadnaught battleships…making it more a rail-bound warship than train-tank hybrid.

203 (Type I): Some of the toys produced in 1917 were painted olive and featured motor nameplates reading "THE LIONEL MANUFACTURING COMPANY".

RARITY
Too rarely traded to establish accurate pricing.

Price Guide Key: VG = Very Good, EX = Excellent, LN = Like New | *Values for each condition are in U.S. dollars.* | **Rarity** = Scale from 1-8 with 8 being the hardest to find.

177

O GAUGE ELECTRIC LOCOMOTIVES

203 (Type II): Other 1917 production was painted battleship gray.

VG	EX	LN	RARITY
1500	2000	3500	8

203 (Type III): From 1918 through 1921, the armored locomotive continued to be painted battleship gray. Now, however, the nameplate on the bottom read "THE LIONEL CORPORATION".

VG	EX	LN	RARITY
1100	1600	2500	8

248: This box-cabbed 0-B-0 electric locomotive does not have a readily identifiable prototype, although various actual railroads of the time (1927-1932) operated box cab locomotives. Regardless of cab color, the body of the 248 was mounted on a black frame. The frame was trimmed with brass flag holders and aluminum simulated springs and journal boxes. On the cab was installed an operating headlight, brass doors, and one each of a brass pantograph and brass whistle. The lettering for these locomotives was applied to separately installed inserts, which were made of either brass or painted steel.

248 (Type I): During 1927, the 248 was made with a dark green body and a maroon-painted lettering insert. These locomotives had strap-type headlights.

VG	EX	LN	RARITY
100	140	200	5

248 (Type II): Unpainted brass inserts, stamped with markings, were used in some of the dark green locomotives made in 1927. These too had strap headlights.

VG	EX	LN	RARITY
100	140	200	5

248 (Type III): Peacock-painted inserts were used in some locomotives with orange bodies during 1927. Like the rest of the 248 locomotives made that year, they had a strap-type headlight.

VG	EX	LN	RARITY
50	90	140	2

248 (Type IV): Some of the orange locomotives had rubber-stamped unpainted brass inserts in 1927.

VG	EX	LN	RARITY
50	90	140	2

248 (Type V): Yellow inserts trimmed 1927 locomotives with peacock body paint. These locomotives had strap headlights.

VG	EX	LN	RARITY
50	90	140	2

248 (Type VI): In 1928, a cast headlight was used instead of the strap headlight of the year before. The dark green locomotive with maroon insert was one of the units to get the new headlight.

VG	EX	LN	RARITY
100	140	200	5

248 (Type VII): Locomotives with orange bodies and rubber-stamped peacock inserts were sold in 1928 and 1929. Naturally, they had cast headlights.

VG	EX	LN	RARITY
50	90	140	2

248 (Type VIII): During 1930 and 1931, Lionel made the 248 with a red body and rubber-stamped yellow insert.

VG	EX	LN	RARITY
50	90	140	2

248 (Type IX): Also shipped during 1930-31 was a light olive locomotive with rubber-stamped yellow insert.

VG	EX	LN	RARITY
50	90	140	2

248 (Type X): In 1930, the 248 was made with a terracotta body and cast headlights. Its rubber-stamped insert was first painted yellow.

VG	EX	LN	RARITY
150	225	325	5

248 (Type XI): The terra-cotta locomotive was continued in 1931, however the brass handrails, which had been installed on all previous models, were omitted. The lettering insert was painted yellow.

VG	EX	LN	RARITY
150	225	325	5

250: Electric locomotives with this catalog number were offered in two different years: 1926 and 1934. The 1926 production did not have a reversing unit; the uncataloged 1934 units had manual reversing units–despite the "E" stamping on some units, which is normally indicative of the presence of an electric reversing unit. Once again, the styling of the New York Central's S2 electric was used.

250 (Type I): One of the colors the 0-B-0 was offered in for 1926 was dark green.

VG	EX	LN	RARITY
150	190	250	5

250 (Type II): Peacock versions of the 250 were also sold in 1926.

VG	EX	LN	RARITY
150	190	250	5

250 (Type III): Despite its lackluster sales, the 250 returned in a third color, orange, during 1934. Some of these locomotives, apparently erroneously, have "E" stamped on their doors.

VG	EX	LN	RARITY
150	190	250	5

250 (Type IV): A terra-cotta version of the 250, with a maroon frame, was another uncataloged 1934 item. Some of these locomotives also have "E" stamped on their doors in error.

VG	EX	LN	RARITY
150	190	250	5

250 (Type V): Some of the terra-cotta cabs were mounted on black frames in 1934. These also came both with and without the "E" marking.

VG	EX	LN	RARITY
150	190	250	5

251/251E: This relatively large boxcab locomotive had a 0-B-0 wheel arrangement. Cataloged until 1932, it was introduced as the 251 in 1925. An E-unit equipped version, the 251E was added to the line two years later.

251 (Type I): During the first year of production for the 0-B-0, its body was painted gray. Brass inserts were installed, as were two strap headlights.

VG	EX	LN	RARITY
275	325	400	4

251 (Type II): The second and third years of production, 1926-27, saw the gray locomotive equipped with red inserts. Strap-type headlights continued to be used.

VG	EX	LN	RARITY
275	325	400	4

251 (Type III): From 1928 through 1932, the 0-B-0 continued to be available in gray with red inserts, but now the headlight housings were castings.

VG	EX	LN	RARITY
275	325	400	4

251 (Type IV): A new color combination was introduced for the 251 in 1928 as well. The 0-B-0 was now available in red with ivory inserts and cast headlights. This combination remained in the line through 1932.

VG	EX	LN	RARITY
325	375	450	6

251 (Type V): An ivory stripe was applied to the base of the body of some of the red locomotives. This stripe matched the inserts.

VG	EX	LN	RARITY
325	375	450	6

251E (Type I): When the 251E was introduced in 1927, it was painted gray with red inserts. Strap-type headlight housings were atop each end of its body.

VG	EX	LN	RARITY
325	375	450	6

251E (Type II): From 1928 though 1932, the electrically reversed 0-B-0 was sold in gray with brass inserts and cast headlights.

VG	EX	LN	RARITY
325	375	450	6

251E (Type III): Some of the 1928-32 gray locomotives had red inserts.

VG	EX	LN	RARITY
325	375	450	6

251E (Type IV): Also available during 1928-32 was a red version of the 0-B-0 with ivory inserts and cast headlights.

VG	EX	LN	RARITY
375	425	475	6

251E (Type V): An ivory stripe was applied to the base of the body of some of the red locomotives. This stripe matched the inserts.

VG	EX	LN	RARITY
375	425	475	6

Price Guide Key: **VG** = Very Good, **EX** = Excellent, **LN** = Like New | *Values for each condition are in U.S. dollars.* | **Rarity** = Scale from 1-8 with 8 being the hardest to find.

179

252/252E: This locomotive was essentially a reversible 250. The 252, sold from 1926 through 1932, used a hand-reversing unit, while the 252E, offered from 1933 through 1935, had an electric E-unit. The units had an 0-B-0 wheel arrangement and the styling of New York Central's S2 locomotives.

252 (Type I): During 1926-27, the locomotive was available with a peacock body mounted on a black frame. A strap headlight was installed, as were nickel journal boxes.

VG	EX	LN	RARITY
75	110	150	3

252 (Type II): The 0-B-0 was also made with a maroon body and black frame during 1926-27. These also had strap headlights and nickel journal boxes.

VG	EX	LN	RARITY
300	450	650	8

252 (Type III): Initially sold in 1926, and continuing into 1928, was an olive green version of the 252. It had a strap-type headlight, and nickel journal boxes were mounted on its black frame.

VG	EX	LN	RARITY
75	110	150	3

252 (Type IV): Sometime in 1928, and continuing into 1929, a cast headlight was installed on the olive green locomotive.

VG	EX	LN	RARITY
75	110	150	3

252 (Type V): In 1930, only a terra-cotta version of the 252 was sold. It had a maroon frame, cast headlight and nickel journal boxes.

VG	EX	LN	RARITY
100	140	200	4

252 (Type VI): In 1931, the journal boxes of the 252 were changed to copper. Even more noticeable was the new yellow-orange body/maroon frame color combination. This version was continued into 1932.

VG	EX	LN	RARITY
100	140	200	4

252 (Type VII): The yellow-orange body was also mounted on a terracotta frame during 1931-32. These also had a cast headlight housing and copper journal boxes.

VG	EX	LN	RARITY
100	140	200	4

252 (Type VIII): Black frames were also used beneath the yellow-orange bodies of some of the 1931-32 locomotives.

VG	EX	LN	RARITY
100	140	200	4

252E (Type I): The addition of an E-unit to the 252 in 1933 resulted in a new model number for the 0-B-0: 252E. One version produced during the first year had a yellow-orange body and terra-cotta frame. The locomotive was decorated with a cast headlight and copper journal boxes.

VG	EX	LN	RARITY
100	140	200	4

252E (Type II): Also introduced late in 1933, but continuing through 1935, was a terra-cotta locomotive with maroon frame. These had cast headlights and nickel journal boxes.

VG	EX	LN	RARITY
100	140	200	4

252E (Type III): In 1935, some of the terra-cotta bodies were mounted on black frames with nickel journal boxes.

VG	EX	LN	RARITY
100	140	200	4

253/253E: Though some sources state that the New Haven railroad's class EY-3 boxcab locomotives inspired the styling of the 253, the 253 was in production two years prior to the delivery of the EY-3 locos. Whatever real locomotive served as the pattern for the 253, it certainly wasn't painted in the rainbow of colors Lionel used through the years. The hand-reversed 253 was sold from 1924 through 1932, while the E-unit equipped 253E was in the catalog from 1931 through 1936. Brass nameplates were attached to the sides of these 0-B-0 electrics, and trim inserts added even more color to the units.

253 (Type I): In 1924-25, the locomotive was offered with a maroon body, brass insert. The journal boxes, pantograph whistle and strap-type headlight were all nickel. The loco rode on spoke wheels.

VG	EX	LN	RARITY
175	300	450	6

253 (Type II): Some of the maroon 1924-25 locomotives had a brass pantograph and brass whistle. Otherwise they were identical to the Type I 253.

VG	EX	LN	RARITY
175	300	450	6

253 (Type III): Gray was the other color the body of the 0-B-0 was painted in during 1924-25. A brass trim insert was used, along with a brass pantograph and brass whistle. Nickel journal boxes were installed, as was a strap-type headlight and spoke wheels.

RARITY
Too rarely traded to establish accurate value.

253 (Type IV): Beginning in 1925, and continuing in 1926, was a dark gray version of the locomotive. While the insert in these locomotives was brass, the remainder of the trim, whistle, pantograph and journal boxes, was nickel. Spoke wheels continued to be installed.

RARITY
Too rarely traded to establish accurate value.

253 (Type V): One mojave version of the 253 sold during 1926-27 had a brass insert, with the rest of the trim being nickel. These units had a strap headlight and spoke wheels.

VG	EX	LN	RARITY
100	150	225	3

253 (Type VI): A second type of mojave also used a brass insert, but the pantograph and whistle were brass as well. These had nickel journal boxes and a strap-type headlight. They rode on spoke wheels, and were sold 1926-27.

VG	EX	LN	RARITY
100	150	225	3

253 (Type VII): Apparently sometime during 1927, disk wheels began to be used rather than spoke, and cast headlight housings replaced the strap-type. Among the versions of the 253 getting the new components was the mojave locomotive. But for the brass insert, all the trim on these units was nickel. Production of this version continued through 1928.

VG	EX	LN	RARITY
100	150	225	3

253 (Type VIII): A dark green version with brass insert, nickel journal boxes, brass pantograph, brass whistle, strap-type headlight and spoke wheels was made, probably in 1927.

VG	EX	LN	RARITY
100	150	225	3

253 (Type IX): Cast headlights and disk wheels were used on a peacock version of the 253 sold in 1928 and 1929. The locomotives had orange inserts, nickel journal boxes, and brass pantographs and whistles.

VG	EX	LN	RARITY
100	150	225	3

253 (Type X): The terra-cotta body with cream insert of this 1929-only production unit made for an attractive locomotive. Riding on disk wheels, it was decorated with nickel journal boxes, brass pantograph, brass whistle and cast headlight.

VG	EX	LN	RARITY
200	300	400	5

253 (Type XI): Also offered only in 1929 was a dark green locomotive with orange insert, nickel journal boxes, brass pantograph, brass whistle, cast headlight and disk wheels.

VG	EX	LN	RARITY
200	300	400	5

253 (Type XII): Another new color in 1929 was red. Made for one year only, these locomotives had yellow inserts, nickel journal boxes, brass pantographs, brass whistles, cast headlights and disk wheels.

VG	EX	LN	RARITY
225	325	475	6

253 (Type XIII): The year 1930 saw the 253 produced in pea green for the only time during its run. An orange insert, nickel journal boxes, brass pantograph, brass whistle, cast headlight and disk wheels completed this version.

VG	EX	LN	RARITY
225	325	475	6

253 (Type XIV): The final two years the 253 was offered, 1931-32, saw it produced in a new color scheme. The body was finished in Stephen Girard green, with a cream insert, and mounted on a dark green frame. Nickel journal boxes, brass pantograph, brass whistle, cast headlight and disk wheels finished the unit.

VG	EX	LN	RARITY
100	150	225	5

253E (Type I): Terra cotta was one of three primary body colors in which the 253E debuted. This version had a cream insert, nickel journal boxes, brass pantograph, brass whistle, cast headlight and rode on disk wheels. This color combination was offered only in 1931.

VG	EX	LN	RARITY
200	250	325	6

Price Guide Key: **VG** = Very Good, **EX** = Excellent, **LN** = Like New | *Values for each condition are in U.S. dollars.* | **Rarity** = Scale from 1-8 with 8 being the hardest to find.

181

O GAUGE ELECTRIC LOCOMOTIVES

253E (Type II): Another single-year color offering for the 0-B-0 was pea green with orange insert, also in 1931. This version also had nickel journal boxes, brass pantograph, brass whistle, cast headlight and disk wheels.

VG	EX	LN	RARITY
100	150	225	3

253E (Type III): The third color the 253E was offered in during 1931 was also the only scheme that would stay in the line until the 253E was discontinued in 1936. That scheme was Stephen Girard green, with a cream insert, nickel journal boxes, brass pantograph, brass whistle, cast headlight and disk wheels.

VG	EX	LN	RARITY
100	150	225	3

253E (Type IV): During 1932, and again in 1933, the 253E was available in apple green with a cream insert. This version had nickel journal boxes, brass pantograph, brass whistle, cast headlight and disk wheels.

VG	EX	LN	RARITY
100	150	225	3

254/254E: Like the number 4, the 254 and later 254E were much reduced, heavily stylized caricatures of the Milwaukee Road's famous EP-2 Bi-polar electric locomotives, which worked in the Rockies. Lionel's 254 and 254E had a 0-B-0 wheel arrangement. The 254 was offered from 1924 through 1932, while the 254E was cataloged from 1927 through 1934.

254 (Type I): One version built in 1924-25 was painted dark green. A brass insert, nickel pantograph, nickel whistle, nickel number plates and strap headlight decorated the body. Nickel journal boxes were installed on the one-piece frame and the locomotive rode on spoke wheels.

VG	EX	LN	RARITY
200	250	325	6

254 (Type II): Also shipped during 1924-25 was a mojave version. It also had a brass insert, nickel journal boxes, nickel pantograph, nickel whistle, nickel number plates, strap headlight, spoke wheels and one-piece frame.

VG	EX	LN	RARITY
200	250	300	4

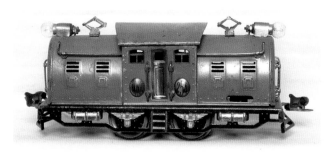

254 (Type III): A change was made to the mojave 254 for 1926-27, when a two-piece frame was added. The brass insert, nickel journal boxes, nickel pantograph, nickel whistle, nickel number plates, strap headlight and spoke wheels, however, were unchanged from the previous edition.

VG	EX	LN	RARITY
200	250	300	4

254 (Type IV): The two-piece frame was also used on the dark green unit beginning in 1926. Through 1927, it had a brass insert, nickel journal boxes, nickel pantograph, nickel whistle, nickel number plates, strap headlight and spoke wheels.

VG	EX	LN	RARITY
200	250	325	6

254 (Type V): A new color, olive green, was added for 1926-27 as well. Like the other locomotives in this series at the time, it had brass inserts, nickel journal boxes, nickel pantograph, nickel whistle, nickel number plates, strap headlight, spoke wheels and two-piece frame.

VG	EX	LN	RARITY
150	200	250	3

254 (Type VI): Sometime during 1927, and continuing into 1928, a brass pantograph and brass whistle began to be used on the olive green locomotive. However, the brass inserts, nickel journal boxes, nickel number plates, strap headlight, spoke wheels and two-piece frame of previous models continued.

VG	EX	LN	RARITY
150	200	250	3

254 (Type VII): Apparently also spanning the 1927-28 timeframe was the introduction of a cast headlight housing to the olive green locomotive. These units had brass inserts, nickel journal boxes, brass pantograph, brass whistle, spoke wheels and two-piece frame.

VG	EX	LN	RARITY
150	200	250	3

254 (Type VIII): A dark olive version of the 0-B-0 was sold in 1928-29. Features of this model included brass inserts, nickel journal boxes, brass pantograph, brass whistle, brass number plates, cast headlight and new disk wheels, as well as a new one-piece frame with gussets.

VG	EX	LN	RARITY
150	200	250	3

254 (Type IX): The new one-piece frame with gussets was also used on locomotives with mojave-painted bodies beginning in 1928. As built through 1929, these units had brass inserts, nickel journal boxes, brass pantograph, brass whistle, brass number plates, cast headlight, as well as disk wheels.

VG	EX	LN	RARITY
200	250	300	4

254 (Type X): New for 1928 was the 254 painted in pea green. Continuing in 1929, the simulated hatches on the side of its hoods were painted orange. Naturally, these locomotives were built on the new-for-1928 one-piece frame with gussets. Further coloration was provided by brass inserts, nickel journal boxes, brass pantograph, brass whistle and brass number plates. The locomotive was equipped with a cast headlight and disk wheels. It was continued in 1929.

VG	EX	LN	RARITY
200	250	300	4

254 (Type XI): Orange paint was applied to the embossed hatches of the olive green 254 in 1930. Through 1934, these units had brass inserts, nickel journal boxes, brass pantograph, brass whistle, brass number plates, cast headlight, disk wheels and a one-piece frame with gussets.

VG	EX	LN	RARITY
150	200	250	3

254 (Type XII): Also sold between 1930 and 1934 was an olive green unit with an orange base stripe. These locomotives had brass inserts, nickel journal boxes, brass pantograph, brass whistle, brass number plates, cast headlight, disk wheels and one-piece frame with gussets.

VG	EX	LN	RARITY
150	200	250	3

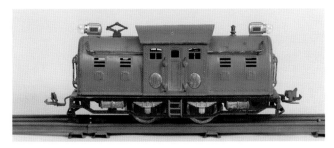

254E (Type I): The first of this series, introduced in 1927, was painted olive green. Through 1929 it had brass inserts, nickel journal boxes, brass pantograph, brass whistle, brass number plates, cast headlight, disk wheels, one-piece frame with gussets and of course an electric reversing unit.

254E (Type II): Beginning in 1928, some of the olive green 0-B-0s had the embossed hood hatches painted orange. Built on one-piece frames with gussets, the locomotives had brass inserts, nickel journal boxes, brass pantograph, brass whistle, brass number plates, cast headlight and disk wheels. This version was last sold in 1929.

VG	EX	LN	RARITY
200	250	300	4

254E (Type III): Also sold in 1928-29 was a pea green version with orange hatches. Like the others, it had brass inserts, nickel journal boxes, brass pantograph, brass whistle, brass number plates, cast headlight, disk wheels and one-piece frame with gussets.

VG	EX	LN	RARITY
250	325	400	6

254E (Type IV): Some of the 1928-29 pea green cabs had an orange base stripe added, in addition to the orange hatches. Brass inserts, nickel journal boxes, brass pantograph, brass whistle, brass number plates, cast headlight, disk wheels and one-piece frame with gussets all were features of this locomotive.

VG	EX	LN	RARITY
250	325	400	6

254E (Type V): Orange hatches were also found on olive green locomotives in 1928-29. Once again brass inserts, nickel journal boxes, brass pantograph, brass whistle, brass number plates, cast headlight, disk wheels and a one-piece frame with gussets were all standard.

VG	EX	LN	RARITY
200	250	300	4

254E (Type VI): Between 1930 and 1934, some of the olive green locomotives had their hatches painted red. They still had brass inserts, nickel journal boxes, brass pantograph, brass whistle, brass number plates, cast headlight, disk wheels and a one-piece frame with gussets.

VG	EX	LN	RARITY
250	325	400	6

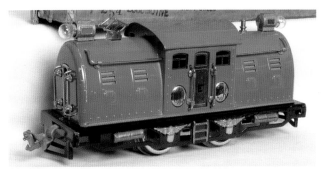

254E (Type VII): A red base stripe was painted along the bottom of some of the olive green cabs between 1930 and 1934. Built on one-piece frames with gussets, these locomotives had brass inserts, nickel journal boxes, brass pantograph, brass whistle, brass number plates, cast headlight and disk wheels.

VG	EX	LN	RARITY
250	325	400	6

254E (Type VIII): Some of the olive green locomotives even had both red base stripes and red hatches. Like the rest of the series, they also had brass inserts, nickel journal boxes, brass

Price Guide Key: **VG** = Very Good, **EX** = Excellent, **LN** = Like New | *Values for each condition are in U.S. dollars.* | **Rarity** = Scale from 1-8 with 8 being the hardest to find.

183

O GAUGE ELECTRIC LOCOMOTIVES

pantograph, brass whistle, brass number plates, cast headlight, disk wheels and a one-piece frame with gussets.

VG	EX	LN	RARITY
250	325	400	6

256: This was the top of the line 0 Gauge locomotive from 1924 through 1930. This orange powerhouse had two motors, one driving each truck. Its wheel arrangement was 0-B+B-0.

256 (Type I): In 1924, the orange body of this locomotive was rubber-stamped "LIONEL" inside a rectangle also rubber-stamped on the side of the body. Both motors had spoke wheels and one nickel, non-operating pantograph was mounted on the cab roof.

VG	EX	LN	RARITY
600	1000	1500	7

256 (Type II): In 1925, the rubber-stamped rectangle was eliminated from the "LIONEL" markings, which continued to be rubber-stamped. The same type of wheels and pantograph arrangement was retained.

VG	EX	LN	RARITY
400	750	1125	5

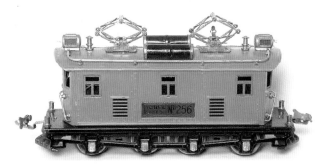

256 (Type III): From 1926 through 1928, the flanks of the orange locomotive were adorned with brass plates reading "LIONEL LINES – No. 256". A rectangle, surrounding the legend, was also stamped on the plate. The locomotive now had disk wheels and two brass operating pantographs.

VG	EX	LN	RARITY
500	800	1200	6

450 (Type I): This red locomotive was merely a 253 0-B-0 with brass plates specially marked for Macy's, which was the exclusive retailer for the unit sometime between 1928 and 1931.

VG	EX	LN	RARITY
400	750	1125	8

450 (Type II): Macy's was also the exclusive seller of this apple green, specially marked locomotive; again, merely a remarked 253 with brass trim. This version, with its "Macy's" lettering, was sold between 1928 and 1931.

VG	EX	LN	RARITY
500	800	1200	8

700: Sold in 1915 and 1916, this was another of the many locomotives that Lionel produced that were styled loosely on the lines of the New York Central's S2 electrics. The 7" long toy even had the oval logo reading "NEW YORK CENTRAL LINES" rubber stamped to the left of the cabside door. To the right of the door was rubber-stamped "700".

700 (Type I): Its 5 1/2" long body painted dark green during its first year of production, the 700 rolled on cast iron wheels. Its windows were trimmed in red.

VG	EX	LN	RARITY
500	625	775	8

700 (Type II): Die-cast wheels were used during the second year. Dark green with red window trim continued to be the only color available.

VG	EX	LN	RARITY
500	625	775	8

701: With a 6" cab and 8" overall length, the 701 was slightly larger than the 700, with which it shared similar styling and markings. It also had the same two-year production span, 1915-1916. Unlike the 700, the 701 had an operating headlight.

701 (Type I): Painted dark green during its first year of production, the 0-B-0 rolled on cast iron wheels. Its windows were trimmed in red and its ventilators in gold.

VG	EX	LN	RARITY
400	500	625	7

701 (Type II): Die-cast wheels were used during the second year. Dark green with red window trim and gold ventilators remained the only paint scheme available.

VG	EX	LN	RARITY
400	500	625	7

703: This 2-B-2 was the top of the line locomotive in 1915 and 1916. Like the 700 and 701, it was styled along the lines of the New York Central S2 and carried the "NEW YORK CENTRAL LINES" oval logo. However, the overall length of the 703 was 10", and its cab was 7" long. It had an operating pedestal-type headlight.

703 (Type I): Cast iron drive wheels were used on the dark green locomotive in 1915. The cab had red windows and gold-painted ventilators.

VG	EX	LN	RARITY
1100	1700	2500	8

703 (Type II): During its second year, the dark green locomotive used die-cast drive wheels. The paint and decoration were unchanged.

VG	EX	LN	RARITY
1100	1700	2500	8

706: The 706, offered in 1915-1916, was simply a 701 equipped with a manual reversing switch.

706 (Type I): Painted dark green during its first year of production, the 0-B-0 rolled on cast iron wheels. Its windows were trimmed in red and its ventilators in gold.

VG	EX	LN	RARITY
325	475	650	7

706 (Type II): Die-cast wheels were used during the second year. Dark green with red window trim and gold ventilators remained the only paint scheme available.

VG	EX	LN	RARITY
325	475	650	7

706 (Type III): Some of the dark green locomotives were rubber-stamped CPR rather than NYC.

RARITY
Too infrequently traded to establish accurate values.

728: This uncataloged 1916 locomotive was simply a 700 0-B-0 rubber-stamped "Quaker" rather than "NEW YORK CENTRAL LINES".

RARITY
Too infrequently traded to establish accurate values.

732: Also produced in 1916 was this uncataloged version of the 701, also rubber-stamped "Quaker".

RARITY
Too infrequently traded to establish accurate values.

1010: Cataloged as part of the Winner line in 1931-32, this locomotive had previously been produced, though uncataloged, in 1930. Its headlight was non-functional and it had no reverse. Only one axle of this lithographed 0-B-0 was powered.

1010 (Type I): Some of these locomotives had orange bodies and green roofs. A cream-colored panel was centered beneath each window.

VG	EX	LN	RARITY
75	110	150	3

1010 (Type II): Other units were a darker shade of orange and lacked the cream panels on the side. The roof of this version was blue-green.

VG	EX	LN	RARITY
75	110	150	3

1010 (Type III): The blue-green roof was also used on locomotives with tan lithographed bodies.

VG	EX	LN	RARITY
85	125	175	4

1651E: Sold only in 1933, this red lithographed 0-B-0 was marked "LIONEL-IVES LINES". It had a brown roof, black frame, and brass and copper trim.

VG	EX	LN	RARITY
100	140	200	4

O GAUGE ELECTRIC LOCOMOTIVES

Price Guide Key: VG = Very Good, EX = Excellent, LN = Like New | *Values for each condition are in U.S. dollars.* | **Rarity** = Scale from 1-8 with 8 being the hardest to find.

185

CHAPTER 17
O GAUGE CABOOSES

For most of the 20th century, the caboose was an essential component of freight trains, both real and toy. Some feel that should still be the case. Lionel naturally included a caboose in every 0 gauge freight set it produced from 1915 through 1942. It is no surprise then that most cabooses are relatively common, and that there is a considerable variety of them.

657 (Type I): This red caboose with cream windows, brass railing and copper journal boxes was produced in 1933. It had brass identification plates.

VG	EX	LN	RARITY
15	25	35	1

657 (Type II): In 1934-35, nickel journal boxes began to be used on the red caboose with cream windows. It continued to have a brass railing and brass plates.

VG	EX	LN	RARITY
15	25	35	1

657 (Type III): From late 1935 through 1938, a lighter shade of red paint was used. At the same time, the railing began to be aluminum and the journal boxes nickel-plated. The windows remained cream, but the identification plates became nickel.

VG	EX	LN	RARITY
15	25	35	1

657 TYPE V

657 (Type IV): In 1939, the railing of the caboose began to be painted light red like the body. Its windows were now white and its journal boxes black. The plates continued to be nickel.

VG	EX	LN	RARITY
15	25	35	1

657 (Type V):  From 1940 through 1942, the caboose looked much different than previously. Its body was painted a very light red with tuscan roof. At the same time, its markings began to be rubber-stamped on the body rather than applied to separately installed plates. Unchanged were its white windows, light red railing and black journal boxes.

VG	EX	LN	RARITY
25	35	45	3

717: As part of Lionel's full-scale marketing effort, this magnificent detailed scale replica of a New York Central caboose was created. Beware, many are found today with warped or replaced roof walkways. This caboose was sold from 1940 through 1942.

VG	EX	LN	RARITY
350	475	650	6

717K: The scale caboose was also offered as an unpainted, unassembled kit from 1940 through 1942. The unpainted kit is much more highly prized to collectors than is the assembled version, and the quality of the assembly affects the value of the ones that have been put together.

Assembled:

VG	EX	LN	RARITY
300	400	550	7

Unassembled:

VG	EX	LN	RARITY
600	1000	1500	8

801 (Type I): This caboose, as produced in 1915, had a brown body and cupola. Its main roof was painted black, and New York Central System markings were rubber-stamped on the body. The underside of the car indicated that this item was a product of the Lionel Mfg. firm.

VG	EX	LN	RARITY
75	100	125	6

801 (Type II): Cars bearing the "Mfg." mark were also made with their brown sides rubber-stamped "Wabash – RR – 4890". The cupola was brown and the main roof black on these 1915-16 cabooses.

VG	EX	LN	RARITY
30	40	65	3

801 (Type III): In 1917, maroon bodies and cupolas began to be used on the cabooses, which continued to have "Wabash – RR – 4890" rubber-stamped on their flanks, and the "Mfg." mark on their underside. The main roof was painted black.

VG	EX	LN	RARITY
30	40	65	3

801 (Type IV): From 1918 through 1926, the caboose continued to have a maroon body and cupola, with black main roof. "Wabash – RR – 4890" was still rubber-stamped on the sides, but underneath "Corp." replaced "Mfg."

VG	EX	LN	RARITY
30	40	65	3

Price Guide Key: **VG** = Very Good, **EX** = Excellent, **LN** = Like New | *Values for each condition are in U.S. dollars.* | **Rarity** = Scale from 1-8 with 8 being the hardest to find.

187

O GAUGE CABOOSES

807 TYPE I

807 (Type I):  When introduced in 1927, this caboose had a peacock body with maroon insert. Its roof was painted dark green, and brass plates and brass railings decorated the car. There were no journal boxes on its trucks.

VG	EX	LN	RARITY
40	50	65	4

807 (Type II): In 1928, a more traditional red enamel began to be applied to the body. Peacock was now used for the insert and there was a peacock roof. Brass plates and brass railings were installed on the car, which continued to have no journal boxes.

VG	EX	LN	RARITY
20	30	40	2

807 (Type III): In 1929, nickel journal boxes began to be installed on the caboose, which continued to have a red body, peacock insert and roof, brass plates and brass rails. This car was continued in 1930.

VG	EX	LN	RARITY
20	30	40	2

807 (Type IV): Sometime during 1931, copper journal boxes began to be used. The red body, peacock insert and roof, as well as brass plates and brass rails, were unchanged.

VG	EX	LN	RARITY
20	30	40	2

807 (Type V): In 1934, the colors of the caboose changed. Now, the body was light red as was the roof. A cream insert was used, as were brass plates and brass rails. The journal boxes were copper.

VG	EX	LN	RARITY
30	40	50	3

807 (Type VI): Some of the 1934 light red-bodied cabooses used nickel plates and aluminum-colored railings. The inserts were cream and the journal boxes copper.

VG	EX	LN	RARITY
30	40	50	3

807 (Type VII): In 1935, nickel journal boxes began to be used on the light red caboose. The plates and railings were also nickel, while the inserts were cream. It continued to be built this way through 1938.

VG	EX	LN	RARITY
30	40	50	3

807 (Type VIII): In 1939, rubber-stamping replaced the use of plates on the light red caboose. It continued to have nickel journal boxes, but now the railings were painted aluminum color. The insert remained cream.

VG	EX	LN	RARITY
35	45	55	3

807 (Type IX): During 1939-40, the caboose had a light red body, cream insert, light red roof, rubber-stamped markings and aluminum-painted rails. But now, its journal boxes were black.

VG	EX	LN	RARITY
35	45	55	3

817 TYPE I

807 (Type X): From 1940 through 1941, the journal boxes remained black. While the body continued to be light red, the body, which previously had matched, was now painted tuscan. The railings, however, now were painted light red to match the body. The markings were rubber-stamped directly on the body and a white window insert was used.

VG	EX	LN	RARITY
35	45	55	3

807 (Type XI): The 1942 caboose was essentially unchanged from that of the previous two years, however the railing was now black rather than red.

VG	EX	LN	RARITY
50	75	100	5

817 (Type I): 🖼 From the time it was introduced in 1926 through 1931, this caboose had a peacock body with dark green roof. Its cupola was peacock, and orange windows and brass rails and plates trimmed the car. Its trucks had nickel journal boxes.

VG	EX	LN	RARITY
35	55	75	2

817 (Type II): Copper journal boxes were used for part of 1931, but the balance of the car was unchanged from prior years' production.

VG	EX	LN	RARITY
35	55	75	2

817 (Type III): The basic peacock/dark green color scheme of the 1931 caboose was carried over into 1932, including the copper journal boxes. The notable exception to this, however, were the windows, which were now brass.

VG	EX	LN	RARITY
35	55	75	2

817 (Type IV): In 1933, the caboose was given a new color scheme. Its body was now red with a peacock roof and red cupola. Brass windows, brass rails, brass plates and copper journal boxes completed the decoration.

VG	EX	LN	RARITY
50	75	100	4

817 (Type V): Nickel journal boxes replaced the copper ones in 1934, but the rest of the caboose was unchanged.

VG	EX	LN	RARITY
50	75	100	4

817 (Type VI): From 1935 through 1939, the caboose had a light red body, roof and cupola. It had aluminum painted rails, nickel windows, nickel journal boxes and nickel plates.

VG	EX	LN	RARITY
20	30	45	1

817 (Type VII): The 1940 edition had a flat red body topped with a brown roof and cupola. Its windows were white, its railings flat red. Nickel was used for its plates and journal boxes.

VG	EX	LN	RARITY
200	300	400	6

817 (Type VIII): Sometime during the 1940 production, the nickel plates gave way to rubber-stamped markings applied directly to the flat red body paint. The brown roof and cupola, white windows, flat red rails and nickel journal boxes all continued.

VG	EX	LN	RARITY
75	100	125	5

817 (Type IX): During 1941-42, black journal boxes were fitted to the trucks, but the rest of the rubber-stamped caboose was unchanged from its late 1940 configuration.

VG	EX	LN	RARITY
75	100	125	5

1517 (Type I): This 1931 caboose bore no Lionel markings. Its orange body was mounted on a black frame. It had a brown

Price Guide Key: **VG** = Very Good, **EX** = Excellent, **LN** = Like New | *Values for each condition are in U.S. dollars.* | **Rarity** = Scale from 1-8 with 8 being the hardest to find.

189

O GAUGE CABOOSES

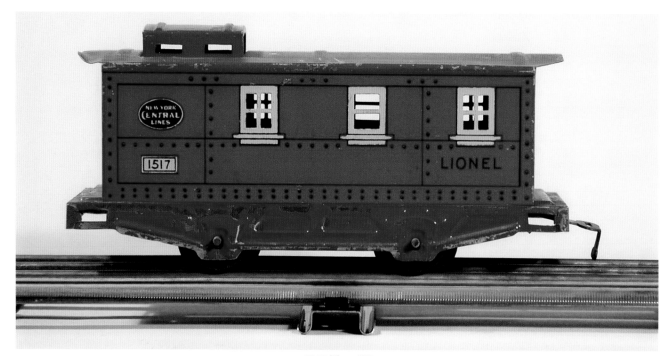

1517 Type IV

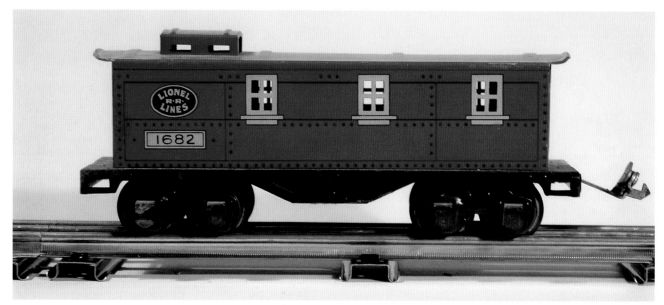

1682 Type V

roof and cupola, and the cupola sides were red. On the side of the car was the "NEW YORK – CENTRAL – LINES" legend.

VG	EX	LN	RARITY
20	30	40	2

1517 (Type II): A red-bodied version of the 1517 was produced from 1931 through 1935. It had a black frame, brown roof and cupola, red cupola sides and "NEW YORK – CENTRAL – LINES" markings, but no Lionel markings.

VG	EX	LN	RARITY
20	30	40	2

1517 (Type III): Some cabooses produced 1936-37 had their red bodies mounted on red and gold frames. These cars had a brown roof and cupola, with red cupola sides. The cars were marked "NEW YORK – CENTRAL – LINES" and were embossed "MADE IN U.S. – OF AMERICA", but had no Lionel markings.

VG	EX	LN	RARITY
20	30	40	2

1517 (Type IV): ■ Other 1936-37 cabooses had red frames and cream cupola sides. The remainder of the car was identical to the Type III 1517.

VG	EX	LN	RARITY
20	30	40	2

1682 (Type I): As delivered in 1933-34, this caboose had a vermilion body with brown roof and cream windows. It rode on trucks with copper journal boxes and had Lionel Lines markings.

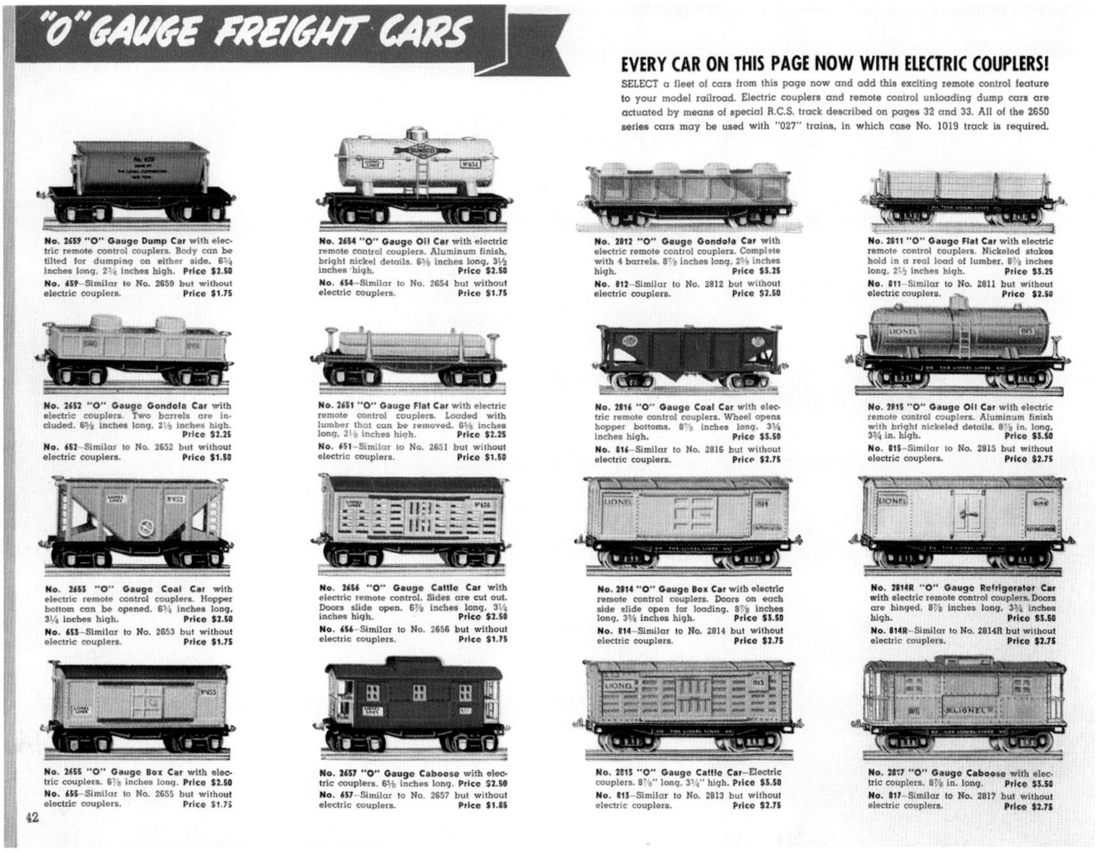

"O" GAUGE FREIGHT CARS

EVERY CAR ON THIS PAGE NOW WITH ELECTRIC COUPLERS!

SELECT a fleet of cars from this page now and add this exciting remote control feature to your model railroad. Electric couplers and remote control unloading dump cars are actuated by means of special R.C.S. track described on pages 32 and 33. All of the 2650 series cars may be used with "027" trains, in which case No. 1019 track is required.

No. 2659 "O" Gauge Dump Car with electric remote control couplers. Body can be tilted for dumping on either side. 6¾ inches long, 2¾ inches high. **Price $2.50**
No. 659–Similar to No. 2659 but without electric couplers. **Price $1.75**

No. 2654 "O" Gauge Oil Car with electric remote control couplers. Aluminum finish, bright nickel details. 6⅝ inches long, 3½ inches high. **Price $2.50**
No. 654–Similar to No. 2654 but without electric couplers. **Price $1.75**

No. 2812 "O" Gauge Gondola Car with electric remote control couplers. Complete with 4 barrels. 8⅞ inches long, 2⅝ inches high. **Price $3.25**
No. 812–Similar to No. 2812 but without electric couplers. **Price $2.50**

No. 2811 "O" Gauge Flat Car with electric remote control couplers. Nickeled stakes hold in a real load of lumber. 8⅞ inches long, 2½ inches high. **Price $3.25**
No. 811–Similar to No. 2811 but without electric couplers. **Price $2.50**

No. 2652 "O" Gauge Gondola Car with electric couplers. Two barrels are included. 6⅝ inches long, 2⅛ inches high. **Price $2.25**
No. 652–Similar to No. 2652 but without electric couplers. **Price $1.50**

No. 2651 "O" Gauge Flat Car with electric remote control couplers. Loaded with lumber that can be removed. 6⅝ inches long, 2⅛ inches high. **Price $2.25**
No. 651–Similar to No. 2651 but without electric couplers. **Price $1.50**

No. 2816 "O" Gauge Coal Car with electric remote control couplers. Wheel opens hopper bottoms. 8⅞ inches long, 3¾ inches high. **Price $3.50**
No. 816–Similar to No. 2816 but without electric couplers. **Price $2.75**

No. 2815 "O" Gauge Oil Car with electric remote control couplers. Aluminum finish with bright nickeled details. 8⅞ in. long, 3¾ in. high. **Price $3.50**
No. 815–Similar to No. 2815 but without electric couplers. **Price $2.75**

No. 2653 "O" Gauge Coal Car with electric remote control couplers. Hopper bottom can be opened. 6¾ inches long, 3¼ inches high. **Price $2.50**
No. 653–Similar to No. 2653 but without electric couplers. **Price $1.75**

No. 2656 "O" Gauge Cattle Car with electric remote control. Sides are cut out. Doors slide open. 6⅞ inches long, 3¼ inches high. **Price $2.50**
No. 656–Similar to No. 2656 but without electric couplers. **Price $1.75**

No. 2814 "O" Gauge Box Car with electric remote control couplers. Doors on each side slide open for loading. 8⅞ inches long, 3¾ inches high. **Price $3.50**
No. 814–Similar to No. 2814 but without electric couplers. **Price $2.75**

No. 2814R "O" Gauge Refrigerator Car with electric remote control couplers. Doors are hinged. 8⅞ inches long, 3¾ inches high. **Price $3.50**
No. 814R–Similar to No. 2814R but without electric couplers. **Price $2.75**

No. 2655 "O" Gauge Box Car with electric couplers. 6⅞ inches long. **Price $2.50**
No. 655–Similar to No. 2655 but without electric couplers. **Price $1.75**

No. 2657 "O" Gauge Caboose with electric couplers. 6⅝ inches long. **Price $2.50**
No. 657–Similar to No. 2657 but without electric couplers. **Price $1.85**

No. 2813 "O" Gauge Cattle Car–Electric couplers. 8⅞" long, 3¾" high. **Price $3.50**
No. 813–Similar to No. 2813 but without electric couplers. **Price $2.75**

No. 2817 "O" Gauge Caboose with electric couplers. 8⅞ in. long. **Price $3.50**
No. 817–Similar to No. 2817 but without electric couplers. **Price $2.75**

42

1938 CATALOG

LIONEL GAUGE

EVERY LIONEL "O" GAUGE TRAIN HAS ELECTRIC COUPLERS

—and Any Outfit Can Be Obtained with a Built-in Locomotive Whistle

LIONEL is the one and only builder of trains able to give you all the thrilling, exciting, action features that have been invented for *remote control operation* of the model railroad. Every one of these developments is included in this year's great, new fleet of Lionel "O" gauge outfits:

built-in electric couplers;
built-in locomotive whistles;
freight cars that unload electrically,
electric, remote control train reversing.

But, railroading with Lionel "O" gauge trains has even more than these new, amazing remote control features. It is the enthusiastic first choice of men and boys everywhere because it includes:

scale-proportioned, fully detailed engines;
all-steel, enameled cars; illuminated Pullmans;
faultless, time-tested, heavy duty motors;
patented, non-derailing, electric switches;

Even more important – in "O" gauge there are Lionel signals, semaphores, crossing gates, stations, bridges, tunnels and everything else that is needed to assemble a modern, completely equipped railroad system.

This is the reason why boys throughout America are now using more Lionel Electric Trains than all other makes combined. It is also the reason why "O" gauge is more popular than any other size or style.

Millions of Lionel locomotives have, in nearly forty years, been operated many millions of miles. Out of this vast experience has come a Lionel motor design of incomparable excellence – sturdy, rugged, powerful – built with as much engineering forethought as if it were to drive a real engine and be responsible for the safety of real passengers. A cut-away illustration and description of the motor appears on the following page.

"O" gauge locomotives are accurate, authentic copies of real railroad equipment, made from real railroad blueprints. There is no skimping of detail and no crude, unfinished abbreviations. Every pipe or handrail is in its place and every pump, seam or rivet head as clean, sharp and clearly defined as if it were cut with a jeweler's tool.

Lionel "O" gauge cars are all-steel and finished in rich, lustrous enamel that is baked in by a secret, intense-heat process. Colors will not chip, check or fade.

The word "gauge" is used to indicate the distance between the running rails of track. The word "scale" describes the proportion of the model to the original.

"O" gauge is 1¼ inches. The gauge of real track in America is 56½ inches. "O" gauge is therefore approximately one forty-eighth actual size – a quarter-inch in the model being equal to a foot in the original. It is commonly called "quarter-inch scale". Eight sections of Lionel "O" gauge track form a circle occupying a space 30⅞ inches square.

If you have sufficient room for building an "O" gauge railroad with all the loops and switches and sidings you want it to have, then by all means choose "O" gauge. In this catalog are "O" gauge outfits of every type, style and price. There is one to fit your needs—exactly.

1939 CATALOG

1722 TYPE II

VG	EX	LN	RARITY
20	30	40	2

1682 (Type II): In 1935, nickel journal boxes replaced the copper ones. The balance of the car was unchanged.

VG	EX	LN	RARITY
20	30	40	2

1682 (Type III): In 1936, the body and roof began to be medium red. Its windows and cupola stripe were cream. The car continued to have Lionel Lines markings and nickel journal boxes.

VG	EX	LN	RARITY
20	30	40	2

1682 (Type IV): In 1937-39, the car had a medium red body and roof, no cupola stripe, cream windows, Lionel Lines markings and nickel journal boxes.

VG	EX	LN	RARITY
20	30	40	2

1682 (Type V): During 1940-41, the cabooses were built with medium red bodies and roofs, no cupola stripes and black journal boxes. The windows were cream and the car had Lionel Lines markings and a box coupler.

VG	EX	LN	RARITY
20	30	40	2

1682 (Type VI): Also in 1940, the caboose was made with a tuscan body and roof, with terracotta windows. These cars had New York Central markings, no cupola stripe, black journal boxes and a latch coupler.

VG	EX	LN	RARITY
20	30	40	2

1682 (Type VII): Box couplers were used in 1940-41 on some of the cars with tuscan bodies and roofs. These cars had terracotta windows, New York Central markings, no cupola stripe and black journal boxes.

VG	EX	LN	RARITY
20	30	40	2

1682X: This number was assigned to caboose variants that had either no journal boxes or two couplers. Because this variation is easily manufactured in the aftermarket, the box is critical for authentication.

VG	EX	LN	RARITY
30	45	60	4

1722 (Type I): Produced 1933-34, this orange caboose had a maroon roof, and copper journal boxes.

VG	EX	LN	RARITY
20	30	40	2

1722 (Type II): From 1935 through 1940, nickel journal boxes were used on the orange cars with maroon roofs.

VG	EX	LN	RARITY
20	30	40	2

1722 (Type III): Also built in 1935-40 were light red cabooses. They too had maroon roofs and nickel journal boxes.

VG	EX	LN	RARITY
20	30	40	2

1722 (Type IV): During 1940, a light red caboose was made. It had a maroon roof and black journal boxes.

VG	EX	LN	RARITY
20	30	40	2

1722 (Type IV): The color of the body changed to orange-red in 1941-42, although it continued to have a maroon roof and black journal boxes.

VG	EX	LN	RARITY
20	30	40	2

1722X: Sold in 1939-1940, this caboose had an orange-red body, maroon roof and black journal boxes.

VG	EX	LN	RARITY
20	30	40	2

2657 (Type I): In 1938, Lionel began making this light red caboose with cream windows. It had an aluminum railing, nickel journal boxes and nickel plates.

VG	EX	LN	RARITY
15	22	30	1

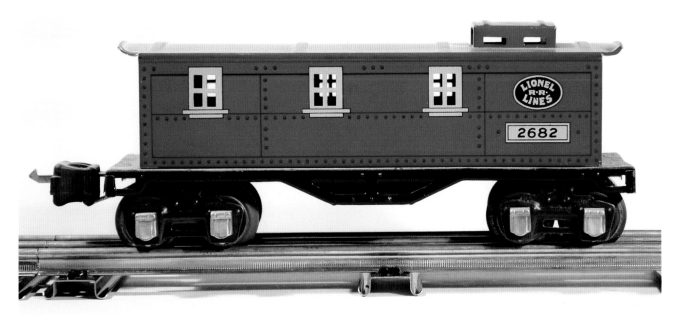

2682 Type I

2657 (Type II): The journal boxes became black in 1939. Cars continued to be made with bodies painted light red, cream windows, aluminum railings and nickel plates.

VG	EX	LN	RARITY
15	22	30	1

2657 (Type III): Some of the cars were painted light red, with white windows, light red railing, black journal boxes and nickel plates. It is believed these were 1939 production.

VG	EX	LN	RARITY
15	22	30	1

2657 (Type IV): Some cars were made from 1940-1942 with very light red bodies, tuscan roofs, white windows and light red railings. Their trucks had black journal boxes. Notably, the markings were rubber-stamped on the body, rather than having separately applied plates.

VG	EX	LN	RARITY
15	22	30	1

2657X (Type I): This light red caboose had cream windows, aluminum railings, nickel journal boxes and nickel plates. It was equipped with electrocouplers for use with switcher sets during 1938.

VG	EX	LN	RARITY
20	30	40	2

2657X (Type II): For 1939, the 2657X caboose packed in switcher sets was changed slightly. Still light red, it had white windows, light red railings, black journal boxes, nickel plates and electrocouplers.

VG	EX	LN	RARITY
20	30	40	2

2657X (Type III): The 1940-42 switcher sets included a very light red caboose with tuscan roof and white windows. Its markings were rubber-stamped on the body, rather than using plates, and it had light red railings, black journal boxes and electrocouplers.

VG	EX	LN	RARITY
20	30	40	2

2672: More realistic appearing than most of Lionel's prewar cabooses, this 1942 Pennsylvania unit was painted tuscan. It did not have separately installed window frames, smokejack or steps.

VG	EX	LN	RARITY
20	30	40	2

2682 (Type I): First appearing in the 1938 catalog, this caboose was finished in medium red. Its roof matched the body, and it had cream windows and cupola stripes. Its trucks had nickel journal boxes and at the front an automatic coupler was installed. It ran again unchanged in 1939.

VG	EX	LN	RARITY
15	22	30	1

2682 (Type II): In 1940, the cupola stripe was eliminated and the journal boxes became black. This version continued through 1941.

VG	EX	LN	RARITY
15	22	30	1

O GAUGE CABOOSES

Price Guide Key: **VG** = Very Good, **EX** = Excellent, **LN** = Like New | *Values for each condition are in U.S. dollars.* | **Rarity** = Scale from 1-8 with 8 being the hardest to find.

193

2757

2682 (Type III): Another version made in 1940-41 had New York Central markings rather than Lionel Lines. Even more noticeable, rather than red, it had a tuscan body and roof, terracotta windows, black journal boxes and automatic coupler.

VG	EX	LN	RARITY
15	22	30	1

2682X: Included with some 1940-41 switcher sets was this caboose with two automatic couplers. It had a medium red body and roof, no cupola stripe, cream windows and black journal boxes.

VG	EX	LN	RARITY
20	30	40	2

2722 (Type I): For its first two years, 1938-39, this car had an orange-red body, maroon roof and nickel journal boxes.

VG	EX	LN	RARITY
20	30	45	2

2722 (Type II): During 1940-42, black journal boxes were used on its trucks.

VG	EX	LN	RARITY
20	30	45	2

2757: Part of Lionel's effort to make more realistic looking trains was this 1941-1942 tuscan caboose with Pennsylvania markings. Separately installed steps, smokejack and red window frames decorated the car.

VG	EX	LN	RARITY
20	30	45	2

2757X: Essentially the same as the 1941-1942 2757, this car differs by having automatic box couplers on both ends. It requires box for full value.

VG	EX	LN	RARITY
30	45	60	4

2817 (Type I): This 1938-39 caboose came with a light red body, roof and cupola, aluminum windows, aluminum painted rails, nickel journal boxes and nickel plates.

VG	EX	LN	RARITY
75	100	125	4

2817 (Type II): In 1940, the color scheme was changed. It then had a flat red body, brown roof and cupola. The windows were white and the railings flat red. Nickel journal boxes and nickel plates continued to be used.

VG	EX	LN	RARITY
300	450	600	7

2817 (Type III): Later in 1940, the plates were eliminated in favor of heat-stamped markings directly on the flat red body.

2957

These cars also had a brown roof and cupola, white windows, flat red rails and nickel journal boxes.

VG	EX	LN	RARITY
100	200	300	6

2817 (Type IV): Essentially the same as the rubber-stamped 1940 cars, those shipped during 1941-42 had black journal boxes in lieu of the nickel ones previously installed.

VG	EX	LN	RARITY
100	200	300	6

2957: This large caboose, offered 1940-42, was essentially the scale caboose with box couplers and conventional trucks installed.

VG	EX	LN	RARITY
125	250	400	5

O GAUGE CABOOSES

Price Guide Key: **VG** = Very Good, **EX** = Excellent, **LN** = Like New | *Values for each condition are in U.S. dollars.* | **Rarity** = Scale from 1-8 with 8 being the hardest to find.

195

CHAPTER 18
O GAUGE DERRICK & CRANE CARS

Just as had been the case first with 2 7/8-inch gauge trains and later Standard Gauge trains, a derrick or crane car was added to Lionel's 0 gauge line. These cars provided youthful railroaders an opportunity to interact directly with the trains.

810 (Type I): When introduced in 1930, the 810 derrick was finished in terra cotta with cream windows. The car had brass identification plates and rode on trucks with nickel journal boxes. Two brass-finished and one nickel-finished knobs controlled the derrick's movements.

VG	EX	LN	RARITY
175	210	250	6

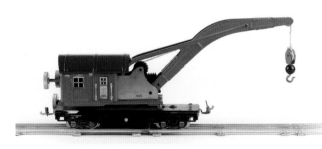

810 (Type II): The following year, the derrick cab continued to be painted terra cotta, but the window inserts were now made of brass, like the nameplates. Two brass-finished and one nickel-finished knobs controlled the derrick's movements.

VG	EX	LN	RARITY
175	210	250	6

810 (Type III): From 1932 through 1934, the coloration of the 810 was unchanged. However, the journal boxes on its trucks were now copper-finished rather than nickel. All three control knobs were now nickel-finished.

VG	EX	LN	RARITY
150	175	225	5

810 (Type IV): In 1935, the color of the derrick cab became cream and its roof was finished in vermilion. The boom, which previously had been painted peacock, now was covered with the same light green enamel that was used on the base of the 45N gateman. The windows were now nickeled and the control knobs were black. Nickel journal boxes returned to use on the trucks.

VG	EX	LN	RARITY
125	150	175	4

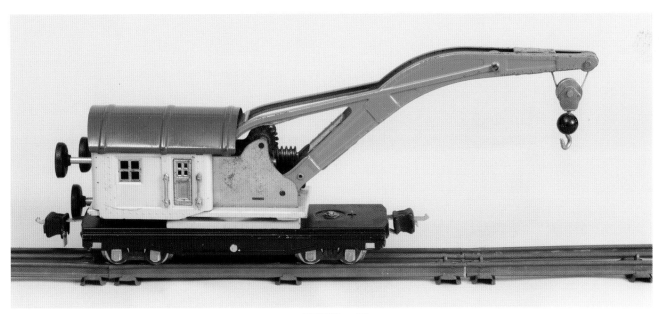

2810 TYPE II

810 (Type V): In 1938, light red replaced vermilion for the roof color, though the rest of the colors and trim were unchanged. This scheme was repeated in 1939.

VG	EX	LN	RARITY
125	150	175	3

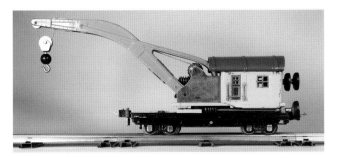

810 (Type VI): In 1940, the cab of the derrick began to be painted in yellow, the color that would be used through the end of production. The roof continued to be red and the boom light green.

VG	EX	LN	RARITY
175	210	250	6

810 (Type VII): During 1941 and 1942, black journal boxes replaced the nickel-finished ones that had been in use since 1935.

VG	EX	LN	RARITY
175	210	250	5

2660 (Type I): Offered from 1938-42, this crane had a cream cab with a red roof. Its two-part boom was unpainted green plastic.

VG	EX	LN	RARITY
60	75	100	4

2660 (Type II): Some of the cranes came with booms painted green.

VG	EX	LN	RARITY
60	75	100	4

2660 (Type III): Some of the cranes were equipped with two-piece booms made of unpainted black plastic. This is not the same style boom used on postwar 2460/6460/6560 cranes. This version is usually found with black journal boxes.

VG	EX	LN	RARITY
60	75	100	4

2810 (Type I): First offered in 1938, the 2810 had a cream cab and light red roof. Its boom was the same light green enamel that was used on the base of the 45N gateman. The windows were nickel finished and the control knobs were black. Nickel journal boxes were used on the trucks. This scheme was repeated in 1939.

VG	EX	LN	RARITY
175	210	250	5

2810 (Type II): In 1940, the cab of the derrick began to be painted in yellow, the color that would be used through the end of production. The roof continued to be red and the boom light green.

VG	EX	LN	RARITY
185	225	275	6

2810 (Type III): During 1941 and 1942, black journal boxes replaced the nickel-finished ones that had been in use since the 2810 was introduced.

VG	EX	LN	RARITY
175	210	250	5

O GAUGE DERRICK & CRANE CARS

Price Guide Key: **VG** = Very Good, **EX** = Excellent, **LN** = Like New | *Values for each condition are in U.S. dollars.* | **Rarity** = Scale from 1-8 with 8 being the hardest to find.

197

CAR LOADING AND UNLOADING

For track to operate the electric, tilting dump car, see Pages 32 and 33.

Other detail pictures of the Coal Elevator will be found on Page 19.

ELECTRIC, REMOTE CONTROL COAL ELEVATOR

No. 97. At last, Lionel has created an accessory which will actually load model freight cars by remote control! Imitation coal placed in a well in the base of this structure is scooped up by a series of buckets traveling on an endless chain. The chain-conveyor lifts the buckets to the top of building where they are turned upside down, dumping their contents into the loft. The remote controls that are provided contain two hand levers. One lever controls the electric motor which operates the endless chain. The other lever opens and closes a gate in the loft. When the gate is opened, the contents of the loft pour down through a chute into your waiting freight car. With each elevator, a half pound of imitation coal is included. Height 12 inches. Base, 6 by 11½ inches. **Price $5.95**

No. 96. Similar to No. 97, but with endless-chain buckets operated by means of hand crank. The gate in loft, however, is opened and shut electrically, by remote control. **Price $3.95**

A SACK OF IMITATION COAL

With each coal elevator and electric dump car, a sack of realistic, imitation coal is included. Not only does this imitation coal provide remarkable resemblance to the real thing, but it is also easy to handle and dustless. Be sure to obtain extra quantities, for no real railroad ever runs low on coal and your surplus can be used as packaged freight and to form realistic coal piles. **Price $.25**
No. 206 Half pound of imitation coal.

With every electric, remote control dump car an unloading bin is included. The bin is made of moulded plastic and has a permanent finish.

ELECTRICALLY OPERATED REMOTE CONTROL DUMP CARS

No. 3659. Car body can be tilted by electric, remote control, for discharging its contents into an unloading bin alongside the track. Must be used with R.C.S. or No. 1019 controlling track described on Pages 32 and 33. Car is also equipped with electric couplers which can be actuated from a distance by the same R.C.S. track and controls. With each car is packed one unloading bin, pictured above, and one quarter pound of imitation coal. The electric dump car is a fascinating addition for any "O" gauge or "027" series outfits. Length 6¾ inches. For use with "027" cars and with the 2650 series of "O" gauge freight cars. **Price $3.25**

No. 3859. Similar to No. 3659 but 8⅞ inches long. Equipped with electric, remote control couplers. For use with the 2800 series freight cars. **Price $4.25**

No. 188 "O" GAUGE COAL ELEVATOR, CAR AND TRACK SET. Consists of one No. 97 Coal elevator, operated by means of built-in electric motor; one No. 3659 Electric, tilting dump car; one section of R.C.S. Special control track; one No. 160 Unloading bin; one No. 206 half pound sack of imitation coal. **Price $10.75**

1938 CATALOG

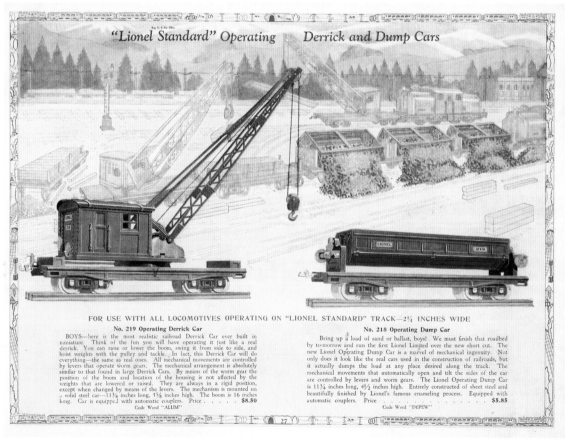

"Lionel Standard" Operating Derrick and Dump Cars

FOR USE WITH ALL LOCOMOTIVES OPERATING ON "LIONEL STANDARD" TRACK—2¼ INCHES WIDE

No. 219 Operating Derrick Car

BOYS—here is the most realistic railroad Derrick Car ever built in miniature. Think of the fun you will have operating it just like a real derrick. You can raise or lower the boom, swing it from side to side, and hoist weights with the pulley and tackle. In fact, this Derrick Car will do everything—the same as real ones. All mechanical movements are controlled by levers that operate worm gears. The mechanical arrangement is absolutely similar to that found in large Derrick Cars. By means of the worm gear the position of the boom and location of the housing is not affected by the weights that are lowered or raised. They are always in a rigid position, except when changed by means of the levers. The mechanism is mounted on a solid steel car—11¾ inches long, 5⅜ inches high. The boom is 16 inches long. Car is equipped with automatic couplers. Price **$8.50**
Code Word "ALUM"

No. 218 Operating Dump Car

Bring up a load of sand or ballast, boys! We must finish that roadbed by to-morrow and run the first Lionel Limited over the new short cut. The new Lionel Operating Dump Car is a marvel of mechanical ingenuity. Not only does it look like the real cars used in the construction of railroads, but it actually dumps the load at any place desired along the track. The mechanical movements that automatically open and tilt the sides of the car are controlled by levers and worm gears. The Lionel Operating Dump Car is 11¾ inches long, 4½ inches high. Entirely constructed of sheet steel and beautifully finished by Lionel's famous enameling process. Equipped with automatic couplers. Price **$5.85**
Code Word "DEPEW"

1927 CATALOG

CHAPTER 19
O GAUGE FLAT & SEARCHLIGHT CARS

The success of the flat car, both from a manufacturing economy and from a play value standpoint in Lionel's Standard Gauge line, meant its inclusion in the new 0 gauge system was a sure thing. Similarly, their adaptation for use as searchlight cars was assured as well.

Today, flat cars, like gondolas, are often found in a well-worn condition. Youngsters could allow their imaginations to work with these cars and twigs, toy trucks and metal soldiers all are known to have gotten train rides. Sometimes bits of paint were unloaded with the cargo as well.

VG	EX	LN	RARITY
50	65	85	3

620 Searchlight Car (Type II): In 1939, though the rest of the car was unchanged, black journal boxes began to be used. This configuration lasted only one year.

VG	EX	LN	RARITY
50	65	85	3

620 Searchlight Car (Type III): In 1940, the light housing began to be painted gray. The red body and black journals were continued. Now the brake stand was black as well. This version of the car continued to be shipped through 1942.

VG	EX	LN	RARITY
70	90	125	5

620 Searchlight Car (Type I): As introduced in 1937 and continued in 1938, this car had a red body and nickel journal boxes. Attached to the body was an aluminum-colored illuminated searchlight.

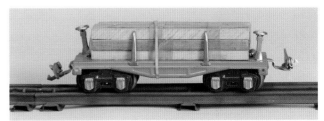

Price Guide Key: **VG** = Very Good, **EX** = Excellent, **LN** = Like New | *Values for each condition are in U.S. dollars.* | **Rarity** = Scale from 1-8 with 8 being the hardest to find.

199

651 Flat Car: This car, with its two four-wheeled trucks and latch couplers, was a staple of the Lionel line through the latter half of the 1930s.

651 Flat Car (Type I): From 1935 through 1938, this green flat car was equipped with nickel journal boxes.

VG	EX	LN	RARITY
20	30	45	2

651 Flat Car (Type II): During 1939, its journal boxes began to be black, but its body remained green.

VG	EX	LN	RARITY
25	35	50	3

651 Flat Car (Type III): The final production of the car had black brake stands as well as journal boxes.

VG	EX	LN	RARITY
25	35	50	3

811 Flat Car (Type I): As introduced in 1926, this car had a maroon body. Along its sides were brass stakes, acting as if they were restraining its load of lumber. The load, in reality, was a single block milled to represent individual timbers. The brake stands and journal boxes were nickel.

VG	EX	LN	RARITY
35	45	60	2

811 Flat Car (Type II): In 1931, the flat car got a makeover. Its body was now painted an aluminum color and its journal boxes changed to copper. The brass stakes, block load and nickel brake stands were retained, however.

VG	EX	LN	RARITY
60	75	100	4

811 Flat Car (Type III): Some of the aluminum-colored cars shipped in 1931 had nickel stakes. The other details were the same as those listed for type II.

VG	EX	LN	RARITY
60	75	100	4

811 Flat Car (Type IV): Cars shipped beginning in 1932 continued to be aluminum-colored and have nickel stakes and copper journal boxes, but the brake stands were changed to brass.

VG	EX	LN	RARITY
60	75	100	4

811 Flat Car (Type V): In 1935, many of the details of the aluminum-colored car changed again. The journal boxes as well as the brake stands reverted to nickel, matching the stakes. The load was composed of individual beams, rather than a solid block. This configuration was continued through 1939.

VG	EX	LN	RARITY
60	75	100	4

811 Flat Car (Type VI): From 1940 through 1942, the journal boxes of the 811 were finished in black. The balance of the car was unchanged.

VG	EX	LN	RARITY
60	75	100	4

820 Searchlight Car: This car was a part of the Lionel product line from 1931 until shipments of trains stopped in 1942 due to World War II. The car always had a black body, onto which was mounted a subfloor supporting twin searchlights. Its dual light assembly was also adapted for use on the Standard Gauge 220 searchlight car.

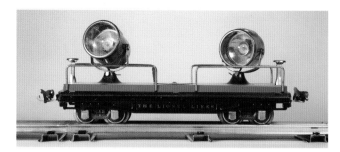

820 Searchlight Car (Type I): The version of the car that entered production in 1931 had a terra-cotta light base and brass searchlights. The trucks had copper journals, and latch couplers were provided. This version remained in production through 1934.

VG	EX	LN	RARITY
100	125	160	3

820 Searchlight Car (Type II): In 1935, several changes were made to the car. The color of the subbase changed to light green and manual box couplers replaced the latch couplers. Nickel-finished lights and journal boxes replaced those previously used. The car ran unchanged through 1937.

VG	EX	LN	RARITY
100	125	160	3

820 Searchlight Car (Type III): A lighter green base, along with nickel lights and nickel journals, was used in 1938. Box couplers began to be used on the 820 at this time.

VG	EX	LN	RARITY
125	160	200	4

820 Searchlight Car (Type IV): Gray die-cast lights and black journal boxes began to be used in 1939. The light green base and box couplers were continued.

VG	EX	LN	RARITY
200	350	600	7

831: Inexpensive to make, this small, four-wheeled flat car was part of Lionel's cataloged product line from 1927 through 1934, and was included in uncataloged sets from 1935 through 1942. The cars came with nickel posts and a block of wood milled to look like eight pieces of lumber.

831 Flat Car (Type I): The 1927 edition of the car was painted black and had no journal boxes.

VG	EX	LN	RARITY
75	110	150	6

831 Flat Car (Type II): In 1928, the color of the car changed to dark green and it continued to be produced without journal boxes.

VG	EX	LN	RARITY
75	110	150	6

831 Flat Car (Type III): From 1928 through 1931, the car continued to be dark green, but now it featured nickel journal boxes.

VG	EX	LN	RARITY
20	30	40	2

831 Flat Car (Type IV): Between 1932 and 1934, the journal boxes were copper, although the car was still painted dark green.

VG	EX	LN	RARITY
20	30	40	2

831 Flat Car (Type V): A pale green car with nickel journal boxes was produced in 1935.

VG	EX	LN	RARITY
20	30	40	2

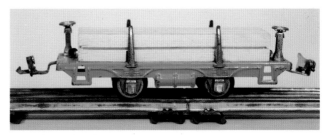

831 Flat Car (Type VI): Also introduced in 1935 was a car painted 45N green. It had nickel journal boxes as well.

VG	EX	LN	RARITY
20	30	40	2

831 Flat Car (Type VII): Dark green returned in 1940, only at this time journal boxes were changed to black. This car was included in some uncataloged sets through 1942.

VG	EX	LN	RARITY
20	30	40	2

2620 Searchlight Car (Type I): First offered in 1938, the 2620 differed from the 620 by having automatic box couplers instead of latch couplers. Like the 620, the 2620 had a red body and nickel journal boxes. Attached to the body was an aluminum-colored illuminated searchlight.

VG	EX	LN	RARITY
50	80	120	3

2620 Searchlight Car (Type II): In 1939, though the rest of the car was unchanged, black journal boxes began to be used. This configuration lasted only one year.

VG	EX	LN	RARITY
50	80	120	3

2620 Searchlight Car (Type III): In 1940, the light housing began to be painted gray. The red body and black journals were continued. Now the brake stand was black as well. This version of the car continued to be shipped through 1942.

VG	EX	LN	RARITY
80	110	150	5

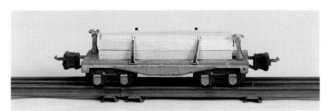

2651 (Type I): In 1938, this green flat car was equipped with nickel journal boxes and electric box couplers. Its four nickel stakes retained a block of wood which had been milled to simulate a lumber load.

VG	EX	LN	RARITY
25	35	50	2

2651 (Type II): During 1939, its journal boxes began to be black, but its body remained green.

VG	EX	LN	RARITY
25	35	50	2

2651 (Type III): In 1940, black paint began to be used on the body. It had black journals and black brake stands.

VG	EX	LN	RARITY
50	75	115	5

Price Guide Key: **VG** = Very Good, **EX** = Excellent, **LN** = Like New | *Values for each condition are in U.S. dollars.* | **Rarity** = Scale from 1-8 with 8 being the hardest to find.

201

2811 (Type I): Introduced in 1938, this aluminum-colored flat car differed from the 811 by being equipped with box couplers. The journal boxes as well as the brake stands were nickel, matching the stakes. The load was composed of individual beams. This configuration was continued again in 1939.

VG	EX	LN	RARITY
65	95	135	6

2811 (Type II): Cars shipped from 1940 through 1942 had black rather than nickel journal boxes. The rest of the car was unchanged.

VG	EX	LN	RARITY
65	95	135	6

2820 (Type I): A light green base, along with nickel lights, nickel journals and electromagnetic couplers were used on this 1938 searchlight car.

VG	EX	LN	RARITY
125	175	225	4

2820 (Type II): Gray die-cast lights began to be used in 1939, as were black journal boxes. The light green base and electromagnetic couplers were continued.

VG	EX	LN	RARITY
200	275	350	6

2820 (Type III): In 1940, solenoid couplers began to be used. Cars so equipped, and having light green base, gray die-cast lights and black journal boxes, continued to be shipped into 1942.

VG	EX	LN	RARITY
200	275	350	6

3651 (Type I): This black log dump car was introduced in 1939. Its dump mechanism was activated by use of Lionel's special electric uncoupling track section. It had nickel stakes and black journal boxes. Two ridges ran the length of the top of its box couplers.

VG	EX	LN	RARITY
20	35	60	2

3651 (Type II): Beginning in 1940, and continuing through the end of the 3651's production, the top of the coupler box was cast to resemble a railroad knuckle coupler.

VG	EX	LN	RARITY
20	35	60	2

3811 (Type I): Also introduced in 1939 was this black operating log dump car with couplers the correct height to match the 2810 series cars. The tops of its coupler boxes had two ridges running their length.

VG	EX	LN	RARITY
35	50	80	3

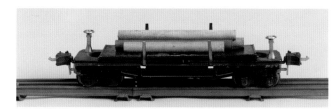

3811 (Type II): From 1940 through 1942, the tops of the coupler boxes were cast to look like actual railroad couplers.

VG	EX	LN	RARITY
35	50	80	3

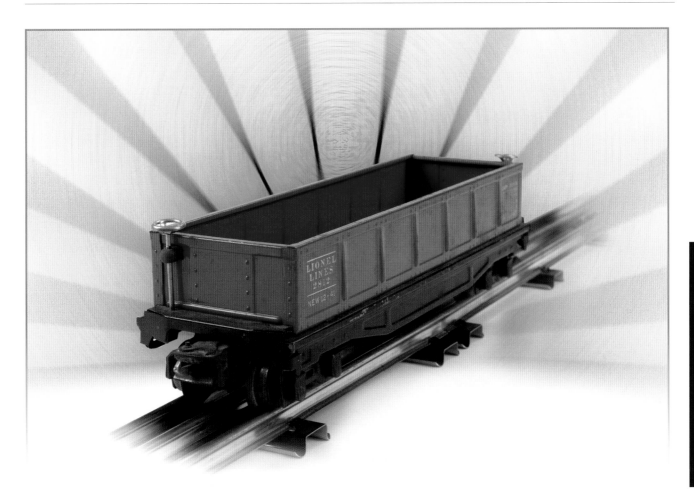

CHAPTER 20
O GAUGE GONDOLA & ORE DUMP CARS

The ubiquitous gondola was produced in a variety of colors and designs during the prewar era. This is hardly surprising, as these cars were included in the majority of 0 gauge freight outfits offered during this time. While the designs of these cars are considered boring by some collectors today, and the majority of these are so common even 60 years since the newest was made they can still be bought inexpensively, their inclusion in these outfits was a shrewd marketing maneuver. As original owners of these trains recall playing with the trains in their youth, with a smile crossing their weathered faces, the common gondola is often mentioned. Marbles became payload to be hauled to distant cities, rocks, sneaked into the house, formed cargo transported from quarries of their imaginations. Lead soldiers defended freedom protected by the bulwark of the car sides. The humble gondola was a fertile field for children's play. The scratched and battered appearance of many of these cars today give mute testimony to their storied past.

652: The 652 gondola was a fixture in the Lionel catalog from 1935 through 1942. Though its body was variously painted yellow or orange, it always had a black frame.

652 Gondola (Type I): From 1935 through 1937, the body of the gondola was painted yellow. Nickel identification plates were installed in the sides of the body and nickel brake stands on each end. The journal boxes were also nickel. Latch couplers were used.

VG	EX	LN	RARITY
25	35	50	2

652 Gondola (Type II): In 1938 and 1939, box couplers equipped the car, which was otherwise unchanged.

VG	EX	LN	RARITY
25	35	50	2

652 Gondola (Type III): A minor change was made to the yellow car in 1940, when the journal boxes began to be black.

VG	EX	LN	RARITY
25	35	50	2

Price Guide Key: **VG** = Very Good, **EX** = Excellent, **LN** = Like New | *Values for each condition are in U.S. dollars.* | **Rarity** = Scale from 1-8 with 8 being the hardest to find.

203

652 GONDOLA TYPE IV

652 Gondola (Type IV):  A new color, orange, was also introduced in 1940. In addition to having black journal boxes, these cars also had black brake stands. But, second to the change in color, the most noticeable change was the use of rubber-stamped lettering instead of the previously used nickel plates. This car continued to be available through 1942.

VG	EX	LN	RARITY
25	35	50	3

659 Ore Dump (Type I): This manually operated ore dump car had a black frame and dark green ore dump bin. From 1935 through 1938, it had nickel journal boxes and brake stands, and was equipped with latch couplers.

VG	EX	LN	RARITY
50	60	75	4

659 Ore Dump (Type II): In late 1938, black journal boxes began to be used on the cars. The rest of the car was unchanged.

VG	EX	LN	RARITY
50	60	75	5

659 Ore Dump (Type III): In 1940, the color of the brakestands changed to black, matching the journal boxes. The dump bin continued to be dark green and the frame of the car was painted black.

VG	EX	LN	RARITY
50	60	75	5

659 Ore Dump (Type IV): Box couplers replaced the latch couplers for the last two years of this model's life, 1941-42. The rest of the car was the same as it had been in 1940.

VG	EX	LN	RARITY
50	60	75	5

809 Dump Car: This small dump car was part of the inexpensive series of four-wheel 0 gauge freight cars Lionel debuted in the 1920s. However, the 809 itself was a late addition, not entering the line until 1930.

809 Dump Car (Type I): When initially offered, the car had a black frame and an orange manually tilted dump body. The car had nickel journal boxes and nickel-plated wheels.

VG	EX	LN	RARITY
50	60	75	5

809 Dump Car (Type II): In 1932, copper journal boxes were used rather than nickel ones, but the rest of the car continued unchanged.

VG	EX	LN	RARITY
50	60	75	5

809 Dump Car (Type III): New in 1932 was a car with a green dump bin. Like its orange-binned counterpart, it had copper journal boxes and nickeled wheels.

VG	EX	LN	RARITY
60	70	85	5

809 Dump Car (Type IV): Some of the cars produced in 1932 with green dump bins had nickel journal boxes and nickeled wheels.

VG	EX	LN	RARITY
60	70	85	5

809 Dump Car (Type V): Strangely, the green dump car returned in 1932. While it still had nickel journal boxes, it now came with black wheels.

VG	EX	LN	RARITY
60	70	85	5

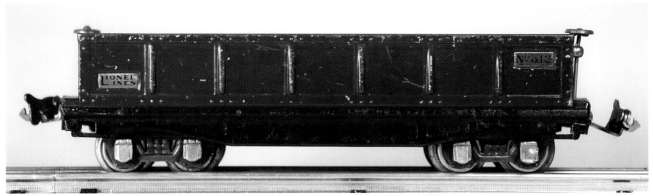

652 GONDOLA TYPE IV

812 GONDOLA TYPE IV

O GAUGE GONDOLA & ORE DUMP CARS

812 Gondola (Type I): Wearing a mojave paint scheme, this gondola with its brass plates and nickel journal boxes graced the pages of Lionel's catalogs every year from 1926 through 1930. Latch couplers allowed this to connect to the rest of the train.

VG	EX	LN	RARITY
50	60	75	4

812 Gondola (Type II): Between 1931 and 1935, the mojave gondola had copper journal boxes. The brass plates and latch couplers, however, continued to be used.

VG	EX	LN	RARITY
50	60	75	4

812 Gondola (Type III): 🔲 Added to the line in 1927 was a dark green version of the 812. Until 1931, it came with brass plates, nickel journal boxes and latch couplers.

VG	EX	LN	RARITY
25	35	45	3

812 Gondola (Type IV): 🔲 The journal boxes on the dark green were changed to copper in 1931. The car continued to be so equipped, along with sporting brass plates and latch couplers, through 1934.

VG	EX	LN	RARITY
25	35	45	3

812 Gondola (Type V): A third color, Stephen Girard green, began to be used on the 812 in 1931. Like its mojave and dark green counterparts, it had brass plates, copper journal boxes and latch couplers.

VG	EX	LN	RARITY
60	75	100	6

812 Gondola (Type VI): The 812 debuted in a new color, the same shade of light green as used on the base of 45N gateman, in 1935. This car had nickel journal boxes and latch couplers.

VG	EX	LN	RARITY
35	45	60	4

812 Gondola (Type VII): In 1936, box couplers began to be installed on the 45N green gondola. It continued in this form, with nickel journal boxes on its trucks, through 1940.

VG	EX	LN	RARITY
35	45	60	4

812 Gondola (Type VIII): A number of changes were made in 1941. The body began to be painted dark orange and the markings were now rubber-stamped in white directly on the body of the car. Black journal boxes and brake wheels began to be used as well. Cars like this were available again in 1942.

VG	EX	LN	RARITY
60	75	100	6

Price Guide Key: **VG** = Very Good, **EX** = Excellent, **LN** = Like New | *Values for each condition are in U.S. dollars.* | **Rarity** = Scale from 1-8 with 8 being the hardest to find.

205

902 GONDOLA TYPE V

901 Gondola (Type I): Believed to have been produced in 1917, this brown four-wheeled gondola was rubber-stamped "LAKE SHORE" in black. No journal boxes were installed on this car.

VG	EX	LN	RARITY
60	75	100	6

901 Gondola (Type II): Cars painted maroon are believed to have been built during 1918. These cars were also rubber-stamped "LAKE SHORE" in black.

VG	EX	LN	RARITY
35	45	60	4

901 Gondola (Type III): Also believed to have been made in 1918 was a 901 painted gray and rubber-stamped "LAKE SHORE" in gold. These cars also had the number 901 rubber-stamped on each end.

VG	EX	LN	RARITY
35	45	60	4

901 Gondola (Type IV): Gray was also the choice for the body color of a car rubber-stamped "PENNSYLVANIA". Believed to have been made in 1918, the rubber-stamped lettering, including the 901 on the ends, was stamped in gold.

VG	EX	LN	RARITY
35	45	60	4

901 Gondola (Type V): Between 1919 and 1927, the 901 was produced in various shades of green. These cars were rubber-stamped "LAKE SHORE" in black.

VG	EX	LN	RARITY
35	45	60	4

902 Gondola (Type I): Introduced in 1927, the 902 like the previous 901 had only four wheels. However, it was larger and

had considerably more detail. As first produced, it was painted dark green and had no journal boxes.

VG	EX	LN	RARITY
20	30	40	3

902 Gondola (Type II): Also introduced in 1927, but carrying over into 1928 as well, was a peacock-painted version, again with no journal boxes.

VG	EX	LN	RARITY
20	30	40	4

902 Gondola (Type III): For 1929, nickel journal boxes were added to the peacock gondola.

VG	EX	LN	RARITY
15	25	35	2

902 Gondola (Type IV): Beginning in 1930, the gondola was painted Stephen Girard green. Through 1931. it was made in the new color with nickel journal boxes.

VG	EX	LN	RARITY
20	30	40	3

902 Gondola (Type V): Sometime during 1931, copper journal boxes began to be used on the Stephen Girard green cars. This combination continued through 1935.

VG	EX	LN	RARITY
20	30	40	3

902 Gondola (Type VI): Nickel journal boxes returned to Stephen Girard green gondola for 1936, its final year of production. The frame of these cars was slightly different than previous editions.

VG	EX	LN	RARITY
20	30	40	3

1512 Gondola (Type I): This was an inexpensively produced, four-wheeled gondola built for use in Lionel's Winner line as well as for Ives sales. As produced during 1931-32, this 6" gondola had a medium blue lithographed body mounted on a black frame with black wheels.

VG	EX	LN	RARITY
5	10	20	3

1512 Gondola (Type II): Beginning in 1933, the body, still lithographed, was dark blue. The frame and wheels were still black. This version was also shipped in 1934.

VG	EX	LN	RARITY
5	10	20	3

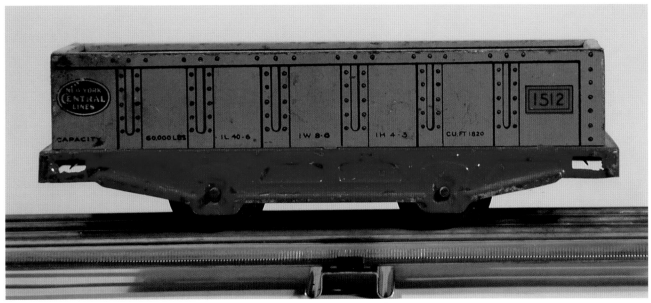

1512 GONDOLA TYPE V

1512 Gondola (Type III): Also, apparently during 1933-34, the light blue lithographed car was made with nickel-plated wheels.

VG	EX	LN	RARITY
5	10	20	3

1512 Gondola (Type IV): From 1935 through 1937, the light blue lithographed body was mounted on a red frame with nickel-plated wheels.

VG	EX	LN	RARITY
5	10	20	3

1512 Gondola (Type V): Some of the 1935-37 cars had blue-green bodies.

VG	EX	LN	RARITY
5	10	20	3

1677 Gondola (Type I): This car, added to the line in 1933, had a lithographed medium blue body and rode on two conventional trucks with copper journal boxes. It is believed that production of this version carried over into 1934 as well.

VG	EX	LN	RARITY
20	30	40	3

1677 Gondola (Type II): Also introduced in 1933-34 was this peacock lithographed gondola. Its trucks had copper journal boxes.

VG	EX	LN	RARITY
30	40	50	5

1677 Gondola (Type III): In 1935-36, the medium blue lithographed car had nickel journal boxes.

VG	EX	LN	RARITY
20	30	40	3

1677 Gondola (Type IV): From 1936 through 1938, the medium blue lithographed car had no journal boxes.

VG	EX	LN	RARITY
20	30	40	3

1677 Gondola (Type V): During 1940, the car was lithographed in dark red and equipped with black journal boxes. As with the previous versions, it was provided with latch couplers.

VG	EX	LN	RARITY
15	20	30	2

1677 Gondola (Type VI): Beginning sometime in 1940, and continuing through 1942, the dark red lithographed gondola was equipped with box couplers.

VG	EX	LN	RARITY
15	20	30	2

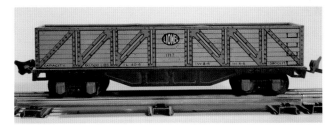

1717 Gondola (Type I): Originally marketed as part of the Ives Line, beginning in 1933 this car, with its yellow body lithographed to simulate wooden slats, was sold as a Lionel product. During the 1933-34 production, copper journal boxes were used.

VG	EX	LN	RARITY
15	25	35	4

1717 Gondola (Type II): The 1935-38 cars had nickel journal boxes, but the yellow body remained the same.

VG	EX	LN	RARITY
15	25	35	4

1717 Gondola (Type III): Black journal boxes were used on the 1939-40 production, which also was equipped with box couplers.

Price Guide Key: **VG** = Very Good, **EX** = Excellent, **LN** = Like New | *Values for each condition are in U.S. dollars.* | **Rarity** = Scale from 1-8 with 8 being the hardest to find.

207

2677 GONDOLA

VG	EX	LN	RARITY
15	25	35	4

1717X Gondola: Some of the lithographed yellow gondolas sold in 1940 were equipped with latch couplers. The boxes for these cars were marked with an X suffix.

VG	EX	LN	RARITY
30	45	60	6

2652 Gondola (Type I): As introduced in 1939, this car was identical to the yellow 652 produced the same year, except it had magnetic box couplers rather than latch couplers.

VG	EX	LN	RARITY
25	35	50	2

2652 Gondola (Type II): A minor change was made to the yellow car in 1940, when the journal boxes began to be black.

VG	EX	LN	RARITY
25	35	50	2

2652 Gondola (Type III): Major changes were also made in 1940. Cars began to be made that were painted orange and had rubber-stamped lettering in lieu of the plates previously used. These cars had black brakestands and journal boxes. They were available through 1942.

VG	EX	LN	RARITY
40	50	65	4

2659 Dump Car (Type I): Based on the 659, this car with dark green dump bin had magnetic couplers and black journal boxes when initially introduced in 1938.

VG	EX	LN	RARITY
75	100	125	7

2659 Dump Car (Type II): From 1939 through 1942, the car continued to be produced, now with solenoid-operated couplers.

VG	EX	LN	RARITY
75	100	125	6

2677 Gondola: ▉ Production of this car began in 1940 and continued through 1942. The dark red lithographed gondola was almost identical to the 1677, except it was equipped with electric box couplers.

VG	EX	LN	RARITY
35	50	70	5

2717 Gondola (Type I): This lithographed gondola was identical to the 1717, except for the couplers installed. During 1938, its first year of production, the 2717 was equipped with magnetic couplers and nickel journal boxes.

VG	EX	LN	RARITY
20	30	40	4

2717 Gondola (Type II): During the second year of production, the magnetic couplers were replaced with solenoid-operated box couplers.

VG	EX	LN	RARITY
20	30	40	4

2717 Gondola (Type III): The only change made for 1940 and later production was the use of black journal boxes on the trucks.

VG	EX	LN	RARITY
20	30	40	4

2812 Gondola (Type I): When the 2812 debuted in 1938, its body was painted the same shade of light green as used on the base of 45N gateman. The cars had nickel journal boxes and box couplers, and continued to be offered this way again the next year.

VG	EX	LN	RARITY
30	40	50	3

2812X GONDOLA TYPE II

2812 Gondola (Type II): In 1940, the car began to be painted dark orange. Nickel plates were still used, but the journal boxes were now black.

VG	EX	LN	RARITY
40	50	70	5

2812 Gondola (Type III): Rather quickly the lettering on the orange gondola began to be rubber-stamped in white rather than using the separately applied plates. This version continued to be shipped through 1942.

VG	EX	LN	RARITY
40	50	60	4

2812X Gondola (Type I): This dark orange car, produced in 1940, used black journal boxes and nickel lettering plates.

VG	EX	LN	RARITY
40	50	70	5

2812X Gondola (Type II): 🖐 Rather quickly the lettering on the orange gondola began to be rubber-stamped in white rather than using the separately applied plates. This version continued to be shipped through 1942.

VG	EX	LN	RARITY
40	50	70	5

3652 Operating Gondola (Type I): As introduced in 1939, this car had a yellow body with nickel plates and black journal boxes.

VG	EX	LN	RARITY
30	50	75	3

3652 Operating Gondola (Type II): During 1940, red rubber-stamped lettering replaced the nickel plates. The body continued to be yellow and the trucks had black journal boxes.

VG	EX	LN	RARITY
50	70	100	6

3652 Operating Gondola (Type III): Starting in 1941, the rubber-stamped lettering began to be black.

VG	EX	LN	RARITY
50	70	100	5

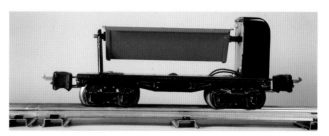

3659 Operating Dump Car (Type I): The light red dump bin of this car stood out against its black chassis. During

Price Guide Key: VG = Very Good, EX = Excellent, LN = Like New | Values for each condition are in U.S. dollars. | Rarity = Scale from 1-8 with 8 being the hardest to find.

209

O GAUGE GONDOLA & ORE DUMP CARS

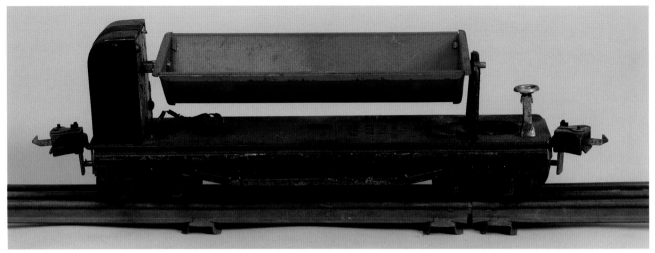

3859 OPERATING DUMP CAR TYPE III

1938, its first year of production, the 3659 was equipped with magnetic couplers and nickel journal boxes.

VG	EX	LN	RARITY
30	50	75	3

3659 Operating Dump Car (Type II): During the second year of production, the magnetic couplers were replaced with solenoid-operated box couplers.

VG	EX	LN	RARITY
30	50	75	3

3659 Operating Dump Car (Type III): The only change made for 1940 and later production was the use of black journal boxes on the trucks.

VG	EX	LN	RARITY
30	50	75	3

3859 Operating Dump Car (Type I): Introduced in 1938 was this operating dump car with couplers the correct height to match the 2810 series cars. The tops of its coupler boxes had two ridges running their length, and the trucks had nickel journal boxes. The dump bin was painted light red.

VG	EX	LN	RARITY
60	85	115	5

3859 Operating Dump Car (Type II): As was the case for the rest of Lionel's product line, the 1939 production cars had solenoid-operated couplers rather than the unreliable electromagnetically operated couplers used in 1938.

VG	EX	LN	RARITY
60	85	115	5

3859 Operating Dump Car (Type III): Those cars shipped during 1940-42 had black journal boxes.

VG	EX	LN	RARITY
60	85	115	5

CHAPTER 21
O GAUGE BOX, STOCK & REFRIGERATOR CARS

During the first half of the 20th century, boxcars were the mainstay of interstate commerce in the United States. In addition to shipping carloads of goods ranging from nails to automobiles, railroads used boxcars to move less than carload lots as well. Just as today a few odd boxes are delivered to merchants via tractor trailer, in times past those few boxes would have arrived at the local depot in a boxcar, along with goods for dozens of other merchants.

Similarly, fresh and frozen foods moved from coast to coast in refrigerator cars. Large bunkers on each end stored ice, making these cars huge iceboxes on wheels. Massive facilities in major rail yards restocked these ice bunkers.

Livestock moved in specialized railcars as well. Cattle, pigs, sheep, poultry and horses all moved by rail. Corrals were provided at trackside to allow the animals to be exercised and inspected, before being reloaded to continue their journey.

Naturally Lionel replicated cars of each of these types in 0 gauge.

655 Boxcar (Type I): For the first two years of this car's production, 1933-34, it had a cream body, maroon roof, copper journal boxes, brass plates and brass ladders.

VG	EX	LN	RARITY
30	40	55	2

655 Boxcar (Type II): Nickel journal boxes, as well as nickel plates and ladders, were introduced in 1935. Until 1938, the cream cars with maroon roofs were equipped with these details.

VG	EX	LN	RARITY
30	40	55	2

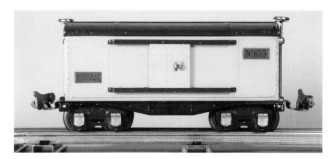

655 Boxcar (Type III): A couple of changes were made in 1939, the most noticeable of which was color of the roof

Price Guide Key: **VG** = Very Good, **EX** = Excellent, **LN** = Like New | *Values for each condition are in U.S. dollars.* | **Rarity** = Scale from 1-8 with 8 being the hardest to find.

211

656 STOCK CAR TYPE I

becoming tuscan. At the same time, the journal boxes started to be finished in black rather than nickel. The cream body, nickel plates and nickel ladders were all continued.

VG	EX	LN	RARITY
45	60	80	4

655 Boxcar (Type IV): In 1940, rubber-stamping replaced the use of plates on the cars. The color scheme of the car and its trim were unchanged.

VG	EX	LN	RARITY
45	60	80	4

655 Boxcar (Type V): When the 1941 edition of the car debuted, it had box couplers rather than the latch couplers previously used. In addition to having black journal boxes, the ladders were now black as well. Its body was cream, the roof tuscan and the markings rubber-stamped. A limited number of this version was also shipped in 1942.

VG	EX	LN	RARITY
45	60	80	4

656 Stock Car (Type I): 🖼 The body of this car, which was punched to simulate the slat-sided construction of stock cars, was painted light gray. A red roof was installed, as were latch couplers, nickel journal boxes, nickel plates and nickel ladders. The car was sold in this configuration from 1935 through 1938.

VG	EX	LN	RARITY
60	75	100	5

656 Stock Car (Type II): In 1939, the nickel journal boxes gave way to black ones, but the rest of the car was unchanged.

VG	EX	LN	RARITY
60	75	100	5

656 Stock Car (Type III): The subsequent year, 1940, saw many changes. The color of the body was now burnt orange and the roof tuscan. Rubber-stamping replaced the nickel plates. Black journal boxes and nickel ladders continued to be used.

VG	EX	LN	RARITY
75	100	140	5

656 Stock Car (Type IV): In 1941, the burnt orange car was equipped with box couplers. At the same time, the ladders became black rather than nickel. Its tuscan roof, black journal boxes and rubber-stamped markings were all unchanged.

714 Boxcar: As part of Lionel's full-scale marketing effort, this magnificently detailed scale replica of a Pennsylvania boxcar was created. Beware, many are found today with warped or replaced roof walkways. This boxcar was sold 1940 through 1942.

VG	EX	LN	RARITY
425	575	750	5

714K Boxcar: The scale boxcar was also offered as an unpainted, unassembled kit from 1940 through 1942. The unpainted kit is much more highly prized to collectors than is the assembled version, and the quality of the assembly affects the value of the ones that have been put together.

Assembled:

VG	EX	LN	RARITY
300	400	550	7

Unassembled:

VG	EX	LN	RARITY
600	1000	1500	8

802 STOCK CAR TYPE III

800 Boxcar (Type I): Introduced in 1915, this 5 1/2" long four-wheeled boxcar was painted light orange with a maroon roof. It was rubber-stamped with Wabash lettering and the number 6399 on its sides.

VG	EX	LN	RARITY
60	75	100	7

800 Boxcar (Type II): An otherwise identical car was also produced about 1915, except for its Pennsylvania lettering. The number on the sides remained 6399.

VG	EX	LN	RARITY
60	75	100	7

800 Boxcar (Type III): About 1917, the number on the boxcar changed to 4862. Although still lettered for the Pennsylvania Railroad, the paint was a slightly lighter shade of orange, with the roof painted to match. The floor of the car was marked Lionel Mfg.

VG	EX	LN	RARITY
25	40	50	5

800 Boxcar (Type IV): From 1918 through 1925, the light orange Pennsylvania boxcar with orange roof had the number "800" stamped on its end.

VG	EX	LN	RARITY
25	40	50	4

800 Boxcar (Type V): In 1926-27, the number 800 moved to the side of the car. The roof and body continued to be orange.

VG	EX	LN	RARITY
25	40	50	4

802 Stock Car (Type I): Introduced in 1915, this 5 1/2" long four-wheeled stock car was painted dark green. Lettered "UNION – STOCK – LINES", the car continued unchanged in 1916.

VG	EX	LN	RARITY
25	40	55	4

802 Stock Car (Type II): In 1917, Lionel Mfg. markings were added to the bottom of the car, which was now painted light green.

VG	EX	LN	RARITY
25	40	55	4

802 Stock Car (Type III): From 1918 through 1925, the stock car was painted medium green and had the number 802 stamped on its end. The underside markings now read Lionel Corp. rather than Mfg.

VG	EX	LN	RARITY
25	40	55	4

802 Stock Car (Type IV): In 1926-27, the number 802 moved to the side of the car. The medium green paint and "Corp." markings were unchanged.

VG	EX	LN	RARITY
25	40	55	4

805 Boxcar: This four-wheeled boxcar was produced from 1927 through 1934. During this span it was produced in a variety of colors, but it always had brass ladders and lettering plates.

805 Boxcar (Type I): Initially, this car had a pea green body, terra-cotta roof and no journal boxes.

Price Guide Key: **VG** = Very Good, **EX** = Excellent, **LN** = Like New | *Values for each condition are in U.S. dollars.* | **Rarity** = Scale from 1-8 with 8 being the hardest to find.

213

O GAUGE BOX, STOCK & REFRIGERATOR CARS

805 BOXCAR TYPE IV

VG	EX	LN	RARITY
30	45	65	4

805 Boxcar (Type II): An early variation had a cream body, orange roof and no journal boxes.

VG	EX	LN	RARITY
25	40	55	4

805 Boxcar (Type III): Some of the cars had a pea green body with maroon roof. No journal boxes were installed on these cars.

VG	EX	LN	RARITY
40	55	75	6

805 Boxcar (Type IV):  The small boxcar was also made with an orange body. These cars had a maroon roof and, not surprisingly, no journal boxes.

VG	EX	LN	RARITY
40	55	75	6

805 Boxcar (Type V): Dark pea green paint was applied to the body of some cars. These cars had orange roofs and no journal boxes.

VG	EX	LN	RARITY
20	35	50	3

805 Boxcar (Type VI): About 1929, nickel journal boxes began to be used on the dark pea green boxcars with orange roofs.

VG	EX	LN	RARITY
20	35	50	3

805 Boxcar (Type VII): Around 1931, copper journal boxes were used on some dark pea green cars with orange roofs.

VG	EX	LN	RARITY
20	35	50	3

805 Boxcar (Type VIII): More abundant, and produced through 1934, were dark pea green cars with maroon roofs and copper journal boxes.

VG	EX	LN	RARITY
20	30	45	2

806 Cattle Car: This stock car rode on four wheels from 1927 through 1934; its entire cataloged life. During this time, it was equipped with brass lettering plates as well as brass ladders.

806 Cattle Car (Type I): In 1927, the cattle car had a pea green body and terra-cotta roof. No journal boxes were installed on the car.

806 CATTLE CAR TYPE IV

VG	EX	LN	RARITY
60	90	125	6

806 Cattle Car (Type II): Also in 1927, or perhaps beginning in 1928, the car was also made with an orange body and maroon roof. No journal boxes were installed on this version either.

VG	EX	LN	RARITY
40	55	75	5

806 Cattle Car (Type III): About 1929, a pea green roof began to be used on the orange-bodied cattle car. Not as noticeable was the nickel journal boxes that were installed.

VG	EX	LN	RARITY
30	45	65	4

806 Cattle Car (Type IV):  In 1930, the roof color changed again, this time to maroon. The orange body and nickel journal boxes were unchanged into 1931.

VG	EX	LN	RARITY
30	45	65	4

806 Cattle Car (Type V): In 1931, copper journal boxes began to be mounted on the orange cattle car. A maroon roof covered the car, which was sold in this form into 1934.

VG	EX	LN	RARITY
25	40	55	4

806 Cattle Car (Type VI): Produced only in 1934 was an orange cattle car with orange roof and copper journal boxes.

VG	EX	LN	RARITY
50	65	85	6

813 Stock Car (Type I): When this stock car was introduced in 1926, it had an orange body, pea green roof, brass plates and nickel journal boxes. It continued to be produced in this form into 1931.

VG	EX	LN	RARITY
75	110	150	4

813 Stock Car (Type II): Sometime in 1931, copper journal boxes began to be installed on the trucks of the 813. This version remained in Lionel's product line through 1934.

VG	EX	LN	RARITY
75	110	150	4

813 Stock Car (Type III): In 1935, nickel journal boxes returned to the stock car, which also now had nickel plates. The body and roof continued to be orange and pea green, respectively.

VG	EX	LN	RARITY
75	110	150	4

813 Stock Car (Type IV): From 1936 through 1939, the body of the stock car was cream and its roof tuscan. The journal boxes and plates were nickel.

VG	EX	LN	RARITY
150	225	300	7

813 Stock Car (Type V): In 1940, another major facelift was given to the stock car. Both the body and roof were now

Price Guide Key: **VG** = Very Good, **EX** = Excellent, **LN** = Like New | *Values for each condition are in U.S. dollars.* | **Rarity** = Scale from 1-8 with 8 being the hardest to find.

215

814 Boxcar Type II

painted a uniform shade of tuscan. Reportedly, some of these cars were made with nickel journal boxes and nickel plates.

RARITY
Unable to establish authenticity of this variation.

813 Stock Car (Type VI): Certainly produced, but difficult to find, are the 1941-42 versions of the 813. This car was built with a tuscan body and roof, but rather than plates, this car had white rubber-stamped lettering. Black journal boxes were installed on the trucks.

VG	EX	LN	RARITY
1500	2250	3250	8

814 Boxcar (Type I): Introduced in 1926, the boxcar with cream body and orange roof would continue essentially

unchanged through 1931. Its cream doors slid in orange door guides, brass nameplates were mounted in its sides and nickel journal boxes were installed on its trucks.

VG	EX	LN	RARITY
60	90	125	3

814 Boxcar (Type II): During 1931, copper journal boxes began to replace the nickel ones used previously. Some of these cars had door guides that were painted apple green. The bodies of the cars were cream and the nameplates continued to be brass.

VG	EX	LN	RARITY
60	90	125	3

814 Boxcar (Type III): Most of the cars with copper journal boxes had orange door guides, which matched the roof. Brass nameplates were attached to the cream body. This configuration was shipped from 1931 through 1934.

VG	EX	LN	RARITY
60	90	125	3

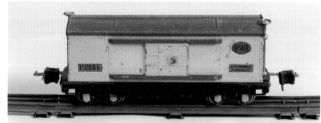

814 Boxcar (Type IV): The color scheme of the boxcar changed dramatically in 1935. The body began to be painted yellow, and a brown roof and brown door guides were installed. Brass plates continued to be used and nickel journal boxes returned.

VG	EX	LN	RARITY
75	110	150	4

814 Boxcar (Type V): From later 1935 through 1938, nickel plates were used on the yellow and brown boxcars. Nickel journal boxes were installed on these cars as well.

VG	EX	LN	RARITY
75	110	150	4

814 Boxcar (Type VI): Cream returned as a body color in 1938-39, this time with a maroon roof and door guides. Nickel nameplates and journal boxes were used on this version of the boxcar.

VG	EX	LN	RARITY
100	150	225	6

814 Boxcar (Type VII): In 1940, the color changed yet again, while the brown roof and door guides were familiar, the orange body color was new. Also, this version lacked nameplates, its markings instead being rubber-stamped directly on the car body. Black journal boxes were found on the trucks of this version, which was shipped into 1942.

VG	EX	LN	RARITY
100	150	225	6

814R (Type I): The 814R refrigerator car was added to the Lionel line in 1929. Similar to the 814 boxcar, the refrigerator had hinged rather than sliding doors. Its body was painted ivory, the roof peacock. The frame of the car was painted black. Its trucks had nickel journal boxes and brass nameplates were on the car's sides. Hinges and latches made of brass were attached to the doors. The car was made in this configuration through 1931.

VG	EX	LN	RARITY
100	150	225	4

814R (Type II): From 1931 through 1934, copper journal boxes were installed, but the remainder of the car was unchanged.

VG	EX	LN	RARITY
100	150	225	4

814R (Type III): In 1935, the color of the body changed to gloss white and the roof began to be painted blue. The nameplates were made of aluminum. Nickel journal boxes began to be used again and the door latches were nickel as well. The hinges, however, continued to be brass.

VG	EX	LN	RARITY
200	275	400	6

814R (Type IV): About 1936, the hinges became nickel as well, although the rest of the car was unchanged. This configuration was repeated in 1937 as well.

VG	EX	LN	RARITY
200	275	400	6

814R (Type V): In 1938, the color of the frame of the refrigerator car changed from black to aluminum. The body itself continued to be gloss white, the roof was painted blue and aluminum plates were mounted on the car. The door hardware and journal boxes were nickel. This style continued into the next year.

VG	EX	LN	RARITY
375	475	600	7

814R (Type VI): The year 1940 saw the most dramatic change in the appearance of the refrigerator car. The color of the body shifted slightly to semi-gloss white, but the roof was now painted brown. The doors, though they still had nickel latches, were now mounted with black hinges. Aluminum nameplates were still used, but the journal boxes were now black.

VG	EX	LN	RARITY
1500	2000	2750	8

814R (Type VII): In 1941, the aluminum plates previously used on the refrigerator car were replaced with heat-stamped lettering (often mistaken for rubber-stamped lettering). The body was painted semi-gloss white with a brown roof, black hinges, nickel latches and black journal boxes. Cars like this were shipped into 1942.

VG	EX	LN	RARITY
1500	2000	2750	8

820 Boxcar: The 820 boxcar was among Lionel's earliest 0 gauge pieces. It was sold from 1915 through 1926 in a variety of colors and road names. Like many of these early pieces, it is difficult in retrospect to determine their sequence of production, hence these are listed alphabetically.

820 Boxcar (Type I): A dark olive boxcar with "A.T. & S.F. – 45822" markings is believed to be among the earliest versions of this car.

VG	EX	LN	RARITY
175	225	300	7

820 Boxcar (Type II): Another early version was painted yellow-orange and wore "ILLINOIS CENTRAL RAILROAD" markings. The weight markings rubber-stamped on this car listed a capacity of "50,000 LBS" and the car number stamped on the side was "65784".

VG	EX	LN	RARITY
40	55	80	4

820 Boxcar (Type III): The yellow-orange Illinois Central car was also produced with capacity markings of "20000 LBS".

VG	EX	LN	RARITY
40	55	80	4

820 Boxcar (Type IV): Some of the yellow-orange Illinois Central boxcars even listed capacity "60000 LBS".

VG	EX	LN	RARITY
40	55	80	4

820 Boxcar (Type V): Orange boxcars with "UNION PACIFIC" markings are reasonably abundant, indicative of a long production run.

Price Guide Key: VG = Very Good, EX = Excellent, LN = Like New | *Values for each condition are in U.S. dollars.* | Rarity = Scale from 1-8 with 8 being the hardest to find.

217

O GAUGE BOX, STOCK & REFRIGERATOR CARS

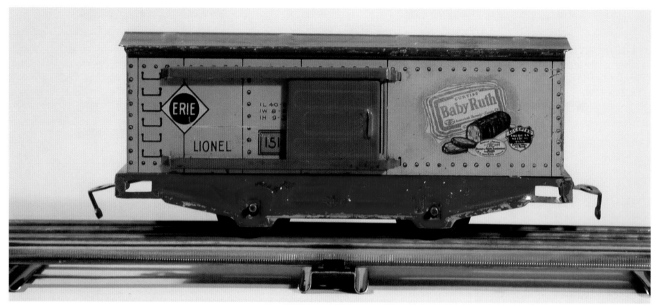

1514 BOXCAR TYPE VI

VG	EX	LN	RARITY
40	55	80	4

820 Boxcar (Type VI): Less common are Union Pacific boxcars painted dark orange.

VG	EX	LN	RARITY
50	65	90	6

821 Stock Car: This was the livestock-hauling counterpart of the 820. Though cataloged as early as 1915, the construction details of these cars indicate that production did not begin until much later, perhaps as late as 1925! The car was made in various shades of green, with production halting in 1926.

VG	EX	LN	RARITY
50	65	90	6

900 Ammunition Boxcar: This unlettered gray boxcar was included in the outfit with the 203 armored motor car from 1917 through 1921.

VG	EX	LN	RARITY
125	225	350	5

1514 Boxcar: This 6" long, four-wheel lithographed boxcar initially was a part of the Ives and Winner lines, before finally moving into the normal Lionel product range, where it remained through 1937.

1514 Boxcar (Type I): When first manufactured in 1931, the light yellow sides of the boxcar were lithographed with Erie markings, but not Lionel. The car had State brown doors and a dark blue roof.

VG	EX	LN	RARITY
15	20	30	3

1514 Boxcar (Type II): Some of the light yellow cars had medium blue roofs. Again, these cars had State brown doors, and Erie but not Lionel markings.

VG	EX	LN	RARITY
15	20	30	3

1514 Boxcar (Type III): About 1935, the word "LIONEL" began to appear on the side of the car, beneath the Erie logo. The sides were still yellow, but now the roof was dark blue and the doors orange.

VG	EX	LN	RARITY
15	20	30	3

1514 Boxcar (Type IV): Brown doors were used on some of the yellow boxcars with both Erie and Lionel markings. These cars had dark blue roofs as well.

VG	EX	LN	RARITY
15	20	30	3

1514 Boxcar (Type V): Medium blue roofs were installed on some of the Lionel/Erie cars with brown doors.

VG	EX	LN	RARITY
15	20	30	3

1514 Boxcar (Type VI): About 1936, the Baby Ruth logo was added to the car, in addition to the Erie medallion and Lionel name. The frames of these cars were red, and the cars had yellow sides, medium blue roofs and brown doors.

VG	EX	LN	RARITY
12	18	25	2

1679 Boxcar: This 8" eight-wheeled lithographed boxcar was produced in a number of variations. Our contributors have documented no less than 14 versions of the basic car, with additional 1679X and 2679 varieties as well. To minimize confusion, only the essential information is documented in the individual listings below. "LIONEL – RR – LINES" indicates that an oval herald with that legend appeared on the left side of the car. "Baby Ruth" is indicative of a printed illustration of a candy bar appearing on the right side of the car, while "CURTISS BABY RUTH" indicates the corporate name was spelled out on the car side, but the candy bar illustration was omitted. All cars have yellow bodies.

1679 Boxcar (Type I): Dark blue roof, brown doors, "LIONEL – RR – LINES", copper journal boxes, 1933-34.

VG	EX	LN	RARITY
12	18	25	2

1679 Boxcar (Type II): Dark blue roof, orange doors, "LIONEL – RR – LINES", copper journal boxes, 1933-34.

VG	EX	LN	RARITY
12	18	25	2

1719 BOXCAR TYPE IV

1679 Boxcar (Type III): Medium blue roof, brown doors, "LIONEL – RR – LINES", copper journal boxes, 1935.

VG	EX	LN	RARITY
12	18	25	2

1679 Boxcar (Type IV): Medium blue roof, Baby Ruth, orange doors, "LIONEL – RR – LINES", nickel journal boxes, 1936-38.

VG	EX	LN	RARITY
12	18	25	2

1679 Boxcar (Type V): Light blue roof, Baby Ruth, brown doors, "LIONEL – RR – LINES", nickel journal boxes, 1936-38.

VG	EX	LN	RARITY
12	18	25	2

1679 Boxcar (Type VI): Light blue roof, Baby Ruth, orange doors, "LIONEL – RR – LINES", nickel journal boxes, 1936-38.

VG	EX	LN	RARITY
12	18	25	2

1679 Boxcar (Type VII): Light blue roof, Baby Ruth, turquoise roof, brown doors, "LIONEL – RR – LINES", black journal boxes, 1939.

VG	EX	LN	RARITY
12	18	25	2

1679 Boxcar (Type VIII): Turquoise roof, Baby Ruth, orange doors, "LIONEL – RR – LINES", black journal boxes, 1939.

VG	EX	LN	RARITY
12	18	25	2

1679 Boxcar (Type IX): Maroon roof, Curtiss Baby Ruth, orange doors, "LIONEL LINES", black journal boxes.

VG	EX	LN	RARITY
12	18	25	2

1679 Boxcar (Type X): Maroon roof, Curtiss Baby Ruth, orange doors, "LIONEL LINES", nickel journal boxes.

VG	EX	LN	RARITY
12	18	25	2

1679 Boxcar (Type XI): Brown roof, Curtiss Baby Ruth, orange doors, "LIONEL LINES", black journal boxes, latch couplers.

VG	EX	LN	RARITY
25	30	40	5

1679 Boxcar (Type XII): Brown roof, Curtiss Baby Ruth, orange doors, "LIONEL LINES", nickel journal boxes, latch couplers.

VG	EX	LN	RARITY
25	30	40	5

1679 Boxcar (Type XIII): Brown roof, Curtiss Baby Ruth, orange doors, "LIONEL LINES", black journal boxes, manual box couplers.

VG	EX	LN	RARITY
25	30	40	5

1679 Boxcar (Type XIV): Brown roof, Curtiss Baby Ruth, orange doors, "LIONEL LINES", nickel journal boxes, manual box couplers.

VG	EX	LN	RARITY
25	30	40	5

1679X Boxcar: Included in some uncataloged sets shipped from 1936 through 1942, the 1679X differed from the normal production by lacking journal boxes, which saved a few cents of the manufacturing cost of the car.

VG	EX	LN	RARITY
20	25	30	4

1679X Boxcar (Type I): Light blue roof, yellow body, Baby Ruth, brown doors, "LIONEL – RR – LINES", no journal boxes, 1936.

VG	EX	LN	RARITY
20	25	30	4

1679X Boxcar (Type II): Turquoise roof, yellow body, Baby Ruth, brown doors, "LIONEL – RR – LINES", no journal boxes, 1937.

Price Guide Key: **VG** = Very Good, **EX** = Excellent, **LN** = Like New | *Values for each condition are in U.S. dollars.* | **Rarity** = Scale from 1-8 with 8 being the hardest to find.

219

O GAUGE BOX, STOCK & REFRIGERATOR CARS

2655 BOXCAR TYPE IV

VG	EX	LN	RARITY
20	25	30	4

1679X Boxcar (Type III): Maroon roof, yellow body, Baby Ruth, orange doors, "LIONEL – RR – LINES", no journal boxes, 1939.

VG	EX	LN	RARITY
20	25	30	4

1719 Boxcar: Production of this car actually began in 1932, but it was an Ives product at that time and wore the number 1709. In 1933, the car moved into the Lionel line and the number changed to 1719. However, the lithographed car did not appear in the Lionel catalog, instead being used as a component of uncataloged sets, a role it filled through 1942.

1719 Boxcar (Type I): In 1933 and 1934, the lithographed sides of the car were Stephen Girard green. The car had a blue roof, brass ladders and copper journal boxes.

VG	EX	LN	RARITY
20	30	40	4

1719 Boxcar (Type II): In 1935, the ladders and journal boxes began to be nickel. This version continued to be produced through 1940.

VG	EX	LN	RARITY
20	30	40	4

1719 Boxcar (Type III): Also built between 1935 and 1940 were cars with lithographed light green sides and peacock roofs. These cars also had nickel ladders and nickel journal boxes.

VG	EX	LN	RARITY
20	30	40	4

1719 Boxcar (Type IV): Black journal boxes were mounted on the lithographed light Stephen Girard green boxcars in 1941 and 1942. The roofs on these cars were light blue and nickel ladders were installed.

VG	EX	LN	RARITY
25	35	45	5

1719X Boxcar: This lithographed light Stephen Girard green boxcar was equipped with truck-mounted box couplers. Shipped in 1942, it had a light blue roof, nickel ladders and black journal boxes.

VG	EX	LN	RARITY
25	35	45	5

2655 Boxcar (Type I): This yellow boxcar with nickel journal boxes, as well as nickel plates and ladders, was introduced in 1938. A maroon roof was installed on these cars, which had magnetic couplers.

VG	EX	LN	RARITY
40	55	75	3

2655 Boxcar (Type II): A couple of changes were made in 1939, the most noticeable of which was color of the roof becoming tuscan. At the same time, the journal boxes started to be finished in black rather than nickel. The yellow body, nickel plates and nickel ladders were all continued.

VG	EX	LN	RARITY
50	65	85	4

2655 Boxcar (Type III): In 1940, rubber-stamping replaced the use of plates on the cars. The yellow and tuscan color scheme of the car and its trim were unchanged.

VG	EX	LN	RARITY
60	75	100	6

2655 Boxcar (Type IV): In 1941, in addition to having black journal boxes, the ladders were now black as well. Its body was yellow, the roof tuscan and the markings rubber-stamped. A limited number of this version was also shipped in 1942.

VG	EX	LN	RARITY
60	75	100	6

2656 Stock Car (Type I): The body of this car, introduced in 1938, was punched to simulate the slat-sided construction of stock cars and was painted light gray. A red roof was installed, as were latch couplers, nickel journal boxes, nickel plates and nickel ladders.

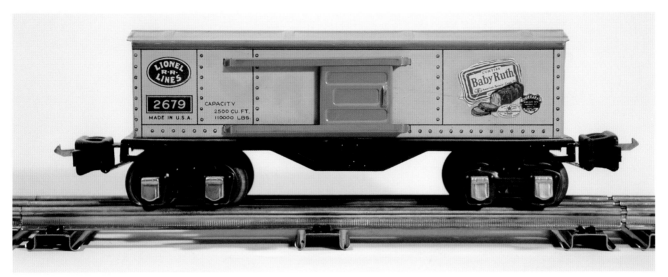

2679 BOXCAR TYPE I

VG	EX	LN	RARITY
60	75	100	4

2656 Stock Car (Type II): In 1939, the nickel journal boxes gave way to black ones and solenoid actuated couplers replaced the older electromagnetic ones, but the rest of the car was unchanged.

VG	EX	LN	RARITY
60	75	100	6

2656 Stock Car (Type III): The subsequent year, 1940, saw many changes. The color of the body was now burnt orange and the roof tuscan. Rubber-stamping replaced the nickel plates. Black journal boxes and nickel ladders continued to be used.

VG	EX	LN	RARITY
100	125	165	7

2656 Stock Car (Type IV): In 1941, the burnt orange car was equipped with black ladders rather than nickel. Its tuscan roof, black journal boxes and rubber-stamped markings were all unchanged.

VG	EX	LN	RARITY
100	125	165	7

2679 Boxcar: This yellow lithographed boxcar was essentially a 1679 equipped with automatic box couplers. It was available from 1938 until sometime in 1942.

2679 Boxcar (Type I): Initially the boxcar was yellow with a lithographed Baby Ruth illustrated advertisement on its sides. It had orange doors and a light peacock roof. A "LIONEL – R.R. – LINES" logo appeared on the left end of the car. Its trucks had nickel journal boxes.

VG	EX	LN	RARITY
15	25	40	3

2679 Boxcar (Type II): Some of the cars built in 1938 had a medium blue roof.

VG	EX	LN	RARITY
15	25	40	3

2679 Boxcar (Type III): In 1939, black journal boxes began to be used on the yellow Baby Ruth boxcar. The roof was medium blue and the doors orange. Solenoid-operated couplers replaced the electromagnetic ones previously used.

VG	EX	LN	RARITY
15	25	40	3

2679 Boxcar (Type IV): During 1939, the decoration of the car was changed. Although it was still yellow, the candy bar illustration was deleted and a "Curtiss Baby Ruth Candy" logo applied instead. Also deleted was the oval "Lionel R.R. Lines" logo and a simple "LIONEL LINES" text appeared instead. Each of these cars had a maroon roof and orange doors, as well as black journal boxes. This configuration was produced through 1941.

VG	EX	LN	RARITY
15	25	40	3

2719 Boxcar: This lithographed boxcar was essentially a 1719 equipped with automatic box couplers. It was available from 1938 until sometime in 1942.

2719 Boxcar (Type I): When made in 1938, this car had lithographed light peacock sides and a blue roof. Its ladders and journal boxes were nickel-finished. It was equipped with electromagnetic couplers.

VG	EX	LN	RARITY
15	25	40	4

2719 Boxcar (Type II): In 1939, solenoid-operated couplers were installed, but the rest of the car was unchanged. These cars were continued in 1940.

VG	EX	LN	RARITY
15	25	40	4

2719 Boxcar (Type III): Black journal boxes were mounted on the lithographed light peacock boxcars in 1941 and 1942. The roofs on these cars were light blue roof, and nickel ladders and black journal boxes were installed.

VG	EX	LN	RARITY
15	25	40	4

Price Guide Key: VG = Very Good, EX = Excellent, LN = Like New | *Values for each condition are in U.S. dollars.* | Rarity = Scale from 1-8 with 8 being the hardest to find.

221

2719 Boxcar Type III

2758 Automobile Boxcar: This tuscan double door boxcar had scale-like detail and proportions, but was overall much smaller than a full-scale car. Nevertheless, this car was attractive and was sold in 1941-42. It was one of the few cars whose body was returned to production after World War II.

VG	EX	LN	RARITY
40	50	65	4

2813 Stock Car (Type I): This electromagnet coupler-equipped stock car was offered in 1938 and 1939. The body of the stock car was cream and its roof tuscan. The journal boxes and plates were nickel.

VG	EX	LN	RARITY
150	225	350	6

2813 Stock Car (Type II): In 1940, a major facelift was given to the stock car. Both the body and roof were now painted a uniform shade of tuscan. Reportedly, some of these cars were made with nickel journal boxes and nickel plates.

RARITY
Unable to establish authenticity of this variation.

2813 Stock Car (Type III): Certainly produced, but difficult to find, are the 1941-42 versions of the 813. This car was built with a tuscan body and roof, but rather than plates, this car had rubber-stamped lettering. Black journal boxes were installed on the trucks.

VG	EX	LN	RARITY
250	325	450	7

2814 Boxcar (Type I): This boxcar, with a cream body and remote control couplers, was offered in 1938-39 with a maroon roof and door guides. Nickel nameplates and journal boxes were used.

VG	EX	LN	RARITY
75	150	250	5

2814 Boxcar (Type II): In 1940, the color changed; now the car had an orange body, and brown roof and door guides. Also, this version lacked nameplates, its markings instead being rubber-stamped directly on the car body. Black journal boxes were found on the trucks of this version, which was shipped into 1942.

VG	EX	LN	RARITY
750	1500	2500	8

2814R Refrigerator Car (Type I): Introduced in 1938, this refrigerator car was equipped with electromagnetic couplers. The body itself was painted gloss white, the frame was painted aluminum, the roof was painted blue roof and aluminum plates were mounted on the car. The door hardware and journal boxes were nickel. This style continued into the next year.

VG	EX	LN	RARITY
250	325	450	7

2814R Refrigerator Car (Type II): The year 1940 saw the most dramatic change in the appearance of the refrigerator car. The color of the body shifted slightly to semi-gloss white, but the roof was now painted brown. The doors, though they still had nickel latches, were now mounted with black hinges. Aluminum nameplates were still used, but the journal boxes were now black.

VG	EX	LN	RARITY
400	550	700	7

2814R Refrigerator Car (Type III): In 1941, the aluminum plates previously used on the refrigerator car were replaced with heat-stamped lettering (often mistaken for rubber-stamped lettering). The body was painted semi-gloss white with a brown roof, black hinges, nickel latches and black journal boxes. Cars like this were shipped into 1942.

VG	EX	LN	RARITY
750	1500	2500	8

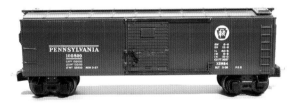

2954 Boxcar: This was a semi-scale version of Lionel's magnificently detailed scale replica of a Pennsylvania boxcar. It differed from the full-scale version, the 714, by having tinplate rather than scale trucks. Beware, many are found today with warped or replaced roof walkways. This boxcar was sold 1940 through 1942.

VG	EX	LN	RARITY
150	250	400	6

3814 Merchandise Car (Type I): This tuscan boxcar contained an operating mechanism, which ejected cube-like plastic "boxes" when activated by a remote control track section. As first built in 1939, the markings on this car were applied with decals and its trucks were equipped with nickel journal boxes.

VG	EX	LN	RARITY
125	175	225	4

3814 (Type II): Later 1939 production had black journal boxes.

VG	EX	LN	RARITY
125	175	225	4

3814 (Type III): In 1940, the lettering was stamped onto the car body, rather than being applied with decals. The black journal boxes continued to be used.

VG	EX	LN	RARITY
175	225	275	4

Price Guide Key: **VG** = Very Good, **EX** = Excellent, **LN** = Like New | *Values for each condition are in U.S. dollars.* | **Rarity** = Scale from 1-8 with 8 being the hardest to find.

223

CHAPTER 22
O GAUGE HOPPER & BALLAST CARS

Among the types of freight cars most often seen on real railroads are hopper cars. Used to move bulk commodities, the cars are loaded from the top and emptied, largely by gravity, through the bottom. Covered hopper cars are totally enclosed and are used to transport products such as grains and dry chemicals that must be sheltered from the weather. Open hoppers lack this roof and are used to haul cargo that does not need protection from the weather, such as coal or gravel. Lionel did not produce a covered hopper during the prewar era, however they did produce numerous versions of the open-top hopper, fitting for an era when coal, hauled in hopper cars, fueled much of America's industry.

These cars in particular are often found today in well-worn condition. This is a result of the great play value they afforded children. Marbles, dominoes, pebbles and the like all made excellent cargo for these cars, and damaged the paint along the way, just as is the case with real hopper cars.

653 Hopper (Type I): When introduced in 1933, the 653 was painted Stephen Girard green and had brass nameplates. Copper journal boxes were affixed to its trucks.

VG	EX	LN	RARITY
30	50	75	3

653 Hopper (Type II): In 1934, nickel journal boxes began to be used on the Stephen Girard green hopper. The plates continued to be brass.

VG	EX	LN	RARITY
30	50	75	3

653 Hopper (Type III): Starting in 1935, nickel plates began to be used on the hopper, whose body continued to be painted Stephen Girard green. The hopper was cataloged through 1940 with nickel journal boxes.

VG	EX	LN	RARITY
30	50	75	3

803 HOPPER TYPE III

653 Hopper (Type IV): Though not cataloged beyond 1940, it is believed that the 653 continued to be shipped into 1942, perhaps with black journal boxes.

RARITY
Existence not confirmed.

716 Hopper: This massive die-cast hopper was offered from 1940 through 1942 as part of Lionel's scale product line. It was painted black and bore Baltimore and Ohio markings.

VG	EX	LN	RARITY
300	450	625	6

716K Hopper: The scale hopper was also offered in primer-only kit form. Unassembled cars bring a premium, while the value of assembled cars is greatly affected by the quality of the hobbyist-applied paint and lettering job.

Unassembled

VG	EX	LN	RARITY
600	900	1500	8

Assembled

VG	EX	LN	RARITY
275	425	575	7

803 Hopper (Type I): As first produced in 1923, this four-wheel dark green hopper car was equipped with hook-type couplers. It also had rubber-stamped markings and no journal boxes.

VG	EX	LN	RARITY
25	35	50	3

803 Hopper (Type II): Later in 1923, the dark green, rubber-stamped hopper began to be supplied with latch couplers. Still, no journal boxes were fitted. It was supplied this way into 1924.

VG	EX	LN	RARITY
25	35	50	3

803 Hopper (Type III): Starting in 1925, nickel journal boxes began to be installed on the dark green hopper. The rubber-stamped car continued to be manufactured this way in 1926.

VG	EX	LN	RARITY
25	35	50	3

803 Hopper (Type IV): In 1927, brass ladders were added to the dark green hopper. Its rubber-stamped lettering, latch couplers and nickel journal boxes all continued into 1928.

VG	EX	LN	RARITY
25	35	50	3

803 Hopper (Type V): In 1929, the car began to be painted peacock. While the latch coupler, nickel journal boxes and brass ladders were all familiar, brass nameplates were new. Cars produced in 1930 were identical to 1929 production.

VG	EX	LN	RARITY
25	35	55	4

803 Hopper (Type VI): In 1931, the peacock car received copper journal boxes, along with its brass plates, latch couplers and brass ladders. It continued to be produced through 1934, when it was dropped.

VG	EX	LN	RARITY
25	35	55	4

Price Guide Key: **VG** = Very Good, **EX** = Excellent, **LN** = Like New | *Values for each condition are in U.S. dollars.* | **Rarity** = Scale from 1-8 with 8 being the hardest to find.

225

803 HOPPER TYPE III

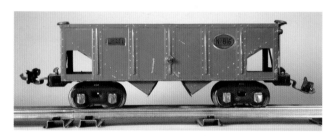

816 Hopper (Type I): From 1927 through 1931, Lionel cataloged this olive green hopper. The car was equipped with brass name and number plates, and nickel journal boxes.

VG	EX	LN	RARITY
80	125	175	4

816 Hopper (Type II): Sometime in 1931, copper journal boxes began to be used on the olive green hopper.

VG	EX	LN	RARITY
80	125	175	6

816 Hopper (Type IV): Nickel journal boxes appeared on the red hopper in 1935. Initially brass plates were on this car as well.

VG	EX	LN	RARITY
60	100	150	3

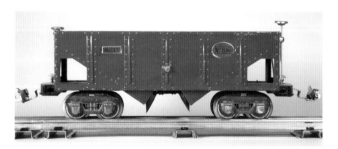

816 Hopper (Type III): Also, beginning in 1931 and destined to continue through 1934, the 816 began to be offered in red. These cars had copper journal boxes and brass plates as well.

VG	EX	LN	RARITY
60	100	150	3

816 Hopper (Type V): Later in 1935, and continuing until sometime about 1941, nickel plates were used on the red hopper. Nickel journal boxes were used on these cars.

VG	EX	LN	RARITY
80	125	175	4

2653 Hopper Type III

816 Hopper (Type VI): Black journal boxes appeared on the red hopper in 1941. More significant, however, was the elimination of the name and number plates in favor of lettering stamped directly on the car's side.

RARITY
Existence questioned.

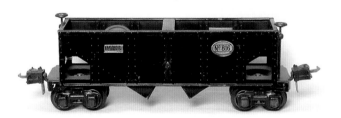

816 Hopper (Type VII): New for 1941 only was the 816 painted black, with nickel plates and black journal boxes.

VG	EX	LN	RARITY
1400	2500	3500	8

816 Hopper (Type VII): Later in 1941, a more significant change was made, however. The name and number plates were eliminated in favor of lettering stamped directly on the car's side. This car, which had black journal boxes, was also shipped in 1942.

VG	EX	LN	RARITY
400	600	1000	7

2653 Hopper (Type I): Differing from the 653 by the inclusion of electromagnetic couplers, this Stephen Girard green hopper debuted in 1938. It had nickel journal boxes and nickel plates.

VG	EX	LN	RARITY
30	50	75	3

2653 Hopper (Type II): In 1939, the electromagnetic couplers were eliminated in favor of solenoid-type automatic couplers. The remainder of the car was unchanged.

VG	EX	LN	RARITY
30	50	75	3

2653 Hopper (Type III): The car got an extensive makeover in 1941. The paint color changed to black, and the marking method changed from plates to heat-stamping. Black journal boxes were installed on the trucks. The car continued in this form until supplies were exhausted in 1942.

VG	EX	LN	RARITY
75	200	350	7

2816 Hopper (Type I): Differing from the 816 by the inclusion of electromagnetic couplers, this red hopper debuted in 1938. It had nickel journal boxes and nickel plates.

VG	EX	LN	RARITY
125	175	250	5

Price Guide Key: **VG** = Very Good, **EX** = Excellent, **LN** = Like New | *Values for each condition are in U.S. dollars.* | **Rarity** = Scale from 1-8 with 8 being the hardest to find.

227

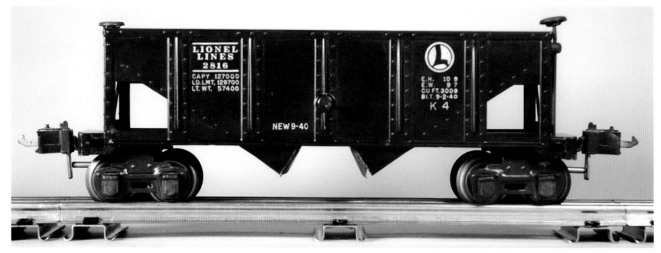

2816 HOPPER TYPE III

2956 HOPPER TYPE I

2816 Hopper (Type II): In 1939, the electromagnetic couplers were eliminated in favor of solenoid-type automatic couplers. The remainder of the car was unchanged.

VG	EX	LN	RARITY
125	175	250	5

2816 Hopper (Type III): 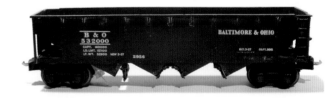 The car got an extensive makeover in 1941. The paint color changed to black, and the marking method changed from plates to heat-stamping. Black journal boxes were installed on the trucks. The car continued in this form until supplies were exhausted in 1942.

VG	EX	LN	RARITY
125	250	425	7

2956 Hopper (Type I): Though it used the same body as the full-scale 716, this semi scale hopper used conventional tinplate trucks with copper journal boxes when it premiered in 1940.

VG	EX	LN	RARITY
200	400	625	7

2956 Hopper (Type II): Later production had trucks with black journal boxes.

VG	EX	LN	RARITY
200	400	625	7

CHAPTER 23
O GAUGE TANK CARS

Lionel's prewar selection of 0 gauge tank cars came in a variety of body types, but a relatively narrow range of reporting marks, with Shell and Sun the only two oil companies represented. However, some cars were also built with the markings of the world-famous "Lionel Lines" railroad.

654 Tank (Type I): This aluminum-colored tank bore Sunoco markings when issued in 1933. It was equipped with copper journal boxes, brass and copper domes, brass plates and brass ladders. It continued unchanged in 1934.

VG	EX	LN	RARITY
25	35	50	3

654 (Type II): From 1935 through 1938, the aluminum Sunoco tank had several nickel-plated components. Among them were the journal boxes, domes, ladders and nameplates.

VG	EX	LN	RARITY
25	35	50	3

654 (Type III): In 1939, the tanker got a new color, orange, and a new oil company name, Shell. The nickel ladders, journal boxes, domes and plates all continued.

VG	EX	LN	RARITY
35	50	70	4

654 (Type IV): In 1940, black journal boxes were used on the orange Shell tanker. The nickel plates were eliminated in favor of additional decals, but the nickel domes and ladders continued.

VG	EX	LN	RARITY
35	50	70	4

654 (Type V): The aluminum-colored tank returned in 1941, as did the Sunoco logo. These cars had black journal boxes, but nickel ladders and domes.

VG	EX	LN	RARITY
30	45	60	4

654 (Type VI): In 1941-42, the tank body was painted gray, and the Sunoco herald and reporting marks were applied with

Price Guide Key: **VG** = Very Good, **EX** = Excellent, **LN** = Like New | *Values for each condition are in U.S. dollars.* | **Rarity** = Scale from 1-8 with 8 being the hardest to find.

229

804 Type V

decals. Ladders and domes were nickel, and the journal boxes black.

VG	EX	LN	RARITY
35	50	70	4

654 (Type VII): Sometime in 1942, an otherwise identical gray car was produced, with black ladders rather than nickel.

VG	EX	LN	RARITY
35	50	70	4

715 (Type I): This beautifully detailed scale model tank car was sold with Shell markings in 1940.

VG	EX	LN	RARITY
300	500	725	6

715 (Type II): During 1941-42, Sunoco markings were used on the scale tanker.

VG	EX	LN	RARITY
400	600	850	7

715K (Type I): The scale tanker was also offered as a kit with Shell decals in 1940. Unassembled cars command a premium;

assembled cars are less desirable. How much is dependent upon the quality of the paint and assembly work.

Unassembled:

VG	EX	LN	RARITY
500	850	1300	8

Assembled:

VG	EX	LN	RARITY
350	550	800	6

715K (Type II): Some of these kits have also been reported with Sunoco decals.

Unassembled:

VG	EX	LN	RARITY
600	950	1450	8

Assembled:

VG	EX	LN	RARITY
400	600	900	7

804 (Type I): This was Lionel's earliest 0 Gauge tanker. Introduced in 1923, its body was painted dark gray and topped with a red dome. It had no journal boxes and its markings were rubber-stamped.

VG	EX	LN	RARITY
20	30	40	3

804 (Type II): Also produced in 1923 was a dark gray tanker with a brass dome. It also had no journal boxes and rubber-stamped markings.

VG	EX	LN	RARITY
20	30	40	3

804 (Type III): In 1924, a lighter shade of gray paint was used on the tank. The lack of journal boxes, brass dome and rubber-stamped markings were unchanged.

VG	EX	LN	RARITY
20	30	40	3

804 TYPE V

804 (Type IV): New in 1925 was the 804 painted terra cotta. The car had no journal boxes, a brass dome and rubber-stamped markings.

VG	EX	LN	RARITY
15	25	35	2

804 (Type V): 🖼 From 1926 through 1928, the terra cotta tanker had nickel journal boxes. It also had rubber-stamped lettering and a brass dome.

VG	EX	LN	RARITY
15	25	35	2

804 (Type VI): Nickel journal boxes were also used on some tank cars with aluminum-painted bodies. These cars had brass domes and rubber-stamped lettering as well, and were sold from 1926 through 1928.

VG	EX	LN	RARITY
15	25	35	2

804 (Type VII): 🖼 During 1929-1930, brass nameplates were used on the aluminum-painted tanker. Nickel journal boxes and a brass dome were features as well.

VG	EX	LN	RARITY
15	25	35	2

painted aluminum, and had brass domes and brass plates. A Sunoco decal decorated the tank as well.

VG	EX	LN	RARITY
15	25	35	2

804 (Type IX): Sometime in 1935, nickel journal boxes returned, replacing the copper ones in use since 1931. A Sunoco decal continued to be applied to the aluminum tank, which was now trimmed with nickel domes, and nickel plates.

VG	EX	LN	RARITY
15	25	35	2

804 (Type X): In 1939, the color of the tank changed to yellow-orange, and Shell decals with reporting marks began to be used. The plates, domes and journal boxes were all nickel finished.

VG	EX	LN	RARITY
35	45	60	5

804 (Type XI): During 1940-41, the yellow-orange tank continued, but now the decal read simply "SHELL". These cars had nickel domes, journal boxes and plates.

VG	EX	LN	RARITY
35	45	60	5

804 (Type VIII): From 1931 until sometime in 1935, copper journal boxes were used on the 804. The tank continued to be

815 (Type I): During its first two years of production, 1926-27, the 815 had a pea green tank, maroon frame, brass dome, nickel journal boxes and brass plates.

Price Guide Key: VG = Very Good, EX = Excellent, LN = Like New | *Values for each condition are in U.S. dollars.* | **Rarity** = Scale from 1-8 with 8 being the hardest to find.

231

815 TYPE II

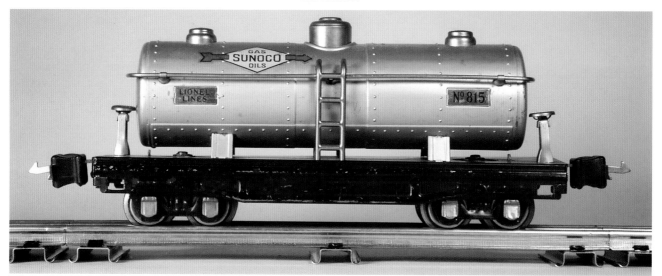

815 TYPE VII

VG	EX	LN	RARITY
300	500	750	7

815 (Type II): 🖼 From 1927 through 1931, the pea green tank was mounted on a black frame. The brass dome, nickel journal boxes and brass plates all continued to be used.

VG	EX	LN	RARITY
50	75	110	2

815 (Type III): In 1931, copper journal boxes were first used on the 815. The tank continued to be pea green and the frame black. Also continuing were the brass dome and brass plates.

VG	EX	LN	RARITY
50	75	110	2

815 (Type IV): Sometime in 1931, the tank began to be painted aluminum. The black frame, copper journal boxes, and brass dome and plates were all used on this version as well.

VG	EX	LN	RARITY
75	110	150	4

815 (Type V): A Sunoco decal was added to the aluminum tank in 1932. Along with the black frame, copper journal

boxes, brass plates and dome, it continued to be used through 1934.

VG	EX	LN	RARITY
75	110	150	3

815 (Type VI): In 1935, nickel journal boxes returned and, at the same time, the nameplates became nickel as well. The tank continued to be finished in aluminum paint and mounted on a black frame. A brass dome was used, as was a Sunoco decal.

VG	EX	LN	RARITY
75	110	150	3

815 (Type VII): 🖼 From 1936 through 1938, an actual aluminum dome was mounted on top of the aluminum-painted tank. Nickel journal boxes and plates were used. The car had a black frame and used Sunoco decals.

VG	EX	LN	RARITY
75	110	150	3

815 (Type VIII): In 1939, the color of the tank changed to orange and, rather than Sunoco, Shell decals were affixed to its sides. Unchanged were its black frame, aluminum dome,

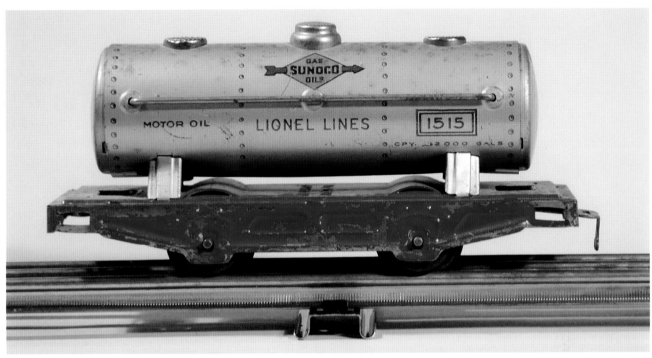

1515 TYPE V

and nickel journal boxes and plates. This car continued to be offered in 1940 as well.

VG	EX	LN	RARITY
200	300	550	7

815 (Type IX): The orange Shell tanker was changed for 1941-42. The nameplates were eliminated in favor of stamped markings, and black journal boxes were introduced. Carried over was the black frame and aluminum dome.

VG	EX	LN	RARITY
200	300	550	7

1515: This four-wheel lithographed tanker was first issued in 1931-32 as part of the Winner and Ives lines. It moved to the Lionel line for the remainder of its production, which ended in 1937.

1515 (Type I): During 1930-32, the aluminum-colored tank was lithographed "Union Tank Lines, Fuel Oil". It was mounted on a black frame, and had a brass center dome, and copper end domes and handrails.

VG	EX	LN	RARITY
25	45	70	7

1515 (Type II): Sometime during 1931, Sunoco began to be applied to the aluminum-colored tank. The lithographed body was mounted on a black frame and decorated with a brass center dome, and copper end domes and handrails, through 1932.

VG	EX	LN	RARITY
15	25	35	4

1515 (Type III): In 1933, the Lionel name began to appear on the car in addition to Sunoco. The base color of the lithographed tank was still aluminum, and it still had a brass center dome, and copper end domes and handrails. This version was built on a black frame through 1934.

VG	EX	LN	RARITY
15	25	35	4

1515 (Type IV): Production in 1935 and 1936 included nickel domes and handrails. Both the Sunoco and Lionel names continued to appear on the aluminum-colored lithographed tank, which was mounted on a black frame.

VG	EX	LN	RARITY
15	25	35	4

1515 (Type V): In 1936 and 1937 a red frame was used on the otherwise unchanged Sunoco/Lionel tanker.

VG	EX	LN	RARITY
15	25	35	4

1680: Another of Lionel's lithographed tank cars was the 1680, offered from 1931 through 1942. Unlike the 1515, the 1680 rode on two four-wheel trucks. Prior to 1933, the same car was produced, with the same number, as part of the Ives line.

1680 (Type I): For its first year in the Lionel line, the lettering on the side of the aluminum-colored lithographed tank read "Motor Oil". Extensive use of copper was made, with the end domes, handrails and journal boxes all made of the material. The center dome was brass and the frame was painted black.

VG	EX	LN	RARITY
15	22	30	3

1680 (Type II): In 1933, Sunoco markings were added to the otherwise unchanged car.

VG	EX	LN	RARITY
15	22	30	3

1680 (Type III): For 1934, the domes of the Sunoco tanker were changed to nickel. The tank itself was still finished in aluminum and mounted on a black frame. The handrails and journal boxes were copper.

VG	EX	LN	RARITY
15	22	30	3

Price Guide Key: **VG** = Very Good, **EX** = Excellent, **LN** = Like New | *Values for each condition are in U.S. dollars.* | **Rarity** = Scale from 1-8 with 8 being the hardest to find.

233

1680 Type VII

1680 (Type IV): During 1935-36, "LIONEL LINES" began to appear beneath the Sunoco herald. The tank was still lithographed in aluminum color, and the frame remained black, but now the handrails as well as the domes were nickel.

VG	EX	LN	RARITY
15	22	30	3

1680 (Type V): Some Sunoco tankers were made with nickel center domes, copper end domes, copper handrails and nickel journal boxes in the 1936-38 period.

VG	EX	LN	RARITY
15	22	30	3

1680 (Type VI): Starting in 1939, the tank began to be lithographed in orange with Shell markings. These cars had black frames, nickel domes and nickel journal boxes.

VG	EX	LN	RARITY
15	22	30	3

1680 (Type VII): ◼ Black journal boxes were used on the orange Shell tankers in 1940, perhaps as early as 1941. These cars had black frames, and nickel domes and handrails.

VG	EX	LN	RARITY
15	22	30	3

1680 (Type VIII): Produced only in 1941, this car lacked any oil company markings, lithographed instead "PETROLEUM – PRODUCTS" and "LIONEL LINES". The aluminum-colored tank had nickel handrails and domes, and was mounted on a black frame with black journal boxes.

VG	EX	LN	RARITY
15	22	30	3

1680 (Type IX): An aluminum-colored tank car with "Gas-Sunoco-Oils" lithography was sold in 1941-42. It had a black frame, nickel domes and handrail, and black journal boxes.

VG	EX	LN	RARITY
15	22	30	3

1680 (Type X): Sometime in late 1941 or early 1942, gray replaced aluminum as the primary color of the "Gas-Sunoco-Oils" tank car. This car had black journal boxes, but no ladders or handrails were ever installed.

VG	EX	LN	RARITY
30	40	55	6

1680X: Created for use in uncataloged sets, this car differed from standard production 1680 tank cars by lacking journal boxes. It appeared in various such sets sporadically from 1936 to 1942.

1680X (Type I): Those cars assembled in 1938 and prior had aluminum-colored lithographed tanks with Sunoco markings. These had nickel center domes, copper end domes and were mounted on black frames.

VG	EX	LN	RARITY
15	22	30	3

1680X (Type II): Spanning 1939-1940 was an orange tank car with Shell markings. Mounted on a black frame, this car had nickel domes.

VG	EX	LN	RARITY
15	22	30	3

1680X (Type III): An aluminum-colored tank car with "Gas-Sunoco-Oils" lithography was sold in 1941-42. It had a black frame, and nickel domes and handrails.

VG	EX	LN	RARITY
15	22	30	3

1680X (Type IV): Sometime in late 1941 or early 1942, gray replaced aluminum as the primary color of the "Gas-Sunoco-

2654 TYPE IV

Oils" tank car. This car had black journal boxes, but no ladders or handrails were ever installed.

VG	EX	LN	RARITY
30	40	55	6

2654 (Type I): Differing from the 654 by having electromagnetic couplers, this aluminum-colored 1938 Sunoco tank car had several nickel-plated components. Among them were the journal boxes, domes, ladders and nameplates.

VG	EX	LN	RARITY
30	40	55	2

2654 (Type II): A few of these aluminum-colored Sunoco tank cars were assembled in 1939 with solenoid-type couplers.

VG	EX	LN	RARITY
30	40	55	4

2654 (Type III): The bulk of 1939 production was in a new color, orange. In addition to nickel journal boxes domes, and plates, the car was decorated with Shell decals.

VG	EX	LN	RARITY
35	45	60	3

2654 (Type IV): Black journal boxes were used on some of the orange Shell tank cars with nickel plates and domes.

VG	EX	LN	RARITY
35	45	60	3

2654 (Type V): In 1940, the nickel plates were deleted. All the markings were applied to the orange with decals. Black journal boxes and nickel domes continued to be used.

VG	EX	LN	RARITY
35	45	60	3

2654 (Type VI): Aluminum returned as the tank color in 1941, as did the Sunoco logo. Nickel domes and black journal boxes completed these cars.

VG	EX	LN	RARITY
30	40	55	4

2654 (Type VII): In 1941-42, the tank body was painted gray, and the Sunoco herald and reporting marks were applied with decals. Ladders and domes were nickel and the journal boxes black.

VG	EX	LN	RARITY
45	55	70	4

2654 (Type VIII): Sometime in 1942, an otherwise identical gray car was produced, with black ladders rather than nickel.

VG	EX	LN	RARITY
45	55	70	4

2680: Differing from the 1680 by use of automatic box couplers rather than manual box or latch couplers, the 2680 was sold from 1938 through 1942.

2680 (Type I): Some of the 1938 production used trucks with nickel journal boxes. The aluminum-painted tank had Sunoco markings and nickel domes, and was mounted on a black frame. Electromagnetic couplers were used on this car.

VG	EX	LN	RARITY
15	25	35	4

2680 (Type II): Other 1938 cars used black journal boxes. The remainer of the car was identical to the Type I.

VG	EX	LN	RARITY
15	25	35	4

2680 (Type III): Starting perhaps as early as late 1938, but probably in 1939, the tank began to be lithographed in orange with Shell markings. These cars had black frames, nickel domes and black journal boxes. The car continued in this version, with solenoid-type couplers, through 1940.

VG	EX	LN	RARITY
15	25	35	4

2680 (Type IV): An aluminum-colored tank car with "Gas-Sunoco-Oils" lithography was sold in 1941. It had a black frame, nickel domes and handrail, and black journal boxes.

Price Guide Key: **VG** = Very Good, **EX** = Excellent, **LN** = Like New | *Values for each condition are in U.S. dollars.* | **Rarity** = Scale from 1-8 with 8 being the hardest to find.

235

2680 TYPE I

VG	EX	LN	RARITY
15	25	35	4

2680 (Type V): Sometime in late 1941 or early 1942, gray replaced aluminum as the primary color of the "Gas-Sunoco-Oils" tank car. This car had black journal boxes, but no ladders or handrails were ever installed.

VG	EX	LN	RARITY
15	25	35	4

2680 (Type VI): During 1942, black domes were used on some of the gray Sunoco tank cars. These cars had black frames and journal boxes, but no ladders or handrails.

VG	EX	LN	RARITY
15	25	35	4

2755 (Type I): More authentic appearing than most of the Lionel prewar freight cars, this tank car had a realistic looking die-cast frame. Atop that was mounted a rolled sheet-metal tank with Sunoco markings. This car was offered in 1941.

VG	EX	LN	RARITY
50	80	125	4

2755 (Type II): The color of the sheet metal tank changed to gray for 1941-42, but the Sunoco markings continued.

VG	EX	LN	RARITY
100	150	225	6

2815: Differing from the 815 by use of automatic box couplers rather than manual box or latch couplers, the 2815 was sold from 1938 through 1942.

2815 (Type I): Incorporating electromagnetic couplers, this car was first produced in 1938. At that time it had an aluminum-colored tank with Sunoco decal, black frame, aluminum dome, and nickel journal boxes and nameplates.

VG	EX	LN	RARITY
100	150	225	3

2955 TYPE I

2815 (Type II): As built in 1939, this car had Shell decals applied to its orange tank. Other features included a black frame, aluminum dome, and nickel journal boxes and plates as well as solenoid-type couplers. This car continued to be offered in 1940 as well.

VG	EX	LN	RARITY
100	150	225	3

2815 (Type III): The orange Shell tanker was changed for 1941-42. The nameplates were eliminated in favor of stamped markings and black journal boxes were introduced as well. Carried over was the black frame and aluminum dome.

VG	EX	LN	RARITY
100	150	225	3

2955 (Type I): Based on the scale 715 tank car, this version used conventional tinplate trucks with automatic box couplers. Its black die-cast body was decorated with Shell markings in 1940.

VG	EX	LN	RARITY
200	350	525	6

2955 (Type II): Sunoco marking were used on the die-cast tanker in 1941-42. It continued to be painted black.

VG	EX	LN	RARITY
350	525	725	7

Price Guide Key: VG = Very Good, EX = Excellent, LN = Like New | *Values for each condition are in U.S. dollars.* | Rarity = Scale from 1-8 with 8 being the hardest to find.

237

CHAPTER 24
O Gauge Passenger & Streamliner Cars

During the prewar era, passenger trains were the primary means of intercity travel in this country. In the most populous areas of the nation, rail service provided the daily means of commuting to work for many people. Thus, many Americans formed some type of bond with this type of train.

With the advent of streamlined passenger trains in the 1930s, many railroads sent their new equipment "barnstorming" across their systems, or indeed the entire nation–eager for publicity.

It is not surprising, then, that the most extensive group of 0 gauge rolling stock offered by Lionel was passenger cars. Initially the primary color for such equipment was the deep green made familiar by the nation-wide Pullman system, but later, a rainbow of colors decorated Lionel's offerings.

529 Pullman: This four-wheel passenger car, stamped "PULLMAN", was part of Lionel's product line from 1926 through 1932.

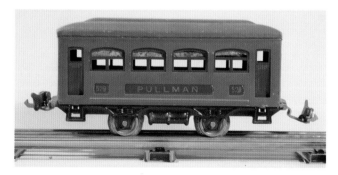

529 Pullman (Type I): In 1926, the little passenger car was painted olive, with a maroon insert. No journal boxes were attached to its black frame.

VG	EX	LN	RARITY
20	30	40	2

529 Pullman (Type II): During 1927 and 1928, red inserts were used in the olive Pullman bodies. The lack of journal boxes continued, as did the black frame.

VG	EX	LN	RARITY
20	30	40	2

530 OBSERVATION TYPE I

529 Pullman (Type III): In 1929. the insert was orange, and nickel journal boxes were installed on the car. The olive body and black frame were unchanged.

VG	EX	LN	RARITY
20	30	40	2

529 Pullman (Type IV): Terra cotta was introduced as a body color in 1930. These cars had cream inserts and a maroon frame with nickel journal boxes.

VG	EX	LN	RARITY
30	40	60	5

529 Pullman (Type V): For 1931 and 1932, copper journal boxes were installed on the terra-cotta, cream and maroon Pullman.

VG	EX	LN	RARITY
30	40	60	5

530 Observation: This four-wheel passenger car, stamped "OBSERVATION", was part of Lionel's product line from 1926 through 1932.

530 Observation (Type I): In 1926, the little passenger car was painted olive with a maroon insert. No journal boxes were attached to its black frame.

VG	EX	LN	RARITY
20	30	40	2

530 Observation (Type II): During 1927 and 1928, red inserts were used in the olive Observation bodies. The lack of journal boxes continued, as did the black frame.

VG	EX	LN	RARITY
20	30	40	2

530 Observation (Type III): In 1929, the insert was orange and nickel journal boxes were installed on the car. The olive body and black frame were unchanged.

VG	EX	LN	RARITY
20	30	40	2

530 Observation (Type IV): Terra cotta was introduced as a body color in 1930. These cars had cream inserts and a maroon frame, with nickel journal boxes.

VG	EX	LN	RARITY
30	40	60	5

Price Guide Key: **VG** = Very Good, **EX** = Excellent, **LN** = Like New | *Values for each condition are in U.S. dollars.* | **Rarity** = Scale from 1-8 with 8 being the hardest to find.

239

O GAUGE PASSENGER & STREAMLINER CARS

600 PULLMAN TYPE V

530 Observation (Type V): For 1931 and 1932, copper journal boxes were installed on the terra-cotta, cream and maroon observation car.

VG	EX	LN	RARITY
30	40	60	5

600 Pullman: This number was assigned to two different passenger cars. The first, made in 1915-25, had only four wheels. The later, offered 1933 though 1942, had eight wheels.

600 Pullman (Type I): This four-wheel Pullman car, originally produced in 1915, was dark green. This color continued in 1916 as well.

VG	EX	LN	RARITY
90	115	150	6

600 Pullman (Type II): Brown four-wheel Pullmans were built in 1917.

VG	EX	LN	RARITY
40	55	75	4

600 Pullman (Type III): From 1918 through about 1924, the four-wheel cars were painted maroon.

VG	EX	LN	RARITY
30	40	50	3

600 Pullman (Type IV): The final color for the four-wheel Pullmans was dark brown, a color they wore through 1926.

VG	EX	LN	RARITY
35	45	55	4

600 Pullman (Type V):  The number 600 returned in 1933, with an all-new body and riding on eight wheels. Through 1934, these cars had a light gray body, red roof and ivory window insert. They were decorated with brass trim, copper journal boxes and red underframe.

VG	EX	LN	RARITY
40	60	90	3

600 Pullman (Type VI): In 1935, the body of the eight-wheeled Pullman was painted light blue. Attached were an aluminum-painted roof and window insert. Nickel trim, nickel journal boxes and an aluminum-painted underframe completed the car.

VG	EX	LN	RARITY
50	75	110	5

600 Pullman (Type VII): In 1936, the light blue and aluminum colored eight-wheeled car was equipped with box rather than latch couplers. It continued to have nickel trim, nickel journal boxes and an aluminum-painted underframe.

VG	EX	LN	RARITY
50	75	110	5

600 Pullman (Type VIII): Latch coupler-equipped Pullmans painted light red with dark red roofs and ivory inserts were sold in 1936 and 1937. These cars had nickel trim, nickel journal boxes and red underframes.

VG	EX	LN	RARITY
40	60	90	3

600 Pullman (Type IX): The light red cars sometimes had box couplers during 1936 and 1937. Like the latch coupler-equipped cars, these also had dark red roofs, ivory inserts, nickel trim, nickel journal boxes and red underframes.

VG	EX	LN	RARITY
40	60	90	3

601 Passenger car: This number was assigned to two vastly different passenger cars. The first, sold from 1915 through 1923, was a Pullman car. The number returned in 1933, this time used on an observation car, which like its matching 600 Pullman stayed in the product line through 1937.

601 Pullman (Type I): This dark green Pullman was cataloged in 1915 and 1916. Rubber-stamped "NEW YORK

601 Pullman Type IV

CENTRAL LINES", the car also had maroon window inserts. No number was stamped on the end of the car, unlike later editions.

VG	EX	LN	RARITY
50	60	75	4

601 Pullman (Type II): The dark green Pullman with maroon inserts was continued through 1917 and 1918. Now, in addition to the "NEW YORK CENTRAL LINES" rubber-stamping on the car sides, "601" was stamped on one end.

VG	EX	LN	RARITY
50	60	75	4

601 Pullman (Type III): Some of the 1917-18 dark green Pullmans had celluloid window glazing. These cars also had maroon window inserts, and "NEW YORK CENTRAL LINES" and "601" rubber-stamping.

VG	EX	LN	RARITY
50	60	75	4

601 Pullman (Type IV):  From 1918 through 1923, the bottom of the Pullman floor was rubber-stamped "MADE IN U.S.A. – THE LIONEL CORPORATION – NEW YORK". The dark green paint, maroon inserts, "601" and "NEW YORK CENTRAL LINES" stamping, and celluloid windows were all carried over.

VG	EX	LN	RARITY
50	60	75	4

601 Observation (Type V): The number 601 returned in 1933, with an all-new body. Through 1934, these cars had a light gray body, red roof and ivory window insert. They were decorated with brass trim, copper journal boxes and red underframe.

VG	EX	LN	RARITY
40	60	90	3

601 Observation (Type VI): Sometime in the 1935-36 period, the light gray observation was made with nickel trim and journal boxes. These cars had red underframes and roofs, and ivory window inserts.

VG	EX	LN	RARITY
40	60	90	3

601 Observation (Type VII): In 1935, the body of the observation car was painted light blue. Attached were an aluminum-painted roof and window insert. Nickel trim, including observation railings, nickel journal boxes and an aluminum-painted underframe completed the car.

VG	EX	LN	RARITY
50	75	110	5

601 Observation (Type VIII): The observation railings on some of the light blue cars were painted the same color as the body. These cars had aluminum-painted roofs, window inserts and underframes. The remainder of the trim, including the journal boxes, was nickel.

VG	EX	LN	RARITY
50	75	110	5

601 Observation (Type IX): In 1936, the light blue and aluminum colored car was equipped with box rather than latch couplers. It continued to have nickel trim, nickel journal boxes and an aluminum-painted underframe. Its observation railing was aluminum.

VG	EX	LN	RARITY
50	75	110	5

Price Guide Key: **VG** = Very Good, **EX** = Excellent, **LN** = Like New | *Values for each condition are in U.S. dollars.* | **Rarity** = Scale from 1-8 with 8 being the hardest to find.

241

O GAUGE PASSENGER & STREAMLINER CARS

601 OBSERVATION TYPE XI

601 Observation (Type X): Latch coupler-equipped observations, painted light red with dark red roofs and ivory inserts, were sold in 1936 and 1937. These cars had nickel trim, nickel journal boxes and red underframes. The observation railings of these cars were painted light red to match the body.

VG	EX	LN	RARITY
40	60	90	3

601 Observation (Type XI):  The light red cars sometimes had box couplers during 1936 and 1937. Like the latch coupler-equipped cars, these also had dark red roofs, ivory inserts, nickel trim, nickel journal boxes and red underframes. Their observation railings were aluminum.

VG	EX	LN	RARITY
40	60	90	3

602 Baggage car: This number was assigned to two vastly different baggage cars. The first version was sold from 1915 through 1923. The number returned in 1933 and, along with the matching 600 Pullman and 601 observation, stayed in the product line through 1937.

602 Baggage (Type I): This dark green baggage car was cataloged in 1915 and 1916. Rubber-stamped "NEW YORK CENTRAL LINES", the car also had maroon baggage doors. No number was stamped on the end of the car, unlike later editions.

VG	EX	LN	RARITY
25	40	60	3

602 Baggage (Type II): The dark green baggage car with maroon doors was continued through 1917 and 1918. Now, in addition to the "NEW YORK CENTRAL LINES" rubber-stamping on the car sides, "602" was stamped on one end.

VG	EX	LN	RARITY
25	40	60	3

602 Baggage (Type III): Some of the 1917-18 dark green baggage cars had celluloid window glazing. These cars also had maroon baggage doors, and "NEW YORK CENTRAL LINES" and "602" rubber-stamping.

VG	EX	LN	RARITY
25	40	60	3

602 Baggage (Type IV): From 1918 through 1923, the bottom of the baggage car floor was rubber-stamped "MADE IN U.S.A. – THE LIONEL CORPORATION – NEW YORK". The dark green paint, maroon baggage doors, "602" and "NEW YORK CENTRAL LINES" stamping and celluloid windows were all carried over.

VG	EX	LN	RARITY
25	40	60	3

602 Baggage (Type V): The baggage car was also painted yellow-orange. These cars had simulated wood-grained doors, and were rubber-stamped "NEW YORK CENTRAL LINES".

VG	EX	LN	RARITY
25	40	60	3

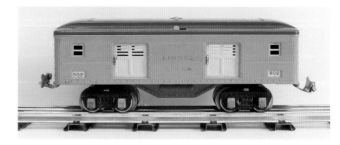

602 Baggage (Type VI): The number 602 returned in 1933, with an all-new body. Through 1934, these cars had a light gray body, red roof and ivory window insert. They were decorated with brass trim, copper journal boxes and red underframe.

VG	EX	LN	RARITY
50	75	110	5

603 PULLMAN TYPE IV

602 Baggage (Type VII): In 1935, the body of the baggage was painted light blue. Attached were an aluminum-painted roof and window insert. Nickel trim, nickel journal boxes and an aluminum-painted underframe completed the car.

VG	EX	LN	RARITY
50	75	110	5

602 Baggage (Type VIII): In 1936, the light blue and aluminum colored baggage car was equipped with box rather than latch couplers. It continued to have nickel trim, nickel journal boxes and an aluminum-painted underframe.

VG	EX	LN	RARITY
80	100	135	5

602 Baggage (Type IX): Latch coupler-equipped baggage cars painted light red, with dark red roofs and ivory inserts, were sold in 1936 and 1937. These cars had nickel trim, nickel journal boxes and red underframes.

VG	EX	LN	RARITY
50	75	110	5

602 Baggage (Type X): The light red cars sometimes had box couplers during 1936 and 1937. Like the latch coupler-equipped cars, these also had dark red roofs, ivory inserts, nickel trim, nickel journal boxes and red underframes.

VG	EX	LN	RARITY
50	75	110	5

603 Pullman: Three different body types were used during the course of the production of this car. One, of indeterminate date, was 7" long, the second was 6 1/2" long and the third was 7 1/2" long.

603 Pullman (Type I): As an uncataloged item in the early 1920s, this car used the same 7" long body as the 601. It was painted yellow-orange and equipped with wood-grained doors. The sides of the car were rubber-stamped "NEW YORK CENTRAL LINES".

VG	EX	LN	RARITY
40	60	80	5

603 Pullman (Type II): During 1920-25, a 6 1/2" long Pullman painted yellow-orange was made. The car was equipped with simulated wood-grained doors and was rubber-stamped "Pullman".

VG	EX	LN	RARITY
25	35	50	3

603 Pullman (Type III): Some of the 1920-25 6 1/2" long Pullmans had maroon doors. They too were painted yellow-orange and rubber-stamped "Pullman".

VG	EX	LN	RARITY
25	35	50	3

603 Pullman (Type IV): The underside of some of the 6 1/2" long cars was rubber-stamped "MADE IN USA – THE LIONEL CORPORATION – NEW YORK". The car bodies were painted yellow-orange and maroon doors were installed. The sides of the cars were marked "PULLMAN". This car was discontinued in 1925 or earlier.

VG	EX	LN	RARITY
25	35	50	3

603 Pullman (Type V): In 1930, the number 603 returned, once again assigned to a Pullman. Continued through 1931, each of these red cars was equipped with a black roof, cream trim and nickel journal boxes.

Price Guide Key: **VG** = Very Good, **EX** = Excellent, **LN** = Like New | *Values for each condition are in U.S. dollars.* | **Rarity** = Scale from 1-8 with 8 being the hardest to find.

243

603 PULLMAN TYPE VIII

VG	EX	LN	RARITY
30	45	60	4

603 Pullman (Type VI): Produced in 1931, this maroon Pullman had a black roof, cream trim and copper journal boxes.

VG	EX	LN	RARITY
75	100	140	6

603 Pullman (Type VII): Believed to have been sold in 1931 and 1934 were red cars with yellow trim. These cars had black roofs and copper journal boxes.

VG	EX	LN	RARITY
30	45	60	4

603 Pullman (Type VIII): 🖼 In 1932, cream trim was used on the red and black Pullman. Copper journal boxes and a black roof completed the car.

VG	EX	LN	RARITY
30	45	60	4

603 Pullman (Type IX): A yellow-orange version of the Pullman was sold in 1931-33. These cars had terra-cotta roofs and cream trim. Their trucks had nickel journal boxes.

VG	EX	LN	RARITY
30	45	60	4

603 Pullman (Type X): In 1933, a green Pullman with green roof was produced. These cars had cream trim and copper journal boxes.

VG	EX	LN	RARITY
30	45	60	4

603 Pullman (Type XI): Sold in 1935-36 was a red Pullman with black roof, yellow trim and nickel journal boxes.

VG	EX	LN	RARITY
30	45	60	4

603 Pullman (Type XII): Copper journal boxes were used on a light red Pullman with light red roof. This car had cream trim.

VG	EX	LN	RARITY
30	45	60	4

603 Pullman (Type XIII): In 1935 and 1936, white trim was used on a light red Pullman with light red roof. This car's trucks had nickel journal boxes.

No. 1090E REMOTE CONTROL PASSENGER OUTFIT

Locomotive in this outfit is more accurately detailed than any ever made before for a moderately priced set. Tender and cars have remote control couplers. Outfit consists of: No. 1666E Locomotive, No. 2689T Tender, two No. 2630 Passenger cars, No. 2631 Observation car, eight sections of No. 1013 curved track, three sections of No. 1018 straight track, No. 1019 track set, Lockon and No. 1039 Transformer. Train is 49¼ inches long. Track supplied forms an oval 27 by 43 inches. **Price $13.75**

No. 1090W. Same as No. 1090E but with built-in whistle and No. 1040 60-watt, combination transformer and whistle controller. **Price $17.50**

No. 1089E REMOTE CONTROL FREIGHT OUTFIT

New, 6-wheel drive steam type locomotive with fascinating driving gear action. Remote Control couplers are built into tender and all cars. Outfit consists of: No. 1666E Locomotive, No. 2689T Tender, No. 2679 Box car, No. 2680 Oil car, No. 2682 Caboose, eight sections of No. 1013 curved track, three sections of No. 1018 straight track, No. 1019 track set, Lockon and No. 1039 Transformer. Train measures 44 inches. Track supplied forms an oval 27 by 43 inches. **Price $11.95**

No. 1089W. Same as No. 1089E but with built-in whistle and No. 1040 combination transformer and whistle controller. **Price $15.75**

All "027" series outfits include a heavy duty transformer.

No. 1666EW LOCOMOTIVE-TENDER OUTFIT
Complete with electric coupler, built-in whistle and No. 1040 transformer-whistle controller. For use with "027" cars. Length, overall, 17½ inches. **Price $10.75**

ELECTRIC COUPLERS
At a touch of the control button, used at any distance from the track, cars uncouple . . . any car, just as your finger dictates.

No. 1093E COMPLETE RAILROAD

Electric remote control switches and electric couplers combine to add extreme interest to the operation of this train. Outfit consists of No. 1666E Locomotive, No. 2689T Tender, No. 2679 Box car, No. 2680 Oil car, No. 2682 Caboose, ten sections of No. 1013 curved track, five sections of No. 1018 straight track, No. 1019 track set, Lockon, No. 1039 Transformer and one pair of No. 1121 Switches. Train is 44 inches long. **Price $16.50**

No. 1093W. Same as No. 1093E but with built-in whistle and with No. 1040 combination transformer and whistle controller. **Price $20.25**

1938 CATALOG

HEAVY DUTY 2·6·2 STEAM TYPE LOCOMOTIVE WITH DISC WHEELS

NEW 12-INCH, ILLUMINATED PULLMANS · ENAMELED, FOUR-WHEEL TRUCK FREIGHT CARS

No. 178E "O" GAUGE REMOTE CONTROL PASSENGER TRAIN OUTFIT

Three new, illuminated, 12-inch cars are finished in brilliant enamel, have removable roofs and electric couplers. Locomotive is powered by an "O" gauge motor. Outfit consists of: No. 224E 6-wheel locomotive, No. 2689T Tender, two No. 2640 Illuminated passenger cars, No. 2641 Observation car, eight sections of OC curved track, three sections of OS straight track, R.S.C. track set, Lockon and No. 88 Controller. Train is 49¼ inches long. Track supplied forms an oval 50 by 30 inches. **Price $15.00**

Type "B" Transformer will operate either 178E or W. Type "T" will provide for accessories.

No. 178W. Same as No. 178E, described above, but equipped with built-in whistle and whistle controller. **Price $18.75**

No. 177E "O" GAUGE REMOTE CONTROL FREIGHT TRAIN OUTFIT

A heavy-duty "O" gauge motor supplies the power for this realistic 6-wheel drive locomotive. All cars are enameled and have electric couplers. Outfit consists of: No. 224E Locomotive, No. 2689T Tender, No. 2652 Gondola car, No. 2654 Oil car, No. 2657 Caboose, eight sections of OC curved track, three sections of OS straight track, Lockon and No. 88 Controller. Train is 42¼ inches long. Track supplied forms an oval 50 by 30 inches. **Price $13.75**

Type "L" Transformer will operate the above train. Type "B" is recommended for 177W.

No. 177W. Same as No. 177E, described above, but equipped with built-in whistle and whistle controller. **Price $17.50**

No. 2224EW LOCOMOTIVE-TENDER OUTFIT
Tender No. 02689W has remote control coupler at car end. Equipped with built-in locomotive whistle. For use with cars of the 2640 and 2651 series, also with cars of the 651 series which do not have electric couplers. Locomotive and tender are 17½ inches long. Locomotive and tender, with whistle controller. **Price $15.00**

ELECTRIC REMOTE CONTROL COUPLERS

13

1938 CATALOG

Price Guide Key: **VG** = Very Good, **EX** = Excellent, **LN** = Like New | *Values for each condition are in U.S. dollars.* | **Rarity** = Scale from 1-8 with 8 being the hardest to find.

245

O GAUGE PASSENGER & STREAMLINER CARS

604 OBSERVATION TYPE III

VG	EX	LN	RARITY
30	45	60	4

604 Observation: Two different body types were used during the course of the production of this car. The first, offered from 1920 through 1925, was 6 1/2" long and the second, spanning 1931-1936, was 7 1/2" long.

604 Observation (Type I): During 1920-25, a 6 1/2" long observation painted yellow-orange was made. The car was equipped with simulated wood-grained doors, and was rubber-stamped "Observation".

VG	EX	LN	RARITY
30	45	60	4

604 Observation (Type II): Some of the 1920-25 6 1/2" long observations had maroon doors. They too were painted yellow-orange and rubber-stamped "Observation".

VG	EX	LN	RARITY
30	45	60	4

604 Observation (Type III): 🔲 The underside of some of the 6 1/2" long cars was rubber-stamped "MADE IN USA – THE LIONEL CORPORATION – NEW YORK". The car bodies were painted yellow-orange and maroon doors were installed. The sides of the cars were marked "OBSERVATION". This car was discontinued in 1925 or earlier.

VG	EX	LN	RARITY
30	45	60	4

604 Observation (Type IV): In 1930, the number 604 returned, once again assigned to an observation. Continued through 1931, each of these red cars was equipped with a black roof, cream trim and nickel journal boxes.

VG	EX	LN	RARITY
30	45	60	4

604 Observation (Type V): Produced in 1931, this maroon observation had a black roof, cream trim and copper journal boxes.

VG	EX	LN	RARITY
75	100	140	6

604 Observation (Type VI): Believed to have been sold in 1931 and 1934 were red cars with yellow trim. These cars had black roofs and copper journal boxes.

VG	EX	LN	RARITY
30	45	60	4

604 Observation (Type VII): In 1932, cream trim was used on the red and black observation. Copper journal boxes and a black roof completed the car.

604 OBSERVATION TYPE XI

VG	EX	LN	RARITY
30	45	60	4

604 Observation (Type VIII): A yellow-orange version of the observation was sold in 1931-33. These cars had terra-cotta roofs and cream trim. Their trucks had nickel journal boxes.

VG	EX	LN	RARITY
30	45	60	4

604 Observation (Type IX): In 1933, a green observation with green roof was produced. These cars had cream trim and copper journal boxes.

VG	EX	LN	RARITY
30	45	60	4

604 Observation (Type X): Sold in 1935-36 was a red observation with black roof, yellow trim and nickel journal boxes.

VG	EX	LN	RARITY
30	45	60	4

604 Observation (Type XI): ⁎ Copper journal boxes were used on a light red observation with light red roof. This car had cream trim.

VG	EX	LN	RARITY
30	45	60	4

604 Observation (Type XII): In 1935 and 1936, white trim was used on a light red observation with light red roof. This car's trucks had nickel journal boxes.

VG	EX	LN	RARITY
30	45	60	4

605 Pullman: At 10 1/2" long, this Pullman was among the largest 0 gauge passenger cars produced by Lionel in the prewar era. First appearing in the 1925 edition, these cars were fixtures in the Lionel catalog through 1932. The cars were decorated with brass steps and opening doors.

605 Pullman (Type I): From 1925 through 1928, this 10 1/2" long Pullman had a gray body, roof and clerestory. "NEW YORK CENTRAL LINES" was rubber-stamped above the windows. Maroon doors and trim, as well as nickel journal boxes, were installed.

VG	EX	LN	RARITY
75	110	175	4

605 Pullman (Type II): Beginning in 1928, and continuing through 1930, red trim was installed on the car. The body, roof and clerestory all remained gray, and the nickel journal boxes continued to be installed.

VG	EX	LN	RARITY
75	110	175	4

605 Pullman (Type III): In 1926, "ILLINOIS CENTRAL" markings began to be applied the gray car sides. The roof was

Price Guide Key: **VG** = Very Good, **EX** = Excellent, **LN** = Like New | *Values for each condition are in U.S. dollars.* | **Rarity** = Scale from 1-8 with 8 being the hardest to find.

247

O GAUGE PASSENGER & STREAMLINER CARS

605 PULLMAN TYPE XI

gray and the trim maroon. Nickel journal boxes were used on this car, which was offered into 1927.

VG	EX	LN	RARITY
75	110	175	4

605 Pullman (Type IV): Between 1926 and 1927, cars with red bodies and roofs were lettered "ILLINOIS CENTRAL" as well. These cars had ivory trim and nickel journal boxes.

VG	EX	LN	RARITY
250	300	350	6

605 Pullman (Type V): "ILLINOIS CENTRAL" was also the road name applied to cars that had orange bodies and roofs, ivory trim and nickel journal boxes. Such cars were offered 1926-27.

VG	EX	LN	RARITY
300	350	400	7

605 Pullman (Type VI): During 1927-28, "THE LIONEL LINES" began to be rubber-stamped on some cars. The body roof and clerestory of these cars was painted gray. The trim was painted maroon trim and nickel journal boxes were installed.

VG	EX	LN	RARITY
75	110	175	4

605 Pullman (Type VII): Red trim was used on some cars marked "THE LIONEL LINES" with gray body, roof and clerestory. Sold in 1927 and the following year, these cars had nickel journal boxes.

VG	EX	LN	RARITY
75	110	175	4

605 Pullman (Type VIII): Another version of the gray "THE LIONEL LINES" Pullman car had an apple green clerestory on its gray roof. The rest of the trim was maroon and nickel journal boxes were used. This version is believed to date from 1927-28.

VG	EX	LN	RARITY
75	110	175	4

605 Pullman (Type IX): Some of the red cars with ivory trim were marked "THE LIONEL LINES" as well. In 1928-29, these cars were equipped with a red roof and nickel journal boxes.

VG	EX	LN	RARITY
150	200	250	6

605 Pullman (Type X): Later production red "THE LIONEL LINES" cars used copper journal boxes. Until discontinued in 1932, red roofs and ivory trim were used on these cars.

VG	EX	LN	RARITY
150	200	250	6

605 Pullman (Type XI): Orange paint was used on the body and roof of some of Pullman cars lettered "THE LIONEL LINES". The doors of these cars were green and the trim cream. Believed to have been produced during the 1929-30 period, these cars had copper journal boxes.

VG	EX	LN	RARITY
150	200	250	6

605 Pullman (Type XII): Other orange cars lettered "THE LIONEL LINES" had dark olive trim and maroon doors. The roofs of these cars were orange as well, and nickel journal boxes were installed. These cars date from 1929-30.

VG	EX	LN	RARITY
150	200	250	6

605 Pullman (Type XIII): The last cars of the series were painted olive green and rubber-stamped "THE LIONEL LINES". Red trim and copper journal boxes are found on these 1932-33 passenger cars.

VG	EX	LN	RARITY
250	300	350	7

605 Pullman (Type XIV): A special production version of the 605 was rubber-stamped "MACY SPECIAL" on the sides of its orange body. Dark red trim and pea green doors decorated this 1929-30 car, which had an orange roof and nickel journal boxes.

VG	EX	LN	RARITY
250	300	350	7

606 Observation: This 10 1/2" long observation car was built to match the 605 Pullman. First appearing in the 1925 edition, these cars were a fixture in the Lionel catalog through 1932. The cars were decorated with brass steps and opening doors.

606 Observation (Type I): From 1925 through 1928, this 10 1/2" long observation had a gray body, roof and clerestory. "NEW YORK CENTRAL LINES" was rubber-

606 OBSERVATION TYPE I

stamped above the windows. Maroon doors and trim, as well as nickel journal boxes, were installed.

VG	EX	LN	RARITY
75	110	175	4

606 Observation (Type II): Beginning in 1928, and continuing through 1930, red trim was installed on the car. The body, roof and clerestory all remained gray, and the nickel journal boxes continued to be installed.

VG	EX	LN	RARITY
75	110	175	4

606 Observation (Type III): In 1926, "ILLINOIS CENTRAL" markings began to be applied to the gray car sides. The roof was gray and the trim maroon. Nickel journal boxes were used on this car, which was offered into 1927.

VG	EX	LN	RARITY
75	110	175	4

606 Observation (Type IV): Between 1926 and 1927, cars with red bodies and roofs were lettered "ILLINOIS CENTRAL" as well. These cars had ivory trim and nickel journal boxes.

VG	EX	LN	RARITY
250	300	350	7

606 Observation (Type V): "ILLINOIS CENTRAL" was also the road name applied to cars that had orange bodies and roofs, ivory trim and nickel journal boxes. Such cars were offered in 1926-27.

VG	EX	LN	RARITY
150	200	250	6

606 Observation (Type VI): During 1927-28, "THE LIONEL LINES" began to be rubber-stamped on some cars. The body roof and clerestory of these cars was painted gray. The trim was painted maroon and nickel journal boxes were installed.

VG	EX	LN	RARITY
75	110	175	4

606 Observation (Type VII): Red trim was used on some cars marked "THE LIONEL LINES" with gray body, roof and clerestory. Sold in 1927 and the following year, these cars had nickel journal boxes.

VG	EX	LN	RARITY
75	110	175	4

606 Observation (Type VIII): Another version of the gray "THE LIONEL LINES" observation car had an apple green clerestory on its gray roof. The rest of the trim was maroon and nickel journal boxes were used. This version is believed to date from 1927-28.

VG	EX	LN	RARITY
75	110	175	4

606 Observation (Type IX): Some of the red cars with ivory trim were marked "THE LIONEL LINES" as well. In 1928-29, these cars were equipped with a red roof and nickel journal boxes.

VG	EX	LN	RARITY
150	200	250	6

606 Observation (Type X): Later production red "THE LIONEL LINES" cars used copper journal boxes. Until discontinued in 1932, red roofs and ivory trim were used on these cars.

VG	EX	LN	RARITY
150	200	250	6

606 Observation (Type XI): Orange paint was used on the body and roof of some of observation cars lettered "THE LIONEL LINES". The doors of these cars were green and the trim cream. Believed to have been produced during the 1929-30 period, these cars had copper journal boxes.

VG	EX	LN	RARITY
150	200	250	6

O GAUGE PASSENGER & STREAMLINER CARS

Price Guide Key: **VG** = Very Good, **EX** = Excellent, **LN** = Like New | *Values for each condition are in U.S. dollars.* | **Rarity** = Scale from 1-8 with 8 being the hardest to find.

249

607 Pullman Type I

606 Observation (Type XII): Other orange cars lettered "THE LIONEL LINES" had dark olive trim and maroon doors. The roofs of these cars were orange as well, and nickel journal boxes were installed. These cars date from 1929-30.

VG	EX	LN	RARITY
150	200	250	6

606 Observation (Type XIII): The last cars of the series were painted olive green and rubber-stamped "THE LIONEL LINES". Red trim and copper journal boxes are found on these 1932-33 passenger cars.

VG	EX	LN	RARITY
250	300	350	7

606 Observation (Type XIV): A special production version of the 606 was rubber-stamped "MACY SPECIAL" on the sides of its orange body. Dark red trim and pea green doors decorated this 1929-30 car, which had an orange roof and nickel journal boxes.

VG	EX	LN	RARITY
250	300	350	7

607 Pullman: This 7 1/2" long Pullman car was sold from 1926 through 1937. It utilized the same body stamping as the 609 and the final series 603 cars.

607 Pullman (Type I):  From 1926 through 1930, the body and roof of the car were painted peacock. Orange trim and nickel journal boxes were installed.

VG	EX	LN	RARITY
40	50	65	3

607 Pullman (Type II): During 1931, the cars were made with a red body and roof. These cars had cream trim and nickel journal boxes.

VG	EX	LN	RARITY
75	85	100	5

607 Pullman (Type III): In 1931, the body and roof of these cars began to be painted Stephen Girard green. At the same time, the trim was painted yellow and copper journal boxes began to be used. Cars were produced in this manner through 1934.

VG	EX	LN	RARITY
75	85	100	5

607 Pullman (Type IV): The Stephen Girard green passenger cars got nickel journal boxes in 1935, which remained in use through 1937. The trim continued to be painted yellow.

VG	EX	LN	RARITY
75	85	100	5

608 Observation: This 7 1/2" long observation car was sold from 1926 through 1937. It utilized the same body stamping as the 609 and the final series 603 cars, and matched the 607 Pullman.

608 OBSERVATION TYPE III

608 Observation (Type I): From 1926 through 1930, the body and roof of the car were painted peacock. Orange trim and nickel journal boxes were installed.

VG	EX	LN	RARITY
40	50	65	3

608 Observation (Type II): During 1931, the cars were made with a red body and roof. These cars had cream trim and nickel journal boxes.

VG	EX	LN	RARITY
75	85	100	5

608 Observation (Type III): 🖼 In 1931, the body and roof of these cars began to be painted Stephen Girard green. At the same time, the trim was painted yellow and copper journal boxes began to be used. Cars were produced in this manner through 1934.

VG	EX	LN	RARITY
75	85	100	5

608 Observation (Type IV): The Stephen Girard green passenger cars got nickel journal boxes in 1935, which remained in use through 1937. The trim continued to be painted yellow.

VG	EX	LN	RARITY
75	85	100	5

609 Pullman: This uncataloged 7 1/2" long blue and silver Pullman car was sold from 1937 through 1942.

VG	EX	LN	RARITY
60	75	100	5

610 Pullman: Cars numbered 610 were produced in two vastly different styles. The early body was used from 1915 through 1925. The following year, a new body was introduced, which was used variously in cataloged and uncataloged sets through 1942.

610 Pullman (Type I): As built in 1915 and 1916, this Pullman was painted dark green and had maroon doors. The upper windows were glazed with red speckled celluloid. "NEW YORK CENTRAL LINES" was rubber-stamped in gold above the windows.

VG	EX	LN	RARITY
45	55	70	3

610 Pullman (Type II): During 1917-18, the doors of the dark green cars were painted to simulate wood-grain. The glazing of the upper windows was changed to blue speckled celluloid. Above the windows continued to be gold rubber-stamped "NEW YORK CENTRAL LINES".

VG	EX	LN	RARITY
45	55	70	3

610 Pullman (Type III): From 1919 through 1922, "610" was rubber-stamped on the end of the dark green Pullman. Both the wood-grained doors and blue speckled celluloid upper windows were continued, as were the gold rubber-stamped "NEW YORK CENTRAL LINES" markings.

VG	EX	LN	RARITY
45	55	70	3

610 Pullman (Type IV): 🖼 Illumination was added to the dark green cars in 1923. The blue speckled celluloid upper windows remained in use, as did the gold rubber-stamped

Price Guide Key: **VG** = Very Good, **EX** = Excellent, **LN** = Like New | *Values for each condition are in U.S. dollars.* | **Rarity** = Scale from 1-8 with 8 being the hardest to find.

251

610 PULLMAN TYPE IV

"NEW YORK CENTRAL LINES" markings. Produced through 1925, some of these cars had maroon doors.

VG	EX	LN	RARITY
45	55	70	3

610 Pullman (Type V): Also sold in the 1923-35 era were illuminated cars painted mojave. These cars had wood-grained doors, blue speckled celluloid upper windows and gold rubber-stamped "NEW YORK CENTRAL LINES" lettering.

VG	EX	LN	RARITY
55	75	100	5

610 Pullman (Type VI): Some of the illuminated mojave passenger cars had maroon doors. Blue speckled celluloid upper windows and gold rubber-stamped "NEW YORK CENTRAL LINES" were used on these cars from 1923 to 1925.

VG	EX	LN	RARITY
55	75	100	5

610 Pullman (Type VII): Also sold during 1923-25 were illuminated cars painted maroon. These cars had dark green doors, blue speckled celluloid upper windows and gold rubber-stamped "NEW YORK CENTRAL LINES".

VG	EX	LN	RARITY
55	75	100	5

610 Pullman (Type VIII): In 1926, a new body style was introduced for the 610. Still illuminated, this design had painted inserts that acted as below-the-windowline lettering and number boards. Lettering above the windows was still rubber-stamped directly on the body. The older body had six large double windows per side, whereas this body had eight single windows per side. One of the color schemes offered in 1926 featured an olive green body and roof, with maroon inserts. Gold rubber-stamped "THE LIONEL LINES" lettering was applied above the windows and "610 PULLMAN 610" was rubber-stamped on the inserts. These cars had nickel journal boxes. They were offered through 1928.

VG	EX	LN	RARITY
50	60	75	3

610 Pullman (Type IX): The new style body was also painted mojave and came with maroon trim. These cars were illuminated, and had gold rubber-stamped "NEW YORK CENTRAL LINES" above the windows and "610 PULLMAN 610" below the windows. Produced this way about 1926, the cars had nickel journal boxes.

VG	EX	LN	RARITY
50	60	75	3

610 Pullman (Type X): Mojave cars with maroon trim were also produced with "ILLINOIS CENTRAL" gold rubber-stamped above the windows in 1926. These cars had "610 PULLMAN 610" visible on the below-the-windows inserts and used nickel journal boxes.

610 PULLMAN TYPE XX

VG	EX	LN	RARITY
100	125	150	6

610 Pullman (Type XI): During 1929, the passenger cars were painted olive green with red trim. "THE LIONEL LINES" was rubber-stamped in gold above the windows. On the inserts below the windows was rubber-stamped "610 PULLMAN 610" in gold. These cars were illuminated and had nickel journal boxes.

VG	EX	LN	RARITY
50	60	75	3

610 Pullman (Type XII): Orange trim was used on some of illuminated, olive green "THE LIONEL LINES" cars. Like the rest of the illuminated cars in this series, these cars had "610 PULLMAN 610" rubber-stamped on the below-the-windows inserts. Nickel journal boxes were used on the trucks during this car's 1929-30 production.

VG	EX	LN	RARITY
50	60	75	3

610 Pullman (Type XIII): In 1930, a new color, pea green, appeared on the body and roof of the 610. Orange trim and nickel journal boxes were installed on these illuminated cars. Gold rubber-stamped "THE LIONEL LINES" lettering was applied above the windows and "610 PULLMAN 610" rubber-stamped on the inserts visible below the windows. This version was sold in 1930.

VG	EX	LN	RARITY
75	95	125	5

610 Pullman (Type XIV): Another 1930-produced version of this illuminated passenger car had "MACY SPECIAL" rubber-stamped in gold above the windows. Its body and roof were red, its trim ivory. This insert was rubber-stamped "610 PULLMAN 610" and nickel journal boxes used.

VG	EX	LN	RARITY
200	300	400	8

610 Pullman (Type XV): During 1931-32, a "THE IVES LINES" decal was applied over the gold rubber-stamped "THE LIONEL LINES lettering on some of the pea green

cars. Below the windows, the "610 PULLMAN 610" lettering was unaltered. These cars had orange trim, nickel journal boxes and were illuminated.

VG	EX	LN	RARITY
75	95	125	5

610 Pullman (Type XVI): A similar treatment was given to some olive green cars with orange trim. Here again, a "THE IVES LINES" decal was placed over the gold rubber-stamped "THE LIONEL LINES" lettering above the windows. These cars also had nickel journal boxes and "610 PULLMAN 610" rubber-stamped on the inserts below the windows. These cars were sold as Ives in 1931-32.

VG	EX	LN	RARITY
75	95	125	5

610 Pullman (Type XVII): Things were even stranger in 1933, when unsold olive green cars, which previously had Ives decals applied over the gold rubber-stamped "THE LIONEL LINES", had yet another decal applied. This decal, placed to cover the Ives decal, restored the "THE LIONEL LINES" lettering. These cars had red trim, nickel journal boxes and, like all the 1926-style cars, were illuminated.

VG	EX	LN	RARITY
100	125	150	6

610 Pullman (Type XVIII): One of the more attractive paint combinations applied to these cars was a terra-cotta body, maroon roof and cream trim. The gold rubber-stamped lettering "THE LIONEL LINES" was above the windows and "610 PULLMAN 610" below the windows. The cars had nickel journal boxes.

VG	EX	LN	RARITY
100	125	150	4

610 Pullman (Type XIX): Some cars were painted pea green with orange trim. They had gold rubber-stamped "THE LIONEL LINES" lettering above the windows and "610 PULLMAN 610" on the inserts below the windows. The trucks on these cars had copper journal boxes.

Price Guide Key: **VG** = Very Good, **EX** = Excellent, **LN** = Like New | *Values for each condition are in U.S. dollars.* | **Rarity** = Scale from 1-8 with 8 being the hardest to find.

253

O GAUGE PASSENGER & STREAMLINER CARS

611 OBSERVATION

VG	EX	LN	RARITY
75	95	125	5

610 Pullman (Type XX): 🖼 Around 1935, Lionel began painting the illuminated cars light red, with aluminum-painted roof and trim. "THE LIONEL LINES" lettering on these cars was rubber-stamped in black. Shipped through 1942, these cars had nickel journal boxes.

VG	EX	LN	RARITY
100	125	150	4

610 Pullman (Type XXI): Some of the light red and aluminum-painted cars had fancy scrollwork stamped on their inserts around the word "PULLMAN". These cars also had nickel journal boxes and were produced sometime between 1935 and 1942.

VG	EX	LN	RARITY
100	125	150	5

610 Pullman (Type XXII): During 1936-37, the body of the illuminated Pullman car was painted light blue. The roof and trim were painted an aluminum color, and "THE LIONEL LINES" and "610 PULLMAN 610" lettering was rubber-stamped in black. These cars had nickel journal boxes.

VG	EX	LN	RARITY
125	175	225	7

611 Observation: 🖼 This uncataloged 7 1/2" long blue and silver observation car matched the 609 Pullman and, like it, was sold from 1937 through 1942.

VG	EX	LN	RARITY
60	75	100	5

612 Observation: Cars numbered 612 were produced in two vastly different styles. The early body was used from 1915 through 1925. The following year, a new body was introduced, which was used variously in cataloged and uncataloged sets through 1942.

612 Observation (Type I): As built in 1915 and 1916, this observation car was painted dark green and had maroon doors. The upper windows were glazed with red speckled celluloid. "NEW YORK CENTRAL LINES" was rubber-stamped in gold above the windows.

VG	EX	LN	RARITY
45	55	70	3

612 Observation (Type II): During 1917-18, the doors of the dark green cars were painted to simulate wood grain. The glazing of the upper windows was changed to blue speckled celluloid. Above the windows continued to be gold rubber-stamped "NEW YORK CENTRAL LINES".

VG	EX	LN	RARITY
45	55	70	3

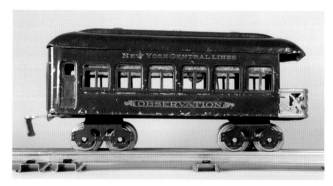

612 Observation (Type III): From 1919 through 1922, "612" was rubber-stamped on the end of the dark green observation. Both the wood-grained doors and blue speckled celluloid upper windows were continued, as were the gold rubber-stamped "NEW YORK CENTRAL LINES" markings.

VG	EX	LN	RARITY
45	55	70	3

612 Observation (Type IV): Illumination was added to the dark green cars in 1923. The blue speckled celluloid upper

612 OBSERVATION TYPE VI

windows remained in use, as did the gold rubber-stamped "NEW YORK CENTRAL LINES" markings. Produced through 1925, some of these cars had maroon doors.

VG	EX	LN	RARITY
45	55	70	3

612 Observation (Type V): Also sold in the 1923-35 era were illuminated cars painted mojave. These cars had wood-grained doors, blue speckled celluloid upper windows and gold rubber-stamped "NEW YORK CENTRAL LINES" lettering.

VG	EX	LN	RARITY
45	55	70	3

612 Observation (Type VI):  Also sold in the 1923-35 era were illuminated cars painted mojave. These cars had wood-grained doors, blue speckled celluloid upper windows and gold rubber-stamped "NEW YORK CENTRAL LINES" lettering.

VG	EX	LN	RARITY
55	75	100	5

612 Observation (Type VII): Some of the illuminated mojave passenger cars had maroon doors. Blue speckled celluloid upper windows and gold rubber-stamped "NEW YORK CENTRAL LINES" were used on these cars as well from 1923 to 1925.

VG	EX	LN	RARITY
55	75	100	5

612 Observation (Type VIII): Also sold during 1923-25 were illuminated cars painted maroon. These cars had dark green doors, blue speckled celluloid upper windows and gold rubber-stamped "NEW YORK CENTRAL LINES".

VG	EX	LN	RARITY
55	75	100	5

612 Observation (Type IX): In 1926, a new body style was introduced for the 612. Still illuminated, this design had painted inserts that acted as below-the-windowline lettering and number boards. Lettering above the windows was still rubber-stamped directly on the body. The older body had six large double windows per side, whereas this body had eight single windows per side. One of the color schemes offered in 1926 featured an olive green body and roof with maroon inserts. Gold rubber-stamped "THE LIONEL LINES" lettering was applied above the windows and "612 OBSERVATION 612" was rubber-stamped on the inserts. These cars had nickel journal boxes. They were offered through 1928.

VG	EX	LN	RARITY
50	60	75	3

612 Observation (Type X): The new style body was also painted mojave and came with maroon trim. These cars were illuminated, and had gold rubber-stamped "NEW YORK CENTRAL LINES" above the windows and "612 OBSERVATION 612" below the windows. Produced this way about 1926, the cars had nickel journal boxes.

VG	EX	LN	RARITY
50	60	75	3

612 Observation (Type XI): Mojave cars with maroon trim were also produced with "ILLINOIS CENTRAL" gold rubber-stamped above the windows in 1926. These cars had "612 OBSERVATION 612" visible on the below-the-windows inserts and used nickel journal boxes.

Price Guide Key: **VG** = Very Good, **EX** = Excellent, **LN** = Like New | *Values for each condition are in U.S. dollars.* | **Rarity** = Scale from 1-8 with 8 being the hardest to find.

255

VG	EX	LN	RARITY
100	125	150	6

612 Observation (Type XII): During 1929, the passenger cars were painted olive green with red trim. "THE LIONEL LINES" was in rubber-stamped in gold above the windows. On the inserts below the windows was rubber-stamped "612 OBSERVATION 612" in gold. These cars were illuminated and had nickel journal boxes.

VG	EX	LN	RARITY
50	60	75	3

612 Observation (Type XIII): Orange trim was used on some of the illuminated, olive green "THE LIONEL LINES" cars. Like the rest of the illuminated cars in this series, these cars had "612 OBSERVATION 612" rubber-stamped on the below-the-windows inserts. Nickel journal boxes were used on the trucks during this car's 1929-30 production.

VG	EX	LN	RARITY
50	60	75	3

612 Observation (Type XIV): In 1930, a new color, pea green, appeared on the body and roof of the 612. Orange trim and nickel journal boxes were installed on these illuminated cars. Gold rubber-stamped "THE LIONEL LINES" lettering was applied above the windows and "612 OBSERVATION 612" rubber-stamped on the inserts visible below the windows. This version was sold in 1930.

VG	EX	LN	RARITY
75	95	125	5

612 Observation (Type XV): Another 1930-produced version of this illuminated passenger car had "MACY SPECIAL" rubber-stamped in gold above the windows. Its body and roof were red, its trim ivory. This insert was rubber-stamped "612 OBSERVATION 612" and nickel journal boxes used.

VG	EX	LN	RARITY
200	300	400	8

612 Observation (Type XVI): During 1931-32, a "THE IVES LINES" decal was applied over the gold rubber-stamped "THE LIONEL LINES" lettering on some of the pea green cars. Below the windows, the "612 OBSERVATION 612" lettering was unaltered. These cars had orange trim, nickel journal boxes and were illuminated.

VG	EX	LN	RARITY
75	95	125	5

612 Observation (Type XVII): A similar treatment was given to some olive green cars with orange trim. Here again, a "THE IVES LINES" decal was placed over the gold rubber-stamped "THE LIONEL LINES" lettering above the windows. These cars also had nickel journal boxes and "612 OBSERVATION 612" rubber-stamped on the inserts below the windows. These cars were sold as Ives in 1931-32.

VG	EX	LN	RARITY
75	95	125	5

612 Observation (Type XVIII): Things were even stranger in 1933, when unsold olive green cars, which previously had Ives decals applied over the gold rubber-stamped "THE LIONEL LINES", had yet another decal applied. This decal, placed to cover the Ives decal, restored the "THE LIONEL LINES" lettering. These cars had red trim, nickel journal boxes and, like all the 1926-style cars, were illuminated.

VG	EX	LN	RARITY
100	125	150	6

612 Observation (Type XIX: One of the more attractive paint combinations applied to these cars was a terra-cotta body, maroon roof and cream trim. The gold rubber-stamped lettering "THE LIONEL LINES" was above the windows and "612 OBSERVATION 612" below the windows. The cars had nickel journal boxes.

VG	EX	LN	RARITY
100	125	150	4

612 Observation (Type XX): Some cars were painted pea green with orange trim. They had gold rubber-stamped "THE LIONEL LINES" lettering above the windows and "612 OBSERVATION 612" on the inserts below the windows. The trucks on these cars had copper journal boxes.

VG	EX	LN	RARITY
75	95	125	5

612 Observation (Type XXI): Around 1935, Lionel began painting the illuminated cars light red, with aluminum-painted roof and trim. The "THE LIONEL LINES" lettering on these cars was rubber-stamped in black. Shipped through 1942, these cars had nickel journal boxes.

VG	EX	LN	RARITY
100	125	150	4

612 Observation (Type XXII): Some of the light red and aluminum-painted cars had fancy scrollwork stamped on their inserts around the word "OBSERVATION". These cars also had nickel journal boxes and were produced sometime between 1935 and 1942.

VG	EX	LN	RARITY
100	125	150	5

612 Observation (Type XXIII): During 1936-37, the body of the illuminated observation car was painted light blue. The roof and trim were painted an aluminum color, and the "THE LIONEL LINES" and "612 OBSERVATION 612" lettering was rubber-stamped in black. These cars had nickel journal boxes.

VG	EX	LN	RARITY
125	175	225	7

613 Pullman: These 10 1/2" illuminated Pullman cars were offered from 1931 through 1940. Matching 614 observation and 615 baggage cars were produced as well. The cars had separately installed doors, and window and letterboard inserts of contrasting colors were installed as well.

613 Pullman (Type I): From 1931 through 1934, the body of the car was painted terra cotta while the roof was a combination of maroon and terra cotta. The inserts and doors were painted cream. The cars had copper journal boxes, and brass trim and steps. They were equipped with latch couplers.

VG	EX	LN	RARITY
100	140	200	6

613 PULLMAN

613 Pullman (Type II): The same car was produced again in 1935, in the same color combination. However, its trucks were now fitted with nickel journal boxes.

VG	EX	LN	RARITY
100	140	200	6

613 Pullman (Type III): New in 1935 was a light red car with light red and aluminum roof. Cream inserts and doors were used, as were nickel trim and steps, and nickel journal boxes. Some of these cars had latch couplers.

VG	EX	LN	RARITY
200	300	400	7

613 Pullman (Type IV): Box couplers were installed on some of the 1935 production light red and aluminum cars with cream inserts. The trim, steps and journal boxes all continued to be nickel.

VG	EX	LN	RARITY
200	300	400	7

613 Pullman (Type V): At some point in the mid-1930s, the cars were produced in blue with two-tone blue and dark blue roofs. These cars had white inserts, nickel trim and steps, and nickel journal boxes. Latch couplers were installed initially.

VG	EX	LN	RARITY
175	250	350	6

613 Pullman (Type VI): Later versions of the blue car with dark blue roof had box couplers. Again, they had white inserts, nickel trim and steps, and nickel journal boxes.

VG	EX	LN	RARITY
175	250	350	6

613 Pullman (Type VII): About 1940, steps and diaphragms were eliminated from the cars. The colors remained blue with white inserts and two-tone blue roof. These cars had nickel trim, nickel journal boxes and box couplers.

VG	EX	LN	RARITY
175	250	350	6

614 Observation: These 10 1/2" illuminated observation cars were offered from 1931 through 1940. They matched the 613 Pullman and 615 baggage cars of the era. The cars had separately installed doors, and window and letterboard inserts of contrasting colors were installed as well.

614 Observation (Type I): From 1931 through 1934, the body of the car was painted terra cotta while the roof was a combination of maroon and terra cotta. The inserts and doors were painted cream. The cars had copper journal boxes, and brass trim and steps. It was equipped with latch couplers.

VG	EX	LN	RARITY
100	140	200	6

614 Observation (Type II): The same car was produced again in 1935, in the same color combination. However, its trucks were now fitted with nickel journal boxes.

VG	EX	LN	RARITY
100	140	200	6

614 Observation (Type III): New in 1935 was a light red car with light red and aluminum roof. Cream inserts and doors were used, as were nickel trim and steps, and nickel journal boxes. Some of these cars had latch couplers.

VG	EX	LN	RARITY
200	300	400	7

Price Guide Key: **VG** = Very Good, **EX** = Excellent, **LN** = Like New | *Values for each condition are in U.S. dollars.* | **Rarity** = Scale from 1-8 with 8 being the hardest to find.

257

614 Observation Type VI

614 Observation (Type IV): Box couplers were installed on some of the 1935 production light red and aluminum cars with cream inserts. The trim, steps and journal boxes all continued to be nickel.

VG	EX	LN	RARITY
200	300	400	7

614 Observation (Type V): At some point in the mid-1930s, the cars were produced in blue with two-tone blue and dark blue roofs. These cars had white inserts, nickel trim and steps, and nickel journal boxes. Latch couplers were installed initially.

VG	EX	LN	RARITY
175	250	350	6

614 Observation (Type VI): Later versions of the blue car with dark blue roof had box couplers. Again, they had white inserts, nickel trim and steps, and nickel journal boxes.

VG	EX	LN	RARITY
175	250	350	6

614 Observation (Type VII): About 1940, steps and diaphragms were eliminated from the cars. The colors remained blue with white inserts and two-tone blue roof. These cars had nickel trim, nickel journal boxes and box couplers.

VG	EX	LN	RARITY
175	250	350	6

615 Baggage: These 10 1/2" baggage cars were offered from 1931 through 1940. They matched the 613 Pullman and 614 observation cars of the era. The cars had separately installed doors, and window and letterboard inserts of contrasting colors were installed as well.

615 Baggage (Type I): From 1931 through 1934, the body of the car was painted terra cotta while the roof was a combination of maroon and terra cotta. The inserts and doors were painted cream. The cars had copper journal boxes, and brass trim and steps. They were equipped with latch couplers.

VG	EX	LN	RARITY
100	140	200	6

615 Baggage (Type II): The same car was produced again in 1935, in the same color combination. However, its trucks were now fitted with nickel journal boxes.

VG	EX	LN	RARITY
100	140	200	6

615 Baggage (Type III): New in 1935 was a light red car with light red and aluminum roof. Cream inserts and doors were used, as were nickel trim and steps, and nickel journal boxes. Some of these cars had latch couplers.

VG	EX	LN	RARITY
200	300	400	7

615 Baggage (Type IV): Box couplers were installed on some of the 1935 production light red and aluminum cars with cream inserts. The trim, steps and journal boxes all continued to be nickel.

VG	EX	LN	RARITY
200	300	400	7

615 Baggage (Type V): At some point in the mid-1930s, the cars were produced in blue with two-tone blue and dark blue roofs. These cars had white inserts, nickel trim and steps, and nickel journal boxes. Latch couplers were installed initially.

VG	EX	LN	RARITY
175	250	350	6

615 Baggage (Type VI): Later versions of the blue car with dark blue roof had box couplers. Again, they had white inserts, nickel trim and steps, and nickel journal boxes.

VG	EX	LN	RARITY
175	250	350	6

616 FLYING YANKEE TYPE I

615 Baggage (Type VII): About 1940, steps and diaphragms were eliminated from the cars. The colors remained blue with white inserts and two-tone blue roof. These cars had nickel trim, nickel journal boxes, and box couplers.

VG	EX	LN	RARITY
175	250	350	6

616 Flying Yankee: The 616E and similar whistle-equipped 616W headed replicas of the streamlined, articulated Boston and Maine "Flying Yankee." These were sold in various color combinations, as well as various numbers, of matching 617 and 618 cars. These cars, in other paint colors, were also sold in other outfits, and those are listed separately.

616 Flying Yankee (Type I): As manufactured in 1935, the power unit was chrome-plated and had a black die-cast top. It came with two chrome 617 coaches with four doors each, and one chrome 618 observation car. All had fluted sides and chrome skirts.

Complete train:

VG	EX	LN	RARITY
300	400	550	4

616 Flying Yankee (Type II): During 1936-37, a gunmetal painted die-cast top was installed on the chrome-plated diesel locomotive body. The two chrome 617 coaches now had only two doors each. The chrome 618 observation had a gunmetal-painted rear casting. The outfit had fluted sides and chrome skirts.

Complete train:

VG	EX	LN	RARITY
275	375	500	4

616 Flying Yankee (Type III): From 1938 through 1941, the chrome and gunmetal outfit had gunmetal painted skirts. The remainder of the construction was identical to the type II.

Complete train:

VG	EX	LN	RARITY
275	375	500	4

616 Flying Yankee (Type IV): The 616 top and 618 rear die-castings were painted olive green in some cases. In such outfits, the chrome-plated locomotive towed two chrome 617 coaches with two doors each and a chrome 618. All had fluted sides and chrome skirts.

Complete train:

VG	EX	LN	RARITY
275	375	500	4

616 Flying Yankee (Type V): Red paint was used on the die-cast components of other outfits. Rather than being

Price Guide Key: **VG** = Very Good, **EX** = Excellent, **LN** = Like New | *Values for each condition are in U.S. dollars.* | **Rarity** = Scale from 1-8 with 8 being the hardest to find.

259

chrome-plated, this locomotive and matching cars, one-each coach and observation, was painted aluminum color. The 617 coach was equipped with four doors, and the sides of all were smooth rather than fluted.

Complete train:

VG	EX	LN	RARITY
275	375	500	4

616 Flying Yankee (Type VI): But for its fluted sides painted aluminum, this 1935 outfit was identical to the type V listed previously.

Complete train:

VG	EX	LN	RARITY
275	375	500	4

617 Coach (Type I): This chrome coach with four doors, fluted sides and chrome skirts was built in 1935.

VG	EX	LN	RARITY
50	60	75	4

617 Coach (Type II): During 1936-37, the chrome coach had two doors, fluted sides and chrome skirts.

VG	EX	LN	RARITY
50	60	75	4

617 Coach (Type III): Gunmetal skirts were used from 1938 through 1941. The chrome coach had two doors and fluted sides.

VG	EX	LN	RARITY
50	60	75	4

617 Coach (Type IV): The coach was also with made an aluminum-painted two-door body and fluted sides.

VG	EX	LN	RARITY
50	60	75	4

617 Coach (Type V): A painted-aluminum coach with four doors and smooth sides was also built, probably in 1935.

VG	EX	LN	RARITY
50	60	75	4

617 Coach (Type VI): Built for inclusion in the 1936-38 Blue Streak, this two-door coach was, naturally enough, painted blue with a white window band. Its sides were fluted.

VG	EX	LN	RARITY
60	70	85	4

617 Coach (Type VII): About 1936-37, an uncataloged version of the 617 two-door coach was made. This car was painted medium blue overall, with no contrasting window band. It had fluted sides and gunmetal skirts.

VG	EX	LN	RARITY
75	85	100	6

618 Observation (Type I): During 1935-37, the chrome observation had fluted sides, and chrome skirts and tail casting.

VG	EX	LN	RARITY
50	60	75	4

618 Observation (Type II): The skirts and die-cast observation end were painted gunmetal from 1938 through 1941. The chrome observation had two doors and fluted sides.

VG	EX	LN	RARITY
50	60	75	4

618 Observation (Type III): The observation was also with made an aluminum-painted body and fluted sides.

VG	EX	LN	RARITY
50	60	75	4

618 Observation (Type IV): A painted-aluminum coach with smooth sides was also built, probably in 1935.

VG	EX	LN	RARITY
50	60	75	4

618 Observation (Type V): Built for inclusion in the 1936-38 Blue Streak, this observation car was, naturally enough, painted blue with a white window band. Its sides were fluted.

VG	EX	LN	RARITY
60	70	85	4

618 Observation (Type VI): About 1936-37, an uncataloged version of the 618 observation was made. This car was painted medium blue overall, with no contrasting window band. It had fluted sides and gunmetal skirts.

VG	EX	LN	RARITY
75	85	100	6

619 Combination (Type I): This chrome combination baggage-coach had fluted sides and chrome skirts. Made in 1935, it matched the chrome 617 and 618 of the period.

629 PULLMAN

VG	EX	LN	RARITY
100	140	200	5

619 Combination (Type II): The combination car was also made in blue with a white window band.

VG	EX	LN	RARITY
100	140	200	6

629 Pullman: * Introduced in 1924, this 6 1/2" long, four-wheel car was the least expensive Lionel Pullman of the time. It remained in production through 1932. The 630 observation car was sold as its companion.

629 Pullman (Type I): From 1934 through 1927, these cars were painted dark green with maroon trim and doors. No journal boxes were installed on the car, which had hook couplers.

VG	EX	LN	RARITY
25	32	40	3

629 Pullman (Type II): A new color combination, orange with peacock trim, was made in 1927. These cars also had no journal boxes and were equipped with hook couplers.

VG	EX	LN	RARITY
25	32	40	3

629 Pullman (Type III): Latch couplers were used on some of the 1927 orange and peacock Pullman cars. No journal boxes were installed.

VG	EX	LN	RARITY
25	32	40	3

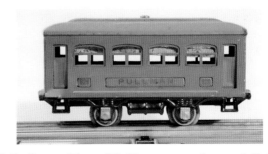

629 Pullman (Type IV): The orange and peacock Pullman with latch couplers was continued in 1928-29, but now had nickel journal boxes.

VG	EX	LN	RARITY
25	32	40	3

629 Pullman (Type V): Beginning in 1930, the Pullman began to be painted red with cream trim. Latch couplers were installed and some of the cars had nickel journal boxes.

VG	EX	LN	RARITY
18	22	30	2

629 Pullman (Type VI): Other red and cream cars had copper journal boxes, as well as latch couplers.

VG	EX	LN	RARITY
18	22	30	2

Price Guide Key: **VG** = Very Good, **EX** = Excellent, **LN** = Like New | *Values for each condition are in U.S. dollars.* | **Rarity** = Scale from 1-8 with 8 being the hardest to find.

261

O GAUGE PASSENGER & STREAMLINER CARS

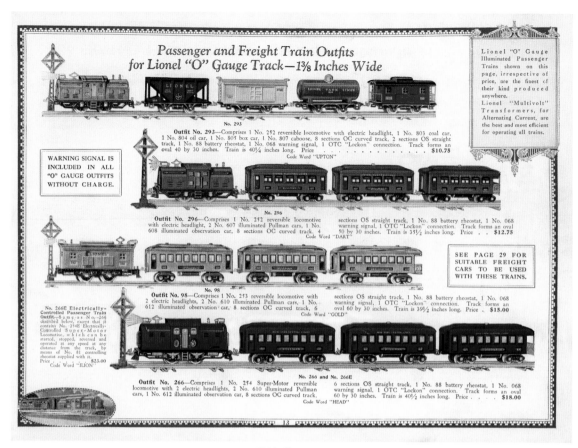

1927 Catalog

1939 Catalog

No. 2763EW WORM-DRIVEN LOCOMOTIVE-TENDER OUTFIT
Modified scale model with tender containing built-in whistle and electric coupler. Locomotive is driven by worm gears. Cab and boiler are a single-piece die casting containing a wealth of accurate detail. For use only on "O72" series track with cars in 2613, 2810, 613, 810 series. Outfit includes whistle-controller. **Price $58.25**

No. 769W	No. 767W	No. 768W
$52.50	$42.50	$45.00

No. 768W PASSENGER TRAIN
Equipped with *built-in whistle and electric couplers*. Outfit consists of: No. 763 Locomotive, No. 2263W Tender, No. 2615 Illuminated baggage car, two No. 2613 Illuminated Pullman cars, No. 2614 Illuminated observation car, sixteen sections of No. 761 curved track, two sections of No. 762 straight track, one section of OS straight track, R.C.S. track set, UTC Lockon and a whistling controller. Train is 68¾ inches long. Track supplied forms an oval 98⅞ by 74¼ inches. **Price $45.00**

No. 767W "O" GAUGE FREIGHT TRAIN
Powered by six-wheel-drive modified scale model Hudson with *built-in whistle*. Cars are equipped with electric couplers. Outfit consists of: No. 763 Locomotive, No. 2263W Tender, No. 2814 Box car, No. 2812 Gondola car, No. 2815 Oil tank car, No. 2817 Caboose, sixteen sections of No. 761 Curved track, two sections of No. 762 Straight track, one section of OS straight track, R.C.S. track set, UTC Lockon and a whistling controller. Train is 65½ inches long. Track supplied forms an oval 98⅞ by 74¼ inches. **Price $42.50**

No. 769W "O" GAUGE WORK TRAIN OUTFIT
Six-wheel-drive modified Hudson *with whistle-tender*. Equipped with electric couplers. Outfit consists of: No. 763 Locomotive, No. 2263W Tender, No. 2820 Floodlight car, No. 2812 Gondola car with tools, No. 2810 Crane, No. 2817 Caboose, sixteen No. 761 Curved track, two No. 762 Straight track, OS track, R.C.S., Lockon and whistling controller. Train, 65¾ inches long. Track oval, 98⅞ by 74¼ inches. **Price $52.50**

Type "R" Trainmaster Transformer will operate any one of these trains. Type "V", of greater capacity, will provide for the addition of numerous automatic and illuminated accessories.

1939 CATALOG

No. 267E "O" GAUGE REMOTE CONTROL STREAMLINE TRAIN OUTFIT
Chromium plated replica of the Boston and Maine's fast Flying Yankee. Built of steel and richly embellished by a wealth of accurate detail. Outfit consists of: No. 616E Power car, two No. 617 Coaches, No. 618 Observation car, No. 88 Reversing controller, eight sections of OC curved track, four sections of OS straight track and Lockon. Train is 42 inches long. Track forms oval 50 by 30 inches. **Price $12.50**

No. 267W. Same as No. 267E but with built-in whistle and whistle controller. **Price $16.50**
Type "B" Transformer will operate this train. Type "T" will provide for many accessories.
No. 616W. Motor car unit only, with built-in whistle and whistle controller. **Price $10.00**
No. 617. Coach with one vestibule. **Price $3.75**

Lionel streamline cars couple into vestibules by an ingenious lock-tight method. Vestibules contain lamps for interior illumination.

LIONEL UNION PACIFIC
"CITY OF DENVER"
No. 299W REMOTE CONTROL STREAMLINE TRAIN
Authentic reproduction of the yellow and golden-brown Pride of the West, the Union Pacific's "City of Denver". Equipped with built-in, remote control whistle. Outfit consists of: No. 636W Power car, two No. 637 Illuminated coaches, No. 638 Illuminated observation car, one Remote control for whistling and reversing, eight sections of OC curved track, four sections of OS straight track and Lockon. Train measures 42½ inches. Track forms an oval 50 by 30 inches. **Price $16.50**
Type "B" Lionel Multivolt Transformer will operate this train. Type "T", of greater capacity, will provide for the addition of numerous accessories.
No. 636W. Power car with whistle and whistle controller. **Price $10.00**
No. 637. Coach with one vestibule. **Price $3.75**

1938 CATALOG

Price Guide Key: **VG** = Very Good, **EX** = Excellent, **LN** = Like New | *Values for each condition are in U.S. dollars.* | **Rarity** = Scale from 1-8 with 8 being the hardest to find.

263

O GAUGE PASSENGER & STREAMLINER CARS

630 OBSERVATION TYPE I

630 Observation: Introduced in 1924, this 6 1/2" long, four-wheel car was the least expensive Lionel observation of the time. It remained in production through 1932. The 630 observation car was sold as a companion to the 629 Pullman.

630 Observation (Type I): From 1934 through 1927, these cars were painted dark green with maroon trim and doors. No journal boxes were installed on the car, which had hook couplers.

VG	EX	LN	RARITY
25	32	40	3

630 Observation (Type II): A new color combination, orange with peacock trim, was made in 1927. These cars also had no journal boxes and were equipped with hook couplers.

VG	EX	LN	RARITY
25	32	40	3

630 Observation (Type III): Latch couplers were used on some of the 1927 orange and peacock observation cars. No journal boxes were installed.

VG	EX	LN	RARITY
25	32	40	3

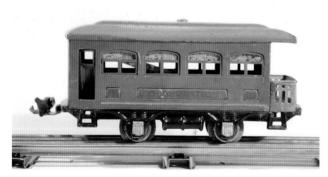

630 Observation (Type IV): The orange and peacock observation with latch couplers was continued in 1928-29, but now had nickel journal boxes.

VG	EX	LN	RARITY
25	32	40	3

630 Observation (Type V): Beginning in 1930, the observation began to be painted red with cream trim. Latch couplers were installed, and some of the cars had nickel journal boxes.

VG	EX	LN	RARITY
18	22	30	2

630 Observation (Type VI): Other red and cream cars had copper journal boxes, as well as latch couplers.

VG	EX	LN	RARITY
18	22	30	2

636W UP City of Denver power unit (Type I): This streamlined diesel was painted yellow with a brown roof. It came with two 637 coaches and one 638 observation car from 1936 through 1939. The roofs of vestibules were brown. The value listed is for the locomotive with matching cars.

VG	EX	LN	RARITY
500	650	1100	6

636W UP City of Denver power unit (Type II): Some of the later vestibules lacked the brown paint on top, being overall yellow instead. The remainder of the City of Denver, the power unit, two 637 coaches and one 638 observation, were unchanged, having yellow sides and brown roofs. Value listed is for a set.

VG	EX	LN	RARITY
300	450	650	4

636W UP City of Denver power unit (Type III): An uncataloged version of the City of Denver set was painted two-tone green. This version included only one 637 coach, in addition to the power unit and 638 observation. Value listed is for a set.

VG	EX	LN	RARITY
4000	5200	7000	8

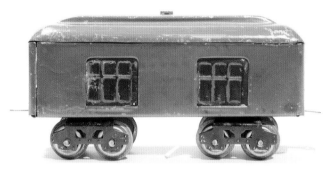

702 Baggage car: This unlettered gray baggage car was built for use in the 1917-21 armored train.

VG	EX	LN	RARITY
125	200	300	7

710 Pullman: These attractive 11 1/2" long passenger cars were sold new from 1924 through 1934.

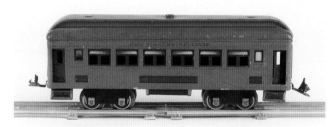

710 Pullman (Type I): When introduced in 1924, and carrying over into 1925, the new cars were painted orange and had dark olive inserts. The doors had a simulated wood-grained finish. Rubber-stamped "NEW YORK CENTRAL LINES" lettering was applied above the windows.

VG	EX	LN	RARITY
125	175	225	4

710 Pullman (Type II): During 1925-27, the orange "NEW YORK CENTRAL LINES" Pullman had maroon doors. The inserts remained dark olive.

VG	EX	LN	RARITY
125	175	225	4

710 Pullman (Type III): Also introduced in 1924 were cars lettered "ILLINOIS CENTRAL LINES". The bodies of these cars were orange and they had brown inserts. Through 1925, they had wood-grained doors.

VG	EX	LN	RARITY
225	275	325	6

710 Pullman (Type IV): Maroon doors were installed in some of the orange "ILLINOIS CENTRAL LINES" cars from 1925 through 1927. The inserts installed in these cars were brown.

VG	EX	LN	RARITY
225	275	325	6

710 Pullman (Type V): During 1927, six-wheel trucks were installed on some of the orange "ILLINOIS CENTRAL LINES" cars. These cars had brown inserts and maroon doors.

VG	EX	LN	RARITY
225	275	325	6

710 Pullman (Type VI): "THE LIONEL LINES" name appeared on orange Pullmans with dark olive green inserts during 1927-28. These cars had maroon doors and nickel journal boxes.

VG	EX	LN	RARITY
125	175	225	4

710 Pullman (Type VII): Some of the orange "THE LIONEL LINES" had pea green inserts and doors in 1929. These cars used nickel journal boxes.

VG	EX	LN	RARITY
125	175	225	4

710 Pullman (Type VIII): In 1930, the orange "THE LIONEL LINES" had cream inserts and Stephen Girard green doors. Nickel journal boxes continued to be used.

VG	EX	LN	RARITY
125	175	225	4

710 Pullman (Type IX): Six-wheel trucks with nickel journal boxes were installed on some of the orange 1929 "THE LIONEL LINES" cars. These cars had pea green inserts and doors.

VG	EX	LN	RARITY
225	275	325	6

710 Pullman (Type X): In 1930, the 12-wheeled "THE LIONEL LINES" passenger cars still had orange bodies, but now they had cream inserts and Stephen Girard green doors. Nickel journal boxes continued to be used.

VG	EX	LN	RARITY
225	275	325	6

710 Pullman (Type XI): Also in 1930, red 12-wheel passenger cars lettered "THE LIONEL LINES" began to be produced. These cars had cream inserts and Stephen Girard green doors. Nickel journal boxes were installed on their six-wheel trucks.

VG	EX	LN	RARITY
300	375	475	7

710 Pullman (Type XII): Red paint was also applied to some eight-wheeled "THE LIONEL LINES" Pullman cars in 1930. They also had cream inserts, Stephen Girard green doors and nickel journal boxes.

VG	EX	LN	RARITY
225	275	325	6

Price Guide Key: VG = Very Good, EX = Excellent, LN = Like New | *Values for each condition are in U.S. dollars.* | Rarity = Scale from 1-8 with 8 being the hardest to find.

265

710 Pullman (Type XIII): Some red eight-wheel cars were made with copper journal boxes during 1931-32. Lettered "THE LIONEL LINES", these cars had ivory inserts and Stephen Girard green doors.

VG	EX	LN	RARITY
225	275	325	6

710 Pullman (Type XIV): Ivory-colored doors were installed on some red cars during 1931-32. These cars were otherwise identical to the type XIII cars listed above.

VG	EX	LN	RARITY
225	275	325	6

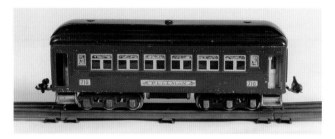

710 Pullman (Type XV): For 1933-34 the car was painted medium blue with a dark blue roof. Cream inserts and doors were installed, as were six-wheel trucks with copper journal boxes. "THE LIONEL LINES" was rubber-stamped above the windows.

VG	EX	LN	RARITY
300	375	475	7

712 Observation: These attractive 11 ½-inch long passenger cars were sold new from 1924 through 1934. During this time, indeed along with the matching 710 Pullman, these were Lionel's largest 0 gauge cars until the 1941 advent of the "Madison" series.

712 Observation (Type I): When introduced in 1924, and carrying over into 1925, the new cars were painted orange and had dark olive inserts. The doors had a simulated wood-grained finish. Rubber-stamped "NEW YORK CENTRAL LINES" lettering was applied above the windows.

VG	EX	LN	RARITY
125	175	225	4

712 Observation (Type II): During 1925-27, the orange "NEW YORK CENTRAL LINES" observation had maroon doors. The inserts remained dark olive.

VG	EX	LN	RARITY
125	175	225	4

712 Observation (Type III): Also introduced in 1924 were cars lettered "ILLINOIS CENTRAL LINES". The bodies of these cars were orange and they had brown inserts. Through 1925, they had wood-grained doors.

VG	EX	LN	RARITY
225	275	325	6

712 Observation (Type IV): Maroon doors were installed in some of the orange "ILLINOIS CENTRAL LINES" from 1925 through 1927. The inserts installed in these cars were brown.

VG	EX	LN	RARITY
225	275	325	6

712 Observation (Type V): During 1927, six-wheel trucks were installed on some of the orange "ILLINOIS CENTRAL LINES" cars. These cars had brown inserts and maroon doors.

VG	EX	LN	RARITY
225	275	325	6

712 Observation (Type VI): "THE LIONEL LINES" name appeared on orange observations with dark olive green inserts during 1927-28. These cars had maroon doors and nickel journal boxes.

VG	EX	LN	RARITY
125	175	225	4

712 Observation (Type VII): Some of the orange "THE LIONEL LINES" had pea green inserts and doors in 1929. These cars used nickel journal boxes.

VG	EX	LN	RARITY
125	175	225	4

712 Observation (Type VIII): In 1930, the orange "THE LIONEL LINES" had cream inserts and Stephen Girard green doors. Nickel journal boxes continued to be used.

VG	EX	LN	RARITY
125	175	225	4

712 Observation (Type IX): Six-wheel trucks with nickel journal boxes were installed on some of the orange 1929 "THE LIONEL LINES" cars. These cars had pea green inserts and doors.

VG	EX	LN	RARITY
225	275	325	6

712 Observation (Type X): In 1930, the 12-wheeled "THE LIONEL LINES" passenger cars still had orange bodies, but now they had cream inserts and Stephen Girard green doors. Nickel journal boxes continued to be used.

VG	EX	LN	RARITY
225	275	325	6

712 Observation (Type XI): Also in 1930, red 12-wheel passenger cars lettered "THE LIONEL LINES" began to be produced. These cars had cream inserts and Stephen Girard green doors. Nickel journal boxes were installed on their six-wheel trucks.

VG	EX	LN	RARITY
300	375	475	7

712 Observation (Type XII): Red paint was also applied to some eight-wheeled "THE LIONEL LINES" observation cars in 1930. They also had cream inserts, Stephen Girard green doors and nickel journal boxes.

VG	EX	LN	RARITY
225	275	325	6

712 OBSERVATION TYPE XV

712 Observation (Type XIII): Some red eight-wheel cars were made with copper journal boxes during 1931-32. Lettered "THE LIONEL LINES", these cars had ivory inserts and Stephen Girard green doors.

VG	EX	LN	RARITY
225	275	325	6

712 Observation (Type XIV): Ivory-colored doors were installed on some cars during 1931-32. These cars were otherwise identical to the type XIII cars listed previously.

VG	EX	LN	RARITY
225	275	325	6

712 Observation (Type XV): 🖼 For 1933-34, the car was painted medium blue with a dark blue roof. Cream inserts and doors were installed, as were six-wheel trucks with copper journal boxes. "THE LIONEL LINES" was rubber-stamped above the windows.

VG	EX	LN	RARITY
300	375	475	7

752 Union Pacific M10000: Although often used to describe the entire streamlined, articulated passenger train with diesel locomotive, the number 752 refers specifically to the locomotive, which was initially cataloged as 752E in 1934. This was a replica of Union Pacific's revolutionary M10000 streamliner that was capturing headlines at the time. In 1935, a whistle-equipped model became available with a catalog number of 752W. The non-whistle version was last cataloged in 1936, while the improved version remained in the product line through 1941. The set was painted yellow and brown throughout this time, as well as in painted aluminum finish from 1934 through 1936. The trains were sold in both three- and four-car sets.

752 (Type I): This was a four-car yellow and brown set.

VG	EX	LN	RARITY
700	1100	1600	6

Price Guide Key: **VG** = Very Good, **EX** = Excellent, **LN** = Like New | *Values for each condition are in U.S. dollars.* | **Rarity** = Scale from 1-8 with 8 being the hardest to find.

752 (Type II): A four-car set was aluminum-finished.

VG	EX	LN	RARITY
600	1000	1400	7

752 (Type III): This was a three-car yellow and brown set.

VG	EX	LN	RARITY
600	1000	1400	6

752 (Type IV): A three-car aluminum-finished set was also available.

VG	EX	LN	RARITY
500	850	1200	7

753 Coach (Type I): This yellow and brown coach with vestibule matching the 752 was produced from 1934 through 1941.

VG	EX	LN	RARITY
100	140	200	6

753 Coach (Type II): An aluminum-finished coach with vestibule was made from 1934 through 1926 to correspond with the aluminum-colored 752.

VG	EX	LN	RARITY
100	140	200	7

754 Observation (Type I): This yellow and brown observation, with vestibule matching the 752 and 753, was produced from 1934 through 1941.

VG	EX	LN	RARITY
75	125	160	6

754 (Type II): An aluminum-finished observation with vestibule was made from 1934 through 1926 to correspond with the aluminum-colored 752 and 753.

VG	EX	LN	RARITY
75	125	160	7

782/783/784 Hiawatha cars: Created using much of the same tooling used to manufacture the M10000, these cars were painted in stylized Milwaukee Road colors and sold with the 250E Hiawatha steam locomotive.

1011 PULLMAN TYPE III

782 Combination Car: Painted with orange sides, gray roof and maroon frame, this was part of a streamlined articulated Hiawatha passenger set pulled by a 250E locomotive. It matches the 783 coach and 784 observation, but does not include a vestibule.

VG	EX	LN	RARITY
200	300	400	6

783 Coach: Built using the tooling developed for the 753, this car had painted orange sides, gray roof and maroon frame. It was part of a streamlined articulated Hiawatha passenger set pulled by a 250E locomotive. It matches the 782 combination and 784 observation, and includes a vestibule.

VG	EX	LN	RARITY
200	300	400	5

784 Observation: Built using the tooling developed for the 754, this car had painted orange sides, gray roof and maroon frame. It was part of a streamlined articulated Hiawatha passenger set pulled by a 250E locomotive. It matches the 782 and 783, and includes a vestibule.

VG	EX	LN	RARITY
200	300	400	6

792 Combination Car: This car had red sides, maroon roof and maroon frame. It was part of a streamlined articulated Rail Chief passenger set pulled by a 700E locomotive. It matches the 793 and 794, but does not include a vestibule.

VG	EX	LN	RARITY
250	375	525	7

793 Coach: Built using the tooling developed for the 753, this car had painted red sides, maroon roof and maroon frame. Part of a streamlined articulated Rail Chief passenger set pulled by a 700E locomotive, it matches the 792 combination and 794 observation. This car does include a vestibule.

VG	EX	LN	RARITY
250	375	525	6

794 Observation: Built using the tooling developed for the 754, this car had painted red sides, maroon roof and maroon frame. Part of a streamlined articulated Rail Chief passenger set pulled by a 700E locomotive, it matches the 792 combination and 793 coach. This car does include a vestibule.

VG	EX	LN	RARITY
250	375	525	7

1011 Pullman (Type I): This lithographed 1931-32 Pullman car had a light orange body and green roof. Its number boards matched its roof.

VG	EX	LN	RARITY
50	60	75	4

Price Guide Key: **VG =** Very Good, **EX =** Excellent, **LN =** Like New | *Values for each condition are in U.S. dollars.* | **Rarity =** Scale from 1-8 with 8 being the hardest to find.

269

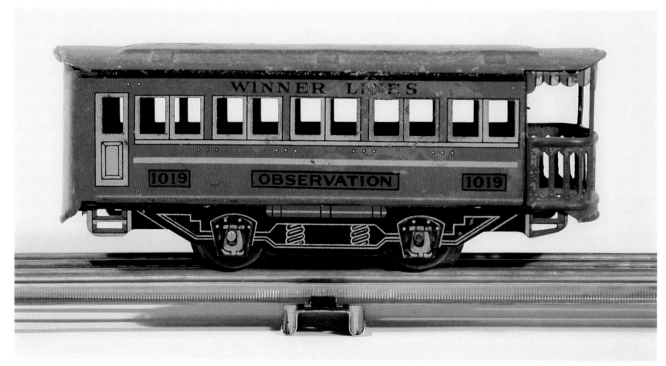

1011 Pullman Type III

1011 Pullman Type II): Some of the light orange lithographed Pullman cars had dark olive roofs. The number boards on these cars matched the roofs.

VG	EX	LN	RARITY
50	60	75	4

1011 Pullman (Type III): 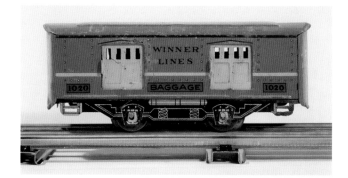 Some of the cars had lithographed dark orange bodies, along with green roofs. The number boards matched the roofs.

VG	EX	LN	RARITY
50	60	75	4

1019 Observation (Type I): This lithographed observation car had a light orange body and green roof. Its number boards matched its roof.

VG	EX	LN	RARITY
50	60	75	4

1019 Observation Type II): Some of the light orange lithographed observation cars had dark olive roofs. The number boards on these cars matched the roofs.

VG	EX	LN	RARITY
50	60	75	4

1019 Observation (Type III): Some of the cars had lithographed dark orange bodies, along with green roofs. The number boards matched the roofs.

VG	EX	LN	RARITY
50	60	75	4

1020 Baggage (Type I): This lithographed baggage car had a light orange body and green roof. Its number boards matched its roof.

VG	EX	LN	RARITY
60	75	100	5

1020 Baggage Type II): Some of the light orange lithographed baggage cars had dark olive roofs. The number boards on these cars matched the roofs.

VG	EX	LN	RARITY
60	75	100	5

1518 Circus Dining Car: This four-wheeled passenger car with elaborate lithographed decoration was part of an uncataloged Mickey Mouse-themed circus outfit sold in 1935.

VG	EX	LN	RARITY
100	150	225	7

1630 PULLMAN TYPE III

1519 Mickey Mouse Band: This four-wheeled passenger car with elaborate lithographed decoration was part of an uncataloged Mickey Mouse-themed circus outfit sold in 1935.

VG	EX	LN	RARITY
100	150	225	7

1520 Mickey Mouse Circus: This four-wheeled car with elaborate lithographed decoration was part of an uncataloged Mickey Mouse-themed circus outfit sold in 1935.

VG	EX	LN	RARITY
100	150	225	7

1630 Pullman: This was the first of a series of 9 1/2" long cars Lionel introduced in 1938. The body stampings for these cars, along with the companion 1631 observation, were also used for the 2630 and 2631 as well as to create some of the early postwar passenger cars.

1630 Pullman (Type I): During 1938-39, the body of the car was painted blue. It had aluminum-colored windows, roof and underframe. "PULLMAN" was rubber-stamped in black on the silver insert, along with the catalog number 1630. Latch couplers were installed.

VG	EX	LN	RARITY
30	45	65	3

1630 Pullman (Type II): Box couplers were mounted during 1940-41, but the balance of the car was unchanged.

VG	EX	LN	RARITY
30	45	65	3

1630 Pullman (Type III):  As the winds of war gathered, aluminum paint pigment became scarce. As a result, gray replaced the aluminum color, resulting in a blue and gray scheme. Box couplers continued to be used.

VG	EX	LN	RARITY
40	55	75	3

1631 Observation (Type I): During 1938-39, the body of the car was painted blue. It had aluminum-colored windows, roof and underframe. "OBSERVATION" was rubber-stamped in black on the silver insert, along with the catalog number 1631. Latch couplers were installed.

VG	EX	LN	RARITY
30	45	65	3

1631 Observation (Type II): Box couplers were mounted during 1940-41, but the balance of the car was unchanged.

VG	EX	LN	RARITY
30	45	65	3

1631 Observation (Type III): As was the case with the Pullman, gray paint replaced aluminum on the observation, resulting in a blue and gray scheme. Box couplers continued to be used.

VG	EX	LN	RARITY
40	55	75	3

1685 Passenger Car: Though designed and built by Lionel, these 12" long cars were sold as Ives products in 1932. After the Ives name was dropped at the end of that year, the cars were given new color schemes and numbers, and the Lionel name was applied. Along with the matching 1686 baggage car and 1687 observation car, they were used exclusively in uncataloged sets from 1933 through 1937.

Price Guide Key: **VG** = Very Good, **EX** = Excellent, **LN** = Like New | *Values for each condition are in U.S. dollars.* | **Rarity** = Scale from 1-8 with 8 being the hardest to find.

271

1686 BAGGAGE CAR TYPE II

1685 Passenger Car (Type I): During 1933, the body of the passenger car was painted gray. The roof and underframe were finished in maroon. Cream windows and doors, along with brass trim, were installed. The car rode on six-wheel trucks with copper journal boxes.

VG	EX	LN	RARITY
250	350	500	7

1685 Passenger Car (Type II): In 1934, the passenger car was painted red. It had a maroon roof and underframe, yellow windows and doors, and brass trim. Four-wheel trucks with copper journal boxes were installed on these cars.

VG	EX	LN	RARITY
175	275	350	5

1685 Passenger Car (Type III): The red body continued in 1935-36, along with the maroon roof and underframe.

However, cream was now the color of choice for the windows and doors. The trim attached to the car was nickel, including the journal boxes on the four-wheel trucks.

VG	EX	LN	RARITY
175	275	350	5

1685 Passenger Car (Type IV): A blue-bodied car was built between 1935 and 1936. It had an aluminum-painted roof, windows, doors and underframe. The trim attached to the car was nickel, including the journal boxes on the four-wheel trucks.

VG	EX	LN	RARITY
175	275	350	5

1685 Passenger Car (Type V): Also produced in 1935-36 was a vermilion passenger car with maroon roof and underframe. Cream windows and doors, and nickel trim were installed on this car. It rode on four-wheel trucks with nickel journal boxes.

VG	EX	LN	RARITY
175	275	350	5

1686 Baggage Car (Type I): During 1933, the body of the baggage car was painted gray. The roof and underframe were finished in maroon, and cream baggage doors, along with brass trim, were installed. The car rode on six-wheel trucks with copper journal boxes.

VG	EX	LN	RARITY
250	350	500	7

1686 Baggage Car (Type II): In 1934, the baggage car was painted red. It had a maroon roof and underframe, yellow baggage doors and brass trim. Four-wheel trucks with copper journal boxes were installed on these cars.

VG	EX	LN	RARITY
175	275	350	5

1686 Baggage Car (Type III): The red body continued in 1935-36, along with the maroon roof and underframe. However, cream was now the color of choice for the baggage doors. The trim attached to the car was nickel, including the journal boxes on the four-wheel trucks.

VG	EX	LN	RARITY
175	275	350	5

1686 Baggage Car (Type IV): A blue-bodied car was built between 1935 and 1936. It had an aluminum-painted roof, baggage doors and underframe. The trim attached to the car

1687 OBSERVATION CAR TYPE IV

was nickel, including the journal boxes on the four-wheel trucks.

VG	EX	LN	RARITY
175	275	350	5

1686 Baggage Car (Type V): Also produced in 1935-36 was a vermilion baggage car with maroon roof and underframe. Cream baggage doors and nickel trim were installed on this car. It rode on four-wheel trucks with nickel journal boxes.

VG	EX	LN	RARITY
175	275	350	5

1687 Observation Car (Type I): During 1933, the body of the observation car was painted gray. The roof and underframe were finished in maroon. Cream windows and doors, along with brass trim, were installed. The car rode on six-wheel trucks with copper journal boxes.

VG	EX	LN	RARITY
250	350	500	7

1687 Observation Car (Type II): In 1934, the observation car was painted red. It had a maroon roof and underframe, yellow windows and doors, and brass trim. Four-wheel trucks with copper journal boxes were installed on these cars.

VG	EX	LN	RARITY
175	275	350	5

1687 Observation Car (Type III): The red body continued in 1935-36, along with the maroon roof and underframe. However, cream was now the color of choice for the windows and doors. The trim attached to the car was nickel, including the journal boxes on the four-wheel trucks.

VG	EX	LN	RARITY
175	275	350	5

1687 Observation Car (Type IV): 🔲 A blue-bodied car was built between 1935 and 1936. It had an aluminum-painted roof, windows, doors and underframe. The trim attached to the car was nickel, including the journal boxes on the four-wheel trucks.

VG	EX	LN	RARITY
175	275	350	5

1687 Observation Car (Type V): Also produced 1935-36 was a vermilion observation car with maroon roof and underframe. Cream windows and doors, and nickel trim were installed on this car. It rode on four-wheel trucks with nickel journal boxes.

VG	EX	LN	RARITY
175	275	350	5

1690-1693: Two other groups of lithographed cars with origins in Lionel's Ives division were the 1690-1691, and 1692 and 1693. The 1690-1691 were sold as Ives during 1931 and 1932, before adding them to the Lionel line in 1933, where they remained through 1942. The 7 1/2" long cars rode on two conventional trucks.

1690 Pullman (Type I): The first two years, these cars were part of the Lionel line. In 1933-1934, their bodies were dark red with yellow windows and the roofs. Brass handrails and copper journal boxes were used on these cars.

VG	EX	LN	RARITY
30	40	55	4

1690 Pullman (Type II): For 1935, the handrails and journal boxes were nickel, but the rest of the car was unchanged.

VG	EX	LN	RARITY
30	40	55	4

1690 Pullman (Type III): Beginning in 1936, the body and roof was lithographed medium red and cream windows were installed. Nickel journal boxes and handrails were found on these cars as well through 1939.

VG	EX	LN	RARITY
30	40	55	4

Price Guide Key: **VG** = Very Good, **EX** = Excellent, **LN** = Like New | *Values for each condition are in U.S. dollars.* | **Rarity** = Scale from 1-8 with 8 being the hardest to find.

273

O GAUGE PASSENGER & STREAMLINER CARS

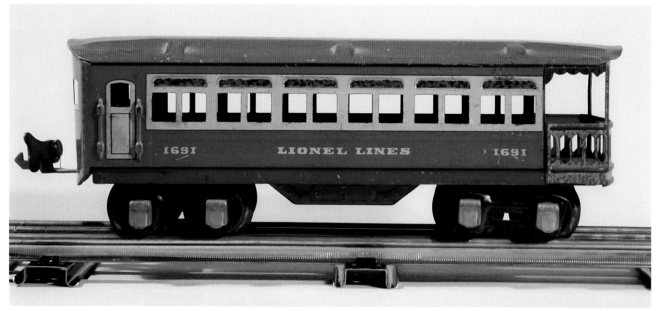

1691 OBSERVATION TYPE III

1690 Pullman (Type IV): Some of the cars with medium red body and roof did not have handrails or simulated underframe installed. The windows of these cars were cream and the trucks had nickel journal boxes.

VG	EX	LN	RARITY
30	40	55	4

1690 Pullman (Type V): Orange-red cars with matching roofs were also made without handrails or underframe details. Again, these cars had nickel journal boxes and cream windows.

VG	EX	LN	RARITY
30	40	55	4

1690 Pullman (Type VI): About 1940, black journal boxes began to be used on the medium red cars. The roof matched the body and cream windows were installed. No handrails or underframe details were used.

VG	EX	LN	RARITY
30	40	55	4

1691 Observation (Type I): The first two years, these cars were part of the Lionel line, 1933-1934, their bodies were dark red with yellow windows and the roofs. Brass handrails and copper journal boxes were used.

VG	EX	LN	RARITY
30	40	55	4

1691 Observation (Type II): For 1935, the handrails and journal boxes were nickel, but the rest of the car was unchanged.

VG	EX	LN	RARITY
30	40	55	4

1691 Observation (Type III): ⁕ Beginning in 1936, the body and roof were lithographed medium red and cream windows were installed. Nickel journal boxes and handrails were found on these cars as well through 1939.

VG	EX	LN	RARITY
30	40	55	4

1691 Observation (Type IV): Some of the cars with medium red body and roof did not have handrails or simulated underframe installed. The windows of these cars were cream and the trucks had nickel journal boxes.

VG	EX	LN	RARITY
30	40	55	4

1691 Observation (Type V): Orange-red cars with matching roofs were also made without handrails or underframe details. Again, these cars had nickel journal boxes and cream windows.

VG	EX	LN	RARITY
30	40	55	4

1691 Observation (Type VI): About 1940, black journal boxes began to be used on the medium red cars. The roof matched the body and cream windows were installed. No handrails or underframe details were used.

VG	EX	LN	RARITY
30	40	55	4

1692 Pullman (Type I): This uncataloged lithographed blue passenger car was made in 1939. Its construction was nearly identical to the 1690. The car had yellow windows and nickel journal boxes installed.

VG	EX	LN	RARITY
40	50	65	5

1692 Pullman (Type II): Some cars were assembled without journal boxes.

VG	EX	LN	RARITY
40	50	65	5

1700E Type VI

1693 Observation (Type I): Also made in 1939, this uncataloged blue lithographed Observation car matched the 1692 Pullman with nickel journal boxes.

VG	EX	LN	RARITY
40	50	65	5

1693 Observation (Type II): Another version of the blue car lacked journal boxes.

VG	EX	LN	RARITY
40	50	65	5

1700E (Type I): This chrome-finished streamlined locomotive was part of the Lionel Junior line in 1935. The diesel had a smooth body, with a red painted nose, frame and vestibules. It came with one matching 1701 coach and one 1702 observation in 1935.

VG	EX	LN	RARITY
150	200	250	4

1700E (Type II): The chrome-finished body was fluted in 1936-37. Light red paint was applied to the nose, vestibules and frame. This version came with two matching 1701 coaches and one 1702 observation.

VG	EX	LN	RARITY
150	200	250	4

1700E (Type III): An aluminum-painted, fluted version was also made. Aluminum paint was applied to the body and nose, while the vestibules and frames were painted light red. One matching 1701 coach and one 1702 observation came with the locomotive in 1936-37.

VG	EX	LN	RARITY
175	225	300	4

1700E (Type IV): Smooth-bodied locos were also painted aluminum. These came with light red vestibules and frames. One matching 1701 coach and one 1702 observation were furnished.

VG	EX	LN	RARITY
150	200	250	4

1700E (Type V): The aluminum and light red locomotive was also shipped with two matching 1701 coaches and one 1702 observation.

VG	EX	LN	RARITY
175	225	300	4

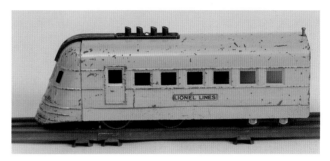

1700E (Type VI):  Some of the smooth-bodied locomotives were painted Hiawatha orange. The locomotive had an orange nose, and used orange vestibules and gray frames. It came with one matching 1701 coach and one 1702 observation.

VG	EX	LN	RARITY
225	275	350	5

1700E (Type VII): An extremely difficult to find version of this outfit was painted Armour yellow. The units had smooth bodies, and the nose and vestibules were also painted Armour yellow. The 1700E came with one matching 1701 coach and one 1702 observation.

Price Guide Key: **VG** = Very Good, **EX** = Excellent, **LN** = Like New | *Values for each condition are in U.S. dollars.* | **Rarity** = Scale from 1-8 with 8 being the hardest to find.

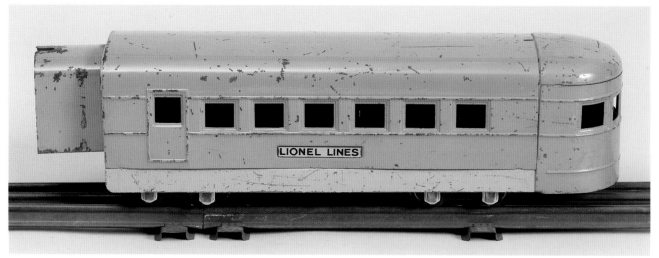

1702 OBSERVATION TYPE V

RARITY
Too rarely traded to establish accurate value.

1701 Coach (Type I): Chrome-finished, smooth body, red vestibule and frame, this car came with a 1700E locomotive and 1702 observation in 1935.

VG	EX	LN	RARITY
25	35	50	4

1701 Coach (Type II): Chrome-finished, fluted body, light red vestibule and frame, this car came with a 1700E locomotive and 1702 observation during 1936-37.

VG	EX	LN	RARITY
25	35	50	4

1701 Coach (Type III): Aluminum-painted, fluted body, with light red vestibule and frame, this car came with a 1700E locomotive and 1702 observation in 1935-37.

VG	EX	LN	RARITY
25	35	50	4

1701 Coach (Type IV): Smooth body, aluminum-painted, with light red vestibule and frame, this car came with a 1700E locomotive and 1702 observation.

VG	EX	LN	RARITY
25	35	50	4

1701 Coach (Type V): This car had a smooth body painted orange, with orange vestibule and gray frame. It came with a 1700E locomotive and 1702 observation.

VG	EX	LN	RARITY
50	75	100	5

1701 Coach (Type VI): Armour yellow paint on a smooth body, included Armour yellow vestibule, this car came with a matching 1700E locomotive and 1702 observation car.

RARITY
Too rarely traded to establish accurate value

1701 Coach (Type VII): This car had a smooth body painted red. The frame and vestibule was maroon. It came with a 1703 front end car and 1702 observation car.

VG	EX	LN	RARITY
25	35	50	4

1702 Observation (Type I): This car was chrome-finished, smooth body, with red painted tail, vestibule and frame. It came with a 1700E locomotive and 1701 coach in 1935.

VG	EX	LN	RARITY
25	35	50	4

1702 Observation (Type II): Chrome-finished, this car had a fluted body, light red painted tail, vestibule and frame. It was furnished with a 1700E locomotive and 1701 coach during 1936-37.

VG	EX	LN	RARITY
25	35	50	4

1702 Observation (Type III): This car had a fluted body painted aluminum, an aluminum-painted tail, and a light red vestibule and frame. It came with a 1700E locomotive and 1701 coach.

VG	EX	LN	RARITY
25	35	50	4

1702 Observation (Type IV): This car had an aluminum-painted smooth body. It had an aluminum-painted tail, with light red vestibule and frame. It came with a 1700E locomotive and 1701 coach.

VG	EX	LN	RARITY
25	35	50	4

1702 Observation (Type V): The smooth body, tail and vestibule were all painted orange on this car, which had a gray frame. It came with a matching 1700E locomotive and 1701 coach.

VG	EX	LN	RARITY
50	75	100	5

1702 Observation (Type VI): Armour yellow paint was applied to the smooth body, tail and vestibule of this observation. It was supplied with a matching 1700E locomotive and 1701 coach.

1702 PULLMAN TYPE V

RARITY
Too rarely traded to establish accurate value.

1702 Observation (Type VII): The smooth body of this car was painted red. The tail, vestibule and frame were painted maroon. It came with a 1703 front end car and 1701 coach 1935-37.

VG	EX	LN	RARITY
25	35	50	4

1703 Front End Car (Type I): This chrome-finished, smooth bodied front end car was made in 1935. It had a red vestibule and frame. The car came with a 1701 coach and 1702 observation.

VG	EX	LN	RARITY
50	75	100	5

1703 Front End Car (Type II): In 1936-37, the chrome-finished front end car had a fluted body. The vestibule and frame were painted light red. It came in sets with a 1701 coach and 1702 observation car.

VG	EX	LN	RARITY
50	75	100	5

1703 Front End Car (Type III): Front end cars with smooth bodies were also painted red. These cars had maroon vestibules and frames, and came with a 1701 coach and 1702 observation.

VG	EX	LN	RARITY
50	75	100	5

1811 Pullman (Type I): 📷 This four-wheel lithographed car had a peacock body, orange roof, black frame and cream windows. This version was made in 1934.

VG	EX	LN	RARITY
30	45	65	3

1811 Pullman (Type II): In 1935, the body was lithographed in gray, and the car had a gray and red roof, red frame and cream windows.

VG	EX	LN	RARITY
30	45	65	3

1811 Pullman (Type III): During 1936-37, the car had a light red body, roof and frame, and cream windows.

VG	EX	LN	RARITY
30	45	65	3

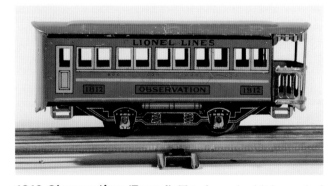

1812 Observation (Type I): This four-wheel lithographed car had a peacock body, orange roof, black frame and cream windows. This version was made in 1934.

VG	EX	LN	RARITY
30	45	65	3

1812 Observation (Type II): In 1935, the body was lithographed in gray, and the car had a gray and red roof, red frame and cream windows.

VG	EX	LN	RARITY
30	45	65	3

1812 Observation (Type III): During 1936-37, the car had a light red body, roof and frame, and cream windows.

Price Guide Key: **VG** = Very Good, **EX** = Excellent, **LN** = Like New | *Values for each condition are in U.S. dollars.* | **Rarity** = Scale from 1-8 with 8 being the hardest to find.

277

2600 PULLMAN TYPE I

VG	EX	LN	RARITY
30	45	65	3

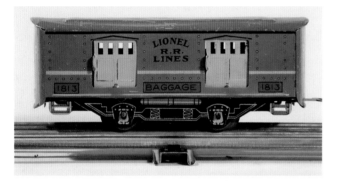

1813 Baggage (Type I): This four-wheel lithographed car had a peacock body, orange roof, black frame and cream windows. This version was made in 1934.

VG	EX	LN	RARITY
30	45	65	3

1813 Baggage (Type II): In 1935, the body was lithographed in gray, and the car had a gray and red roof, red frame and cream windows.

VG	EX	LN	RARITY
30	45	65	3

1813 Baggage (Type III): During 1936-37, the car had a light red body, roof and frame, and cream windows.

VG	EX	LN	RARITY
30	45	65	3

1816 Diesel: This clockwork-powered, chrome-finished diesel had a fluted body and aluminum-painted nose. It had a bell and battery-powered headlight, but no whistle. A brass nameplate was on its nose. During 1935, it came with a matching 1817 coach and 1818 observation with orange vestibules and frames.

VG	EX	LN	RARITY
100	150	200	5

1816W: This 1936-37 version added a whistle to the chrome-finished diesel. The bell and headlight were deleted. It had a fluted body, aluminum-painted nose with nickel nameplate. It came with a matching 1817 coach and 1818 observation with orange vestibules and frames.

VG	EX	LN	RARITY
110	160	225	6

1817 Coach (Type I): This car had a chrome-finished, fluted body, orange vestibules and lower skirt. It was sold in sets with matching 1816 or 1816W locomotive and 1818 observation during 1935-36.

VG	EX	LN	RARITY
20	35	50	5

1817 Coach (Type II): Featuring a chrome-finished, fluted body, red vestibules and lower skirt, this car was sold in 1937 sets with matching 1816 or 1816W locomotive and 1818 observation.

VG	EX	LN	RARITY
20	35	50	5

1818 Observation (Type I): This car had a chrome-finished, fluted body, orange vestibules and lower skirt. It was offered as a set with matching 1816 or 1816W locomotive and 1817 coach during 1935-36.

VG	EX	LN	RARITY
20	35	50	5

1818 Observation (Type II): Chrome-finished, with a fluted body, red vestibules and lower skirt, this car was included during 1937 in sets with matching 1816 or 1816W locomotive and 1817 coach.

VG	EX	LN	RARITY
20	35	50	5

2600-2601-2602: These cars were basically equivalent to the later production 600 series cars, only with the addition of electrically operated couplers. They were always painted light red with dark red roofs and ivory inserts. The cars had simulated underframes painted red and rode on four-wheel trucks.

2600 Pullman (Type I): During 1938-39, this car had nickel trim, nickel steps and nickel journal boxes. It was equipped with electromagnetic box couplers.

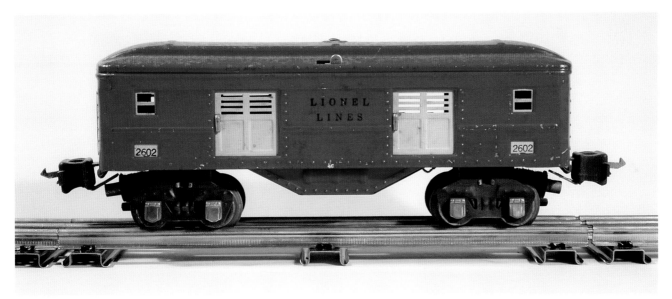

2602 BAGGAGE TYPE II

VG	EX	LN	RARITY
80	125	175	5

2600 Pullman (Type II): In 1940, the car had black journal boxes and solenoid-actuated couplers. No steps were installed on the car, but it did have nickel trim.

VG	EX	LN	RARITY
80	125	175	5

2601 Observation (Type I): During 1938-39, this car had nickel trim, nickel steps and nickel journal boxes. It was equipped with electromagnetic box couplers. The observation railing was painted light red.

VG	EX	LN	RARITY
80	125	175	5

2601 Observation (Type II): In 1940, the car had black journal boxes and solenoid-actuated couplers. No steps were installed on the car, but it did have nickel trim. The observation railing was painted aluminum color.

VG	EX	LN	RARITY
80	125	175	5

2601 Observation (Type III): Also produced in 1940, this car had its observation railing actually made of aluminum. The rest of the car was identical to the type II.

VG	EX	LN	RARITY
80	125	175	5

2602 Baggage (Type I): During 1938-39, this car had nickel trim and nickel journal boxes. It was equipped with electromagnetic box couplers. It had 5 11/16" wheelbase.

VG	EX	LN	RARITY
80	125	175	5

2602 Baggage (Type II): In 1940, the car had black journal boxes and solenoid-actuated couplers. This car had a 6 7/8" wheelbase.

VG	EX	LN	RARITY
80	125	175	5

2613 Pullman: These 10 1/2" illuminated Pullman cars were offered from 1938 through 1942. They were essentially 613-series cars equipped with remote-control couplers. Matching 2614 observation and 2615 baggage cars were produced as well. The cars had separately installed doors, and window and letterboard inserts of contrasting colors were installed.

2613 Pullman (Type I): In 1938-39, these cars were made with blue bodies and two-tone blue roofs. White inserts, nickel trim and steps, and nickel journal boxes completed the cars, which had magnetic couplers.

VG	EX	LN	RARITY
90	165	250	4

2613 Pullman (Type II): From 1940 through 1942, the cars were sold in State green with a two-tone State green and dark green roof. White inserts were installed and the underframe detail was painted dark green. The cars had nickel trim and nickel journal boxes. These cars had no steps or diaphragms installed.

VG	EX	LN	RARITY
200	300	400	6

2614 Observation (Type I): In 1938-39, these cars were made with blue bodies and two-tone blue roofs. The observation railing was painted blue. White inserts, nickel trim and steps, and nickel journal boxes completed the cars, which had magnetic couplers.

VG	EX	LN	RARITY
90	165	250	4

2614 Observation (Type II): Aluminum observation railings were installed on some of the 1938-39 blue cars. The rest of the car was unchanged.

Price Guide Key: **VG** = Very Good, **EX** = Excellent, **LN** = Like New | *Values for each condition are in U.S. dollars.* | **Rarity** = Scale from 1-8 with 8 being the hardest to find.

279

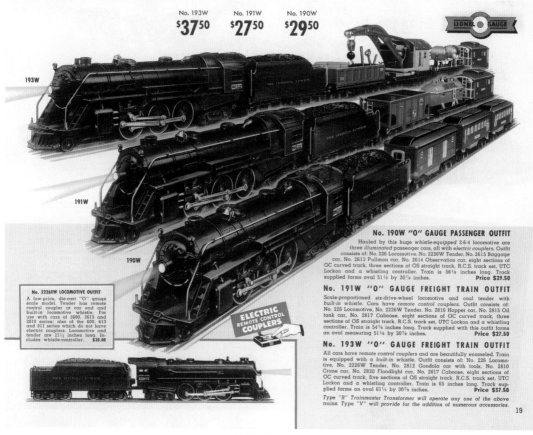

No. 193W $37.50   No. 191W $27.50   No. 190W $29.50

193W

191W

190W

No. 2226EW LOCOMOTIVE OUTFIT
A low-price, die-cast "O" gauge scale model. Tender has remote control coupler at car end and built-in locomotive whistle. For use with cars of 2600, 2613 and 2810 series; also of the 600, 613 and 811 series which do not have electric couplers. Locomotive and tender are 21½ inches long. Includes whistle-controller. **$20.00**

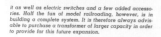

ELECTRIC REMOTE CONTROL COUPLERS

No. 190W "O" GAUGE PASSENGER OUTFIT
Hauled by this huge *whistle-equipped* 2-6-4 locomotive are three *illuminated* passenger cars, all with *electric couplers.* Outfit consists of: No. 226 Locomotive, No. 2226W Tender, No. 2615 Baggage car, No. 2613 Pullman car, No. 2614 Observation car, eight sections of OC curved track, three sections of OS straight track, R.C.S. track set, UTC Lockon and a whistling controller. Train is 56⅛ inches long. Track supplied forms oval 51⅛ by 30⅞ inches. **Price $29.50**

No. 191W "O" GAUGE FREIGHT TRAIN OUTFIT
Scale-proportioned six-drive-wheel locomotive and coal tender with *built-in whistle.* Cars have *remote control couplers.* Outfit consists of: No. 226 Locomotive, No. 2226W Tender, No. 2816 Hopper car, No. 2815 Oil tank car, No. 2817 Caboose, eight sections of OC curved track, three sections of OS straight track, R.C.S. track set, UTC Lockon and a whistling controller. Train is 54⅞ inches long. Track supplied with this outfit forms an oval measuring 51⅛ by 30⅞ inches. **Price $27.50**

No. 193W "O" GAUGE FREIGHT TRAIN OUTFIT
All cars have *remote control couplers* and are beautifully enameled. Train is equipped with a *built-in whistle.* Outfit consists of: No. 225 Locomotive, No. 2226W Tender, No. 2812 Gondola car with tools, No. 2810 Crane car, No. 2820 Floodlight car, No. 2817 Caboose, eight sections of OC curved track, five sections of OS straight track, R.C.S. track set, UTC Lockon and a whistling controller. Train is 65 inches long. Track supplied forms an oval 61¼ by 30⅞ inches. **Price $57.50**
Type "R" Trainmaster Transformer will operate any one of the above trains. Type "V" will provide for the addition of numerous accessories.

19

1939 CATALOG

---

it as well as electric switches and a few added accessories. Half the fun of model railroading, however, is in building a complete system. It is therefore always advisable to purchase a transformer of larger capacity in order to provide for this future expansion.

No. 267 $12.50   No. 267W $16.50   No. 299W $16.50

267W

299W

Lionel streamline cars couple into vestibules which contain lights for inside illumination.

No. 267W FLYING YANKEE STREAMLINE PASSENGER TRAIN OUTFIT
Chromium-plated replica of the Boston and Maine's fast Flying Yankee. Built of steel and richly embellished by a wealth of accurate detail. Equipped with *built-in whistle.* Outfit consists of: No. 616W Power car, two No. 617 Coaches, No. 618 Observation car, whistling controller, eight sections of OC curved track, four sections of OS straight track and UTC Lockon. Train is 42 inches long. Track supplied forms an oval measuring 51⅛ by 30⅞ inches. **$16.50**

No. 267. Similar to No. 267W outfit, as described above, but without built-in whistle and whistle-controller. **Price $12.50**
No. 616W—Power car complete with whistle and whistle-controller.   Price $10.00
No. 617—"Flying Yankee" Coach complete with one vestibule.   Price $ 3.75

No. 299W UNION PACIFIC STREAMLINE PASSENGER TRAIN OUTFIT
Authentic reproduction of the yellow and golden-brown Pride of the West, the Union Pacific's "City of Denver". Equipped with *built-in remote control whistle.* Outfit consists of: No. 636W Power car, two No. 637 Illuminated coaches, No. 638 Illuminated observation car, whistling controller, eight sections of OC curved track, four sections of OS straight track and UTC Lockon. Train measures 42½ inches. Track oval, 51⅛ by 30⅞ inches. **Price $16.50**
No. 636W—Power car complete with whistle and whistle-controller.   Price $10.00
No. 637—Union Pacific Coach with one vestibule.   Price $ 3.75

Type "Q" Trainmaster Transformer will operate either train illustrated above. Type "R", of greater capacity, will provide for numerous accessories.

1939 CATALOG

2623 Pullman Type II

VG	EX	LN	RARITY
90	165	250	4

2614 Observation (Type III): From 1940 through 1942, the observation cars were sold in State green with a two-tone State green and dark green roof. Even the observation railing was painted State green. White inserts were installed, and the underframe detail was painted dark green. The cars had nickel trim and nickel journal boxes. These cars had no steps or diaphragms installed.

VG	EX	LN	RARITY
200	300	400	6

2614 Observation (Type IV): Some of the State green cars had aluminum observation railings installed.

VG	EX	LN	RARITY
200	300	400	6

2615 Baggage (Type I): In 1938-39, these cars were made with blue bodies and two-tone blue roofs. White inserts, nickel trim and steps, and nickel journal boxes completed the cars, which had magnetic couplers.

VG	EX	LN	RARITY
90	165	250	4

2615 Baggage (Type II): From 1940 through 1942, the cars were sold in State green with a two-tone State green and dark green roof. White inserts were installed, and the underframe detail was painted dark green. The cars had nickel trim and nickel journal boxes. These cars had no steps or diaphragms installed.

VG	EX	LN	RARITY
200	300	400	6

2623 Pullman (Type I): Built in 1941-42, this 14 1/2" long scale-detailed Pullman had a Bakelite body painted tuscan. The same body moldings were also used from 1946 through 1950. These cars were lettered "2623 IRVINGTON 2623" in white.

VG	EX	LN	RARITY
200	300	425	6

2623 Pullman (Type II): Some of the scale-detailed Bakelite Pullman cars were lettered "2623 MANHATTAN 2623" in white. The body was painted tuscan.

VG	EX	LN	RARITY
125	200	300	6

2624 Pullman: A few of the big Bakelite cars were also made with "2624 MANHATTAN 2624" white lettering.

VG	EX	LN	RARITY
800	1500	3000	8

2630 Pullman (Type I): During 1938-41, the body of this car was painted blue. It had aluminum-colored windows, roof and underframe. "PULLMAN" was rubber-stamped in black on the silver insert, along with the catalog number 2630.

VG	EX	LN	RARITY
25	50	75	2

2630 Pullman (Type II): As the winds of war gathered, aluminum paint pigment became scarce. As a result, gray replaced the aluminum color in 1942, resulting in a blue and gray scheme.

VG	EX	LN	RARITY
35	60	90	4

2631 Observation (Type I): During 1938-41, the body of the car was painted blue. It had aluminum-colored windows, roof and underframe. "OBSERVATION" was rubber-stamped in black on the silver insert, along with the catalog number 1631.

VG	EX	LN	RARITY
25	50	75	2

2631 Observation (Type II): As was the case with the Pullman, gray paint replaced aluminum on the observation, resulting in a blue and gray scheme.

VG	EX	LN	RARITY
35	60	90	4

Price Guide Key: **VG** = Very Good. **EX** = Excellent. **LN** = Like New | *Values for each condition are in U.S. dollars.* | **Rarity** = Scale from 1-8 with 8 being the hardest to find.

281

O GAUGE PASSENGER & STREAMLINER CARS

2641 OBSERVATION TYPE II

2640 Pullman (Type I): During 1938-41, this illuminated blue passenger car was sold. It had aluminum-colored windows, roof and underframe. "PULLMAN" was rubber-stamped in black on the silver insert, along with the catalog number 2640. But for the lighting and number, it was identical to the 2630 of those years.

VG	EX	LN	RARITY
25	50	75	2

2641 Observation (Type II):  About 1942, the cars were sold in State green with a dark green roof. Cream inserts were installed, and the underframe detail was painted State green. The cars had black journal boxes, but no steps or diaphragms.

VG	EX	LN	RARITY
25	50	75	2

2642 Pullman: This 1941-42 illuminated passenger car used the same body stampings as the 1630, 2630 and 2640. However, its body, roof and underframe were painted tuscan. Gray windows and electric couplers were installed.

VG	EX	LN	RARITY
40	60	85	4

2640 Pullman (Type II): About 1942, the cars were sold in State green with a dark green roof. Cream inserts were installed and the underframe detail was painted State green. The cars had black journal boxes, but no steps or diaphragms.

VG	EX	LN	RARITY
25	50	75	2

2641 Observation (Type I): During 1938-41, this illuminated blue observation car was sold. It had aluminum-colored windows, roof and underframe. "PULLMAN" was rubber-stamped in black on the silver insert, along with the catalog number 2640. But for the lighting and number, it was identical to the 2631 of those years.

VG	EX	LN	RARITY
25	50	75	2

2643 Observation: This 1941-42 illuminated observation car matched the 2642 Pullman. Its body, roof and underframe were painted tuscan. Gray windows and electric couplers were installed.

VG	EX	LN	RARITY
40	60	85	4

OO GAUGE
OVERVIEW

Most likely two forces within the toy train hobby came together in the early 1930s, resulting in Lionel's introduction of OO gauge trains. First was the increasing demand for more realistic trains. Whereas during the first three decades of the company, the trains were unmistakably toys aimed at children, there was a growing demand for realistic model trains for use by hobbyists, who were primarily adult males. In 0 gauge, this manifested itself in the fabulous 700E locomotive and related cars, as well as the Pennsylvania B-6 switcher.

The second force was closely related to the first. Whereas many children were perfectly content to play with their trains on the floor, as so often depicted in the catalogs of the period, this wouldn't do for adult hobbyists. They envisioned their trains traversing complete miniature worlds, with realistic scenery and landscaping, an environment that required a permanent, tabletop display. Lionel's Standard and 0 gauge trains required vast amounts of space to accomplish this. But OO, and the slightly smaller HO, trains required only about 1/8 the volume of space for a given display (the wider radius of Lionel's two-rail OO track violates this principle).

Unfortunately, the Depression, World War II and Lionel's somewhat timid entry into this market combined to undermine this effort. Despite its popularity in Europe, OO never took hold in the U.S. and, consequently, OO did not return to Lionel's catalogs in the postwar era.

CAR KITS AND ASSEMBLED MODELS

LIONEL OO GAUGE

Construction kits for "OO" gauge cars contain everything required for rapid and simple assembly. The only tools needed are a small hammer, screw driver and nail set. Car frames and bodies are ready for painting. Trucks contain assembled wheels and axles. Authentic decalcomania car markings, paint brush and enamel are included. Cars made from Kits may be used on either 2-rail or 3-rail track. The box car is 6⅞ inches long; oil tank car, 5¾ inches; hopper car, 5½ inches; caboose, 4⅝ inches. All cars have approved scale model wheels and scale model couplers. Frames and bodies are die cast in steel dies.

CAR KITS FOR 2-RAIL OR 3-RAIL TRACK
No. 0044K—Box car Kit. $2.75
No. 0045K—Oil tank car Kit. $2.75
No. 0046K—Hopper car Kit. $2.75
No. 0047K—Caboose Kit. $2.75

ASSEMBLED CARS FOR 2-RAIL TRACK
No. 0044—Box car. Price $3.00
No. 0045—Oil tank car. Price $3.00
No 0046—Hopper car. Price $3.00
No. 0047—Caboose. Price $3.00

ASSEMBLED CARS FOR 3-RAIL TRACK
No. 0014—Box car. Price $3.00
No. 0015—Oil tank car. Price $3.00
No. 0016—Hopper car. Price $3.00
No. 0017—Caboose. Price $3.00

Built by Lionel

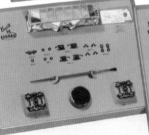

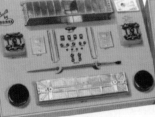

3-RAIL TRACK, SWITCHES AND CROSSOVERS

"OO" gauge has one great advantage over larger sizes in that it permits the reproduction of a considerable amount of track in a moderately small space. Use this advantage by planning a system with switches and crossovers that will give you not only realistic appearance but operating fun as well. Build a freight yard, double-track a part of your line, add sidings—and you will discover an increasing pleasure and gratification in railroading.

"OO" gauge has been designed scientifically to offer the greatest variety of layouts that can be constructed with standard lengths of track. Because curved track is only a 30-degree segment, it is possible to use two parallel lines with reasonably close clearances and switch from one to the other. By the use of five-sixth length and half-length track together or in multiples, a stretch of straight track of practically any length may be obtained.

Lionel 3-rail track is mounted on black Bakelite base containing moulded, closely-spaced ties. One section is joined to the next by a self-contained, lock-tight clip. A special section of curved track contains terminals for wire connections to the transformer.

Curved track is 7 inches long; straight track, 6¾ inches.

"OO" GAUGE 3-RAIL TRACK
No. 0051—Curved track. Price $.40
No. 0052—Straight track. Price $.40
No. 0054—Connection curved track, 7 inches long. Price $.75
No. 0063—½-Curved track, 3½ inches long. Price $.35
No. 0065—½-Straight track, 3⅜ inches long. Price $.35
No. 0066—5/6 size straight track. $.40

"OO" GAUGE 3-RAIL, REMOTE CONTROL SWITCHES
Switch motors are small so they will not interfere with parallel tracks. Red or green lights on controller and on switch base indicate whether switch is open or closed. Equipped with automatic non-derailing device.
No. 0072—Pair, right and left. Price $10.00
No. 0072L—Left Hand Switch. Price $ 5.50
No. 0072R—Right Hand Switch. Price $ 5.50

"OO" GAUGE 3-RAIL CROSSOVER
No. 0070—Crossovers are always invaluable aids in the construction of interesting track formations. The length of the "OO" gauge crossover is equal to one section of straight track. 90-degree intersection. Solid Bakelite block in center prevents short circuits. Price $2.50

New
2-RAIL TRACK

New Lionel "OO" 2-rail track is the most realistic ever manufactured for quick assembly. Ties, tie plates and bolts are strictly true-to-scale. Ties are spaced accurately for a heavy-duty main line. Rails are solid steel and shaped in the traditional T. The base is Bakelite and may be covered easily with realistic rock ballast.

Track is joined by a lock-tight clip that snaps closed quickly and surely. Twelve sections of curved track form a circle with a 24-inch radius. A circle of track, including base, occupies a space of 50 by 50 inches.

No. 0031—Curved track, 13 inches long. Price $.60
No. 0032—Straight track, 12 inches long. Price $.60
No. 0034—Connection curved track. Price $.75

CHAPTER 25
OO GAUGE

001 STEAM LOCOMOTIVE: The first, and only, style of locomotive produced by Lionel in OO gauge was a replica of a New York Central J-3a 4-6-4 Hudson. The 001 was a super-detailed representation designed to be operated on three-rail track. A feedwater pump, booster steam pipes, flag stanchions, boiler turret caps, front coupler, simulated turbo generator and full valve gear adorned the locomotive. The tender featured hand rails on each corner and around the tank top. The locomotive and tender were 15 1/2" long and the number "5342" was rubber-stamped beneath the cab window. "New York Central" was rubber-stamped in silver on the sides of the 12-wheel tender.

001 STEAM LOCOMOTIVE (Type I): In 1938, its first year of production, the locomotive and tender were joined by a miniature drawbar pin with its own retaining chain. The catalog number "001" was not stamped on the product. It was offered with either the 001W tender with whistle integral to the body, or with the 001T tender, which lacked a whistle. Locomotives with non-whistling tenders are today estimated at $70 less than the values listed here.

VG	EX	LN	RARITY
250	450	700	5

001 STEAM LOCOMOTIVE (Type II): From 1939 through the end of production in 1942, a spring-loaded pin was used to connect the tender drawbar to the locomotive, rather than the separate pin and chain used initially. The locomotives were rubber-stamped "001" on the inside of the cab roof. It was offered with either the 001W tender with whistle integral to the body, or with the 001T tender, which lacked a whistle. The appropriate catalog number, "001W" or "001T", was rubber-stamped on the underside of the tender. Locomotives with non-whistling tenders are today estimated at $70 less than the values listed here.

VG	EX	LN	RARITY
200	400	600	4

002 STEAM LOCOMOTIVE: In 1939, this less-detailed and hence less-expensive version of the three-rail OO Hudson was offered. Though the same size, and having the same external markings as the fully-detailed 001, the 002 was quite different. The 002 lacked the elaborate piping and valve gear, as well as many smaller details found on the 001. Similarly,

003 STEAM LOCOMOTIVE

its tender was bereft of handrail and brake details found on the 001T and 001W. Like the 1939 and later 001, the stock numbers of the 002 engine and tender were rubber-stamped inside the cab and under the tender frame. Locomotives with non-whistling tenders are today estimated at $70 less than the values listed here.

VG	EX	LN	RARITY
175	350	550	4

003 STEAM LOCOMOTIVE: Released in 1939 in an effort to tap into the growing scale model railroading market, this Hudson was designed to operate on two-rail track. Its left-side drivers were made of Bakelite, its pilot, trailing and tender trucks were insulated, and naturally there were no center rail pickups. A plug and jack, as well as the tender drawbar, provided the electrical connection between locomotive and tender. Like the three-rail 001, the 003 was a super-detailed representation of this famous locomotive. A feedwater pump, booster steam pipes, flag stanchions, boiler turret caps, front coupler, simulated turbo generator and full valve gear adorned the locomotive. The tender featured hand rails on each corner and around the tank top. The locomotive and tender were 15 1/2" long and the number "5342" was rubber-stamped beneath the cab window. "New York Central" was rubber-stamped in silver on the sides of the 12-wheel tender. The locomotives were rubber-stamped "003" on the inside of the cab roof. It was offered with either the 003W tender with whistle integral to the body, or with the 004T tender, which lacked a whistle. The appropriate catalog number, "003W" or "003T", was rubber-stamped on the underside of the tender. The locomotive was discontinued in 1942. Locomotives with non-whistling tenders are today estimated at $70 less than the values listed here.

VG	EX	LN	RARITY
250	450	700	5

004 STEAM LOCOMOTIVE: As was done with the three-rail engines, from 1939-42 a less-detailed replica of the 4-6-4 Hudson, designed for operation on two-rail track, was offered. It had the same external markings as the other locomotives, but was stamped "004" inside the cab roof, and either "004W" or "004T" as appropriate beneath the tender. Its detailing was identical to that of the 002, but electrically it was identical to the 003. Interestingly, while this seems to be the most difficult of the OO Hudsons to find, it is the least valuable.

VG	EX	LN	RARITY
150	300	500	6

Note: The 1938 Lionel catalog illustrated two other OO Hudsons, the 0081KW and 0081K. These were to be kits, with and without whistles, respectively. To date, no evidence has surfaced that these were actually produced.

Note on Lionel OO freight cars: "Super-detailed" freight cars have a simulated air brake reservoir, whereas semi-scale cars do not. Interestingly, no semi-scale hopper cars were produced. All kit cars came with insulated wheels, permitting them to be operated on two-rail track. These cars, as well as two-rail cars, could also be run on three-rail track. However, cars designed for three-rail operation cause a short circuit if placed on two-rail track.

0014 BOXCAR: From 1938 through 1942, this 6 7/8" long super-detailed boxcar designed for use on three-rail track graced the pages of the Lionel catalogs.

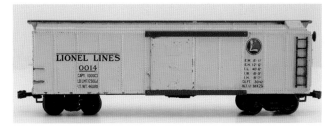

0014 BOXCAR (Type I): Not only was 1938 the introductory year for Lionel's OO, it was also a troublesome year for its rolling stock, marred by a couple of faux pas. One of these was the decorating of its scale-detailed boxcar in the yellow and maroon "Lionel Lines" paint scheme taken directly from its toy line. Though attractive, the red and blue Lionel circle "L" decal was not what model railroaders wanted. It is not unusual to find these cars repainted today.

VG	EX	LN	RARITY
75	125	200	6

0014 BOXCAR (Type II): In 1939 and subsequent years through 1942, the 0014 wore a much more realistic tuscan paint scheme with white decal "PENNSYLVANIA 0014" lettering.

VG	EX	LN	RARITY
50	65	80	4

0015 TANK CAR: Offered from 1938 through 1942, this 5 3/4" long, super-detailed, die-cast tanker was designed for operation on three-rail track. In addition to the cars listed later, two other versions were cataloged, but not manufactured. The first of these, shown in the 1938 catalog, was lettered "Lionel Lines 601614". The second non-existent tank car was shown in the 1941 catalog, and was a BLACK tanker marked "S.U.N.X. 0015".

0015 TANK CAR (Type I): In 1938, despite what was shown in the catalog, the only tank car offered was silver with a black frame. Its black decal lettering read "THE SUN OIL CO." and "S.O.C.X. 0015"; the familiar Sunoco logo appeared on the opposite end of the car. Unlike tank cars

Price Guide Key: **VG** = Very Good, **EX** = Excellent, **LN** = Like New | *Values for each condition are in U.S. dollars.* | **Rarity** = Scale from 1-8 with 8 being the hardest to find.

285

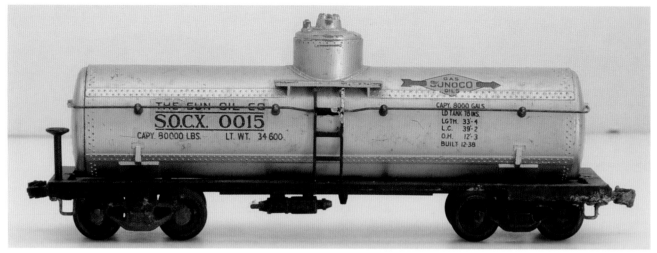

0015 TANK CAR TYPE I

made in subsequent years, no catalog number was stamped on the bottom of the frame.

VG	EX	LN	RARITY
50	75	100	6

0015 TANK CAR (Type II): In 1939 and 1940, the tank as well as the frame was black, and a white decal lettered "SHELL", "S.E.P.X. 8126" was applied to its sides. On the underside of the frame "0015" was rubber-stamped in silver.

VG	EX	LN	RARITY
40	60	80	5

0015 TANK CAR (Type III): In 1941, the Sunoco herald returned and was carried over into 1942. However, it differed from the 1938 edition. While the frame was still black and the tank was again silver, the black decal lettering now read "S.U.N.X. 2599" and the Sunoco herald was larger. The underside of the frame was rubber-stamped "0015" in silver.

VG	EX	LN	RARITY
40	60	80	5

0015 TANK CAR (Type IV): A fourth variation of the 0015 existed, which was almost identical to the Type III. However on the bottom it was stamped "G 0015" rather than simply "0015".

VG	EX	LN	RARITY
40	60	80	5

0016 HOPPER CAR: Offered from 1938-42, this detailed die-cast replica of a hopper car was 5 1/2" long and designed for use with three-rail track. In addition to the cars listed here, two other versions were cataloged, but not manufactured. The first of these, shown in the 1938 catalog, was lettered "Lionel Lines." The second of the aborted hopper cars was shown in the 1941 catalog, and was marked "Reading".

0016 HOPPER CAR (Type I): The hopper actually produced in 1938 was painted gray and its black decal lettering read "SP 0016". A round "SOUTHERN PACIFIC LINES" herald, also decaled in black, was near the right-hand end of car.

VG	EX	LN	RARITY
75	125	175	6

0016 HOPPER CAR (Type II): From 1939 through 1942, the Southern Pacific hopper was black. Its decal lettering still read "SP 0016" and it still sported a "SOUTHERN PACIFIC LINES" herald, which was round. But now the markings were white and slightly smaller than they had been in 1938.

VG	EX	LN	RARITY
60	100	150	4

0017 CABOOSE: Every train needs a caboose, or at least it did in the 1930s and 1940s. So naturally, Lionel provided one to finish off its OO train. The 4 5/8" long car, introduced in 1938, was nicely detailed, including a smokejack and underframe piping, and it remained in the product line through 1942. There was, however, one error in Lionel's strategy. The only OO locomotive it offered was the instantly recognizable New York Central Hudson. The caboose it chose to model was the equally recognizable Pennsylvania Railroad N5 cabin car. Although appearing in the 1938 catalog wearing "Lionel Lines" garb, the first year it was actually properly lettered "Pennsylvania". Recognizing its strategic error, in 1939 Lionel partially recovered by lettering the caboose "NYC", but that could not hide its distinctive Pennsy lines.

0017 CABOOSE (Type I): Despite appearing again in the 1940 catalog, this "PENNSYLVANIA 0017"-lettered version of the 0017 was only available in 1938. The caboose had a red body, slightly lighter than those of later years, and a maroon roofwalk. The car's lettering was done with white decals.

VG	EX	LN	RARITY
75	115	150	5

0017 CABOOSE (Type II): From 1939 through 1942, the car body was painted a darker shade of red, as was the roofwalk, and the white decal lettering was changed to read "N.Y.C. 0017".

VG	EX	LN	RARITY
50	75	100	3

0024 BOXCAR: During 1939-42, this semi-scale 6 7/8" long Pennsylvania boxcar with white decal lettering reading "PENNSYLVANIA 0024" was available. It was designed for operation on three-rail track. Sometimes it surfaces with black ladders, but this does not warrant a premium.

VG	EX	LN	RARITY
45	60	75	4

0025 TANK CAR: In 1939, Lionel began offering its tanker in a semi-scale version as well. Although still 5 3/4" long, these three-rail cars did not have the brake reservoir found on the 0015.

0025 TANK CAR (Type I): Debuting in 1939, this car was all black except for the white decal lettering on its flanks reading "SHELL, S.E.P.X. 8126". Beneath the car, "0025" was rubber-stamped on the frame in silver. In 1940, it continued unchanged, then disappeared for a year in 1941. It returned again in 1942, very likely as Lionel was using up leftover and repair parts inventory of decals and decorated bodies in a desperate attempt at supplying product despite War Production Board Order L-81, which prohibited the use of war materials (metals) in models.

VG	EX	LN	RARITY
40	60	80	3

0025 TANK CAR (Type II): In 1941 and 1942, the 0025 was offered with a bright silver tank and a new oil brand, Sunoco. The silver tank, with black decals featuring a large Sunoco logo and "S.U.N.X. 2599" reporting marks, was mounted on a black frame with "0025" silver-stamped on its bottom.

VG	EX	LN	RARITY
40	60	80	3

0027 CABOOSE: Cataloged between 1939 and 1942, the 4 5/8" long semi-scale three-rail caboose always sported white decal lettering emblazoned "N.Y.C. 0027" on its red body.

VG	EX	LN	RARITY
40	60	80	3

0031 CURVED TRACK: The 0031 was the standard two-rail 24" radius OO curved track, with Bakelite base and integral crossties. It was available from 1939 through 1942. Twelve sections were required to form a circle.

VG	EX	LN	RARITY
8	14	20	4

0034 CURVED TRACK: During 1939 through 1942, Lionel offered 00 Gauge trains in both two- and three-rail versions. The 0034 was based on the standard two-rail 24" radius curved track, with Bakelite base and integral crossties. However, it had the addition of two electrical connections, which permitted the 0034 to be used as the "Lockon" for a 00 outfit.

VG	EX	LN	RARITY
12	18	25	5

0044 BOXCAR: From 1939 through 1942, this 6 7/8" long super-detailed die-cast boxcar designed for use on two-rail track appeared on the pages of the Lionel catalogs. The 0044 wore a realistic tuscan paint scheme with white "PENNSYLVANIA 0044" decal lettering.

VG	EX	LN	RARITY
45	70	100	5

Price Guide Key: VG = Very Good, EX = Excellent, LN = Like New | *Values for each condition are in U.S. dollars.* | **Rarity** = Scale from 1-8 with 8 being the hardest to find.

287

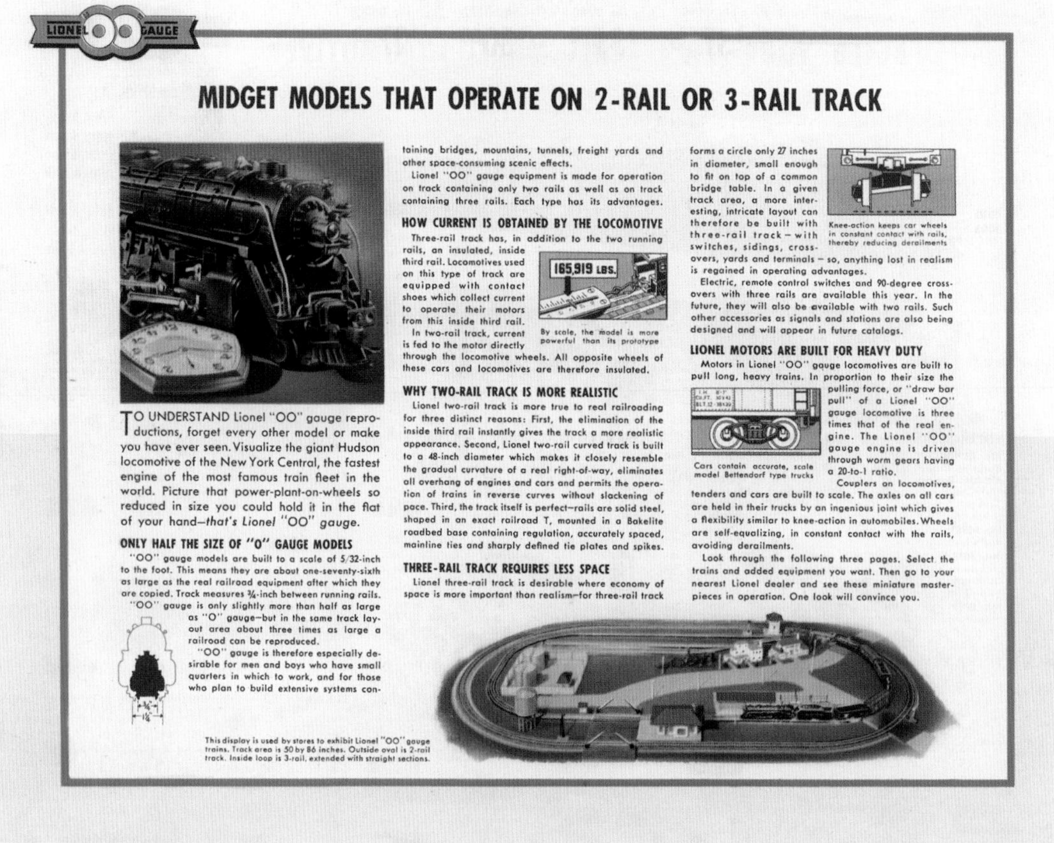

LIONEL OO GAUGE

MIDGET MODELS THAT OPERATE ON 2-RAIL OR 3-RAIL TRACK

TO UNDERSTAND Lionel "OO" gauge reproductions, forget every other model or make you have ever seen. Visualize the giant Hudson locomotive of the New York Central, the fastest engine of the most famous train fleet in the world. Picture that power-plant-on-wheels so reduced in size you could hold it in the flat of your hand—*that's Lionel "OO" gauge.*

ONLY HALF THE SIZE OF "O" GAUGE MODELS

"OO" gauge models are built to a scale of 5/32-inch to the foot. This means they are about one-seventy-sixth as large as the real railroad equipment after which they are copied. Track measures ¾-inch between running rails.

"OO" gauge is only slightly more than half as large as "O" gauge—but in the same track layout area about three times as large a railroad can be reproduced.

"OO" gauge is therefore especially desirable for men and boys who have small quarters in which to work, and for those who plan to build extensive systems containing bridges, mountains, tunnels, freight yards and other space-consuming scenic effects.

Lionel "OO" gauge equipment is made for operation on track containing only two rails as well as on track containing three rails. Each type has its advantages.

HOW CURRENT IS OBTAINED BY THE LOCOMOTIVE

Three-rail track has, in addition to the two running rails, an insulated, inside third rail. Locomotives used on this type of track are equipped with contact shoes which collect current to operate their motors from this inside third rail.

In two-rail track, current is fed to the motor directly through the locomotive wheels. All opposite wheels of these cars and locomotives are therefore insulated.

165,919 LBS.

By scale, the model is more powerful than its prototype

WHY TWO-RAIL TRACK IS MORE REALISTIC

Lionel two-rail track is more true to real railroading for three distinct reasons: First, the elimination of the inside third rail instantly gives the track a more realistic appearance. Second, Lionel two-rail curved track is built to a 48-inch diameter which makes it closely resemble the gradual curvature of a real right-of-way, eliminates all overhang of engines and cars and permits the operation of trains in reverse curves without slackening of pace. Third, the track itself is perfect—rails are solid steel, shaped in an exact railroad T, mounted in a Bakelite roadbed base containing regulation, accurately spaced, mainline ties and sharply defined tie plates and spikes.

THREE-RAIL TRACK REQUIRES LESS SPACE

Lionel three-rail track is desirable where economy of space is more important than realism—for three-rail track forms a circle only 27 inches in diameter, small enough to fit on top of a common bridge table. In a given track area, a more interesting, intricate layout can therefore be built with three-rail track—with switches, sidings, crossovers, yards and terminals—so, anything lost in realism is regained in operating advantages.

Knee-action keeps car wheels in constant contact with rails, thereby reducing derailments

Electric, remote control switches and 90-degree crossovers with three rails are available this year. In the future, they will also be available with two rails. Such other accessories as signals and stations are also being designed and will appear in future catalogs.

LIONEL MOTORS ARE BUILT FOR HEAVY DUTY

Motors in Lionel "OO" gauge locomotives are built to pull long, heavy trains. In proportion to their size the pulling force, or "draw bar pull" of a Lionel "OO" gauge locomotive is three times that of the real engine. The Lionel "OO" gauge engine is driven through worm gears having a 20-to-1 ratio.

Cars contain accurate, scale model Bettendorf type trucks

Couplers on locomotives, tenders and cars are built to scale. The axles on all cars are held in their trucks by an ingenious joint which gives a flexibility similar to knee-action in automobiles. Wheels are self-equalizing, in constant contact with the rails, avoiding derailments.

Look through the following three pages. Select the trains and added equipment you want. Then go to your nearest Lionel dealer and see these miniature masterpieces in operation. One look will convince you.

This display is used by stores to exhibit Lionel "OO" gauge trains. Track area is 50 by 86 inches. Outside oval is 2-rail track. Inside loop is 3-rail, extended with straight sections.

1939 CATALOG

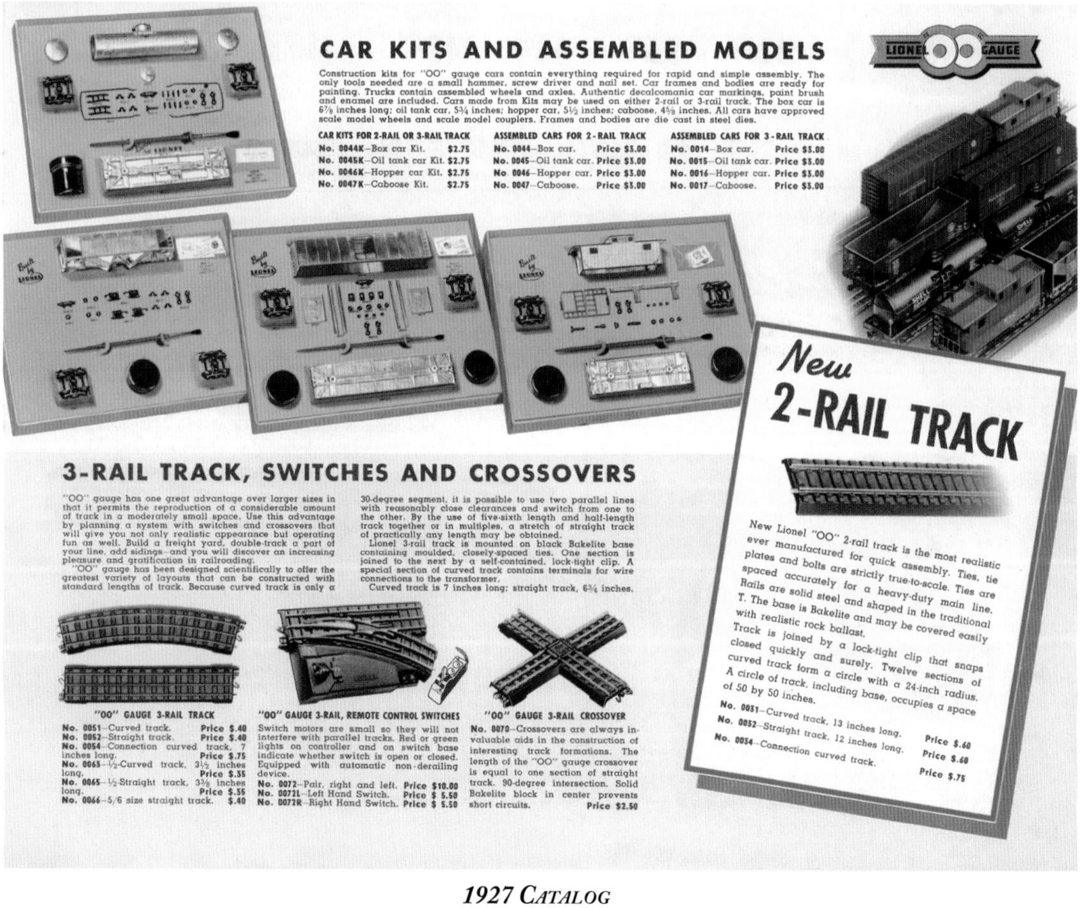

CAR KITS AND ASSEMBLED MODELS

LIONEL OO GAUGE

Construction kits for "OO" gauge cars contain everything required for rapid and simple assembly. The only tools needed are a small hammer, screw driver and nail set. Car frames and bodies are ready for painting. Trucks contain assembled wheels and axles. Authentic decalcomania car markings, paint brush and enamel are included. Cars made from Kits may be used on either 2-rail or 3-rail track. The box car is 6⅞ inches long; oil tank car, 5¾ inches; hopper car, 5½ inches; caboose, 4⅝ inches. All cars have approved scale model wheels and scale model couplers. Frames and bodies are die cast in steel dies.

CAR KITS FOR 2-RAIL OR 3-RAIL TRACK

No. 0044K—Box car Kit. $2.75
No. 0045K—Oil tank car Kit. $2.75
No. 0046K—Hopper car Kit. $2.75
No. 0047K—Caboose Kit. $2.75

ASSEMBLED CARS FOR 2-RAIL TRACK

No. 0044—Box car. Price $3.00
No. 0045—Oil tank car. Price $3.00
No. 0046—Hopper car. Price $3.00
No. 0047—Caboose. Price $3.00

ASSEMBLED CARS FOR 3-RAIL TRACK

No. 0014—Box car. Price $3.00
No. 0015—Oil tank car. Price $3.00
No. 0016—Hopper car. Price $3.00
No. 0017—Caboose. Price $3.00

New 2-RAIL TRACK

New Lionel "OO" 2-rail track is the most realistic ever manufactured for quick assembly. Ties, tie plates and bolts are strictly true-to-scale. Ties are spaced accurately for a heavy-duty main line. Rails are solid steel and shaped in the traditional T. The base is Bakelite and may be covered easily with realistic rock ballast.

Track is joined by a lock-tight clip that snaps closed quickly and surely. Twelve sections of curved track form a circle with a 24-inch radius. A circle of track, including base, occupies a space of 50 by 50 inches.

No. 0031—Curved track, 13 inches long. Price $.60
No. 0032—Straight track, 12 inches long. Price $.60
No. 0034—Connection curved track. Price $.75

3-RAIL TRACK, SWITCHES AND CROSSOVERS

"OO" gauge has one great advantage over larger sizes in that it permits the reproduction of a considerable amount of track in a moderately small space. Use this advantage by planning a system with switches and crossovers that will give you not only realistic appearance but operating fun as well. Build a freight yard, double-track a part of your line, add sidings—and you will discover an increasing pleasure and gratification in railroading.

"OO" gauge has been designed scientifically to offer the greatest variety of layouts that can be constructed with standard lengths of track. Because curved track is only a 30-degree segment, it is possible to use two parallel lines with reasonably close clearances and switch from one to the other. By the use of five-sixth length and half-length track together or in multiples, a stretch of straight track of practically any length may be obtained.

Lionel 3-rail track is mounted on black Bakelite base containing moulded, closely-spaced ties. One section is joined to the next by a self-contained, lock-tight clip. A special section of curved track contains terminals for wire connections to the transformer.

Curved track is 7 inches long; straight track, 6¾ inches.

"OO" GAUGE 3-RAIL TRACK

No. 0051—Curved track. Price $.40
No. 0052—Straight track. Price $.40
No. 0054—Connection curved track, 7 inches long. Price $.75
No. 0063—½-Curved track, 3½ inches long. Price $.35
No. 0065—½-Straight track, 3⅜ inches long. Price $.35
No. 0066—5/6 size straight track. $.40

"OO" GAUGE 3-RAIL, REMOTE CONTROL SWITCHES

Switch motors are small so they will not interfere with parallel tracks. Red or green lights on controller and on switch base indicate whether switch is open or closed. Equipped with automatic non-derailing device.

No. 0072—Pair, right and left. Price $10.00
No. 0072L—Left Hand Switch. Price $ 5.50
No. 0072R—Right Hand Switch. Price $ 5.50

"OO" GAUGE 3-RAIL CROSSOVER

No. 0070—Crossovers are always invaluable aids in the construction of interesting track formations. The length of the "OO" gauge crossover is equal to one section of straight track. 90-degree intersection. Solid Bakelite block in center prevents short circuits. Price $2.50

1927 CATALOG

0045 Tank Car

VG	EX	LN	RARITY
40	60	80	3

0044K BOXCAR: Also available 1939-42, this version of the 6 7/8" long super-detailed die-cast boxcar came unassembled and painted with gray primer. Paint, brush and decals were included in the kit. The pricing here for Very Good and Excellent assumes an unassembled kit, and Excellent assumes the original packaging is present.

VG	EX	LN	RARITY
70	125	350	6

0045 TANK CAR: Its wheels insulated for two-rail operation, this super-detailed 5 3/4" long tank car was cataloged 1939-42. During that time, it was produced in three variations.

0045 TANK CAR (Type I):  In 1939 and 1940, the tank as well as the frame was black, and a white decal lettered "SHELL", "S.E.P.X. 8126" was applied to its sides. On the underside of the frame "0045" was rubber-stamped in silver. It returned again in 1942, very likely as Lionel was using up leftover and repair parts inventory of decals and decorated bodies in a desperate attempt at supplying product despite wartime restrictions.

VG	EX	LN	RARITY
40	60	80	5

0045 TANK CAR (Type II): In 1941 and 1942, the 0025 was offered with a bright silver tank and a new oil brand, Sunoco. The silver tank, with black decals featuring a large Sunoco logo and "S.U.N.X. 2599" reporting marks, was mounted on a black frame with "0045" rubber-stamped in silver on its bottom.

0045K TANK CAR: Available 1939-42, this version of the 5 3/4" long super-detailed die-cast tank car came unassembled and painted with gray primer. Paint, brush and decals were included in the kit. The pricing for Very Good and Excellent assumes an unassembled kit, and Excellent assumes the original packaging is present.

VG	EX	LN	RARITY
70	125	350	6

0046 HOPPER CAR: From 1939 through 1942, the 5 1/2" long super-detailed Southern Pacific hopper was offered with insulated wheels for two-rail operation. Its body was painted black and it still sported a round "SOUTHERN PACIFIC LINES" herald. But now the markings were white and read "SP 0046".

VG	EX	LN	RARITY
40	70	100	4

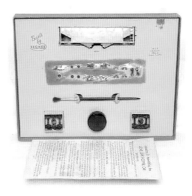

Price Guide Key: VG = Very Good, EX = Excellent, LN = Like New | *Values for each condition are in U.S. dollars.* | Rarity = Scale from 1-8 with 8 being the hardest to find.

289

0046K HOPPER CAR: Also available 1939-42, this version of the 5 1/2" long super-detailed die-cast hopper car came unassembled and painted with gray primer. Paint, brush and decals were included in the kit. The pricing for Very Good and Excellent assumes an unassembled kit, and Excellent assumes the original packaging is present.

VG	EX	LN	RARITY
70	125	350	6

0047 CABOOSE: This 4 5/8" long super-detailed caboose, with smoke jack and piping, had insulated wheels for two-rail operation. It was cataloged from 1939 through 1942. Despite being cataloged differently in 1940, it was always made with a red body and catwalk, and featured white decal lettering reading "N.Y.C. 0047".

VG	EX	LN	RARITY
30	60	90	4

0047K CABOOSE: Available 1939-42, this version of the 4 5/8" long super-detailed die-cast caboose came unassembled, and painted with gray primer. Paint, brush and decals were included in the kit. The pricing for Very Good and Excellent assumes an unassembled kit, and Excellent assumes the original packaging is present.

VG	EX	LN	RARITY
70	125	350	6

0051 CURVED TRACK: The 0051 was the standard three-rail 27" radius OO curved track offered from 1939 through 1942, with Bakelite base and integral crossties. The rail had a tubular cross-section. Twelve sections were required to form a circle.

The 0051 differed from the earlier 0061 production in that the under roadbed spring clip of the electrical connection was dispensed with. Instead, a blade-type collection was attached to the center rail. Similar connectors replaced the round pins in the outer rails. Lionel did not change the engraving on the molds, so "061-2" continued to appear on the track itself.

VG	EX	LN	RARITY
6	12	18	4

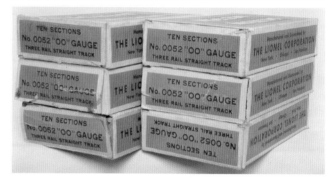

0052 STRAIGHT TRACK: During 1939 through 1942, Lionel offered 00 Gauge trains in both two- and three-rail versions. The 0052 was the standard three-rail 7" long straight track, with tubular rails, Bakelite base and integral crossties.

The 0052 differed from the earlier 0062 production in that the under roadbed spring clip of the electrical connection was dispensed with. Instead, a blade-type collection was attached to the center rail. Similar connectors replaced the round pins in the outer rails. Lionel did not change the engraving on the molds, so "062-2" continued to appear on the track itself.

VG	EX	LN	RARITY
12	18	30	5

0054 CURVED TERMINAL TRACK: During 1939 through 1942, Lionel offered 00 Gauge trains in both two- and three-rail versions. The 0054 was based on the standard 0051 three-rail 27" radius curved track, with tubular rails, Bakelite base with integral crossties and no under track spring clip connectors for the center rails. However, it had the addition of two side-mounted electrical connections, which permitted the 0054 to be used as the "Lockon" for the 00 outfit.

VG	EX	LN	RARITY
12	18	25	5

0061 CURVED TRACK: All the OO track produced in 1938 (despite the catalog listings, evidence indicates only straight, curved and terminal sections were made in 1938) had a spring clip electrical connector joining the center rails. The outer rails used round mating pins, much like 0 and Standard Gauge. Twelve sections of the track, which featured a molded Bakelite base with integral crossties, could form a 27" diameter circle.

VG	EX	LN	RARITY
5	10	15	4

0062 STRAIGHT TRACK: All the OO track produced in 1938 (despite the catalog listings, evidence indicates only straight, curved and terminal sections were made in 1938) had a spring clip electrical connector joining the center rails. The outer rails used round mating pins, much like 0 and Standard Gauge. This was the standard three-rail 7" long straight OO track, with tubular rails, Bakelite base and integral crossties included in first year sets.

VG	EX	LN	RARITY
6	12	18	6

0063 CURVED TRACK: Although cataloged in 1938, the 0063 was not actually produced until the following year. Therefore, none exist with the spring clip center rail connection. This was a 3" long "half section" of three-rail tubular OO curved track, with molded Bakelite base including realistically close-spaced crossties. It remained in the lineup through 1942.

VG	EX	LN	RARITY
12	18	24	6

0064 CURVED TERMINAL TRACK: This terminal track was only offered in 1938. The 0064 was based on the standard 0061 three-rail 27" radius curved track, with tubular rails, Bakelite base with integral crossties and no under track spring clip connectors for the center rails. However, it had the addition of two side-mounted electrical connections, which permitted the 0064 to be used as the "Lockon" for the 00 outfit.

VG	EX	LN	RARITY
12	18	25	5

0065 STRAIGHT TRACK: Although cataloged in 1938, the 0065 was not actually produced until the following year. Therefore, none exist with the spring clip center rail connection. This was a 3 3/8" long "half section" of three-rail tubular OO track, with molded Bakelite base including realistically close-spaced crossties. It remained in the lineup through 1942.

VG	EX	LN	RARITY
12	18	24	6

0066 STRAIGHT TRACK: Although cataloged in 1938, the 0065 was not actually produced until the following year. Therefore, none exist with the spring clip center rail connection. This was a 5 5/8" long "5/6" of three-rail tubular OO track, with molded Bakelite base including realistically close-spaced crossties. It remained in the lineup through 1942.

VG	EX	LN	RARITY
12	18	24	6

0070 90-DEGREE CROSSING: This three-rail 00 Gauge 90-degree crossing was cataloged from 1938 through 1942, but was not produced until 1939. It had a molded Bakelite base with representing ballasted closely spaced ties.

VG	EX	LN	RARITY
4	8	12	5

0072 PAIR OF REMOTE CONTROL SWITCHES: Although cataloged in 1938, the 0072 was not actually produced until the following year. Therefore, none exist with the spring clip center rail connection. This was a pair of illuminated remote control turnouts for three-rail tubular OO track. Their molded Bakelite base included realistically close-spaced crossties. The 0072, and their lighted controllers, remained in the lineup through 1942.

VG	EX	LN	RARITY
125	200	300	6

0072L REMOTE CONTROL SWITCH: Produced from 1939 through 1942, this was a single left-hand OO gauge turnout and controller only.

VG	EX	LN	RARITY
60	90	140	6

0072R REMOTE CONTROL SWITCH: Produced from 1939 through 1942, this was a single right-hand OO gauge turnout and controller only.

Price Guide Key: **VG** = Very Good, **EX** = Excellent, **LN** = Like New | *Values for each condition are in U.S. dollars.* | **Rarity** = Scale from 1-8 with 8 being the hardest to find.

291

VG	EX	LN	RARITY
60	90	140	6

0074 BOXCAR: From 1939 through 1942, this 6 7/8" long semi-scale die-cast boxcar designed for use on two-rail track appeared on the pages of the Lionel catalogs. The 0074 wore a realistic tuscan paint scheme with white "PENNSYLVANIA 0074" decal lettering.

VG	EX	LN	RARITY
45	70	100	5

0075 TANK CAR: Its wheels insulated for two-rail operation, this semi-scale 5 3/4" long tank car was cataloged 1939-42. During that time it was produced in two, or perhaps three, variations.

0075 TANK CAR (Type I): In 1939 and 1940, the tank as well as the frame was black and a white decal lettered "SHELL", "S.E.P.X. 8126" was applied to its sides. On the underside of the frame, "0075" was rubber-stamped in silver. It returned again in 1942, very likely as Lionel was using up leftover and repair parts inventory of decals and decorated bodies in a desperate attempt at supplying product despite wartime restrictions.

VG	EX	LN	RARITY
20	40	60	3

0075 TANK CAR (Type II): In 1941 and 1942, the 0025 was offered with a bright silver tank and a new oil brand, Sunoco. The silver tank, with black decals featuring a large Sunoco logo and "S.U.N.X. 2599" reporting marks, was mounted on a black frame with "0075" rubber-stamped in silver on its bottom.

VG	EX	LN	RARITY
20	40	60	3

0075 TANK CAR (Type III): A few examples of gray semi-scale two-rail tank cars have been found with white decal "SHELL S.E.P.X. 8126" lettering, and "0075" rubber-stamped in silver on the bottom. Some collectors believe that Lionel created these in 1942 by factory-assembling unsold kits and applying the kit decals. However, no documentation has surfaced to support this.

RARITY
No value established.

0077 CABOOSE: This red 4 5/8" long semi-scale caboose with insulated wheels for two-rail operation was cataloged from 1939-1942. It had white decal lettering reading "N.Y.C. 0077".

VG	EX	LN	RARITY
20	40	60	3

1939 Catalog

ACCESSORIES, CATALOGS & TOYS, ETC.
OVERVIEW

Though Lionel was always a diversified manufacturing firm, also producing appliances, defense products, chemistry sets and a host of other items, the one thing beyond trains the firm's first century is remembered for is its catalogs.

Though the first catalogs were humble, by the 1920s the Lionel catalog had grown into an extravagant full-color masterpiece of marketing. Typically, boys – with their all-American companion, a puppy – were shown playing gleefully with Lionel products while their families, including sisters, looked on approvingly.

Contrasting with the apple-pie imagery was boastful rhetoric that would make even today's most ardent Fifth Avenue copywriter blush. Not only were trains that obviously weren't labeled "realistic scale models" in the catalogs, competitors' trains were shown and labeled "shaky, flimsy and rickety."

Accessories filled page after page of these catalogs, representing added fun for the junior engineer and added profits for the company. The accessory market was much less competitive than the market for sets, allowing hefty profit margins. Because fewer accessories were sold than outfits, it is much harder to build a complete accessory collection today than many realize.

Though, as mentioned earlier, Lionel produced a myriad of non-train products through the years, some are of special note and are discussed in the final chapter. Also included are a few trains that defy categorization in other areas, notably handcars.

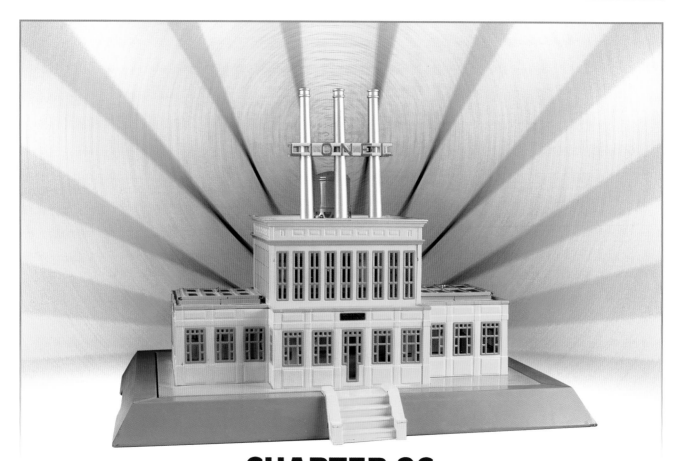

CHAPTER 26
ACCESSORIES, TRACK &
TRANSFORMERS

One of the key elements in Lionel's success, both prewar and postwar, was its numerous operating accessories. Joshua Cowen felt it was important to provide a means for children and adults to interact with the trains, as well as provide a semi-realistic setting to operate them in.

Today Lionel's accessories retain their appeal to operators and collectors alike. Children, young or old, still delight in watching day to day tasks being performed in miniature by these accessories.

Despite their appeal compared to trains, and starter sets in particular, all accessories are relatively scarce. The rarity ratings given in this chapter are relative to other accessories, not the Lionel product line as a whole. Even the most common of accessories, like the 45 gateman, is more difficult to locate than a common train car, such as the 1679 boxcar.

1 BILD-A-MOTOR: Shown in the 1928 and 1929 catalogs with a reverse lever, these 0 Gauge motors were sold separately for use powering other projects.

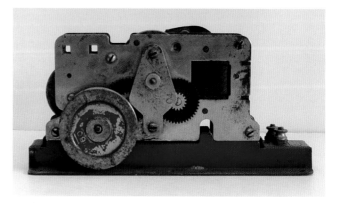

1 BILD-A-MOTOR (Type I): As described previously.

VG	EX	LN	RARITY
60	90	150	7

1 BILD-A-MOTOR (Type II): In 1930, the 0 Gauge Bild-A-Motor was improved, and this version was carried over into 1931 as well. The motor had nickel-plated sides and was mounted on a red or black base. When sold separately, the 5 1/2" x 3" x 3" motors were supplied in a two-piece box with a label reading "No. 1 - 'BILD-A-MOTOR' -TRADEMARK PATENTS PENDING."

VG	EX	LN	RARITY
60	90	150	7

2 BILD-A-MOTOR: During 1928-29, the Standard Gauge 2 Bild-A-Motor was offered separately. This motor was similar to the 0-sized number 1 motor, and was provided with either a red or black base. These motors were 7" long, 3 1/2" wide and 4" high.

2 BILD-A-MOTOR (Type I): As described previously.

VG	EX	LN	RARITY
100	125	225	7

2 BILD-A-MOTOR (Type II): During 1930-31, the No. 2 Bild-A-Motor was equipped with a three-speed gear mechanism and reversing device.

VG	EX	LN	RARITY
100	125	225	7

011 PAIR OF REMOTE CONTROL SWITCHES: From 1933 through 1937, this pair of illuminated 0 Gauge turnouts, with controllers, was offered.

VG	EX	LN	RARITY
20	30	40	3

011L LEFT HAND REMOTE CONTROL SWITCH: This was a 0 Gauge, illuminated, left-hand, non-derailing switch, built in 1933-37. It was similar to 012, but with solenoid mechanism in housing beneath the lantern stand, raised to provide clearance for lever mechanism, three screw-type terminals for wire connections, with controller and three-wire cable; non-derailing feature activated by grounding switch machine solenoid to insulated rails on straight and curved approach tracks.

011L LEFT HAND REMOTE CONTROL SWITCH (Type I): The 1933 catalog showed this turnout to have a green-enameled base. The control housing was nickel-plated and the lantern support was painted maroon.

VG	EX	LN	RARITY
10	15	20	3

011L LEFT HAND REMOTE CONTROL SWITCH (Type II): In the catalogs from 1934-37, these turnouts were shown with a black-painted base. While the nickel-plated control housing was retained, the lantern support was now painted red rather than maroon. Due to the imprecise nature of the catalog, those illustrations cannot be used to establish the exact dates of manufacturing or color changes.

VG	EX	LN	RARITY
10	15	20	3

011L LEFT HAND REMOTE CONTROL SWITCH (Type III): A third variation was produced, which differed from the Type II by featuring a black lantern support and a black-enameled nickel plate reading: "011 -AUTOMATICALLY CONTROLLED-ILLUMINATED SWITCH-THE LIONEL CORPORATION, N.Y."

VG	EX	LN	RARITY
10	15	20	3

011L LEFT HAND REMOTE CONTROL SWITCH (Type IV): During 1931-32, the Lionel 011 was marketed under the Ives name (Ives by that time was wholly owned by Lionel). The turnouts were assigned the Ives catalog number 1897.

VG	EX	LN	RARITY
10	15	20	3

011R RIGHT HAND REMOTE CONTROL SWITCH: Produced 1933-37, this turnout naturally was the mirror image of the 011L. It was produced in the same variety of types as its left-hand brother.

VG	EX	LN	RARITY
10	15	20	3

012 PAIR OF REMOTE CONTROL SWITCHES: This pair of 012L and 012R illuminated 0 Gauge turnouts with controllers was cataloged from 1927 through 1933.

VG	EX	LN	RARITY
25	30	40	3

012L LEFT HAND REMOTE CONTROL SWITCH: Cataloged from 1927 through 1933, these steel-based illuminated 0 Gauge remote control turnouts look very similar to the later 011, although they lack the non-derailing feature of the new turnouts. The lighted simulated lantern had rounded corners and housed two red and two green celluloid disks through which the light shown. A trio of screw-type terminals were provided to connect the three-wire cable from the controller.

VG	EX	LN	RARITY
12	15	20	3

012R RIGHT HAND REMOTE CONTROL SWITCH: The mirror-image of the 012L was the 012R right hand remote control turnout, also offered 1927-33.

VG	EX	LN	RARITY
12	15	20	3

013 REMOTE CONTROL SWITCH SET: During the period 1929-31, a deluxe pairing of 012 0 Gauge turnouts was offered, packaged with a 439 control panel. The value of this accessory lies almost solely in the original packaging.

Price Guide Key: **VG** = Very Good, **EX** = Excellent, **LN** = Like New | *Values for each condition are in U.S. dollars.* | Rarity = Scale from 1-8 with 8 being the hardest to find.

295

VG	EX	LN	RARITY
100	140	200	6

20 90-DEGREE CROSSING: One of the most basic accessory items for trains is the 90-degree crossing. In 1909, Lionel introduced the number 20 crossing to its line of Standard Gauge track. It would remain in the catalog through 1942, although through the intervening years it was produced in three distinctive variations, as detailed here.

20 90-DEGREE CROSSING (Type I): Introduced in 1909, the 20 crossing featured a small square base. The approaching rails extended beyond this base, and a single crosstie was present on each set of approach rails. The earliest production lacked a pickup shoe support at the junction of the rails, but this feature was added later, preventing damage to pickups on locomotives and cars.

VG	EX	LN	RARITY
3	7	10	1

20 90-DEGREE CROSSING (Type II): Later in the production, probably sometime between 1917 and 1925, the #20 crossing was redesigned such that it resembled the 0 Gauge crossing. The steel baseplate was reshaped so that it extended to the ends of the approach rails. The course negated the need for the individual crossties on the ends of each approach. Each of these approaches was joined to their adjacent approaches by a steel web or filet integral with the baseplate, which was painted either pea green or black, the latter from 1932 onward.

A nameplate, made of either brass or nickel plate proudly proclaimed "No 20 - CROSSING - THE - LIONEL CORP. - NEW YORK".

VG	EX	LN	RARITY
3	7	10	1

20 90-DEGREE CROSSING (Type III): During 1931-32, when Lionel made and marketed trains under the Ives label, the 20 appeared in the Ives catalog as the number 1899.

VG	EX	LN	RARITY
3	7	10	1

20 DIRECT CURRENT REDUCER: Listed in the 1906, this device, with integral on-off switch, was designed to vary the speed of the train.

RARITY
Too rarely, if ever, traded to establish market pricing, or even confirm existence.

20X 45-DEGREE CROSSING: This Standard Gauge crossing, introduced in 1928, was similar in design to the second series 20 crossing. However it created a 45-degree junction rather than the 90-degree junction of the 20.

VG	EX	LN	RARITY
5	10	15	2

020 90-DEGREE CROSSING: This 0 gauge accessory was introduced in 1915. Except for the interruption of production during World War II, it was available continuously through 1961.

020 90-DEGREE CROSSING (Type I): Despite catalog descriptions, which began in 1915, as being similar to the contemporary number 20 Standard Gauge crossing (i.e.. approach rails extending beyond the baseplate), no evidence has surfaced of this crossing actually being produced in this configuration. Rather, all observed examples include baseplates that extend to the ends of the rails. Each of these approaches are joined to their adjacent approaches by a steel web or filet integral with the baseplate, which was painted either pea green or black, the latter from 1932 onward. A brass or nickel plate was affixed to one web, the plate bearing the legend "No 020 -CROSSING - THE - LIONEL CORP. - NEW YORK".

VG	EX	LN	RARITY
4	6	8	2

020 90-DEGREE CROSSING (Type II): Later production omitted the separately installed nameplate in favor of molding the same information into a pickup shoe support.

VG	EX	LN	RARITY
4	6	8	2

020X 45-DEGREE CROSSING: This 0 gauge accessory was introduced in 1915 and, except for the interruption of production during World War II, was available continuously through 1959.

VG	EX	LN	RARITY
4	7	10	3

21 90-DEGREE CROSSING: Cataloged in 1906, this Standard Gauge crossing appeared similar to the number 20 but had an 8" rather than 12" square base. It is not believed to have been manufactured.

RARITY
Too rarely, if ever, traded to establish market pricing, or even confirm existence

21 MANUAL SWITCH: From 1915 through 1925, Lionel offered this Standard Gauge manual turnout made of steel. On top of its control housing was mounted a square lamp housing with two each red and green celluloid lenses simulating a switch stand lamp. This lamp housing was removable and is often missing.

21 MANUAL SWITCH (Type I): From 1915-22, the control lever mechanism support featured two cut-out areas.

VG	EX	LN	RARITY
12	20	35	2

21 MANUAL SWITCH (Type II): Beginning in 1923, the control mechanism support was closed and two heavy fiber strips added where the rails meet. Turnouts of this design were produced through 1925.

VG	EX	LN	RARITY
12	20	35	3

021 PAIR OF MANUAL SWITCHES: These were the earliest 0 gauge turnouts, being introduced in 1915. They remained in the product line through 1937.

VG	EX	LN	RARITY
15	25	40	2

021L LEFT HAND MANUAL SWITCH: Available 1915-37, these illuminated 0 Gauge turnouts were modeled after Standard Gauge 21 turnouts, including the lantern assemblies.

021L LEFT HAND MANUAL SWITCH (Type I)
From 1915 through 1922, like the 21, the 021 control lever support baseplate was punched out, allowing the surface beneath the turnout to be visible.

VG	EX	LN	RARITY
7	12	20	2

021L LEFT HAND MANUAL SWITCH (Type II)
Beginning in 1923, the control mechanism support was solid and two heavy fiber strips added where the rails meet. A brass plate marked "021-LIONEL RAILROAD -ILLUMINATED-FOR USE WITH '0' GAUGE TRACK-THE LIONEL CORPORATION, N.Y." was mounted near the control lever housing. Turnouts of this design were produced through 1925.

VG	EX	LN	RARITY
7	12	20	3

021L LEFT HAND MANUAL SWITCH (Type III)
During 1931-32, when Lionel made and marketed trains under the Ives label, the 021 appeared in the Ives catalog as the number 1895.

VG	EX	LN	RARITY
10	15	25	3

021R RIGHT HAND MANUAL SWITCH
From 1915-37, naturally right hand turnouts were made as well, in the same variations as found in left hand turnouts. The catalog number of the right hand turnout was 021R.

22 MANUAL SWITCH
Introduced in 1906, the number 22 was the first turnout produced for Lionel's then-new Standard Gauge trains. Initially these turnouts incorporated a very realistic-looking cast iron switch stand, however it was replaced in 1916 with a less expensive switch stand formed from sheet metal.

22 MANUAL SWITCH (Type I)
From 1906 through 1913, the turnout was manufactured with its switch stand mounted on two extra-long crossties, as was done in prototype practice. Installed on top of the switch stand were red and white signal disks, which indicated the position of the points, or swivel rails. The center rails terminated in a diamond-shaped pickup shoe support.

VG	EX	LN	RARITY
30	40	50	7

22 MANUAL SWITCH (Type II)
The 1914 catalog illustration indicated that the turnout had been redesigned. The individual ties, which had previously supported the rails of the turnout as well as the switch stand, were supplanted by a formed sheet metal base with integral switch stand support. The juncture of the center rails was widened, but lacked the earlier diamond-shape. The signal disks continued to be described as red and white in the catalog.

VG	EX	LN	RARITY
20	30	40	5

22 MANUAL SWITCH (Type III)
In both the 1915 and 1916 catalog, the signal disks were described as red and green instead of red and white.

VG	EX	LN	RARITY
20	30	40	5

22 MANUAL SWITCH (Type IV)
From 1917 through 1922, the switch shown in the catalog was a new style turnout. The signal disks were replaced with a lantern housing like the one used on the 21. This was mounted on a sheet metal switch stand, which also acted as the control lever support. Although this lantern was lighted on the 21, on the 22 it was purely decorative.

VG	EX	LN	RARITY
17	25	35	3

22 MANUAL SWITCH (Type V)
In 1923, the control mechanism base was closed, and a y-shaped metal plate replaced the wires previously used to connect the center rails. Two heavy fiber strips were added where the rails cross. The turnout continued to be produced in this configuration through 1925.

VG	EX	LN	RARITY
17	25	35	3

022 PAIR OF MANUAL SWITCHES
These were among the earliest 0 gauge turnouts, being introduced in 1915. However, they were sold as a pair only from 1922 until they were discontinued in 1926. A pair consisted of one 022L and one 022R. They differed from the 021 in that they lacked illumination.

VG	EX	LN	RARITY
25	40	65	6

022L LEFT HAND MANUAL SWITCH
Offered from 1915 through 1926, this 0 Gauge manually operated turnout was non-illuminated. Its baseplate and mechanism were of steel construction, and included a sheet metal switch stand supporting a simulated lantern. The lantern was removable, and hence is often missing today. Two red and two green disks, retained by circular frames, depicted the lens of an actual switch stand lantern.

022L LEFT HAND MANUAL SWITCH (Type I)
From 1915 through 1922, like the 021, the 022 control lever support baseplate was punched out, allowing the surface beneath the turnout to be visible.

VG	EX	LN	RARITY
12	20	32	6

022L LEFT HAND MANUAL SWITCH (Type II)
Beginning in 1923, the control mechanism support was solid and two heavy fiber strips added where the rails meet. A brass plate marked "022 - LIONEL RAILROAD SWITCH - NOT ILLUMINATED - FOR USE WITH '0' GAUGE TRACK-THE LIONEL CORPORATION, N.Y." was mounted near the control lever housing. Turnouts of this design were produced through 1925.

VG	EX	LN	RARITY
12	20	32	7

022R RIGHT HAND MANUAL SWITCH
Naturally, from 1915 through 1926, right hand turnouts were offered as well. They were made in the same variations, and have the same values, as their left-hand brothers.

022 REMOTE CONTROL SWITCHES
Introduced in 1938, the 022 became the mainstay of Lionel's 0 gauge turnouts for most of the rest of the 20th century. Discontinued in 1942 due to war production, the turnouts were extensively redesigned internally after World War II. Yet they retained the same catalog number as their prewar counterparts upon their 1945 reintroduction and retained it throughout the run,

Price Guide Key: VG = Very Good, EX = Excellent, LN = Like New | *Values for each condition are in U.S. dollars.* | **Rarity** = Scale from 1-8 with 8 being the hardest to find.

297

which ending in 1966. When reintroduced in 1980, finally the stock numbers were changed. Each pair of turnouts came with a pair of illuminated 022C controllers. These were simple, rugged reliable turnouts and included a non-derailing feature as well as an illuminated position indicator. By removing two screws, the operating mechanism could be shifted from side to side of the turnouts' Bakelite base to allow greater flexibility in track planning.

VG	EX	LN	RARITY
60	75	90	2

022L LEFT HAND REMOTE CONTROL SWITCH: During 1938-1942, and 1950-61, Lionel sold 022 turnouts individually as well as in pairs. The value of this left-hand 0 gauge turnout with controller is enhanced by its separate-sale box.

VG	EX	LN	RARITY
35	45	55	4

022R RIGHT HAND REMOTE CONTROL SWITCH: Of course, the right-hand turnout was also sold separately during 1938-1942 and 1950-61. The value of this right-hand 0 gauge turnout with controller is enhanced by its separate-sale box.

VG	EX	LN	RARITY
35	45	55	4

23 BUMPER: Made in 1906-33, this was Standard Gauge, steel construction, with two spring-loaded plunger assemblies.

23 BUMPER (Type I): As shown in the 1906-07 catalogs, this bumper consisted of two spring-loaded shafts that acted as buffers supported by two U-shaped steel straps.

RARITY
Too rarely, if ever, traded to establish market pricing, or even confirm existence.

23 BUMPER (Type II): From 1908 through 1913, the 23 was shown with triangular-shaped side panels supporting a pair of black spring-loaded rectangular buffers. The bumper, the sides of which were painted either black or red, was sold mounted on section of type "S" Standard Gauge track.

VG	EX	LN	RARITY
20	30	40	5

23 BUMPER (Type III): The 23 was also produced with open, triangular-shaped sides from 1914 through 1933. It was painted either red, black, green or yellow-orange.

VG	EX	LN	RARITY
20	30	40	5

23 90-DEGREE CROSSING: The same as the 20 Crossing, this appears only in the 1912 catalog with an illustration identical to the 20.

RARITY
Too rarely, if ever, traded to establish market pricing, or even confirm existence.

023 BUMPER: A 0 gauge bumper was offered from 1915 through 1933, which was styled much like the Standard Gauge number 23. Naturally it was smaller, and it had only one spring-loaded buffer bar. These bumpers were made in both red and black colors.

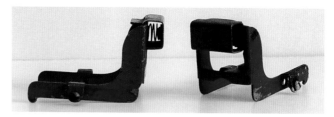

023 BUMPER (Type I): As described previously.

VG	EX	LN	RARITY
15	25	35	4

023 BUMPER (Type II): Painted yellow-orange and marked as Ives, this had Ives catalog number 340-0.

VG	EX	LN	RARITY
15	25	35	6

24 RAILWAY STATION: Shown in the 1906 and 1907 catalogs, this station, with ivory sides simulating brick, was mounted on a dark red base. Separating the walls from the base was a black simulated-brick foundation. The station had a traditional projecting bay window, painted maroon, on the track side. A maroon-painted door was on either side of the bay window, and on the gable above the bay was a sign reading "OCEANSIDE". The roof was red and black, and was topped with an ivory chimney. Although marketed by Lionel, it is believed that this 11" x 7 1/2" x 8" item was actually purchased by the firm from an outside vendor.

RARITY
Too rarely, if ever, traded to establish market pricing.

25 OPEN RAILWAY STATION: Depicted in the 1906 and 1907 catalogs, this 11" x 11" x 8" station came as two sections. One section had four pillars supporting a roof; the opposite section included a fence. It is believed that this item, which included a miniature figure, was actually purchased by the firm from an outside vendor.

RARITY
Too rarely, if ever, traded to establish market pricing, or even confirm existence.

25 ILLUMINATED BUMPER: Introduced in 1927, this Standard Gauge die-cast bumper was offered through 1942. Two buffers were cast into the face of the bumpers, and on each side of the bumper two vertical ribs were cast. In the top of the casting, a light socket was mounted, which was protected by a brass or nickel light guard.

25 ILLUMINATED BUMPER (Type I): During 1927-33, the bumper casting was painted a cream color and the cast ribs were highlighted in red. The light guard was natural brass.

VG	EX	LN	RARITY
25	33	45	5

25 ILLUMINATED BUMPER (Type II): Beginning in 1934, and continuing through 1942, the casting was painted overall black. The light guard was nickel colored.

VG	EX	LN	RARITY
20	25	35	3

25 ILLUMINATED BUMPER (Type III): Ives offered the number 25 bumper from 1928-30, assigning it catalog number 339. The 339 came in either solid black or yellow with the cast ribs highlighted in red.

VG	EX	LN	RARITY
20	25	35	4

025 ILLUMINATED BUMPER: Styled along the lines of the 25, the 0 Gauge 025 was offered from 1928-1942.

025 ILLUMINATED BUMPER (Type I): As with the 25, from 1928-33, 025 was painted cream with a brass light guard.

VG	EX	LN	RARITY
20	25	30	5

025 ILLUMINATED BUMPER (Type II): Also available in 1928-33 was a black bumper with nickel light guard.

VG	EX	LN	RARITY
20	25	30	5

025 ILLUMINATED BUMPER (Type III): Beginning in 1934, the 025 was painted semi-gloss black. Through 1942 it continued in this color, with either a nickel or brass light guard.

VG	EX	LN	RARITY
15	20	25	3

Price Guide Key: **VG** = Very Good, **EX** = Excellent, **LN** = Like New | *Values for each condition are in U.S. dollars.* | **Rarity** = Scale from 1-8 with 8 being the hardest to find.

025 ILLUMINATED BUMPER (Type IV): Some of the semi-gloss black bumpers were adorned with a vertical red stripe painted on each side.

VG	EX	LN	RARITY
20	25	30	5

025 ILLUMINATED BUMPER (Type V): Ives offered the number 25 bumper from 1928-30, assigning it catalog number 339-0.

VG	EX	LN	RARITY
15	20	25	5

26 PASSENGER FOOTBRIDGE: This imposing Standard Gauge structure was cataloged in both 1906 and 1907, but is believed to have been only marketed by Lionel, but made by another firm. Two semaphores and two miniature figures adorned the elevated portion of the bridge, and a set of steps was mounted on each end.

RARITY
Too rarely, if ever, traded to establish market pricing, or even confirm existence.

27 STATION: This lithographed station was offered from 1908 through 1914. It is suspected that this station was manufactured for Lionel by Ives. The track side had a bay window, three conventional windows and two doors. The opposite side had four windows and two doors.

RARITY
Too rarely traded to establish market pricing.

27 LIGHTING SET: This item, offered from 1911 through 1923, was used to add interior illumination to passenger cars. The set included three sockets, associated bulbs and contacts, and 5' of wire. A 30 percent premium should be added for original packaging.

VG	EX	LN	RARITY
15	30	45	3

28 STATION: From 1908 through 1914, the number 28 was the ultimate Lionel station. A leaded glass train shed was supported over the track by two number 27 stations, one on each side. The catalogs gave its size as 18" x 22 1/2" by 11", coincidentally (or not) the same as the hauntingly similar Ives 123 double station.

RARITY
Too rarely traded to establish market pricing.

30 CURVED RUBBER ROADBED: This roadbed, made of rubber, was sold from 1931 through 1937. Molded to simulate ballast, it muffled the sound of the train, as well as kept the Standard Gauge track from "creeping" across the hardwood floors popular at the time. Each section of roadbed supported one section of track.

RARITY
Too rarely traded to establish market pricing.

030 CURVED RUBBER ROADBED: This was the 0 Gauge equivalent of the 30 roadbed. It was offered from 1931 through 1939.

RARITY
Too rarely traded to establish market pricing.

31 STRAIGHT RUBBER ROADBED: Just as the case with the 30 curved Standard Gauge roadbed, the straight roadbed was sold from 1931 through 1937.

RARITY
Too rarely traded to establish market pricing.

031 STRAIGHT RUBBER ROADBED: The 0 Gauge straight rubber roadbed with simulated ballast was available from 1931 through 1939.

RARITY
Too rarely traded to establish market pricing.

0031 CURVED TRACK: The 0031 was the standard two-rail 24" radius OO curved track, with Bakelite base and integral crossties. It was available from 1939 through 1942. Twelve sections were required to form a circle.

VG	EX	LN	RARITY
8	14	20	4

32 MINIATURE FIGURES: This assortment of a dozen seated molded Standard Gauge passengers was sold from 1909 through 1918. Holes were provided in the figurines to receive pins in trolley or Pullman cars, keeping the figures in place. The figures were painted various colors.

VG	EX	LN	RARITY
70	100	150	5

32 90-DEGREE CROSSING RUBBER ROADBED: Standard Gauge rubber roadbed was made to support 90-degree crossings as well. This was cataloged from 1931 through 1937.

RARITY
Too rarely traded to establish market pricing.

032 90-DEGREE CROSSING RUBBER ROADBED: 0 Gauge rubber roadbed was made to support 90-degree crossings as well. This was cataloged from 1931 through 1939.

RARITY
Too rarely traded to establish market pricing.

0032 STRAIGHT TRACK: The 0032 was the standard two-rail 12" long 00 Gauge straight track, with Bakelite base and integral crossties. The 0032 was available from 1939 through 1942.

VG	EX	LN	RARITY
12	18	30	6

33 45-DEGREE CROSSING RUBBER ROADBED: Standard Gauge rubber roadbed was made to support 45-degree crossings as well. This was cataloged from 1931 through 1937.

RARITY
Too rarely traded to establish market pricing.

033 45-DEGREE CROSSING RUBBER ROADBED: 0 Gauge rubber roadbed was made to support 45-degree crossings as well. This was cataloged from 1931 through 1939.

RARITY
Too rarely traded to establish market pricing.

34 PAIR OF SWITCH RUBBER ROADBED: Sold by the pair from 1931 through 1937, this rubber roadbed accommodated Standard Gauge turnouts.

RARITY
Too rarely traded to establish market pricing.

034 PAIR OF SWITCH RUBBER ROADBED SECTIONS: Rubber roadbed was also made for 0 Gauge turnouts. Offered from 1931 through 1939, it was sold by the pair.

RARITY
Too rarely traded to establish market pricing.

0034 CURVED TRACK: During 1939 through 1942, Lionel offered 00 Gauge trains in both two- and three-rail versions. The 0034 was based on the standard two-rail 24" radius curved track, with Bakelite base and integral crossties. However, it had the addition of two electrical connections, which permitted the 0034 to be used as the "Lockon" for a 00 outfit.

VG	EX	LN	RARITY
12	18	25	5

35 BOULEVARD LAMP: Offered first in 1940, this attractive lamp was in the lineup through 1942, then returned postwar in 1945-49. Its post and top were painted aluminum color, except in 1942, when they were gray. The lamp housing itself is made of translucent white plastic and has eight sides. An intricate molded plastic cap with eight fragile points sits atop the lamp housing. This cap is often found with one or more of its points broken off. The lamp is 6 1/8" high and the postwar versions have a nickel-plated finial.

35 BOULEVARD LAMP (Type I): This was a 1940-41 production post painted aluminum color.

VG	EX	LN	RARITY
20	35	55	5

35 BOULEVARD LAMP (Type II): This was a 1942 production post painted 92 gray.

VG	EX	LN	RARITY
30	45	65	6

41 CONTACTOR : When this pressure-operated, under track, single-pole, single-throw (SPST) switch was introduced in 1936, it was perhaps of greater benefit to Lionel and its dealers than it was to the consumer. Prior to this time, many otherwise identical lineside accessories were packaged in both 0 and Standard Gauge due to the differing control tracks. The 41 was universal with respect to trackage, allowing only one version of the accessory and controller to be sold, and hence stocked, for use with all track types. It was offered through 1942.

VG	EX	LN	RARITY
1	5	8	1

042 PAIR OF MANUAL SWITCHES: During 1938-1942, and again from 1946 through 1959, Lionel sold this pair of illuminated, manually operated 0 gauge turnouts. In 1950, the screw-base 1447 bulb was replaced with a bayonet base 1445.

VG	EX	LN	RARITY
40	50	60	4

042L LEFT HAND MANUAL SWITCH: First offered in 1938, the 042 was at a glance very similar to the 1938 022. However, rather than having a plastic housing with solenoid-operated "motor," the 042 had a die-cast housing with a red-painted die-cast operating lever. Although both the 022 and 042 were illuminated, the 042's lack of automatic anti-derailing feature meant the base's two turnouts were electrically much different. This turnout was offered as a separate sale item through 1942.

VG	EX	LN	RARITY
20	25	30	4

042R RIGHT HAND MANUAL SWITCH: This was a mirror image of the 042L, and was sold during the same years.

VG	EX	LN	RARITY
20	25	30	4

43/043 BILD-A-MOTOR GEAR SET: This accessory, offered in 1929, could be used to convert the mechanism from a 43 Standard Gauge or 043 0 Gauge Bild-A-Loco into a Bild-A-Motor.

VG	EX	LN	RARITY
40	60	90	5

45 AUTOMATIC GATEMAN, 045 AUTOMATIC GATEMAN, 45N AUTOMATIC GATEMAN: These three catalog numbers all represent essentially the same accessory, the ever-popular

gateman. The 45 and 045 included control tracks for Standard Gauge and 0 Gauge respectively, and were offered in 1935 and 1936. With the introduction of the 41 contactor in 1936, one accessory could be sold for either gauge, and the gateman was given the new catalog number of 45N, which it carried from 1937 until 1942, and again in 1945. The accessory was of virtually all-steel construction, with its base painted a shade of green, now known as "45N green," which was also used on numerous other accessories for as long as the Lionel Corporation manufactured trains. A simple gateman's shanty, painted white or ivory, provided shelter for the Standard Gauge-sized attendant, who held a translucent red plastic lantern in his right hand. The building's door was painted red until 1942, when it was painted white to match the building. An attached coal bin, sometimes referred to as a toolbox, had a matching lid, which was marked "AUTOMATIC GATEMAN-MADE IN U.S. OF AMERICA-THE LIONEL CORPORATION-NEW YORK" either by embossing or with a decal. The roof was red, and on prewar versions included a chimney painted to match the house. A bulb was mounted within the base, which shown into the gateman's lantern when he emerged from the house.

45 AUTOMATIC GATEMAN, 045 AUTOMATIC GATEMAN (Type I): When introduced in 1935, the gateman accessory had an ivory-painted building. Its brass, diamond-shaped warning sign was supported by an aluminum-painted girder pole topped with a brass or nickel finial. The warning sign had the legend "RAILROAD CROSSING" and "LOOK OUT - FOR LOCOMOTIVE" in black on its face. The catalog number "45" or "045" was rubber-stamped in black on the underside of the accessory inside the depression where the post joins the base. These came with the early gateman figure, which had two swinging arms. This item was packaged with the appropriate gauge of insulated track section, lockon, wire and instructions, all of which naturally necessitated an oversized box, which today adds a premium to the value of the piece.

VG	EX	LN	RARITY
30	45	60	2

45 AUTOMATIC GATEMAN, 045 AUTOMATIC GATEMAN (Type II): In 1936, the warning on the brass sign was changed slightly. Now it read "RAILROAD CROSSING" and "LOOK OUT-FOR THE LOCOMOTIVE". On the underside of the accessory, the rubber-stamped catalog numbers were larger.

VG	EX	LN	RARITY
30	45	60	2

45N AUTOMATIC GATEMAN (Type III): In 1937, several minor changes were made. Foremost was the renumbering and inclusion of the 41 contactor, which resulted in much smaller packaging. (Note: the contactor was introduced in 1936, however, the 1936 Lionel sales manual specifies that the 1936 Gateman production was completed prior to the introduction of the contactor.) Concurrently, the aluminum-colored, girder-type post supporting the warning sign pole was replaced with a solid pole painted 92 gray, to which the sign was affixed.

VG	EX	LN	RARITY
30	45	60	2

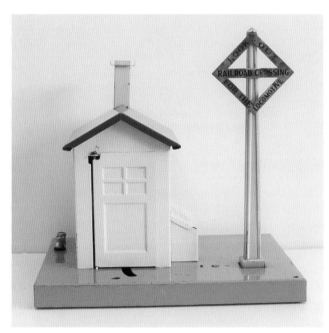

45N AUTOMATIC GATEMAN (Type IV): The 1938 45N was essentially the same as the 1937 edition, however the signpost was now painted aluminum color, rather than 92 gray.

VG	EX	LN	RARITY
30	45	60	2

45N AUTOMATIC GATEMAN (Type V): In 1939, the most visible change was the replacement of the brass warning sign with a die-cast crossbuck. The crossbuck, which was painted white with black lettering, was mounted midway up an aluminum-painted pole with nickel finial. The building continued to be ivory-colored, and now a silver decal was on the coalbox lid reading "No. 45" in blue sans-serif lettering.

VG	EX	LN	RARITY
30	45	60	2

45N AUTOMATIC GATEMAN (Type VI): In 1940, the pole changed colors again, back to the familiar 92 gray. Its finial now sometimes was black, although the nickel finial continued to be used intermittently as well. The lettering on the decal was now serif type. The figure was changed, now having only one swinging arm and a simplified paint scheme.

VG	EX	LN	RARITY
30	45	60	2

45N AUTOMATIC GATEMAN (Type VII): In 1941, once again the pole reverted to aluminum color, but this was overshadowed by the building now being painted white rather than the previously used ivory. The door was painted light red and the sign pole was topped with a black finial.

VG	EX	LN	RARITY
40	60	80	5

45N AUTOMATIC GATEMAN (Type VIII): In 1942, the annual shift in pole color occurred again, with once more 92 gray being the color of choice. The white building continued, now with a matching white door. Once again the coalbox lid was embossed rather than having a separately applied decal. The crossbuck was dispensed with and the brass warning sign reappeared. Very probably, most of these changes were a result of Lionel using previously manufactured spare parts to produce this accessory, rather than new materials restricted by the war effort.

VG	EX	LN	RARITY
40	60	80	5

45 AUTOMATIC GRADE CROSSING: This was shown in the 1936 catalog, but not manufactured.

46 SINGLE CROSSING GATE: This elaborate and attractive accessory, introduced in 1939, was based on the previously introduced number 47 double crossing gate. Its steel base was formed to create a highway grade crossing sloping up to track level. The roadway area was painted ivory; the remainder of the accessory base was painted 45N green. The support for the gate itself was painted light red. A solenoid lowered the red and white main gate, which in turn lowered the small pedestrian gate. Naturally the 46 had only a single gate, which protected a narrower roadway.

A decal reading "AUTOMATIC - CROSSING GATE - No. 46 - MADE IN THE U.S. OF AMERICA-THE LIONEL CORP., NEW YORK" was applied to the accessory. A tiny bulb hung from the gate, and onto it was clipped a die-cast and wire base, causing the bulb to resemble a kerosene lantern. These items are often missing and, when that is the case, the value of the accessory is greatly reduced.

46 SINGLE CROSSING GATE (Type I): Most of these accessories had aluminum-painted pedestrian gates and nickel terminal posts.

Price Guide Key: **VG** = Very Good, **EX** = Excellent, **LN** = Like New | *Values for each condition are in U.S. dollars.* | **Rarity** = Scale from 1-8 with 8 being the hardest to find.

303

VG	EX	LN	RARITY
75	100	125	3

46 SINGLE CROSSING GATE (Type II): However, some had 92 gray pedestrian gates and black terminal posts. The decal lettering was smaller on this version.

VG	EX	LN	RARITY
100	125	150	6

47 DOUBLE CROSSING GATE: This very attractive, well-proportioned accessory was offered from 1938 through 1942. Its steel base was formed to create a highway grade crossing sloping up to track level, with a gate on each side of the roadway. The roadway area was painted ivory, the remainder of the accessory base was painted 45N green. The support for the gates themselves were painted light red. A solenoid lowered the red and white main gates, which in turn lowered the small pedestrian gates. A tiny bulb hung from each main gate, and onto the bulbs was clipped a die-cast and wire base causing the bulb to resemble a kerosene lantern. These items are often missing, and when that is the case the value of the accessory is greatly reduced.

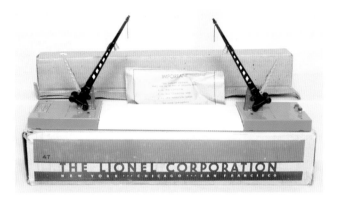

47 DOUBLE CROSSING GATE (Type I): Most of these accessories had aluminum-painted pedestrian gates.

VG	EX	LN	RARITY
60	100	150	3

47 DOUBLE CROSSING GATE (Type II): The pedestrian gates on some were painted 92 gray, however.

VG	EX	LN	RARITY
100	150	200	6

48W WHISTLE STATION: From 1937 until production halted in 1942, this lithographed steel station with whistle was sold. Removing the roof exposed a standard Lionel air whistle,

without relay. Instead of the DC relay, a simple momentary contact switch was installed in one end of the building. On the opposite end of the structure, a pair of terminal posts was mounted in the base. These provided a means by which the accessory was connected to its power supply. "LIONEL" appeared above the windows on both ends.

VG	EX	LN	RARITY
30	45	60	4

0051 CURVED TRACK: The 0051 was the standard three-rail 27" radius OO curved track offered from 1939 through 1942, with Bakelite base and integral crossties. The rail had a tubular cross-section. Twelve sections were required to form a circle.

The 0051 differed from the earlier 0061 production in that the under roadbed spring clip of the electrical connection was dispensed with. Instead, a blade-type collection was attached to the center rail. Similar connectors replaced the round pins in the outer rails. Lionel did not change the engraving on the molds, so "061-2" continued to appear on the track itself.

VG	EX	LN	RARITY
6	12	18	4

0052 STRAIGHT TRACK: During 1939 through 1942, Lionel offered 00 Gauge trains in both two- and three-rail versions. The 0052 was the standard three-rail 7" long straight track, with tubular rails, Bakelite base and integral crossties.

The 0052 differed from the earlier 0062 production in that the under roadbed spring clip of the electrical connection was dispensed with. Instead, a blade-type collection was attached to the center rail. Similar connectors replaced the round pins in the outer rails. Lionel did not change the engraving on the molds, so "062-2" continued to appear on the track itself.

VG	EX	LN	RARITY
12	18	30	5

52 LAMP POST: New in the 1933 catalog was this lamp post consisting of a one-piece die-cast combination base and post topped with a frosted white bulb. The post was painted the color of aluminum and two terminal posts projected from the base. "Made by The Lionel Corporation No. 52" was integral with the base. It remained in the product line through 1941.

VG	EX	LN	RARITY
35	55	75	5

53 LAMP POST: This lamp post was developed by Ives in 1928. It was sold through 1930 by Ives as its item number 308. In 1931, it moved to the Lionel catalog, where it remained through 1942. Lionel assigned it the item number 53. The base and post were a one-piece die-casting topped with a large decoratively-shaped bulb. The lamps sold as Lionel had "53-1" in the underside of the base.

53 LAMP POST (Type I): The colors the lamp post are most commonly found in are ivory, aluminum, light mojave, gray or white. All these are valued equally.

VG	EX	LN	RARITY
25	35	45	3

53 LAMP POST (Type II): In 1931 and 1932, the lamp post continued to be offered in the Ives catalog, now with the item number 1882.

VG	EX	LN	RARITY
40	65	90	6

53 LAMP POST (Type III): The lamp post was painted State green.

RARITY
Too rarely, if ever, traded to establish market pricing.

0054 CURVED TERMINAL TRACK: During 1939 through 1942, Lionel offered 00 Gauge trains in both two- and three-rail versions. The 0054 was based on the standard 0051 three-rail 27" radius curved track, with tubular rails, Bakelite base with integral crossties and no under track spring clip connectors for the center rails. However, it had the addition of two side-mounted electrical connections, which permitted the 0054 to be used as the "Lockon" for the 00 outfit.

VG	EX	LN	RARITY
12	18	25	5

54 LAMP POST: This lamp post, known as a double gooseneck lamp, consisted of a rolled-steel post supporting two lamps, with brass reflectors suspended from steel brackets, and resting on a cast-iron base. It was first sold in 1929. Two pear-shaped frosted bulbs provided the illumination for the 9 1/2" tall post. Oftentimes the stock number "54" was rubber-stamped on the underside of the base. It was last cataloged in 1935. Through the years, it was made three different colors: maroon, pea green and State brown. Today, these colors are equally desirable and valuable.

54 LAMP POST (Type I): As described previously.

VG	EX	LN	RARITY
40	60	80	5

54 LAMP POST (Type II): In 1932, the 54 also appeared in the Ives catalog, with stock number 1905.

VG	EX	LN	RARITY
60	80	100	6

56 LAMP POST: This long-running item was available from 1924 through 1942, and again in 1946-49. A die-cast base, which is usually rubber-stamped "Lionel #56" or "56" on the bottom, supports the rolled-steel shaft. A pair of terminal posts was installed on the base, and a lantern with bulb enclosure was mounted on the opposite end of these 7 3/4" tall lamp posts. Whereas the prewar versions came in a variety of colors, postwar the 56 came only in green.

56 LAMP POST (Type I): This type was in copper. This version does not appear to have been offered for separate sale. Rather, it was mounted on scenic plots only.

VG	EX	LN	RARITY
40	55	90	6

56 LAMP POST (Type II): This type was pea green.

VG	EX	LN	RARITY
30	45	60	4

56 LAMP POST (Type III): This type was dark green.

VG	EX	LN	RARITY
30	45	60	4

56 LAMP POST (Type IV): This type was painted 45N green.

VG	EX	LN	RARITY
30	45	60	4

56 LAMP POST (Type V): This type was aluminum-painted.

VG	EX	LN	RARITY
30	45	60	4

56 LAMP POST (Type VI): This type was painted gray.

VG	EX	LN	RARITY
30	45	60	4

56 LAMP POST (Type VII): In 1939, this type was painted dark gray.

VG	EX	LN	RARITY
30	45	60	4

57 LAMP POST: Introduced in 1922, this 7 1/2" tall lamp post appeared in the catalog for 20 years. It had a die-cast base, on which stood a rolled sheet metal post topped with a distinctive lamp housing. This cubical housing, with formed sheet-metal base and top, had white celluloid sides that the light shown through. Onto these sides were rubber-stamped street names,

Price Guide Key: VG = Very Good, EX = Excellent, LN = Like New | *Values for each condition are in U.S. dollars.* | Rarity = Scale from 1-8 with 8 being the hardest to find.

305

usually Main Street and Broadway. A nickel finial held the top in place, and two terminal posts were attached to the die-cast base of the post itself. On the underside of the base usually "Lionel #57" was rubber-stamped. Excellent reproduction posts and parts have been made. Be particularly wary of those with unusual street names.

57 LAMP POST (Type I): The most common variation of the 57 lamp post was painted 9E orange. "MAIN" and "BROADWAY" were printed alternately on each of the four light panels. Lamp posts were made with either serif or sans-serif lettering in apparently equal numbers, and today there is no difference in value.

VG	EX	LN	RARITY
30	45	60	2

57 LAMP POST (Type II): Just like the previous entry, this lamp post was painted 9E orange. However, rubber-stamped on the sides of its lamp shade were alternately "FIFTH AVENUE" and "42ND STREET".

VG	EX	LN	RARITY
35	50	70	3

57 LAMP POST (Type III): Just like the previous entry, this lamp post was painted 9E orange. However, the lamp shade was rubber-stamped on the sides with a new combination of names: alternately "BROADWAY" and "21ST STREET".

VG	EX	LN	RARITY
35	50	70	3

57 LAMP POST (Type IV): This type was the same as the previous lamps, only with four different street names. Date of production has not been positively identified, although it is possible that this was early production, then someone realized how unrealistic the sign arrangement was. In any event, the lamp posts reading "BROADWAY", "42ND STREET",

"FIFTH AVENUE", "21ST STREET", are much harder to find than the two-name signs.

VG	EX	LN	RARITY
60	85	115	6

57 LAMP POST (Type V): Like the first three versions listed, this post was painted 9E orange and displayed a new combination of street names: "21ST STREET" and "FIFTH AVENUE". For some reason, however, this combination is much more difficult to find.

RARITY
Too rarely traded to establish market pricing.

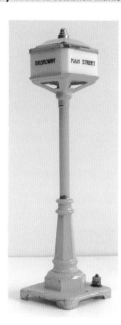

57 LAMP POST (Type VII): American Flyer sold the Lionel 57 lamp post under its own catalog number of 2013. The Flyer version came in Flyer packaging and was painted yellow, and the panels were lettered alternately "MAIN" and "BROADWAY".

VG	EX	LN	RARITY
45	65	85	4

58 LAMP POST: Another of the lamp posts introduced in 1922 was this attractive gooseneck lamp. The lamp post with a die-cast base with the rounded back and squared off front remained in the product line through 1942, then returned after the war until 1950. With its finely-crafted steel post, it stood 7 3/8" high. A pear-shaped, frosted bulb hung beneath a small reflector by means of an elegantly filigreed steel bracket. Cast into the base was the inscription "The Lionel Corporation New York", and often "LIONEL #58" was rubber-stamped on the underside of the base.

Lamp posts produced postwar can be distinguished by their flush-sitting baseplates and less elaborate filigree.

58 LAMP POST (Type I): During the first two years in production, the lamp posts were available in dark green.

VG	EX	LN	RARITY
30	40	60	3

58 LAMP POST (Type II): In 1927, the lamp post was offered in 9E orange.

VG	EX	LN	RARITY
30	40	60	3

58 LAMP POST (Type III): From 1928 through 1934, pea green was the predominate color for 58 lamp post production.

VG	EX	LN	RARITY
30	40	60	3

58 LAMP POST (Type IV): Beginning in 1940, the lamp post was produced with a cream-colored finish.

VG	EX	LN	RARITY
30	40	60	3

58 LAMP POST (Type V): At some point in the late 1930s, some 58s were painted peacock.

VG	EX	LN	RARITY
30	40	60	3

58 LAMP POST (Type II):) Another 58 color for which dating is vague was maroon.

VG	EX	LN	RARITY
30	40	60	3

59 LAMP POST: Somewhat taller than the 58 at 8 5/8", the 59, introduced in 1920, also had a much more substantial base made of cast iron. Its gooseneck lamp support and shade resembled that used on the later 54 and 58 posts. Beneath its sheet metal reflector hung a pear-shaped frosted, or occasionally a round, bulb. The round bulbs were not always frosted.

The 59 lamp post was produced in basically two groups of colors, one group all equally common, the second group all exceedingly difficult to find. The common colors were dark green, olive green, light green, maroon, State brown and red. Their values are recorded here.

VG	EX	LN	RARITY
35	55	75	3

The uncommon colors, all of which are too infrequently sold to establish market values, include peacock, aluminum and cream.

60 PAIR OF AUTOMATIC TRACK TRIPS: Between 1906 and 1912, Lionel cataloged these Standard Gauge track trips. They consisted of flat metal strips, which were to be mounted outside the rails in order to activate the reversing mechanism in use at the time.

RARITY
Too rarely, if ever, traded to establish market pricing.

Price Guide Key: **VG** = Very Good, **EX** = Excellent, **LN** = Like New | *Values for each condition are in U.S. dollars.* | **Rarity** = Scale from 1-8 with 8 being the hardest to find.

307

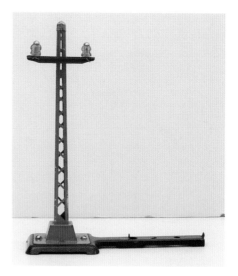

60 TELEGRAPH POST: Although properly sized for Standard Gauge, from its 1920 introduction these telegraph posts were marketed to both Standard Gauge and 0 Gauge enthusiasts. After the introduction of the smaller, 0 Gauge sized 060 in 1929, the 60 was marketed for Standard Gauge use until it was dropped from the catalog after its 1935 appearance.

The construction of the 60 included a square stamped-steel base, with a steel latticework post attached. Its crossarm supported two white porcelain or clear glass insulators. A finial, either brass, nickel or black, topped the post. After 1929, the 60 was packaged with a clip to be used to attach the 8 1/2" tall telegraph pole to the track.

Various color combinations were produced, none of which are more valued than others. As mentioned previously, there were two types of insulators and three types of finials. Additionally, the crossarms were painted either red or maroon. The base and post were made in the following colors: Peacock, Stephen Girard green, dark gray, apple green and aluminum color.

VG	EX	LN	RARITY
20	25	30	3

060 TELEGRAPH POST: In 1929, a smaller telegraph post, only 6 7/8" tall, was introduced for use with 0 Gauge trains. Available through 1942, its construction was similar to the 60, with a square, stamped-steel base, separate finial and crossarm with two porcelain insulators. The post was furnished with a clip to be used to attach it to the train track. The pole itself on early production units replicated steel latticework, while later versions were solid. The base and post of the 060 were painted one of the following colors: 9E orange, gray, 45N green, aluminum or 92 gray. Regardless of post color, the 060 had either maroon or red crossarms, and brass finials.

VG	EX	LN	RARITY
20	25	30	3

61 LAMP POST: After its initial appearance in the 1914 catalog, this 12 1/2" tall lamp post appeared in each succeeding catalog through 1936, except for a curious absence in 1933. Its cast iron base was often rubber-stamped "LIONEL #61" on the underside. A rolled-metal post supported, via an elegant filigreed steel gooseneck, a sheet metal lamp reflector shade, which housed a frosted pear-shaped or frosted or unfrosted round bulb.

The base of early units was 2 3/8" x 2 1/2", while later production bases were 2 1/2" square. A variety of colors including olive green, mojave, dark green, pea green, maroon, State brown and black were produced. All are equally desirable, though the black seems to command a 10 percent premium.

1939 Catalog

1938 Catalog

Price Guide Key: **VG** = Very Good, **EX** = Excellent, **LN** = Like New | *Values for each condition are in U.S. dollars.* | **Rarity** = Scale from 1-8 with 8 being the hardest to find.

309

VG	EX	LN	RARITY
40	50	60	4

0061 CURVED TRACK: All the OO track produced in 1938 (despite the catalog listings, evidence indicates only straight, curved and terminal sections were made in 1938) had a spring clip electrical connector joining the center rails. The outer rails used round mating pins, much like 0 and Standard Gauge. Twelve sections of the track, which featured a molded Bakelite base with integral crossties, could form a 27" diameter circle.

VG	EX	LN	RARITY
5	10	15	4

62 AUTOMATIC TRACK TRIP: Between 1914 and 1916, Lionel cataloged these track trips for use with Standard Gauge track. Like the previous 60, these were mounted outside the rails, and engaged the reverse mechanism lever. Only rather than by means of the previously used flat strips, a cam was employed.

RARITY
Too rarely, if ever, traded to establish market pricing.

62 SEMAPHORE: This semaphore-type 8 1/2" tall railroad block signal was cataloged from 1920 through 1932. The manually operated semaphore arm was supported by a tapered steel latticework post capped with a brass finial. The post in turn was attached to a square sheet-metal base. Though non-illuminated, the red semaphore arm did have simulated light disks in green, yellow and red.

62 SEMAPHORE (Type I): This type had a yellow pole mounted on a dark green base.

VG	EX	LN	RARITY
30	40	50	4

62 SEMAPHORE (Type II): The pole and base were painted olive green.

VG	EX	LN	RARITY
30	40	50	4

62 SEMAPHORE (Type III): The pole and base were painted apple green.

VG	EX	LN	RARITY
30	40	50	4

62 SEMAPHORE (Type IV): The pole and base were painted pea green.

VG	EX	LN	RARITY
30	40	50	4

62 SEMAPHORE (Type V): A red pole was mounted on a yellow base.

VG	EX	LN	RARITY
40	50	60	6

0062 STRAIGHT TRACK: All the OO track produced in 1938 (despite the catalog listings, evidence indicates only straight, curved and terminal sections were made in 1938) had a spring clip electrical connector joining the center rails. The outer rails used round mating pins, much like 0 and Standard Gauge. This was the standard three-rail 7" long straight OO track, with tubular rails, Bakelite base and integral crossties included in first year sets.

VG	EX	LN	RARITY
6	12	18	6

63 SEMAPHORE: One of the earliest signals produced by Lionel was this semaphore, cataloged 1915-21. Although the catalog proudly proclaimed the black simulated relay box at the base of the orange rolled-steel pole was a casting, all observed examples were made of stamped steel.

Though unlighted, the manually-operated red and black semaphore arm included two colored celluloid disks simulating lenses. A wooden finial and dark green ladder completed the unit's trim.

VG	EX	LN	RARITY
25	40	55	6

63 LAMP POST: One of the most attractive and best proportioned lamp posts ever produced by Lionel was introduced in 1933. Although it remained in the catalog through 1942, sadly it was not reintroduced postwar. The base and post of the 63 were die-cast as a single unit and painted aluminum color. The top-mounted crossarm terminated in elaborate torch-like sockets, into which were installed opalescent bulbs, the globes of which were formed to replicate the shape of street lamp globes. The 12 1/2" tall post looked at home adjacent to the scale 700E.

VG	EX	LN	RARITY
150	200	250	6

0063 CURVED TRACK: Although cataloged in 1938, the 0063 was not actually produced until the following year. Therefore, none exist with the spring clip center rail connection. This was a 3" long "half section" of three-rail tubular OO curved track, with molded Bakelite base including realistically close-spaced crossties. It remained in the line-up through 1942.

VG	EX	LN	RARITY
12	18	24	6

0064 CURVED TERMINAL TRACK: This terminal track was only offered in 1938. The 0064 was based on the standard 0061 three-rail 27" radius curved track, with tubular rails, Bakelite base with integral crossties and no under track spring clip connectors for the center rails. However, it had the addition of two side-mounted electrical connections, which permitted the 0064 to be used as the "Lockon" for the 00 outfit.

VG	EX	LN	RARITY
10	15	20	4

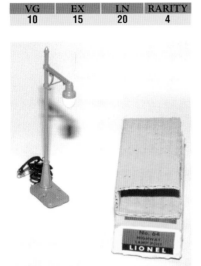

64 HIGHWAY LAMP POST: Last appearing in the Lionel catalog in 1949, this attractive lamp post had been introduced in 1940. It was produced through 1942, discontinued for the war, and reintroduced in 1945. This 45N green, 6 3/4" tall lamp used a special 64-15 bulb, which has not been exactly reproduced, current lamps are not as flat.

VG	EX	LN	RARITY
45	60	75	6

64 SEMAPHORE: Another early signal produced by Lionel was this 14" tall semaphore, also cataloged 1915-21. As it did with the 63, the catalog stated the black simulated relay box at the base of the orange rolled-steel pole was a casting, yet all observed examples were made of stamped steel.

The 64 was equipped with two semaphore arms. The upper arm was red and black, while the lower arm was green and black. Though unlighted, both of the manually-operated semaphore arms included two colored celluloid disks simulating lenses. A wooden finial and dark green ladder completed the unit's trim, and two control levers were installed in the base.

VG	EX	LN	RARITY
30	45	65	5

65 SEMAPHORE: The 65 semaphore, offered from 1915 through 1926, was essentially an illuminated version of the 63. Construction techniques were the same, with a black two-piece stamped-steel base and simulated relay box holding an orange rolled-steel pole and dark green ladder. The pole was topped with a wooden finial. The red and black manually operated semaphore arm, some notched at the ends and others not, included two celluloid disks that acted as lenses for the bulb. The semaphore was 14" tall.

VG	EX	LN	RARITY
30	45	65	6

0065 STRAIGHT TRACK: Although cataloged in 1938, the 0065 was not actually produced until the following year. Therefore, none exist with the spring clip center rail connection. This was a 3 3/8" long "half section" of three-rail tubular OO track, with molded Bakelite base including realistically close-spaced crossties. It remained in the line-up through 1942.

VG	EX	LN	RARITY
12	18	24	6

65 WHISTLE CONTROLLER: In 1935, this whistle controller, housed in a black steel box, was offered for separate sale, as well as being included in train sets with whistle tenders. On the top of the controller, were three red control buttons, four binding posts and nickel instruction/nameplate with black border and print.

VG	EX	LN	RARITY
3	5	7	2

0066 STRAIGHT TRACK: Although cataloged in 1938, the 0065 was not actually produced until the following year. Therefore, none exists with the spring clip center rail connection. This was a 5 5/8" long "5/6" of three-rail tubular OO track, with molded Bakelite base including realistically close-spaced crossties. It remained in the line-up through 1942.

VG	EX	LN	RARITY
12	18	24	6

Price Guide Key: **VG** = Very Good, **EX** = Excellent, **LN** = Like New | *Values for each condition are in U.S. dollars.* | **Rarity** = Scale from 1-8 with 8 being the hardest to find.

311

66 SEMAPHORE: The 66 semaphore, offered from 1915 through 1926, was essentially an illuminated version of the double arm 64. Construction techniques were the same, with a black two-piece stamped-steel base and simulated relay box holding an orange rolled-steel pole and dark green ladder. The pole was topped with a wooden finial.

The upper arm was red and black, while the lower arm was green and black, some were notched at the ends and others were not. Both of the manually operated semaphore arms included two colored celluloid disks that acted as lenses for the bulbs. The semaphore was 14" tall and two control levers were mounted in the base.

VG	EX	LN	RARITY
30	45	65	5

66 WHISTLE CONTROLLER: In 1936-38, this whistle controller, housed in a black steel box, was offered for separate sale, as well as being included in Standard Gauge train sets with whistle tenders. On the top of the controller were three red control buttons, four binding posts and nickel instruction/ nameplate with black border and print. The instructions on this plate were somewhat more comprehensive than the ones on the earlier 65 whistle controller, which was also different internally.

VG	EX	LN	RARITY
3	5	7	2

67 LAMP POST: After its initial appearance in the 1915 catalog, this 12 1/2" tall lamp post appeared in each succeeding catalog through 1932. Its cast iron base was often rubber-stamped "LIONEL #67" on the underside. A rolled-metal post supported, via a pair of elegant filigreed steel goosenecks, two sheet metal lamp reflector shades that each housed a frosted pear-shaped or frosted or unfrosted round bulb.

The base of early units was 2 9/16" x 2 1/2", while later production bases were 2 1/2" square and somewhat more finely cast. Likewise, the cast filigree gooseneck of the later lamps was more delicate and hence more ornate than on the early posts.

67 LAMP POST (Type I): This type was dark green.

VG	EX	LN	RARITY
75	115	150	5

67 LAMP POST (Type II): This type was State green.

VG	EX	LN	RARITY
75	115	150	5

67 LAMP POST (Type III): This type was peacock.

RARITY
Too rarely, if ever, traded to establish market pricing.

67 WHISTLE CONTROLLER: In 1936-38, this whistle controller, housed in a black steel box, was offered for separate sale, as well as being included in 0 Gauge train sets with whistle tenders. On the top of the controller were three red control buttons, four binding posts and nickel instruction/ nameplate with black border and print. This controller appears identical to the 66, but differs internally, producing a slightly lower voltage.

VG	EX	LN	RARITY
3	5	7	2

68 WARNING SIGNAL: From 1920 through 1939, Lionel Standard Gauge railroaders could purchase this warning sign to protect crossings. It had a square stamped sheet metal base supporting a tapered steel lattice post. The post was capped with a nickel or brass finial. Hung from the post was an open diamond sign made of brass. A strip horizontally bisecting the diamond across its 3 1/2" extremity bore the legend "RAILROAD CROSSING," while the admonition "LOOK OUT FOR THE LOCOMOTIVE" wrapped around the border. These words were embossed in either black or red. The accessory was 8 7/8" tall, and was often rubber-stamped #68 or #69 on the bottom of the base.

68 WARNING SIGNAL (Type I): This type had dark olive paint and black lettering.

VG	EX	LN	RARITY
5	10	15	1

68 WARNING SIGNAL (Type II): This type featured 9E orange paint with black lettering.

VG	EX	LN	RARITY
5	10	15	1

68 WARNING SIGNAL (Type III): Type III had maroon paint with black lettering.

VG	EX	LN	RARITY
5	10	15	1

68 WARNING SIGNAL (Type IV): This type was pea green with black lettering.

VG	EX	LN	RARITY
5	10	15	1

68 WARNING SIGNAL (Type V): Type V was painted white with lettering stamped in red.

VG	EX	LN	RARITY
5	10	15	1

68 WARNING SIGNAL (Type VI): This type was painted white with lettering stamped in black.

VG	EX	LN	RARITY
5	10	15	1

68 WARNING SIGNAL (Type VII): This type featured peacock paint and red lettering.

VG	EX	LN	RARITY
5	10	15	1

068 WARNING SIGNAL: Lionel 0 Gauge railroaders got their own warning signal in 1925 and it stayed in the product line through 1942. It had a square-stamped sheet metal base that initially supported a tapered steel lattice post, though in later years the post became solid. A nickel or brass finial capped the post. Hanging from the post was an open diamond sign made of brass. A strip horizontally bisecting the diamond across its 2 3/16" extremity bore the legend "RAILROAD CROSSING", while the admonition "LOOK OUT FOR THE LOCOMOTIVE" wrapped around the border. These words were embossed in either black or red. The accessory was 6 1/2" tall, and was often rubber-stamped "LIONEL / #068" on the bottom of the base.

068 WARNING SIGNAL (Type I): This type featured orange paint.

VG	EX	LN	RARITY
5	10	15	1

068 WARNING SIGNAL (Type II): This type was pea green with sans-serif lettering.

VG	EX	LN	RARITY
5	10	15	1

068 WARNING SIGNAL (Type III): A third type was pea green with serif lettering.

VG	EX	LN	RARITY
5	10	15	1

068 WARNING SIGNAL (Type IV): This type was dark pea green with serif lettering.

VG	EX	LN	RARITY
5	10	15	1

068 WARNING SIGNAL (Type V): Shown only in the 1926 catalog, this pea green signal's diamond was painted orange (rather than being unpainted), and had rubber-stamped lettering. This is the most difficult variant of the 068 to locate.

VG	EX	LN	RARITY
25	40	60	5

Price Guide Key: **VG** = Very Good, **EX** = Excellent, **LN** = Like New | *Values for each condition are in U.S. dollars.* | **Rarity** = Scale from 1-8 with 8 being the hardest to find.

313

69 ELECTRIC WARNING BELL SIGNAL, 069 ELECTRIC WARNING BELL SIGNAL, 69N ELECTRIC WARNING BELL SIGNAL: From 1921 through 1935, this signal with operating bell was cataloged in both Standard Gauge (69) and 0 Gauge (069) versions, with the appropriate control track. It was Lionel's first track-actuated accessory. Beginning in 1936, however, the accessory was renumbered 69N and was packaged with a 41 pressure-actuated control switch.

It had a square stamped sheet metal base that supported a tapered steel lattice post. The post was capped with a nickel or brass finial. Attached to the post was an open diamond sign made of brass. A strip horizontally bisecting the diamond across its 3 1/2" extremity bore the legend "RAILROAD CROSSING," while the admonition "LOOK OUT FOR THE LOCOMOTIVE" wrapped around the border. These words were embossed in either black or red. Also attached to the post were the warning bells. Only one bell was used through 1926, but beginning in 1927 two bells were installed, and that remained the case through 1942.

69/069/069N WARNING BELL (Type I): This type had olive paint and black lettering.

VG	EX	LN	RARITY
30	45	60	4

69/069/069N WARNING BELL (Type II): This type featured 9E orange paint with black lettering.

VG	EX	LN	RARITY
30	45	60	4

69/069/069N WARNING BELL (Type III): This type had maroon paint with black lettering.

VG	EX	LN	RARITY
30	45	60	4

69/069/069N WARNING BELL (Type IV): This type had a dark green base with yellow post.

VG	EX	LN	RARITY
30	45	60	4

69/069/069N WARNING BELL (Type V): This type was painted white with lettering stamped in red.

VG	EX	LN	RARITY
30	45	60	4

69/069/069N WARNING BELL (Type VI): This type was painted red with lettering stamped on nickel sign in black.

VG	EX	LN	RARITY
30	45	60	4

69/069/069N WARNING BELL (Type VII): This type was painted aluminum with lettering stamped on a nickel sign in black.

VG	EX	LN	RARITY
30	45	60	4

0070 90-DEGREE CROSSING: This three-rail 00 Gauge 90-degree crossing was cataloged from 1938 through 1942, but was not produced until 1939. It had a molded Bakelite base with representing ballasted closely spaced ties.

VG	EX	LN	RARITY
4	8	12	5

70 ACCESSORY OUTFIT: This prepackaged accessory outfit was offered from 1921 through 1932. Each set contained one 59 Lamp Post, two 62 Semaphores, one 68 Warning Signal and two spare bulbs. Through the years, various color combinations of accessories were packaged in this outfit. The value of this is almost entirely in the original box.

VG	EX	LN	RARITY
75	125	175	7

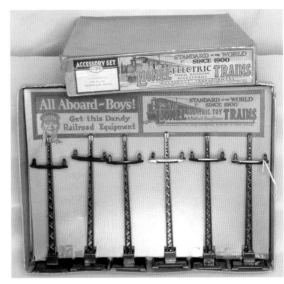

71 TELEGRAPH POST SET: Cataloged 1921-31, this set contained six matching conventional 60 Telegraph Posts, making the original box by far the most difficult part of this set to obtain. The color combinations included gray with maroon crossarms, apple green with maroon crossarms, and peacock with maroon crossarms. All are equally valuable.

VG	EX	LN	RARITY
75	125	175	7

071 TELEGRAPH POST SET: Cataloged 1929-42, this set contained six matching conventional 060 Telegraph Posts, making the original box by far the most difficult part of this set to obtain. The color combinations included 92 gray with light red crossarms, green with red crossarms, and 9E orange with maroon crossarms. Post and insulator construction, of course, changed as it did with separate sale 060 telegraph poles.

VG	EX	LN	RARITY
75	125	175	7

Price Guide Key: **VG** = Very Good, **EX** = Excellent, **LN** = Like New | *Values for each condition are in U.S. dollars.* | **Rarity** = Scale from 1-8 with 8 being the hardest to find.

315

0072 PAIR OF REMOTE CONTROL SWITCHES 0066 STRAIGHT TRACK

Although cataloged in 1938, the 0072 was not actually produced until the following year. Therefore, none exist with the spring clip center rail connection. This was a pair of illuminated remote control turnouts for three-rail tubular OO track. Their molded Bakelite base included realistically close-spaced crossties. The 0072, and their lighted controllers, remained in the line-up through 1942.

VG	EX	LN	RARITY
125	200	300	6

0072L REMOTE CONTROL SWITCH

Produced from 1939 through 1942, this was a single left-hand OO gauge turnout and controller only.

VG	EX	LN	RARITY
60	90	140	6

0072R REMOTE CONTROL SWITCH

Produced from 1939 through 1942, this was a single right-hand OO gauge turnout and controller only.

VG	EX	LN	RARITY
60	90	140	6

76 BLOCK SIGNAL, 076 BLOCK SIGNAL

Two individual nickel lamp bases were supported by a tapered steel lattice post on this 8 1/2" tall accessory, which was cataloged from 1923 through 1928 as both Standard Gauge (76) and 0 Gauge (076). One lamp had red celluloid lenses, the other green. Rubber-stamped lettering labeled the three terminals attached to the signal's square sheet-metal base as "A", "B" and "B". These terminals were connected to lockons attached to the two insulated track sections, which were furnished with the accessory. The intention was that the activating sections be placed such that the red and green lamps would light sequentially. The Standard Gauge signals had black lamp housings, while the 0 Gauge versions had mojave housings. The bases and poles were offered in both gauges in either white or mohave. Today, there is no difference in value.

VG	EX	LN	RARITY
30	50	80	4

76 WARNING BELL AND SHACK

Using the same building as the 45 gateman, this accessory, offered from 1939 through 1942, had a new color combination. While the walls of the building were white, the base was red and the roof, which was without a chimney, was painted Hiawatha orange. Early editions had a brass warning sign lettered "LOOK OUT/FOR THE LOCOMOTIVE" suspended from an aluminum-painted solid post, much like the sign on the 45. Later production versions had a white-painted die-cast crossbuck. In either event, a black simulated bell was also mounted on the post.

Inside the shanty was the actual bell and its solenoid mechanism. A label on the coal bunker lid read: "No. 76 WARNING BELL- AND SHACK - MADE IN THE U.S. OF AMERICA-THE LIONEL CORP.-NEW YORK" in blue against a silver background.

76 WARNING BELL AND SHACK (Type I)

This type was an early production with a brass warning sign.

VG	EX	LN	RARITY
100	175	275	6

76 WARNING BELL AND SHACK (Type II)

This was a later production with a die-cast warning sign.

VG	EX	LN	RARITY
85	150	250	5

77 AUTOMATIC CROSSING GATE, 077 AUTOMATIC CROSSING GATE, 77N AUTOMATIC CROSSING GATE

(1923-35): (1936-39): This was for both Gauges. When initially introduced in 1923, this accessory was cataloged in both Standard Gauge and 0 Gauge versions. Beginning in 1936, it was shipped with a contactor, eliminating the need for the packaging of two versions. Its 11" long steel gate was supported by a sheet metal base, which enclosed the operating solenoid. Cutouts in the gate exposed a paper insert, inexpensively producing a multicolored gate.

77 (Type I)

The 1923 production had a black base with nickel cover. White paper inserts were installed in the black gate and a brass identification plate reading "77 FOR STANDARD GAUGE TRACK" "PATENTED SEPT. 21, 1915-THE LIONEL CORPORATION, N.Y." was affixed to Standard Gauge versions. The 0 Gauge version was identical except the plate read "077 FOR 0 GAUGE TRACK".

VG	EX	LN	RARITY
30	45	60	5

77 (Type II)

In 1924, a circular cutout was added to the gate, which exposed a paper label with "STOP" printed in red.

VG	EX	LN	RARITY
30	45	60	5

77 (Type III)

Beginning in 1927 and continuing through 1930, the base was painted pea green and the mechanism housing maroon or terra cotta rather than the drab black previously used. The gate itself was now pea green with a white paper insert, with a red circular warning sign and with "STOP" in white.

VG	EX	LN	RARITY
30	40	50	4

77 (Type IV): In 1931, a major change was made. An operating red warning light was added to the gate and the counterweights changed to offset the added weight. Coloration of the accessory remained as it was in 1927-1930. Production continued in this form through 1934.

VG	EX	LN	RARITY
30	40	50	4

77 (Type V): In 1935, the colors of the accessory were changed. The base was either black with a red or pea green mechanism housing with black cover, or dark green base with a maroon mechanism housing. The gate itself was black.

VG	EX	LN	RARITY
30	40	50	4

77 (Type VI): In 1936, the nameplate was changed from brass to nickel, and the lettering on it changed to reflect the now universal 0 and Standard Gauge nature of the item. It now read "77N CROSSING GATE / MADE IN U.S. OF AMERICA/THE LIONEL CORPORATION, N.Y." The gate and base were black and the mechanism housing was red. The accessory was furnished with a No. 41 contactor.

VG	EX	LN	RARITY
30	40	50	4

77 (Type VII): In 1926-29, American Flyer Manufacturing Co. sold this gate as its item number 2032.

VG	EX	LN	RARITY
30	45	60	5

77 (Type VIII): Like many Lionel accessories, the 77 and 077 appeared in the 1931-32 Ives catalogs as the 1879 (Wide Gauge) and 1878 (0 Gauge) gates.

VG	EX	LN	RARITY
30	45	60	5

78 TRAIN CONTROL BLOCK SIGNAL, 078 TRAIN CONTROL BLOCK SIGNAL: The block signal with integral train control was offered in both Standard Gauge and 0 Gauge versions from 1924 through 1932. Its die-cast base, which was shaped to simulate a relay box, housed the train stop circuit. A pole, made of rolled steel, supported a die-cast signal head, which enclosed two bulbs. Red and green celluloid lenses were installed in each of three sides of the light housing.

Like several of Lionel's early die-cast items, the impurities in the castings of many of these signals have caused them to deteriorate. Reproduction castings are readily available, most of which do not have "MADE BY-THE-LIONEL CORP.-NEW YORK-PATENTED" cast into them. But to complicate matters, some reproductions do have these markings, and a few originals do not.

78 (Type I): Produced lettered both "78" and "078", this variation had a maroon base, white signal head and a terra-cotta pole.

VG	EX	LN	RARITY
40	70	100	6

78 (Type II): Also offered in both Standard Gauge (78) and 0 Gauge (078), this version had an orange base, white signal head and a cream pole. Two colors of ladders have been found on this signal, pea green and dark green, but there is no difference in value.

VG	EX	LN	RARITY
40	70	100	6

78 (Type III): Produced lettered both "78" and "078", this variation had a maroon base, white signal head, green ladder and a mojave pole.

VG	EX	LN	RARITY
40	70	100	6

78 (Type IV): In 1926-29, American Flyer Manufacturing Co. sold this signal as its item number 2033.

VG	EX	LN	RARITY
40	70	100	6

78 (Type V): As with other Lionel accessories, the 78 and 078 appeared in the 1932 Ives catalog. The numbers assigned the signals were 1908 (Wide Gauge) and 1907 (0 Gauge).

VG	EX	LN	RARITY
40	70	100	6

79 FLASHING HIGHWAY SIGNAL: This grade crossing signal had an unusually shaped base resembling a Mayan pyramid, the sides of which were perforated with square holes. A rolled-steel pole stood atop this base, and supported a crossbuck made of brass or nickel. Two red bulbs hung from a fancy crossarm mounted beneath the crossbuck. A bimetallic strip in the base was used to alternately light the bulbs.

79 FLASHING HIGHWAY SIGNAL (Type I): Many of these signals were made with a cream base, and a pole painted either cream or mojave.

VG	EX	LN	RARITY
100	125	150	5

79 FLASHING HIGHWAY SIGNAL (Type II): On some signals, the pole and base were painted white, while the crossarm was painted gold. The crossbuck and finial were brass.

VG	EX	LN	RARITY
100	125	150	5

79 FLASHING HIGHWAY SIGNAL (Type III): In a step toward realism, some signals were produced with an aluminum-painted base and pole. However, the crossarm continued to be gold-painted and the sign and finial were unpainted brass.

VG	EX	LN	RARITY
125	150	175	6

79 FLASHING HIGHWAY SIGNAL (Type IV): On this variation, the front of the brass sign was nickel plated. The

Price Guide Key: VG = Very Good, EX = Excellent, LN = Like New | *Values for each condition are in U.S. dollars.* | **Rarity** = Scale from 1-8 with 8 being the hardest to find.

317

base, pole and crossarm were all painted ivory color. A nickel finial topped the pole.

VG	EX	LN	RARITY
100	125	150	5

79 FLASHING HIGHWAY SIGNAL (Type V): The brass crossbuck with nickel-plated face was also installed on some of the overall aluminum-colored signals. Once again, a nickel finial was used.

VG	EX	LN	RARITY
125	150	175	6

79 FLASHING HIGHWAY SIGNAL (Type VI): Ultimately, the aluminum cover signal was fitted with a crossbuck that was all nickel.

VG	EX	LN	RARITY
125	150	175	6

79 FLASHING HIGHWAY SIGNAL (Type VIII): The 79 was also sold by Ives. During 1929-30, it was assigned catalog number 349, which was changed to 1880 for 1931-32.

VG	EX	LN	RARITY
125	150	175	6

80 SEMAPHORE, 080 SEMAPHORE: From 1926 through 1935, this attractive 15" tall semaphore was offered as both Standard Gauge (80) and 0 Gauge (080). An appropriate insulated track section was furnished for each gauge. Its die-cast square base included a simulated relay box with case-in detail and open back. The rolled steel post was topped with a finial that was made of either brass or nickel. A black and red semaphore arm was actuated by a solenoid mechanism, and its movement determined whether a red or green celluloid lens was presented to the lamp.

80 (Type I): The most common variant of this signal had a terra-cotta base, mojave pole and a dark pea green ladder.

VG	EX	LN	RARITY
50	75	110	5

80 (Type II): Probably the most realistic coloring applied to these signals was a black base, mojave pole and dark green ladder.

VG	EX	LN	RARITY
50	85	125	6

80 (Type III): An orange pole was installed in a dark green base, along with a green ladder, on some of these signals.

VG	EX	LN	RARITY
50	75	110	5

80 (Type IV): Other signals had an orange base, mojave pole and dark green ladder.

VG	EX	LN	RARITY
50	75	110	5

80 (Type V): The 1932 Ives catalog included the 80 semaphore, referring to the Wide Gauge (Standard Gauge) version as the 1903 and the 0 Gauge version as the 1904.

VG	EX	LN	RARITY
50	85	125	6

80N SEMAPHORE: In 1936, the contactor was introduced to control line side accessories. The 80 and 080 were replaced with the 80N, which was the same accessory, now packaged with the universal contactor, rather than the gauge-specific insulated track section. It remained in the catalog through 1942. It was produced with a light red base, aluminum-painted pole and black ladder. A nickel finial topped the post.

VG	EX	LN	RARITY
50	75	110	5

Specifications of Lionel "Multivolt" Transformers

Lionel "Multivolt" Transformers are made completely at our own factories. The only parts purchased are the raw materials. We correctly wind and insulate the coils, make the cases, laminations, switch handles, and in fact do every operation. Lionel "Multivolt" Transformers are listed as standard by the Underwriters' Laboratories.

Sub-Base—A metal sub-base is attached to the bottom. The air, circulating between this sub-base and the transformer case, keeps it cool while in operation. Holes in this sub-base provide means for fastening to wall or table.

Separable Plug—All "Multivolt" Transformers are fitted with an approved, separable plug, which is a distinct advantage over the one-piece plug, because the circuit can be immediately broken.

Plug Protecting Device—A unique receptacle for protecting the plug against breakage in shipment. This device consists of a wooden container entirely covering the plug. It is sealed with a conspicuous label which draws attention to the fact that the transformer must be used **only** on **alternating** current of the number of cycles designated. This obviates the possibility of connecting the transformer with wrong current and avoids mishandling.

Double Contact Control Switch—This is infinitely superior to the one-piece switch, which is easily bent and does not make positive contact. Our double switch has a flexible, phosphor-bronze contact arm under the rigid switch, so that positive contact with the points is assured. This flexible contact is protected from injury by the rigid brass handle to which it is attached. An exclusive feature of "Multivolt" Transformers.

Laminations—The laminations are made of the best grade of electrical sheets and the windings are perfectly insulated.

Rigid Supports for Coils—The coils and laminations of Lionel "Multivolt" Transformers are rigidly supported inside the case by means of metal bands which prevent these parts from moving and eliminate the possibility of broken lead wires. In addition to these supports, the interior of the case is fitted with an insulating receptacle and the case is air cooled.

Metal Case—The case is beautiful in design and is stamped of heavier steel than is required by the Underwriters' Laboratories.

Finish—"Multivolt" Transformer cases are covered with a rubberoid composition which is applied at 390 degrees Fahrenheit. This is much greater heat than the case is ever subjected to, and the finish cannot be scratched and will not peel off during the entire life of the transformer.

Visible Connections—All contacts and switches are mounted on one piece of heavy insulating material and are at the top of the transformer, right before the user.

Lamp Cord—All "Multivolt" Transformers are fitted with 7 feet of flexible lamp cord which enters the transformer case through an approved porcelain bushing.

It will be seen that "Multivolt" Transformers incorporate every device that will increase their efficiency.

LIONEL DIRECT CURRENT REDUCERS
(Not to Be Used on Alternating Current)

No. 107 Lionel Current Reducer for 110-Volt Circuit—This is constructed of four porcelain tubes wound with best quality of resistance wire. These porcelain tubes are mounted on a substantial base measuring 8 by 10 inches and ¾ inches thick. The porcelain tubes are protected and ventilated by a perforated steel cover lined with heavy asbestos. The sliding lever regulates the voltage so that train will just crawl along or go ahead at express speed. The reducer is connected with the house current by a separable plug with 7 feet of flexible cord. Four porcelain supports with screws are supplied so that the reducer can be screwed to wall or table. Price $10.00
Code Word "KENTUCKY"

No. 170 Lionel Direct Current Reducer for 220-Volt Circuit—This reducer is identical in appearance with No. 107, mentioned above, but is for use on 220 volts. Price $14.50
Code Word "ASBURY"

CONTROLLING RHEOSTATS FOR BATTERIES

No. 88 Rheostat for Dry Cells or Storage Batteries—It provides a gradual increase or decrease of current. A heat-resisting unit on a porcelain tube is mounted on a steel frame which has a sliding finger that increases or decreases the speed of the train. All parts are of the best quality. The steel base is enameled and other parts are nickel-plated. Size 5 inches long, 2½ inches wide. Price $1.50
Code Word "BANNER"

No. 81 Controlling Rheostat—With this rheostat you can operate all Lionel Trains at various speeds as well as start or stop them at any distance from the track. By sliding the finger from side to side, various speeds can be obtained, and by manipulating a small lever up and down, the current is turned on and off, so that train can be started or stopped at will. The porcelain coil is protected by a perforated steel cover, and air holes prevent overheating. Size 5 inches long, 2½ inches wide. Code Word "BONE" Price $2.50

32

1927 CATALOG

Lionel All-Steel Flag-Staffs—Illuminated Bungalows, Villas and Sets

BUILD a model village, boys, with these substantial, handsomely finished illuminated houses. They will greatly enhance the appearance of your Lionel Model Railroad.

No. 89 Flag-Staff and Flag—For use with Lionel model villages or to place in front of a Lionel Station. Flag-staff is 14 inches high. Silk flag may be lowered by cord attached, which can be fastened to hook near the base. Price . . . . $.75
Code Word "ARTHUR"

No. 90 Flag-Staff and Flag—The flag-staff (14 inches high) is removable, and fits into an ornamental base mounted on a miniature grass plot with flower border. Price $1.25
Code Word "PLOT"

No. 191 Illuminated Villa—Beautifully designed. 7½ inches long, 5½ inches wide and 5¼ inches high. Roof is removable. Complete with interior lighting fixture, lamp and connecting wires. Price $3.35
Code Word "SOLID"

No. 192 Illuminated Villa Set—A handsome assortment of model houses. Comprises 1 No. 191 villa, 1 No. 189 villa and 2 No. 184 bungalows. All complete with interior lights and connecting wires. Very attractively packed. Price $8.75
Code Word "VILLAGE"

No. 186 Illuminated Bungalow Set—Comprises 4 No. 184 bungalows, beautifully finished in assorted colors. Complete with interior lights and connecting wires. Attractively packed. Price $7.50
Code Word "HAMLET"

No. 184 Illuminated Bungalow—4 inches high, 4¾ inches wide. Beautifully decorated. Complete with interior light and connecting wires. Price $1.50
Code Word "HOME"

No. 189 Illuminated Villa—A model that is architecturally perfect. 5½ inches high, 4¾ inches wide and 5½ inches high. Complete with interior light and connecting wires. Price $2.95
Code Word "MANSE"

37

1927 CATALOG

Price Guide Key: **VG** = Very Good, **EX** = Excellent, **LN** = Like New | *Values for each condition are in U.S. dollars.* | **Rarity** = Scale from 1-8 with 8 being the hardest to find.

319

81 RHEOSTAT: Offered in 1927-33, this device was intended to regulate the speed of trains. A ceramic core wrapped with resistance wire was housed in a black steel frame with a green steel cover. A spring steel slide with on-off switch could be moved along the core to vary the voltage, up to 18 volts AC.

VG	EX	LN	RARITY
5	10	15	3

82 TRAIN CONTROL SEMAPHORE, 082 TRAIN CONTROL SEMAPHORE: This semaphore, cataloged in both Standard Gauge (82) and 0 Gauge (082) from 1927 through 1935, featured an elaborate three-tiered die-cast base. Three sides had rivet detail cast in, and the front had simulated door and hinge detail. The casting back was open and covered with a fiber (early) or Bakelite (late) panel.

An appropriate insulated track section was furnished for each gauge, and the number plate attached to the rolled steel post indicated the catalog number. Its post was topped with a finial that was made of either brass or nickel. A black and red semaphore arm was actuated by a solenoid mechanism, and its movement determined whether a red or green celluloid lens was presented to the lamp. The solenoid mechanism and train control circuit were housed in the base.

82(Type I): The earliest production had a peacock base, cream pole and orange ladder. Initially the finial and name plate were brass, but nickel was used later.

VG	EX	LN	RARITY
50	80	110	6

82(Type II): Later production semaphores all had nickel trim and the base was painted 45N, while the pole was aluminum-painted with a black ladder.

VG	EX	LN	RARITY
50	80	110	5

82N SEMAPHORE: Like most of Lionel's line side accessories, beginning in 1936 the 82 was no longer packaged and sold as gauge-specific. A universal contactor was included, allowing it to be used with either Standard Gauge or 0 Gauge. This remained the case through 1942. The coloration, 45N green base, aluminum-painted pole, black ladder and nickel finial, was the same as used with the late 82 and 082.

VG	EX	LN	RARITY
50	80	110	5

83 TRAFFIC AND CROSSING SIGNAL: Sold from 1927 through 1942, the light housing at the top of the die-cast base of this signal resembled a diver's helmet. Red celluloid disks cover the openings in the light housing, and the light itself flashes through the action of a bimetallic strip. Three sides of the base bare in black the rubber-stamped legend "CAUTION - DRIVE – SLOWLY", the fourth side is marked "MADE BY- THE - LIONEL - CORPORATION - NEW YORK".

83 TRAFFIC AND CROSSING SIGNAL (Type I): From 1927 through 1934, the base of the signal was mojave, with a cream relay box, and white signal head.

VG	EX	LN	RARITY
75	150	250	6

83 TRAFFIC AND CROSSING SIGNAL (Type II): Beginning in 1935, and continuing through 1942, the base was painted light red, the relay box cream and the signal head white.

VG	EX	LN	RARITY
50	110	190	4

83 TRAFFIC AND CROSSING SIGNAL (Type III): At some point the accessory was also produced with a red base, cream box, and mojave signal head.

VG	EX	LN	RARITY
50	100	175	3

84 SEMAPHORE, 084 SEMAPHORE: This signal was offered in both Standard Gauge, and 0 Gauge from 1927 through 1932. Its die-cast base was formed to resemble a relay box, with appropriate detail cast in. The exception to this was the rear, which consisted of a fiberboard or Bakelite terminal strip.

At the top of the pole was a bulb mounted beneath a sheet metal lamp cover. Attached to this cover was a black and red semaphore arm with red and green celluloid lenses. A ladder extended most of the signal's 15" height. Some of these signals were equipped with a manually-operated train control mechanism.

84 SEMAPHORE, 084 SEMAPHORE (Type I): This had two electrical terminals on the rear, without the manual train-stop circuit. A rolled steel pole, painted cream and topped with a brass finial extended up from the dark green base.

VG	EX	LN	RARITY
40	80	130	5

84 SEMAPHORE, 084 SEMAPHORE (Type II): Equipped with the manual train control, this type was distinguished by three electrical terminals on the back. A cream pole, mounted in a dark green base and topped with a brass finial, was used on this version as well.

VG	EX	LN	RARITY
40	80	130	5

84 SEMAPHORE, 084 SEMAPHORE (Type III): Constructed with a maroon base and peacock ladder, this signal had three electrical terminals.

VG	EX	LN	RARITY
40	80	130	5

84 SEMAPHORE, 084 SEMAPHORE (Type IV): Signals, also equipped with three terminals, were made with the dark green base, orange pole and peacock ladder as well.

VG	EX	LN	RARITY
40	80	130	5

85 TELEGRAPH POST: Designed to be attached to the track, these stamped steel telegraph posts had tapered open girder posts. On the crossarm was mounted two porcelain insulators. These 9" tall posts were part of the product line from 1929 through 1942.

85 TELEGRAPH POST (Type I): The early posts were painted orange. The crossarm was maroon and orange insulators were installed.

VG	EX	LN	RARITY
12	25	45	2

85 TELEGRAPH POST (Type II): Later posts were painted an aluminum color. Red crossarms with white insulators were used on these.

VG	EX	LN	RARITY
20	40	65	5

86 TELEGRAPH POST SET: Also cataloged 1929-42 was this set of six 85 telegraph posts. The original box is crucial for the values stated here.

86 TELEGRAPH POST SET (Type I): The early sets included posts that were painted orange. The crossarm was maroon and orange insulators were installed.

VG	EX	LN	RARITY
100	200	400	5

86 TELEGRAPH POST SET (Type II): Later, the aluminum-painted posts were included in the sets. Red crossarms with white insulators were used on these.

VG	EX	LN	RARITY
125	250	500	6

87 RAILROAD CROSSING SIGNAL: Sold from 1927 through 1942, this crossing signal had styling similar to that of the 83. However, rather than having a "diver's helmet" lamp housing on top, it had a simple target-type lamp housing.

Three sides of the die-cast base bear in black the rubber-stamped legend "CAUTION - DRIVE – SLOWLY", the fourth side is marked "MADE BY- THE - LIONEL - CORPORATION - NEW YORK". The bulb housed inside the drum-shaped target at top blinks due to a bimetallic strip.

87 RAILROAD CROSSING SIGNAL (Type I): The most common and longest-produced version of the signal had an orange base and relay box, topped with an ivory-colored drumhead.

VG	EX	LN	RARITY
75	125	200	5

87 RAILROAD CROSSING SIGNAL (Type II): Some of the signals were made with a light tan base, orange relay box and ivory-colored drumhead.

VG	EX	LN	RARITY
75	125	200	5

87 RAILROAD CROSSING SIGNAL (Type III): A white drumhead with red bull's eyes was mounted atop a Stephen Girard green relay box, which in turn rested on a dark green base.

VG	EX	LN	RARITY
125	225	350	6

87 RAILROAD CROSSING SIGNAL (Type IV): Some of the signals had a mojave base, orange relay box and a white signal head with orange bull's eyes.

VG	EX	LN	RARITY
75	125	200	5

87 RAILROAD CROSSING SIGNAL (Type V): A black arc joined the light orange bull's eye on some of the signals that had a mojave base, orange relay box and ivory drumhead.

Price Guide Key: VG = Very Good, EX = Excellent, LN = Like New | Values for each condition are in U.S. dollars. | Rarity = Scale from 1-8 with 8 being the hardest to find.

321

VG	EX	LN	RARITY
75	125	200	5

87 RAILROAD CROSSING SIGNAL (Type VI): Some of the signals were built with a dark green base and cream relay box. Mounted on top was a white signal head with red bull's eyes.

VG	EX	LN	RARITY
125	225	350	6

88 BATTERY RHEOSTAT: This control, sold from 1915 through 1927 to control the speed of the train, was rated up to 12 volts DC.

VG	EX	LN	RARITY
5	10	15	5

88 DIRECTION CONTROLLER: Pushing the button of this control opened a set of contacts and disconnected the flow of current to the rails. This caused the reversing mechanism of most locomotives to cycle. It was produced from 1933 through 1942.

VG	EX	LN	RARITY
5	10	15	2

89 FLAG POLE: Mounted on the square steel base of this accessory was a 14" tall pole supporting a silk American flag. The base and pole were painted either white or ivory – the color has no effect on the item's value. It was sold by Lionel from 1923 through 1934, and an identical item was sold as Ives from 1930 through 1932.

VG	EX	LN	RARITY
50	75	110	2

90 FLAG POLE: This flag pole had a round base decorated with simulated grass and flowers. The pole stood 14 1/2" tall and supported a silk American flag. It was sold from 1927 through 1942.

90 FLAG POLE (Type I): On the earliest version, the pole stood in a brass pedestal.

VG	EX	LN	RARITY
75	110	150	3

90 FLAG POLE (Type II): Later versions used a nickel pedestal.

VG	EX	LN	RARITY
75	110	150	3

90 FLAG POLE (Type III): The final version had a black pedestal.

VG	EX	LN	RARITY
75	110	150	3

91 CIRCUIT BREAKER: The die-cast base of this accessory housed a circuit breaker. The light above illuminated to indicate trouble had caused the circuit breaker to open. It was sold continuously from 1930 through 1942.

91 CIRCUIT BREAKER (Type I): As first produced, the die-cast base was painted mojave and topped with a brass light cover. Two electrical terminals were provided.

VG	EX	LN	RARITY
25	35	45	3

91 CIRCUIT BREAKER (Type II): A similar version was made with the die-cast base painted State brown.

VG	EX	LN	RARITY
25	35	45	3

91 CIRCUIT BREAKER (Type III): The final version of the circuit breaker was also painted State brown on the base. However, it had a nickel light cover and three terminals installed.

VG	EX	LN	RARITY
25	35	45	3

092 ILLUMINATED SIGNAL TOWER: This illuminated tower, sold from 1923 through 1927, was essentially a 438 less its supports. The base of the 092 tower measured 4 1/8" x 2 13/16".

092 ILLUMINATED SIGNAL TOWER (Type I): The first version of the signal tower had a mojave base, terra-cotta walls, pea green roof, maroon doors and cream windows.

VG	EX	LN	RARITY
50	90	150	4

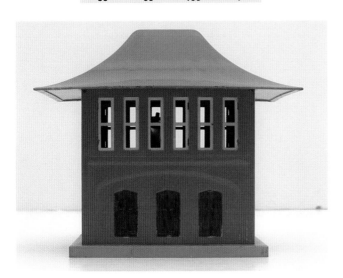

092 ILLUMINATED SIGNAL TOWER (Type II): Some of these towers were made with the doors painted to simulate wood grain. They were otherwise identical to the Type I.

VG	EX	LN	RARITY
50	90	150	4

092 ILLUMINATED SIGNAL TOWER (Type III): Another version of the tower had a brown base, terra-cotta walls, pea green roof, cream windows and brown doors with black lines.

VG	EX	LN	RARITY
50	90	150	4

092 ILLUMINATED SIGNAL TOWER (Type IV): Another version, similar to the type III, had a pea green roof and red doors.

VG	EX	LN	RARITY
50	90	150	4

092 ILLUMINATED SIGNAL TOWER (Type IV): A mojave base supported a tower with white walls, red roof, red doors and pea green windows.

VG	EX	LN	RARITY
90	150	225	6

92 FLOODLIGHT TOWER: The 5" square base of this 1931-42 accessory supported a 20 1/2" tall floodlight tower. At the top of the accessory was a platform supporting two lamp housings surrounded by a handrail.

92 FLOODLIGHT TOWER (Type I): From 1931 through 1934, the unit had a terracotta base and pea green tower structure. The lamp housings and nameplate were brass.

VG	EX	LN	RARITY
75	125	175	4

92 FLOODLIGHT TOWER (Type II): Beginning in 1935, this accessory had a red base and an aluminum-painted tower. The lamp housings and nameplate were nickel. It was available in this configuration into 1941.

VG	EX	LN	RARITY
100	150	200	4

92 FLOODLIGHT TOWER (Type III): During 1941-42, the tower was made with a light red base and gray tower. The lamp housings and nameplate were nickel.

VG	EX	LN	RARITY
125	175	225	6

93 WATER TOWER: This little 8 3/8" high sheet-metal tower was cataloged from 1931 through 1942. Returning after the war, it was in a somewhat secondary role, being dwarfed by the massive and detailed 30 and 38. It nevertheless was available in 1946-49. The postwar production was painted silver, with a black manually lowered spout and a red base. A large "LIONEL TRAINS" decal with red letters outlined in black was applied to the tank. The decal had a thin black border.

93 WATER TOWER (Type I): When introduced in 1931, the 93 water tower had a pea green tank and matching pipe, mounted on a burnt orange tower, which in turn was attached to a maroon base. A brass spout was installed, but there was no "Lionel" decal. It continued to be offered in this color scheme through 1934.

VG	EX	LN	RARITY
25	35	60	3

Price Guide Key: **VG** = Very Good, **EX** = Excellent, **LN** = Like New | *Values for each condition are in U.S. dollars.* | **Rarity** = Scale from 1-8 with 8 being the hardest to find.

323

VG	EX	LN	RARITY
25	35	60	3

94 HIGH TENSION TOWER: The 5" square base of this accessory supported a realistic-looking open girder high-tension electrical tower. Each of its three crossarms supported two hanging porcelain insulators. From 1932 through 1942, each of these towers was shipped with a spool of copper wire. The complete tower stood two feet tall.

93 WATER TOWER (Type II): In 1935, a new color scheme was introduced, which would remain available through 1941. In this scheme, the tower, tank and pipe were all painted an aluminum color and mounted on a vermilion base. A black spout and silver decal outlined in black, displaying "LIONEL / TRAINS" in red, completed the tower.

VG	EX	LN	RARITY
30	45	65	4

93 WATER TOWER (Type III): This variation differed from the Type II tower only in having a maroon base.

VG	EX	LN	RARITY
25	35	60	3

93 WATER TOWER (Type IV): In 1941-42, towers were assembled that featured a green tank, pipe and tower, mounted on a vermilion base. Its "LIONEL/TRAINS" decal had light red lettering. A black spout completed the tower.

VG	EX	LN	RARITY
25	35	60	3

94 HIGH TENSION TOWER (Type I): An early version of the accessory had a terra-cotta base and gunmetal tower. A brass builder's plate was installed on this version.

VG	EX	LN	RARITY
150	300	500	6

94 HIGH TENSION TOWER (Type II): Another early version again used a terra-cotta base with brass builder's plate, this time supporting a mojave tower.

VG	EX	LN	RARITY
150	300	500	6

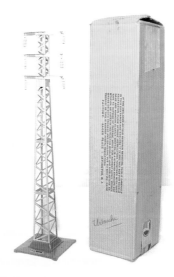

93 WATER TOWER (Type V): In 1942, gray replaced the aluminum paint on the tower, tank and pipe. The base continued to be vermilion.

VG	EX	LN	RARITY
25	35	60	3

93 WATER TOWER (Type VI): Some water towers were produced with aluminum-colored tanks and pipes, but gray towers.

94 HIGH TENSION TOWER (Type III): Later units had red bases, aluminum-painted tower structures and nickel builder's plates.

VG	EX	LN	RARITY
100	175	275	3

94 HIGH TENSION TOWER (Type IV): The final version produced substituted gray paint for the aluminum color previously used. Its base was red.

VG	EX	LN	RARITY
150	300	500	6

95 RHEOSTAT: Sold from 1934 through 1942, this black rheostat had a red push button on its control slide. This button was used to momentarily interrupt the current flow in order to cycle three-position remote-control reverse units.

95 RHEOSTAT (Type I): The early units had brass instruction plates.

VG	EX	LN	RARITY
10	15	20	2

95 RHEOSTAT (Type II): Later versions replaced the brass plate with a nickel one.

VG	EX	LN	RARITY
10	15	20	2

096 TELEGRAPH POST: These 0 Gauge stamped steel telegraph posts had a pea green tapered open girder post. On the red crossarm were mounted two white porcelain insulators. These 6 1/2" tall posts were part of the product line in 1934-35. Rather than being sold individually, these were available only in the 097 Telegraph Post and Signal Set.

VG	EX	LN	RARITY
15	20	25	4

96 COAL ELEVATOR: Sold from 1938 through 1940, this was essentially a non-motorized version of the famous 97 coal loader. It had a black Bakelite base to which was attached an aluminum-colored tower supporting a cream coal bunker. The windows and roof of the bunker were red. A hinged coal-receiving bin was attached. A hand crank operated the chain-type conveyor, which had black sheet-metal buckets attached. The dumping mechanism, however, was electrically actuated.

VG	EX	LN	RARITY
100	175	275	6

097 TELEGRAPH POST AND SIGNAL SET: This accessory set, sold in 1934 and 1935, contained six 096 telegraph posts and one 068 warning signal. The original box is a key to attaining the values listed.

VG	EX	LN	RARITY
200	275	375	5

97 MOTORIZED COAL ELEVATOR (Type I): This elaborate operating accessory was first produced in 1938 and remained in production until World War II suspended toy manufacturing. It was revived again in 1946 and was produced through 1950. The accessory had a Bakelite base and sheet-metal superstructure. A motor, hidden beneath the base, drove a chain conveyor with sheet metal buckets. This lifted the simulated coal from a track-level dump bin into the yellow sheet metal coal bunker on the opposite side. There it was stored until the remote-controlled solenoid opened a door, discharging the coal down a chute into a car waiting below.

This rugged, reliable accessory worked well, but required a lot of space and two parallel tracks about 15" on center to operate. Its controller had one knob and one pushbutton, and was housed in a derivative of the UCS controller housing. The supporting structure for the yellow bunker and the conveyor was painted aluminum.

VG	EX	LN	RARITY
100	175	225	5

Price Guide Key: VG = Very Good, EX = Excellent, LN = Like New | *Values for each condition are in U.S. dollars.* | Rarity = Scale from 1-8 with 8 being the hardest to find.

325

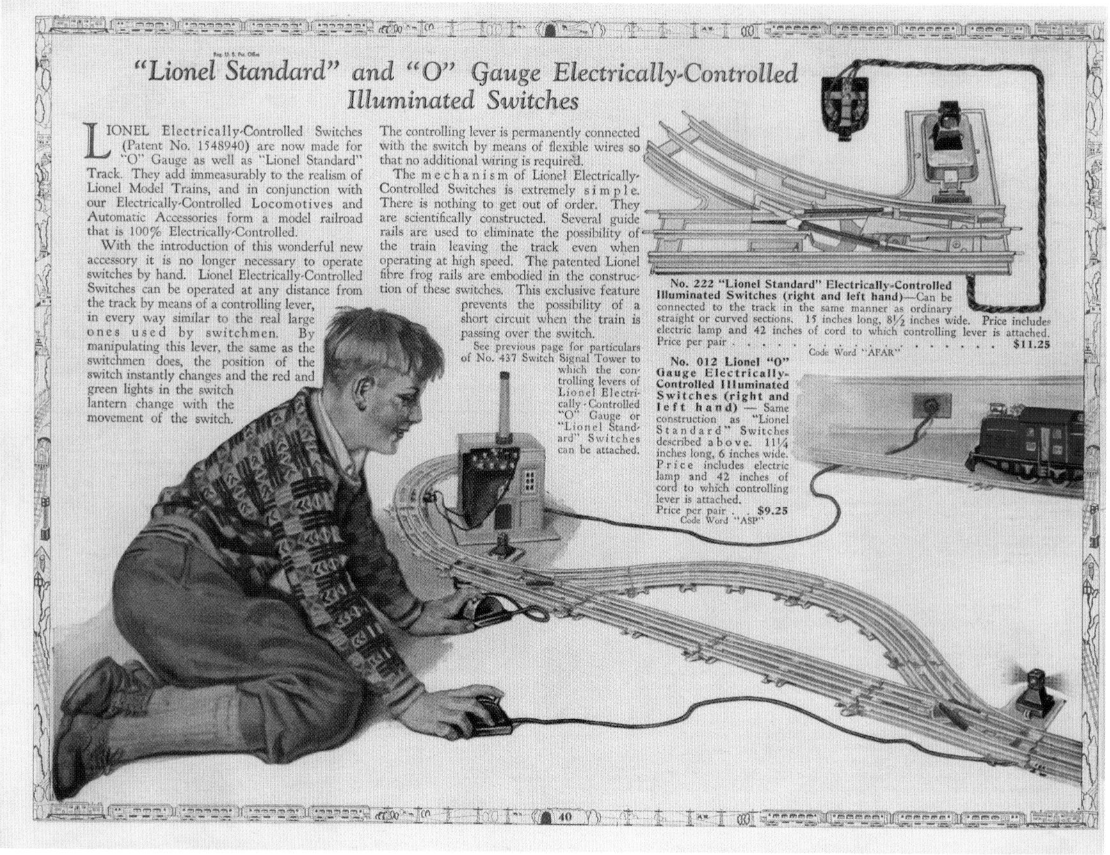

Reg. U. S. Pat. Office

"Lionel Standard" and "O" Gauge Electrically-Controlled Illuminated Switches

LIONEL Electrically-Controlled Switches (Patent No. 1548940) are now made for "O" Gauge as well as "Lionel Standard" Track. They add immeasurably to the realism of Lionel Model Trains, and in conjunction with our Electrically-Controlled Locomotives and Automatic Accessories form a model railroad that is 100% Electrically-Controlled.

With the introduction of this wonderful new accessory it is no longer necessary to operate switches by hand. Lionel Electrically-Controlled Switches can be operated at any distance from the track by means of a controlling lever, in every way similar to the real large ones used by switchmen. By manipulating this lever, the same as the switchmen does, the position of the switch instantly changes and the red and green lights in the switch lantern change with the movement of the switch.

The controlling lever is permanently connected with the switch by means of flexible wires so that no additional wiring is required.

The mechanism of Lionel Electrically-Controlled Switches is extremely simple. There is nothing to get out of order. They are scientifically constructed. Several guide rails are used to eliminate the possibility of the train leaving the track even when operating at high speed. The patented Lionel fibre frog rails are embodied in the construction of these switches. This exclusive feature prevents the possibility of a short circuit when the train is passing over the switch.

See previous page for particulars of No. 437 Switch Signal Tower to which the controlling levers of Lionel Electrically-Controlled "O" Gauge or "Lionel Standard" Switches can be attached.

No. 222 "Lionel Standard" Electrically-Controlled Illuminated Switches (right and left hand)—Can be connected to the track in the same manner as ordinary straight or curved sections. 15 inches long, 8½ inches wide. Price includes electric lamp and 42 inches of cord to which controlling lever is attached. Price per pair **$11.25**
Code Word "AFAR"

No. 012 Lionel "O" Gauge Electrically-Controlled Illuminated Switches (right and left hand) — Same construction as "Lionel Standard" Switches described above. 11¼ inches long, 6 inches wide. Price includes electric lamp and 42 inches of cord to which controlling lever is attached. Price per pair . . **$9.25**
Code Word "ASP"

40

1927 CATALOG

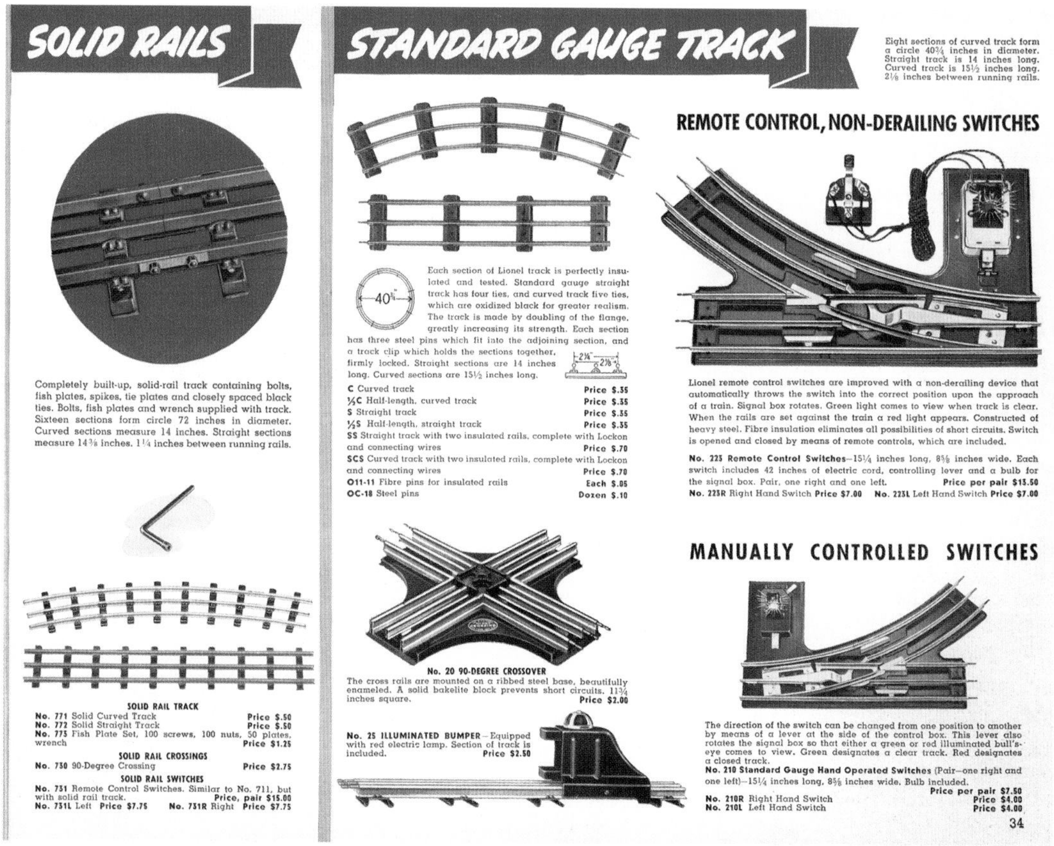

SOLID RAILS

Completely built-up, solid-rail track containing bolts, fish plates, spikes, tie plates and closely spaced black ties. Bolts, fish plates and wrench supplied with track. Sixteen sections form circle 72 inches in diameter. Curved sections measure 14 inches. Straight sections measure 14⅜ inches. 1¼ inches between running rails.

SOLID RAIL TRACK

No. 771 Solid Curved Track **Price $.50**
No. 772 Solid Straight Track **Price $.50**
No. 773 Fish Plate Set, 100 screws, 100 nuts, 50 plates, wrench **Price $1.25**

SOLID RAIL CROSSINGS

No. 730 90-Degree Crossing **Price $2.75**

SOLID RAIL SWITCHES

No. 731 Remote Control Switches. Similar to No. 711, but with solid rail track. **Price, pair $15.00**
No. 731L Left **Price $7.75** **No. 731R** Right **Price $7.75**

STANDARD GAUGE TRACK

Eight sections of curved track form a circle 40¾ inches in diameter. Straight track is 14 inches long. Curved track is 15½ inches long. 2⅛ inches between running rails.

40¾"

Each section of Lionel track is perfectly insulated and tested. Standard gauge straight track has four ties, and curved track five ties, which are oxidized black for greater realism. The track is made by doubling of the flange, greatly increasing its strength. Each section has three steel pins which fit into the adjoining section, and a track clip which holds the sections together, firmly locked. Straight sections are 14 inches long. Curved sections are 15½ inches long.

2¼" 2⅛"

C Curved track **Price $.35**
½C Half-length, curved track **Price $.35**
S Straight track **Price $.35**
½S Half-length, straight track **Price $.35**
SS Straight track with two insulated rails, complete with Lockon and connecting wires **Price $.70**
SCS Curved track with two insulated rails, complete with Lockon and connecting wires **Price $.70**
O11-11 Fibre pins for insulated rails **Each $.05**
OC-18 Steel pins **Dozen $.10**

No. 20 90-DEGREE CROSSOVER
The cross rails are mounted on a ribbed steel base, beautifully enameled. A solid bakelite block prevents short circuits. 11¾ inches square. **Price $2.00**

No. 25 ILLUMINATED BUMPER—Equipped with red electric lamp. Section of track is included. **Price $2.50**

REMOTE CONTROL, NON-DERAILING SWITCHES

Lionel remote control switches are improved with a non-derailing device that automatically throws the switch into the correct position upon the approach of a train. Signal box rotates. Green light comes to view when track is clear. When the rails are set against the train a red light appears. Constructed of heavy steel. Fibre insulation eliminates all possibilities of short circuits. Switch is opened and closed by means of remote controls, which are included.

No. 223 Remote Control Switches—15¼ inches long, 8⅝ inches wide. Each switch includes 42 inches of electric cord, controlling lever and a bulb for the signal box. Pair, one right and one left. **Price per pair $13.50**
No. 223R Right Hand Switch **Price $7.00** **No. 223L** Left Hand Switch **Price $7.00**

MANUALLY CONTROLLED SWITCHES

The direction of the switch can be changed from one position to another by means of a lever at the side of the control box. This lever also rotates the signal box so that either a green or red illuminated bull's-eye comes to view. Green designates a clear track. Red designates a closed track.

No. 210 Standard Gauge Hand Operated Switches (Pair—one right and one left)—15¼ inches long, 8⅝ inches wide. Bulb included. **Price per pair $7.50**
No. 210R Right Hand Switch **Price $4.00**
No. 210L Left Hand Switch **Price $4.00**

34

1938 CATALOG

ACCESSORIES, TRACK & TRANSFORMERS

VG	EX	LN	RARITY
40	75	125	3

97 MOTORIZED COAL ELEVATOR (Type II): In 1942, the supporting structure for the coal bunker and conveyor was painted gray.

VG	EX	LN	RARITY
125	200	275	7

98 COAL BUNKER: A second non-motorized coal bunker was also made from 1938 through 1940. Though similar to the 96, this unit had a sheet metal base that was smaller than the Bakelite units used on the other coal bunkers. Its aluminum nameplate read "No. 98 COAL HOUSE - MADE IN U.S. OF AMERICA" and "THE LIONEL CORPORATION, N.Y." in black. This bare-bones bunker had no conveyor or receiving bin.

Simulated coal was loaded in the bunker manually through a chute on the back of the cream-colored coal bunker. A solenoid-operated trap door allowed the coal to be discharged.

VG	EX	LN	RARITY
200	325	500	6

99/099 TRAIN CONTROL BLOCK SIGNAL: Offered in Standard Gauge as the 99 and in 0 Gauge as the 099, this block signal used a bimetallic strip to automatically stop and restart passing trains. It was sold from 1932 through 1935, when it was replaced with the 99N. Depending on gauge, the brass plate on the signal mast read "99" or "099". Including its die-cast combination base and relay box, the accessory was 12" tall.

99/099 TRAIN CONTROL BLOCK SIGNAL (Type I): From 1932 through 1934, the signal was sold with a black base and cream pole.

99/099 TRAIN CONTROL BLOCK SIGNAL (Type II): In 1935, the signal had a red base with cream pole.

VG	EX	LN	RARITY
40	75	125	3

99/099 TRAIN CONTROL BLOCK SIGNAL (Type III): Some signals were produced that had black bases and mojave poles.

VG	EX	LN	RARITY
40	75	125	3

99N TRAIN CONTROL BLOCK SIGNAL: In 1936, the train control block signal became universal, rather than being built gauge-specific. This was accomplished by including a pressure-actuated switch rather than insulated track section with the signal. It was sold this way through 1942. The plate attached to its mast was nickel and numbered "99N".

99N TRAIN CONTROL BLOCK SIGNAL (Type I): Some of these signals had light red bases and ladders, and aluminum-painted poles.

VG	EX	LN	RARITY
40	75	125	3

99N TRAIN CONTROL BLOCK SIGNAL (Type II): Other signals retained the aluminum-painted pole, but the base and ladder were vermilion.

Price Guide Key: VG = Very Good. EX = Excellent. LN = Like New | *Values for each condition are in U.S. dollars.* | **Rarity** = Scale from 1-8 with 8 being the hardest to find.

327

VG	EX	LN	RARITY
40	75	125	3

100 BRIDGE APPROACHES: Sold from 1920 through 1931, these standard gauge sheet-metal ramps, sold in pairs, gradually elevated the track to the height of the 104 Bridge Center Span. Each ramp held one section of type S straight track.

100 BRIDGE APPROACHES (Type I): On early units, the roadbed was lithographed speckled-gray to resemble ballast.

VG	EX	LN	RARITY
10	20	40	2

100 BRIDGE APPROACHES (Type II): Later, the roadbed was merely painted light gray.

VG	EX	LN	RARITY
10	20	40	2

100 BRIDGE APPROACHES (Type III): In some cases, the roadbed was painted black.

VG	EX	LN	RARITY
10	20	40	2

101 BRIDGE: The catalog number 101 was assigned to the Standard Gauge 104 Bridge Center Span and one pair of 100 approaches when sold as a combination. The combined length of the bridge was 42". The 101 was cataloged from 1920 through 1931. The original box is a significant portion of the value listed.

101 BRIDGE (Type I): On early units, the roadbed was lithographed speckled-gray to resemble ballast.

VG	EX	LN	RARITY
100	150	225	4

101 BRIDGE (Type II): Later, the roadbed was merely painted light gray.

VG	EX	LN	RARITY
100	150	225	4

101 BRIDGE (Type III): In some cases, the roadbed was painted black.

VG	EX	LN	RARITY
100	150	225	4

102 BRIDGE: Reaching 56" in length, this Standard Gauge bridge consisted of two 104 Bridge Center Spans and one pair of 100 approaches. It was cataloged from 1920 through 1931. The original box is a significant portion of the value listed.

102 BRIDGE (Type I): On early units, the roadbed was lithographed speckled-gray to resemble ballast.

VG	EX	LN	RARITY
125	175	250	4

102 BRIDGE (Type II): Later, the roadbed was merely painted light gray.

VG	EX	LN	RARITY
125	175	250	4

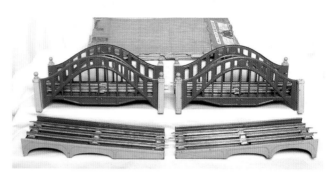

102 BRIDGE (Type III): In some cases the roadbed was painted black.

VG	EX	LN	RARITY
125	175	250	4

103 BRIDGE: Cataloged from 1913 through 1915, this 28" long Standard Gauge, papier-mâché bridge was intended to look like a stone bridge. However, it is believed none were ever manufactured.

RARITY
Too rarely, if ever, traded to establish market pricing.

103 BRIDGE: Reaching 70" in length, this Standard Gauge bridge consisted of three 104 Bridge Center Spans and one pair of 100 approaches. It was cataloged from 1920 through 1931. The original box is a significant portion of the value listed.

103 BRIDGE (Type I): On early units, the roadbed was lithographed speckled-gray to resemble ballast.

VG	EX	LN	RARITY
150	200	275	5

103 BRIDGE (Type II): Later, the roadbed was merely painted light gray.

VG	EX	LN	RARITY
150	200	275	5

103 BRIDGE (Type III): In some cases, the roadbed was painted black.

VG	EX	LN	RARITY
150	200	275	5

104 BRIDGE CENTER SPAN: This pea green sheet-metal bridge with cream posts was a miniature version of Lionel's 300 Hellgate bridge. Its elevated roadbed was designed to accept a single section of Standard Gauge. It was sold from 1920 through 1931.

104 BRIDGE CENTER SPAN (Type I): On early units, the roadbed was lithographed speckled-gray to resemble ballast.

VG	EX	LN	RARITY
20	30	40	2

104 BRIDGE CENTER SPAN (Type II): Later, the roadbed was merely painted light gray.

VG	EX	LN	RARITY
20	30	40	2

104 BRIDGE CENTER SPAN (Type III): In some cases, the roadbed was painted black.

VG	EX	LN	RARITY
20	30	40	2

104 TUNNEL: Between 1909 and 1914, this 13" long, 9" tall hand-painted papier-mâché tunnel was sold for use with Standard Gauge trains.

VG	EX	LN	RARITY
50	80	125	5

105 BRIDGE: Despite being listed in the catalog every year from 1911 through 1914, it is not believed this papier-mâché Standard Gauge was actually produced.

RARITY
Too rarely, if ever, traded to establish market pricing.

105 BRIDGE APPROACHES: Sold from 1920 through 1931, these 0 gauge sheet-metal ramps, sold in pairs, gradually elevated the track to the height of the 110 Bridge Center Span. Each ramp held one section of OS straight track.

105 BRIDGE APPROACHES (Type I): On early units, the roadbed was lithographed speckled-gray to resemble ballast. The sides of the approaches were painted cream.

VG	EX	LN	RARITY
10	20	30	4

105 BRIDGE APPROACHES (Type II): Later, the roadbed was merely painted light gray. They continued to have cream sides.

VG	EX	LN	RARITY
10	20	30	4

105 BRIDGE APPROACHES (Type III): The sides of some of the late production units were painted a light mustard color. The roadbed of these approaches was light gray.

VG	EX	LN	RARITY
10	20	30	4

106 BRIDGE: The catalog number 106 was assigned to the 0 Gauge 110 Bridge Center Span and one pair of 105 approaches when sold as a combination. The combined length of the bridge was 31". The 106 was cataloged from 1920 through 1931.

106 BRIDGE (Type I): On early units, the roadbed was lithographed speckled-gray to resemble ballast. The sides of the approaches were painted cream, as were the pillars on the center span.

VG	EX	LN	RARITY
50	75	110	4

106 BRIDGE (Type II): Later, the roadbed was merely painted light gray. They continued to have cream sides.

VG	EX	LN	RARITY
50	75	110	4

106 BRIDGE (Type III): The sides of some of the late production units were painted a light mustard color, as were the pillars of the center span. The roadbed of these approaches was light gray.

VG	EX	LN	RARITY
50	75	110	4

106 BRIDGE (Type IV): Other units had gray roadbed and pea green sides. The pillars on the center span were painted cream.

VG	EX	LN	RARITY
50	75	110	4

106 AC REDUCER: Sold 1909-14, this was a reducer for 110-volt AC.

RARITY
Too infrequently traded to establish accurate value.

106 RHEOSTAT: This was a step-type voltage reducer for 110- or 220-volts sold from 1911 through 1914.

RARITY
Too infrequently traded to establish accurate value.

107 DC REDUCER: This item was sold in two versions between 1911 and 1938. From 1911 through 1913, this was made to reduce 220 volts DC to levels required to run toy trains. A 110-volt DC version was sold from 1911 through 1938. During these periods, some parts of New York City had Direct Current, rather than the alternating current now standard throughout the United States.

107 DC REDUCER (Type I): This type was 110-volt.

RARITY
Too infrequently traded to establish accurate value.

Price Guide Key: **VG** = Very Good, **EX** = Excellent, **LN** = Like New | *Values for each condition are in U.S. dollars.* | **Rarity** = Scale from 1-8 with 8 being the hardest to find.

329

107 DC REDUCER (Type II): This type was 220-volt.

RARITY
Too infrequently traded to establish accurate value.

108 BATTERY RHEOSTAT: This rotary speed control was sold from 1912 through 1914 for use with large storage batteries.

RARITY
Too infrequently traded to establish accurate value.

108 BRIDGE: The catalog number 106 was assigned when two of the 0 gauge 110 bridge center spans and one pair of 105 approaches were sold as a combination. The combined length of the bridge was 42". The 108 was cataloged from 1920 through 1931. The presence of the original box is important to achieving these values.

108 BRIDGE (Type I): On early units, the roadbed was lithographed speckled-gray to resemble ballast. The sides of the approaches were painted cream, as were the pillars on the center span.

VG	EX	LN	RARITY
75	100	150	5

108 BRIDGE (Type II): Later, the roadbed was merely painted light gray. They continued to have cream sides.

VG	EX	LN	RARITY
75	100	150	5

108 BRIDGE (Type III): The sides of some of the late production units were painted a light mustard color, as were the pillars of the center span. The roadbed of these approaches was light gray.

VG	EX	LN	RARITY
75	100	150	5

109 BRIDGE: The catalog number 106 was assigned when three of the 0 gauge 110 bridge center spans and one pair of 105 approaches were sold as a combination. The combined length of the bridge was 52 1/2". The 108 was cataloged from 1920 through 1931. The presence of the original box is important to achieving these values.

109 BRIDGE (Type I): On early units, the roadbed was lithographed speckled-gray to resemble ballast. The sides of the approaches were painted cream, as were the pillars on the center span.

VG	EX	LN	RARITY
100	150	200	5

109 BRIDGE (Type II): Later, the roadbed was merely painted light gray. They continued to have cream sides.

VG	EX	LN	RARITY
100	150	200	5

109 BRIDGE (Type III): The sides of some of the late production units were painted a light mustard color, as were the pillars of the center span. The roadbed of these approaches was light gray.

VG	EX	LN	RARITY
100	150	200	5

109 TUNNEL: Sold in 1913, this Standard Gauge hand-painted papier-mâché tunnel was 12 1/2" tall and 25" long.

VG	EX	LN	RARITY
75	125	200	6

110 BRIDGE CENTER SPAN: This pea green sheet-metal bridge was a miniature version of Lionel's 300 Hellgate bridge. Its elevated roadbed was designed to accept a single section of OS Standard Gauge. It was sold from 1920 through 1931.

110 BRIDGE CENTER SPAN (Type I): On early units, the roadbed was lithographed speckled-gray to resemble ballast. The pillars were painted cream.

VG	EX	LN	RARITY
20	30	40	2

110 BRIDGE CENTER SPAN (Type II): Later, the roadbed was merely painted light gray. The pillars were painted cream.

VG	EX	LN	RARITY
20	30	40	2

110 BRIDGE CENTER SPAN (Type III): The pillars of some of the late production units were painted a light mustard color. The roadbed of these approaches was gray.

VG	EX	LN	RARITY
20	30	40	2

111 BULB ASSORTMENT: Intended for dealers, the assortment of replacement 12- and 18-volt bulbs was sold from 1920 through 1931.

111 BULB ASSORTMENT (Type I): Initially, the bulbs were packed in wooden containers, which were then packed in a wooden box.

VG	EX	LN	RARITY
500	1000	2000	8

111 BULB ASSORTMENT (Type II): A yellow cardboard box replaced the wooden outer box in later shipments. Likewise, the bulbs were also packed in cardboard rather than wood.

VG	EX	LN	RARITY
250	500	1000	7

112 STATION: This large pressed-steel station was sold from 1931 through 1934. Constructed to resemble a major metropolitan terminal of stone construction, "LIONEL CITY" was embossed over its doors. Also above the doors were embossed ornamental clocks with celluloid faces. The station had interior illumination.

112 STATION (Type I): An early version of the station had cream walls and a terra-cotta base. Its roof was pea green, as was its skylight and window inserts. Maroon doors and brass clock inserts were installed.

VG	EX	LN	RARITY
150	250	375	5

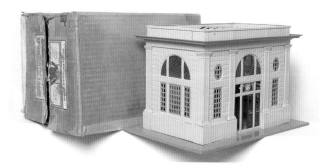

112 STATION (Type II): Also built on a terra-cotta base was a station with beige walls. The terminal roof was apple green as were the window inserts, while the skylight could be either apple green or pea green. Maroon doors and brass clock inserts were used.

VG	EX	LN	RARITY
150	250	375	5

112 STATION (Type III): A mojave base was used in conjunction with ivory walls to build this terminal. Its roof and window inserts were apple green and it had a pea green skylight. Maroon doors and brass clock inserts were used on this version as well.

VG	EX	LN	RARITY
150	250	375	5

112 STATION (Type IV): A station with ivory walls was also built on a light red base. Light red was also the color of the roof, skylight, window inserts and doors. White metal clock inserts were used on this version.

VG	EX	LN	RARITY
150	250	375	5

113 STATION: Also sold from 1931 through 1934 was this station, whose structure was the same as the 112. However, gold-painted outside light fixtures holding tulip-shaped bulbs upright were installed flanking the doors on the front of the station.

VG	EX	LN	RARITY
200	400	600	6

114 STATION: This lengthened version of the 113 was sold during 1931-34. Its front and back walls were stretched by an additional panel width. Like the 113, it had light fixtures flanking the front door, and the interior was illuminated. On its roof were two green skylights.

114 STATION (Type I): An early version of the station had cream walls and a terra-cotta base. Its roof was pea green, as were its skylights and window inserts. Maroon doors and brass clock inserts were installed.

VG	EX	LN	RARITY
500	1000	1600	6

114 STATION (Type II): Also built on a terra-cotta base was a station with beige walls. The terminal roof was apple green as were the window inserts, while the skylights could be either apple green or pea green. Maroon doors and brass clock inserts were used.

VG	EX	LN	RARITY
500	1000	1600	6

114 STATION (Type III): A mojave base was used in conjunction with ivory walls to build this terminal. Its roof, skylights and window inserts were apple green. Maroon doors and brass clock inserts were used on this version as well.

VG	EX	LN	RARITY
500	1000	1600	6

115 STATION: First offered from 1935 through 1942, the 115 returned after the war and was cataloged again from 1946-49. This imposing building was similar to the 112, but had light fixtures on either side of the doors. It was essentially all steel, with embossed stonework. In addition to the two silver-colored die-cast lamp brackets that were on the front of the station, there was an interior light.

Underneath the removable skylight was an automatic train control. This device, with an adjustable bimetallic strip, was intended to be wired to an insulated center rail three or four track sections long. After disengaging the E-unit, a train would circle the track and come to a rest in front of the station and, in a few moments, resume its journey. This action could be bypassed if so desired. Beware, this entire station and all of its components have been expertly reproduced.

115 STATION (Type I): A mojave base was used in conjunction with dark cream walls to build the initial version of this terminal. Its roof and window inserts were pea green and it had a pea green skylight. Maroon doors and brass clock inserts were used.

RARITY
Too rarely, if ever, traded to establish market pricing.

Price Guide Key: VG = Very Good, EX = Excellent, LN = Like New | Values for each condition are in U.S. dollars. | Rarity = Scale from 1-8 with 8 being the hardest to find.

331

115 STATION (Type II): Later production featured a vermilion base, roof, skylight, window inserts and doors. The walls of the terminal were painted ivory.

VG	EX	LN	RARITY
250	350	500	5

115 STATION (Type III): Otherwise identical stations were produced with light red paint substituted for the vermilion of the type II station.

VG	EX	LN	RARITY
250	350	500	5

116 STATION: This 1935-42 station was the same as 114, with the addition of a train-stop circuit.

116 STATION (Type I): The first two years' production used a mojave base and cream walls. The trim was pea green.

VG	EX	LN	RARITY
800	1400	2000	7

116 STATION (Type II): Subsequent production stations had walls that were almost white and were built on a red base.

VG	EX	LN	RARITY
700	1200	1800	6

117 STATION: But for the lack of exterior lights, this model sold in 1935-42 was the same as the 115.

VG	EX	LN	RARITY
100	200	300	4

118 TUNNEL: Cataloged from 1915 through 1932, this 0 Gauge tunnel was produced in a number of variations.

118 TUNNEL (Type I): From 1915 until about 1920, the 118 was made of hand-painted papier-mâché. It was 10" long and was reinforced with a steel brace. A building appeared to be standing on the mountainside.

118 TUNNEL (Type II): About 1920, steel began to be used to manufacture the tunnel. All the 118 tunnels built hence would be of metal construction. The ends of the tunnel were embossed to simulate stone portals. The entire unit was hand-painted.

VG	EX	LN	RARITY
20	35	50	2

118 TUNNEL (Type III): Some of the tunnels were made of brass rather than steel. But for the material, these were identical to the Type II.

VG	EX	LN	RARITY
20	35	50	2

118L TUNNEL: This tunnel was made with the same dies as was the metal 118. However, it was illuminated, with the light shining not only from the portals but also from the houses on each side.

VG	EX	LN	RARITY
40	75	150	6

119 TUNNEL: Cataloged from 1915 through 1942, this tunnel was designed for use with either Standard or 0 Gauge trains. During this time, it was produced in a number of variations.

119 TUNNEL (Type I): From 1915 until about 1919, the 119 was made of hand-painted papier-mâché. It was 16" long and was reinforced with a steel brace. A house appeared to be standing on the mountainside.

119 TUNNEL (Type II): About 1920, steel began to be used for the interior of the tunnel, with brass for the exterior. All the 119 tunnels built hence would be of metal construction. The ends of the tunnel were embossed to simulate stone portals. The entire unit was hand-painted. This version continued to be produced through 1923.

VG	EX	LN	RARITY
20	35	50	2

119 TUNNEL (Type III): About 1924, representations of a house and bridge were added to the mountainside. The tunnel continued unchanged through 1942.

VG	EX	LN	RARITY
20	35	50	2

119L TUNNEL: This illuminated version of the metal 119 was sold from 1927 through 1933. A white two-story house stood on the mountainside.

VG	EX	LN	RARITY
40	75	150	6

120 TUNNEL: Cataloged from 1915 through 1927, this tunnel was designed for use with either Standard or 0 Gauge trains. During this time, it was produced in a number of variations.

120 TUNNEL (Type I): From 1915 until 1921, the 119 was made of hand-painted papier-mâché. It was 20" long and was reinforced with a steel brace. A house appeared to be standing on the mountainside.

120 TUNNEL (Type II): In 1922, the tunnel began to be made of steel, the material it continued to be produced with through 1927. Its length was reduced to 17". A hand-painted waterfall appeared on its side, as well as a separately installed white two-story house with maroon roof.

VG	EX	LN	RARITY
35	75	125	4

120 TUNNEL (Type III): Later versions of the tunnel added a chimney to the house, which also sported a red roof.

VG	EX	LN	RARITY
35	75	125	4

120L TUNNEL: This metal tunnel, sold in 1927-42, was the same as the metal 120, but had two bulbs lighting its interior.

120L TUNNEL (Type I): As first produced, the tunnel was painted in rather drab colors. Two houses with cream walls stood on the mountainside.

VG	EX	LN	RARITY
50	100	200	4

120L TUNNEL (Type II): Later production used more vivid colors and the walls of the houses were yellow.

VG	EX	LN	RARITY
50	100	200	4

121 STATION: Lionel cataloged stations with this number from 1908 through 1926, but there were several distinct varieties sold during that time.

121 STATION (Type I): From 1908 through 1917, Lionel cataloged this lithographed station, which was in fact made by Ives. The Lionel version was lettered "TICKET OFFICE" above its door, whereas the Ives version was lettered "TELEGRAPH – OFFICE".

RARITY
Too rarely, if ever, traded to establish market pricing.

121 STATION (Type II): In 1917, Lionel changed suppliers for the 121 station, going to Schoenhut, who supplied a structure made of wood and composition board. The 13 1/2" wide, 9" deep, 13" tall station was sold through 1920.

VG	EX	LN	RARITY
175	225	275	5

121 STATION (Type III): In 1920, Lionel brought the manufacture of the 121 in-house. Sold through 1926, the building was made of steel that had been embossed to represent brick walls. Brass signs were installed: a hanging sign reading "LIONEL CITY", and a sign on the door lettered "WAITING – ROOM". No lights were installed in the 13 1/2" wide station. The station had a gray base, pea green roof, doors and windows, and brown walls.

VG	EX	LN	RARITY
150	200	250	4

121 STATION (Type IV): Some of the stations had doors painted to resemble wood grain. This version had a gray-speckled base.

VG	EX	LN	RARITY
150	200	250	4

121X STATION: An illuminated version of the early 121 was cataloged as well from 1917 through 1919. It too was made for Lionel by Schoenhut.

RARITY
Too rarely, if ever, traded to establish market pricing.

122 STATION: Cataloged from 1920 through 1931, this was the illuminated version of the Lionel-produced 121.

122 STATION (Type I): The station had a gray base, pea green roof, doors and windows, and brown walls.

VG	EX	LN	RARITY
75	150	225	4

122 STATION (Type II): Some of the stations had doors painted to resemble wood grain. This version had a gray-speckled base.

VG	EX	LN	RARITY
75	150	225	4

123 STATION: Once again using the sheet metal components of the Lionel-produced 121, this 1920-23 station was like the 122 illuminated – but this time with a 110-volt bulb! It was provided with a power cord to connect it to household current.

VG	EX	LN	RARITY
150	225	350	6

123 TUNNEL: This fiber 18" wide curved 0 Gauge tunnel was sold from 1933 through 1942.

VG	EX	LN	RARITY
75	150	225	4

124 STATION: The 121 tooling was used yet again to create this station, first from 1920 to 1930, then again from 1933 through 1936. With this version, not only were there interior lights, but it also had two light fixtures under the eaves on corners. It used the same brass "WAITING – ROOM" and "LIONEL CITY" signs as did the 121.

Price Guide Key: **VG** = Very Good, **EX** = Excellent, **LN** = Like New | *Values for each condition are in U.S. dollars.* | **Rarity** = Scale from 1-8 with 8 being the hardest to find.

124 STATION (Type I): One version of the 124 had terra-cotta walls and cream trim, and was mounted on a tan base. Its roof and windows were pea green, its doors red. It had brass light fixtures and black cardstock arrival signs.

VG	EX	LN	RARITY
100	200	300	4

124 STATION (Type II): Identical stations were assembled on dark gray bases.

VG	EX	LN	RARITY
100	200	300	4

124 STATION (Type III): Some stations were even built with pea green bases. These stations had red roofs and cream trim.

VG	EX	LN	RARITY
200	300	400	5

124 STATION (Type IV): Some of the stations with gray bases had pea green doors. These stations had no cardstock arrival signs.

VG	EX	LN	RARITY
100	200	300	4

124 STATION (Type V): Nickel light fixtures were mounted on some of the stations with pea green bases.

VG	EX	LN	RARITY
100	200	300	4

124 STATION (Type VI): Nickel light fixtures were used on stations with speckled tan bases as well.

VG	EX	LN	RARITY
100	200	300	4

125 STATION: Sold from 1923 through 1925, this station's walls were lithographed to represent red brick and were attached to a dark mojave base. Two chimneys stood over the pea green roof, which had two arched dormers. The station had an arched brass ticket window; the rest of the windows were white. A brass sign reading "LIONELVILLE" was attached to the front of the station, while an "EXPRESS" sign was attached above one end door, and a "BAGGAGE" sign above the other. The 10" wide, 7" deep, 7 1/2" tall station was not illuminated.

VG	EX	LN	RARITY
100	150	225	4

125 TRACK TEMPLATE: This 1938 template included patterns to use when designing layouts made with 072, 0 or 027 track, switches and crossovers.

VG	EX	LN	RARITY
2	5	10	7

126 STATION: This was an illuminated version of the 125. Sold from 1923 through 1936, the early stations were lithographed while later versions were painted.

126 STATION (Type I): A station with lithographed brick walls and pea green roof was built on a light gray base. The front and rear doors were Stephen Girard green, while the baggage and express doors were maroon. The station had an arched brass ticket window; the rest of the windows were white. A brass sign reading "LIONELVILLE" was attached to the front of the station, while an "EXPRESS" sign was attached above one end door, and a "BAGGAGE" sign above the other. The station was 10" wide, 7" deep, and 7 1/2" tall.

VG	EX	LN	RARITY
75	125	200	4

126 STATION (Type II): Another version of the station still had lithographed brick walls and pea green roof, but was built on a dark gray base. These stations had dark green door frames, and mojave front and rear doors. The baggage and express doors continued to be maroon. Also used on this version were the brass ticket window, white window inserts and brass signs.

VG	EX	LN	RARITY
75	125	200	4

126 STATION (Type III): Rather than being lithographed, the walls of this station were painted with red crackle enamel. The station had a pea green roof and doors, and was mounted on a mojave base. Its door frames were ivory as were its windows, except for the brass ticket window. A brass sign reading "LIONELVILLE" was attached to the front of the station, while an "EXPRESS" sign was attached above one end door, and a "BAGGAGE" sign above the other. The station was 10" wide, 7" deep and 7 1/2" tall.

VG	EX	LN	RARITY
100	150	225	4

126 STATION (Type IV): This station was identical to the one listed previously as Type III, but its window inserts were pea green.

VG	EX	LN	RARITY
100	150	225	4

126 STATION (Type VI): Stations were built with white window inserts as well. The remainder of the station was identical to the Type III.

VG	EX	LN	RARITY
100	150	225	4

126 STATION (Type VII): Some stations were built with mustard-colored painted walls. These had light red roofs, doors and ticket windows. They were attached to green bases. They had white door frames and other windows.

VG	EX	LN	RARITY
200	275	375	6

126 STATION (Type VIII): In 1930, Ives sold this station as its catalog number 226. Attached to the maroon walls of the station was a brass sign reading "THE IVES RAILWAY LINES". The roof was maroon, and the building had white door frames and green doors.

VG	EX	LN	RARITY
200	275	375	6

127 STATION: Sold from 1923 through 1936, this structure was intended to represent a small rural or suburban station. Its walls were stamped to look like clapboard siding and a sign reading "LIONELTOWN" hung above the door frames. Two chimneys rose over the roof. There was an arched window on either side of the front and rear doors, and rectangular windows on the end of the building. The 8 1/2" wide, 4 1/2" deep, 5" tall station was illuminated.

127 STATION (Type I): This white station was attached to a cream base. It had a red roof, yellow doors and windows, and door and window frames painted 45N green. The signs were nickel. Rubber-stamped on the underside of the base was "No. 127 STATION - MADE BY - THE LIONEL CORPORATION - NEW YORK - U.S. OF AMERICA".

VG	EX	LN	RARITY
75	110	150	3

127 STATION (Type II): The station was also made with mustard walls, maroon roof and dark gray base. This version had dark green door and window frames, and simulated wood-grained doors. The window inserts were Stephen Girard green. The signs were brass.

VG	EX	LN	RARITY
100	150	225	6

127 STATION (Type III): Ivory-colored walls were used on some stations. These stations were attached to gray bases and had red roofs. Dark green door and window frames were

Price Guide Key: **VG** = Very Good, **EX** = Excellent, **LN** = Like New | *Values for each condition are in U.S. dollars.* | **Rarity** = Scale from 1-8 with 8 being the hardest to find.

335

installed, as were maroon doors and peacock window inserts. Brass signs were used on this station.

VG	EX	LN	RARITY
75	110	150	3

127 STATION (Type IV): Stations were made with white walls attached to mustard-colored bases. The door and window frames of these stations were green. The doors themselves, as well as the window inserts, were yellow. White chimneys rose above the red roof. The signs above the doors were nickel.

VG	EX	LN	RARITY
75	110	150	3

127 STATION (Type V): Mustard-colored bases were also used with cream walls. These stations had red roofs and lithographed brick chimneys. The door and window frames were painted peacock. The doors themselves were red and the window inserts light yellow. Brass signs were used on this station.

VG	EX	LN	RARITY
100	150	225	4

127 STATION (Type VI): The station was also made with dark ivory walls, maroon roof and dark gray base. This version had dark green door and window frames, and simulated wood-grained doors. The window inserts were Stephen Girard green. The signs were brass.

VG	EX	LN	RARITY
75	110	150	3

127 STATION (Type VII): Apple green replaced Stephen Girard green on the window inserts of some stations with mustard walls, maroon roofs and dark gray bases. This version had dark green door and window frames, and simulated wood-grained doors. The signs were brass.

VG	EX	LN	RARITY
75	110	150	3

127 STATION (Type VIII): Light mojave bases were used with cream walls. These stations had red roofs and yellow-painted chimneys. The door and window frames were painted peacock. The doors themselves were red and the window inserts cream. Brass signs were used on this station.

VG	EX	LN	RARITY
75	110	150	3

127 STATION (Type IX): Stations were made with white walls attached to mustard-colored bases. The door and window frames of these stations were peacock. The doors themselves, as well as the window inserts, were cream. White chimneys rose above the red roof. The signs above the doors were nickel.

VG	EX	LN	RARITY
75	110	150	3

128 STATION AND TERRACE: From 1928 through 1942, Lionel sold this combination accessory made up of a 129 terrace and a station.

128 STATION AND TERRACE (Type I): From 1928 through 1930, a 124 station was packaged with the terrace.

VG	EX	LN	RARITY
1000	1500	2100	6

128 STATION AND TERRACE (Type II): Between 1931 and 1934, the 113 station was combined with the terrace.

VG	EX	LN	RARITY
1050	1600	2200	6

128 STATION AND TERRACE (Type III): From 1935 until production ended in 1942, the 115 station was placed on the terrace.

VG	EX	LN	RARITY
1200	1800	2500	6

128 TUNNEL: This tunnel was cataloged in 1920, but is not known to have been produced.

RARITY
Too rarely, if ever, traded to establish market pricing.

129 TERRACE: This massive structure was offered from 1928 through 1942. Its elaborate raised oval platform was designed to support a station, replicating a major metropolitan station. Elegant railings on each end supported lamp posts, and partially enclosed landscaped plots holding an urn on one end and a flagpole on the other. This landscaping is fragile and is often damaged or missing today. The terrace is 18" wide and 31 1/2" long.

129 TERRACE (Type I): As first produced, the terrace was light mojave. It had white railings with pea green decoration. The lamp posts were painted gold and the flagpole pedestal was brass.

VG	EX	LN	RARITY
600	900	1200	6

129 TERRACE (Type II): Light cream base and railings were used on later production terraces. Red trim was installed on the railings, as were aluminum-painted lamp posts. The flagpole pedestal was nickel.

VG	EX	LN	RARITY
800	1200	1700	7

129 TUNNEL: This tunnel was cataloged in 1920, but is not known to have been produced.

RARITY
Too rarely, if ever, traded to establish market pricing.

130 TUNNEL: This tunnel was cataloged in 1920, but is not known to have been produced.

RARITY
Too rarely, if ever, traded to establish market pricing.

130 TUNNEL: Sold in 1926, this 0 Gauge tunnel formed a 90-degree curve. Though made of steel, it represented a snow-capped mountain that was home to five small houses. Its ends were embossed to resemble stone tunnel portals. It was 14 1/2" tall and had a 26" x 23" footprint.

VG	EX	LN	RARITY
200	400	1000	8

130L TUNNEL: This illuminated 0 Gauge curved tunnel was cataloged from 1927 through 1933.

130L TUNNEL (Type I): The 1927 edition was merely the 1926 130 with the addition of lighting.

VG	EX	LN	RARITY
200	400	1000	8

130L TUNNEL (Type II): From 1928 through 1933, the tunnel was resized. It became 14 1/2" tall with an 18 1/2" x 14 1/2" footprint.

VG	EX	LN	RARITY
100	200	500	6

131 CORNER ELEVATION: Offered from 1924 through 1928, this plot was sold individually as well as being used as a component of the scenic railway. It was made of steel.

VG	EX	LN	RARITY
125	250	500	6

132 CORNER GRASS PLOT: Another segment that was also offered from 1924 through 1928, this plot was sold individually as well as being used as a component of the scenic railway. It was made of steel.

VG	EX	LN	RARITY
125	250	500	6

133 HEARTSHAPE GRASS PLOT: Another segment that was also offered from 1924 through 1928, this plot was sold individually as well as being used as a component of the scenic railway. It was made of steel.

VG	EX	LN	RARITY
125	250	500	6

134 OVAL GRASS PLOT: Another segment that was also offered from 1924 through 1928, this plot was sold individually as well as being used as a component of the scenic railway. It was made of steel.

VG	EX	LN	RARITY
125	250	500	6

134 STATION: Sold from 1937 until World War II forced the cessation of toy train sales, this station was merely a 124 with the addition of a bimetallic train-stop circuit. The colors of the building were changed as well.

134 STATION (Type I): Initially, nickel exterior light fixtures were attached on the outside of the station, which had tan walls, a red roof and a 45N green base. The windows had ivory frames with white inserts. The doors were white as well. Nickel was used for the signs.

VG	EX	LN	RARITY
175	275	450	5

134 STATION (Type II): On later stations, the exterior light fixtures were painted an aluminum color.

VG	EX	LN	RARITY
175	275	450	5

135 SMALL CIRCULAR GRASS PLOT: Another segment that was also offered from 1924 through 1928, this plot was sold individually as well as being used as a component of the scenic railway. It was made of steel.

VG	EX	LN	RARITY
100	200	400	6

136 LARGE ELEVATION: Another segment that was offered from 1924 through 1928 was this plot, again sold individually as well as being used as a component of the scenic railway. It was made of steel.

VG	EX	LN	RARITY
125	250	500	6

136 STATION: Sold from 1937 until World War II forced the cessation of toy train sales, this station was merely a 126 with the addition of a bimetallic train-stop circuit.

136 STATION (Type I): Initially, the station had cream walls, a red roof and a 45N green base. The windows had white inserts. The doors were red with white frames. Brass was used for the signs.

VG	EX	LN	RARITY
75	125	175	4

Price Guide Key: **VG** = Very Good, **EX** = Excellent, **LN** = Like New | *Values for each condition are in U.S. dollars.* | **Rarity** = Scale from 1-8 with 8 being the hardest to find.

136 STATION (Type II): On later stations, the signs were nickel.

VG	EX	LN	RARITY
75	125	175	4

136 STATION (Type III): Some stations were made with mustard walls and chimneys, red roof and 45N green base. The signs on these stations were made of aluminum with "LIONELVILLE" picked out in red, while "BAGGAGE" and "EXPRESS" were picked out in black.

VG	EX	LN	RARITY
125	250	400	6

136 STATION (Type IV): The station was also made with dark cream walls and chimneys. This version had vermilion doors, windows and roof. The signs were made of nickel.

VG	EX	LN	RARITY
100	225	350	5

137 STATION: Sold from 1937 until World War II forced the cessation of toy train sales, this station was merely a 127 with the addition of a bimetallic train-stop circuit.

137 STATION (Type I): This station had ivory walls and a vermilion roof. It was mounted on a tan base. The door and window frames were pea green, while the doors themselves were cream, as were the window inserts.

VG	EX	LN	RARITY
100	150	225	4

137 STATION (Type II): Other stations were built with white walls and a vermilion roof. The bases on these stations were tan, but the windows and doors were yellow.

VG	EX	LN	RARITY
100	150	225	4

137 STATION (Type III): Ivory walls were also used to build a station on a dark cream base. Its roof was light red. And the window frames and door were painted 45N green.

VG	EX	LN	RARITY
100	150	225	4

140L TUNNEL: Sold for use with both 0 and Standard Gauge trains from 1927 through 1932, this tunnel forms a 90-degree curve. Though made of steel, it represented a snow-capped mountain that was home to seven small houses. Its ends were embossed to resemble stone tunnel portals. It was 20" tall and had a 24 1/2" x 37" footprint. One bulb was installed near each portal for illumination.

VG	EX	LN	RARITY
600	1200	2000	7

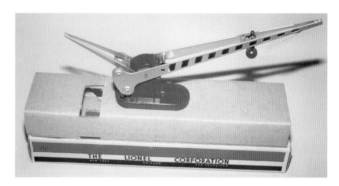

152 AUTOMATIC CROSSING GATE (Type I): Available in 1940-42, this gate was reissued postwar. Up until 1941, all the gates were painted silver, as they were postwar. The die-cast base was painted red. A red bulb hung beneath the gate and a small pedestrian gate extended from the back of the base. Today this small gate is often missing.

VG	EX	LN	RARITY
20	40	55	5

152 AUTOMATIC CROSSING GATE (Type II): During 1942, the gates themselves were painted 92 gray. The die-cast base continued to be painted red.

VG	EX	LN	RARITY
25	50	60	6

153 AUTOMATIC BLOCK SIGNAL AND CONTROL: Although initially offered in 1940-42, the 153 returned in 1945 for a much longer run, staying in the catalog through 1959. It had a green die-cast base, an orange ladder and a black signal head mounted on a silver-colored post. It was furnished with a 153C contactor.

Signals produced prior to World War II used screw-base bulbs operating on six to eight volts. This required the installation of a resistor by Lionel, which is visible on the underside of the signal.

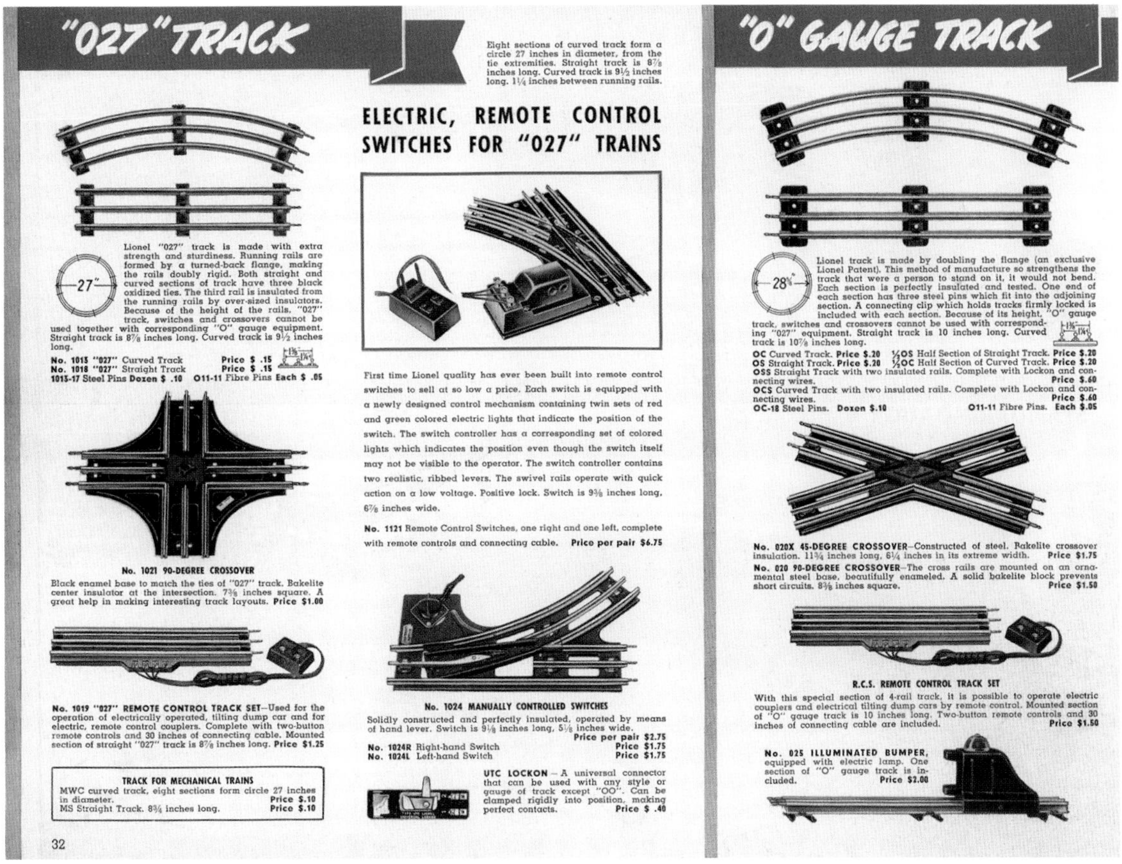

"027" TRACK

Eight sections of curved track form a circle 27 inches in diameter, from the tie extremities. Straight track is $8\frac{7}{8}$ inches long. Curved track is $9\frac{1}{2}$ inches long. $1\frac{1}{4}$ inches between running rails.

27"

Lionel "027" track is made with extra strength and sturdiness. Running rails are formed by a turned-back flange, making the rails doubly rigid. Both straight and curved sections of track have three black oxidized ties. The third rail is insulated from the running rails by over-sized insulators. Because of the height of the rails, "027" track, switches and crossovers cannot be used together with corresponding "O" gauge equipment. Straight track is $8\frac{7}{8}$ inches long. Curved track is $9\frac{1}{2}$ inches long.

No. 1013 "027" Curved Track **Price $ .15**
No. 1018 "027" Straight Track **Price $ .15**
1013-17 Steel Pins **Dozen $ .10** **O11-11** Fibre Pins **Each $ .05**

No. 1021 90-DEGREE CROSSOVER

Black enamel base to match the ties of "027" track. Bakelite center insulator at the intersection. $7\frac{3}{8}$ inches square. A great help in making interesting track layouts. **Price $1.00**

No. 1019 "027" REMOTE CONTROL TRACK SET—Used for the operation of electrically operated, tilting dump car and for electric, remote control couplers. Complete with two-button remote controls and 30 inches of connecting cable. Mounted section of straight "027" track is $8\frac{7}{8}$ inches long. **Price $1.25**

TRACK FOR MECHANICAL TRAINS

MWC curved track, eight sections form circle 27 inches in diameter. **Price $.10**
MS Straight Track. $8\frac{3}{4}$ inches long. **Price $.10**

ELECTRIC, REMOTE CONTROL SWITCHES FOR "027" TRAINS

First time Lionel quality has ever been built into remote control switches to sell at so low a price. Each switch is equipped with a newly designed control mechanism containing twin sets of red and green colored electric lights that indicate the position of the switch. The switch controller has a corresponding set of colored lights which indicates the position even though the switch itself may not be visible to the operator. The switch controller contains two realistic, ribbed levers. The swivel rails operate with quick action on a low voltage. Positive lock. Switch is $9\frac{3}{8}$ inches long, $6\frac{7}{8}$ inches wide.

No. 1121 Remote Control Switches, one right and one left, complete with remote controls and connecting cable. **Price per pair $6.75**

No. 1024 MANUALLY CONTROLLED SWITCHES

Solidly constructed and perfectly insulated, operated by means of hand lever. Switch is $9\frac{1}{8}$ inches long, $5\frac{1}{8}$ inches wide. **Price per pair $2.75**
No. 1024R Right-hand Switch **Price $1.75**
No. 1024L Left-hand Switch **Price $1.75**

UTC LOCKON—A universal connector that can be used with any style or gauge of track except "OO". Can be clamped rigidly into position, making perfect contacts. **Price $ .40**

32

"O" GAUGE TRACK

28⅝"

Lionel track is made by doubling the flange (an exclusive Lionel Patent). This method of manufacture so strengthens the track that were a person to stand on it, it would not bend. Each section is perfectly insulated and tested. One end of each section has three steel pins which fit into the adjoining section. A connecting clip which holds tracks firmly locked is included with each section. Because of its height, "O" gauge track, switches and crossovers cannot be used with corresponding "027" equipment. Straight track is 10 inches long. Curved track is $10\frac{7}{8}$ inches long.

OC Curved Track. **Price $.20** **½OS** Half Section of Straight Track. **Price $.20**
OS Straight Track. **Price $.20** **½OC** Half Section of Curved Track. **Price $.20**
OSS Straight Track with two insulated rails. Complete with Lockon and connecting wires. **Price $.60**
OCS Curved Track with two insulated rails. Complete with Lockon and connecting wires. **Price $.60**
OC-18 Steel Pins. **Dozen $.10** **O11-11** Fibre Pins. **Each $.05**

No. 020X 45-DEGREE CROSSOVER—Constructed of steel. Bakelite crossover insulation. $11\frac{3}{4}$ inches long, $6\frac{1}{4}$ inches in its extreme width. **Price $1.75**

No. 020 90-DEGREE CROSSOVER—The cross rails are mounted on an ornamental steel base, beautifully enameled. A solid bakelite block prevents short circuits. $8\frac{3}{8}$ inches square. **Price $1.50**

R.C.S. REMOTE CONTROL TRACK SET

With this special section of 4-rail track, it is possible to operate electric couplers and electrical tilting dump cars by remote control. Mounted section of "O" gauge track is 10 inches long. Two-button remote controls and 30 inches of connecting cable are included. **Price $1.50**

No. 025 ILLUMINATED BUMPER, equipped with electric lamp. One section of "O" gauge track is included. **Price $2.00**

1938 CATALOG

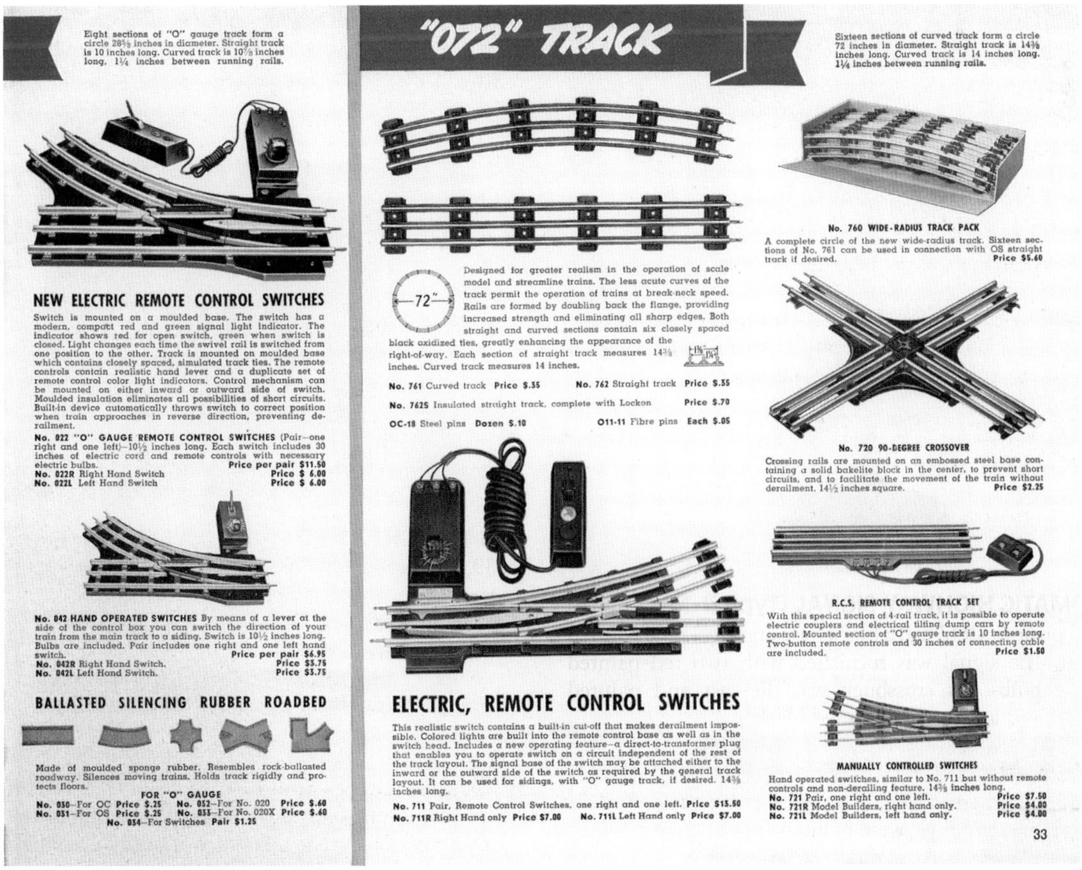

Eight sections of "O" gauge track form a circle $28\frac{5}{8}$ inches in diameter. Straight track is 10 inches long. Curved track is $10\frac{7}{8}$ inches long, $1\frac{1}{4}$ inches between running rails.

NEW ELECTRIC REMOTE CONTROL SWITCHES

Switch is mounted on a moulded base. The switch has a modern, compact red and green signal light indicator. The indicator shows red for open switch, green when switch is closed. Light changes each time the swivel rail is switched from one position to the other. Track is mounted on moulded base which contains closely spaced, simulated track ties. The remote controls contain realistic hand lever and a duplicate set of remote control color light indicators. Control mechanism can be mounted on either inward or outward side of switch. Moulded insulation eliminates all possibilities of short circuits. Built-in device automatically throws switch to correct position when train approaches in reverse direction, preventing derailment.

No. 022 "O" GAUGE REMOTE CONTROL SWITCHES (Pair—one right and one left)—$10\frac{1}{2}$ inches long. Each switch includes 30 inches of electric cord and remote controls with necessary electric bulbs. **Price per pair $11.50**
No. 022R Right Hand Switch **Price $ 6.00**
No. 022L Left Hand Switch **Price $ 6.00**

No. 042 HAND OPERATED SWITCHES By means of a lever at the side of the control box you can switch the direction of your train from the main track to a siding. Switch is $10\frac{1}{2}$ inches long. Bulbs are included. Pair includes one right and one left hand switch. **Price per pair $6.95**
No. 042R Right Hand Switch. **Price $3.75**
No. 042L Left Hand Switch. **Price $3.75**

BALLASTED SILENCING RUBBER ROADBED

Made of moulded sponge rubber. Resembles rock-ballasted roadway. Silences moving trains. Holds track rigidly and protects floors.

FOR "O" GAUGE
No. 030—For OC **Price $.25** **No. 032**—For No. 020 **Price $.60**
No. 031—For OS **Price $.25** **No. 033**—For No. 020X **Price $.60**
No. 034—For Switches **Pair $1.25**

"072" TRACK

72"

Designed for greater realism in the operation of scale model and streamline trains. The less acute curves of the track permit the operation of trains at break-neck speed. Rails are formed by doubling back the flange, providing increased strength and eliminating all sharp edges. Both straight and curved sections contain six closely spaced black oxidized ties, greatly enhancing the appearance of the right-of-way. Each section of straight track measures $14\frac{3}{8}$ inches. Curved track measures 14 inches.

No. 761 Curved track **Price $.35** **No. 762** Straight track **Price $.35**
No. 762S Insulated straight track, complete with Lockon **Price $.70**
OC-18 Steel pins **Dozen $.10** **O11-11** Fibre pins **Each $.05**

ELECTRIC, REMOTE CONTROL SWITCHES

This realistic switch contains a built-in cut-off that makes derailment impossible. Colored lights are built into the remote control base as well as in the switch head. Includes a new operating feature—a direct-to-transformer plug that enables you to operate switch on a circuit independent of the rest of the track layout. The signal base of the switch may be attached either to the inward or the outward side of the switch as required by the general track layout. It can be used for sidings, with "O" gauge track, if desired. $14\frac{3}{8}$ inches long.

No. 711 Pair, Remote Control Switches, one right and one left. **Price $13.50**
No. 711R Right Hand only **Price $7.00** **No. 711L** Left Hand only **Price $7.00**

Sixteen sections of curved track form a circle 72 inches in diameter. Straight track is $14\frac{3}{8}$ inches long. Curved track is 14 inches long. $1\frac{1}{4}$ inches between running rails.

No. 760 WIDE-RADIUS TRACK PACK

A complete circle of the new wide-radius track. Sixteen sections of No. 761 can be used in connection with OS straight track if desired. **Price $5.60**

No. 720 90-DEGREE CROSSOVER

Crossing rails are mounted on an embossed steel base containing a solid bakelite block in the center, to prevent short circuits, and to facilitate the movement of the train without derailment. $14\frac{1}{2}$ inches square. **Price $2.25**

R.C.S. REMOTE CONTROL TRACK SET

With this special section of 4-rail track, it is possible to operute electric couplers and electrical tilting dump cars by remote control. Mounted section of "O" gauge track is 10 inches long. Two-button remote controls and 30 inches of connecting cable are included. **Price $1.50**

MANUALLY CONTROLLED SWITCHES

Hand operated switches, similar to No. 711 but without remote controls and non-derailing feature. $14\frac{3}{8}$ inches long.
No. 721 Pair, one right and one left. **Price $7.50**
No. 721R Model Builders, right hand only. **Price $4.00**
No. 721L Model Builders, left hand only. **Price $4.00**

33

1938 CATALOG

VG	EX	LN	RARITY
40	55	70	6

153 AUTOMATIC BLOCK SIGNAL AND CONTROL (Type I): From 1940 until early 1942, the signal head of the 153 was mounted on an aluminum-colored pole.

VG	EX	LN	RARITY
30	40	50	3

153 AUTOMATIC BLOCK SIGNAL AND CONTROL (Type II): Due to a shortage of aluminum pigment, signals produced in 1942 had their masts painted 92 gray.

VG	EX	LN	RARITY
40	55	70	6

153C CONTACTOR: Introduced in 1940, this was a single pole, double throw pressure-activated momentary contact switch for use actuating signals. It could also be used to control a second train on a loop. The collectable value is in the box.

VG	EX	LN	RARITY
1	2	10	1

154 AUTOMATIC HIGHWAY SIGNAL: This signal has the distinction of being shown in every consumer catalog produced from 1940 through 1969. Even more remarkable are the relatively few variations in such a long-lived item. The signal was always furnished with a 154C contactor, which used a split contact to make the two red bulbs of the 154 flash alternately.

154 AUTOMATIC HIGHWAY SIGNAL (Type I): Most signals produced prior to 1942 had a black base and steel pole painted aluminum. The signal was furnished with two red-painted screw-base bulbs. Its crossbuck was die-cast and painted white. Its raised letters were painted black.

VG	EX	LN	RARITY
30	40	50	3

154 AUTOMATIC HIGHWAY SIGNAL (Type II): Due to a shortage of aluminum pigment, signals produced in 1942 had their masts painted 92 gray.

154 AUTOMATIC HIGHWAY SIGNAL (Type III): A few signals were produced that had the die-cast base painted Hiawatha orange. The poles for these signals, capped with a nickel finial, were painted aluminum color.

VG	EX	LN	RARITY
50	75	100	7

155 FREIGHT SHED: Cataloged from 1930 through 1942, the 155 represented the simple covered freight dock, typical of those that would have handled less-than-carload shipments of the era. The floor of the dock, which would have been at boxcar-floor height, was replicated by the 155's raised steel base. Three die-cast poles support the roof, with three finials holding it in place. Two light fixtures were mounted beneath the roof for nighttime operation. The freight shed was 18" long, 8 1/2" wide and 11" tall.

155 FREIGHT SHED (Type I): For its first nine years, 1930-39, the base of the freight shed was painted yellow with a terra-cotta floor. Its maroon roof was supported by pea green posts and retained with brass finials. A brass builder's plate was installed.

VG	EX	LN	RARITY
175	250	350	5

VG	EX	LN	RARITY
90	150	225	6

155 FREIGHT SHED (Type II): In 1940, the color scheme changed. Now, the base was painted white with a red floor. The roof color was changed to gray with red trim, and aluminum-colored posts supported it. A brass builder's plate was installed. This version was cataloged into 1942.

VG	EX	LN	RARITY
225	325	450	6

155 FREIGHT SHED (Type III): At some point, the builder's plate began to be made of nickel.

VG	EX	LN	RARITY
225	325	450	6

155 FREIGHT SHED (Type IV): The aluminum pigment shortage of 1942 caused the color of the posts to be changed to 92 gray. At the same time, black finials began to be used as well.

VG	EX	LN	RARITY
325	425	550	6

156 ILLUMINATED STATION PLATFORM (Type I): This station platform was cataloged prewar 1939-42, but was also available postwar 1946-51. The base and roof were Bakelite, painted green and red respectively, while the posts supporting the roof were silver-painted die-cast parts. Sections of black plastic picket fence connected the posts, and a separately provided fence section could be used to connect two or more platforms together. Two lights were installed under the roof and four lithographed tin miniature billboards hung from the picket fences.

VG	EX	LN	RARITY
60	100	150	4

156 ILLUMINATED STATION PLATFORM (Type II): The aluminum pigment shortage of 1942 caused the color of the posts to be changed to 92 gray. At the same time, black finials began to be used as well.

157 HAND TRUCK: This red die-cast two-wheel hand truck was sold separately during 1930-32, and included in 163 Freight Accessory Sets through 1942.

VG	EX	LN	RARITY
20	30	40	2

158 STATION SET: Sold from 1940 through 1942, this combination consisted of a 136 station and two 156 platforms packaged together. The original box is crucial for the values listed.

VG	EX	LN	RARITY
400	700	1000	7

159C BLOCK CONTROL CONTACTOR SET: Introduced in 1940, this was a single pole, double throw pressure-activated momentary contact switch for use actuating signals. It could also be used to control a second train on a loop. Packaged with it were a lockon and two fiber pins. It was discontinued in 1942.

VG	EX	LN	RARITY
10	15	25	4

160 UNLOADING BIN: This plastic tray, usually black although sometimes mottled, was produced from 1938 through 1942, and into the postwar era. It was designed to receive coal and logs from various operating cars.

VG	EX	LN	RARITY
1	1	2	1

161 BAGGAGE TRUCK: This metal four-wheel hand truck, sold separately during 1930-32 and included in 163 Freight Accessory Sets through 1942, was produced in both pea green and 45N green. There is no difference in value due to color.

VG	EX	LN	RARITY
30	40	55	3

Price Guide Key: **VG** = Very Good, **EX** = Excellent, **LN** = Like New | *Values for each condition are in U.S. dollars.* | **Rarity** = Scale from 1-8 with 8 being the hardest to find.

341

162 DUMP TRUCK: This metal four-wheel hand truck was sold separately during 1930-32, and included in 163 Freight Accessory Sets through 1942.

162 DUMP TRUCK (Type I): This was a red hand truck with gray dump bin.

RARITY
Too rarely, if ever, traded to establish market pricing.

162 DUMP TRUCK (Type II): An orange hand truck had a blue dump bin.

VG	EX	LN	RARITY
30	50	75	4

162 DUMP TRUCK (Type III): A terra-cotta hand truck had a peacock dump bin.

VG	EX	LN	RARITY
30	50	75	4

162 DUMP TRUCK (Type IV): This yellow hand truck had a green dump bin.

VG	EX	LN	RARITY
35	60	90	6

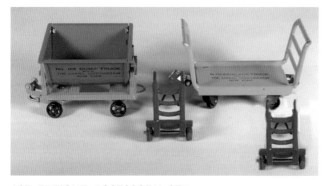

163 FREIGHT ACCESSORY SET: Packaged as a unit in a special box from 1930 through 1942, this set contained many items typically found at freight sheds. The accessory set consisted of two 157 hand trucks, one 161 baggage truck and one 162 dump truck. The presence of the original box is crucial for the values listed.

VG	EX	LN	RARITY
175	250	350	5

164 LOG LOADER: This imposing accessory was first offered from 1940 through 1942. Revived after WWII, it was produced again from 1946 through 1950. Like the 97 coal elevator, the 164 was designed to be placed between two tracks 15" on center. The accessory used the same controller as the 97. Turning it "on" started a motor, which drove a conveyor and lifted the logs up into a loading bin. Pushing the "dump" button lowered two posts and allowed the logs to roll into the car waiting below.

When first produced in 1940, the power terminals protruded through the side of the green-painted Bakelite base. Beginning in 1941, the terminals were relocated to the top, adjacent to the loading bin. The postwar version can be distinguished by having two small holes in the base directly under the conveyor chains.

164 LOG LOADER (Type I): Initially the roof supporting structure was painted silver.

VG	EX	LN	RARITY
150	225	350	4

164 LOG LOADER (Type II): The die-cast struts supporting the roof were painted gray in 1942 because of wartime shortages of aluminum pigment.

VG	EX	LN	RARITY
200	275	400	5

164 LOG LOADER (Type III): Some of the log loaders packed in the 186 Accessory Set had orange roofs.

VG	EX	LN	RARITY
225	325	450	7

165 MAGNETIC CRANE: Produced from 1940 into 1942, this crane shares many components with the 2660 crane. It had a green-painted Bakelite base with a sheet-metal tower structure. On top of the tower was mounted a crane cab. An elaborate gearbox and clutch mechanism converted the power from the unit's motor, based on that used in the 00 gauge Hudson, into up and down cable and revolving crane movements. The position of the boom was controlled manually, just as it was on the 2660. The nicely detailed electro-magnet, which lifted the 182-22 scrap steel supplied with the crane, was marked "Cutler Hammer". The boom was green and had "LIONEL CRANE" molded in its sides.

165 MAGNETIC CRANE (Type I): As first produced, the crane had an aluminum-painted tower and top, and glossy green base.

VG	EX	LN	RARITY
200	275	375	4

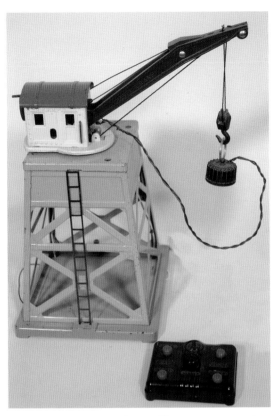

165 MAGNETIC CRANE (Type II): During 1942, the tower and tower top were painted gray. The base was matte green.

VG	EX	LN	RARITY
300	375	475	6

166 WHISTLE CONTROLLER: Sold in 1938-39, this whistle controller resembled the 66.

VG	EX	LN	RARITY
5	7	10	1

167 WHISTLE AND DIRECTION CONTROLLER: Produced in assorted versions between 1939 and 1942 (none particularly collectible), this two-button controller could be used to control the operation of the train's E-unit and whistle/horn.

VG	EX	LN	RARITY
4	8	15	1

167X WHISTLE AND DIRECTION CONTROLLER: Intended specifically for use with 00 Gauge trains, this item was produced from 1940 through 1942.

VG	EX	LN	RARITY
10	20	30	6

168 MAGIC ELECTROL CONTROLLER: Production of the two-train Magic-Electrol sets of 1940-42 brought about the creation of this special controller. Its two buttons could selectively be used to cycle the reversing mechanism of either locomotive.

168 MAGIC ELECTROL CONTROLLER (Type I): Some of the Magic Electrol controllers resembled the 167 Whistle Controller.

VG	EX	LN	RARITY
10	20	30	6

168 MAGIC ELECTROL CONTROLLER (Type II): Others looked much like the control for a 1019 remote-control track section.

VG	EX	LN	RARITY
10	20	30	6

169 DIRECTION CONTROLLER: Another special controller developed for use with the semiscale switchers was this 1940-42 product. Its two buttons were used to control Teledyne couplers and Magic Electrol reversing mechanisms.

VG	EX	LN	RARITY
10	20	30	6

170 DC REDUCER: This item was made to reduce 220 volts DC to levels required to run toy trains. It was sold from 1914 through 1938. During this period, some parts of New York City had Direct Current, rather than the alternating current now standard throughout the United States.

VG	EX	LN	RARITY
10	20	30	6

171 DC TO AC INVERTER: Sold from 1936 through 1942, this unit converts 115-volt DC current to 2- to 30-volt variable AC output.

VG	EX	LN	RARITY
4	8	15	5

172 DC TO AC INVERTER: Sold from 1936 through 1942, this unit converts 220-volt DC current to 2- to 30-volt variable AC output.

VG	EX	LN	RARITY
4	8	15	5

Price Guide Key: **VG** = Very Good, **EX** = Excellent, **LN** = Like New | *Values for each condition are in U.S. dollars.* | **Rarity** = Scale from 1-8 with 8 being the hardest to find.

343

186 ILLUMINATED BUNGALOW SET: The 184 bungalows were also sold in sets of five from 1923 through 1932. The presence of the original box is required for the values listed here.

VG	EX	LN	RARITY
400	1000	1800	6

184 BUNGALOW: This illuminated sheet-metal house was sold individually from 1923 through 1932. It remained available, though installed on Scenic Plots, through 1942. This little (4 1/2" by 2 1/2" by 4" tall) structure was produced in far too many variations to list in this book. Both enamel and lithographed finishes were used during the course of this unit's production.

VG	EX	LN	RARITY
40	90	150	5

186 LOG LOADER OUTFIT: This elaborate accessory set was sold only in 1940 and 1941. The large original box, which is required for the values listed here, contained the following: 164 log loader, 3651 lumber dump car, 160 unloading bin, RCS remote control track section and logs.

VG	EX	LN	RARITY
500	800	1200	6

187 BUNGALOW SET: The 185 bungalows were also sold in sets of five during 1931-32. The presence of the original box is required for the values listed here.

VG	EX	LN	RARITY
400	1000	1800	7

185 BUNGALOW: During 1923-24, this non-illuminated version of the 184 was available. It came in many variations, but not as many as the longer-lived 184.

VG	EX	LN	RARITY
50	100	175	6

188 COAL ELEVATOR OUTFIT: This elaborate accessory set was sold from 1938 through 1941. The large original box, which is required for the values listed here, contained the following: 97 coal loader, 3659X coal dump car, 160 unloading bin, RCS remote control track section and two 206 sacks of coal.

VG	EX	LN	RARITY
500	800	1200	6

191 VILLA: This large illuminated sheet-metal house is readily identified by its two-story, hip roof construction. It was sold individually from 1923 through 1932. It remained available, though installed on Scenic Plots, through 1942. This 7 1/8" by 5" by 5 1/4" tall structure was produced in too many variations to list in this book. Both enamel and lithographed finishes were used during the course of the villa's production.

VG	EX	LN	RARITY
150	275	400	4

189 VILLA: This large illuminated sheet-metal house was sold individually from 1923 through 1932. It remained available, though installed on Scenic Plots, through 1942. This 5 3/8" by 4 7/8" by 5 1/2" tall structure was produced in too many variations to list in this book. Both enamel and lithographed finishes were used during the course of the villa's production.

VG	EX	LN	RARITY
150	250	375	4

192 ILLUMINATED VILLA SET: Offered from 1923 through 1932, this set contained two 184 bungalows, a 189 villa and a 191 villa. The original set packaging is critical to establishing the set's authenticity.

VG	EX	LN	RARITY
1500	2500	4000	8

193 AUTOMATIC ACCESSORY SET: This 0 Gauge combination pack was sold only from 1927 until 1929. Packed in a single box, which is now critical to its value, were one each: 069 warning bell, 076 block signal, 077 crossing gate, 078 train control signal, 080 semaphore, as well as five sections of insulated OSS track to control the myriad of devices.

VG	EX	LN	RARITY
250	500	800	6

194 AUTOMATIC ACCESSORY SET: Also sold during 1927-29, this was the Standard Gauge equivalent of the 193: This set contained one each of the 69 warning bell, 76 block signal, 77 crossing gate, 78 train control signal, 80 semaphore and five sections SS insulated control track. Like the 193, the original box is key to attaining these values.

VG	EX	LN	RARITY
200	400	700	5

195 ILLUMINATED TERRACE: Attached to the scenic-detailed 22" x 19" plywood base of this accessory were the

Price Guide Key: **VG** = Very Good, **EX** = Excellent, **LN** = Like New | *Values for each condition are in U.S. dollars.* | **Rarity** = Scale from 1-8 with 8 being the hardest to find.

345

following items: 191 villa, 185 villa, 184 bungalow, 90 flagpole and two 56 lamp posts. It was sold from 1927 through 1930.

VG	EX	LN	RARITY
400	800	1600	8

196 ACCESSORY SET: These items were sold as a set only in1927. Like all this type combination pack, the original box holds the key to the value. This set contained the following: 127 station, two 58 lamp posts, six 60 telegraph poles, one 62 semaphore and one 68 warning signal.

VG	EX	LN	RARITY
250	500	800	6

200 TURNTABLE: From 1928 into 1933, Lionel sold this Standard Gauge turntable. It was 17" in diameter, ironically meaning it couldn't handle steam locomotives, but only electrics, which didn't need to be turned anyway! A brass knob and gear, cranked by hand, turned the center disk, which held a section of straight track. It was designed to accommodate eight approach tracks.

200 TURNTABLE (Type I): Most of these turntables had a red rotating platform mounted in a pea green base.

VG	EX	LN	RARITY
75	125	200	4

200 TURNTABLE (Type II): Some of the pea green base units had a mojave rotating platform installed.

VG	EX	LN	RARITY
75	125	200	4

200 TURNTABLE (Type III): A few units were made with a red platform mounted on a black base.

VG	EX	LN	RARITY
200	350	550	6

205 MERCHANDISE CONTAINERS: Lionel cataloged this set of three less than carload lot (LCL) containers from 1930 through 1938. The sheet-metal boxes, with hinged, opening doors, were painted dark green. The trim, as well as a nameplate above the door reading "LIONEL - RAILWAY EXPRESS", was made of brass. Inserted in a holder attached to the door was a slip of paper printed with "The L.C.L. Corporation - Merchandise Container – Patented".

VG	EX	LN	RARITY
125	225	350	6

206 ARTIFICIAL COAL: From 1938 through 1942, these half-pound cloth bags filled with ground Bakelite "coal" were sold by Lionel dealers. The white bags were lettered with red "No. 206" "ARTIFICIAL COAL" and Lionel markings.

VG	EX	LN	RARITY
5	10	15	3

207 SACK OF COAL: This larger bag of artificial coal was also sold from 1938 through 1942. It held about three-fourths pound of ground Bakelite.

VG	EX	LN	RARITY
5	10	15	3

208 TOOL SET: This tool box, containing miniatures of the tools used by section gangs, was included in Lionel work train sets from 1928 through 1932. It was also cataloged separately through 1942. The cast iron tools were nickel-plated.

208 TOOL SET (Type I): As first produced, the toolbox was painted gray and had a brass handle. It had rubber-stamped lettering "TOOL BOX" in gold.

VG	EX	LN	RARITY
50	150	275	5

208 TOOL SET (Type II): The next version of the toolbox produced was rubber-stamped in black rather than gold.

VG	EX	LN	RARITY
50	150	275	5

208 TOOL SET (Type III): The third version produced was painted an aluminum color. Its handle was nickel and it was rubber-stamped in black.

VG	EX	LN	RARITY
50	150	275	5

208 TOOL SET (Type IV): The toolbox of the final version was painted 92 gray. It had black rubber-stamped "TOOL BOX" lettering.

VG	EX	LN	RARITY
75	200	350	6

209 BARRELS: This set of four hollow Standard Gauge barrels was included in Lionel work train sets from 1930 through 1932. It was also cataloged separately through 1942. The drums pulled apart in the center. The values indicated presume the presence of the original box.

209 BARRELS (Type I): From 1930 through 1934, the sides of the barrels were arced, as they were on full-sized wooden barrels.

VG	EX	LN	RARITY
150	225	300	6

209 BARRELS (Type II): Beginning in 1935, the design of the barrels was changed to resemble that of steel drums. It continued this way through 1942.

VG	EX	LN	RARITY
150	225	300	6

0209 BARRELS: An 0 gauge version of Lionel's wooden replica of a steel drum was sold as well. Packaged as a set of six, these also pulled open in the middle. Barrels were sold after World War II with the same catalog number, but they were solid wood turnings.

VG	EX	LN	RARITY
100	175	250	5

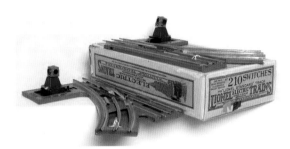

210 PAIR OF MANUAL TURNOUTS: Cataloged from 1926 through 1942 was this pair of illuminated manual Standard Gauge turnouts, consisting of one 210L and one 210R.

VG	EX	LN	RARITY
20	30	40	3

210L LEFT HAND MANUAL TURNOUT: Lionel's replacement for the 21 left hand Standard Gauge turnout was the 210L. Made from sheet metal, the illuminated turnout was operated by a control lever affixed to a short steel tower, the top of which housed the bulb in a removable cubical housing. The light shone through two red and two green celluloid disks. These turnouts were sold from 1926 into 1942.

210L LEFT HAND MANUAL TURNOUT (Type I): During the first two years of production, 1926-27, the turnout base was unpainted metal with a black lantern support and control housing.

VG	EX	LN	RARITY
10	15	20	3

210L LEFT HAND MANUAL TURNOUT (Type II): Some of the 1926-27 turnouts had their bases painted pea green. On this turnout, the control housing and lantern support was painted red.

VG	EX	LN	RARITY
10	15	20	3

210L LEFT HAND MANUAL TURNOUT (Type III): From 1928 through 1933, the turnout again had a pea green base. But the control lever housing was dark green.

VG	EX	LN	RARITY
10	15	20	3

210L LEFT HAND MANUAL TURNOUT (Type IV): Starting in 1934, the base of the turnout was black.

VG	EX	LN	RARITY
10	15	20	3

210R RIGHT HAND MANUAL TURNOUT: Naturally, a right hand turnout was produced from 1926 through 1942 as well. It was made in the same variations as the left hand turnout.

VG	EX	LN	RARITY
10	15	20	3

217 LIGHTING SET: This item was sold to allow interior illumination to be added to passenger cars from 1914 through 1923. The set consisted of three wooden sockets with 14-volt bulb, connected by wire insulated with green cloth. Clamps were included to aid installation.

VG	EX	LN	RARITY
20	35	50	4

220 PAIR OF MANUAL TURNOUTS: This pair of manually operated, non-illuminated Standard Gauge turnouts was sold in 1926.

VG	EX	LN	RARITY
20	40	70	5

222 PAIR OF REMOTE CONTROL TURNOUTS: Starting in 1926, and continuing until the 1931 edition, the Lionel catalog listed these Standard Gauge turnouts. The pair consisted of one each illuminated 222L and one 222R turnouts with a pair of controllers.

VG	EX	LN	RARITY
40	60	100	3

222L LEFT HAND REMOTE CONTROL TURNOUT: Production of this Standard Gauge turnout began in 1926 and continued through 1931. Though similar to the 210, these illuminated turnouts differed in having a solenoid-actuated operating mechanism. These were each furnished with a controller, which was connected by means of a three-wire cable.

222L LEFT HAND REMOTE CONTROL TURNOUT (Type I): During the first two years of production, 1926-27, the turnout base was unpainted metal with a red lantern support and nickel control housing. The controller wiring permanently attached.

VG	EX	LN	RARITY
20	30	50	3

Price Guide Key: **VG** = Very Good, **EX** = Excellent, **LN** = Like New | *Values for each condition are in U.S. dollars.* | **Rarity** = Scale from 1-8 with 8 being the hardest to find.

347

222L LEFT HAND REMOTE CONTROL TURNOUT (Type II): Some of the 1926-27 turnouts had their bases painted pea green. On these turnouts the control housing and lantern support were painted red. The turnout came with a red lantern support and nickel control housing. The controller wiring permanently attached.

VG	EX	LN	RARITY
20	30	50	3

222L LEFT HAND REMOTE CONTROL TURNOUT (Type III): In 1928, the turnout was redesigned. Now, three screw-type terminals were provided, to which the controller wires were attached. The turnout continued to be produced in this form through 1930.

VG	EX	LN	RARITY
20	30	50	3

222L LEFT HAND REMOTE CONTROL TURNOUT (Type IV): In 1931, a non-derailing feature was added to the turnout. The feature utilized an insulated approach rail to energize the turnout solenoid. Normally, the circuit was open, but the wheels and axle of the approaching train served to "make" the ground leg of the control circuit.

VG	EX	LN	RARITY
30	45	60	5

222R RIGHT HAND REMOTE CONTROL TURNOUT: Naturally, a right hand 222 remote control turnout was produced from 1926 through 1931 as well. It was made in the same variations as the left hand turnout listed above.

RARITY
Each variation valued the same as the corresponding 222L variation.

223 PAIR OF REMOTE CONTROL TURNOUTS: From 1932 into 1942, Lionel sold these illuminated Standard Gauge remote control turnouts. The pair consisted of one each illuminated 223L and one 223R turnouts with two controllers.

VG	EX	LN	RARITY
60	90	125	3

223L LEFT HAND REMOTE CONTROL TURNOUT: In 1932, the non-derailing Standard Gauge turnout was given a new catalog number, 223. It was still illuminated, and came with a separate controller. It continued to be available into 1942.

223L LEFT HAND REMOTE CONTROL TURNOUT (Type I): During 1932-33, the base of the turnout was pea green.

VG	EX	LN	RARITY
30	45	60	3

223L LEFT HAND REMOTE CONTROL TURNOUT (Type II): About 1934, the base of the turnout became black, the color it would be for the remainder of its production.

VG	EX	LN	RARITY
30	45	60	5

223R RIGHT HAND REMOTE CONTROL TURNOUT: Of course, a right hand 223 remote control turnout was sold during 1932-42. It was made in the same variations as the left hand turnout.

VG	EX	LN	RARITY
30	45	60	5

225 REMOTE CONTROL TURNOUT SET: One of Lionel's more elaborate packagings of turnouts was this 1929-32 pair of remote control Standard Gauge, 222 turnouts with a 439

control panel. The original box is a significant portion of the value listed.

VG	EX	LN	RARITY
125	250	400	7

270 BRIDGE: Between 1931 and 1942, this 0 Gauge truss bridge was sold. Made of sheet metal, it simulated open girder-type construction with pedestrian walkways on each side. The side members of the bridge were low and rectangular. The bridge was 10" long, 6 3/8" wide, 3" high and accommodated one section of OS track.

270 BRIDGE (Type I): One of the earliest versions of this bridge was painted light red. A brass builder's plate was installed on each side.

VG	EX	LN	RARITY
25	35	50	4

270 BRIDGE (Type II): Another early version of the bridge was maroon. It too had builder's plates made of brass.

VG	EX	LN	RARITY
25	35	50	4

270 BRIDGE (Type III): The maroon version was also built with nickel builder's plates, probably in 1935-36.

VG	EX	LN	RARITY
25	35	50	4

270 BRIDGE (Type IV): Aluminum plates replaced the nickel ones about 1937, and continued to be used through the end of production.

VG	EX	LN	RARITY
25	35	50	4

270 BRIDGE (Type V): Probably in 1942, some bridges were painted vermilion. These had aluminum or nickel plates.

VG	EX	LN	RARITY
25	35	50	4

270 BRIDGE (Type V): Another 1942 aberration was a red bridge with no plate at all. Instead yellow decals with a green "LIONEL" were applied where the plates normally were installed.

VG	EX	LN	RARITY
50	75	125	7

270 LIGHTING SET: This item was sold to allow interior illumination to be added to passenger cars from 1915 through 1923. The set consisted of two wooden sockets with eight-volt bulbs, connected by wire insulated with green cloth. This set was intended for use with DC current.

VG	EX	LN	RARITY
20	35	50	4

271 LIGHTING SET: This item was sold to allow interior illumination to be added to passenger cars from 1915 through 1923. The set consisted of two wooden sockets with 14-volt bulb, connected by wire insulated with green cloth. This set was intended for use with AC current.

VG	EX	LN	RARITY
20	35	50	4

271 BRIDGES: Cataloged from 1931 through 1940, except 1934, this was a set of two matching 270 Bridges. Much of the value is in the original packaging.

VG	EX	LN	RARITY
150	250	400	6

272 BRIDGES: Cataloged from 1931 through 1940, except 1934, this was a set of three matching 270 Bridges. Much of the value is in the original packaging.

VG	EX	LN	RARITY
250	450	750	8

280 BRIDGE: This Standard Gauge truss bridge was sold from 1931 through 1942. A pedestrian walkway was on either side of the tapered truss. The bridge was 14" long and accepted a single piece of type S track.

280 BRIDGE (Type I): As first produced, the bridge was gray and had brass nameplates installed.

VG	EX	LN	RARITY
50	80	125	4

280 BRIDGE (Type II): The bridge was also made in red, again with brass nameplates.

VG	EX	LN	RARITY
50	80	125	4

280 BRIDGE (Type III): About 1936, the bridge began to be painted pea green. Soon thereafter, the nameplate changed from brass to nickel.

VG	EX	LN	RARITY
50	80	125	4

280 BRIDGE (Type IV): About 1939, the color of green changed to the same shade used on the base of the 45N gateman and many other accessories. The nameplate was nickel.

VG	EX	LN	RARITY
50	80	125	4

281 BRIDGES: Cataloged from 1931 through 1940, except 1934, this was a set of two matching 280 Bridges. Much of the value is in the original packaging.

VG	EX	LN	RARITY
150	250	400	6

282 BRIDGES: Cataloged from 1931 through 1940, except 1934, this was a set of three matching 280 Bridges. Much of the value is in the original packaging.

VG	EX	LN	RARITY
250	450	750	8

300 HELL GATE BRIDGE: This was the largest of Lionel's bridges. Stretching 28 1/2" long and 11" wide, while standing 10 1/2" tall, it was designed to accept Standard Gauge trains, but clearly 0 Gauge track could be used instead. Styled along the lines of New York's famed Hell Gate bridge (spanning the East River), its four towers, though made of pressed steel, simulated stone. Like the real Hell Gate (an abomination for the old Dutch name given to the body of water beneath it "Hellegat" or "beautiful strait"), Lionel's bridge was a steel arch bridge (not a suspension bridge as many believe).

300 HELL GATE BRIDGE (Type I): Though the steelwork of the real bridge was (and is) red, Lionel chose to paint the arch on its replica green when it was introduced in 1928. The simulated stone towers were painted cream, and the base of the bridge, which was flat–allowing to be placed directly on the floor–was orange. The bridge was trimmed in brass and continued in this color scheme through 1934.

VG	EX	LN	RARITY
800	1100	1400	6

Price Guide Key: **VG** = Very Good, **EX** = Excellent, **LN** = Like New | *Values for each condition are in U.S. dollars.* | **Rarity** = Scale from 1-8 with 8 being the hardest to find.

349

300 HELL GATE BRIDGE (Type II): Some of these bridges were built with a terra-cotta base.

VG	EX	LN	RARITY
800	1100	1400	6

300 HELL GATE BRIDGE (Type III): Though the real bridge has only been painted twice, when it was new in 1917 and again in the late 1980s, in 1935 Lionel changed the color scheme of its replica. The steel work of the bridge became aluminum-colored, while the base was red. The towers remained ivory. At the same time, the trim material was changed to nickel. This version was shipped into 1941, or perhaps early 1942.

VG	EX	LN	RARITY
1000	1500	2100	7

300 HELL GATE BRIDGE (Type IV): The very last of these bridges produced, perhaps in late 1941 or early 1942, had black oxide railings and stanchions.

VG	EX	LN	RARITY
1200	1800	2500	8

301 BATTERIES: Home electrical service was not common in the early years of the 20th century. For this reason, Lionel listed sets of four dry cell batteries in its 1903-05 catalogs. "Everbest Dry Cell" batteries were shown in the 1903 catalog, in 1904 the type changed to "Eastern Dry Cell No. 3", and in 1905 the "Climax Dry Cell" was shown.

RARITY
No known surviving examples.

302 PLUNGE BATTERY: Offered in 1901 and 1902, the plunge battery was described in the latter catalog as four glass jars containing a carbon cylinder and pencil-shaped zinc in a wood box. Water and three pounds of "electric sand" charged the four cells, which were connected in series.

RARITY
No known surviving examples.

303 CARBON CYLINDERS: This electrical component was listed in the 1902 catalog.

RARITY
No known surviving examples.

304 COMPOSITE ZINCS: This electrical component was listed in the 1902 catalog.

RARITY
No known surviving examples.

305 ELECTRIC SAND: This electrical component was listed in the 1902 catalog.

RARITY
No known surviving examples.

306 GLASS JARS: This electrical component was listed in the 1902 catalog.

RARITY
No known surviving examples.

308 RAILROAD SIGN SET: This item, initially sold 1940-42, returned to the Lionel catalog in 1945-49. The set included five different die-cast sign posts. They were painted white with black lettering. The original box is important to the value of this item.

308 RAILROAD SIGN SET (Type I): Initially the bases of the signs were painted green and had artificial grass added.

VG	EX	LN	RARITY
35	50	75	5

308 RAILROAD SIGN SET (Type II): In later production, the rectangular bases were painted white.

VG	EX	LN	RARITY
35	50	75	5

308 RAILROAD SIGN SET (Type III): For the final production, the white bases were round.

VG	EX	LN	RARITY
35	50	75	5

310 TRACK (Type I): The track available in 1901 and 1902 can best be described as primitive. It is the only Lionel track that can be truly termed rare. Loose tinplated straight steel rails about 13 3/8" long were furnished with wooden cross ties. The rails, which were all straight, were 3/8" high and 1/16" wide. The crossties were actually made of wood and stained red. They were 4" long, 1" wide and 1/16" tall. Grooves were cut across the ties 2 7/8" apart to accept the rails.

Brass plates on the outer two of the five ties per "section" were equipped with brass plates that provided electrical contact to the next section. A tack held each brass plate in place. Curved track was created by bending the rails, then trimming the inner rail to the proper length.

RARITY
Too rarely, if ever, traded to establish market pricing.

310 TRACK (Type II): From 1903 through 1905, an improved version of the 2 7/8-inch gauge track was offered. Still assembled from component parts by the owner, it was now packaged as 24 tinplated steel rails with 60 wooden cross ties. Still 3/8" tall and 1/16" wide, the rails were shortened to about 12" long. The crossties were natural wood color and wood 4" long, 1/2" wide and 1/2" tall. The ties continued to be routed to accept the steel rails.

The ends of the rails were now bent to form hooks, which engaged abutting rail sections. The rails were now furnished in two different lengths, eliminating the need for the owner to trim the inner rail on curves to length, although the curve itself still had to be manually formed.

VG	EX	LN	RARITY
75	125	200	-

313 BASCULE BRIDGE: Debuting in 1940, this impressive accessory was discontinued in 1942, returning in 1946 before being discontinued again in 1949. The prewar version is distinguished by having a square gearbox inside the support tower nearest the bridge tender's house. Postwar, the gearbox was L-shaped. The base of the lifting span was green-painted Bakelite, whereas the fixed base was green-painted die-cast. Note on some examples, impurities in the zinc alloy have caused crystallization and disintegration. Also, the tension of the counterbalancing spring can cause the base to warp over time. It is recommended that this tension be relieved prior to storing the bridge for an extended period of time. A black steel alignment frame was originally supplied with this bridge. Its purpose was to maintain the alignment of the lift span and adjoining track when neither the track nor the bridge were permanently fastened down. Prewar, and for the first two years postwar, the warning lamp lens on the lift span was a smooth-topped R-68 red lens. The bridge tender's house was painted a pale yellow with orange windows and a red roof.

313 BASCULE BRIDGE (Type I): In 1940 and 1941, the superstructure of the bridge was painted silver.

VG	EX	LN	RARITY
300	525	675	5

313 BASCULE BRIDGE (Type II): Bridges assembled in 1942 had their upper works painted gray.

VG	EX	LN	RARITY
400	625	775	7

314 PLATE GIRDER BRIDGE: Another prewar carry-over bridge was this 10" single-track span. Sold prewar in 1940-42, it returned postwar in 1945-50. Its rounded-end die-cast girder sides were painted gray during the postwar era and were riveted to the heavy sheet-metal base. The word "LIONEL" was rubber-stamped in black on each side of the bridge.

314 PLATE GIRDER BRIDGE (Type I): In 1940-41, the bridge was painted silver with 9/32" tall "LIONEL" lettering.

VG	EX	LN	RARITY
25	35	50	3

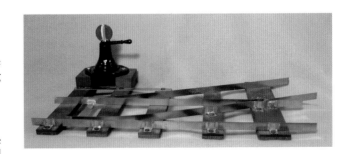

314 PLATE GIRDER BRIDGE (Type II): During 1942, the bridge was painted 92 gray and the rubber-stamped lettering was 5/16" tall.

VG	EX	LN	RARITY
25	35	50	3

315 ILLUMINATED TRESTLE BRIDGE: First available before World War II in 1940-42, this 24 1/2" long bridge returned in 1946-47. Painted silver every year but 1942, when it was

gray, the 315 had the added feature of a glowing red light mounted on top of its superstructure mid-span. The crosspiece supporting the R-68 red lamp cover was stamped with the Lionel name and "315".

315 ILLUMINATED TRESTLE BRIDGE (Type I): This aluminum-colored bridge was sold in 1940-41.

VG	EX	LN	RARITY
75	100	125	5

315 ILLUMINATED TRESTLE BRIDGE (Type II): During 1942, the bridge was painted 92 gray.

VG	EX	LN	RARITY
100	125	150	6

316 TRESTLE BRIDGE: This item, uncataloged in 1941 and 1942, had a one-year reprise in 1949. This 24" long steel bridge had the Lionel nomenclature and stock number embossed in the bottom plate after World War II. This information was rubber-stamped on the prewar version.

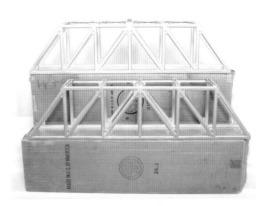

316 TRESTLE BRIDGE (Type I): Initially the bridge was painted an aluminum color.

VG	EX	LN	RARITY
25	40	55	4

316 TRESTLE BRIDGE (Type II): The final versions, likely assembled in 1942, were painted 92 gray.

VG	EX	LN	RARITY
30	50	70	6

Price Guide Key: **VG** = Very Good, **EX** = Excellent, **LN** = Like New | *Values for each condition are in U.S. dollars.* | **Rarity** = Scale from 1-8 with 8 being the hardest to find.

351

320 SWITCH AND SIGNAL: From 1902 through 1905, this 17 1/2" long turnout was marketed. A working cast iron switchstand was included, with red and white signal targets. A single lever moved both the points and the target, just as on a real turnout.

RARITY
Too rarely, if ever, traded to establish market pricing.

330 CROSSING: This 90-degree crossover was cataloged from 1902 through 1905. It mated with the Type II 310 track, and had a square solid base rather than individual crossties.

RARITY
Too rarely, if ever, traded to establish market pricing.

340 SUSPENSION BRIDGE: This hard to find 24" long bridge was sold unassembled during 1902-05. It was cast iron and wooden construction. "LIONEL MFG. CO. - NEW YORK" was cast into the beams forming the top of the sides. Numbers to aid in assembly were also cast into the side members.

340 SUSPENSION BRIDGE (Type I): The 1902 edition of the 340 was 10" high and the beams above the ends of the bridge were straight. The bridge was 6" wide.

RARITY
Too rarely, if ever, traded to establish market pricing.

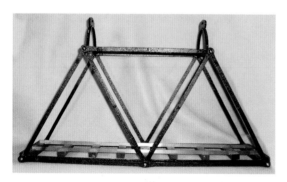

A properly marked reproduction 340 made by Joe Mania Trains. This firm's reproductions are carefully and permanently marked, but beware, others have made unmarked reproductions.

340 SUSPENSION BRIDGE (Type II): From 1903-05, the height of the bridge was increased to 14" high in order to clear the derrick car. The beams over the ends of the bridge were arched on this version to permit greater clearance. The bridge continued to be 6" wide.

RARITY
Too rarely, if ever, traded to establish market pricing.

350 BUMPER: From 1902 through 1905, this end-of-track bumper was offered. Styled after bumpers found in contemporary big city terminals, it was about 4" tall and 4" long, and stood about 3" tall.

350 BUMPER (Type I): The 1902 edition came with a crosstie to be used instead of the normal end tie of the adjoining track. The new tie did not include the brass contact plate, creating an electrically dead section of track in order to stop the train.

RARITY
Too rarely, if ever, traded to establish market pricing.

350 BUMPER (Type II): From 1903 through 1905, the bumper came pre-installed on a short straight section of track. Rather than insulating this section, a spring-loaded striker was incorporated to cushion the blow of the stopping train.

RARITY
Too rarely, if ever, traded to establish market pricing.

370 JARS AND PLATES: During 1902 and 1903, Lionel offered a wet-cell battery consisting of two glass jars containing lead plates and electrolytes.

RARITY
No known surviving examples.

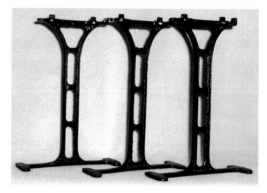

380 ELEVATED PILLARS: In 1904-05, Lionel sold a set of 12 8 1/2" tall cast iron posts to be used in creating an elevated railway. Hardware was included with which to attach the wooden 2 7/8-inch gauge crossties to the pillars.

VG	EX	LN	RARITY
450	850	1200	-

TYPE L
110 Volts — 60 Cycles — 50 Watt Capacity

TYPE B
110 Volts — 60 Cycles — 75 Watt Capacity

Type H
110-115 Volts — 25 to 40 Cycles — 75 Watt Capacity

38 years of Experience
IS BUILT INTO LIONEL TRANSFORMERS

Lionel engineers and craftsmen have been making Lionel Electric Trains since the turn of the century. What they have learned about boys and trains and transformers in all that time is packed inside the case of a Lionel Multivolt Transformer. Here is the very heart of the railroad and here Lionel craftsmanship is at its best. Lionel Electric Trains operate on harmless low voltage. It is necessary to reduce house current, which is usually 110 volts, to as low as 12 volts. When the house current is alternating, called A.C., a transformer is required for this function.*

For this purpose Multivolt Transformers are built in Lionel's own factories, under the skilled supervision of Lionel engineers and with the highest degree of uniformity and accuracy.

Look at the cut-away illustration of a Multivolt. It tells the inside story of transformers. There is no doubtful efficiency and no doubtful safety in the service a Multivolt gives. And a guarantee of proper service is behind it.

Laminations are made of silicon steel. Coils are windings of enameled copper wire, protected by layers of heavy insulation. When the coils are completely wound, they are dipped in varnish and baked to form a hard, moisture-proof unit. Because of the use of these materials and this scientific electrical design, Lionel Multivolt Transformers can withstand many continuous overloads and even temporary short circuits with less danger of "burn-outs". They give the greatest range of fixed voltage, with intervals, or steps, of one or two volts.

The chart below will help you in selecting the proper Lionel Multivolt Transformer for your train. Your local lighting company will tell you the type of current you have in your home; the voltage and the cycles.

Remember, transformers operate only on alternating current (A.C.).

This chart specifies transformers for trains only. If you intend to add many accessories, get a larger unit than that specified.

*If your house is supplied with Direct Current you cannot use a transformer to operate an electric train but must use either a No. 171 Inverter or a No. 107 Reducer. See Page 38 for description and application of these devices.

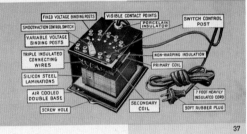

TYPE T
110 Volts — 60 Cycles — 100 Watt Capacity

TYPE K
110 Volts — 60 Cycles — 150 Watt Capacity

Transformer	Cycles	Watts	Range of Voltage	Will Operate	Size	Price
Type "L"	60	50	6 to 15	175E, 176E, 177E, 179E, 181E	3⅜x3½x4"	3.50
Type "B"	60	75	8 to 12-14 to 18 21 to 25	175W, 176W, 177W, 178W, 178E, 179W, 181W, 299W, 267E, 267W, 182E, 182W, 183E, 183W, 295W, 185W, 186W, 187W, 189W, 190W, 191W, 0080, 0080W	4½x5½x3¾"	5.75
Type "H"	25 to 40	75	3 to 7-8 to 12 13 to 17	175E, 176E, 177E, 178E, 179E, 181E 267E, 182E, 183E, 0080	4½x5½x3¾"	6.00
Type "T"	60	100	2 to 10-10 to 18 17 to 25	193W, 194W, 195W, 197W, 758W, 759W, 755W, 767W, 768W, 769W, 366W, 377W, 367W, 369W, 371W, 378W	4½x6x4¼"	8.00
Type "K"	60	150	2 to 10-10 to 18 17 to 25	709W, 356W, 386W	4⅝x6x5"	11.00

Types "L," "B," "T" and "K" are for 110 volts, A.C., 60 cycles. Type "H" is for 110 to 120 volts, A.C., 25 to 40 cycles.

FIXED VOLTAGE BINDING POSTS
VISIBLE CONTACT POINTS
SMOOTHACTION CONTROL SWITCH
PORCELAIN INSULATOR
SWITCH CONTROL POST
VARIABLE VOLTAGE BINDING POSTS
TRIPLE INSULATED CONNECTING WIRES
NON-WARPING INSULATION
SILICON STEEL LAMINATIONS
PRIMARY COIL
AIR COOLED DOUBLE BASE
7 FOOT HEAVILY INSULATED CORD
SECONDARY COIL
SCREW HOLE
SOFT RUBBER PLUG

37

1938 CATALOG

Lionel "Multivolt" Transformers For 110 Volts and 220 Volts— 60, 40 and 25 Cycles

This illustration shows transformer contained within the new Lionel Power Station. They are made in two sizes to accommodate every type of Lionel "Multivolt" Transformer. Full description of this desirable new accessory will be found on Page 39.

The Lionel Power Station is placed over the Transformer, and you can manipulate the controlling switch by simply raising the grating on the roof.

LIONEL "Multivolt" Transformers have been on the market for a great many years and operate all makes of Electric Trains. We justly claim they are best. Don't experiment with other makes of doubtful value. Remember, that all transformers look alike outside, but their imperfections will only be discovered after they are in actual use for a length of time. Lionel "Multivolt" Transformers will last indefinitely and are guaranteed unconditionally as long as they are used on the current for which they are intended. They are absolutely safe and will give steady, even power.

LIONEL "MULTIVOLT" TRANSFORMERS are for use only on Alternating Current. Do not use them on Direct Current.

Type "A" Transformer will operate any "O" gauge outfit.
For 110 volts, 60 cycles. 40 watts capacity.
Gives 4, 7, 10, 13, 15.
Size: 4½ by 2¾ by 4¼ inches. Sub-base: 3¾ by 4½ inches.
Price **$3.75**
Code Word "STRONG"
Note: Type "A" Transformer is recommended for use with the train outfits shown on Page 12.

Type "B" Transformer will operate any "O" gauge outfit, and in addition the extra binding posts enable the user to light up lamp-posts, semaphores and other electrically illuminated accessories.
For 110 volts, 60 cycles. 50 watts capacity.
Gives 25 volts in following steps:
Permanent: 7, 8, 15.
Variable: 2, 4, 6, 8, 9, 10, 11, 12, 13, 17, 19, 21, 23, 25.
Size: 4½ by 3¾ by 3 inches. Sub-base: 5 by 4½ inches.
Price **$5.00**
Code Word "BRADLEY"
A fully guaranteed transformer at a very popular price.

Type "T" Transformer will operate any "O" gauge or "Lionel Standard" outfit; also has extra binding posts for attaching illuminated electrical accessories.
For 110 volts, 60 cycles. 100 watts capacity.
Gives 25 volts in following steps:
Permanent: 2, 4, 6, 7, 8, 10, 12, 14, 11, 16, 17, 18, 19, 21, 23, 25.
Variable: 2, 6, 8, 10, 12, 14, 16, 17, 18, 19, 21, 23, 25.
Size: 5 by 4 by 5½ inches. Sub-base: 4½ by 5½ inches.
Price **$7.50**
Code Word "BIRCH"

Type "K" Transformer will operate any outfit as well as illuminated accessories. This transformer has sufficient wattage capacity to operate two trains at once.
For 110 volts, 60 cycles. 150 watts capacity. Sub-base: 4½ by 5½ inches.
"K"—For 110 volts, 60 cycles, 150 watts capacity. Specifications same as Type "T", but has higher wattage capacity. Price **$11.00**
Code Word (110 V.) "BINGHAM"
"K"—For 220 volts, 60 cycles, 110 watts capacity. Specifications same as Type "K", but is for use on 220-volt circuit.
Price **$14.50**
Code Word (220 V.) "BROOK"

Type "C" Transformer will operate any outfit and illuminated accessories on 25 or 40 cycle current.
For 110 volts, 25 to 40 cycles. 75 watts capacity. Specifications same as Type "T," but is for use on 25 or 40 cycle current.
Size: 5 by 4 by 5½ inches. Sub-base: 4½ by 5½ inches.
Price **$7.50**
Code Word "LAWRENCE"
This transformer is the best obtainable for use on 25 or 40 cycle current.

TYPE A
TYPE B
TYPE T
TYPE K
TYPE C

33

1927 CATALOG

Price Guide Key: **VG** = Very Good, **EX** = Excellent, **LN** = Like New | *Values for each condition are in U.S. dollars.* | **Rarity** = Scale from 1-8 with 8 being the hardest to find.

353

435 POWER STATION: This building, 5" tall, was mounted on a 7 1/2" x 6" base. Built to look like a power substation, it was designed to house a Lionel A or B transformer. A sign was mounted above the door that read "POWER STATION". The 435 was cataloged from 1926 through 1938.

435 POWER STATION (Type I): One of the earliest versions of this power station had terra-cotta walls and mustard roof cornices. It was mounted on a gray base and had a green skylight. Its doors were maroon and mounted in dark green frames, as were the pea green windows. A brass "EDISON SERVICE" sign was over the door rather than a "POWER STATION" sign.

VG	EX	LN	RARITY
300	600	1000	7

435 POWER STATION (Type II): Other stations reversed the colors of the walls and cornices, with the former being mustard and the later terra cotta. These too were mounted on gray bases. The dark green door and window frames were used, but the doors were wood-grained doors. The building had pea green windows and a green skylight.

VG	EX	LN	RARITY
125	250	400	3

435 POWER STATION (Type III): In some cases, the walls were painted ivory with cream roof cornices. The gray base continued to be used, as did the green skylight, and dark green door and window frames. The doors were now red and the windows orange.

VG	EX	LN	RARITY
125	250	400	3

435 POWER STATION (Type IV): Terra-cotta walls were also used in conjunction with light cream roof cornices, with the entire structure mounted on a gray base. These buildings had green skylights and window frames.

VG	EX	LN	RARITY
125	250	400	3

435 POWER STATION (Type V): Ivory walls were combined with terra-cotta roof cornices and a gray base to make some of the power stations. This version had pea green window frames and skylight. The door frame was dark green.

VG	EX	LN	RARITY
125	250	400	3

435 POWER STATION (Type VI): Terra-cotta roof cornices were also used with cream walls and a gray base. A light green skylight and matching window frames were added. The doors were red and mounted with dark green door frames, while the windows were orange. This version lacked the "POWER STATION" sign.

VG	EX	LN	RARITY
150	275	425	4

435 POWER STATION (Type VII): Late in the production life of the 435, the base plate began to be painted 45N green. The walls were cream with mustard roof cornices. The door and window frames, as well as the skylight, were painted red. The doors and windows themselves were painted white. The chimney was painted aluminum color. A brass "POWER STATION" sign was over the door.

VG	EX	LN	RARITY
200	400	700	6

435 POWER STATION (Type VIII): An otherwise identical building was made with a nickel "POWER STATION" sign.

VG	EX	LN	RARITY
200	400	700	6

436 POWER STATION: A larger version of the 435 was the 436. This structure was 5 7/8" tall and was mounted on a 9 1/8" x 7 5/8" base. Built to look like a power substation, it was designed to house a Lionel C, K or T transformer. A sign was mounted above the door that read "POWER STATION". The 436 was cataloged from 1926 through 1937.

436 POWER STATION (Type I): One of the earliest versions of this power station had terracotta walls and yellow roof cornices. It was mounted on a gray base and had a light green skylight. Its doors were maroon and mounted in dark green frames, as were the light green windows. A brass "POWER STATION" sign was over the door.

VG	EX	LN	RARITY
200	400	700	5

436 POWER STATION (Type II): Terra-cotta walls were also used in conjunction with cream roof cornices, with the entire structure mounted on a gray base. These buildings had pea green skylights. The door and window frames were dark green, and the doors themselves red. Orange windows were installed, as was a brass "POWER STATION" sign.

VG	EX	LN	RARITY
150	275	425	4

436 POWER STATION (Type III): Another early version of this power station had terracotta walls and light cream cornices. It was mounted on a gray base and had a pea green skylight. Its doors were maroon and mounted in dark green frames, as were the pea green windows. A brass "EDISON SERVICE" sign was over the door rather than a "POWER STATION" sign.

VG	EX	LN	RARITY
500	900	1700	8

436 POWER STATION (Type IV): Terra-cotta roof cornices were also used with cream walls and a gray base, and a pea green skylight. The door and window frames were dark green. The doors themselves were red, while the windows were orange. A brass "POWER STATION" sign was attached to the building.

VG	EX	LN	RARITY
150	275	425	4

436 POWER STATION (Type V): Late in the production life of the 436, the base plate began to be painted 45N green. The walls were cream with mustard roof cornices. The door and window frames, as well as the skylight, were painted red. The doors and windows were painted white. The chimney was painted aluminum color. A brass "POWER STATION" sign was over the door.

VG	EX	LN	RARITY
150	275	425	4

436 POWER STATION (Type VI): An otherwise identical building was made with a nickel "POWER STATION" sign.

VG	EX	LN	RARITY
150	275	425	4

437 SWITCH SIGNAL TOWER: This large and imposing structure replicated the look of a tower housing a large interlocking plant, like one might have seen during this time in a major metropolitan area. The 10 1/4" x 8 3/8" x 8 7/8" tall tower was sold from 1926 through 1937. The interior was illuminated, and knife switches were mounted on the back for the miniature railroader to use in controlling power to various "blocks" of his railroad. Brackets for mounting switch controllers were also on the rear of the tower. Lionel's towers were painted in elaborate schemes.

437 SWITCH SIGNAL TOWER (Type I): One version of the tower had terra-cotta lower walls, mustard upper walls and an ivory band between floors. The roof was pea green. It had a red door, peacock windows, vermilion trim under the dormer and a red chimney.

VG	EX	LN	RARITY
200	350	550	4

437 SWITCH SIGNAL TOWER (Type II): Another version also had terra-cotta lower walls, but the upper walls were cream. Ivory trim was between the floors. The roof was painted peacock and the tower was mounted on a mojave base. It had orange windows and a red door.

VG	EX	LN	RARITY
300	475	700	5

437 SWITCH SIGNAL TOWER (Type III): Burnt orange lower walls were combined with mustard upper walls for this version. Ivory trim was installed between the floors. The roof was pea green, the base mojave. It had a red door, peacock windows, vermilion trim under the dormer and a red chimney.

VG	EX	LN	RARITY
200	350	550	4

437 SWITCH SIGNAL TOWER (Type IV): White trim separated the burnt orange lower walls from the light mustard upper walls of this version. Its roof and windows were pea green and its base mojave. The door was maroon and there was vermilion trim under the dormer.

VG	EX	LN	RARITY
200	350	550	4

437 SWITCH SIGNAL TOWER (Type V): Looking radically different from the other versions, this tower had yellow lower and upper walls, with brown trim separating them. Its roof was orange and it was mounted on a red base. It had green windows, red doors and a cream chimney.

Price Guide Key: **VG** = Very Good, **EX** = Excellent, **LN** = Like New | *Values for each condition are in U.S. dollars.* | **Rarity** = Scale from 1-8 with 8 being the hardest to find.

355

VG	EX	LN	RARITY
1200	1800	2500	8

438 SIGNAL TOWER: This tower was introduced in 1927 and remained in the product line through 1939. The 12" tall sheet-metal structure was mounted on a 6" x 4 3/4" base. Except for the first year's production, knife switches were mounted on the rear of the building.

438 SIGNAL TOWER (Type I): As built in 1927, the tower had an orange building mounted atop pea green supports that, in turn, were attached to a mojave base

A cream upper base separated the orange from the green. The roof and doors were red and the windows white. Brass ladders and number plate were installed, as was a lithographed brick chimney.

VG	EX	LN	RARITY
300	475	700	6

438 SIGNAL TOWER (Type II): The following year, knife switches were mounted on the rear of the tower, and the color of the chimney changed to cream. The balance of the tower was unchanged.

VG	EX	LN	RARITY
200	325	500	4

438 SIGNAL TOWER (Type III): Later towers had aluminum-painted supporting structures, ivory walls, and gray upper and lower bases. These towers had red roofs, doors, ladders and windows. An ivory chimney was installed, as was a nickel number plate.

VG	EX	LN	RARITY
300	475	700	6

438 SIGNAL TOWER (Type IV): Another late version had white walls and black upper and lower bases. The supporting structure was painted aluminum color. The roof, doors, windows and ladder were red, the chimney white and the nameplate nickel.

VG	EX	LN	RARITY
300	475	700	6

439 PANEL BOARD: Sold from 1928 until World War II halted toy train production, this accessory, similar to the 440C Panel Board, was made of stamped-steel construction. Six knife switches were mounted on a simulated marble control panel. Provision was made for the installation of two switch controllers. Two simulated meters decorated the panel as well, which was illuminated by a hooded lamp at the center top.

439 PANEL BOARD (Type I): Some of these panels had white simulated marble backgrounds mounted on crackle red supports. The switches, meter rims, lamp hood and identification plates were all brass.

VG	EX	LN	RARITY
100	150	200	5

439 PANEL BOARD (Type II): Other boards were identical except they had black simulated marble panels.

VG	EX	LN	RARITY
75	125	175	4

439 PANEL BOARD (Type III): Still others had black simulated marble panels mounted to a maroon supporting structure.

VG	EX	LN	RARITY
75	125	175	4

439 PANEL BOARD (Type IV): Some of these maroon supports had a crackle finish.

VG	EX	LN	RARITY
75	125	175	4

439 PANEL BOARD (Type V): Others had the basic structure painted bright red. These units had black control panel boards. The switches, meter rims, lamp hood and nameplate were all nickel.

VG	EX	LN	RARITY
75	125	175	4

439 PANEL BOARD (Type VI): Nickel trim was also used on some of the maroon painted units.

VG	EX	LN	RARITY
75	125	175	4

440 SIGNAL BRIDGE/0440 SIGNAL BRIDGE: Sold between 1932 and 1935, the 440 Standard Gauge and the 0440 0 Gauge bridge were the same structures. They differed in the gauge of the insulated tracks furnished with each. This imposing structure was designed to span two parallel Standard Gauge tracks, and worked just as well with 0 gauge. Its die-cast bases supported a sheet-metal structure, upon which were installed two black die-cast signal heads. Five lamps shown from each signal head. The bridge came with a 440C Panel Board, which was used to control it.

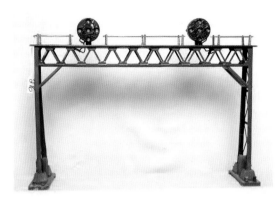

440 SIGNAL BRIDGE/0440 SIGNAL BRIDGE (Type I):
Initially, the bridge was mojave and was supported by die-cast terra-cotta-colored bases. It had a maroon walkway and brass trim.

VG	EX	LN	RARITY
175	250	350	3

440 SIGNAL BRIDGE/0440 SIGNAL BRIDGE (Type II):
Later bridges were painted aluminum. They were attached to two red die-cast bases and had red walkways. The trim on these units was nickel.

VG	EX	LN	RARITY
200	325	450	6

440C PANEL BOARD:
Sold from 1932 until World War II halted toy train production, this accessory, similar to the 440C Panel Board, was made of stamped-steel construction. Four knife switches were mounted on a simulated marble control panel, as were two special switches, which controlled the indication of the signals mound on a 440 Signal Bridge. These two levers were mounted with a plate reading "TRACK" as well as "Go" and "Stop". Provision was made for the installation of two switch controllers as well. Two decorative simulated meters were attached to the panel as well, which was illuminated by a hooded lamp at the center top.

440C PANEL BOARD (Type I):
Some of these panels were made with the supporting structure painted light red. These units had brass nameplates and trim.

VG	EX	LN	RARITY
75	125	175	4

440C PANEL BOARD (Type II):
Others were painted with a glossy red, crackle finish paint. They too had brass trim and nameplates.

VG	EX	LN	RARITY
75	125	175	4

440C PANEL BOARD (Type III):
Flat red paint with a light crackle finish was used on some of the 440C boards as well. These also used brass nameplates and trim.

VG	EX	LN	RARITY
75	125	175	4

440C PANEL BOARD (Type V):
Some of these units were painted red and their switches, meter rims, lamp hood and nameplate were all nickel.

VG	EX	LN	RARITY
75	125	175	4

440C PANEL BOARD (Type VI):
Others had the basic structure painted 92 gray. These units had black control panel boards. The switches, meter rims, lamp hood and nameplate were all nickel.

VG	EX	LN	RARITY
100	150	200	5

440N SIGNAL BRIDGE:
In 1936, the signal bridge began to be cataloged as a universal item, rather than making Standard and 0 Gauge-specific items. It continued to be sold this way, and with the new number "440N", into 1942.

440N SIGNAL BRIDGE (Type I):
Most 440N bridges were painted aluminum. They were attached to two red die-cast bases and had red walkways. The trim on these units was nickel.

VG	EX	LN	RARITY
175	225	275	3

440N SIGNAL BRIDGE (Type II):
In 1942, 92 gray paint replaced the aluminum-colored paint used previously. The rest of the signal bridge was unchanged.

VG	EX	LN	RARITY
250	450	650	6

Price Guide Key: **VG** = Very Good. **EX** = Excellent. **LN** = Like New | *Values for each condition are in U.S. dollars.* | **Rarity** = Scale from 1-8 with 8 being the hardest to find.

357

441 WEIGHING STATION: This unusual Standard Gauge item was sold from 1932 through 1936. The weight of actual railroad cars, and their cargo, is important to real railroads. It affects not only the transportation charges collected, but also motive power selection. Lionel created this miniature weigh station to replicate this action. It had a green die-cast base that included a platform scale. The adjacent cream structure housed the balance beam and separate brass weights, which were accessible through the opening double doors on its rear. Today these weights are often missing. The scale house had a maroon crackle finish roof and terra-cotta window frames. The accessory was 29 1/2" long.

VG	EX	LN	RARITY
500	1000	1500	7

442 LANDSCAPED DINER: This roadside diner was sold from 1938 into 1942. A 610 Pullman roof and body was mounted on a fiberboard foundation and pressed-wood base. Wood and cardboard steps were added, and bits of artificial "shrubbery" provided landscaping. Rather than being rubber-stamped "Pullman", the big letterboard read "DINER", and "EAT" replaced "610" on the two small boards. It was equipped with interior illumination.

442 LANDSCAPED DINER (Type I): Some of these diners had ivory bodies with light red roofs. The doors, windows and plates were red, with silver rubber-stamped lettering. They were mounted on light tan bases, and had pink foundations and steps.

VG	EX	LN	RARITY
150	250	375	5

442 LANDSCAPED DINER (Type II): A duplicate diner was made with red foundation and steps.

VG	EX	LN	RARITY
150	250	375	5

442 LANDSCAPED DINER (Type III): Other diners had cream walls. On these, the roof, doors, windows and letterboards were red. Gold rubber-stamped lettering was applied. They were mounted on a light brown base and had a pink foundation and steps.

VG	EX	LN	RARITY
150	250	375	5

444 ROUNDHOUSE: Sold from 1932 through 1935, this large illuminated roundhouse stall was designed to be combined with others like it to make an even larger structure. It could be used in conjunction with the 200 turntable. It had terracotta walls and a pea green roof with two green skylights, and maroon windows.

VG	EX	LN	RARITY
1200	2000	3000	7

444-18 CLIP: This item was used to join roundhouse sections together.

RARITY
Too rarely traded to establish market pricing.

500 PINE BUSHES: Sold during 1927-28, they were also used on some Scenic Railways.

RARITY
Too rarely traded to establish market pricing.

501 SMALL PINE TREES: Sold during 1927-28, they were also used on some Scenic Railways.

RARITY
Too rarely traded to establish market pricing.

502 MEDIUM PINE TREES: Sold during 1927-28, they were also used on some Scenic Railways.

RARITY
Too rarely traded to establish market pricing.

503 LARGE PINE TREES: Sold during 1927-28, they were also used on some Scenic Railways.

RARITY
Too rarely traded to establish market pricing.

504 ROSE BUSHES: Sold during 1927-28, they were also used on some Scenic Railways.

RARITY
Too rarely traded to establish market pricing.

505 OAK TREES: Sold during 1927-28, they were also used on some Scenic Railways.

RARITY
Too rarely traded to establish market pricing.

506 PLATFORM: A two-section landscaped platform sold during 1924-28, it was also used as part of 198 Scenic Railway.

RARITY
Too rarely traded to establish market pricing.

507 PLATFORM: A three-section landscaped platform sold during 1924-28, it was also used as part of 199 Scenic Railway.

RARITY
Too rarely traded to establish market pricing.

508 SKY: A two-section painted backdrop sold during 1924-28, it was also used as part of 198 and 199 Scenic Railways.

RARITY
Too rarely traded to establish market pricing.

509 COMPOSITION BOARD MOUNTAINS: This hand-painted mountain range sold during 1924-28, and was also used as part of 198 and 199 Scenic Railways.

RARITY
Too rarely traded to establish market pricing.

510 CANNA BUSHES: Sold during 1927-28, they were also used on some Scenic Railways.

RARITY
Too rarely traded to establish market pricing.

550 MINIATURE RAILROAD FIGURES: For four years beginning in 1932, Lionel sold this set of six 3" tall hollow cast figures made by "J. HILL & CO., ENGLAND". The set contained the following figures: 551 Engineer, 552 Conductor, 553 Porter with detachable footstool, 554 Male Passenger, 555 Female Passenger, 556 Red Cap with removable luggage. The original box is a significant part of the values listed here.

VG	EX	LN	RARITY
225	375	550	6

551 ENGINEER: Sold separately in 1932 and as part of the 550 Figure set during 1932-36, this cast engineer figure wore medium or dark blue clothing and carried an aluminum-painted oil can.

VG	EX	LN	RARITY
20	30	40	4

552 CONDUCTOR: Sold separately in 1932 and as part of the 550 Figure set during 1932-36, this cast conductor figure wore black clothing.

VG	EX	LN	RARITY
20	30	40	4

553 PORTER: Sold separately in 1932 and as part of the 550 Figure set during 1932-36, this cast porter figure wore dark blue clothing and came with a removable yellow step box.

VG	EX	LN	RARITY
20	30	40	4

554 MALE PASSENGER: Sold separately in 1932 and as part of the 550 Figure set during 1932-36, this cast man wore brown or mojave clothing.

VG	EX	LN	RARITY
20	30	40	4

555 FEMALE PASSENGER: Sold separately in 1932 and as part of the 550 Figure set during 1932-36, this cast female passenger was produced wearing a variety of different colored clothing.

VG	EX	LN	RARITY
20	30	40	4

556 RED CAP: Sold separately in 1932 and as part of the 550 Figure set during 1932-36, this cast red cap figure wore dark blue clothing and, of course, a red cap. Naturally, he was supplied with luggage.

VG	EX	LN	RARITY
20	30	40	4

711 PAIR OF REMOTE CONTROL TURNOUTS: Sold from 1935 into 1942, these turnouts, one each 711L and 711R, with controllers, matched 0 gauge cross-sectional track. One side was curved to match the radius of 072 track.

VG	EX	LN	RARITY
75	125	200	4

711L LEFT HAND REMOTE CONTROL TURNOUT: Cataloged continuously from 1935 through 1942, these turnouts were similar in appearance to the late O22 turnouts, but had a much wider radius diverging track. Like the O22, they incorporated a non-derailing feature, and their mechanism could be placed on either side of the approaching track. The turnout was 14 3/8" long.

VG	EX	LN	RARITY
40	60	100	4

711R RIGHT HAND REMOTE CONTROL TURNOUT: This was the right-hand version of the 711L, and was also sold from 1935 through 1942.

VG	EX	LN	RARITY
40	60	100	4

720 90-DEGREE CROSSING: This crossing, sold in 1935-42, was manufactured to the same proportions as 072 Gauge track. Its construction was similar to that of the standard 020. It was 14 1/2" across either segment.

VG	EX	LN	RARITY
25	35	45	4

721 PAIR OF MANUAL TURNOUTS: These were non-motorized versions of the 711 turnouts sold from 1935 through 1942.

VG	EX	LN	RARITY
50	75	125	6

721L LEFT HAND MANUAL TURNOUT: This was a left-hand only manual version of the 711.

VG	EX	LN	RARITY
25	40	60	6

Price Guide Key: **VG** = Very Good, **EX** = Excellent, **LN** = Like New | *Values for each condition are in U.S. dollars.* | **Rarity** = Scale from 1-8 with 8 being the hardest to find.

359

721R RIGHT HAND MANUAL TURNOUT: This was a right-hand only manual version of the 711.

VG	EX	LN	RARITY
25	40	60	6

730 90-DEGREE CROSSING: This crossing, sold in 1935-42, was manufactured to the same specifications as Lionel's scale-like T-rail track. It was 14 1/2" across either segment.

VG	EX	LN	RARITY
30	45	60	6

731 PAIR OF REMOTE CONTROL TURNOUTS: Sold in 1935-42, this pair of remote control turnouts was manufactured to the same specifications as Lionel's scale-like T-rail track. Packed in the box were one 731L and one 731R and two controllers.

VG	EX	LN	RARITY
75	125	200	6

731L LEFT HAND REMOTE CONTROL TURNOUT: Like the 711, this was a 072 switch. However, rather than tubular rails, its rails had a realistic solid T-shaped cross-section. It was available from 1935 into 1942.

VG	EX	LN	RARITY
40	60	100	6

731R RIGHT HAND REMOTE CONTROL TURNOUT: This was the right-hand version of the 731L, and was also sold from 1935 through 1942.

VG	EX	LN	RARITY
40	60	100	4

760 072 TRACK: This box of 16 sections of 072 track was available 1938-42, again in 1950 and finally from 1954-58. The 072 designation refers to its 0-gauge cross section and 72 center to center diameter. The prices are predicated on the presence of the original box.

VG	EX	LN	RARITY
50	75	120	5

761 CURVED TRACK: This was a 14" long curved track section. The 072 designation refers to its 0-gauge cross section and 72 center to center diameter.

VG	EX	LN	RARITY
1	2	3	4

762 STRAIGHT TRACK: This was a 15" long straight track section.

VG	EX	LN	RARITY
1	2	3	5

762S STRAIGHT TRACK: This was a 15" long straight track section with one outside rail insulated for control purposes.

VG	EX	LN	RARITY
1	2	3	6

771 CURVED TRACK: This was a 14" long curved track section made with rail that had a T-shaped cross section. Each section of track had 10 crossties. Introduced in 1935, it was sold into 1942.

VG	EX	LN	RARITY
5	10	15	6

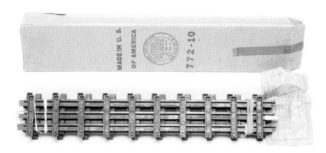

772 STRAIGHT TRACK: This was a 15" long section of T-rail straight track sold from 1935 into 1942.

VG	EX	LN	RARITY
10	15	20	6

772S STRAIGHT TRACK: This was a 15" long section of T-rail straight track with one outside rail insulated for control purposes, which was sold in 1935-42.

VG	EX	LN	RARITY
20	30	40	7

773 FISHPLATE SET: This set of 50 fishplates, 100 bolts, 100 nuts and a wrench was sold from 1935 into 1942. This hardware was used for connecting sections of T-rail track. As opposed to conventional tubular track that used pins, the T-rail track was joined together in a realistic manner.

VG	EX	LN	RARITY
25	50	75	8

812T TOOL SET: This set of oversized section tools was packed with certain 0 gauge work trains between 1930 and 1941.

VG	EX	LN	RARITY
50	100	150	4

840 INDUSTRIAL POWER STATION: Cataloged from 1928 through 1940, this massive structure was Lionel's biggest powerhouse. At 26" wide, 21 1/2" deep and 18" tall, it was the largest accessory in the line. The power station included several loose parts, which are often missing or replaced today. The huge cardboard box did not hold up well, resulting in it adding more than the usual premium when present.

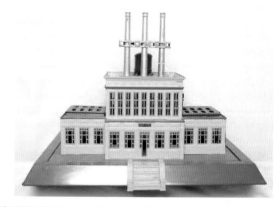

840 INDUSTRIAL POWER STATION (Type I): As originally produced and most commonly found, the 840 had cream walls, an orange roof with matching removable skylights, green windows and was mounted on a green base. Above the station stood a red water tower and three smokestacks supporting a "LIONEL" sign. The power station was illuminated and designed to house Lionel transformers. Six knife switches were installed to control power distribution.

VG	EX	LN	RARITY
1000	1700	2500	7

840 INDUSTRIAL POWER STATION (Type II):
A later version of the power station had white walls, and a red roof and trim.

VG	EX	LN	RARITY
1500	2500	3500	8

910 GROVE OF TREES:
Sold for 10 years beginning in 1932, this scenic accessory had a wooden base about 8" x 16" onto which was mounted a varying number of trees and shrubs. The base was covered in artificial grass and sometimes included "felt" rocks.

VG	EX	LN	RARITY
100	250	500	5

912 SUBURBAN HOME:
Another house sold on a landscaped lot was the 912. In this instance, a 189 villa was mounted on the 16" x 8" wooden base. Once again artificial grass, trees and shrubbery were installed. These were sold from 1932 into 1942, with the houses appearing in a variety of color combinations.

VG	EX	LN	RARITY
200	500	1000	6

913 LANDSCAPED BUNGALOW:
A third variety of pre-landscaped plots with houses was also sold from 1932 into 1942. The 913 came with a 184 bungalow mounted on a 16" x 8" wooden base. Artificial grass, trees and bushes were added to the base. A variety of color combinations of bungalows were used, but that has little effect on the value today.

VG	EX	LN	RARITY
150	300	550	5

911 COUNTRY ESTATE:
This accessory, sold from 1932 into 1942, consisted of a 191 villa mounted on a 16" x 8" wooden base. Artificial grass, trees and bushes were added for landscaping. A variety of color combinations of villas were used, but that has little effect on the value today.

VG	EX	LN	RARITY
200	500	1000	5

914 PARK LANDSCAPE:
One of the many scenic accessories sold by Lionel in the 1930s was this 16" x 8 1/2" oval plot. Cataloged from 1932 through 1936, its plywood base was painted cream, representing concrete walkways amongst the

Price Guide Key: **VG** = Very Good, **EX** = Excellent, **LN** = Like New | *Values for each condition are in U.S. dollars.* | **Rarity** = Scale from 1-8 with 8 being the hardest to find.

361

imitation grass, shrubbery and flowers. A cream-colored urn was mounted in the center.

VG	EX	LN	RARITY
150	350	650	5

915 TUNNEL: This felt composition tunnel, mounted on a wooden base. was designed to accommodate a 90-degree curve of Standard Gauge track. It was sold during 1932-35 and was detailed with bushes, trees and small houses.

915 TUNNEL (Type I): Initially, the tunnel was 65" by 28 1/2" by 23 1/2" tall.

VG	EX	LN	RARITY
150	300	650	8

915 TUNNEL (Type II): Later editions were 60" by 28 3/4" by 20 1/2" tall.

VG	EX	LN	RARITY
100	200	300	5

916 TUNNEL: This felt composition tunnel, mounted on a base, was designed to accommodate a 90-degree curve of 0 Gauge track. It was sold during 1932-42 and was detailed with bushes, trees and three small chalets.

916 TUNNEL (Type I): During its first year of production 1932, the 916 was 37" by 30" and stood 13 1/2" tall.

VG	EX	LN	RARITY
150	300	550	7

916 TUNNEL (Type II): Starting in 1933 and on into 1942, the dimensions changed to 29 1/4" by 24" by 13 1/2" tall.

VG	EX	LN	RARITY
100	200	300	5

917 SCENIC HILLSIDE: This 34" long, 15" wide felt composition hillside was sold during 1932-36. It was detailed with bushes, trees and two small houses.

VG	EX	LN	RARITY
150	200	250	5

918 SCENIC HILLSIDE: (1932-36): This smaller hillside was also sold from 1932 through 1936. It was constructed similarly

to the 917, but had only one house attached rather than two, and was only 30" long and 10" wide.

VG	EX	LN	RARITY
150	200	250	5

919 ARTIFICIAL GRASS: From 1932 through 1942, and again postwar, Lionel offered for sale half-pound bags of green-dyed sawdust, which they marketed as artificial grass. It was sold in white cloth drawstring closure bags, typically with red lettering on the bag.

VG	EX	LN	RARITY
7	7	25	2

920 SCENIC PARK: This large (57" x 31 1/2") two-piece scenic plot was elaborately landscaped with grass, bushes, trees and two 184 bungalows, a 189 villa, and a 191 villa. It was sold in 1932-33.

VG	EX	LN	RARITY
1000	2000	3000	8

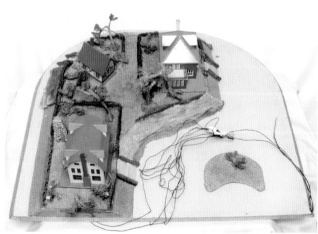

921 SCENIC PARK: Sold during the same time period as the 920, this was the same accessory with the addition of a third panel. The addition of the 921C Park Center Section increased the length to 85", but the width remained 31 1/2".

VG	EX	LN	RARITY
2000	3200	4500	8

921C PARK CENTER SECTION: Sold in 1932-33, this 28" by 31" panel was decorated with artificial grass, bushes and trees. Among the scenic items attached to it were the 184 bungalow, 189 villa, 191 villa and a 922 lamp terrace. It was designed to expand a 920 scenic park into a 921 scenic park.

VG	EX	LN	RARITY
750	1500	2250	8

922 LAMP TERRACE: Another of the scenic accessories sold by Lionel in the 1930s was this 13" x 3 3/4" oval plot with a 56 lamp post mounted at its center. Cataloged from 1932 through 1936, its plywood base was painted cream, representing concrete walkways amongst the imitation grass, shrubbery and flowers.

922 LAMP TERRACE (Type I): Some of these plots came with a copper-colored lamp post. This color lamp was not available for separate sale.

VG	EX	LN	RARITY
200	350	550	8

922 LAMP TERRACE (Type II): Other plots were made which had either a green, mojave or pea green lamp post installed.

VG	EX	LN	RARITY
100	150	200	6

923 TUNNEL: This felt composition tunnel, mounted on a base, was designed to accommodate a 90-degree curve of either Standard or 0 Gauge track. It was sold during 1933-42 and was detailed with bushes, trees and three small chalets. It was 40 1/2" long, 23" wide and 14 1/2" tall.

VG	EX	LN	RARITY
100	200	400	6

924 TUNNEL: Another felt composition tunnel was the 924, made to accommodate 072 curved track. It was detailed with bushes, trees etc., and was sold from 1935 into 1942.

924 TUNNEL (Type I): In 1935, the 924 was 29 1/2" x 20 1/2", and stood 13 1/2" tall.

VG	EX	LN	RARITY
200	350	550	8

924 TUNNEL (Type II): From 1936 onward, the tunnel was 30 1/8" x 21 1/2", and was 12 1/2" tall.

VG	EX	LN	RARITY
100	200	400	6

925 LUBRICANT: This two-ounce tube of grease was available from 1935 into 1942.

VG	EX	LN	RARITY
1	4	10	1

927 ORNAMENTAL FLAG PLOT: Another of the scenic accessories sold by Lionel in the 1930s was this 16" x 8 1/2" oval plot with an ivory-colored flag post mounted at its center, making its overall height 14 1/2". A silk American flag flew from the post. Cataloged from 1937 through 1942, its plywood base was painted cream, representing concrete walkways amongst the imitation grass, shrubbery and flowers.

VG	EX	LN	RARITY
100	200	400	6

1012 WINNER STATION: Shipped during 1931-33, this station was similar to the 48W. The lithographed station had cream walls and an orange roof. It was mounted on a green base. Inside the station was a transformer.

Price Guide Key: **VG** = Very Good, **EX** = Excellent, **LN** = Like New | *Values for each condition are in U.S. dollars.* | **Rarity** = Scale from 1-8 with 8 being the hardest to find.

363

1012 WINNER STATION (Type I): Some of these stations had "1012" lithographed above the "WINNERTOWN" sign. These stations had two binding posts.

VG	EX	LN	RARITY
40	55	75	4

1012 WINNER STATION (Type II): Other stations had three binding posts, but lacked the "1012" on the end.

VG	EX	LN	RARITY
40	55	75	4

1012K WINNER STATION: Sold during 1932-33, this was the same structure as the 1012, but without the internal transformer.

VG	EX	LN	RARITY
40	55	75	4

1013 CURVED TRACK: Sold from 1933 into 1942, and throughout the duration of the postwar era, 027 curved track is easily the most common single item Lionel produced. The crossties came in black, gray and brown, depending upon the era.

VG	EX	LN	RARITY
.25	.50	1.00	1

1017 WINNER STATION: Sold in 1932 and 1933, this was the same as the 1012, but was lettered "STATION" rather than "WINNERTOWN".

VG	EX	LN	RARITY
40	55	75	4

1018 STRAIGHT TRACK: Sold from 1933 through 1942, and throughout the duration of the postwar era, the only thing more common than this 027 straight track is 027 curved track. The 8 7/8" long sections came with black, gray and brown crossties, depending upon the era.

VG	EX	LN	RARITY
.25	.50	1.00	1

1019 REMOTE CONTROL TRACK SET: First sold from 1938 through 1942, and then 1946-50, this 027 uncoupling track with controller would operate coil-coupler equipped cars through its control rail, but had no electromagnet for magnetic couplers.

VG	EX	LN	RARITY
5	8	10	3

1021 90-DEGREE CROSSING: First offered from 1933 through 1942, this steel 027 90-degree crossing returned to the catalog from 1945 through 1954.

VG	EX	LN	RARITY
2	4	8	3

1022 TUNNEL: This felt composition tunnel, sold 1935-42, was basically an economy version of the 123 90-degree curved tunnel. The savings were achieved by the omission of the house and tree detailing. It was 18 3/4" by 16 1/2" and 9 1/4" tall.

VG	EX	LN	RARITY
20	40	75	3

1023 TUNNEL: This tunnel, cataloged from 1934 through 1942 was 14 3/8" long, 10 1/2" wide, and stood 5 7/8" tall.

VG	EX	LN	RARITY
20	40	75	3

1024 PAIR OF MANUAL TURNOUTS: Sold prewar from 1935 through 1942, this pair of metal-based 027 manual turnouts returned in 1946 and remained in the line through 1952. Circular red- and green-painted direction markers are provided to indicate the position of the switch points.

VG	EX	LN	RARITY
10	15	25	3

1024L LEFT-HAND MANUAL TURNOUT: Cataloged from 1934 through 1942, this 027 turnout was equipped with circular red- and green-painted direction markers to indicate the position of the switch points.

VG	EX	LN	RARITY
5	8	10	3

1024R RIGHT-HAND MANUAL TURNOUT: This was the right-hand mate to the 1024L.

VG	EX	LN	RARITY
5	8	10	3

1025 ILLUMINATED BUMPER: This die-cast black illuminated bumper, attached to a section of 027 straight track, was sold from 1940 through 1942 and again in 1946-47.

VG	EX	LN	RARITY
10	15	20	4

1027 LIONEL JUNIOR TRANSFORMER STATION: This was the same transformer-equipped station as the 1017, but it was yellow rather than cream. It was sold during 1933-34.

VG	EX	LN	RARITY
40	60	85	4

1028 LIONEL JUNIOR TRANSFORMER STATION: The former 1027 was given this number in 1935.

VG	EX	LN	RARITY
40	60	85	4

1029 LIONEL JUNIOR TRANSFORMER STATION: The former 1027 was given yet another number in 1936.

VG	EX	LN	RARITY
40	60	85	4

1038 TRANSFORMER: This was an uncataloged 30-watt, 60-cycle transformer from the late 1930s or early 1940s.

VG	EX	LN	RARITY
5	10	20	4

1039 TRANSFORMER: This 35-watt, 60-cycle transformer was sold from 1937 through 1940.

VG	EX	LN	RARITY
5	10	20	2

1040 TRANSFORMER: Sold during 1937-39, this 60-watt, 60-cycle transformer was equipped with a whistle control.

VG	EX	LN	RARITY
20	35	50	4

1041 TRANSFORMER: This 60-watt, 110-volt primary transformer with speed, whistle and direction controls was offered from 1939 into 1942, and again postwar.

VG	EX	LN	RARITY
20	35	50	4

1045 OPERATING WATCHMAN: First available in 1938-42, the 1045 operating gateman returned to the catalog in 1946-50. It had a huge, oversize blue plastic man who held up a white signal flag as the train passed. Beside him was a signpost with a diamond-shaped nickel or brass sign affixed to it reading, "Look out for the Locomotive."

1045 OPERATING WATCHMAN (Type I): The earliest versions used a brass sign mounted on an aluminum-painted pole topped with a nickel finial. The flagman wore a dark blue uniform and details of his uniform were painted on.

VG	EX	LN	RARITY
20	35	50	4

1045 OPERATING WATCHMAN (Type II): On some of these early accessories, the flagman wore a black uniform with dark blue right arm.

VG	EX	LN	RARITY
30	45	65	6

1045 OPERATING WATCHMAN (Type III): Other early versions had a brown figure and arm.

VG	EX	LN	RARITY
25	40	60	5

1045 OPERATING WATCHMAN (Type IV): A later version used a nickel sign. The flagman's uniform was a lighter shade of blue uniform and lacked the painted details.

VG	EX	LN	RARITY
20	35	50	4

1045 OPERATING WATCHMAN (Type V): Some versions, probably assembled in 1942, had the sign post painted 92 gray rather than aluminum.

VG	EX	LN	RARITY
30	45	65	6

1121 REMOTE CONTROL TURNOUTS: This pair of turnouts was originally sold from 1937 to 1942. Reintroduced in 1946 and cataloged through 1951, the postwar version can be differentiated from the prewar version by its plastic rather than metal controller and mechanism covers. A single 1121C-60 controller operated both turnouts. Prior to 1950, screw-based lamps were used; later turnouts used bayonet-based bulbs. Early turnouts had flat plastic direction indicator lenses; later ones used a protruding ribbed rubber lens.

VG	EX	LN	RARITY
20	35	45	3

1550 PAIR OF MANUAL TURNOUTS: Sold from 1933 through 1937 as part of the Lionel Junior line, these lightweight sheet-metal manual turnouts had only two rails and were used by clockwork trains.

VG	EX	LN	RARITY
1	2	5	4

1555 90-DEGREE CROSSING: This was the two-rail 90-degree crossing used by Lionel Junior clockwork trains from 1933 through 1937.

VG	EX	LN	RARITY
1	2	5	4

1560 LIONEL JUNIOR STATION: Sold from 1933 through 1937 as part of the Lionel Junior line, this station was identical to the 1012K.

VG	EX	LN	RARITY
15	25	35	3

1569 LIONEL JUNIOR ACCESSORY SET: Not wanting to miss out on lucrative accessory sales, even for the Lionel Junior line, Lionel created this set. Sold during 1933-37, it consisted of four 1571 telegraph poles, a 1572 semaphore, a 1573 warning signal, a 1574 clock and a 1575 crossing gate. The original box is required for the values listed.

1569 LIONEL JUNIOR ACCESSORY SET (Type I): This version included accessories with black bases.

Price Guide Key: **VG** = Very Good, **EX** = Excellent, **LN** = Like New | *Values for each condition are in U.S. dollars.* | **Rarity** = Scale from 1-8 with 8 being the hardest to find.

365

VG	EX	LN	RARITY
100	200	400	6

1569 LIONEL JUNIOR ACCESSORY SET (Type II): This version included accessories with red bases.

VG	EX	LN	RARITY
100	200	400	6

1571 TELEGRAPH POLE: This telegraph pole was a component of the previously listed 1569 Lionel Junior Accessory Set. The channel-shaped sheet metal pole was painted green or gray, and attached to a square sheet metal base. Two red crossarms were attached near the top. While it was a component of the accessory set in 1933-37, it had been sold as an Ives item in 1931-32.

VG	EX	LN	RARITY
5	10	15	4

1572 SEMAPHORE: Another component of the 1933-37 1569 Lionel Junior Accessory Set was this semaphore signal with two cream-colored manually operated semaphore arms.

1572 SEMAPHORE (Type I): Some of these signals had gray masts and were mounted on black bases with a pea green post and light red base.

VG	EX	LN	RARITY
5	10	15	4

1572 SEMAPHORE (Type II): Other signals had a pea green post and a light red base.

VG	EX	LN	RARITY
5	10	15	4

1575 CROSSING GATE: Another item that was sold as part of the 1933-37 1569 Lionel Junior Accessory Set was this 5 1/2" long gate.

1575 CROSSING GATE (Type I): The red, white and black gate of this accessory was attached to a gray post and supported by a black base.

VG	EX	LN	RARITY
5	10	15	4

1575 CROSSING GATE (Type II): Other gates were made using a pea green post and light red base. The gate was red, white and black.

VG	EX	LN	RARITY
5	10	15	4

A MINIATURE MOTOR: This was sold in 1904.

VG	EX	LN	RARITY
50	75	100	7

Most of the transformers that Lionel produced during the prewar era were lettered rather than numbered. There are a few generalizations that can be made about these items. TRAINmaster transformers had Bakelite cases, whereas others had steel cases, except those made prior to 1922. These earlier transformers used cast iron cases.

A TRANSFORMER (Type I): Produced from 1921 through 1931, this was a 40-watt, 60-cycle, stepped voltage output transformer.

VG	EX	LN	RARITY
5	10	15	4

A TRANSFORMER (Type II): From 1931 through 1937, the output was boosted to 60 watts.

VG	EX	LN	RARITY
10	15	20	4

B NEW DEPARTURE MOTOR: This was sold from 1906 through 1916.

VG	EX	LN	RARITY
75	110	150	6

B TRANSFORMER (Type I): This 50-watt, Multivolt, 60-cycle, stepped voltage output transformer was sold in 1916 and 1917.

VG	EX	LN	RARITY
5	10	25	5

B TRANSFORMER (Type II): During 1917, and continuing into 1921, the output was increased to 75 watts.

VG	EX	LN	RARITY
5	10	25	3

B TRANSFORMER (Type III): During 1921, the output was again reduced to 50 watts, where it remained through 1931.

VG	EX	LN	RARITY
5	10	20	3

B TRANSFORMER (Type IV): In 1932, the output returned to 75 watts and it continued to be produced with that rating through 1938.

VG	EX	LN	RARITY
5	10	25	3

C CURVED TRACK: Standard Gauge curved track was sold from 1906 into 1942 in a variety of lengths. The 1906 track formed a 36" diameter circle, later track formed a 42" diameter.

VG	EX	LN	RARITY
1.00	1.50	2.50	1

CC CURVED TRACK: This curved terminal track section was sold from 1915 through 1922.

VG	EX	LN	RARITY
1.00	1.50	2.50	2

C NEW DEPARTURE MOTOR: Sold from 1906 through 1916, this was similar to the B.

VG	EX	LN	RARITY
100	130	175	6

C TRANSFORMER: This 75-watt Multivolt transformer was designed to operate on 25- to 40-cycle current and was sold from 1922 through 1931. It had stepped voltage output.

VG	EX	LN	RARITY
5	10	25	5

D NEW DEPARTURE MOTOR: Also sold from 1906 through 1916, this was equipped with a reversing mechanism and on-off switch.

VG	EX	LN	RARITY
100	130	175	6

E NEW DEPARTURE MOTOR: This two-speed motor was sold from 1906 through 1916.

VG	EX	LN	RARITY
100	130	175	6

F NEW DEPARTURE MOTOR: This two-speed motor was sold from 1906 through 1916 and was equipped with a reversing device.

VG	EX	LN	RARITY
100	130	175	6

F TRANSFORMER: This 40-watt Multivolt transformer was designed to operate on 25- to 40-cycle current and was sold from 1931 through 1937. It had stepped voltage output.

VG	EX	LN	RARITY
5	10	25	5

G FAN MOTOR: This battery-operated fan motor was sold in 1909-14.

VG	EX	LN	RARITY
100	130	175	6

H TRANSFORMER: This 75-watt Multivolt transformer was designed to operate on 25- to 40-cycle current and was sold in 1938-39.

VG	EX	LN	RARITY
5	10	25	5

K SEWING MACHINE MOTOR: This was sold from 1904 through 1906.

VG	EX	LN	RARITY
100	130	175	6

K TRANSFORMER (Type I): This 60-cycle, 150-watt, 29-volt stepped output, slate top Multivolt transformer was sold from 1913 into 1917.

VG	EX	LN	RARITY
20	40	60	5

K TRANSFORMER (Type II): During 1917, the output was raised to 200-watts, where it remained into 1921.

VG	EX	LN	RARITY
20	40	60	5

K TRANSFORMER (Type III): During 1921, the output was again reduced to 150 watts, where it remained through 1938. A brass identification plate was installed.

VG	EX	LN	RARITY
15	20	25	3

K TRANSFORMER (Type IV): Some of the late 150-watt transformers had nickel identification plates rather than brass.

VG	EX	LN	RARITY
15	20	25	3

L SEWING MACHINE MOTOR: This was sold in 1905.

VG	EX	LN	RARITY
75	100	125	5

L TRANSFORMER (Type I): As sold from 1913 through 1916, this 75-watt, 60-cycle transformer had six fixed voltage taps.

VG	EX	LN	RARITY
10	15	20	3

L TRANSFORMER (Type II): When the "L" designation returned from 1933-38, it was assigned to a 50-watt, 60-cycle, stepped voltage output Multivolt transformer.

VG	EX	LN	RARITY
10	15	20	1

Price Guide Key: **VG** = Very Good, **EX** = Excellent, **LN** = Like New | *Values for each condition are in U.S. dollars.* | **Rarity** = Scale from 1-8 with 8 being the hardest to find.

367

ACCESSORIES, TRACK & TRANSFORMERS

M PEERLESS MOTOR: This battery-operated, single speed motor was sold in 1915-20.

VG	EX	LN	RARITY
50	75	100	4

MS STRAIGHT TRACK: This two-rail, 027-style track was produced from 1933 through 1938 for use with clockwork trains.

VG	EX	LN	RARITY
.50	1.00	2.00	4

MWC CURVED TRACK: This two-rail, 027-style track was produced from 1933 through 1938 for use with clockwork trains.

VG	EX	LN	RARITY
.50	1.00	2.00	4

N TRANSFORMER: This 50-watt, 60-cycle, stepped voltage output, Multivolt transformer was sold during 1941-42.

VG	EX	LN	RARITY
5	10	15	3

OC CURVED TRACK: This was the catalog identification used for 0 gauge curved track from 1915 to 1961.

VG	EX	LN	RARITY
.25	,50	1.00	1

OCC CURVED TRACK: This 0 gauge curved terminal track was sold from 1915 through 1922.

VG	EX	LN	RARITY
. .25	.50	1.00	4

OCS CURVED TRACK: Cataloged from 1933 through 1942, this section of OC curved track had one outside rail insulated for use in controlling accessories.

VG	EX	LN	RARITY
.25	.50	1.00	4

OS STRAIGHT TRACK: This was the catalog identification used for 10" long 0 gauge straight track from 1915 to 1961.

VG	EX	LN	RARITY
.50	1	2	1

OSC STRAIGHT TRACK: This 0 gauge straight terminal track was sold from 1915 through 1922.

VG	EX	LN	RARITY
.50	1	2	4

OSS STRAIGHT TRACK: Cataloged from 1933 through 1942, this section of OS straight track had one outside rail insulated for use in controlling accessories.

VG	EX	LN	RARITY
.50	1	2	4

OTC LOCKON: This 0 Gauge lockon was sold from 1923 through 1936. It provided a means of connecting the transformer output to the track.

VG	EX	LN	RARITY
.25	.50	1.00	1

Q TRANSFORMER (Type I): Sold during 1914-15, this 50-watt, 60-cycle transformer had three fixed voltage taps.

VG	EX	LN	RARITY
10	20	40	4

Q TRANSFORMER (Type II): This very basic 75-watt, 110-volt primary transformer had a speed control and circuit breaker, but no whistle or directional controls, nor fixed voltage taps. It was available from 1938 into 1942, and again in 1946.

VG	EX	LN	RARITY
10	20	40	4

R PEERLESS MOTOR: This battery-powered, reversible, two-speed motor was sold in 1915-20.

VG	EX	LN	RARITY
75	100	125	5

R TRANSFORMER: This transformer had two independent throttles and numerous fixed voltage taps. Its variable voltage posts went up to 24 volts. It did not have whistle or direction controls.

R TRANSFORMER: Those transformers produced in 1939-42 and in 1946 had nameplates giving a 100-watt rating.

VG	EX	LN	RARITY
50	75	100	4

RCS REMOTE CONTROL TRACK: This remote control section of 0 gauge track was available in 1938-42 and again in 1946-48. It has two control rails in addition to the normal three rails. These control rails make contact with the head of a rivet housed in a sliding shoe on operating cars and on coil-coupler trucks. This track does not include the electromagnet needed for the later style magnetic couplers.

VG	EX	LN	RARITY
5	10	15	3

S STRAIGHT TRACK: Standard Gauge straight track was sold from 1906 into 1942. It was 12" long in 1906, 14" thereafter.

VG	EX	LN	RARITY
1.00	2.00	3.00	2

S TRANSFORMER (Type I): This 50-watt, 60-cycle, stepped voltage Multivolt transformer was sold from 1914 through 1917.

VG	EX	LN	RARITY
20	35	60	5

S TRANSFORMER (Type II): This 80-watt, 110-volt primary transformer had built-in speed, direction and whistle controls. It was available from 1938 through 1942, and again in 1947.

VG	EX	LN	RARITY
20	35	60	5

SC STRAIGHT TRACK: This Standard Gauge straight terminal track was sold from 1915 through 1922.

VG	EX	LN	RARITY
1.00	2.00	3.00	2

SCS CURVED TRACK: Cataloged from 1933 through 1942, this section of Standard Gauge curved track had one outside rail insulated for use in controlling accessories.

VG	EX	LN	RARITY
1.00	2.00	3.00	2

SMC CURVED TRACK: This section of curved, two-rail, 027-style track had trips that activated a Mickey Mouse stoker in the clockwork trains with which it was furnished during 1935-36.

VG	EX	LN	RARITY
1.00	2.00	3.00	5

SS STRAIGHT TRACK: Cataloged from 1933 through 1942, this section of Standard Gauge straight track had one outside rail insulated for use in controlling accessories.

VG	EX	LN	RARITY
1.00	2.00	3.00	3

STC LOCKON: This Standard Gauge lockon was sold from 1923 through 1936. It provided a means of connecting the transformer output to the track.

VG	EX	LN	RARITY
.25	.50	1.00	1

T TRANSFORMER (Type I): This 60-cycle, 75-watt, 29-volt stepped output, Multivolt transformer was sold from 1914 into 1917.

VG	EX	LN	RARITY
10	15	25	6

T TRANSFORMER (Type II): During 1917, the output was raised to 150 watts, where it remained into 1921.

VG	EX	LN	RARITY
15	25	35	6

T TRANSFORMER (Type III): During 1921, the output was reduced to 110 watts, where it remained into 1922. A brass identification plate was installed.

VG	EX	LN	RARITY
10	15	25	6

T TRANSFORMER (Type IV): During 1922, the output was further reduced to 100 watts, where it remained into 1922. A brass identification plate was installed.

VG	EX	LN	RARITY
10	15	25	2

T TRANSFORMER (Type V): Some of the late 100-watt transformers had nickel identification plates, rather than brass, and rubber-insulated supply cords.

VG	EX	LN	RARITY
10	15	25	2

U TRANSFORMER: This 50-watt, 60-cycle, stepped voltage output "ALLADIN" transformer was sold in 1932-33. An identical transformer was sold as the Ives model "Y".

VG	EX	LN	RARITY
10	15	25	4

UTC LOCKON: This Universal lockon was sold from 1936 into 1942. Its universal design allowed it to be connected to Standard Gauge, 0 gauge, 072 or 027 track.

VG	EX	LN	RARITY
.25	.50	1.00	1

V TRANSFORMER: This four-throttle 150-watt transformer was first offered in 1938-1942, then returned after World War II for 1946-47. These transformers have no fixed voltage, direction or whistle controls, but they are rated at 24 volts.

VG	EX	LN	RARITY
100	125	150	4

W CURVED TRACK (Type I): A half section of Standard Gauge curve track, 7" long, was sold only in 1906.

VG	EX	LN	RARITY
2	5	10	6

W CURVED TRACK (Type II): A half section of Standard Gauge curve track, 8" long, sold from 1934 into 1942.

VG	EX	LN	RARITY
1.00	2.00	3.00	2

W TRANSFORMER: This was a 75-watt, 60-cycle, Multivolt transformer sold from 1933 into 1942. It was also made for Ives.

VG	EX	LN	RARITY
10	15	25	4

WX TRANSFORMER: Also cataloged from 1933 through 1942 was this 25-cycle version of the 75-watt, 25-cycle, Multivolt transformer.

VG	EX	LN	RARITY
10	15	25	4

Y PEERLESS MOTOR: This battery-powered reversible, three-speed motor was sold in 1915-20.

VG	EX	LN	RARITY
50	75	100	4

Z TRANSFORMER: This four-throttle 250-watt transformer was first offered in 1938-1942, then returned after World War II for 1945-47. These transformers have no fixed voltage, direction or whistle controls, but they are rated at 24 volts.

VG	EX	LN	RARITY
100	125	150	4

Price Guide Key: **VG** = Very Good, **EX** = Excellent, **LN** = Like New | *Values for each condition are in U.S. dollars.* | **Rarity** = Scale from 1-8 with 8 being the hardest to find.

369

CHAPTER 27
CATALOGS & PAPER PRODUCTS

For many, the collecting of Lionel paper goods is a hobby unto itself. Indeed, so vast was Lionel's production of trains, it is difficult to comprehend that in fact there were more different paper products produced than trains. A large display area indeed is required to display a "complete"–whatever that means–collection of both.

Beyond the celebrated color consumer catalog, during the latter portion of the prewar era, Lionel published a dealer advance catalog. Though often similar to the consumer catalog, dealer catalogs also illustrated store displays and promotional items that were not shown in the regular catalog. Also, these dealer catalogs often give us insight into how pieces evolved, for the illustrations in the dealer publication were often based on pre-production samples. Some items are shown that were never produced.

Far from the full-color 1942 catalog full of trains that closed the prewar era, the 1900 Lionel catalog was black and white, and illustrated no trains at all.

Virtually every operating piece Lionel produced had its own instructional document, often several editions as production continued on good-selling items.

Booklets were printed for department store and hobby shop salespeople, teaching the "right" way to extol the virtues of Lionel's products.

Rather than trying to list and illustrate each paper product issued, which would require a massive volume, these listings will be confined to catalogs: consumer, dealer and accessory. A few other items of special interest are listed as well.

Unlike the trains, only two values are listed for paper products, Very Good and Excellent. Paper in less than excellent condition is not generally considered collectible. Beware, however, that like the trains, rare and valuable catalogs have been reproduced. Those that are not marked as such are sometimes hard to distinguish.

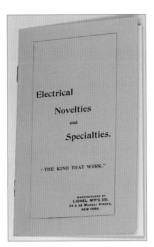

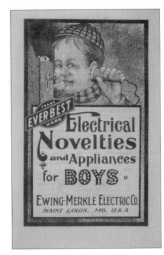

1900 Catalog: The first catalog Lionel issued was a 12-page 3 1/2" x 5 7/8" flier filled with medical devices and electric novelties–all kinds of materials, but no trains.

RARITY
Too rarely traded to establish pricing.

1901 Catalog: This four-page catalog was the first catalog to illustrate trains.

RARITY
Too rarely traded to establish pricing.

1903 Catalog (Type I): This 16-page 6" x 9" vertical format catalog bore the name "Ewing-Merkle Electric Co., Saint Louis, Mo. U.S.A.", which was an early Lionel distributor.

RARITY
Too rarely traded to establish pricing.

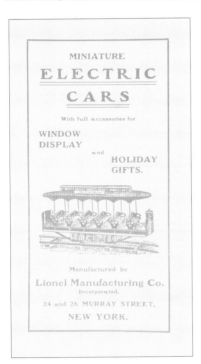

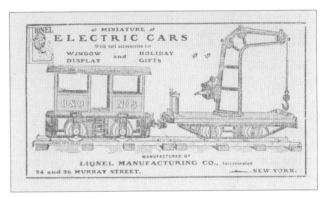

1903 Catalog (Type II): This was a 20-page, 6 1/2" x 3 1/2" horizontal format catalog with a 24-26 Murray Street address listed for Lionel.

RARITY
Too rarely traded to establish pricing

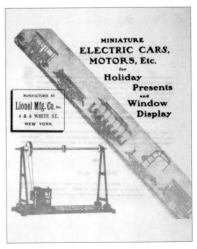

1902 Catalog: This was a 16-page 3 1/2" x 6 1/2" vertical format catalog with a cover made of light green paper, printed with red ink.

RARITY
Too rarely traded to establish pricing.

1904 Catalog: This was a 6" x 6 1/2" 12-page booklet promoting Lionel products, with a diagonal stripe on cover.

RARITY
Too rarely traded to establish pricing.

Price Guide Key: **VG** = Very Good, **EX** = Excellent, **LN** = Like New | *Values for each condition are in U.S. dollars.* | **Rarity** = Scale from 1-8 with 8 being the hardest to find.

371

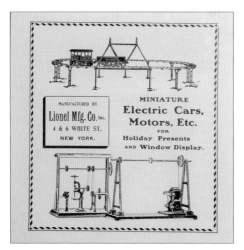

1905 Catalog: This was a 6" x 6" 12-page catalog. The cover shows a 100 locomotive towing a 400 gondola over a 340 suspension bridge.

RARITY
Too rarely traded to establish pricing.

1906 Catalog: This was a 4 1/2" x 6 1/2" 24-page black and white catalog.

RARITY
Too rarely traded to establish pricing.

1907 Catalog: This catalog was 28 pages in a 6" x 9" horizontal format.

RARITY
Too rarely traded to establish pricing.

1908 Catalog: This catalog was also 28 pages in a 6" x 9" horizontal format.

RARITY
Too rarely traded to establish pricing.

1909 Catalog: In 1909, the catalog grew to 32 pages in a 6" x 9" format.

RARITY
Too rarely traded to establish pricing.

1910 Catalog (Type I): This catalog was 28 pages in an 8" x 10" vertical format with an illustration of the Lionel factory centered at the bottom of the front cover.

RARITY
Too rarely traded to establish pricing.

1910 Catalog (Type II): The factory illustration was omitted in favor of a blank where dealers could print their addresses.

RARITY
Too rarely traded to establish pricing.

1910 Catalog (Type III): This was the same catalog with a full-color wraparound cover showing many trains.

RARITY
Too rarely traded to establish pricing.

1911 Catalog (Type I): This was a 32-page 8" x 10" vertical format catalog.

RARITY
Too rarely traded to establish pricing.

1911 Catalog (Type II): The same catalog featured a full-color wraparound cover showing many trains.

RARITY
Too rarely traded to establish pricing.

1912 Catalog (Type I): In 1912, the catalog was 36 pages in an 8" x 10" vertical format.

RARITY
Too rarely traded to establish pricing.

1912 Catalog (Type II): This was the same catalog with full-color wraparound cover showing many trains.

RARITY
Too rarely traded to establish pricing.

1913 Catalog (Type I): This was a 36-page 8" x 10" vertical format catalog.

RARITY
Too rarely traded to establish pricing.

1913 Catalog (Type II): Another 1913 version was 16 pages in a 6" x 6 1/2" format. Note: Reproduction shown above.

RARITY
Too rarely traded to establish pricing.

1914 Catalog (Type I): This 8" x 10" vertical format catalog was 36 pages.

RARITY
Too rarely traded to establish pricing.

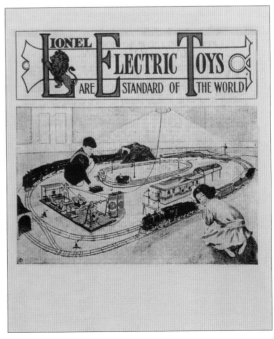

1914 Catalog (Type II): Another type was 16 pages, 6" x 6 1/2" and printed with green ink.

RARITY
Too rarely traded to establish pricing.

Price Guide Key: **VG** = Very Good, **EX** = Excellent, **LN** = Like New | *Values for each condition are in U.S. dollars.* | **Rarity** = Scale from 1-8 with 8 being the hardest to find.

373

1914 Catalog (Type III): At 16 pages, this 6" x 6 1/2" catalog was printed with brown and orange ink.

RARITY
Too rarely traded to establish pricing.

1917 Catalog (Type II): This is a 6" x 9" vertical format catalog. The cover on this version reads, "1917 – CATALOGUE OF – LIONEL – ELECTRIC – TOYS".

RARITY
Too rarely traded to establish pricing.

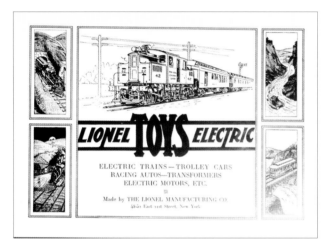

1915 Catalog (Type I): The 1915 catalog grew to 40 pages, with a 10" x 7" horizontal format. Price of set 421 on the left centerfold is $32.50.

RARITY
Too rarely traded to establish pricing.

1915 Catalog (Type II): This type of catalog was also 40 pages, with a 10" x 7" horizontal format. Price of set 421 on the left centerfold is $40.

RARITY
Too rarely traded to establish pricing.

1916 Catalog: The 1916 catalog was also 40 pages, 10" x 7" horizontal format.

RARITY
Too rarely traded to establish pricing.

1917 Catalog (Type I): In 1917, the catalog was 40 pages, 10" x 7" horizontal format.

RARITY
Too rarely traded to establish pricing.

1917 Catalog (Type III): This version was a 6" x 9" vertical format catalog. The cover on this version reads, "1917 – CATALOGUE OF – LIONEL – ELECTRIC – TOY TRAINS". Note: reproduction shown above.

RARITY
Too rarely traded to establish pricing.

1918 Folder: This was a 6" x 9" vertical format catalog. The cover on this folder reads, "LIONEL – ELECTRIC – TOY TRAINS – and Multivolt transformers – SOLD BY – MANUFACTURED AND GUARANTEED BY – The Lionel Manufacturing Company, 48-52 East 21st Street, New York".

RARITY
Too rarely traded to establish pricing.

1919 Folder: This was a 6" x 9" vertical format catalog. The cover on this folder reads "LIONEL – ELECTRIC – TOY TRAINS – and Multivolt transformers – SOLD BY – MANUFACTURED AND GUARANTEED BY – The Lionel Corporation, 48-52 East 21st Street, New York".

RARITY
Too rarely traded to establish pricing.

1920 Folder: This was a 7" x 5" double-sided, full-color folder representing a 32-page catalog. One "page" of the folder had the headline "STANDARD of the WORLD FOR TWENTY YEARS".

RARITY
Too rarely traded to establish pricing.

1921 Folder: This was a 7" x 5" double-sided, full-color folder representing 32-page catalog. One "page" of the folder had the headline "STANDARD of the WORLD FOR TWENTY-ONE YEARS".

RARITY
Too rarely traded to establish pricing.

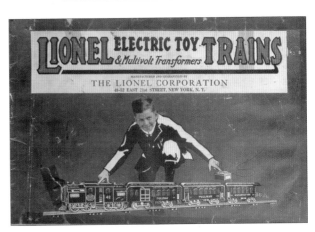

1922 Catalog: At 40 pages, this was a 10" x 6 3/4" horizontal format color catalog with a gray cover.

VG	EX	LN	RARITY
200	300	—	6

1920 Catalog: At 46 pages, this was a 10" x 6 3/4" horizontal format catalog with a gray cover.

RARITY
Too rarely traded to establish pricing.

Price Guide Key: **VG** = Very Good, **EX** = Excellent, **LN** = Like New | *Values for each condition are in U.S. dollars.* | **Rarity** = Scale from 1-8 with 8 being the hardest to find.

375

1923 Catalog: In 1923, the catalog was 48 pages, in a 10" x 7" horizontal color format with a color cover.

VG	EX	LN	RARITY
200	300	—	6

1924 Catalog: This was a 44-page, 10 1/2" x 8" horizontal format color catalog with a color cover.

VG	EX	LN	RARITY
175	250	—	5

1924 Folder: This 3 5/16" x 6 1/2" folder was printed in orange and black.

VG	EX	LN	RARITY
40	75	—	4

1925 Catalog: This catalog was 44 pages, 10 1/2" x 8" horizontal format, in color with a color cover.

VG	EX	LN	RARITY
125	200	—	5

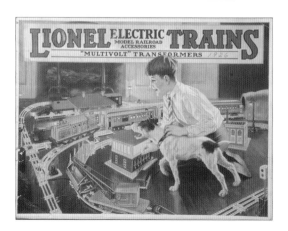

1926 Catalog: This color catalog was 48 pages, 10 1/2" x 8" horizontal format with a color cover.

VG	EX	LN	RARITY
125	200	—	5

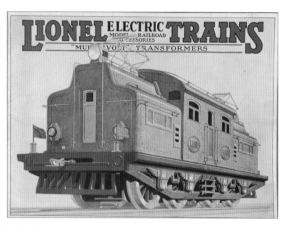

1927 Catalog: This was a 46-page, 11 1/2" x 8 1/2" horizontal format, color catalog with a color cover.

VG	EX	LN	RARITY
125	200	—	5

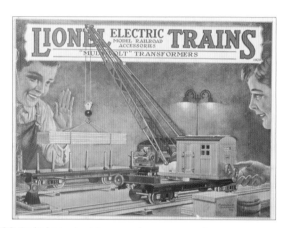

1928 Catalog: At 46 pages, this was an 11" x 8 1/2" horizontal format, color catalog with a color cover.

VG	EX	LN	RARITY
125	200	—	5

1929 Catalog: The 1929 color catalog was again 46 pages, 11 1/2" x 8 1/2" horizontal format with a color cover.

VG	EX	LN	RARITY
175	250	—	5

1929 Miniature Catalog: A smaller version was 32 pages, 7 5/8" x 5 3/4" horizontal format with a color cover.

VG	EX	LN	RARITY
40	50	—	5

1930 Advance Catalog: This version for 1930 was black and white.

RARITY
Too rarely traded to establish accurate pricing.

1930 Trade Price List: In an 8 1/2" x 11 1/2" format, this price list was in black and red ink on white paper, and was effective in February 1930.

RARITY
Too rarely traded to establish accurate pricing.

1930 Consumer Catalog: The full catalog was 48 pages, 11 1/2" x 8 1/2" horizontal format, in color with a color cover.

VG	EX	LN	RARITY
175	250	—	5

1930 Miniature Folder: The Blue Comet was on this cover in 1930.

VG	EX	LN	RARITY
40	50	—	5

1930 Winner Brochure: This brochure was 11 1/2" x 17".

RARITY
Too rarely traded to establish accurate pricing.

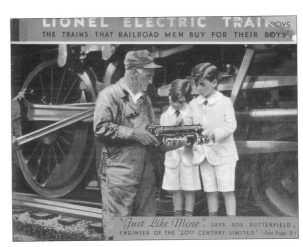

1931 Consumer Catalog: Growing again to 52 pages, this color catalog was 11 1/2" x 8 1/2" horizontal format with a color cover.

VG	EX	LN	RARITY
125	200	—	5

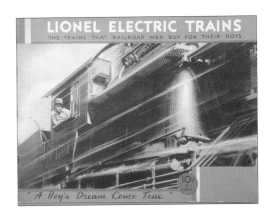

Price Guide Key: **VG** = Very Good, **EX** = Excellent, **LN** = Like New | *Values for each condition are in U.S. dollars.* | **Rarity** = Scale from 1-8 with 8 being the hardest to find.

377

1932 Consumer Catalog: The 1932 version was a 52-page, 11 1/2" x 8 1/2" horizontal format color catalog with a color cover.

VG	EX	LN	RARITY
100	175	—	4

1933 Consumer Catalog: The 1933 catalog was 52 pages, 11 1/4" x 8 3/8" horizontal format, in color with a color cover.

VG	EX	LN	RARITY
100	175	—	4

1934 Consumer Catalog: This was a 36-page, 11 1/2" x 7 1/2" horizontal format, color catalog with a color cover.

VG	EX	LN	RARITY
100	175	—	4

1935 Consumer Catalog: In 1935, the catalog was 44 pages, 11 1/4" x 8 3/8" horizontal format, in color with a color cover.

VG	EX	LN	RARITY
75	150	—	3

1936 Advance Catalog: This catalog was a 10" x 7 1/2" horizontal format, and in black and white.

VG	EX	LN	RARITY
175	250	—	7

1936 Consumer Catalog: The full 1936 catalog was 48 pages, 11 1/4" x 8 3/8" horizontal format, in color with a color cover.

VG	EX	LN	RARITY
100	175	—	4

1937 Master Catalog: Spiral bound with a stiff blue cover, this catalog was intended for use by the Lionel sales force.

VG	EX	LN	RARITY
300	500	—	8

1937 Advance Catalog: At 28 pages, this catalog was in a 10 1/8" x 7 1/2" black and white horizontal format.

VG	EX	LN	RARITY
175	250	—	7

1937 Consumer Catalog (Type I): This version of the 1937 catalog was 48 pages, 11 1/4" x 8 3/8" horizontal format, in color with a color cover.

VG	EX	LN	RARITY
75	150	—	3

1937 Consumer Catalog (Type II): Another version of the catalog was 24 pages, 10 1/2" x 7 1/2" horizontal format, in black and white with a black and white cover.

VG	EX	LN	RARITY
20	40	—	3

1938 Master Catalog: This catalog, 58 pages spiral bound with a stiff shiny silver cover, was intended for use by the Lionel sales force.

VG	EX	LN	RARITY
400	700	—	8

1938 Advance Catalog: This version was 20 pages, 8 1/2" x 10 7/8" vertical format, in black and white.

VG	EX	LN	RARITY
175	250	—	7

1938 Consumer Catalog (Type I): The color version of the 1938 catalog was 52 pages, 11 1/2" x 8 1/2" horizontal format with a color cover.

VG	EX	LN	RARITY
75	150	—	3

1938 Consumer Catalog (Type II): The black and white catalog was 32 pages, 10 1/4" x 7 1/2" horizontal format, with a black and white cover.

Price Guide Key: VG = Very Good, EX = Excellent, LN = Like New | *Values for each condition are in U.S. dollars.* | **Rarity** = Scale from 1-8 with 8 being the hardest to find.

379

VG	EX	LN	RARITY
20	40	—	3

1938 Lionel Sales Aids and Complete Retail Price List: This price list for 1938 was 12 pages, 8 3/8" x 10 7/8" vertical format, in blue and white with a blue and red cover.

VG	EX	LN	RARITY
50	100	—	6

1939 Master Catalog: At 68 pages spiral bound with stiff bright red cover, this was intended for use by the Lionel sales force.

VG	EX	LN	RARITY
300	500	—	8

1939 Consumer Catalog: This was a 52-page, 10 3/4" x 8 3/8" horizontal format, color catalog with a color cover.

VG	EX	LN	RARITY
60	125	—	3

1939 Lionel Assortments and Dealer Displays Price List: This price list had a red cover.

VG	EX	LN	RARITY
250	400	—	8

1940 Executive Catalog: Spiral bound with a cloth-covered cover, this catalog was intended for use by the Lionel sales force.

VG	EX	LN	RARITY
300	500	—	8

1940 Consumer Catalog: Growing again to 64 pages, this was an 11 1/4" x 8 1/8" horizontal format color catalog with a color cover.

VG	EX	LN	RARITY
60	125	—	3

1941 Consumer Catalog: This catalog was 64 pages, 11 1/4" x 7 3/8" horizontal format, in color with a color cover.

VG	EX	LN	RARITY
60	125	—	3

1941 Lionel Dealer Displays Price List (Type I): This vertical format price list was 16 pages, with red stripes on the cover.

VG	EX	LN	RARITY
50	100	—	6

1941 Lionel Dealer Displays Price List (Type II): Another vertical format price list was 16 pages, with blue stripes on cover.

VG	EX	LN	RARITY
50	100	—	6

1941 Replacement Parts for Lionel Trains and Accessories: A brown soft-cover binder contained lists of train parts.

RARITY
Too rarely traded to establish accurate pricing.

1942 Advance Catalog: This was a 12-page, 10" x 11" red and black on white catalog.

VG	EX	LN	RARITY
250	400	—	8

1942 Consumer Catalog: The 1942 catalog was just 32 pages, 11" x 8 1/2" horizontal format, in color with a color cover.

VG	EX	LN	RARITY
60	125	—	3

Price Guide Key: **VG** = Very Good, **EX** = Excellent, **LN** = Like New | *Values for each condition are in U.S. dollars.* | **Rarity** = Scale from 1-8 with 8 being the hardest to find.

381

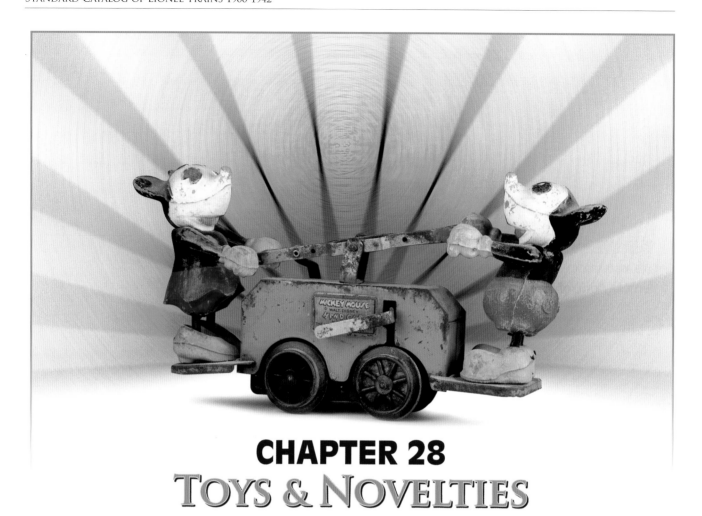

CHAPTER 28
TOYS & NOVELTIES

In addition to its extensive line of electric trains, and limited line of wind-up trains, Lionel also produced other track-bound toys before World War II. Unrelated to trains at all were other toys, most of which are described here.

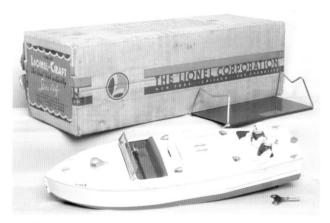

43 Lionel Craft Pleasure Boat: Lionel took to the waves with the 1933 introduction of this pleasure boat. A clockwork motor propelled this sheet-metal beauty, which came with its own display stand for storage. Above the water line, its hull was painted white, below vermilion, and its deck was tan. The 17" long boat continued to be cataloged through 1936.

VG	EX	LN	RARITY
325	550	750	5

44 Lionel Craft Racing Boat: A replica of the racing boats of the prewar era, such as those made famous by Gar Wood, this 17" long boat was powered by a clockwork motor. Its hull was white and green, and topped by a dark brown deck with large simulated engine. The catalog number, 44, appeared as racing numbers on the hull sides.

VG	EX	LN	RARITY
500	800	1250	7

49 Airport: This lithographed 58" diameter two-piece cardboard mat was sold separately for use with the 50 and 55 airplanes from 1937 through 1939.

VG	EX	LN	RARITY
400	700	1100	5

50 Remote Control Airplane: A steel pylon supported this red fabric airplane. A rubber propeller appeared to pull the aircraft through the air as directed by the joystick mounted on the tethered control box. This was sold in 1936.

VG	EX	LN	RARITY
425	650	850	6

51 Airport: This lithographed two-piece cardboard square was made for use with the 50 and 55 airplanes in 1936 and 1938.

VG	EX	LN	RARITY
200	300	500	6

55 Remote Control Airplane: Differing mechanically and cosmetically from the previous model 50, the silver-winged 55 was offered from 1937 through 1939.

VG	EX	LN	RARITY
325	550	750	5

80 Racing Automobile Set: Lionel took to the streets in 1912 with this race set. Arguably one of the first slot car sets made, the 8 1/2" long sheet metal car, painted either orange or red, cruised around a 36" diameter sheet metal track. It was sold from 1912 through 1916.

VG	EX	LN	RARITY
1500	2200	3500	8

81 Racing Automobile Set: Identical to the 80, this race set had 30" diameter track and was designed so it could be combined with the 80 to form a two-lane race track. It was sold from 1912 through 1916.

VG	EX	LN	RARITY
1500	2200	3500	8

84 Double Racing Automobile Set: Also offered from 1912 through 1916, this circular race course was a combination of the 80 and 81 sets.

VG	EX	LN	RARITY
2500	3300	4500	8

50 Wartime Freight Train: Government controls of steel usage during WWII, as well as military production contracts, effectively put Lionel out of the electric train business until late 1945. Unwilling to let its name disappear from the toy-buying public's mind, Lionel created this "paper train" in 1943. Several sheets of die-cut cardboard were included, along with wooden axles, allowing the diligent and patient parent or child to assemble a representation of a train set. The value shown is predicated on the outfit being complete, unassembled and unpunched.

VG	EX	LN	RARITY
200	300	500	6

Price Guide Key: **VG** = Very Good, **EX** = Excellent, **LN** = Like New | *Values for each condition are in U.S. dollars.* | **Rarity** = Scale from 1-8 with 8 being the hardest to find.

383

85 Double Racing Automobile Set: The deluxe racing outfit cataloged from 1912 through 1916 was this two-lane oval race course with cars. In addition to the curved track pieces of the other racing outfits, this set included eight pieces of straight track.

VG	EX	LN	RARITY
3000	4000	5700	8

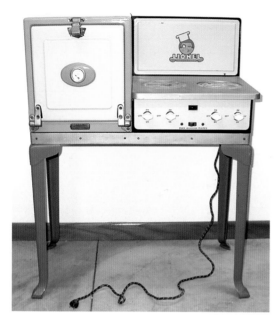

455 Electric Range: Lionel's first attempt at a toy aimed specifically at little girls was this electric range. It debuted in 1930, then returned in 1932 and stayed in the line until 1934. The green and cream porcelain and steel range would certainly not pass today's regulation, as it is an actual working electric stove, only reduced to 25" wide, 11" deep and 33" tall.

VG	EX	LN	RARITY
400	800	1500	6

1100-series Hand Cars: First appearing in 1934, these clockwork toys gave Lionel a product with a low retail price–important in those Depression-torn days. Legend claims these toys were responsible for preventing the collapse of Lionel, but like many legends around the company, a lot of myth added to the mystique. Certainly, however, the profits from the sales of these items were welcomed by the company.

1100 Hand Car (Type I): When introduced as an uncataloged item in 1934, the hand car had a red base. On it rode Mickey and Minnie Mouse, furiously pumping the levers. This was continued through 1937, always packaged with a circle of two-rail track.

VG	EX	LN	RARITY
350	600	1100	6

1100 Hand Car (Type II): Mickey and Minnie Mouse sometimes rode a hand car with an orange base. It came packaged with a circle of two-rail track.

VG	EX	LN	RARITY
500	900	1600	7

1100 Hand Car (Type III): Green bases were sometimes used, once again with Mickey and Minnie Mouse onboard, again riding a circle of two-rail track.

VG	EX	LN	RARITY
400	675	1250	6

1100 Hand Car (Type IV): A fourth base color for the Mickey and Minnie Mouse hand car was maroon. A circle of two-rail track was included with the hand car.

VG	EX	LN	RARITY
450	700	1400	7

1103 Hand Car (Type I): This uncataloged hand car, known as the Peter Rabbit Chick Mobile, was an attempt to increase sales outside the Christmas seasons from 1935 through 1937. At one end of the yellow base stood Peter Rabbit, pumping the levers, while an Easter basket was attached to the other end. It came packaged with a circle of two-rail track.

VG	EX	LN	RARITY
300	600	900	6

1103 Hand Car (Type II): The Peter Rabbit Chick Mobile Hand Car was also sold as a floor toy. Rather than coming with a circle of track, this version had rubber wheels installed.

VG	EX	LN	RARITY
400	675	1250	8

1105 Hand Car (Type I): Santa traded in his sleigh for a hand car for the Christmases of 1935 and 1936. At one end of the base, which was sometimes painted green, stood Santa, with Mickey Mouse peeking from his sack. At the other end stood, fittingly, a Christmas tree.

VG	EX	LN	RARITY
700	1500	2500	8

1105 (Type II): More common is Santa, with Mickey in the bag, riding a red hand car with his Christmas tree.

VG	EX	LN	RARITY
500	1000	2000	7

1106: Santa hand cars were made without Mickey as well. The base of these cars was red.

RARITY
Too rarely traded to establish pricing, exceptionally difficult to locate.

Price Guide Key: **VG** = Very Good, **EX** = Excellent, **LN** = Like New | *Values for each condition are in U.S. dollars.* | **Rarity** = Scale from 1-8 with 8 being the hardest to find.

385

1107 Rail Car (Type I): Donald Duck quacked along behind Pluto in his white dog house on this rail car during 1936-37. The dog house had a red roof.

VG	EX	LN	RARITY
500	700	1000	7

1107 (Type II): Sometimes the white dog house was made with a green roof.

VG	EX	LN	RARITY
400	600	900	6

1107 (Type III): A few of the cars were made with an orange dog house with green roof. Like the other cars, the base of this version was red.

VG	EX	LN	RARITY
700	1000	1500	8

APPENDIX 1
AWAKENING SLEEPING TOYS
HOW TO CLEAN AND PREPARE TRAINS FOR USE AFTER LONG-TERM STORAGE

In the instruction booklet Lionel furnished with its outfits, it recommended to customers that they keep all the original packaging materials to protect the trains during storage or travel. Oftentimes, however, that was not the case, and the boxes went outside or in the fireplace on Christmas morning.

In the passing years, trains were stored in attics, basements or closets, oftentimes in no box at all. Dust and dirt filtered into the working mechanisms of the trains as well as coating the shiny finish Lionel had carefully applied. With trains stored in hot attics, lubricants solidified into solid blocks. In damp basements, humidity allowed rust to work its evil on plated or blackened surfaces and on wheels once worn shiny from use.

If it is your intention to sell your trains to a collector or dealer wholesale (see Chapter 2), then it is my recommendation that you do not attempt to clean the trains. The dealer or collector knows how to clean each piece without damage and can tell even in a dirty state how the item will clean up and what it will be worth. He will pay slightly less for a dirty piece to recoup his time. However, certain trains are easily damaged by inappropriate cleaning and, once the damage is done, the value is permanently diminished. Better that you allow the dealer do the cleanup than for you to take this risk.

If you are keeping the trains for yourself and want to clean them up, following are a few general tips.

The first thing that most people notice that needs cleaning is the track. Do NOT use steel wool or sandpaper to clean the track. Steel wool will deposit fine metal fibers

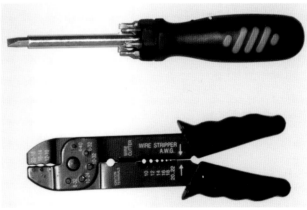

The essential tools for repair of prewar Lionel trains are a screwdriver with various sizes and types of tips, and a wire stripping and crimping tool. Also handy would be a soldering iron and a side-cutting pliers.

Price Guide Key: **VG** = Very Good, **EX** = Excellent, **LN** = Like New | *Values for each condition are in U.S. dollars.* | **Rarity** = Scale from 1-8 with 8 being the hardest to find.

387

Dirty, rusty track is best cleaned by scouring with a Scotchbrite pad, as shown here. Do NOT use steel wool or sandpaper.

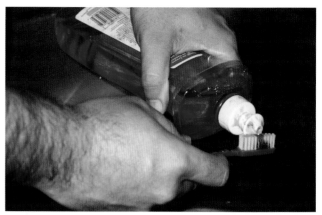

In the case of severe dirt and grime build-up on the bodies of the trains, cautious use of a mild detergent applied with a soft toothbrush or cotton swab sometimes produces excellent results. Be careful, however, as some markings are easily damaged by even the mildest of detergents.

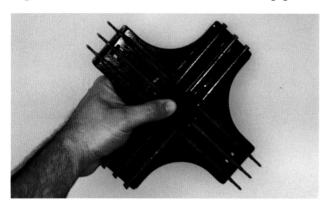

Only the tops of the rails, and the connecting pins, must be clean for good operation of the trains.

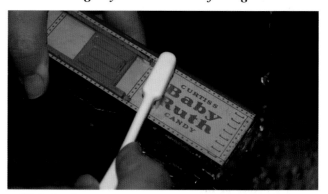

Work slowly, and in a circular motion, for best results. Too vigorous scrubbing risks scratching the paint.

that will cause short circuits and sandpaper will remove the tinplating that protects the track from further rust. Excellent results can be had with 3-M "Scotchbrite" pads available in auto parts stores. Various textures are available. These non-metallic pads make short work of dirt and light rust deposits, especially the courser textures. While the entire exposed surface of the connecting pins needs to be clean, only the tops of the rails require thorough cleaning.

A small piece of the Scotchbrite pad can be used to clean the contact surfaces of the locomotive's wheels as well as the center contact rollers. This will insure good electrical connection and prevent intermittent operation.

Lionel's trains are usually easily disassembled with a screwdriver. In many cases, the bodies of various items are assembled to the frames with sheet metal tabs, which are bent to secure the parts together. It is NOT recommended that you straighten these tabs. They are easily broken, which seriously affects the value of an item, as well as its functionality.

Items that are designed to come apart usually are held together with screws. Trucks are retained with screws, cotter pins or steel clips. If you feel like you have to force something apart–STOP. More than 99 percent of the items fit together easily. If force is required, that is usually a sign that you have not located and removed all the necessary screws or are not following the proper procedure.

If simple dusting does not clean the train, then cautiously use plain tap water. Be particularly careful around decals or lettering. Some collectors use a diluted mild liquid dishwashing

Rinse the train thoroughly, avoiding wetting the paper label (if present) on the bottom, and dry in a warm area before storing.

detergent applied with a soft toothbrush or cotton swab to clean the surfaces, but beware that such techniques risk damaging the item, particularly markings. Rinse the body thoroughly in running water, making sure to keep the paper lubrication labels, if present, dry. Let the body air dry thoroughly. Incomplete rinsing will leave rings and spots on

A light oil and a light plastic-compatible grease, available at most hobby stores, are needed to lubricate your trains.

The locomotive, of course, with its abundance of moving parts, requires the most lubrication. A single drop of oil on the armature shaft, as well as the axle bearings, greatly improves the life and performance of the motor. The spur gears are best lubricated with a light grease.

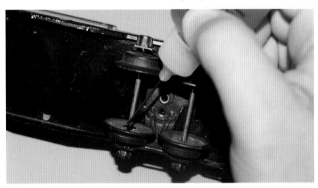

Lubricating the cars' axles and truck pivot points will quiet the train and reduce the load on the locomotive substantially.

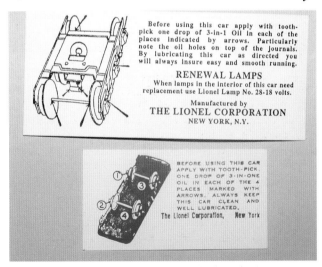

Some of Lionel's prewar cars had lubrication instructions pasted on their bottoms. These instructions are as valid today as they were when the cars were new.

the body. If you are uncomfortable with this, find a shop that specializes in Lionel and have it clean that item for you.

Bare metal components and blued steel car frames can be wiped with a cloth moistened with a product such as WD-40 that will remove built-up dirt and leave a protective petroleum barrier against rust.

While the cars are dismantled, inspect the wiring on any operating cars or whistling tenders. Check for wires that have broken loose or have cracking insulation. Replace them with similar sized, highly flexible wires. Use rosin core solder, not acid core. Do any soldering with the body removed (and preferably on another bench). It is amazing the number of otherwise beautiful collectable trains we see that have been bumped and ruined by a hot soldering iron.

The bodies of most locomotives are removed by first removing screws, although a few are held on by pins driven in place.

On spur gear-driven locomotives, the commutator can be seen. This is usually a three-segmented copper disk. Using a little cigarette lighter fluid on a cotton swab (with appropriate safety measures concerning flammable liquids), wipe this down. A little lighter fluid washed over the brushes will remove excess carbon deposits as well. After the lighter fluid has evaporated, apply a couple of drops of light, plastic-compatible grease to each end of the armature shaft, taking care not to get any lube on the brushes, brush holders or commutator. Some motors are equipped with felt oil wicks to lubricate the armature shaft. On these motors, saturate the wick with a light, plastic-compatible oil.

The 700E, 700K and 763E steam locomotives have internal gearboxes accessed by removing the boiler. These locomotive models are driven through a worm and wheel arrangement. Both the worm and gear should be lubricated with a light grease. Be advised that disassembly and proper reassembly of these locomotives is tedious and time consuming. Once exposed, the old lubricant should be scraped out and disposed of properly. Final clean up of the old lube is aided by the use of cigarette lighter fluid. The gearboxes should be refilled with light plastic-compatible grease, taking time to work it thoroughly into the gear train.

The driving axles of many locomotives turn in porous bronze bushings, which should be lightly lubricated with light oil. While you have your light oil out, it would be a good time to lubricate the junction of the wheels and axles on all your cars. You will be surprised what an improvement

in performance this step will bring.

Reassemble your trains, taking care to put the screws back into their proper holes. None of Lionel's screws should require more than finger effort to install. If they do, make sure you have the proper screw and recheck your alignment. Use caution and do not overtighten any of the screws.

Your trains should now be ready to run.

Price Guide Key: **VG** = Very Good, **EX** = Excellent, **LN** = Like New | *Values for each condition are in U.S. dollars.* | **Rarity** = Scale from 1-8 with 8 being the hardest to find.

389

APPENDIX 2
SETTING UP YOUR TRAIN

Lionel's trains were well-made, reliable toys. Often they will work as well today as the day they were made. However, there are some simple steps you should take to protect the

The power leads from the transformer are connected to the track by means of a lockon. Lockons were produced in multiple styles. Using a pair of wire strippers (shown in Appendix 1, figure 1), carefully remove a short section of the insulation from each end of the hook up wire.

trains and, more importantly you and your family, before plugging in the toys you just hauled down from the attic or home from a garage sale.

The instructions here serve two purposes. They will aid failing memories in the event the train's original instructions have been lost or discarded. They also contain some tips necessary due to the age of the trains. Remember, when Lionel wrote its instruction sheets, they were for use with new toys!

First, and absolutely most importantly, examine the transformer (power pack). If it has been exposed to an obvious roof leak, or has a broken or cracked case, take it in to a qualified Lionel center before proceeding. Next, grasp the power cord and bend it 180 degrees, tightly. If the insulation cracks or breaks off, the transformer needs service. This is a common problem, and the transformer is the only area with much potential for injury. Do not be tempted to wrap the cord in electrical tape or to splice on a new wire. Lionel knotted its power cords inside the transformer case to act as a strain relief, and the insulation there will also be failing if the insulation you can see is.

Next, examine the visible wiring on the underside of illuminated or operating cars such as steam locomotive tenders, cabooses, passenger cars or unloading freight cars. Make sure that none of the tiny wire leads have broken loose, and that the insulation on those leads is still intact and pliable.

Unless the locomotive has been serviced recently, follow

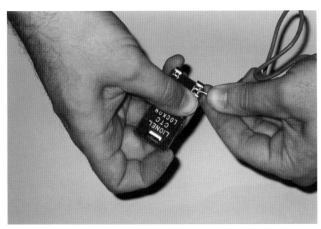

Depress the end of one fahnstock clip on the lockon and slip the end of the wire through the SMALL loop. Releasing the end of the clip locks it in place. Repeat the process with the second wire and the other fahnstock clip, ensuring that not even a single strand of wire touches between the two clips.

the procedure for doing so as outlined in Appendix 1.

Finally, examine the track. Make sure that all the connecting pins are in place (see the special note concerning switches before you begin installing replacements) as well as the insulation between the center rail and the crossties. If any insulation is missing, it must be replaced or that section should be discarded.

If the tops of the rails are dirty or rusty, follow the steps listed in Appendix 1 to clean them. Connect the sections of track into the configuration of your choice. Note that the track-to-track connections should be firm, the firmer the better. It may be necessary to tighten the open ends of the rails to ensure a tight fit. Specially-made track pliers are ideal for this, however conventional needle-nose pliers can be used as well with patience.

Should you choose to permanently attach your train's track to a board, don't do this until it has been test run and then use screws, not nails, to attach the truck. Nails work loose, and a misplaced hammer blow can permanently deform the rails. Even at this, based on the author's years of experience in the hobby shop industry, if the train is for a child, resist the urge to fasten the track to a sheet of plywood. This, in essence, is the same as gluing together Legos. The creativity, as well as the ability to expand the railroad, stops when the track is screwed down. From then on, the child is destined to only watch the train circle round a sheet of plywood, and hence will lose interest rapidly.

Once you have your track sections connected together, attach the wires to the end then the lockon to the track as shown in photos 1 through 4. After checking the condition of the transformer (Appendix 1), connect the other ends of the wires to the appropriate terminals on the transformer. Before placing the trains on the track, plug the transformer into a wall outlet. If your transformer is equipped with lights, the green one should now glow, and the red one, if so equipped, should be off. On transformers equipped with a red light, that lamp's illumination indicates that the circuit breaker has opened due to a short circuit. Advance the throttle again, watching for a change in any indicator lights. A dimming green light or glowing red light is a sign of a short circuit. If your transformer has no lights, it should emit a pleasant hum when plugged in; a clicking is a sign of a short circuit.

The UTC universal lockon can be used with either Standard Gauge or 0 gauge track.

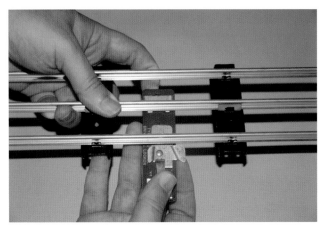

To attach the UTC to Standard Gauge track, hook the tangs furthest from the fahnstock clips over the flange at the bottom of the center rail, as shown here.

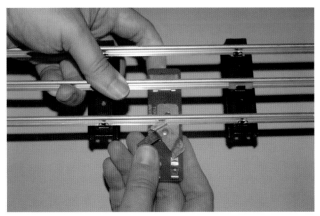

Using the attached lever, swing the short end of the lock plate over the flange of an outer rail, locking the lockon in place.

SHORT CIRCUITS, NO TRAIN

If the short circuit exists with the throttle closed, verify you have connected the leads to the track to the proper posts on the transformer. If they are properly connected, you should take the transformer in for service.

If, with the throttle closed, there is no short, yet there is with the throttle advanced, make sure the two wires are not touching each other at either the lockon or transformer binding posts. Make sure that there are no loose screws, nails or track pins lying on the track. Remove any debris from the track and try again. If the short persists, separate the section of track with the lockon affixed from the others, and begin adding sections one at a time. When a bad section is added, the short

Price Guide Key: VG = Very Good, EX = Excellent, LN = Like New | *Values for each condition are in U.S. dollars.* | **Rarity** = Scale from 1-8 with 8 being the hardest to find.

391

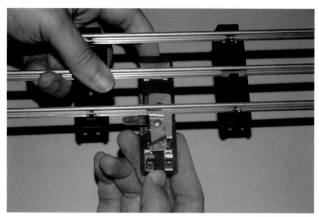

When properly installed, the UTC rigidly spans two rails (wires omitted here for clarity).

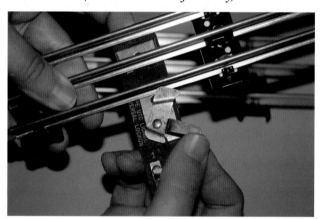

When a UTC lockon is used with 0 gauge track, the connection procedure is the same, except the long extension of the lock plate is swung over the rail flange.

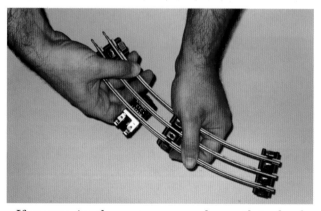

If you are using the more common, and currently produced, CTC lockon with 0 gauge track, place the bar beneath the word "LOCKON" over the lower flange of the outer rail. The tab above the word "LIONEL" will now snap over the opposite flange of the center rail. The lockon will now be securely in place. The lockon can be attached to any section of track, curved or straight.

will return. Either repair or replace the defective section.

PLACE THE TRAINS ON THE TRACK

Put the cars on one at a time, coupling them to each other as you place them on the track. After each one is placed on the track, roll it back and forth to ensure that the wheels

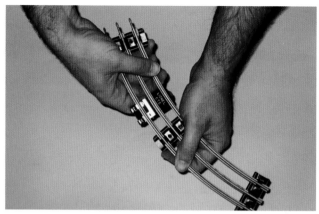

This is how NOT to attach a lockon. This is the number one mistake made in the initial set up. If it is hooked up like this, not only will the train not run, but if allowed to remain this way, serious damage to the transformer can occur.

are properly in place. Turn the power on, again checking for potential short circuits. If a short exists, begin removing cars until the short goes away. When the short is corrected, the most recently removed car was at fault. Examine it for broken wires or low, loose hanging coupler components. If no shorts existed with all the cars on the track, place the locomotive on the track.

OPEN THE THROTTLE

Moving the throttle regulates the speed of the train by increasing and decreasing the track voltage. Voltage is normally somewhere between 6 and 18 volts, although some transformers go up to 24 volts.

REVERSING

Many Lionel locomotives are equipped with a remote reversing mechanism commonly referred to as an "E-unit." This mechanism is operated by current interruptions. These interruptions can be caused by operating the "direction" control on the transformer (if so equipped) or by closing and reopening the throttle. Some locomotives have only two-position E-units, shifting directly from forward to reverse. Many locomotives have a three-position E-unit, which sequences as follows: Forward-neutral-reverse-neutral-forward. The neutral position allows power to flow to the track without moving the train in order to operate special features such as log, coal and merchandise cars that unload.

The E-unit, or reversing mechanism, can be disconnected if so desired. Start the train moving in the desired direction at a low speed. Hold it still with your hand and move the E-unit control lever on the locomotive (NOT a transformer control) to the opposite position. The E-unit control is USUALLY a shiny lever protruding from the top of the locomotive, or in some instances from the bottom or rear of the locomotive.

BLOWING THE WHISTLE

Many of Lionel's steam locomotive replicas included a whistle. The whistle mechanism was actually housed inside the locomotive's tender. It was operated by slowly moving the appropriate control on the transformer. In some instances, it may be necessary to move the control (lever or button) only part way through its travel for best operation. Excessive slowing of the train is an indication that the whistle unit is in need of service.

Many of Lionel's smaller transformers have only two binding posts for attaching the other ends of the track power wires. Once again, the end of each wire is stripped, the binding post nut loosened, the wire wrapped around it in a clockwise manner and the binding post nut retightened.

The binding posts are sometimes located on the back of the transformer near the 110-volt power cord. Additional combinations of posts, labeled appropriately, yield various fixed voltages for powering lights and accessories. It is usually considered that the outer rails are the "ground" and as such terminal 2 on the lockon is generally connected to the "U" post on the transformer, although the train will run with the connections reversed.

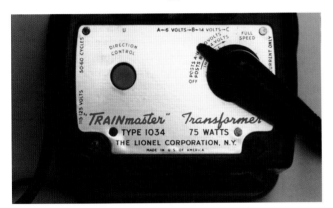

Lionel's larger transformers have multiple binding posts. Lionel solved the problem of remembering which to use by thoughtfully providing that information near the throttle. The letters, such as "A–U" shown here, correspond to the letters adjacent to the binding posts. Often two pairs of posts are indicated for an individual throttle, indicating that two different voltage ranges are available depending on which combination is used.

OPERATING CARS

Electrically operated cars such as the 3652 gondola, 3651 log car or 3659 coal dump car are operated electrically. The current flows from the control rails of the uncoupling track section, through small rivets in the car's sliding shoes and to the car's mechanism, when the proper button is pushed on the controller. These cars reset themselves after use, although most must still be manually reloaded.

INSTALLING TURNOUTS (SWITCHES)

Switches, often referred to as turnouts to prevent confusing them with electrical off-on switches, add considerable play value to a miniature railroad. Lionel made turnouts in both manual and remote control versions. Left-hand turnouts, as the name implies, have the train exit (or enter) from the left side of the straight segment; right-hand turnouts are the opposite.

Manually operated turnouts are installed in the track just like any other piece of track. Remote control switches are only slightly more complicated. Later Lionel 0 Gauge turnouts have

a built in non-derailing feature that automatically aligns the moveable rails to prevent a train from running "against" them.

This non-derailing feature is the cause of Lionel's installation of fiber pins in two rails on these turnouts. These insulating pins are installed on the two-track end of the turnout. On left-hand 022 turnouts, the pins are in the ends of the left-most rails of both the straight and curved segment. On right-hand turnouts, they are in the ends of the right-most rails.

It is very important that these pins not be removed or replaced with steel pins. It will be necessary to either add or remove steel pins from the track sections that connect to the turnouts.

Removing crimped-in pins from Lionel track is easily done using side-cutting pliers. Grip the pin in the jaw of the pliers. Use the flange of the rail as a lever point and ease the pin out slowly. It may be necessary to reshape the rail if it was distorted by the removal of the pin.

VOLTAGE DROP

The rails of the track are the path of the electrical current to the train. The steel rails have a much higher resistance to current flow than does copper wire. Therefore, on larger railroads, it is not unusual for the train to slow as it travels farther from the lockon.

The solution is not, as many people think, buying a larger transformer. The solution is buying more lockons and connecting them equidistant about the railroad. Then all the terminal 1 lockon connections are connected to the same transformer post, and all the terminal 2 lockon connections are connected to the other appropriate transformer post.

ENJOY YOUR TRAINS

Although sometimes mechanically complex, Lionel trains were intended to be primarily children's toys. As such, the connecting and operating of these items were kept deliberately simple. Oftentimes simply sitting down and getting started will bring back old memories of how each step is to be done. Much like riding a bicycle, it is not easily forgotten.

Lionel, through the years, produced detailed instruction sheets and booklets to accompany its train sets, locomotives, accessories and cars. There is no substitute for these original instructions. Fortunately, many of these have been reproduced and are available at hobby shops and train shows.

Price Guide Key: VG = Very Good, EX = Excellent, LN = Like New | *Values for each condition are in U.S. dollars.* | **Rarity** = Scale from 1-8 with 8 being the hardest to find.

393

GLOSSARY

AAR: Association of American Railroads, a full-sized railroad industry standards and lobbying group.

Bakelite: A brand of hard, brittle thermoset plastic. Heating Bakelite does not soften it, making it popular for electrical components. Lionel also used Bakelite occasionally for car bodies.

Cupola: The raised structure on the roof of a caboose that allowed a clear view of the sides of the train, making dragging equipment and "hot boxes" easily spotted regardless of the height of the remainder of the train.

Die-casting: A manufacturing process that involves forcing molten metal, usually a zinc alloy, into a mold, called a die, under high pressure. Rugged, detailed, precisely made parts can be mass-produced in this manner.

E unit: This has two meanings. A) In Lionel trains, the electromechanical switch that selects motor contacts, and thus the motor's direction of rotation, is called an "E-unit." It is usually cycled by interrupting the current flow to the track. These come in two-position (forward-reverse) or three-position versions, as well as a manual version that is two-position, but requires hands-on operation by the operator. Three-position E-units are the most common, and their sequence of operation is forward-neutral-reverse-neutral-forward. B) In real railroading, E-unit is slang for a General Motors Electro-Motive Division E-series twin-engine diesel that rode on two A-1-A trucks. The two terms are not generally confused, as Lionel did not build a miniature E-unit locomotive during the prewar era.

Gauge: The distance between the tops of the rails. On most real U.S. railroads, this is 4', 8 1/2". For Lionel's most popular size of trains, this width is 1 1/4".

Heat stamping: A decorating process in which a heated die is used to transfer and adhere colored decoration to the subject piece. When used on plastics, heat stamping often leaves an impression, the depth of which varies with the temperature of the tool and the duration of contact. When used on painted sheet-metal components, the underlying paint is occasionally softened, and thus the stamping can sometimes be felt.

Hot box: Early railroad wheel bearings were lubricated with oil-soaked cotton called "waste." These bearings, or journals, as well as the "waste," were housed in journal boxes. If the lubrication ran dry, the bearing would overheat, setting fire to the waste. If the train continued to operate, the bearing would fail, derailing the train.

House car: This standard railroad industry term is used for enclosed freight cars such as box, stock, refrigerator and poultry cars. These cars are used for lading requiring protection from weather, and the construction of these cars rather resembled that of a house.

Journal box: The enclosure at the junction of the axle and truck sideframe, which housed the axle bearing, or journal, and the cotton waste that acted as a lubricant reservoir.

Lithography: A printing process often used on metal surfaces. Part of the surface is treated to retain ink while other areas are treated to repel ink. This process allows elaborate and colorful decorations to be applied.

Rubber-stamping: A decorating process that uses an engraved rubber block, which is inked then pressed to the subject. Rubber-stamping tends to not be as bold, or as permanent, as heat stamping. However, rubber-stamping can be used on irregular surfaces which heat-stamping cannot, and the set-up cost is considerably less.

Scale: A numeric ratio describing the relative size of a miniature to an original.

Silk screening: A labor-intensive decorating process. A piece of sheer fabric (originally silk, now polyester) is stretched tight. A thin sheet of plastic, with holes cut out to reveal where ink is to appear on the work piece, is placed over the screen. The screen is pressed to the work piece ink, then forced through the openings in the plastic, and through the screen onto the work surface. Multi-color designs require multiple screens, and the inks are applied sequentially starting with the lightest color and moving up to the darkest.

Sintered Iron: Sintering is a metallurgical process in which powdered metal is poured into a mold and subjected to heat and pressure, thus forming it into a single part.

Tack board: Wooden panels on an otherwise steel door provided a place to attach various notes.

Truck: The structure consisting of paired wheels with axles, side frame, bolster and suspension system beneath railroad cars. This is referred to as a "bogie" in Europe.

INDEX

Price Guide Key: **VG** = Very Good, **EX** = Excellent, **LN** = Like New | *Values for each condition are in U.S. dollars.* | **Rarity** = Scale from 1-8 with 8 being the hardest to find.

INDEX

APPENDIX II

Price Guide Key: **VG** = Very Good, **EX** = Excellent, **LN** = Like New | *Values for each condition are in U.S. dollars.* | **Rarity** = Scale from 1-8 with 8 being the hardest to find.

397

NATIONAL TOY TRAIN MUSEUM
HEADQUARTERS FOR THE TRAIN COLLECTORS ASSOCIATION

Many of the trains shown in this volume are from the collection of the National Toy Train Museum, headquarters for The Train Collectors Association. The TCA is an international organization of men and women dedicated to collecting and preserving toy trains.

The Train Collectors Association, was born from a 1954 meeting in the Yardley, Pennsylvania barn of Ed Alexander. The TCA has grown to nearly 32,000 members today. A national office, along with a museum, was built in Strasburg, Pennsylvania to accommodate the growing needs. The building has undergone 3 expansions since that time.

Toy trains are presented in a colorful and exciting turn-of-the-century setting. The Museum's vast collection of floor toys, electric trains and train-related accessories includes those from the mid-1800s through the present. See Lionel, American Flyer, Marx, Marklin, LGB and many, many others.

The National Toy Train Museum offers five operating layouts: Standard, "0", "S", "G" and HO gauges. The Standard gauge layout highlights tinplate trains from the 1920s and 1930s. The "0" gauge layout presents trains from the 1940s through current production items. The "S" gauge layout highlights American Flyer trains manufactured during the 1950s. The "G" gauge layout shows what one can do with large, durable modern trains which are made for indoor or outdoor use. The HO gauge layout was professionally built by Carstens Publications, Inc. for a series of articles published in its Railroad Model Craftsman magazine.

A continuously running video show in The Museum's Theater area features cartoons and comedy films about toy trains. The Museum Gift Shop offers a wide and unusual selection of toy train-related gifts. Also housed in the Museum is an extensive Toy Train Reference Library, which is open to the public. On file are catalogs, magazines and books devoted to toy trains from 1900 to the present.

Come to Strasburg and visit the National Toy Train Museum where we have 5 different gauge layouts operating and displays of trains dating from 1840 until the present. If you are a person with a few trains or a house full, come join us.

OPEN:
- Weekends in April, November and December
- Daily — May through October
- 10:00 a.m. - 5:00 p.m.

visit their website at
www.traincollectors.org
for additional information.

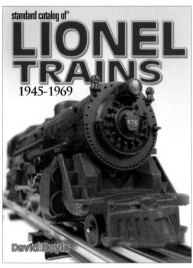

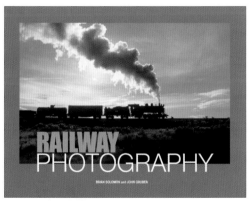
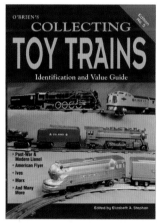

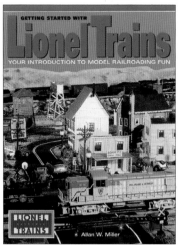
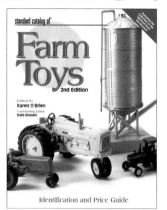
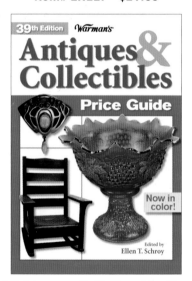